Present and Past
in
Middle Life

Present and Past in Middle Life

Edited by

Dorothy H. Eichorn   John A. Clausen

Norma Haan   Marjorie P. Honzik

Paul H. Mussen

Institute for Human Development
University of California
Berkeley, California

1981

ACADEMIC PRESS
A Subsidiary of Harcourt Brace Jovanovich, Publishers
New York   London   Toronto   Sydney   San Francisco

ACADEMIC PRESS, INC.
111 Fifth Avenue, New York, New York 10003

United Kingdom Edition published by
ACADEMIC PRESS, INC. (LONDON) LTD.
24/28 Oval Road, London NW1   7DX

Library of Congress Cataloging in Publication Data
Main entry under title:

Present and past in middle life.

  Bibliography: p.
  Includes index.
  1. Middle age--Longitudinal studies--Addresses,
essays, lectures. 2. Life cycle, Human--Longitudinal
studies--Addresses, essays, lectures. I. Eichorn,
Dorothy H.
HQ1061.P69   305.2'4   80-70589
ISBN 0-12-233680-1   AACR2

PRINTED IN THE UNITED STATES OF AMERICA

81 82 83 84   9 8 7 6 5 4 3 2 1

*For over half a century, the generous collaboration
of the longitudinal study members and their families
has contributed to knowledge about human development
and has enriched our research efforts with the warmth of
human relationships.
To you, our partners in the study of human lives,
we gratefully dedicate this volume.*

Contents

PART II   INTRAPERSONAL DIMENSIONS

Chapter 3   Health in the Middle Years

LEONA M. BAYER, DOROTHY WHISSELL-BUECHY,
AND MARJORIE P. HONZIK

Chapter 4   Experience, Personality, and IQ: Adolescence
to Middle Age

DOROTHY H. EICHORN, JANE V. HUNT, AND MARJORIE P. HONZIK

Contributors

Numbers in parentheses indicate the pages on which the authors' contributions begin.

LEONA M. BAYER (55), Institute of Human Development, University of California, Berkeley, California 94720

SHERI A. BERENBAUM (435),[1] Dight Institute for Human Genetics, University of Minnesota, Minneapolis, Minnesota 55455

JANE B. BROOKS (243), Department of Psychiatry, Kaiser-Permanente Medical Center, Hayward, California 94545

JOHN A. CLAUSEN (299, 321, 411), Institute of Human Development, University of California, Berkeley, California 94720

DOROTHY H. EICHORN (33, 89, 411), Institute of Human Development, University of California, Berkeley, California, 94720

GLEN H. ELDER, JR. (3), Department of Sociology, Cornell University, Ithaca, New York 14853

NORMA HAAN (117, 391, 411), Institute of Human Development, University of California, Berkeley, California 94720

RICHARD A. HARSHMAN (435),[2] Bell Laboratories, Murray Hill, New Jersey 07974

[1]*Present Address:* Department of Psychology, University of Health Sciences/The Chicago Medical School, North Chicago, Illinois 60064

[2]*Present Address:* Department of Psychology, University of Western Ontario, London, Ontario N6A 5C2, Canada

MARJORIE P. HONZIK (55, 89, 411), Institute of Human Development, University of California, Berkeley, California 94720

JANE V. HUNT (89), Institute of Human Development, University of California, Berkeley, California 94720

MARY COVER JONES (223), Institute of Human Development, University of California, Berkeley, California 94720

JOSEPH KUYPERS (299), School of Social Welfare, University of Manitoba, Winnipeg, Manitoba R3T 2N2, Canada

FLORINE B. LIVSON (195), Institute of Human Development, University of California, Berkeley, California 94720

NORMAN LIVSON (153, 183), Institute of Human Development, University of California, Berkeley, California 94720 and Department of Psychology, California State University, Hayward, California 94542

PAUL H. MUSSEN (299, 391, 411), Institute of Human Development, University of California, Berkeley, California 94720

HARVEY PESKIN (153, 183),[3] Institute of Human Development, University of California, Berkeley, California 94720

ARLENE SKOLNICK (269), Institute of Human Development, University of California, Berkeley, California 94720

JANICE G. STROUD (353), Department of Sociology and Anthropology, University of North Carolina–Charlotte, Charlotte, North Carolina 28223

DOROTHY WHISSELL-BUECHY (55), Institute of Human Development, University of California, Berkeley, California 94720

[3]*Present Address:* Psychology Department, San Francisco State University, San Francisco, California 94132

Preface

Over the half century since multidisciplinary longitudinal studies were established at the University of California, the University of Colorado, Harvard University, the Bush Foundation, and the Fels Research Institute, there have been periods when laboratory studies on specific behaviors were favored, and longitudinal studies, particularly multidisciplinary ones, were denigrated as "shotgun" approaches with poor prognoses for "relevant payoff." By contrast, naturalistic research and a life-span or life-course approach are in vogue today. As described by Abeles and Riley (1976–1977), "life-course development is multidetermined [and] the life-course perspective highlights the need to study interrelationships among the processes of change and stability across various domains of functioning and to study them over time" [p. 3]. These descriptions and others are almost identical to early statements of the premises underlying the longitudinal studies at the Institute of Human Development (see, for example, Macfarlane, 1938).

Fashion in the study of human development thus seems to have come full circle. But the context of a society in which the population distribution is becoming weighted toward the older instead of the younger segment of the life span has introduced a change. For many years, developmental scientists concentrated on the age span from infancy through early adulthood. During the last decade, however, middle and old age have received increasing attention. Nonetheless, to date, most research done under the rubric of "life span" or "life course" actually includes only old age or the span from the middle to the later years. In this volume we bring an interdisciplinary focus to the portion of the life course from adolescence to middle age, extending previous publications from these studies, which dealt either with earlier portions of the life span or primarily with one or two domains.

Our first two chapters describe the background of the research—its sociohistorical context, the persons studied, and the methods of data collection. The substantive chapters present our study members as individuals—their health, intellectual abilities, and personalities— and as members of social groups, that is, as family members, workers, and, less comprehensively, as members of the body politic. Within each domain, we describe the status of our groups at middle age and examine associations with their earlier characteristics. We also stress relationships among domains, for example, the influence of personality on physical health or political attitudes. Whenever possible we indicate how our groups compare to more representative populations—either the general United States population or the standardization samples for a particular measure. These data, together with the information about the social and economic background of our samples and the times in which they lived, should help the reader to judge how applicable our findings are to other groups. Several specialized chapters, such as that on problem drinkers, sharpen the more general focus and illustrate the uses to which such data can be put in addressing specific issues of social or scientific concern.

Our intent has been to present the data in each domain in a way that would be comprehensible to persons trained in another discipline. To this end we have tried to avoid disciplinary "jargon" and to provide brief definitions of terms or descriptions of tests or other methods of data collection and organization. Simultaneously, we provide information, such as tests of significance, needed by our colleagues to evaluate our findings. We hope both the specialist and the general reader will benefit from this approach.

Dorothy H. Eichorn

Acknowledgments

Yahraes (1969) has said that the Institute of Human Development's archives "probably offer the richest collection of data ever assembled on human beings over a long period." This trust induces a great deal of humility; even a group of persons feels unequal to the challenge. The riches also reflect our great debt to many persons, only a few of whom can be named here.

The original investigators—Nancy Bayley, Harold and Mary Jones, Jean Macfarlane, Nathan Shock, and Herbert Stolz—had the vision to undertake these studies and to nurture them by meticulous data collection and recording and by valiant efforts to maintain funding through lean times in both the availability of research funds and the fashionability of longitudinal research. Countless interviewers, testers, coders, clerks, secretaries, and administrative assistants selflessly aided them. This volume owes much to Rose Fox, whose administrative skills in stretching limited budgets and office space recall the miracle of loaves and fishes, and to Christine Godet, Helen Cline, and Corrina Spencer, who skillfully typed and retyped, and with unfailing good nature coped with the idiosyncrasies of many authors. We particularly acknowledge the study members and their families whose dedication and interest have kept the enterprise alive and worthwhile.

These studies could not have begun nor continued without the understanding and support of a number of private foundations and federal agencies. The Laura Spelman Fund provided support for the first 5 years of the Guidance and Oakland Growth Studies. Since that time, the University of California has maintained basic support through facilities and some salaries. Additional funds necessary to continue the studies during the childhood and adolescence of the study members came from the General Education Board. Data collection and analysis for the early adult years was funded by grants from the Ford Foundation, the National Heart and Lung Institute, and the National Institute of Mental Health. The assessments at middle age were supported by the National Institute of Mental Health and the National Institute of Child Health and Human Development (NICHHD). When the National Institute on Aging (NIA) was established, the grant from NICHHD was transferred to NIA, and that institute continued funding for data analyses through March 1981.

The staff of Academic Press has encouraged us with their enthusiasm for this volume and has borne with almost infinite patience the vicissitudes of a multiauthored volume. Murphy's law of publication is that the author most needed to rewrite or to answer a query is the most likely to be out of town.

My own debt to the co-authors and co-editors of this volume is great. They have with grace subordinated their own preferences and needs to the common goal, even taking the next to impossible step for an author—voluntarily cutting favorite phrases or illustrations to meet page limitations. They have also been generous with each others' frailties, particularly mine. Finally, my task would never have been done had not my husband done all manner of "pinch-hitting" while behaving as if an often preoccupied and sometimes irritable wife were the best possible kind.

Part I
BACKGROUND

1

Social History and Life Experience

GLEN H. ELDER, JR.

The imprint of history is one of the most neglected facts in development. Lives are shaped by their settings and by the timing of encounters with historical forces. The state of the labor market when a career begins—plentiful jobs in many lines of work or few of any kind—affect both career prospects and the timing of other life events, such as marriage and parenting. The temporal relations between historical events and life experiences are an essential point of departure for my longitudinal studies of life-span development in two birth cohorts: the Oakland Growth Study (OGS), born in 1920–1921 and growing up in the northeastern sector of Oakland, California, and the Guidance Study sample (GS), born in 1928–1929 and growing up in Berkeley, California (Chapter 2).

THE TIMING OF LIVES

With pre-Depression birthdates that differ by about eight years, those samples may seem to share historical conditions in the 1920s and 1930s. But closer examination shows noteworthy variations in developmental stage at the point of economic strain in the 1930s and in the social timetable of age-related options or roles.

The OGS were children during the prosperous 1920s, a time of unparalleled economic growth for the state as a whole but especially the San Francisco Bay region. Thus, they entered the Depression after a relatively secure phase of early development. Later, they avoided the scars of joblessness after high school by virtue of wartime mobilization.

3

With few exceptions, the men entered the armed services during World War II, thereby delaying entry into regular careers. Most married and started families by the mid-1940s. The OGS timetable minimized exposure to the hardship of the Great Depression, and we find little evidence of such costs up to middle age.

By contrast, the GS encountered hard times in the vulnerable years of early childhood and the pressures of adolescence during the unsettled though prosperous years of World War II. Wartime pressures tended to extend the developmental handicap of Depression hardship for GS males as compared to OGS (Elder & Rockwell, 1978a; Elder, 1979). Some endured economic hardship up to their departure from the family in the mid-1940s, shaping their wartime adolescence and the psychosocial course of their lives to adulthood. Such hardship increased their feelings of inadequacy during the war years and reduced their prospects for higher education at a time of expanding educational opportunity. But by the time they reached the middle adult years, the disadvantage of deprivation had largely disappeared, at least relative to socioeconomic attainment. From adolescence to middle age, we observe increasing convergence between the developmental patterns of men in the two cohorts. Depression hardship did not impair development among the GS women, because of the example and support of their mothers. At mid-life, GS women resemble OGS women in showing no reliable evidence of Depression-related handicaps in social position and health.

As adolescents, OGS members played important roles in the economy of deprived families, girls helped run the household and boys worked at odd jobs in the community (Elder, 1974). For the GS youngsters, such roles were more common at the end of the 1930s and in the War years; they were too young in the worst of the Depression to relieve the burden of hard-pressed parents. Likewise, the military and home fronts of World War II vary in prominence between the OGS and GS. My focus is on the experience of mobilization in the Bay area, particularly those aspects that shaped family life and the social world of the GS adolescents.

Community of origin represents another difference between the early experience of the two cohorts. The University of California dominated the economic and cultural scene of Berkeley, a city of approximately 82,000 residents in 1930. Oakland was a "workingman's town," a rapidly growing transportation and distribution center of 284,000 inhabitants, with a labor force equally divided among service, conversion, and distribution industries. Professionals and semi-professionals were more numerous in Berkeley than in Oakland (20% versus 11%);

Oakland had more merchants and wholesalers. Composition of the working class did not differ, in part because a large segment of the Berkeley labor force (62%) was employed outside the city.

Scattered evidence suggests that the goal of a university education for offspring attracted families to Berkeley. The state offered all residents with a high-school diploma tuition-free higher education (Smelser & Almond, 1974). Only the most able had access to the state universities; junior and state colleges were available to the average or borderline student. As a consequence, well over half of the OGS and GS at least enrolled in a college or university, a figure far above the national average.

Berkeley public schools had no unusual feature except an experimental elementary school. GS members typically attended neighborhood grade schools and then the public high school. By contrast, OGS members were selected from five grade schools in northeast Oakland. They attended experimental secondary schools associated with the School of Education at the University of California in which the educational philosophy minimized class differences and favored educating the "whole child," with emphasis on social development and adjustment, tolerance and good citizenship. Traditional academic subjects and intellectual excellence also were stressed in the high school.

The life courses of OGS and GS members and their families represent a generational bridge spanning a century of American history: from the late-nineteenth-century origins of parents, in villages throughout Eastern Europe, small Midwestern towns, and large cities along the Pacific Coast, to the advanced industrial age of their children and grandchildren in the 1970s. All parents of the OGS were born in the late-nineteenth century, with birthdates as far back as 1870. Only half of the GS parents were born before the turn of the century. Something of the historical distance and intergenerational connections between these times and the 1970s is suggested by the contemporary reflections of a middle-class, middle-aged Berkeley father. Troubled by his offsprings' experimentation with drugs and transcendental religion, he sought explanations in a cross-generational pattern of paternal neglect.

> Grandfather was an unskilled immigrant who took jobs wherever he could get them and ... he was away much of the time ... My father went to work at an early age—after school, on Saturdays and Sundays. The family had little time together, unlike the experience in Europe where all members worked together on a farm; children and parents contributed to a common venture and had cohesiveness ... my father was a self-made man, working his way from janitor-errand boy to the president of a very valuable firm where in his late 60s he still puts in long hours and dominates

everyone.... While I was growing up he worked every night until 10 or 11 p.m. and I saw little of him. In no sense was he even an understanding father. He was strict with me and I saw him only at meals when I kept my mouth shut. No affection was shown; no intimacy existed.... I remember sadly wishing he liked me. [Institute of Human Development interview files, 1960]

Forces set in motion by the swing of boom and bust—the economic growth and opportunity of the pre-Depression era, the economic collapse of the 1930s, and recovery through wartime mobilization to unequaled prosperity during the 1940s and 1950s—influenced the life histories of these study members in ways that have yet to be fully understood. The first and last periods marked the beginning and end of a generational cycle in the lives of the OGS and GS, from their own birth to the birth of their children.

YEARS OF GROWTH

One of the most vivid portraits of late-nineteenth-century America is that of people on the move in search of a more abundant life (Thernstrom, 1973). Within the great westward migration is a striking example of such mobility—migration to California's land of opportunity. The state's population more than trebled between 1900 and 1930. Approximately 80% of this increase were persons born outside the state. By 1930, two of three residents listed birthplaces other than California; 20% were born abroad, and a majority of the United States-born migrants came from urban areas of the Central Plains (Gordon, 1954); farm-to-city migration was not an important source of population. The influx of new families fueled the bouyant consumer economy of the 1920s, and shaped the institutional and aspirational context of families and children in the depressed 1930s.

Between 1900 and 1910 the population in Oakland increased 124% and that of Berkeley 206%, with migration from the Midwest and Europe, from small towns in California and from fire-devastated San Francisco following the 1906 earthquake. Berkeley gained as many as 7000 new residents per year, a staggering expansion for a university town of barely 13,000 in 1900. The number of building permits climbed from less than 200 in 1904 to over 2000 during the year of 1907, and Oakland's growth followed much the same course.

When the study families first settled in Berkeley and Oakland is unknown, but many were undoubtedly part of this large population gain beginning at the turn of the century. Fewer than 10% of the GS parents were native to the Bay region and the birthplaces of GS and OGS parents parallel the demographic record.

From the turn of the century through the 1940s, major increases in the flow of migrants to the state generally accompany periods of extraordinary economic growth (1899–1913, 1918–1930, 1935–1944), "when the rate of economic expansion has exceeded that of the nation" (Gordon, 1954). Industrial mobilization during both World Wars attracted defense workers and nearly doubled per capita income between 1939 and the end of World War II. No industrial growth in the state could compare with what McWilliams (1948, 1971) called the "fabulous boom" of the 1940s. Immigration expanded demand for goods and services, particularly in the area of housing.

Rising consumer demand also spurred evolution of "the debt pattern" (Douglas, 1938) way of life. "The expansion of installment selling indicates the determination of the masses to enjoy the material blessings of life. Industry, mobilized for mass production, has found it necessary to break open mass markets with the tool of debt and the ideal of 'paying-as-you-use.'" The housewife of the 1920s was "solicited to buy for two dollars down and a dollar a month a dozen attractive articles her mother never dreamed of" (President's Research Committee on Social Trends, 1933). By the mid-1920s, economic growth had reached new heights in California (Kidner, 1946); the 1931 edition of *Daily Commercial News* was headlined: "Marvelous San Francisco Bay: Gateway to Prosperity."

The depression of 1913–1915 interrupted generalized prosperity in the East Bay, as did the depression of 1921–1922. Another economic crisis was precipitated by the San Francisco earthquake and fire. On the day after the quake, each train to the East Bay brought literally hundreds of persons, "with barely the clothes on their backs" (*Tribune*, 4/19/1906).[1] At least five study parents are known to have been part of this mass exodus; two of the fathers lost their businesses in the fire. Within a week the number of refugees had about doubled Berkeley's population. Estimates placed Oakland's relief burden well above 100,000 refugees. Both cities quickly responded to the crisis, organizing Relief Committees to coordinate the efforts and resources of churches, service groups, and individual volunteers. Seven tent camps were established throughout the East Bay with the aid of military authorities.

---

[1]The two local newspapers, the *Berkeley Daily Gazette* and the *Oakland Tribune,* are hereafter identified as the *Gazette* and *Tribune* with dates enclosed in parentheses.

The relief burden diminished sharply as San Franciscans returned home or acquired permanent residence in the East Bay, and its drain on local resources was more than equaled by the consumer needs of the new residents. However, the cities' collective response to the refugees established a social work foundation that played an important role in subsequent crises, especially the Depression of the 1930s. The Charity Organization Society, later known as the Berkeley Welfare Society, was organized in direct response to refugee needs. By the depression of 1914–1915, three public agencies were operating in Berkeley: the Welfare Society with direct financial aid for destitute families, the Health Clinic for the sick poor, and the Day Nursery, for children of working mothers. Rising unemployment during the winter of 1914–1915 also led to the creation of labor exchanges to match jobs and job seekers. According to Institute of Human Development (IHD) and official records, less than 6% of OGS and GS families received public aid during the 1920s, and, with few exceptions, these families were in the lower class in 1929.

In many respects the refugee aftermath of the 1906 disaster represents a microcosm of elements during the "years of growth" before 1930 that shaped the career beginnings of the study parents and the social world of their offspring, especially the waves of migrants and their economic stimulus and pressures for a more systematic approach to social welfare. Neither the depression of 1921–1922 nor the great Berkeley fire of 1923 altered for long or in any appreciable degree the region's economic surge following World War I (Table 1.1).

The full impact of the early-1920s depression did not hit the Bay Area until late 1921, and recovery was underway a year later. However, the fire of 1923 posed a severe threat to the economy and human welfare. Fanned by high winds, the fire swept down from the hills to the business district, destroying the homes of over 4000 residents and causing property losses exceeding $10,000,000. Few traces of devastation remained after a 2-year rebuilding effort, except an aggravated shortage of single-unit dwellings. By the end of the decade, new businesses, jobs, and bank deposits had surpassed Berkeley's growth in population. In Oakland and Berkeley, net retail sales climbed by nearly 50% between 1920 and 1928, symbolizing new levels of prosperity in this age of mass advertising and consumption on the installment plan. Most study families, except those headed by laborers, benefited.

Within this economic setting, we see trends and forces altering family patterns, especially in the urban middle class. The 1920 themes of

Table 1.1

Age of Oakland Growth and Guidance Study Members
by Historical Events

Date	Event	Age of study members	
		OGS	GS
1880–1900	Birth years of OGS parents		
1890–1910	Birth years of GS parents		
1921–1922	Depression	Birth (1920–1921)	
1923	Great Berkeley Fire	2–3	
1923–1929	General economic boom; growth of "debt pattern" way of life; cultural change in sexual mores	1–9	Birth (1928–1929)
1929–1930	Onset of Great Depression	9–10	1–2
1932–1933	Depth of Great Depression	11–13	3–5
1933–1936	Partial recovery, increasing cost of living, labor strikes	12–16	4–8
1937–1938	Economic Slump	16–18	8–10
1939–1940	Incipient stage of wartime mobilization	18–20	10–12
1941–1943	Major growth of war industries (shipyards, munitions plants, etc.) and of military forces	20–23	12–15
1945	End of World War II	24–25	16–17
1950–1953	Korean War	29–33	21–25

property mobility (better housing, neighborhood, durable goods) and a debt-pattern life-style were joined, according to some analysts, with an apparent rise in the valuation of humanistic sentiments such as "consideration, tenderness, mutual aid, respect, cooperation." The ideal marriage was said to be that of "genuine partnership," with children valued "less as a family savings bank or form of social insurance and more in and of themselves" (Todd, 1935). Changes in material and humanistic values were paralleled by improvements in the status of women and children generally and among the study families. Since the nineteenth century such improvements include noteworthy gains in women's education and labor force participation even after marriage;

greater knowledge, means, and support for fertility control, coupled with a postwar shift toward sexual openness and understanding among the better educated;[2] and downward trends in infant mortality,[3] health risks of childbirth, and family size.

Generational Differences

The study mothers were far more likely to be advantaged by native-birth and related educational opportunities than were the grandmothers. Less than 20% of the mothers of GS members were foreign-born, but 67% were children of immigrants from abroad. Only two grandmothers are known to have completed college in contrast to 25% of the GS mothers. Mothers were more likely than grandmothers to advocate equality in marriage, to form supportive and less punitive relations with children, to tolerate sex play among children, and to allow children to make their own decisions. These orientations are consistent with observations on the middle-class family of the 1920s (Hill, 1970).

Interviews during World War II suggest that the better-educated study mothers placed strong material and psychological demands on their marriage. One explained, "women today expect an awful lot out of life. They're not content any more to lead a drab existence." Another noted that the contemporary woman "can meet more situations with flexibility than could her mother or grandmother, whose main time was consumed by doing heavy physical work to keep the family going and who grew up in a generation when women didn't have much education and possessed very limited interests."

[2]Though a marked increase in premarital sexual activity seems to have occurred before 1920, judging from sketchy and unrepresentative evidence, one encounters frequent reference to a change in sexual attitudes at this time among the middle classes, a shift away from the sexual denial and repression of the late-nineteenth century (e.g., Dickinson & Beam, 1931, 1970). McGovern (1958) argues that a major shift in manners and morals of American women occurred after 1910, with the urban middle class leading the way. The revolution took the form of "more permissive sexuality and diminished femininity." In a more recent evaluation of the evidence, Filene (1974) identifies the cohort that includes the younger GS women as the path-breaker: "The generation of women born between 1900 and 1909 did indeed mark an abrupt fork in the history of sexual behavior."

[3]Berkeley ranked well below cities of its size in infant mortality during the 1920s, and this observation prompted a study of mothers and newborns in 1928–1929 designed to investigate causal factors. The GS members were selected from this sample, called the Berkeley Survey.

Employment of Women

Gainful employment was more available to the study mothers in the 1920s than it had been to their own mothers, and the well educated had access to a greater range of skilled jobs. Smuts' (1959) description of the typical working woman of 1890 serves as a comparison with employment patterns in the 1920s.

> She was young and single, the daughter of ambitious, hard-working immigrants or native farmers. With little education or training, she was spending the years between school and marriage in one of the many kinds of unskilled jobs available in the city.... Most of the married women who worked outside the home had little choice; they were the victims of one misfortune or another which deprived them of adequate support by a husband.

Economic necessity remained a primary motive for women's employment during the 1920s, but the decade witnessed increasing numbers of working women from the educated middle class. In Berkeley, employment growth among females between 1910 and 1930 (20–28%) occurred mainly in sales, clerical, and professional service occupations. GS mothers who had at least a high-school education were most likely to enter higher-status jobs in the expanding white-collar sector. Nine out of ten of these women reported some gainful employment during their lives, but a majority worked either before marriage or childbearing, or after the children were in school or out of the home. Employment was largely confined to fields of "women's work" and earned meager income relative to male standards. Nevertheless, paid work assumed a more pervasive role in the lives of the Berkeley women at the upper-class levels than it had for their mothers.

Childbearing

The childbearing years of the OGS and GS mothers (1910 to the late 1930s) occurred in a period of declining fertility nationwide (Bane, 1976), raising many questions at the time about the future of the American family and the social options of women.[4]

With origins in relatively large families, some members of the parent generation were undoubtedly disadvantaged in education and life chances, but their lower fertility offered a more positive future for their

[4]Symptomatic of the impact of the fertility decline on projections of the future is Douglas's (1934) conclusion that the population maximum for 1970 "will probably not be more than 170,000,000."

children and a qualitatively different upbringing in a smaller family unit. Compared to their own mothers, study mothers had greater access to medical care (in a region that had reduced infant mortality well below the national average) and to birth control information and devices.

Berkeley mothers born before 1900 grew up in households with an average of 4.5 children and gave birth to an average of 2.8 children. Fertility was somewhat less among younger mothers who encountered the economic constraints of the Great Depression (the mean equals 2.2 versus 4.0 for their mothers). A similar intergenerational decline probably occurred among the OGS mothers who typically gave birth to their first child between 1900 and 1910. Relatively small families were concentrated among the middle-class members of both GS and OGS, but the intergenerational decline appears across all class and ethnic categories. With fewer children, more labor-saving devices, and an appreciable increase in real income relative to the grandparental household, middle-class women of the prosperous 1920s were more able to take advantage of civic, consumption, and earning opportunities.

Overview

Although worlds of mother and daughter in the grandparent and parent generations were vastly different, one senses from IHD records that the changes involved aspirations more than any basic alteration of "women's place in the home" (Chafe, 1972). The soaring aspirations of young women in the 1920s for independence, new opportunities, and a better life were often in conflict with both their upbringing and the constraints of family living. Their desire for independence in marital choice was sometimes ground for conflict with parents, their plans for gainful employment were frequently frustrated by their husbands, and satisfying their material desires by buying on the installment plan conflicted with traditional notions of thrift.

Prosperity during the early phases of the lives of the study families brought great and often conflicting pressures to bear on the traditional pattern of man as principal earner and woman as wife, mother, and homemaker. Rising consumption aspirations imposed a heavy burden on the husband's earning capacity, as well as to altered expectations regarding marital roles, sexuality, and a broader life among educated wives. Effects of these pressures were evident in the issues that truly mattered in the study families when the regional economy tottered in the Great Depression. The most prominent sources of marital and family instability (Macfarlane, 1938) at that time were finances, sexual relations, and child care.

DEPRESSION AND WAR, 1929–1945

No event could have seemed more improbable to Bay Area residents in 1930 than a prolonged economic crisis that eventually displaced over a third of the working population and forced countless families to accept public assistance. Surging population growth muted the effect of the 1921–1922 depression, and economic growth in the mid-1920s was unparalleled, greater than that of the country as a whole. In no other section of the country was there greater justification for the reassuring theme that "prosperity is just around the corner." Yet records show that manufacturing in the state declined to a degree that matched the national average. California and New York were among the states with the highest rates of unemployed and work relief. However, the full brunt of the Depression was felt in the Bay Area approximately 6 months later than among the Eastern industrial states.

The Depression decade is marked by four economic phases that had varying consequences for parents and children in the East Bay: (*a*) the initial collapse that reached a low point during the winter of 1932–1933, when the cost of living dropped by approximately 25%; (*b*) an upswing in the cost of living beginning during early 1933 that aggravated hardship and minimized the benefits of partial recovery, accompanied by political movements (Lewis's "End Poverty in California") and proliferation of crippling labor strikes throughout the region; (*c*) the sharp Depression of 1937–1938 that displaced large numbers of the re-employed; and (*d*) the economic stimulus of war mobilization and industrial development at the end of the decade.

The Depressions (1929–1933, 1937–1938) were distinguished by an extreme loss of resources, whereas recovery may have spurred aspirations to spend beyond one's economic means. With Depression scarcity followed by the economic boom of World War II, a substantial number of the study families experienced both types of strain. Many of the GS children were exposed to an insecure childhood of hardship and then to the pressures of affluence during a wartime adolescence. The depressed 1930s *and* World War II mark off distinct phases of the study members' life experience, and also represent a different slice of history for OGS and GS members.

As indexed by construction activity, retail sales, and level of employment, the pattern of economic decline from 1929 through the mid-1930s in Oakland followed the pattern of six cities selected for comparison—San Francisco, Los Angeles, Cleveland, Detroit, Philadelphia, and Atlanta. Neighboring Berkeley tended to fare better, in part because of the stabilizing influence of its dominant institution, the University of California, whose faculty and officials had only minor cuts in salary. Between 1929 and 1933, building permits in Oakland dropped more (60%) than in Berkeley (31%), but less than in Detroit, Cleveland, and Philadelphia. By 1933, net retail sales fell to an average low of 50% in Oakland and the six comparison cities, but to only 33% in Berkeley.

In general, economic recovery occurred more rapidly on the West Coast than in other parts of the nation. The upswing in building permits from 1933 to 1937 was stronger in Oakland and Berkeley than in the other major cities. However, employment in retail trade, which dropped 33% across all eight cities, also returned to pre-Depression levels in all eight by 1935. Although Berkeley appears relatively advantaged during the Great Depression, most of its working-class members were employed in other communities before the crisis. From this perspective, the regional economy mattered most to Berkeley families.

Such comparisons are useful for locating the East Bay relative to other urban centers, but they are steps removed from the particular hardships of families—drastic income loss, unemployment or reduced work weeks, and the dreaded last resort, public assistance. According to a survey of rural and urban families in California, total family income averaged $1696 in 1929. At the end of 1933 this figure had declined by over 30%, nearly doubling the number of families with income less than $1000. Over this period the average income of GS families dropped from $2220 to $1570, a loss of 29%. OGS families, typically headed by older men employed in merchandising, wholesaling, or construction, entered the Depression with a higher average income and suffered a more substantial loss, from $3179 to $1911—a decline of nearly 40%.

Income loss is the best single measure of Depression hardship across social strata because unemployment was largely the misfortune of manual workers. Salary cuts, demotions, and a short week accounted for more deprivation in the middle class than did actual job loss (Elder, 1974). Nationally and in the East Bay, estimates in 1933 placed unemployment at approximately 30–33% of the normally employed (Huntington, 1939). Among OGS families over half the men who lost more than 33% of their income between 1929 and 1933 also were out of work at some point during this period (Elder, 1974).

Variation in economic loss is one of the most important observations for understanding family life in the 1930s. It serves as the point of departure for examining the effects of economic change on OGS and GS members and their families (Elder, 1974; Elder & Rockwell, 1978a). In OGS, two deprivational groups within the middle and working class of 1929 were identified according to income loss (1929–1933) relative to the decline in cost of living (about 25% over this period). Families suffered asset losses with some frequency only when the economic loss exceeded 40% of 1929 income. Therefore, deprived families were defined in terms of income losses above 34%; all other families were categorized as nondeprived. This division proved equally appropriate for the GS. By this criterion, 36% of the GS middle-class families were economically deprived, compared to 57% of the working-class families. Deprived families were more prevalent in both strata of OGS (56% working class versus 69% working class), a difference that partially reflects the more commercial–industrial character of Oakland's economy. From the early 1930s to the War years, the Depression experience of the study members varied markedly between the nondeprived and deprived. Some key aspects of this variation will be noted in the context of more general economic and social changes of the decade.

In April 1930, 7.4% of the male work force in Oakland was out of work. Early in 1931 some 500 unemployed men from the Bay Area stressed the urgency of the situation by journeying to Sacramento to present a list of relief demands to the Governor. As winter approached, a work campaign in Oakland reported that over 3000 families of the unemployed were destitute and that twice that number were nearing the end of their resources (*Tribune,* 11/1926). More than 10,000 unemployed men were registered over a 2-week period in the city, with the list increasing by as many as 700 cases each day. Special registration of unemployed women was initiated, but all were notified that preference in hiring would be given to married men with families.

Lines of jobless men before the registration desks at fire houses throughout the city told a vivid story of the times, as did eviction notices and the appearance of household possessions on the curb arousing anger and neighborhood protests. Throughout the state, members of the California Unemployment Commission found numerous homes ravaged by loss of job and income.

It has broken the spirits of their members, undermined their health, robbed them of self-respect, destroyed their efficiency and employability.... Many households have been dissolved; little children parcelled out to friends, relatives or charitable homes; husbands and wives, parents and children separated, temporarily or permanently.

Homes in which life savings were invested and hopes bound up have been lost never to be recovered. Men, young and old, have taken to the road ... the army of homeless men grows alarmingly [Bernstein, 1970: 321].

Apart from public aid, a number of schemes for assisting the destitute were proposed spreading the work, making jobs more labor intensive, eliminating female employment, and self-help cooperatives. Such ventures assumed a variety of forms, but generally involved a democratic mobilization of the underemployed and unemployed in an effort to obtain the necessities of life; methods ranged from political pressure to collective barter of labor with bakeries, farms, and the production of commodities for exchange. Though hampered by lack of access to an agricultural surplus, some 20 cooperatives were established in the Bay Area, with two achieving noteworthy benefits for their members (including some from the study sample) through the exchange of things for things, not labor for things—the Berkeley Self-help Cooperative and the Unemployed Exchange Association.

The Depths of the Great Depression

The worsening economic situation in the winter of 1932 pushed the relief burden in Oakland and Berkeley to the crisis stage, threatening a total breakdown of private and public agencies. Between 1928 and 1933, the average number of families receiving public aid in Alameda County (which includes the two cities) increased sevenfold. With over 55,000 citizens wholly dependent on public aid for food, clothing, and shelter, the financial drain exhausted county funds by the end of 1932, requiring emergency transfers from other sources and a special $3,000,000 relief bond election. The bond issue passed, thereby ensuring support of the dependent population until federal funds arrived through the Emergency Relief Administration in March, 1933.

Throughout this period, estimates placed the dependency level at 10% or more of the local population, a figure that roughly corresponds with the annual percentage of relief cases among study families. Principal sources of direct assistance prior to federal aid included the Berkeley Welfare Society and the Alameda Associated Charities Commission. Nearly half the deprived OGS families (Elder, 1974) that suffered unemployment received assistance during this period. This rate increased to 60% after the initiation of public works programs. Among families on relief at the end of 1934, the Depression had increased by a factor of three the number who were forced to live on little more than a dollar a day; nearly 60% were attempting to survive on less than $500 per year, a figure that includes all income, whether earned, borrowed, or donated, and food raised and consumed.

Just as installment buying challenged the virtues of thrift and saving, increased numbers of families dependent on public aid raised the specter of a generation devoid of self-respect and the initiative for self-support. Local editorials criticized "charity politics" for creating "public dependency" through the demoralizing practice of direct relief (see *Gazette,* 12/30/1932), an attitude not inconsistent with the desperate search for jobs among the unemployed and their stubborn resistance to charity and its stigma.

Analysis of the adaptations of OGS families (Elder, 1974) illustrates attempts to remain self-supporting. A substantial number of OGS mothers sought jobs, despite a hostile climate toward women "taking jobs away from men." Families drew on their limited savings, borrowed from kin and friends, and exhausted credit from banks and merchants before taking the last resort, public assistance. Whether their families were on relief or not, the OGS boys usually helped by acquiring paid jobs, and the girls played an important role in the household, frequently taking up the slack caused by their mothers' employment. Instead of fostering unambitious dependents, family hardship tended to strengthen initiative and independence among the children and accelerated their movement toward adult roles. Adversity and work experience among both middle- and working-class boys served to crystallize orientations toward work and adult independence. Acceptance of public aid often proved demoralizing to the parents (less so for work relief than for direct aid) and caused untold emotional strain in the family, but we see no substantial negative effect of this condition or of generalized hardship in the accomplishments and health of these children at middle age.

Though most adaptive strategies observed among OGS families were also employed by GS families, the two groups differ in one important respect—the function and meaning of children. OGS children were old enough to contribute to the family economy, to be counted on and thus to "count" under extreme circumstances; one gains a sense of this personal significance from the subjective details of their lives and interpretations. By contrast, GS children were too young to be much help, and many of their mothers were forced by hardship to give up plans for additional children. The birth rate in Berkeley dropped by 20% between 1931 and 1932, reflecting forces that also curtailed fertility among the younger Berkeley mothers; they ended up with much smaller families than women who were at least 30 years of age when hard times arrived (mean equals 2.1 versus 2.8).

Partial Recovery and Economic Slump

With the advent of New Deal programs, economic prospects began a hesitant rise through higher earnings and new jobs, but the Depression's trough in the winter of 1933 also marked the low point of living costs in the Bay Area. Food costs, in particular, dropped sharply during the Depression and made a significant difference in the welfare of hard-pressed families. However, the cost of food, rent, and clothing moved upward more rapidly than weekly earnings during late 1933. Through 1936 we see a pattern in which living expectations and costs rose faster than real income, producing an "economic squeeze" with issues and discontents that mobilized consumer strikes in various parts of the country. Many of these concerns were also expressed by workers in a long siege of strikes—561 across California between October 1934 and November 1936 (Caughey, 1970).

The San Francisco maritime strike of 1934 marked the beginning of significant labor mobilization in the region to seek bargaining rights, improve wages and working conditions. The anticipated impact of the strike posed a serious threat to the welfare of the East Bay population by curtailing the usual flow of foodstuffs, and the mayors of Oakland and Berkeley set up emergency measures. A more severe crisis occurred during the second maritime strike (October 29, 1936 to February 4, 1937), which displaced thousands of workers. The Berkeley City Council issued a series of urgent appeals requesting federal intervention for a settlement (*San Francisco News*, 12/9/1936).

Twelve Bay Area industries or firms were directly affected by strikes in December 1936 and over 45,000 workers were on strike. But such figures barely suggest the total cost for the region. Other firms were forced to slow production or close, laying off workers, and casting more gloom across thousands of households. Whatever the long-term benefits to labor, the immediate costs in the work lives of blue-collar fathers in the study samples and in hardships suffered by their families were undeniable. A number of these men were laid off just after they had returned to full employment, and they faced another round of joblessness during the Depression of 1937–1938.

From the early 1930s to the end of the decade, three modes of change observed among deprived families in the OGS and GS distinguished them from relatively nondeprived study families: changes in the family economy, relationships, and level of social and psychological stress (Elder, 1974; *The Berkeley Families*, report in progress, 1979). In both cohorts, income loss sharply increased: (*a*) indebtedness as savings diminished, (b) curtailment and postponement of expenditures, (c) replacement of funds for services and goods with family labor (e.g., laundering, clothes making, food preparation), and (d) reliance on earnings of women and older children. As noted earlier, OGS youth were old enough to play important roles in the economy of deprived families, from domestic activities to paid work. These roles were beyond the capacity of GS children until the latter years of the decade.

Changes in family relationships stemmed from father's loss of earnings, withdrawal from family roles, and adaptations in economic support. Economic loss increased the relative power and emotional significance of mother vis-à-vis father for boys and girls—a degree of polarization most evident in the perceptions and relationships of the younger GS boys. Economic deprivation heightened parental discontent, depression about living conditions, likelihood of parental conflicts, inconsistencies in relations with children (as based on the GS data), and the risk of father's behavioral impairment—heavy drinking, demoralization, and health disabilities.

The most adverse effects of these family patterns under deprived circumstances appear in the pre-adult lives of GS boys (Elder, 1979). According to clinical judgments (see Chapters 2 and 4), these boys as adolescents ranked well below the nondeprived on goal orientation, self-competence, social skills, and assertiveness, a difference (most pronounced in the middle class) that is linked to paternal impairment, hostile relations with father, and inconsistent discipline. By contrast, GS girls from deprived families displayed the competence that so many of their mothers exemplified in jobs and household management; these girls were more goal oriented, self-adequate, and assertive than those from nondeprived homes. In psychosocial development OGS boys and girls from deprived families tend to resemble the GS girls of similar background. Toward the end of high school, the OGS show no evidence of a developmental disadvantage from family hardship.

The common impression that hard times in the 1930s brought some families together and shattered others (Lynd & Lynd, 1937) finds empirical support in the GS (Elder, 1979). If parents were relatively close to each other *before* income loss, economic deprivation enhanced warm feelings toward mother *and* father among boys and girls. But when combined with marital discord, deprivation sharply increased hostility toward father among girls and especially boys, while strengthening the relationship between mother and daughter. Marital discord is the only context in which economic loss produced uniformly adverse consequences for the development of boys.

War Mobilization and the "Home Front"

Retail business, capital investments, and housing starts were beyond pre-Depression levels by 1939 and war mobilization had begun on the West Coast. The outbreak of war in Europe stimulated American markets and industries, generating opportunities for the young and their families. Difficult times still lay ahead for some working-class families in the study, but the future looked brighter to most OGS youth at the end of 1938. Though a good many knew firsthand the emotional pain and material deprivations of the 1930s

> nearly three-fourths of the boys felt that the Depression, as they had experienced it, was over. The sons of deprived parents were not more discouraged about their future than members of more affluent families, but they displayed more awareness of potential disappointments in life. Exposure to family hardships and suffering had not shaken their belief in the democratic system of government or in the formula of hard work and talent for getting ahead. [Elder, 1974: 154]

Most OGS youth rejected the notion that "Hitler was doing more good than harm," but they also mirrored the pacifism of the times in opposing American military intervention (University of California Attitude Survey, 1937–1938). Three of every five boys were critical of the argument that "military preparedness is one of the best ways to prevent war," and a larger number (70%) undoubtedly had their own future in mind when they took issue with the plan for universal military training. Little did they know that over 90% would serve in the armed forces before the end of World War II. The most fateful year for the OGS was 1942; the region was declared a war zone and 40% of the young men were called to serve by the end of the year. Most men served for three years and were discharged in 1945–1946.

Though war mobilization put America back to work and marked the beginning of an extraordinary phase of economic prosperity in California, one also detects continuities across the periods of depression and war, as experienced by the study families. These include the family "absence" of fathers, paid work of youth, and employment of mothers. Depression hardship left many homes without an effective father, while a decline in the presence of father in the home occurred among study families during World War II because of the overtime demands of a booming economy and, in a few cases, the separation imposed by military duty. One GS father, a technician for a local oil company, recalled that when the war came "they started us working . . . at 5 a.m. . . . Came home at 9 at night."

Soaring labor needs on ranches and in industries spurred recruitment of teenagers, including those still in school. Gainful employment played an important role in the lives of OGS boys, largely because of family and personal needs; work also assumed prominence among the GS adolescents as lucrative jobs became more available. Having known scarcity firsthand, some older men were understandably appalled at the high wages and carefree habits of youngsters. A GS father remembered "a bunch of kids" at his shop, "earning $1.50 an hour, and they really weren't worth 25 cents. They spend it up as fast as they got it and figured life was pretty easy. I used to tell them, 'some day they'll pull the plug out of the bottom of the boat and then where will you be? It won't be so easy to get a job as it is right now.'"

The dramatic increase of married women in the Bay Area labor force was heralded by the *Gazette* (9/11/1942) as "one of the most notable movements of this war, a development that perhaps not one American in a hundred would have thought possible.... Already there are thousands of women working in factories which formerly confined their employment to men." Although many working women shifted their employment to war-related industries, gainful employment was not foreign to the experience of most study mothers who helped fill labor needs during the War. Approximately half the GS mothers were employed at some point during the war, but a majority had also worked in the 1930s.

Working mothers and overtime or absent fathers inevitably raised serious questions and problems about the care and supervision of children. "What to do with the children of working mothers" became a major issue among local residents and city leaders during the summer and fall of 1942. By the end of the year, shipyards were sponsoring child-care centers and the Berkeley Board of Education had initiated steps to develop a comprehensive plan of operation for the care of children of working mothers. The belief that working women were among the "real winners of this war" was coupled with the fear that their young children would be among the losers if child-care facilities were not forthcoming.

The wartime problem of "street" youth and delinquency bears some resemblance to that of migratory youth in the Great Depression. Arrests of boys in Berkeley more than doubled between 1941 and 1943, and probation records show a pronounced upswing in misconduct among girls as well during the first 7 months of 1942 (*Gazette*, 9/1930). Press releases typically pointed to the disintegration of family life as the major cause. The familiar litany of family ills included the working mother, but a more compelling cause was mass migration of new workers and their families into East Bay communities that were ill-prepared in housing and services. These families, a large percentage from the Black South, were the primary component of population growth up to 1945—a 20% gain between 1940 and the end of 1942 in Berkeley and Oakland. Nearly 600 families moved to the East Bay in October of 1942. Manifestations of the influx of newcomers were visible throughout the East Bay—tent cities, trailer parks, conversion of single housing to multiple units, overcrowded neighborhoods, schools, and recreational facilities.

Community problems of this sort acquired distinctive meaning within the all-encompassing "crises" of depression and war; both historical periods revitalized collective experience as problems were cast within the framework of an emergency so grave that it threatened the common way of life. "Nation saving" assumed priority through the centralization of power and subordination of individual or group interests to the needs of the state. Rooted in such conditions is the experience of solidarity and self-sacrifice. Both values were highlighted during the first four years of the New Deal through mass mobilization and the psychology of war; "the depression, like perhaps no other period in our history, since the days of the frontier . . . rekindled a new sense of collective responsibility for the welfare of all the citizenry" (Wirth in Ogburn, 1943). Though class interests, conflicts, and politics emerged as devisive forces during the later 1930s, entry into the war restored the superordinate goal of defeating a common enemy: "The war fulfilled an important psychological need by giving common purpose to what in 1940 was still a country threatened with serious economic unrest" (Barnett, 1973:46).

Juvenile delinquency, neglect of young children, and racial unrest in the East Bay were characterized as a threat to the common good and the future of community and nation. Judging from letters to the local press and citizen mobilization on such problems, the home front mentality entailed ower tolerance than usual for behavior that undermined the collective good as well as support for new measures of social control—for example, a curfew to keep youngsters off the streets late at night. Exemplary youth, in public opinion, were those who displayed discipline and a willingness to sacrifice through contributions to the war effort. One gains a vivid impression of such behavior in the lives of the Berkeley adolescents from a newsletter published occasionally by the city's Defense Council to inform volunteers about the activities of its 41 departments and committees and to broaden the scope of contributions "to the effort of the home front army."

Signs of consciousness raising and civilian mobilization throughout the city included: a local radio series entitled "My War" that dramatized "the wartime contributions of every man, woman, and child on the home front"; exposure of children at Saturday movies to the reality of war through newsreels; the constant flow of troop trains and ships in the Bay Area; the shared family experience of tragic and good news from the war front; families working Victory gardens on vacant plots—over 40,000 reported in the East Bay during the year 1943; window cards in homes identifying block lieutenants, wardens, and Gold Star mothers; a notice from the Berkeley city library, "This is war. Let's read about it!"; citywide defense drills and "blackouts"; and messages to parents on "family fortifications"—"know where your children are at all times; provide a responsible person to take charge if you must be away from home, arrange a first and second choice of meeting places if separated during an emergency."

The active role of children in the war effort and their resulting sense of significance are most strikingly documented through the seemingly endless round of collection drives: monthly collections of fats for the Grease Bank and of tin cans—nine can collections totaled 604 tons and 45 gondola cars by the end of 1943; yearly scrap metal drives in which Scouts played a major role; waste paper collections organized in large measure by the city schools, students, and Scouts; Victory drives to provide books for servicemen, with collections again managed by the Scouts; and a drive to supply much needed clothing to "liberated countries in Europe." In addition to all this activity, young people served as agents for the distribution of mobilization literature, as volunteers for the harvest season, and as temporary employees in manpower-short firms.

"The War" became the most popular conversational topic with peers among GS boys, outranking girls, school, and "things I want." As military events began to shift in favor of the Allies, GS adolescents were questioned about things they most often talked about with friends. The list included aspects of popular culture (movies, radio programs, hit songs), relations with the opposite sex, family and school affairs, and war items—the war in general, the Armed Services you would choose, the new defense workers and their families, and postwar planning. Over half the boys (versus 37% of the girls) claimed they often talked about the war with friends of the same sex, and the preferred branch of military service was only slightly less popular (41% versus 34% for the girls). The latter topic was most salient among youth who had decided to enlist as soon as possible; such talk and action were concentrated among boys with an older brother in the Armed Forces. For these youth, as one parent put it, the primary issue was how to get in "under age." Rumors circulated about the "entry" success of a classmate who everyone thought was too young.

GS girls reported greater conversational interest in the wave of new defense workers and their families (40% versus 12% of the boys), a preoccupation that may have reflected their mothers' concerns over the moral and social dangers they perceived in this change. Forced removal of Japanese-American families (Thomas & Nishimoto, 1946), virulent anti-Japanese propaganda, and the influx of Black families brought minorities to the fore of domestic concerns and markedly altered the social experience of GS adolescents. The Institute for Human Development (IHD) records describe the upset of one mother who discovered that her daughter was still corresponding with a Japanese friend in a camp. Another mother expressed some consternation about the foul language of children of defense workers, the increasing incidence of behavior problems and assaults on students, and crowded classrooms. With the change in population composition and size, World War II marked the end of "old Berkeley" as the study parents had known it.[5]

The implications for adolescents of historical change between the 1930s and World War II is suggested by variations in the topics included on questionnaires for OGS and GS. Two such instruments, "Things to Be" and "Things to Talk About," were administered to adolescents in both study groups, but the content of each sample's form differs in ways that shed light on what the IHD staff thought most salient to the worlds of OGS and GS youth. Consistent with the pacifist climate of the late 1930s, OGS adolescents were asked to complete a vocational form that did not include a single, explicit military occupation; only "aviator" and "sailor" had potential relevance, and both also applied to peacetime vocations. Some 5 years later, GS adolescents were given the additional choice of "Marine," "soldier," and "Spar" (the Women's Corp of the Coast Guard); and 20% of the boys selected one of the military options as their primary occupational choice.

The OGS version of "Things to Talk About," administered before the United States entry into the war, implies that neither depression nor war (Spanish Civil War, Italy's conquest of Ethiopia, German militarism) was considered sufficiently prominent among adolescent interests to be included (these topics were included in Attitude and Morale Inventories, administered during high-school years). The most popular topics were aspects of teenage culture that may seem to have more in common with preoccupations of the 1950s than of the 1930s—boy–girl relations, the latest song hits (among girls), movies, and

---

[5]The Black population in Berkeley tripled over the 1940s (from 4% to 11.7%); the change was even greater in Oakland (2.8% to 12.4%).

classwork generally (average percentage equals 55). Judging from their response to questions on the Morale Inventory (Elder, 1974), Depression hardship did not reduce aspirations for the future. For GS youth, World War II was very much a conscious reality in adolescent experience, a fact documented by war themes in conversations and by the war topics that the IHD staff added to the list of things to talk about.

From a historical standpoint, this contrast fails to highlight salient features specific to the experience of each cohort and consequently risks a misperception of the relative weight of historical events in lives. The military experience of OGS men in World War II was surely as consequential in their lives (from the trauma of battle to delays in family and career formation) as the home front experience of GS males. The latter encountered World War II within the context of a family environment shaped by events and circumstances of the depressed 1930s. Their wartime adolescence cannot be understood from a developmental perspective apart from a life history that extends across the Depression decade.

In the middle and working classes, GS males from deprived families held lower aspirations during wartime adolescence than the nondeprived (Elder & Rockwell, 1978a); their scholastic performance fell below that of their counterparts from more affluent families (no difference in IQ). Despite expanding opportunities during the War, deprived youth were least likely to be optimistic about their future, self-directed, and assertive. Feelings of victimization, withdrawal from adversity, and self-defeating behavior distinguished their behavioral course from that of boys who grew up in nondeprived homes. At midlife GS men of deprived origins tended to nominate adolescence as the "worst period of their life," as did their counterparts in OGS. Both judgments may reflect the Depression's impact, even though adolescence occurred in very different historical periods for the two groups.

Adolescence entailed very different meanings for women in the two cohorts who grew up in deprived families. During junior and senior high school, OGS females from deprived families were socially disadvantaged relative to the daughters of more affluent parents; the deprived were less well-dressed in school than the nondeprived and more often felt excluded from the groups and social activities of age mates. The deprived were also more self-conscious and characterized by hurt feelings and mood swings. A Depression adolescence was not a gratifying time for a good many OGS women (Elder, 1974). It typically represented a "worst stage of life" in the adult memories of those who experienced economic deprivation.

A strikingly different impression of adolescence appears in the lives of GS women from deprived homes (Elder, 1979). When they reached adolescence in World War II, the financial constraints of the Depression were largely past. Moreover, they were not characterized in adolescence as less goal oriented, self-competent, or assertive than the nondeprived—an outcome that partly reflects the prominence and resilience of mothers in deprived households. As Westin (1976) points out, no one considered the "strong-woman image ... unusual during the thirties." *It is the particular sequence of prosperity, depression and war, and their variable timing in the life course, that distinguish the developmental histories of the two cohorts.*

THE POSTWAR ERA

Both economic and generational cycles are represented in the lives of the study members from childhood to the postwar era of abundance; born in the 1920s, they launched their own families during the economic surge of the 1940s and 1950s. Though OGS and GS encountered depression and war at different points in their lives, in the postwar years they shared the pursuit of adult vocations in a time of opportunity, material well-being, and family preoccupations. Yet, their concerns seem to reflect past deprivations.

Work-life prospects for the men were enhanced by educational opportunity in California that was unknown to the parent generation, and a large percentage made the best of this chance. OGS fathers, for example, were more likely to have completed college than the norm for the period (17%), but their sons more than tripled this proportion. Such intergenerational gains were experienced by GS men, though less impressively, and by the daughters in both samples relative to their mothers. Higher education enabled the men to participate in the postwar growth of a new middle class, one largely college-educated. "It is a class of white-collar employees, managers, professionals, junior executives, and service workers in the higher-status services such as education, recreation, leisure, social work, psychiatry, and the other service occupations" (Bensman & Vidich, 1971).

No section of the nation experienced greater expansion of this class than the Far West, especially California. Between 1950 and 1960 the state's employment in the professional, technical, and kindred worker category increased by 83%, well above the national average of 47%. The "phenomenal increase in scientists, engineers, and technicians," the dominant factor in this development (Manor, 1963), is paralleled by equally impressive gains in the managerial, clerical, and sales categories. Given the advancement prospects in such growth, it is not surprising that half the OGS men were in the upper middle class at 40, though only 25% of all men in the sample grew up in this stratum. By the same age, nearly 60% of the GS men from middle-class homes had entered the professional–managerial category, in addition to 25% of the sons of working-class parents. Although little hope for such a future appeared amidst the Depression hardships of these men, we find no evidence of disadvantage in their work life to date. For both cohorts, occupational status at mid-life is unrelated to family misfortune in the 1930s.

In the postwar years a new middle class emerged with the growth of large-scale organizations or bureaucracies, contrasting with the entrepreneurial character of the "old middle class" of small businessmen and independent craftsmen, a socioeconomic pattern common among OGS fathers. We see this organizational change in the work histories of OGS and GS sons. Self-employment is largely foreign to OGS men; 70% report no such experience up to middle age, and less than 20% devoted as much as half of their work life to entrepreneurial endeavors. Likewise, only 30% of the GS men claim any experience as a self-employed worker up to age 40, and only four managed to remain their own bosses over most of their career.

An unprecedented rise in the marriage rate also followed World War II. More couples married than ever before and did so at an earlier age than in the 1920s or before; the median age at first marriage for women in 1930 was 21.3, in contrast to 20.5 in 1945. These developments, as well as favorable economic conditions, contributed to the baby boom and the pervasive importance of the family in the postwar era. When OGS and GS women married and bore their first children, the home held an unchallenged position in a woman's world. Though more women were working than during the 1920s, this increase did not occur in the most highly skilled occupations. More women were entering college; yet a smaller proportion entered the labor market in professional jobs.

According to a content analysis of the *Ladies Home Journal*, "marriage was portrayed as a full-time job in the late 1940s and early 1950s, a career which entailed 'training, sound preparation, and skills.' Marital stability and family happiness received special emphasis as the presumed (sic) values of women who spend their days in household routines and lacked social outlets beyond the home" (Elder, 1974). The divorce rate seemed to affirm this image (Carter & Glick, 1976), reaching a low point in the mid-1950s after an extraordinary peak in the immediate postwar years. In California, as elsewhere (Carter & Glick,

1976), "marriage was more nearly the universal conjugal state among adult Americans of the 1960s than it ever had been before."

One important feature of postwar domesticity is expressed in the tendency for married women to subordinate their interests to those of children and husbands. We see suggestions of this pattern in a widening disparity after the 1930s between the educational attainments of men and women beyond secondary school (Duncan, 1968). The study mothers were members of a generation in which women were often better educated than their husbands. One might expect a continuation of this pattern among the daughters, who were far more likely than their mothers to enter college. However, the prospective mates of the daughters achieved greater intergenerational gains in higher education. Hence, although only 27% of OGS mothers were less educated than their husbands, this percentage increased to 44% in the marriages of their daughters.

Similarly, GS women were more likely than their mothers to enter college, but less likely to take full advantage of this opportunity by earning a 4-year degree. Not so, however, for their husbands; once in college, most tended to complete their studies, and a substantial number continued into postgraduate work.

OGS and GS women embarked on families at different times in the 1940s and 1950s but under the same guiding ethos of domesticity. Most OGS women married for the first time before the peak manpower demands of World War II, and for some the decision may have been influenced by the anticipated departure of mates or by prospects for achieved status through marriage. Such early marriages, which involved teenagers, marked the beginning of a childbearing career that persisted through most of their forties, produced an average of 3.4 children, and entailed a high risk of marital separation (divorce rate was 35% up to age 40). Women who wed after the age 22 typically gave birth to their first child by the 1950s, reached the end of a relatively short childbearing span with an average of 2.6 children, and were most likely to enter middle age with their marriage intact (94% at age 40). For GS women, the events of first marriage and childbearing generally extended from the late 1940s through the "baby boom" phase of the 1950s. They married at the same age as OGS women (mean equals 21.7 versus 21.6), and the timing of marriage, whether early or late, had similar consequences for childbearing and marital stability.

An expanding economy, a successful husband, and the domestic ethos of the postwar era favored full-time motherhood. The family-centered life-style of many college-educated women in the study embodies much of what seems distinctive of their generation, when compared to the "hard times" experiences of their mothers. This life pattern applies to the 25% of OGS women who gave up jobs at marriage or childbirth and had not returned to the labor force by age 43. Though well above the educational norm for the sample, these women expressed less interest in paid work and attributed greater value to family activity, children, and homemaking than any other group. The college-educated in this category did not put their knowledge and skills to work by customary standards, nor did they "cultivate talents which would enable them to be self-supporting, should the need arise" (Elder, 1974). Their main outlet beyond the family involved associations in the community and friends.

Despite the domestic pattern of the postwar years, the national proportion of working mothers increased over this time span (Ridley, 1969), often in response to economic pressures (an influence that played so important a role in the labor force experience of their mothers and grandmothers). Among OGS women, children represented one focal point of a satisfying marriage, but such preferences did not deter their employment when called for by family need. Two of three women worked after their first child arrived, a proportion that increased under conditions of financial strain. Economic need was less common among GS women, because of their greater advancement through education and marriage; less than half reported gainful employment after the birth of their first child. Financial pressures represent one common impetus to maternal employment across the generations in this study. Another generational link stems from having had a working mother during the 1930s (Bennett & Elder, 1979). Even in the upper middle class this experience increased the likelihood maternal employment among OGS and GS women, as well as dual careers (marriage and work) in the lives of their own daughters.

Though many years removed from the Great Depression, the postwar configuration of family-centered values and maternal employment is most characteristic of OGS and GS women who grew up in deprived households, especially within the middle class. They were more likely than the nondeprived to marry at an early age (Bennett & Elder, 1979), to sacrifice their education for marriage and husband's career, and to coordinate employment with family needs. They married at least as well as the nondeprived in terms of the husband's occupational accomplishments, and those who married into the upper middle class gave birth to more children than the others. Social advancement through marriage enabled women in both cohorts to overcome the limitations of a deprived family background. A large percentage achieved a family situation that provided options for expressing Depression-shaped values in decisions regarding childbearing, material consumption, and gainful employment.

Though a number of OGS and GS men from deprived homes were disadvantaged in education, most countered this handicap through achievement. They were more likely than the nondeprived to enter the labor market at an early age, establish a career at a young age, and follow a stable career over most of the years before mid-life. In both cohorts mid-life status exceeded predictions based on family background and education primarily among men who grew up in deprived families (Elder & Rockwell, 1978a). The significance of this achievement is seen in the long-term consequences of Depression hardship for adult health and values.

Adverse outcomes in health and a preference for security were linked mainly to family deprivation among men who were relatively unsuccessful in work life. The interaction of a Depression childhood and a troublesome work life enhanced the significance of income, job security, and the concept of home as a refuge (Elder, 1974; Elder & Rockwell, 1978b). Such concerns were subordinated to life quality issues in the social world of men who rose above the limitations of family deprivation through occupational attainments. GS men from deprived families valued work as a medium of self-expression and marriage as a primary relationship based on mutual understanding—experiences often missing in their Depression childhood.

In the upper middle class are found the most striking contrasts between the Depression childhoods of the study members and the childhoods of their offspring amidst the affluence and opportunity of the postwar era. The biography of the study members from deprived homes "is unique in the sense that widespread hardship, which enhanced the value of material goods and the desire for children, was soon followed by an economic upswing that often turned these values into reality. In one life span, Americans had moved from scarcity to abundance, from sacrifice to the freedoms made possible by prosperity" (Elder, 1974).

The Great Depression and World War II are known to most offspring of these cohorts only from reading, films, or tales of family and friends. Unlike their parents, these children were generally favored by prosperity through adolescence, and now face, as members of the huge "baby boom" cohort, a future that will be shaped by the harsh realities of limited resources and options, a future that harkens back to Depression life and the challenge of "making the best of what we have." The clash between consumption aspirations and resources may well become as much a part of their lives as it was in the childhood experience of their parents.

OTHER SOURCE MATERIAL

This chapter draws upon an unpublished essay by Frances M. Welch entitled "A Study of the City of Berkeley," 1929, available at the Institute of Human Development; a survey of news accounts, editorials, and letters to the editor in the *Berkeley Daily Gazette* and the *Oakland Tribune,* the primary newspapers for the two cities; and the following documents at the Bancroft Library, University of California, Berkeley.
The Depression decade:
Margery Carpenter. *A study of social work in Berkeley.* Berkeley: Commission of Public Charities, 1926.
Report of the State Unemployment Commission, Sacramento, California, November, 1932.
Paul N. Woolf. Economic trends in California, 1929–34. California Emergency Relief Administration, Sacramento, California, 1934.
Review of activities of the State Relief Administration of California, 1933–35. Sacramento, California, 1936.
California Medical-Economic Survey: Formal report on factual data. San Francisco: California Medical Association, 1937.
Report of a Joint Legislative Fact-finding Committee on Employment. Sacramento, California, 1940.
The War Years:
Berkeley Defense Council. *Messenger,* April 1943 through May 1944 (a newsletter that provided information on war mobilization activities throughout the city).
California State War Council. *War Council Manual.* Sacramento: Office of State Director of Civilian Defense, 1943.
California State Chamber of Commerce. Individual Incomes of Civilian Residents of California by Counties, 1939–1946. Sacramento, California, 1947.

2

Samples and Procedures

DOROTHY H. EICHORN

From the drama—often poignant—of the social history through which our study participants have thus far lived, we turn here to the more prosaic description of the research context. A fact of research history bears importantly on later methodology: the three longitudinal studies now merged as the Intergenerational Studies (IGS) were initiated separately by different investigators and had different major foci (Jones *et al.*, 1971). To set the research stage their separate origins must be traced.

IHD LONGITUDINAL STUDIES

Guidance Study

The Guidance Study (GS), was begun by Jean Walker Macfarlane in January 1928. Planned as a 6-year prospective study of a normal sample, the original purposes were to assess (*a*) how prevalent and severe were behavior problems of the kind reported for preschool children brought to therapeutic clinics, (*b*) biological and environmental factors associated with the presence or absence of such behaviors, and (*c*) the influence of intensive discussions with parents about child-rearing practices on children's problem behavior (Macfarlane, 1938; Macfarlane, Allen, & Honzik, 1954). By the end of the 6 years, more general questions about personality development were intriguing psychologists and psychiatrists, and so the GS continued but with the intent of examining the interactions of psychological, social, and biological factors in personality development.

33

The 248 original participants were drawn from a socioeconomic survey of every third birth in Berkeley between January 1, 1928, and June 30, 1929. Other aspects of this Berkeley Survey are mentioned in Chapter 1. Despite this selection procedure, the GS sample differed from the general United States population (as judged by census data) in ways expectable in a university community. Hospital deliveries exceeded the national average, and the infant mortality rate was lower. Although their incomes were below average, the GS parents were above average in education status and more likely to own their own homes and to have labor-saving appliances.

These and other detailed demographic and socioeconomic data on the family at the time of the child's birth were obtained from the parents by an interviewer trained in economics and social work. Pre- and perinatal data were obtained by a public health nurse from mothers, physicians, and hospital records. From the infant's third through eighteenth month, a public health nurse also visited the home every 3 months to measure height and weight and make systematic records of progress, including health, diet, and behavior. Both parents filled out detailed health histories for themselves and their parents (the infant's grandparents).

Because one purpose of the research was to assess the effect of parental "guidance" by professional staff, the 248 infants selected for the GS were assigned, at 21 months of age, to one of two subsamples—a Guidance or a Control group, each with 124 infants. These two subgroups were matched for sex of child, size of family, family income at birth of the study child, occupation of father, neighborhood, and age, education, nativity, and ethnic derivation of the parents. The groups did not differ in condition at birth nor in developmental status and number of behavior problems at 21 months.

When the study members were 21 months old, intensive data collection at the Institute of Human Development (IHD) began. They were then assessed every 6 months from 2 to 4 years, and annually from 5 to 18 years. At each visit their mothers accompanied them and were interviewed.

Medical examinations, health histories, and a small battery of anthropometric measurements were obtained at 21 months and annually from 3 through 18 years. From 8 to 18, anthropometric measures, strength measures, body photographs and hand–wrist X-rays for assessing skeletal maturity were taken semiannually (Tuddenham & Snyder, 1954). Alternate forms of the California Preschool Schedule (Jaffa, 1934), an intelligence test standardized in Berkeley, were administered at 21 months, semiannually through 4 years, and again at

5. The 1916 Stanford-Binet was given at 6 and 7, alternate forms of the 1937 revision at 8, 9, 10, 12 or 13, and 14 years, and the Wechsler–Bellevue Intelligence Scale (WBIS), Form I, at 18.

Intensive interviews with children and parents distinguished the Guidance group. A retrospective interview with the mother about her child's life to date was done at 21 months, and these reports were checked against data collected during the preceding 21-month period by the public health nurse (Pyles, Stolz, & Macfarlane, 1935). Detailed interviews about the child's habits and regime, social standards, sociability, interpersonal behaviors, interests, and personality characteristics were conducted semiannually from 2 through 8 years and then annually through 16 years. Intensive interviews with the child on the same topics began at 6 years and continued through 16. A less intensive inventory was obtained from the Control group mothers when their children were 21 months, at semiannual intervals through 4 years, and annually through 14. When the Guidance and Control groups were 17, a recapitulation interview was done with them and each of their parents.

At each visit each child was rated on an extensive list of personality characteristics (e.g., irritability, aggressiveness, dependence, introversion, extraversion, anxiety) carefully coded on 5-point scales (Macfarlane *et al.*, 1954). From 5 through 15 years, teachers were interviewed yearly about each child's personality and behavior. To obtain peers' opinions about personality and behavior, a Reputation Test asking for the names of children who best fitted such pairs of descriptions as "ones everybody likes" and "ones nobody likes very much" (Tuddenham, 1951, 1952) was administered to classmates annually from 6 through 13. Both groups took projective tests (TAT and/or Rorschach) almost semiannually from 9½ through 18 as well as occasional interest or vocational inventories.

Socioeconomic data were rechecked annually. For ages 6 through 16 a large number of additional items were added to the interviews. These covered health of family members, interpersonal relations among family members, strains and satisfactions in the home, patterns of displaying affection and anger, closeness of bonds, styles of discipline, and personality appraisals of family members as seen by the participants and their parents.

All types of measures were repeated at age 30 (except X-ray and most of the intelligence test). The medical examination by an internist included a health history, and each participant was interviewed for a total of about 12 hours by two psychologists (from a staff of four). The interview included questions and probes about education, occupation, residence, marriage, and parenting, as well as a "life morale recapitulation," with report of the factors associated with high, low, or variable morale. A concomitant assessment of spouses and children included health, anthropometrics, intelligence tests, interviews, personality ratings, and educational and occupational histories.

Berkeley Growth Study

The Berkeley Growth Study (BGS) was initiated by Nancy Bayley with 61 infants born between September 15, 1928 and May 15, 1929. Thus this sample is of essentially the same birth cohort as the GS. Originally called the Intensive Study, this research was designed to trace normal intellectual, motor, and physical development during the first year.

Infants were located by asking permission of obstetricians to visit their newly delivered patients. Because the sample was to be assessed each month, it was kept small, and homogeneity was achieved by limiting the group to healthy, full-term infants born in hospitals to white, English-speaking parents. The fathers ranged from unskilled laborers who did not complete grammar school to professionals with graduate training, but the families were predominantly middle class, native born, and Protestant. As new questions arose and the study continued past the first year, 13 infants born during the next 3 years were added to augment the sample or replace children who had moved from Berkeley, increasing the sample to 74.

Within 4 days after each infant's birth, anthropometric, neurological, and physiological measures were made in the hospital by the study pediatrician. Pre- and circumnatal histories were obtained from the mother, physician, and hospital records, and socioeconomic data and family histories from the parents, in each instance by the same personnel performing these functions in the GS. Study members were assessed at IHD monthly from 1 through 15 months, every 3 months from 18 through 36 months, annually from 4 through 7 years, semiannually from 8 through 18 years, and again at about 21, 26, and 36 years.

Health histories were taken at all visits. From 2 through 18 years, medical examinations were given annually by the physicians who examined the GS and OGS members, using the same forms and instruments. In addition, blood pressures, pulse rate, respiratory rate, body temperature, and reflexes were recorded at each visit through 18 months by the pediatrician who made the neonatal measures. At 10 years, 30 BGS members received the physiological battery used in the Oakland Growth Study (OGS) (see next section). At 36 years, the medical examination and history were done by an internist. Currently, at about age 50, BGS members are undergoing a health screening (including detailed medical history) similar to that in which the members of the other two studies participated in 1969–1972, when the GS group was about 40 years old and the Oakland Growth Study group (OGS) about 48 (see Chapter 3). A battery of anthropometrics, more extensive than that in GS or OGS, was taken at all ages. Body photographs were made from 1 month through 36 years. X-rays of the knee were taken within the first few days of life and annually for the first 4 years; hand–wrist X-rays were made annually from 8 through 18 years or until the epiphyses were closed, indicating essential skeletal maturity.

Gross motor tests were administered from 1 month through 9 years, strength tests from 8 through 18 years and at each adult recall, and tests of manual skills during infancy and from 4½ through 9 years and periodically through 15 years. The California First Year Mental Scale, forerunner of the Bayley Scales of Infant Development (Bayley, 1969), was administered monthly from 1 through 15 months and the California Preschool Schedule (see the foregoing for GS) at each visit from 18 through 60 months. As did the GS, the BGS children took the 1916 Stanford revision of the Binet at 6 and 7 years. The two forms of the 1937 revision became available when they were 8, so these were alternated through most of the years to 17. Different forms of the Terman–McNemar group test of intelligence were substituted at 13 and 15, and the Wechsler-Bellevue, Form I, at 16. The latter was repeated at 18, 21, and 26 years and then replaced at 36 with the WAIS.

During their children's first 3 years, BGS mothers were interviewed at each visit about the child's routine and feeding using the schedule developed in GS. Mothers were also observed during these visits by a psychologist not involved in the measurements. She and Dr. Bayley independently completed a personality rating scale on each child and made narrative notes of their observations immediately after the visit. When the children were between 9 and 14 years, data on parental child-rearing attitudes and practices and socioeconomic characteristics of the family and their dwelling were obtained by a clinical psychologist who interviewed the parents once or twice in their homes. Later her interviews and the notes made during the first 3 years served as the basis for ratings of maternal personality and child-rearing attitudes and practices made independently by two developmental psychologists (Schaefer, Bell, & Bayley, 1959). The detailed data on the parents and home were also used to update and extend socioeconomic ratings. Most participants have been visited in their adult homes during the longitudinal study of their offspring (Eichorn, 1973).

At all sessions, participants were rated on personality traits from behaviors during the several kinds of examinations (Schaeffer & Bayley, 1963). The Scale of Behavioral Reactions used during childhood and adolescence was identical to that used in both GS and OGS for rating behavior and attitudes during mental tests and included ratings on 5- or 7-point scales for 33 items such as cooperation, attentiveness, activity, independence, shyness, and self-confidence. Notes were also made about behaviors, attitudes, and participants' and their relatives' reports of events in their lives. Projective tests, such as the TAT and Rorschach, and inventories of leisure time, interest, personality, and vocational preference (usually ones also used in GS and/or OGS) were included on an irregular schedule after age 8.

When the participants were about 36, a male clinical psychologist and a female psychiatric social worker, neither of whom had previous acquaintance with the participants nor access to other data about them, conducted intensive interviews covering facts and attitudes about marriage, parenting, education, occupation, residence, recreation, community and political activities, and a "life morale capitulation" (see GS, in the foregoing). This interview was adapted from the one used with GS at 30 and OGS at 38. At their 36-year recall, BGS members also completed the California Psychological Inventory (CPI), a self-report personality questionnaire, also used at adult recalls in GS and OGS (see Chapter 10).

Oakland Growth Study

The OGS was undertaken in 1931 by Harold E. and Mary C. Jones and Herbert R. Stolz, a physician and first director of the Institute of Child Welfare (now IHD). Originally called the Adolescent Growth Study, it was designed to study normal adolescence, particularly physical and physiological maturation and peer relationships. The 212 original participants were recruited from the high fifth and low sixth grades of five elementary schools in Oakland. In addition to the consent of the youngsters and their parents, selection was based on intent to attend the junior high school chosen as the center of observation for the research.

When the initial measures were taken in 1932, the youngsters ranged from 10 to 12 years. Their median birthdate was May 4, 1921, so this sample is, on the average, 7.75 years older than the GS–BGS cohort (median birthdate was October 28, 1928). Although the OGS was limited to Caucasians because other ethnic groups were too small to provide subgroups of adequate size, the sample was reasonably representative of the population attending Oakland schools at the time (92% Caucasian). Data taken in classrooms and other group situations usually included all members of the school class present (both to provide the complete context and to avoid discrimination).

Participants came to IHD semiannually through the 6 years of junior and senior high school. They were scheduled in same-sex groups of six to eight persons who, in addition to being tested and measured, lunched together and engaged in free-play during this period. During these lunch hours three staff members made observational notes and independent ratings (called ICW—Institute of Child Welfare—Ratings) of behaviors and personal characteristics important in social relationships, for example, talkative, active, physically attractive. Other narrative notes and ratings were made in mixed-sex school and social situations, such as picnics, dances, or athletic events, and, particularly, in the clubhouse ("Clubhouse Ratings") established by the study near the school playground (H. E. Jones, 1940; Newman, 1946).

As in GS, teachers' appraisals, school attendance records, and grades were regularly obtained, and a sociometric "Guess Who" test (Tryon, 1939b), similar to the Reputation Test used in GS (see the foregoing), was administered in classrooms each year to get peer judgments of behavior and personality. A year after the participants graduated from high school three staff members who had known them well made independent ratings on 5-point scales of inferred motivations, using a list of nine "drives" (autonomy, social ties, achievement, recognition, abasement, aggression, succorance, dominance, and escape) adapted from Murray's (1938) schema. In Chapter 9, Jones uses a number of these measures, for example, the ICW and Clubhouse Ratings and "Guess Who" scores, to assess the adolescent personalities of problem drinkers.

The OGS youngsters completed inventories of adjustment, interests and attitudes, and vocational preferences, as well as individual and group intelligence and achievement tests (e.g., 1937 Stanford–Binet, Terman–McNemar, Kuhlman–Anderson, Stanford Achievement, and Iowa Reading), and projective tests, including, as in GS and BGS, the TAT and Rorschach. They also provided sociocultural information about their families in classroom tests (Burdick, Heilman–Simas). Sociocultural data from the parents, particularly the mothers, were obtained in interviews at the onset of the study and again when the youngsters were about 14. Photographs and ratings of the dwelling were also made, and a socioeconomic interview with the parents provided data on ethnicity, education, income, and changes in life-style during the Great Depression (Chapter 1). The GS parental interview schedule was used to obtain information about the child and parents from the pregnancy to the time of the interview. Thus this part of the interview covered health, habits and regime, personality characteristics, play, friendships, interests, and parents' attitudes and practices with respect to child-rearing. From these interviews ratings were made of parental attitudes, adequacies, and personality characteristics.

Half of the OGS sample ("physiological panel") received a battery of physiological measures under basal and exercise conditions on 2 successive days every 6 months (Shock, 1944a,b,c, 1946a,b). These assessments included systolic and diastolic blood pressure, pulse rate (these three measures are also available for all participants in all three studies from the medical examinations), oral temperature, respiratory rate, oxygen consumption, carbon dioxide production, breath holding, vital capacity, urinalysis, exercise recovery curves for the respiratory and cardiovascular measures, and galvanic skin responses under a variety of experimental conditions. All OGS members had a medical examination, health history, strength tests, body build photographs, and anthropometrics semiannually. Hand–wrist X-rays were taken semiannually from about 14 through 17 years; optometric examinations and diet and menstrual records were taken on several occasions.

Adult recalls of OGS centered around ages 33 and 38. However, additional mail inquiries or assessments of subgroups were done on several occasions between the ages of about 20 to 42. Data collection at 33 included a repetition of the Terman–McNemar group test of intelligence, anthropometrics, medical and optometric examinations, health histories of self, parents, and siblings; interviews dealing with occupation, marriage and family, recreation, and social adjustment; personality tests (CPI, Edwards Personal Preference Scale, and Minnesota Multiphasic), projective tests (Rorschach, TAT, Draw-a-Person), personality ratings by staff, and galvanic skin responses in situations similar to those used in adolescence A laboratory assessment of the physiological panel, conducted at the University's Cowell Hospital, included analyses of blood and urine, basal metabolism as estimated by both conventional (as in adolescence) and radioactive iodine techniques, oral temperature, various measures of respiratory and cardiovascular functions like those done during adolescence, exchangeable body sodium, chest X-ray, and electrocardiogram. At about age 38, the assessment included self-ratings of personality and an intensive interview (about 12 hours) conducted by one of a staff of six experienced clinical psychologists and one psychiatric social worker.

Summary

Although these three longitudinal studies differed in origins and objectives, they had a number of features in common, each obtaining many assessments of cognitive, personality, social, and biological characteristics. More specifically, all three studies obtained medical examinations (including systolic and diastolic blood pressures and pulse rates), health and dietary histories, anthropometrics, X-rays for assessing skeletal maturation, demographic and socioeconomic data, personality assessment, chronologies of education, occupation, deaths, marriages, births, and other events in the lives of the participants and their families of origin and procreation. In many instances the same staff made the same examinations, tests, and ratings.

Each initial sample was equally divided between males and females, but only the GS, in sampling every third birth in Berkeley, included small numbers (3%) of Blacks, because non-Caucasians constituted only a minor fraction of the Berkeley and Oakland populations in the 1920s and 1930s. Also, the socioeconomic range of the families of origin is similar across samples, although about 40% of the OGS came from working-class homes compared to slightly over 33% of the two Berkeley samples—a difference in keeping with the population characteristics of these two cities at the time. As adults, 90% of all three groups are middle class. Whether as a result of financial restrictions limiting our ability to see participants (see next section), deaths or other causes, some evidence of selective attrition appear in the combined GS and BGS data at adult follow-ups (Table 2.1), that is, middle and lower class men are less well represented. At least suggestive evidence of selective drop-out among lower IQ participants is also found (see Chapter 4).

INTERGENERATIONAL STUDIES

Despite the similarities just summarized, a number of differences existed among studies, and the staff became increasingly concerned that attrition would progressively decrease the adequacy of the separate samples for assessing adult development and aging. Therefore, steps were taken to facilitate pooling data across studies. The first, described in the following under Q-sort assessments, was to find a common means for describing personality characteristics at different ages that could be derived from the diverse sorts of data collected earlier in the three studies. With that task accomplished, it was then

Dorothy H. Eichorn

Table 2.1
Guidance and Oakland Studies
Percent Participation in Adult Follow-ups by Hollingshead
SES Category in 1929–1930

| Level of Adult | Hollingshead SES Category | | | |
Participation	1 & 2	3	4 & 5	Total
	Males			
N	(81)	(70)	(89)	(240)[*]
None	20	29	33	27
Some	22	37	28	29
Full	58	34	39	44
	Females			
N	(75)	(72)	(96)	(243)[**]
None	24	14	26	22
Some	12	33	31	26
Full	64	53	43	52

[*]There are 17 cases for which data on 1929–1930 SES are missing or insufficient to allow coding.

[**]There are 21 cases for which data on 1929–1930 SES are missing or insufficient to allow coding.

possible to plan a follow-up in which identical new data from merged samples could be related to archival data. In 1967 the staff, with Eichorn as principal investigator, submitted such a proposal titled "Intergenerational Studies of Development and Aging" (IGS I).

Sample

As the fortunes of this merger illustrate, sociohistorical events affect research as well as the lives of participants. Originally conceived as including all three generations (participants and their parents and offspring) of all three studies, IGS I had to accommodate to a general reduction in federally funded grants. Only members of GS and OGS, their spouses, and offspring from all three studies were brought to Berkeley for assessment. BGS members and spouses could be omitted with least loss of data because they had so recently (1964–1968) participated in a recall. Parents of GS and BGS were interviewed and tested in their homes; a grant "freeze" so delayed funding that the number of surviving OGS parents was no longer large enough to justify data collection under the reduced budget; widowed fathers, another small group, also had to be omitted. Financial limitations also restricted participants in all generations (subjects, spouses, and offspring) to California residents except when travel plans of the families or staff made data collection at IHD or home locations possible at modest cost. During the period of data collection (1969–1972) 144 members of GS (about age 40), 107 members of OGS (about 48), 190 of their spouses (aged 31–58), 756 children (aged 3–31), and 171 GS and BGS parents (aged 59–81) were assessed.

Procedures

The WAIS was administered to original participants, their spouses and parents. In the earlier BGS follow-up, this test was given to 54 participants and about 67% of their spouses. Offspring of the GS and OGS who were under 18 were tested twice, once with the age-appropriate Wechsler Scale (WPPSI, WISC, or WAIS) and once with the test taken by their study parent when he or she was of the same age. Those over 18 were tested once with the WAIS. As noted earlier, the longitudinal testing program for BGS offspring parallels that of their study parents, but beginning during IGS, the WISC was added at 11, 13, or 15 to augment the sample of offspring with childhood Wechsler Scales.

A health screening examination for GS and OGS members only was done at the East Bay Health Screening Center of Alta Bates Hospital in Berkeley. It included tests of vision, tonometry, audiometry, blood pressures, pulse rate, ECG, forced vital capacity, 1-second forced expiratory volume, chest X-ray, urinalysis, serology, hematology, and blood chemistry. The standardized health history covered primary current and past problems, a systemic review, habits and appetite, general health, exercise, and family history. Hand–wrist X-rays were done at IHD, as was the battery of anthropometric measurements (identical to that used with the BGS at 36 years). GS also completed a food preference list like that used in BGS at 36 years.

The behavioral and social assessments included an interview (the average time being 4 hours) and a detailed questionnaire for study members, their parents and spouses, and offspring aged 14–18. These instruments were the sources of updated histories on residence, education, occupation, and family (health, personality of all family members, attitudes, interactions, and child-rearing practices) and included a life review of changes, stresses, and satisfactions. Data were obtained on both family of origin and family of procreation. Interviews and questionnaires for spouses and offspring paralleled those for study members. Among the topics covered in the interview with parents were current health status; age at, and cause of, death of parents (study members' grandparents) and siblings (study members' aunts and uncles); and interactions with the study member and his or her offspring. Chapter 12 reports some analyses of the cross-generational data.

Other behavioral data included, for study members and spouses, the CPI, (also used in the previous adult recall, see the foregoing), and vocational interest tests for teenage offspring. The personalities of all children were rated after the standardized intelligence test at each visit on the Scale of Behavioral Reactions used under the same circumstances with the original participants during their childhood and adolescence. Kohlberg's Moral Judgment Interview and two of Piaget's tasks for assessing cognitive development were administered to OGS members, their spouses, and their offspring aged 14 or older.

Many of the data collected during IGS I were coded and analyzed during the next grant period (IGS II, May 1, 1974 through December 31, 1978). The following section describes ratings or other derived measures used in more than one of the substantive chapters in this book. Where needed, more detail is provided in the major chapter addressed to the measure. Assessment techniques used in only one chapter are described in that chapter.

Derived Measures

To systematize the medical records, each of the two physicians independently completed the following assessments:

1. physical complaints, taken from the medical histories at approximate ages (depending upon the sample) of 30, 33, 36, 40 and 50; these were organized by organ systems, sex and age in terms both of the percentage of total symptoms classifiable within each system and the percentage of persons with each type of complaint;

2. physicians' physical findings from the medical examinations at these ages, organized in the same way as complaints;

3. laboratory findings at age 34 (OGS only), 40, and 50, similarly organized (these are not available for BGS, who had only physicians' examinations at 36);

4. clinical health ratings of overall health on a 5-point scale (excellent to very poor) for all childhood and adult ages; conference ratings for adult ages were then made;

5. cause of death for the 33 deceased cases;

6. a general health index summarizing all the health screening and physiological data (see Chapter 3);

To avoid bias, ratings on all subjects for one age were done before proceeding to the next age, and no individual's case history across all ages was reviewed until ratings at each age had been completed.

Q Sorts of Personality Characteristics

A very pressing need was a common measure for personality characteristics that could be derived from the diverse sorts of data collected in the three studies. After consideration of the alternatives available, the staff selected the Q sort (Block, 1961; Stephenson, 1953) as the method of choice. A Q sort consists of a set of descriptive items, such as "favors conservative values in a variety of areas" and "seeks reassurance from others." The judge doing a Q sort places the items in a forced normal distribution of nine categories in which the lower scores, that is, 1–3, represent traits or behaviors *least* characteristic of the person being rated, the higher scores, that is, 7–9, those most characteristic, and the middle scores, 4–6, those moderately characteristic. This is an *ipsative* procedure in which the relative saliency of each item is judged *within the individual's personality,* rather than a *normative* one in which the person is judged against age and sex peers. Because the information on which judges base Q-sort ratings can be of various kinds—for example, interviews, case records, observational notes—the method has the marked advantage for pooling across studies that identical information for each sample is not necessary, only source material of sufficient breadth and depth. Other advantages, as well as disadvantages, of this procedure are described in Chapter 5.

Q sorts for different age periods were done in three phases. Work on those for early and late adolescence and early adulthood for GS and OGS was begun in 1960 by a committee of IHD staff chaired by Jack Block. Most of this process was accomplished between 1961 and 1969, first (1961–1966) under a grant to Block and Clausen and subsequently under grants to Block for analyses done by him and Norma Haan. These phases were thoroughly documented by Block, (1971) in collaboration with Haan, so they are only summarized here.

Q sorts were done separately for early adolescence, late adolescence and early adulthood (about age 30 for GS and 38 for OGS). Each of the adolescent sorts was based upon a separate case assembly of most of the archival material for each participant, one for ages 12–14 (early adolescence) and one for ages 15–18 (late adolescence). All data based on parent interviews and certain tests (e.g., the CPI) and ratings (e.g., "drive" ratings, see above) were withheld from judges to permit independent assessments. The early adult sorts were based upon interviews lasting an average of 12 hours distributed over several days. The raters were 26 clinical psychologists (21 held Ph.D.'s) and one psychiatric social worker, all but two of whom had 10 or more years of clinical experience. Many also had research and clinical publications. Eleven were male and 16 were female.

Raters were trained to do three different Q sorts: (*a*) the 104-item Core Q sort of personality characteristics and behaviors; (*b*) the Interpersonal Q sort, a 63-item sort dealing with differential behavior toward peers and adults, roles in peer groups, attitudes toward parents, and the like; and (*c*) an Environmental Q sort of 92 items describing the parents and home. The latter two sorts were done only for the two adolescent periods.

At least three judges rated each adolescent and at least two rated each adult. Combinations of raters were systematically varied, and no judge rated the same case at more than one age. The reliability of the composite Q sorts for each participant at each age was calculated by averaging the z transformations of the interjudge correlations. The Spearman-Brown reliability formula for the appropriate number of observations was then applied. Extra raters were used if the reliability of an individual's composite for *either* the Core or Interpersonal Sort was less than .60, when both were less than .65, or when either was between .60 and .65. Additional raters were required for 35% of the adolescents and 53% of the adults. The mean of the final composite reliabilities ranged from .72 to .78 (Figs. 2.1 and 2.2), depending upon sex and age, with the Interpersonal sorts yielding slightly higher agreements.

Interjudge reliabilities for individual *items,* as opposed to persons, were calculated by intraclass correlation for the 90 items common to the adolescent and adult sorts. The mean item reliabilities (Fig. 2.3) were: .63, early adolescence; .68, late adolescence; and .68, early adulthood.

The middle adult Q sorts are based on interviews averaging 4 hours in length done during IGS I, when GS members were about age 40 and OGS members about 48. The interviewers (all female) were seven clinical psychologists and one psychiatric social worker. None had previous contact with the participants whom they rated. Each case was Q-sorted by the interviewer and, from the verbatim transcript of the interview, by at least one other member of the interviewing staff. If their initial agreement was below .45 for an uncorrected individual Q

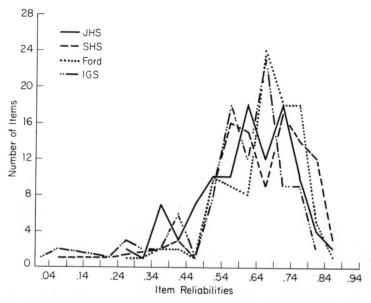

Fig. 2.1 Distribution of Q-sort item reliabilities for females.

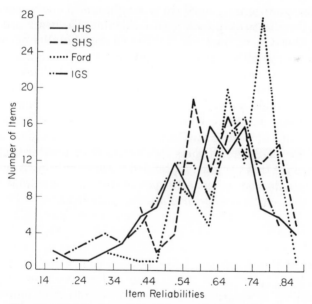

Fig. 2.2 Distribution of Q-sort item reliabilities for males.

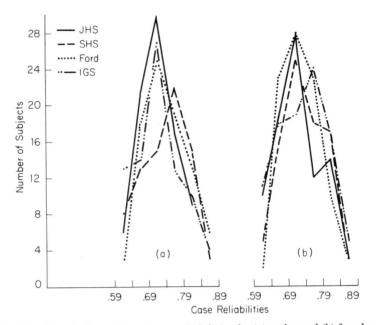

Fig. 2.3   Distribution of Q-sort case reliabilities for (a) males and (b) females.

correlation, additional raters (to a maximum of four) were used to bring the reliability of the composite, calculated as described above for early adulthood, to at least .65–.70. The mean reliability of the composite scores for individual *items* was .60. Figures 2.1 to 2.3 summarize graphically the distribution of case and item reliabilities.

During the last year of IGS II and subsequently, Q sorts for both adolescent periods as well as two childhood periods (early and late) were completed for BGS. In the earlier years of that grant, the two childhood sorts were done for GS (preadolescent data are not available, of course, for OGS). Adult sorts for BGS were done after their 36-year recall. Because this volume is intended to cover only early adolescence through middle age, when all types of data are maximal across all three studies, childhood Q-sorts are not included.

PARAFAC

Individual items are less reliable than composite scores and pose other statistical problems—the number of items becomes large relative to the number of subjects and statistical significance cannot be precisely assessed because many items are intercorrelated, presumably because they reflect the same underlying dimension(s). One method of reducing the many Q-sort items to a smaller number of underlying dimensions is PARAFAC, a form of factor analysis for repeated measurements. Details on this procedure are given in the Appendix A and in Chapter 5.

Cluster Analysis

Another approach to underlying dimensions is represented by the cluster analysis on which Chapters 6 and 7 are based. Using rotational devices that maximize intermatrix agreement N. Livson found patterns of intercorrelations (hence, dimensionality) that were sufficiently similar to justify combining the correlation matrices of eight subsamples (two adolescent periods × two sexes × two cohorts). Then a cluster analysis was done from the single pooled matrix, providing much more reliable correlation estimates. An 11-cluster solution was obtained that accounted for 98% of the reliable covariance among the 90 Q-sort items common to both the adolescent and adult Q sorts. (The BCTRY program accepts only 90 variables.) To extend the solution to the full Q set, items not used in the original clustering were introduced and the analysis rerun. First, however, the intercorrelations between the eliminated and introduced items were examined to ascertain if additional clusters were created by the two subsets. None was. Nor did additional clusters emerge on the rerun with the "new" items. As a final check, the fit of each of the 11 clusters to the original eight intercorrelation matrices was checked by computing all 88 (8 × 11) internal consistency coefficients. Because all were quite high, the initial 11-cluster solution was retained.

Most of the "residual" single variables show poor inter-rater agreement, so failure of these items to appear in the clusters can be attributed to their unreliability. However, eight items showed substantial rater agreement; these probably tap unique facets of personality not "explained" by the clusters. Because the intent of the cluster analysis is to find the minimal number of dimensions necessary to account for all reliable information in the Q sorts, these items were added as separate "clusters," producing a final set of 19 dimensions for the 104-item adolescent Q sort. These 19 variables are used in Chapters 6 and 7 to assess the predictability of adult psychological health.

Psychological Health Index

Four experienced clinical psychologists were asked to do a Q sort that would characterize a psychologically healthy person (Livson & Peskin, 1967). The composite of their independent sorts (reliability, .95; average first-order inter-rater agreement, .82), constituted the criterion of psychological health. The correlation of any study member's Q sort with this composite is his or her "psychological health" score. Within our samples this index has only very low and statistically insignificant correlations with IQ from childhood through adolescence or with indices of socioeconomic status (parental education, family income, father's occupation), and the criterion sort is highly similar for the two sexes. This composite psychological health Q sort is very similar to the criterion Q sort developed independently by Block (1961) for the "optimally adjusted personality"; the two sorts correlate .91.

Marital Relations Q Sort

Skolnick developed a Marital Relations Q sort to describe marriages across a number of dimensions, for example, expectations and assumptions about marriage, satisfactions and dissatisfactions with spouse's performance of marital roles, depth and quality of the personal relationship between spouses, division of labor within the household, patterns of conflict and dominance, leisure activities, and relations with kin, friends, and community. Most items are intended to be descriptive, that is, based on self-reports of behavior or feeling, rather than on a rater's inferences about underlying processes. This Q sort was tested on 50 men and their spouses and 50 women and their spouses selected randomly except that, for each sex, 25 pairs came from GS and 25 from OGS. Reliabilities were satisfactory (.76), and the sorts did not resemble one another in stereotypic fashion.

ORIENTATION TO SUBSTANTIVE CHAPTERS

The analysis and reporting of long-term, multifaceted longitudinal data pose special problems. If one analyzes across a long time span, say from infancy through adulthood, it is almost impossible to present in one report analyses of more than one or two types of data. We have published in the past, and shall continue to publish, papers and monographs that focus on one aspect of human development, such as the influence of child-rearing practices on personality development.

But another perspective is needed—one that describes concurrent development in the major domains of physical health, personality, intellectual abilities, and social relationships and attempts to achieve some integration, some flavor of "whole persons," through examining associations among domains. Only by restricting the time span examined can this even more difficult task be approximated at present, for our tools—instruments and statistics—are still inadequate. Further, were we to wait for time and funds to do all the analyses we think important, including updating analyses as cases from one or another study are finally coded in a particular fashion, publication would be even longer delayed.

For these reasons we restrict our purview primarily to the segment of the life span between early adolescence (12–14) and mid-life (about 36–50). Within this span we have data in each domain for all three of our samples, although not all specific measures were taken in all three, or, for lack of funds, had been rated for all three in time to include them here. We present one general chapter on each domain intended to describe the status of our study members at mid-life, their development within that domain, and some associations across domains. Because our groups are not random samples of the United States population, we include wherever possible comparisons with more representative groups, such as the normative samples for tests or census data on socioeconomic status or divorce. Such data give the reader some basis for judging the extent to which our results can be generalized to other persons of comparable age. To add depth to the more general perspective we report several analyses of selected subgroups, such as Jones's developmental study of problem drinkers and F. Livson's analysis of different paths to "psychological health" in middle age.

Part II

INTRAPERSONAL DIMENSIONS

3

Health in the Middle Years

LEONA M. BAYER, DOROTHY WHISSELL-BUECHY, AND
MARJORIE P. HONZIK

INTRODUCTION

"How are you?" Greetings and toasts quite universally include references to health, implying some popular agreement about its desirability and definition. Yet, great conceptual problems occur in developing indices of health and even in describing health status (Sullivan, 1966). Indeed, the definition of health varies with the society and its goals (Callahan, 1977). The World Health Organization (WHO) defines health as a "state of complete physical, mental, and social well-being, not merely the absence of disease and illness" (1946). In a recent editorial on "total health" Lambo (1975), the deputy general of WHO, points to the need for a balanced consideration of the biological, social, and cultural aspects of health. The present study lends itself well to such multidimensional assessments.

DATA BASE

Physical health is a complex phenomenon that can be assessed from many viewpoints: how the individual feels at the moment of the examination; what the history tells; what the physical examination shows; what the laboratory reveals. We explored all these sources to assess the health status of the study members.

The longitudinal data come from the Berkeley Growth Study (BGS), ages birth to 36; Oakland Growth Study (OGS), ages 11–50; and Guid-

55

ance Study (GS) with its Control Group, birth to 42 years. During childhood and adolescence the data consist primarily of anthropometric measures, medical examinations, and brief health histories since the previous appointment (Macfarlane, 1938). Bayer and Snyder (1950) analyzed the childhood and adolescent illness experiences of the Guidance Group of GS. Half the OGS also had laboratory tests of physiologic functions that have been extensively reported (see, e.g., Shock, 1944a, 1946b).

The GS at 30 years and BGS at 36 had examinations similar to those in childhood and adolescence. The OGS participated in an intensive overnight hospital study at 34 years. Laboratory tests, as well as extensive histories and medical examinations, were done. At 42 years GS underwent a multiphasic health screening at the East Bay Health Screening Center; this included computerized histories, some anthropometric measures, and 35 laboratory procedures. At 50 the OGS had the same health screening as did GS at 42. Ratings on all samples are used to trace health trends from birth to the middle years.

Because of methodological differences among the adult examinations, the data were organized pragmatically. Self-assessments of health status in the middle years were taken from nonmedical interviews or excerpted from computer-taken medical histories. Health histories obtained by physicians or computer were used to determine illness experience and present complaints. Physicians' findings from the medical examinations and physiologic tests were reviewed for information about physical and physiological status at specific ages. From these different sources, overall ratings of physical health (described in a later section) were made for each participant at each adult examination.

Only large representative samples can yield definitive age norms. The small, restricted samples characteristic of long-term longitudinal research serve to provide depth to the necessarily more superficial assessments of large-scale studies by examining health from a number of perspectives, both antecedent and concurrent. Thus we report here not only several ways of evaluating the adult health of our study members from data collected concurrently but also interage correlations for a number of measures to assess continuity and change both within these aspects of health and in their associations with such potential influences on health as socioeconomic status, smoking, drinking, and personality characteristics. In describing participants' status on parameters of adult health, we attempt to set them in the context of reference norms from larger samples, such as United States public health surveys. The reader then has some basis for judging the extent to which the age trends and associations found in our samples represent more general phenomena.

SELF-ASSESSMENTS OF HEALTH

Self-assessments of health were obtained from nonmedical interviews at 30 (GS) and 38 (OGS). (No objective health data were obtained at the time of the OGS 38-year interviews.) At 42 (GS) and 50 (OGS) responses were to computerized questions. More than 80% of the participants considered themselves in good-to-excellent health throughout the middle years. This finding accords with the United States Public Health Service report (1976:243) that "the American people think of themselves as being in good health."

The highest percentages of self-ratings of "good" or "excellent" were among GS women at 30 (92%) and GS men at 42 (98%). Although 80% of OGS women considered themselves in good health at 50, 16% considered themselves in poor health, a higher proportion than at any other age in either sex in either cohort. (Indeed, by age 38, 7% of the OGS women already considered themselves in poor health.) In contrast to self-reports of declining health, overall health ratings by physicians show no mean change between 34 and 50 (see section on health ratings).

Comparing self-reports of both sexes at about 40, we find significantly fewer ($p < .05$) 38-year-old OGS members than 42-year-old GS members assessed their health as good or excellent. This sample or cohort difference also appears in the illness histories and laboratory findings described in the following sections.

MEDICAL ASSESSMENTS

Illness Experience

In spite of the generally favorable self-assessments of health, the 395 adult medical protocols record many and increasing numbers of complaints and illnesses. At 30 (GS) and 34 (OGS) the histories were taken by physicians; at 42 (GS) and 50 (OGS) participants responded to a computer-based history. From these sources, we describe the patterns of illness experience during the middle years.

Responses to questions about health were classified into 18 categories describing organ systems or areas of involvement. In most instances a complaint belonged in only one category. However, some complaints had to be placed in two or three categories: a broken leg was entered under injury, extremity, and musculoskeletal; a cholecystectomy (gall bladder removal) under surgery and gastrointestinal.

Table 3.1 shows the percentage of men and women with complaints in each category at four adult periods. Complaints listed at a given age include the experience of the years since the previous examination. A summary of age trends and sex and cohort differences in organ systems and areas of involvement follows.

Age Changes

The percentage of women with complaints increases with age in both cohorts and for every category of illness (Table 3.1). The pattern is similar for men with two exceptions: in both cohorts, the proportion

Table 3.1

Illness Experience of Men and Women
at Ages 30, 34, 42, and 50 Years
(% of Individuals with Complaints in Each of 18 Categories)

Illness category	Men (%)				Women (%)			
	GS $N=61$	OGS $N=34$	GS $N=41$	OGS $N=25$	GS $N=69$	OGS $N=60$	GS $N=43$	OGS $N=50$
Age	30	34	42	50	30	34	42	50
Eyes	3	13	44	96	1	12	78	96
Ears	7	20	17	32	0	15	14	20
Respiratory	89	50	49	44	65	37	69	64
Cardiovascular	8	12	22	52	10	18	59	60
Gastrointestinal	62	50	80	88	41	45	74	76
Urinary	16	8	51	76	28	27	76	84
Reproductive	7	5	51	28	48	75	98	84
Nervous (CNS-PNS)	44	27	49	52	43	40	63	68
Skin	31	8	49	36	33	13	49	60
Hematologic	2	5	2	4	6	8	16	36
Endocrinologic	2	0	27	28	19	20	57	68
Musculo-skeletal	34	17	56	76	32	10	75	76
Extremities	33	25	63	68	28	3	88	92
Injuries	31	23	51	48	20	7	41	52
Surgery	28	45	71	84	33	53	76	80
Allergies	31	15	32	40	35	15	57	68
Infections	36	50	20	48	45	32	53	48
Emotional	21	23	54	56	17	37	86	84

with respiratory and infectious complaints decreases with age, and hematologic complaints show no real age change.

The predominant categories of malaise and dysfunction also shift with age. Where such shifts are marked, they can be ascribed primarily to a change in the nature of complaints from actue to chronic. At 30 and 34, infections, especially of the upper respiratory and lower urinary tracts, are common complaints. At 42 and 50, urinary malfunction and visual difficulties replace infections as leading sources of complaints. This shift from acute to more chronic problems occurs in all categories. Complaints about the ear, for example, shift from pain and drainage to hearing loss and tinnitus (ringing in the ear); musculoskeletal complaints shift from strains and sprains to chronic pain, stiffness and limitations of movement. Complaints of chronic bronchitis, emphysema, hypertension, arthritis, and metabolic disease make their appearance early and increase with age. Increasing complaints about chronic disorders is characteristic of aging populations. However, the prominence of these complaints in early middle age in these relatively advantaged cohorts is both noteworthy and unexpected because the participants at 40 and 50 appeared at first glance to be in excellent health.

Sex Differences

From late adolescence to age 50, the most common source of complaints among men is the digestive system; among women, it is the reproductive system (see Table 3.1). Men suffer over three times the number of peptic ulcers and complain more often of stomach pain. During the childbearing years, miscarriage is a major source of gynecologic complaints among women. In the later years uterine fibroids and ovarian cysts are an increasing source of malaise. Menstrual problems are common throughout, changing from pain and tension in early maturity to irregular flow later.

In addition to gynecologic difficulties, and with the exception of gastrointestinal problems, women report more illness than men in all categories. The high proportion of women with cardiovascular complaints is noteworthy in view of women's generally lower cardiac morbidity. Inspection of the medical records reveals that many of these complaints are classified as functional or pregnancy related.

The high incidence of the women's complaints contrasts with the known longevity of females. Perhaps the paradox can be explained in part by women's greater awareness of their bodies because of cyclic rhythm and childbearing and child-rearing functions. Similar contrasts have been reported by other investigators (Waldron & Johnston,

1976). In the GS women, illness experiences reported at 42 correlate
with physiologic status at that time ($r = 0.48$); no such correlation was
found for the males, who were judged physiologically less well. Perhaps
men are somatically less aware or more reluctant to report malaise, or
both. Some of the difference is explained by the number of men with
incipient hypertension, which is usually asymptomatic.

Cohort or Sample Differences

A few differences among the samples may reflect dissimilarities in
life experiences as a result of historical events or socioeconomic differences. Half of the OGS men at 34 complained of infections. These
infections include dengue fever, malaria, and bacillary dysentery, con-
tracted during World War II. A different kind of historical contrast is
suggested by the relatively high percentage of GS men reporting deviations in the reproductive system at 42. These include vasectomies,
which have been performed with increasing frequency since the middle
of this century, mirroring changing attitudes toward, and technical
capability for, family planning.

A higher proportion of 34-year-old OGS women than 30-year-old GS
women had complaints about the reproductive system; OGS women
also had more complications of pregnancy and delivery such as fetal
loss and toxemia. In addition, OGS women at 34 reported more
menstrual difficulties than did GS women at 30. These differences are
at least partly explained by the somewhat longer reproductive period
already experienced by the older group. By 42, 98% of GS women had
complaints about the reproductive system, almost half of which concerned the menses. The most common complaint, premenstrual tension, is a disorder that was less clearly recognized as an entity until
after the 30- and 34-year follow-ups.

Comparison with United States Public Health Survey Data

The illness histories of our sample are quite similar to findings reported from a 1975 health survey in the United States. Combining the
two cohorts, we have data for approximate ages of 30 (GS), 34 (OGS),
42 (GS), and 50 (OGS). The best standard against which to judge the
representativeness of these complaint histories should be the United
States Public Health Service interview data. Unfortunately, the authors of the report on those findings point to several problems with the
interview data. Therefore, we used instead the findings they consider
more reliable, that is, hospital discharges in their 15- to 44-year age
group (1976:523). A marked similarity between our areas of common
complaints and their most frequent causes for hospitalization is seen in
this list, presented in order of decreasing frequency.

Sexes Combined

GS and OGS data complaints (30–50 years)	U.S. hospitalizations (15–44 years)
1. Genito-urinary	1. Genito-urinary
2. Gastrointestinal	2. Accidents
3. Respiratory	3. Gastrointestinal
4. Nervous system	4. Respiratory
5. Emotional	5. Mental
6. Musculoskeletal	6. Musculoskeletal
7. Allergy	7. Neoplasm
8. Skin	8. Circulatory
9. Injuries	9. Nervous system or sense organs

The similarities are expectable because, in general, the most common problems are also the most common causes for hospitalization. The differences, which occur in the least frequent categories, may reflect the fact that some less common complaints may be more serious and thus more often require hospitalization. Examples are neoplasms, circulatory disorders, and accidents. In our samples, only 2% had surgery for neoplasms and 3% had cardiovascular surgery; the majority of reported injuries required at least short-term hospitalization.

Comparisons can also be made between acute and chronic disorders in our data and in the United States survey. The total incidence of acute disorders (infections and infestations, acute respiratory ailments, and injuries) reported by our participants during the early adult years was much greater than that reported in the United States interview data for persons aged 17–44 years (United States Public Health Survey, 1976, p. 479). When comparisons are made within the categories of acute illness, only injuries are less frequent among our women than in the national data for women.

If the OGS at 50 are compared to the 45- to 64-year category of the survey (United States Public Health Survey, 1976, p. 485), no significant differences are seen for women. For men, however, respiratory conditions are half as frequent, but injuries twice as common, as in the national survey. Thus, although injuries decrease relative to other complaints in the 50-year-old OGS men, they exceed the national figures at nearly every age period.

For the younger ages (30 and 34), the incidence of chronic conditions agrees fairly well with the United States data (United States Public Health Survey, 1976, p. 483) for persons aged 17–44 years. However, heart conditions and back problems are markedly higher than the United States figures for both sexes. Auditory and visual difficulties are also more prevalent among our younger men than among United States males in general. In the OGS members of both sexes at 50, the incidence of chronic disease is higher than that reported in the United

States 45–64-year age group (United States Public Health Survey, 1976, p. 487), except diabetes, for which the incidence is lower, and hypertension, for which it is about the same.

Greater reporting of both chronic and acute conditions in our samples may be a function of reporting circumstances; our groups have been interviewed frequently and are above average in socioeconomic status.

Summary

Complaints generally increased with age, primarily because of the increasing prevalence of chronic conditions. The trend in both sexes is toward a decrease in complaints of acute disorders and an increase in complaints of a chronic nature. Although patterns differ for men and women, the early age (30-year follow-up) at which chronic complaints appear in both is noteworthy. Also noteworthy is the similarity of major sources of malaise reported by our sample and morbidity statistics reported for the United States.

Physical and Physiological Status

A significant amount of physical and physiologic deviation appears early and makes an often "silent" increase throughout the middle years. The presence and extent of deviation from normal was determined by accepting the evaluations of the examining physicians and then applying generally accepted limits of normal for the standard medical and laboratory procedures (Davidson & Henry, 1969; Harrison, 1974).

Each adult medical examination included measurements of blood pressure, pulse, vision, hearing, and many anthropometric parameters. At 30 and 34 the evaluation included a classic physical examination of all organ systems. At 42 and 50 this kind of examination was largely replaced by laboratory procedures.

The extensive physical examinations document occasional pathology in both sexes. In women, pathology was found most frequently in the breasts and pelvic organs, validating their complaints.

The remainder of this section is confined to a discussion of selected quantitative evaluations. Data on vision and hearing are treated in the following section.

Weight   Change in weight with age is illustrated in Fig. 3.1, where the mean weight/height^3 (linearity) ratios are plotted from 21 months to middle age for the GS and BGS, and from 11 years to 50 for the OGS.

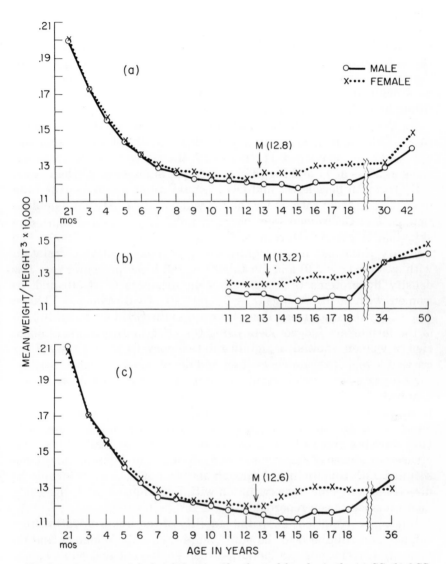

Fig. 3.1 Average weight/height³ ratios of males and females in the (a) GS, (b) OGS, and (c) BGS groups during childhood and at mid-life. M = age at menarche.

Slimming occurs rapidly in both sexes until about 5–7 years and ratios during this period do not differ appreciably for boys and girls. Thereafter, the girls' ratios begin to exceed those of the boys, although until adolescence the rate of change is slow in both sexes. In all three samples the boys' ratios continue to fall until age 15, while the girls' ratios begin to climb between 12 and 15. This weight gain appears in the same year or the year following the onset of menses. Although the boys begin to fill out after 15, the girls remain relatively plumper throughout the second decade.

By the fourth decade the male ratios equal or exceed the female ratios. OGS women, born nearly a decade before the other two samples, are somewhat heavier at 34 than at 17; the GS women are about the same at 30 as at 17 and the BGS women are slimmer at 36 than at 17.

By the fifth decade GS and OGS female ratios again overtake the male. The highest ratio is for the GS women at 42. At that examination, 31% of GS women were obese as judged by weight, height, and skin fold thickness (Durnin & Rahaman, 1967; Vague, 1969). The linearity ratio also has a significant ($p < .001$) positive correlation with systolic ($r = .50$) and diastolic ($r = .60$) blood pressure, very low density lipoproteins ($r = .42$), sleep disturbances ($r = 50$) and, in women, with health ratings ($r = .39$, $p < .01$). OGS women at 50 have essentially the same mean linearity ratio as the GS at 42, but only 11% of the former are judged obese using the criteria already mentioned. Heavy women showed a significant tendency ($p < .05$) toward increased levels of serum cholesterol and decreased vital capacities.

As a group, the middle-aged men were overweight, their *mean* percent body fat exceeding the highest acceptable normal value. No significant correlations of physiological functioning with the linearity ratio were found, perhaps because of reduced variability in these functions. However, the generally poor health of the men, as well as their increased incidence of cardiovascular dysfunction and death, may be associated with this finding. Although obesity has not been shown to be directly atherogenic, its association with hypertension and with early death has long been reported.

Interage correlations show the stability of the linearity ratios from infancy and childhood to the adult years (Fig. 3.2). Moderate and increasing correlations are found between adolescent and adult ratios. The girls' adolescent ratios are more predictive in the GS and BGS, and the boys' in the OGS. Statistically significant prediction of adult ratios is obtained as early as 21 months for GS males ($r = 0.54$, $p < 0.001$) and from 3 years for BGS females ($r = 0.50$, $p < 0.01$). Comparable correlations for GS females and BGS males do not reach significance

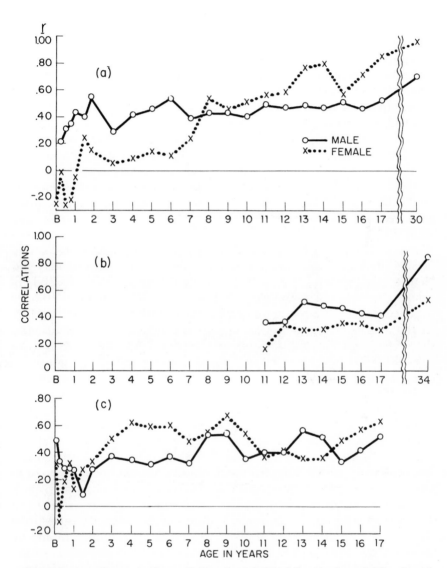

Fig. 3.2 Age changes in the prediction of weight/height³ ratios from childhood to (a) age 42 years in the GS, (b) 50 years in the OGS, and (c) 36 years in the BGS.

until 8 years. Perhaps the most noteworthy finding is the lack of correlation between ratios during the first year (birth, 3, 6, 9, and 12 months) and adult ratios (Girls' correlations are actually negative in both GS and BGS at certain periods during the first year). This failure of prediction is important because of current concern that heavy babies are likely to become obese adults (Bray, 1973).

Table 3.2 contains adult data on 14 physiological measures for GS and OGS. Not shown are pulse rate and blood pressures taken at least yearly (from 21 months to 17 years in BGS and GS and 11–17 years in the OGS).

Table 3.2

Physiologic Measures--Age, Sex, and Cohort Differences

	GS				OGS			
	Age 30		Age 42		Age 34		Age 50	
	Men $N = 61$	Women $N = 69$	Men $N = 41$	Women $N = 52$	Men $N = 60$	Women $N = 60$	Men $N = 25$	Women $N = 25$
	Mean	Mean	Mean	Mean	Mean	Mean	Mean	Mean
Pulse rate (beats/min)	74.1 (8.1)	77.8 (10.0)	67.2 (8.2)	69.6 (10.5)	84.9 (5.6)	85.3 (8.8)	68.5 (8.9)	71.9 (12.3)
Systolic blood pressure (mm Hg)	117.8 (10.8)	112.9 (9.1)	137.5 (15.5)	121.2 (15.6)	131.1 (10.8)	123.0 (9.6)	127.8 (12.9)	117.6 (14.5)
Diastolic blood pressure (mm Hg)	77.4 (7.6)	71.4 (8.3)	87.4 (12.9)	83.8 (11.7)	82.5 (9.0)	77.9 (8.1)	86.7 (8.0)	81.0 (9.9)
Vital capacity (% of predicted)			92.6 (13.9)	91.5 (9.7)	107.7 (15.4)	101.6 (13.2)	91.2 (12.9)	98.6 (32.2)
Timed vital capacity (% of predicted)			77.9 (9.4)	80.1 (7.1)			80.1 (8.3)	75.8 (19.1)
Red blood cells (millions/mm^3)			5.0 (0.4)	4.4 (0.4)	4.9 (0.4)	4.3 (0.4)	5.0 (0.4)	4.4 (0.3)
Hemoglobin (gms/100 ml)			15.6 (1.0)	13.9 (0.9)	14.2 (1.0)	12.7 (1.1)	15.5 (0.9)	14.1 (0.6)
Hematocrit (cc/100 ml)			45.9 (3.1)	41.1 (2.8)	46.5 (2.6)	40.9 (3.2)	45.4 (2.7)	41.5 (1.9)
Cholesterol (mg%)			247.6 (36.1)	218.5 (34.0)	216.1 (36.0)	198.2 (38.3)	250.4 (37.7)	243.4 (48.9)
Total triglycerides (mg%)			163.9 (109.8)	84.1 (35.6)			177.8 (121.6)	128.4 (89.8)
Very low-density lipoproteins (mg%)			147.0 (88.9)	78.9 (33.5)			166.2 (115.7)	113.7 (70.3)
Sf 0 - 12 low-density lipoproteins					356.6 (80.3)	292.3 (84.6)		
Sf 12 - 400 lower and very low-density lipoproteins					150.7 (83.8)	93.8 (73.9)		
Atherogenic index (calculated from plasma lipids)					67.6 (52.1)	45.6 (18.6)		

Note: Numbers in parentheses refer to standard deviations.

Pulse rates fall rapidly in childhood from a range of 115–135 at 21 months to the seventies and eighties in adolescence. Female rates tend to exceed male rates slightly, but this is variable. These findings parallel those described for normal children in pediatric texts. Although in adulthood the female rate is consistently higher than the male rate (Table 3.2), the difference is statistically significant ($p < .05$) only for GS at 30. Table 3.2 indicates a slight tendency toward slowing of the pulse rate as the cohorts enter the middle years. The decrease is statistically significant ($p < .05$) for both sexes between 30 and 42 but not between any of the other adult ages compared. Although pulse rates of a group of 60- to 70-year-olds have been found in one study to be faster than those of a group of 15- to 18-year-olds, suggesting an increase in old age (De Vries & Adams, 1972), cross-sectional data in standard medical and physiological textbooks show declines well into adulthood (Timiras, 1972). Our longitudinal data support a general lowering of the rate at least to 50.

Blood pressure   Mean systolic and diastolic blood pressures rise in both sexes from 21 months to 36 years in BGS and to 42 in GS. The sexes differ little during childhood. Around puberty the curves of the GS and OGS groups begin to diverge, especially those for systolic pressures, with the values for the girls being consistently lower. These sex differences accord with those found in the United States Health Examination Survey of 1966–1970 for children 12–17 years of age (Roberts & Maurer, 1977a). The BGS group differs in two ways from the others—their systolic pressures are lower and the male and female curves are remarkably similar from 21 months through 36 years.

Mean systolic and diastolic pressures for GS and OGS at adult ages are shown in Table 3.2. In all cases the levels are lower in women. This difference is highly significant even to age 50 for systolic pressures. Diastolic pressures show less marked sex differences at 42 and 50 but female values remain lower. In cross-sectional studies of the United States population (Gordon, 1964), female diastolic and systolic values lie below male values until about 50 and above them thereafter. How much of this effect is caused by differential mortality is at present unknown.

At 30 blood pressures in the GS are comparable to age 30 levels in the United States population. However, at 42 GS males have mean diastolic and systolic pressures almost 7 and 10 mm Hg higher, respectively, than United States men aged 35–44 and about 3 mm Hg above that of men aged 45–54. The GS women at 42 have mean diastolic pressures almost 6 mm Hg higher than the United States figures (Gordon, 1964).

In contrast to the GS at 30 and BGS at 36, the mean blood pressures of OGS at 34 were higher than averages for the United States population at either 30 or 40. The 34-year-old "casual" measurements on OGS were made in a hospital situation and may reflect some anxiety, a conjecture supported by their somewhat elevated pulse rates. This possibility may partially explain the decrease in mean systolic pressure from 34–50. However, the systolic pressures are well below the national mean of 133.8 mm Hg for both sexes at an average age of 50 (Gordon, 1964). On the other hand, diastolic pressures rose in OGS from 34 to 50. For men they exceed, and for women they fall short of, the United States mean. In all cases OGS values are below those found for the GS cohort at 42, although only the male systolic pressures differ significantly (ages 34 versus 42, $p < .026$; ages 42 versus 50, $p < .008$).

Because of small numbers, the probably false elevation of systolic pressures at 34 in OGS, and the cohort differences, the failure of OGS blood pressures to rise from 34 to 50 years is difficult to interpret. One explanation may lie in the fact that blood pressure at 34 was lower among those who returned at 50 than those who did not. Also, in several instances hypertension was under treatment at the later age, so the data may mask the true state of affairs—a rise in untreated blood pressure over the years from 21 months to 50 years.

Among GS men at 42, who as a group had the highest mean values, diastolic and systolic pressures were negatively correlated with time spent at sports. For GS women at 42 and OGS men at 50, diastolic pressure was positively correlated with sleep disturbances. Among the GS at 42, diagnosis and treatment of hypertension were rare. The different correlations suggest sex-specific homeostatic mechanisms, which fail when stressed in sex-specific ways and result in hypertension.

The stability of systolic blood pressure measures from early childhood to the adult years was first assessed by correlating adult pressures with earlier levels, beginning at 21 months (GS and BGS) and 12 years (OGS). Although the results, at least for age 6 and older, were positive, some inconsistencies occur among samples and between the sexes. Because of the known lability and, hence, low reliability, of blood pressure measurements, systolic blood pressures were next averaged across age periods and the intercorrelations computed. As illustrated in Fig. 3.3, moderate to high consistency was found except between childhood and adolescence in GS males.

Diastolic pressures from 21 months to 18 years yield low correlations

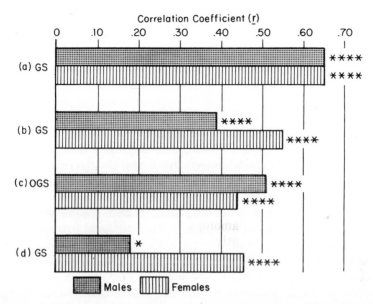

Fig. 3.3 Stability of systolic blood pressure from childhood to the adult years. (a) Childhood × adolescence (5–10 × 11–17 yr); (b) Adolescent × adult years (11–17 × 30–42 yr); (c) Adolescent × adult years (11–17 × 34–50 yr); (d) Childhood × adult (5–10 × 30–42 yr).
   *$p < .10$.
  **$p < .05$.
 ***$p < .01$.
****$p < .001$

with middle-age values. However, there are significant correlations ($p < .05$) between values at 34 and 50 years for both OGS men and women, and for GS women between 30 and 42 years. The essentially zero correlation between diastolic pressures of GS men at 30 and 42 is partially explained by two men whose diastolic pressures rose an average of 44 mm Hg, as compared to 14.6 mm Hg gained on the average by the GS men. When the diastolic pressures are grouped as are the systolic (Fig. 3.3), the results are essentially the same: high consistency except between childhood and adolescence in GS males.

Vital capacity, a test of pulmonary function, was measured at 34 (OGS), 42 (GS) and 50 (OGS). In the men, mean performance is superior at 34, with slightly lower levels in the older groups. In the OGS women little decrease occurs between 34 and 50. The mean for GS at 42, although well within the norm, is lower than the OGS women's means at either adult follow-up.

Timed vital capacity is a test of airway patency. GS men at 42 differ little from OGS men at 50, whereas the OGS women at 50 are slightly lower than GS women at 42. Variability is great, and in all subgroups some individuals fall below the normal range. No significant correlation was found between either of these measures of pulmonary function and smoking.

Red blood cells, hemoglobin, and hematocrit   The average red blood cell counts and red cell indices compare well with normal standards, although a few individuals, especially among the 34-year-old women, were mildly anemic.

Urinalyses in a general screening process are of special interest with regard to metabolic disorders, such as diabetes, and urinary tract disease. Urinalyses were done at 34 (OGS), 42 (GS), and 50 (OGS). Although sugar was found in several instances, it was associated with elevated blood glucose in only one woman. Proteinuria and ketonuria were also found occasionally but did not appear to be clinically significant in context.

Urine cultures were done for most participants at 42 (GS) and 50 (OGS). As expected, suspicious and positive cultures were more common among women than among men and most common among 42-year-old women. Significantly more 42-year-old women had positive cultures than 50-year-old women or either male age group.

Serology tests and Panicolaou smears for syphilis and cervical cancer, respectively, yielded no positive results.

Blood chemistries   Included in the multiphasic examinations (GS at 42, OGS at 50) were thyroid hormone (T4), lipoproteins, and an analysis of 12 blood factors (SMA 12) made on blood drawn 2 hours after an oral dose of 50 g of glucose. The 12 factors were total protein, albumin, calcium, creatinine, inorganic phosphorus, cholesterol, glucose, uric acid, total bilirubin, alkaline phosphatase, lactic acid dehydrogenase and serum transaminase.

Although these data represent only single points on two different time lines and therefore are not longitudinal, some differences between the two age groups are interesting in relation to other studies.

Mean values for total protein, albumin, creatinine, and total bilirubin are significantly lower in the older women. The direction of change is the same in the men but less marked. Mean serum calcium levels are higher in 50-year-old women and lower in 50-year-old men than in the 42-year-old groups. Serum phosphorus and alkaline phosphatase are higher at 50 than at 42. Whether a rise in these values with age is typical is not yet established (Cohen, Giltman, & Lipschutz, 1960).

Decreased tolerance for glucose with age is well established (Andres & Tobin, 1972). In our data the mean glucose levels 2 hours after ingestion of 50 g of glucose are significantly higher in the OGS men at 50 than in the GS men at 42. The levels of the older and younger women do not differ significantly. These findings suggest that ability to respond to the stress of glucose loads decreases sooner in the male than in the female. Such a possibility has not yet been tested in the Baltimore longitudinal study (Andres & Tobin, 1972) because until recently women were not included.

The extent to which the SMA 12 data reflect aging, per se, and how many of the differences depend on age-associated disease or sample differences cannot be determined until repeated measures on the same persons are available. Although the means for all 12 blood chemistries were within normal limits for both cohorts and both sexes, a few abnormalities appeared. Some of these occurred along with well-known disorders such as hypothyroidism or diabetes; others required substantiation and investigation and will not be presented here.

Lipid metabolism   Over 95% of all fat carried in the blood in the postabsorptive state is in the form of lipoproteins. These are a mixture of triglycerides or neutral fat, phospholipids, cholesterol, and protein. High levels of serum lipids are associated with increased risk of atherosclerosis and hence of cardiovascular disease. Abnormally high levels of lipids in the blood (hyperlipidemia) are said to be pandemic in the United States today. Tests of lipid metabolism performed on GS at 42 and OGS at 50 reflect this national pattern.

Many cross-sectional studies have shown that cholesterol levels rise gradually from 20 until about 45–55 in men and until at least 65 in women (Abraham, Johnson, & Carrol, 1977; Kritchevsky, 1972; Werner, Tolls, Hultin, & Mellecker, 1970). In our samples the mean values of cholesterol, although significantly lower for the women, increase in both sexes with age. However, in women the rise seems continuous and gradual whereas in men it appears to be rapid between 34 and 42 and then gradual to 50. The difference between the mean values for men at 42 (GS) and 50 (OGS) is not statistically significant, but that for OGS between 34 and 50 is ($p < .0001$). Differential mortality has been suggested as a cause for the leveling off of cholesterol values at mid-life for men (Finch & Hayflick, 1977). Longitudinal studies, of course, can examine this possibility. In our samples one OGS man with high cholesterol at 34 died of a heart attack later that year.

Although the numbers of individuals in each of our sex and age groups are small and the cholesterol values widely distributed, the data hint at possible subpopulations. Kannel (1976) suggests that individuals with plasma cholesterol levels below 185 mg% are at less risk of developing heart disease than are those with higher levels. This criterion might be expected to distinguish those whose cholesterol levels increase at different rates, or even those whose cholesterol will rise to significant risk levels (over 240 mg%), from those who will not develop pathological elevations.

Twenty-one OGS women had cholesterol measurements at both age 34 and 50. Those who had levels below 185 mg% at 34 had levels below 240 mg% at 50. Those with cholesterol levels above 185mg% at 34 had levels above 240 mg% at 50, the mean level being 270 mg%. In only two women was the cholesterol constant over the 16-year period from 34 to 50 years. For men similar results were obtained. Seventy-one percent of those with cholesterol values below 185 mg% at 34 were below 240 mg% at 50, whereas only 36% of those with cholesterol values above 185 mg% were below 240 mg% at 50.

Cholesterol levels were positively correlated with systolic blood pressure ($r = .23$, $p < .05$), sleep disturbances ($r = .26$, $p < .05$), and smoking ($r = .34$, $p < .01$) in GS women at 42. Among GS men only one variable was significantly associated with cholesterol level—men with high levels engaged in less sport ($r = -.32$, $p < .05$). Among the GS at 50 cholesterol levels were significantly correlated with weight ($r = .36$, $p < .05$) in women and with increased "nervousness" in men ($r = -.45$, $p < .05$). Again, the findings suggest that age and sex, as well as health habits, such as exercise and diet, influence cholesterol metabolism.

The mean levels of total triglycerides and of very low density lipoproteins (VLDL) are significantly higher in both sexes in the 50-year-old OGS sample than in the 42-year-old GS group. However, the male and female distributions of total triglycerides are remarkably different. For women at both ages, the data are distributed unimodally with a tail toward increased values. At 50, the mode is the same, but the tail of high values becomes proportionately larger. For men at both ages, the distributions are relatively flat, suggesting heterogeneity, but have a tail of high values; the latter is larger in the 50-year-olds.

The distributions of pre-Beta lipoproteins (VLDL) also differ for men and women. At 42, both sexes show a unimodal curve with a long tail of high values that is more marked in the men. At 50 the sample is very small, but there is again a suggestion of heterogeneity, raising the possibility of constitutional or environmental differences between individuals whose lipoproteins do or do not increase markedly with age.

Because diseases of the cardiovascular system are known to be the major cause of death in the aging United States population, prediction of cardiovascular disease was attempted for the OGS. The factors considered were historical, physical, and physiologic. History focused on parental deaths from cardiovascular causes, as well as on participants' smoking, personal history, and cardiovascular complaints. Physical findings examined were weight, blood pressure, funduscopic examination, and peripheral pulses. Physiologic data scrutinized were vital capacity, EKG, chest X-ray, cholesterol, triglycerides, atherogenic index (AI) (Gofman, Jones, Lindgren, Lyon, Elliott, & Stresower, 1950), and low density lipoproteins. Using these criteria, women and men at 34 years were sorted into high-, moderate-, and low-risk categories.

Twenty-one OGS women who returned at 50 had all relevant data at 34. Of these, seven fell in the high-risk category, ten in the moderate-risk category, and four in the low-risk category. At 50, four of the seven women in the high-risk group had high blood pressure, one of whom was being treated by her physician; a fifth was normotensive but under treatment for hypertension. All had increased cholesterol; three had increased lipids other than cholesterol. Five of the women had symptoms suggestive of arteriosclerosis at 50, and one had hypertension during pregnancy. Among the four women rated in the low-risk category at 34, none had increased blood pressure, cholesterol, or other lipid components at 50. One had leg cramps at night and mentioned an unspecified heart problem in her computer-taken history.

Fifteen 50-year-old OGS men had data at 34 years sufficiently complete to permit similar prognostic classifications. Six were placed in a high-risk group at 34. At 50 three of these were being treated for hypertension, two others now had untreated hypertension, and one was normotensive. All had increased cholesterol but none had a concomitant increase in other lipids. However, one of the low-risk men gave a definite history of arteriosclerosis. Among both women and men classified in the moderate-risk category at 34, the status at 50 was intermediate.

In summary, some deviations from normal values, pointing to possible later cardiovascular disease, appeared early in adult life and increased with time. For lipid metabolism these changes were marked by 50, more so in men than women. Symptoms became more frequent with age but much pathology remained silent, especially in those areas where preventive measures for individuals at high risk might be helpful. Prognosis of later pathology in the OGS sample was validated more often in women than in men.

Eyes and Ears, Vision and Hearing

Except for GS women at 30, complaints involving eyes and ears were reported by some participants at all adult ages. In both sexes complaints increased with age and included such symptoms as earaches, eye and ear infections, and blurred vision, as well as loss of acuity. At 42 in GS and 50 in OGS, vision and hearing were examined in some detail by computer history and by specific tests. More impairment of function in both senses was found in men than in women.

Eyes and Vision

At 34 years (OGS), 24% of 60 women had abnormalities of the *ocular fundi* ranging from mild deviations to a severe retinopathy with exudate. A similar, somewhat more severe, range of pathology was found in 27% of the men.

Intraocular tension was measured in the multiphasic examinations. No statistically significant differences were found between the GS at 42 and the OGS at 50. At 42, 20% of the GS women and 29% of the men had pressures in one or both eyes at or above the accepted limit. At 50 years, 13% of the OGS women and 32% of the men had borderline elevations.

Visual acuity was also assessed in the screening examinations. At 42, about 25% of the GS wore glasses for distance vision and 30% for near vision. Fifty percent of the women and 39% of the men had at least one pair of glasses. At 50, slighlty more than 40% of the OGS women and 69% of the men required distance corrections and almost 70% of each sex needed correction for near vision. Eighty-eight percent of the women and 100% of the men had at least one pair of glasses.

In tests of visual function, participants used glasses if such was their habit. Each eye was tested separately, as well as both eyes together. All mean and median values in both sexes were within normal limits for near and far visual acuity, although mean acuity was slightly poorer in the older sample. Mean and median values for *lateral* and *vertical phoria* (normal rest positions of eyes) and *stereopsis* (depth perception) were also within normal ranges but at the lower ends, indicating gradually deteriorating function with age.

These findings are consistent with the onset of presbyopia, decreased visual acuity, decreased depth perception, and weakening muscular function, typical of the middle years.

Hearing

Complaints of diminished auditory acuity were absent in women and negligible in men (2%) in the GS at 30. At 42, there were still very few complaints among women but 14% of the men reported noticeable hearing impairment. In the OGS group at 34, only about 3% of women reported hearing difficulties; by 50 this complaint was made by 20%. Among the men at 34, hearing impairment was already noted by 10%; at 50, 32% had this complaint.

Audiometric tests of hearing acuity were also part of multiphasic examinations. Median values are summarized in Fig. 3.4 for each sex and for each ear separately. The appearance of presbycusis is especially apparent in 50-year-old men. High-frequency thresholds at 42 in GS women were below normal in 44% of the tests; among the men, mild to severe impairment was already evident in 66% of the tests. Both sexes in OGS at 50 have more impairment—women had median high-frequency of about 30 decibels, while the thresholds for men were about 40 in the right ear and 50 in the left. Despite increasing complaints of hearing impairment, especially among some men, average thresholds for frequencies in the median voice range (500–2000 cycles per second) were normal for both groups and both sexes at 42 and 50. In contrast with the large number of participants who wore eye glasses, none wore a hearing aid.

If the differences between two cohorts are interpreted as indicating age trends, the audiometric findings parallel data from larger cross-

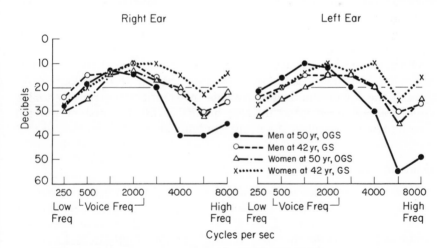

Fig. 3.4 Distributions of median hearing levels of different frequencies.

sectional samples (Gloreg & Roberts, 1965) in showing loss of auditory acuity to be more marked for males and most severe in the high frequency range.

MORTALITY

Thirty-four participants are known to have died. These include six males and five females (3% of 322) through age 49 in the younger cohort (GS and BGS) and 16 males and 7 females (11% of 212) through age 57 in the older cohort (OGS). These deaths have been classified into two broad categories of cause—violence and disease.

Guidance Study

Four of the six male deaths were violence-related (car accident at 3 years, drowning at 35, plane crash at 39, death in a POW camp at 42). One of the five women died at 21 in a motorcycle accident; disease took the lives of the others. One died at 20 of myeloid leukemia and another of breast cancer at 47; neither history was premonitory. For the other two women, the histories are more suggestive. One died at 36 of myocardial ischemia secondary to congenital anomaly of the coronary arteries. A heart murmur was reported throughout her history; a congenital heart lesion was suspected at 14; at the 30-year follow-up, the cardiac signs persisted and the liver was palpable. At 35, the other woman died of uremia caused by pyelonephritis with pyo-hydronephrosis. She had a poor medical history throughout childhood and adolescence and at the 30-year examination, a severe chronic pyelonephritis was noted.

Of the two men who succumbed to disease, one died at 46 of multiple sclerosis, first diagnosed at 32, and the other at 48 of leukemia. Although the latter was below average in weight and strength during childhood and was rated in poor health at 30, his history did not foreshadow the onset of the neoplasm (cancer).

Oakland Growth Study

In this group, followed from about age 11, 23 deaths were reported through age 57. Seven violent deaths occurred among the 16 men, two of which were war-related (POW camp at 21 and crash of a training flight at 22). Two deaths were in auto accidents (ages 26 and 31); two were suicides (ages 36 and 48); one man drowned in a diving accident at 51. Only one woman met a violent end (homicide victim at 27).

Deaths from disease fell into several categories. Among the women, one death at 43 was attributed to a "heart condition." Illnesses in adolescence were considerable but not relevant. Her 34-year examination recorded one miscarriage out of four pregnancies, severe diabetes, and elevated lipids. Two women died of neoplasms—one at 45, site unknown; the other at 47 of leukemia. The remaining female deaths are accounted for by uremic poisoning at 20, unknown cause at 51, and emphysema at 53 years. Only the woman with emphysema had a relevant history; bronchopneumonia was recorded in adolescence, a sharply decreased vital capacity at 50, and heavy cigarette smoking for over 17 years.

Among the men there were four cardiac deaths. One occurred at 26 in a man in whom arrhythmia and hypertension were noted throughout adolescence. Another man died of a heart attack at 34; the only relevant findings was an elevated cholesterol level at 34. In a 47-year-old man, death followed a heart transplant. Heart murmurs were noted in adolescence, and at 34 a diagnosis of rheumatic valvular heart disease was recorded, along with a blood pressure of 140/75. The fourth cardiac death was attributed to a heart attack, stroke, and renal failure at 54. At 17.6 years, this man's blood pressure was 128/80, which is above average for age (upper quartile of the United States survey, Roberts & Maurer, 1977b).

Neoplasm caused the deaths of three men. In only one was the history contributory. This man succumbed to lung cancer at 47 after many respiratory infections in adolescence and years of heavy cigarette smoking. Another died at 51, site of cancer unknown, and the third at 53 of a brain tumor.

Infections were responsible for two deaths. One man, who died at 28 of tuberculosis following service in World War II, had many upper respiratory and ear infections throughout adolescence. Another man died of poliomyelitis at 32.

Summary

We note some marked contrasts between the GS and OGS groups. One is a death rate through the fifth decade that is over 2.5 times higher for the OGS. Through 49, six OGS men but only two GS men died of illness. Although more of the OGS men died of violence during the same time span, two of these deaths were war related. Further, the OGS death from tuberculosis at 28 may also have been war related.

Just as World War II had divergent health impacts on the two cohorts, so did other environmental factors (see Chapter 1). For example, the GS group originally lived in Berkeley, where childhood health care was known to be superior, and were born almost a decade later, during which time medical care improved. Their parents were somewhat more advantaged socioeconomically than those of the OGS. Such factors may enhance longevity in the GS group.

Age 40 is a convenient dividing line for summarizing age and sex differences in mortality. Before 40, 17 deaths occurred. Two of the 6 female deaths and 8 of the 11 male deaths can be attributed to some kind of violence. After 40, 17 more deaths occurred, 4 in the GS and 13 in the OGS. None of the six female deaths was violent, but violence felled 3 of 11 men. Thus, more violent deaths occurred in both sexes before 40 than after. The nonviolent causes of death also demonstrate changing patterns, with cardiac and neoplastic fatalities increasing with age. The higher incidence of violent deaths in men is in accord with the sex difference in accident rate reported by Bayer and Snyder (1950) for the first 18 years in the GS cohort. It is also of interest that two of the three GS men who met violent deaths had a higher than average incidence of accidents and injuries between 2 and 18 years.

In only 4 of the 21 deaths from disease did past histories seem clearly premonitory. One was lung cancer, one was renal, and two were cardiac. Suggestive histories characterized three of the four other cardiac deaths. (Recall also from the section on physiologic data that blood pressures and cholesterol levels showed considerable consistency among individuals across age.) Among the eight persons dying of neoplasms, only the man with lung cancer had a contributory history.

HEALTH RATINGS

Overall ratings of physical health were assigned by physicians to each participant on the basis of each medical examination to assess changes in general health over time, antecedents of such changes and their correlates. Similar rating procedures are being used in several other longitudinal studies for the same reasons (Nowlin, 1979; Schaie & Gribbins, 1979). Except for the physiological panel of OGS, the early data were from examinations by study physicians and included almost no laboratory studies. The adult data (ages 34, 42, and 50) contain substantial laboratory work.

The annual medical examination for the childhood and adolescent years were rated by L. M. Bayer using a scale described in detail in Bayer and Snyder (1950). Because chronic disabilities were rare, ratings were based on the occurrence of acute illness during each year, as well as on the examination findings. The rating scale was: (a) no illness, (b) mild or very little illness, (c) moderate severity or moderate amount of illness, (d) moderate severity *and* moderate amount of illness, (e) severe or much illness. Bayer and Snyder (1950) concluded that "every period of childhood has its special health hazards, none of them ... too serious when ordinary care is given. Only a small percentage of children became affected with permanent ill health." Among the severe disabilities noted before 18 were two which accounted for deaths in the third and fourth decades—myeloid leukemia and congenital heart disease (see section on Mortality).

Although a 5-point scale was also used in rating adult examinations, important differences between childhood and adult data required a change in the criteria. First, intervals between examinations jumped from a year to decades, so adult health pictures were seen as composites rather than as moving frames. Second, chronic conditions gradually became dominant while acute illness receded. Third, laboratory data were introduced into examinations of both GS and OGS at ages of 34 years and older. The adult assessments were thus more related to the concepts of good versus poor health than to the incidence of acute illness.

As in childhood scoring, the adult rating scale included the frequency and duration of illness and complaints as well as the seriousness of the disease category relative to others. Consideration was also given to the degree to which a condition might be expected, on the basis of population studies, to affect the total life span. Finally, the physician raters also took into account the ability of the individual to carry out daily activities unfettered by physical problems.

A rating of 1 described an adult who had no present complaints, an essentially negative history since the preceding follow-up and normal physical, physiological, and laboratory measures. A rating of 5 was given to persons suffering from immediate life-threatening illness and/or a condition judged markedly to decrease life expectancy. A rating of 3 characterized a heterogeneous group, but all had medical and physical problems of intermediate severity or frequency. These were problems which, if adequately attended, would not be expected to shorten the life span appreciably and would only slightly affect daily life.

The inclusion of prognosis based on accepted vital statistics was essential to a realistic effort to appraise adult health status. In general, the intent of the two physicians (LMB and DW-B) who did the ratings was to assess the status of individuals against a standard of "ideal" health, defined as absence of complaints, intervening illness, and current disease rather than on the basis of health relative to age and sex.

Then the effect on health of age, sex, life-style, and secular trends could be assessed.

Reliability of the Adult Ratings

Correlations were computed between the independent ratings of the two physicians' for the men and women in the three cohorts at each adult period. The average inter-rater agreement coefficient is .66. The lowest correlation ($r = .49$) was obtained for GS men at 42; the highest ($r = .77$) for both GS men and women at 30. Availability of laboratory tests accounted for some of the divergence between the two raters because DW-B tended to give greater weight to such evidence. A conference rating subsequently reached by discussion between the two physicians is the actual rating used in all further analyses reported here. The average reliability coefficient for these conference ratings is .79 (using the Spearman-Bowman correction).

Age Changes, Sex and Cohort Differences in the Health Ratings

In the GS and BGS samples, health assessments were made for the pregnancy (prenatal) and for the immediate postnatal (perinatal) period. The average prenatal rating was 2.0 (Good) for BGS and 2.2 (Fairly Good) for GS. The average perinatal ratings were "Very Good" in both samples.

An overview of the health trends in all three samples is shown in Fig. 3.5. Pre-adult ratings reach their lowest ebb in the first and second years for both sexes in GS and for boys in BGS. This period of relatively poor health is followed by a shift toward better health between 3 and 5 years, which is then maintained throughout later childhood by both sexes. During adolescence statistically significant sex differences appear in the GS and OGS cohorts but in opposite directions. GS boys exhibit a period of health superior to their childhood levels and superior to that of the adolescent girls from 12 to 17 years. In contrast, OGS girls enjoyed significantly better health than the boys from 11 to 16. No clear-cut sex differences exist in BGS. Adolescent boys in OGS worked hard and were probably under greater strain because of the Depression (Elder, 1974) than those in GS and BGS, who were adolescent during World War II.

Between 17 years and the fourth decade (i.e., GS at 30, OGS at 34 and BGS at 36), average health declined (mean ratings increase) ex-

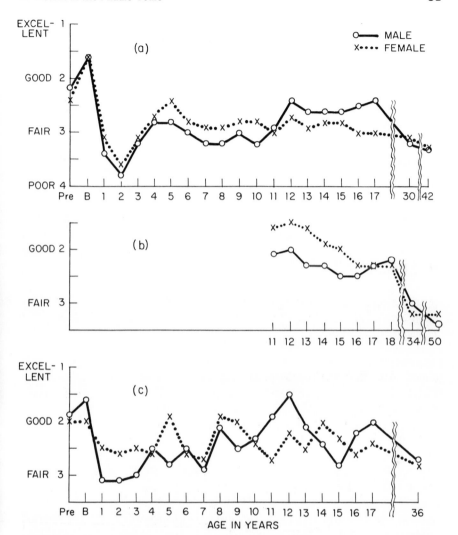

Fig. 3.5 Average health ratings during childhood and the adult years for (a) GS, (b) OGS, and (c) BGS.

cept for GS women at 30. However, the health of GS women declined somewhat more than that of the men between 30 and 42. Health of OGS men between 34 and 50 appears to decline (3.1–3.4), but this difference is not statistically significant. The OGS women maintained the same level of health during these years (34–50).

Stability of the Health Ratings

To assess stability and change, health ratings at all ages were inter-correlated for each sample. The matrices of interage correlations for the first 17 years and the adult ages yield more than a chance number of statistically significant coefficients but few clear-cut trends. Correlations between health ratings at successive adult examinations—30 and 42 (GS) and 34 and 50 (OGS)—are low for men (GS, $r = .28$, $p < .05$; OGS, $r = .09$, ns). For women, however, the correlations are moderate ($r = .60$, $p < .001$ for the GS and $r = .32$, ns for the OGS) during these childbearing years.

Prediction of health in the middle years from illness before 18 was done by correlating the earlier ratings with an adult rating (36 years for BGS; 42 for GS; and 50 for OGS). The prenatal and perinatal ratings in GS and BGS have no significant associations with mid-life ratings. In GS, the girls' health ratings from 1 to 4 years correlate significantly with the 42-year ratings, but in BGS it is the boys whose health ratings during these years correlate significantly with the 36-year ratings. One consistent finding, illustrated in Fig. 3.6, is that health ratings become more stable in women than in men beginning in childhood.

FACTORS RELATED TO HEALTH

Socioeconomic Status

Is health in adulthood related to the socioeconomic status of the home in which the study members were reared? Although the correlations are very low, they are in the direction of better health among adults (36–50 years) whose parents were well educated. Fathers' occupations are less closely associated than their education with their offspring's health in childhood. The only statistically significant association is between fathers' education and ratings of daughters' adult health ($r = .28$, $p < .01$ for the combined GS, BGS, and OGS). This correlation is only .18 for adult sons.

Occupational ratings of the study members themselves have only negligible correlations with health ratings, but the education of the men and of the spouses of the women are positively and significantly correlated with health (r for men $= .31$, $p < .01$, and for spouses of women $= .37$, $p < .001$).

These intriguing though tenuous findings suggest that better edu-

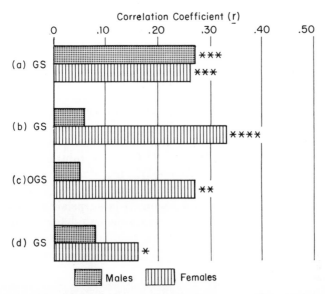

Fig. 3.6 Stability of health ratings from childhood to the adult years. (a) Childhood × adolescence (5–10 × 11–17 yr); (b) Adolescent × adult years (11–17 × 30–42 yr); (c) Adolescent × adult years (11–17 × 34–50 yr); (d) Childhood × adult years (5–10 × 30–42 yr).
   *$p < .10$.
   **$p < .05$.
   ***$p < .01$.
   ****$p < .001$

cated men provide an environment conducive not only to their own health but also to that of their families, whether because of greater knowledge, concern, income, or some combination of these influences.

Smoking and Drinking

Data from large cross-sectional samples (e.g., Bellock and Breslow, 1972) indicate adverse effects of smoking and drinking on health. We examined the longitudinal data on our small normal groups for evidence of progressive effects.

Following the classifications in Chapter 9, we categorized drinking patterns as: (a) abstaining, (b) light, (c) moderate, (d) heavy, and (e) problem. These drinking ratings were correlated with health ratings for the combined GS and OGS cohorts at 30–34 years and 42–50 years. Although very low, the correlations tend to increase—from $-.13$ to $.12$

(ns) for men and from .03 to .16 ($p < .10$) for women. When the correlation includes both males and females, it becomes significant (.16, $p < .04$) for the later age period. Case studies of individuals with decreasing IQs during the adult years (Chapter 4) suggest that heavy drinking is associated with a depressed state in which the drinker neglects his or her health.

Smoking was scored according to the number of cigarettes smoked per day at the time of the last interview (GS at 42 and OGS at 50). For men, negligible relationships obtained between smoking rate and health ratings in the fifth decade (.04 for the combined GS and OGS) and the sixth decade (OGS only, $r = .12$, ns). For women, the correlations were .49 ($p < .002$) in the fifth, and .29 ($p < .02$) in the sixth. Finding stronger associations for women is surprising but in accord with the very slightly higher correlations found for them between drinking and health.

Personality

The possibility that personality characteristics may influence health was explored by correlating the health ratings with two very different personality measures, the California Psychological Inventory (CPI; see Chapter 10) and factor scores derived from the California Q sort (Chapter 5). The CPI, an inventory of 480 items which the respondent answers as true or false, yields 18 scales assessing primarily interpersonal behavior (Gough, 1957). GS and OGS completed this inventory several years before their most recent health evaluation.

Correlations were run between the scores on each scale and the latest health rating (GS, 42; OGS, 50) for men and women separately. Six scales yielded statistically significant correlations for *both* men and women. These were: Well-Being (a sense of physical and emotional well-being—able to enjoy life): $r = .43$, $p < .001$ for women, and .27, $p < .06$ for men; Intellectual Efficiency (feels capable of using intellectual and personal resources in a productive and efficient manner): $r = .41$, $p < .001$ for women; $r = .28$, $p < .05$ for men; and Responsibility (serious in thought and manner, reliable, and dependable) $r = .35$, $p < .002$ for women, and .31, $p < .03$ for men; Achievement via Conformity (strong need for achievement, works well where the criteria for superior performance are clear and unambiguous): $r = .47$, $p < .001$ for men, and .34 $p < .002$ for women; Socialization (comfortable acceptance of social conventions, circumspect, sensitive to the rights and wishes of others): $r = .45$, $p < .001$ for men, and .20, $p < .08$

for women. Most of the associations that hold for both sexes imply that self-control, and easy acceptance of social conventions and folkways promote health. The explanation may be that a degree of serenity is obtained by the person who does not feel compelled to oppose the ordinary constraints of everyday life.

Three other scales were significantly correlated with health ratings for women but not men: Capacity for Status ($r = .42$, $p < .001$), Social Presence ($r = .41$, $p < .001$), and Sociability ($r = .39$, $p < .001$). These results suggest that women who are comfortable in their relationships to others and who view themselves as reasonably competent in coping with interpersonal demands tend to have better health than those less characterized by these attitudes.

Do the health ratings relate to staff Q-sort (Block, 1961) evaluations of the subjects' personalities based on interviews and observations? Q sorts were available for four age periods for members of GS and OGS: early adolescence (12–14 years), late adolescence (15–17 years), early adulthood (30, GS, or 38, OGS), and middle adulthood (40, GS, and 48, OGS). As described in Chapter 5 and Appendix A, the 100-item Q sort has been reduced by Harshman's (1970) PARAFAC method to six factors that are similar at all ages. GS and OGS were combined and factor scores at each age period were correlated with the health ratings in the middle years (age 42 for GS and 50 for OGS). Only Factor 2, Emotionally Under/Overcontrolled, is significantly related to health. Its definers are: calm, emotionally bland, overcontrolled, dependable, sympathetic, arouses liking; does not push limits, not assertive, not rebellious, not irritable; and is satisfied with self. Factor 2 at early adolescence correlates with health in the middle years ($r = .30$, $p < .08$ for men, and $.26$, $p < .09$ for women). In late adolescence the correlations ($.17$ and $.15$) are not statistically significant, but they become so in the thirties for both sexes ($r = .48$, $p < .001$ for men and $r = .28$, $p < .02$ for women). In the forties the correlations are significant for men ($r = .48$, $p < .001$) but not for women ($r = .17$, ns).

The freedom from extreme affect that is a component of Factor 2 is less obvious in the CPI scales that correlate with health. However, the "control" element in several CPI scales is related to the absence of hyperemotionality. On the Q sort, individuals who score high on Factor 2 are not easily aroused, are not irritable or talkative, and have a slow tempo. Apparently, these people are not easily stressed; and as Selye (1956) brilliantly hypothesized, over-reaction to stress may be inimical to health. Particularly noteworthy is the fact that characteristics predictive of health in middle age were observable by early adolescence.

SUMMARY

We analyzed all aspects of the medical data—self-evaluations, medical history, physicians' findings, routine and special tests—in an attempt to portray central tendencies and individual differences in mid-life health, especially as these may be associated with significant antecedents. Despite their socioeconomic advantage, our participants are in the main similar to more representative populations in all these aspects and in the range of individual variability in the processes of aging by the middle years.

Self-assessments of health   These adults tend to assess their health as "good" even in the face of their own reported complaints, illness experience, and objective medical findings.

Illness experience and complaints   The most consistent source of malaise in women throughout the middle years is the reproductive system. In men, it is the digestive system. Problems with the genitourinary system increase as men age. In both sexes, acute complaints diminish with age while chronic complaints increase. Notable among the chronic ailments, especially among men, are afflictions of the eyes and ears and increased infirmities of the extremities and musculoskeletal apparatus. Surgery is a common experience in both sexes. In most organ systems, women register more complaints than do men.

Physical and physiological findings   Paralleling their complaints, pathology in women is noted most frequently in the reproductive system. In the men, the most common abnormality is hypertension, although there is a gradual elevation of blood pressure in both sexes from infancy through middle age. Overweight develops by adulthood in both sexes, and is progressive in men but recedes among the older women. Both blood pressure and weight show some consistency among individuals after infancy. Weight for height is positively and significantly correlated with systolic and diastolic blood pressures, very low density lipoproteins, and sleep disturbances in both sexes and with health ratings in women.

Blood lipid levels tend to increase during adulthood; by 50 this increase is quite marked among the men. Cholesterol levels in adulthood show some predictability for individuals and some associations with physical status and health habits.

Vision and hearing   Diminution of these two perceptual functions with age is so common that it is often regarded as a nonpathological or an involutional sign of aging. Our samples show general loss of function in these areas, but some individuals maintain good sight and hearing into their fifties. Handicaps are more common among the men.

Mortality   Reported causes of death for 34 participants also conform to national trends: men die earlier than women; more male deaths are from violent causes; violence causes more deaths before 40, whereas disease is responsible for more deaths after 40. Cardiac pathology, neoplasm, and renal failure were the most frequent lethal diseases in our cohorts. Premonitory symptoms were noted in the histories of some cardiac cases.

Because only three deaths after the fourth decade were in the GS cohort, while the other 13 occurred in the OGS cohort, it will be important to see whether the experience of the younger group parallels that of the older. Both cohorts are still relatively young. Death is one condition that often carries with it a definition of its cause. It may later be feasible to make predictions from historical and physiologic data for both cohorts that can be tested against a final validation.

Health ratings suggest a slight deterioration between the fourth and fifth decades that continues in the men but not in the women. Stability of ratings over time is greater than would occur by chance. Although ratings of early illness experience are not strong predictors of adult health, some association is evident in childhood and adolescence for women.

Other variables   Several factors besides past health appear to have small to moderate impact upon the health of our study members. The health of men is associated with their own education and perhaps that of their fathers. Women's health is correlated with the education of their fathers and their husbands. Restraint in smoking and drinking shows a very slight but increasing relation to better health. Some cohort differences were noted that may be a function of different life experiences either as a result of historical events or sample differences in socioeconomic status. A provocative finding is that a calm, self-controlled, and responsible personality, manifest as early as 11–13 years, is conducive to adult health. *Mens sana in corpore sano* may be a reversible equation.

Conclusion   The lives of our cohorts spanned the development of chemotherapy, antibiotics, widespread immunization, and better and more widespread knowledge about nutrition. Little morbidity and few

deaths resulted from infectious disease; no serious instances of mal-
nutrition were uncovered. Through age 18 our participants recovered
completely from all but the most severe accidents, disabling diseases,
and congenital defects. By the middle years (30–50) they seem more
vulnerable. They display what Lambo (1975) has described as a "growing incidence of conditions which are linked to the process of technolog-
ical development itself and the rapid and profound social changes
which accompany it. . . ." Applicable to our findings are several conditions listed by Lambo, namely accidents, stress disorders, and alcohol
abuse.

Women report more physical malfunctions, but men evidence more
degenerative disease. Thus the females seem both more aware of debil-
ity and more resilient. These observations are consonant with our findings that little relation exists between people's complaints over the
years and the final causes of their deaths.

From an environmental viewpoint, it appears that mid-life well-
being, even in this relatively favored population, might be enhanced in
a social setting that was less violent and less stressful, and in which
people ate, drank, and smoked less. From an individual viewpoint, our
data support the value of regular medical screening examinations, for
again, even in these economically advantaged groups, we found previously undetected pathologies that herald incipient disease.

4

Experience, Personality, and IQ: Adolescence to Middle Age

DOROTHY H. EICHORN, JANE V. HUNT,
AND MARJORIE P. HONZIK

INTRODUCTION

"One of the most salient questions in the study of the human life span concerns the nature and degree of changes in intelligence" (Eisdorfer, 1969, p. 237). Implicit in this succinct statement are more specific questions, all of which must be asked for each segment of the life span. Is the period characterized by stability or change? Do all types of abilities and all individuals show similar age trends? What factors are associated with stability, improvement, or decrement? Although we address such questions here only for the period from adolescence to middle age, our brief historical review sets this period in the broader context of research on other segments of the life span.

HISTORICAL REVIEW

Following publication of the first Stanford revision of Binet's mental age scale (Terman, 1916), retests of many children in the age range from preschool to high school were done to assess the effects on consistency of IQ scores of factors such as age, sex, social background, and interval between tests. Most retests were over quite short intervals, but some covered periods of up to 7 years. In a volume summarizing the results of such studies, Terman (1919) reported that the average retest

89

correlation was very high (.93) and that 50% of the retest IQs were within 5 points of the first test. Somehow, Terman's table showing the distribution of IQ changes of 10 points or more (42% were of this magnitude) was forgotten. Thus, the concept of the constancy of the IQ was born.

When longitudinal data from the IHD and other samples began to emerge (Bayley, 1940, 1949; Bradway, 1944; Ebert & Simmons, 1943; Honzik, 1938) the concept of IQ constancy had been widely accepted for two decades. Also, evidence had accumulated that correlations with school performance and other indicators of ability and general knowledge were substantially higher with Binet IQ than with other methods of assessing intelligence (e.g., teachers' ratings). Therefore, longitudinal data showing many marked individual changes in IQ were first met with great skepticism. The data showed that until about age 12 retest correlations progressively decreased as the interval between tests increased; total IQ during the first year or so permitted only short-term prediction; during the preschool years, correlations with subsequent IQs became increasingly positive, but not until 6–9 years were they sufficiently high (.80) for reasonably accurate prediction to age 18. Marked shifts in scores were more common than was reported in the early shorter term studies. For example, between ages 6 and 18, 58% of the GS group had at least one shift in IQ of ±15 points or more between any two tests (Honzik, Macfarlane, & Allen, 1948). Individual curves showed all possible patterns, for example, marked fluctuations, stability, steady increases or decreases, or abrupt changes followed by stability.

A succession of longitudinal studies from Berkeley and elsewhere (see Eichorn, 1973, for a review) linked IQ level and change to socioeconomic indicators, preschool attendance, child-rearing practices, and personality characteristics of both parents and child. By the late 1960s, when our study members took their most recent adult tests, professional and public opinion had swung to the other extreme. Preschool intervention programs were being mounted on a nationwide scale with great confidence in the mutability of the IQ, at least during early childhood.

Despite early acceptance of the concept of IQ constancy in children, a quite different concept of adult IQ was, paradoxically, subsequently adopted. In his presidential address to the American Psychological Association, Miles (1932) commented, "The great interest in mental measurement in the first two decades of life still leaves four to six decades of human adult life relatively untouched." The following year Jones and Conrad (1933) published their classic cross-sectional study in which 1000 10- to 60-year-olds from New England villages were tested with the Army Alpha. IQ was highest among the 18- to 21-year-olds and declined progressively among older age groups. These results and similar ones from the standardization sample for the Wechsler-Bellevue (Wechsler, 1939, 1944), led to the conclusion that IQ declined with age in adulthood. This interpretation, reinforced by a growing literature on the poorer performance of older adults on tests of learning, memory and perception (Birren, 1968), provided the view of the course of cognitive abilities during the adult years that was presented in textbooks for several decades. Adult intelligence was believed not to be immutable but to peak early and then diminish with advancing years. The possibility that age-associated cultural differences (such as amount or quality of education) might have influenced these results from cross-sectional samples was not considered, just as cultural differences were not believed to have important effects on childhood IQ.

As longitudinal data on adults became available, the picture changed. Owen's (1953) data came from the same test, the Army Alpha, that Jones and Conrad (1933) used in their cross-sectional study. From a college class whose members had been tested at about 19, Owens (1953, 1966) was able to retest 127 men at about age 50 and 96 of that group again at about 61. Stability of individual differences was indicated by high interage correlations—.79 between 19 and 50 and .78 between 19 and 61—despite the restricted range of scores in this sample of superior ability and education. To control for secular change (i.e., a general increase in IQ among adults of all ages because of shared cultural influences) a random sample of 101 male freshmen enrolled in the same college at the time of the age 61 follow-up were tested. Their scores were used to adjust the initial (age 19) scores of the longitudinal sample. After this adjustment, gains were still found between 19 and 50 on the verbal components of the Army Alpha, but insignificant declines occurred in the numerical and reasoning components. Between 50 and 60 years, further gains were observed in information, analogies, and following directions; all other subtest scores and total score declined. Nevertheless, after adjustment for cultural change, scores at 60 were still significantly higher than at 19 for practical judgment, disarranged sentences, analogies, number series completion, and the total. A significant decline occurred in arithmetical problems.

Corroborating the general tenor of Owen's findings are retests at ages from early to late adulthood of persons first tested sometime between early childhood and early adulthood. The samples range from the gifted (Bayley & Oden, 1955) to the retarded (Charles, 1953). As did Owens, some investigators used group tests, for example, the Concept Mastery (Bayley & Oden, 1955), Terman–McNemar (Haan, 1963), or Primary Mental Abilities (Schaie & Strother, 1968). Others used the individually administered Stanford-Binet and Wechsler scales (Bayley, 1957, 1966; Bradway, Thompson, & Cravens, 1958; Honzik & Macfarlane, 1973; Kangas & Bradway, 1971). All failed to find general decrements in measured intelligence across adult ages and some found increments.

The inference that the IQ decreases noted by Jones and Conrad for cross-sectional samples were associated with cohort differences (perhaps in amount of education) is given some support from the cross-sectional standardization data of the Wechsler adult tests. Comparisons between the Wechsler-Bellevue (1944) and WAIS (1955) show a later onset (after 35–44 years) of decline in verbal IQ (and, hence, to a lesser extent, also in total score) in the more recent standardization.

Against such evidence for the maintenance of intellectual abilities in adults must be set the report of Tuddenham, Blumenkrantz, and Wilkin (1968) on scores on the Army General Classification Test (a group test) for 164 soldiers of average ability tested in their twenties and again in their forties. The interage correlation (.79) equaled that of Owens, but this group showed a significant decrement in perceptual reasoning and insignificant declines in other subtests. These results and some discrepancies among the other studies leave a number of issues to be resolved. For example, reported gains range from very small (Bayley, 1966) to marked (Kangas & Bradway, 1971) in groups assessed with the same tests and having a similar age range. As yet, research on factors associated with different patterns of ability either among subgroups in one sample or across studies is limited. Among potential influences that have been implicated are practice effects, sample attrition, difficulty of the test relative to the abilities of the group, and cohort differences in personality characteristics, education, or other forms of mental stimulation. To date, however, none of these clearly accounts for discrepant results among studies.

Gains into late adulthood have usually been found on subtests such as information and vocabulary, that is, the kinds of items that Horn and Cattell (1967) classify as measures of "crystallized" intelligence. In contrast, declines at least by middle age have been noted on items depending on the speed of motor responses. However, the results for other types of items, including those Horn and Cattell categorize as "fluid" intelligence, are more inconsistent. Much remains to be learned about the kinds of abilities that tend to be maintained or augmented

Table 4.1

IQ Means, Standard Deviations, and Gains

Tests		OGS			GS			BGS	
	Age (yr)	Men (N = 45) Mean	Women (N = 49) Mean	Age (yr)	Men (N = 51) Mean	Women (N = 64) Mean	Age (yr)	Men (N = 21) Mean	Women (N = 20) Mean
Stanford-Binet	17	120.2 (12.5)	111.3 (12.0)						
Wechsler-Bellevue:									
Full-scale IQ				18	121.1 (8.6)	116.9 (10.0)	18	119.1 (19.6)	124.4 (9.5)
Verbal IQ					119.8 (10.9)	113.1 (10.4)		117.7 (19.9)	120.8 (10.7)
Performance IQ					116.4 (8.3)	115.7 (9.6)		114.7 (14.9)	121.6 (8.6)
WAIS:									
Full-scale IQ									
Unadjusted	48	125.6 (11.0)	113.7 (9.4)	40	123.3 (9.3)	122.4 (9.0)	36	124.5 (17.6)	125.8 (8.5)
Adjusted		125.0	113.1		125.9	125.0		128.0	128.9
Verbal IQ									
Unadjusted		124.7 (11.7)	112.1 (10.5)		121.5 (9.6)	120.7 (9.8)		122.5 (19.2)	124.7 (8.7)
Adjusted		127.7	114.9		124.6	123.8		126.0	127.9
Performance IQ									
Unadjusted		123.6 (12.1)	114.3 (9.6)		122.5 (10.7)	121.6 (10.5)		124.4 (15.0)	123.7 (10.4)
Adjusted		119.2	109.0		123.3	122.6		126.5	126.0
IQ gain, 36–48 (Adjusted) – 17 or 18:									
Full-scale					4.8	8.1		8.9	4.5
Verbal		7.5	3.6		4.8	10.7		8.3	7.1
Performance					6.9	6.9		11.8	4.4

Note: Numbers in parentheses are standard deviations.

and those that plateau or decline, about the timing of such patterns, and about possible differences in cohort characteristics that may influence findings. A major focus of this chapter is correlates of adult IQ change in our samples.

SAMPLES AND PROCEDURES

The Wechsler Adult Intelligence Scale (WAIS) was administered to all three samples at their last adult evaluation, that is, at about 36 years for BGS, 40 years for GS, and 48 years for OGS. A total of 250 persons, 117 males and 133 females, tested at these ages had also had IQ tests (see Table 4.1) at about age 17 (OGS) or 18 (GS and BGS). The GS and BGS participants were tested from infancy through late adolescence with individually administered tests, most frequently with alternate forms of the 1937 Stanford-Binet (S-B). Both of these groups had the Wechsler-Bellevue, Form I (W-B) at 18, and this test was also given to BGS at 16, 21, and 26. Because neither the 1937 Binet nor the Wechsler was yet available, OGS members were tested at several ages between 10½ and 14 with group tests (e.g., Terman–McNemar, Form C), as well as with such individual tests as the Kuhlman–Anderson and the 1916 Binet. When they were approximately 17, they took both the new 1937 Stanford-Binet, Form L, and the Terman–McNemar, Form A. In their mid-thirties they were retested with the latter.

Given the differences in the testing schedules of the three samples, we consider here only changes in the period between late adolescence, when both GS and BGS took the W-B, and the last adult tests, when all three samples took the WAIS. Even with these similarities, scores at these two age periods cannot be compared directly because of differences in difficulty between the WAIS and W-B and differences in composition and scoring between the S-B and both Wechsler tests. The 1937 S-B uses a ratio IQ (mental age divided by chronological age), whereas Wechslers are scored in points to yield a standard deviation IQ. To adjust for this difference, IQs of the OGS on the 1937 S-B were converted to standard deviation IQs using Pinneau's (1961) conversion tables. This conversion reduced the original ratio IQs on the S-B at age 17 by an average of 4.7 IQ points for males and 4.5 points for females. The reduction is of the same order (5 points) as that which Wechsler (1944) reports to be the average difference between the 1937 Binet and the W-B. If this general adjustment is specifically applicable to Binet IQs for the OGS at 17 years, then the adjustment makes their S-B IQs comparable to those of the GS and BGS on the W-B at approximately the same age (18 years). In fact, the verbal IQ on the Wechsler Scales probably constitutes the best basis for comparison with the S-B. The S-B is essentially a verbal test and correlations between S-B IQs and Wechsler verbal IQs are high; correlations of S-B IQs with Wechsler performance IQs are much lower and nearer the order of those between the verbal and performance scales on either the W-B or WAIS (Kangas & Bradway, 1971; Wechsler, 1955).

Differences between the W-B and WAIS must be taken into account when comparing the adolescent and adult IQs. The total raw points possible on the verbal, performance, and total scales is greater for the WAIS than for the W-B. Further, a "given weighted score total is worth more (sometimes as much as eight IQ points more) on the WAIS than on the W-B in the lower intelligence range" (Holt, 1968, p. 170). In the higher intelligence range, however, a raw score on the WAIS is converted to a somewhat *lower* weighted score than on the W-B. Holt reports that more able persons (average W-B full scale IQ of 118) earn higher IQs on both the full and performance scales of the W-B than on the WAIS and cites five additional supporting studies (Holt, 1968, p. 170). A seventh study (Rabourn, 1957) reports similar results for 50 persons aged 17 to 27 with educational levels comparable to those of our samples. Because our groups have W-B IQs in late adolescence and WAIS IQs in middle age, the net result would be an *underestimate* of any gain between these two periods.

A further complication arises because IQs on both Wechsler scales allow for the fact that in the standardization populations, point scores were highest in the young adult population and declined at older ages. As Wechsler (1955) notes, IQs as scored from the test manual are suitable for comparing a sample with their age peers, but the age adjustments must be taken into account in assessing score changes across age within a sample. The ages for maximum scores, as well as the timing and extent of the declines, differ for the W-B and WAIS and for verbal, performance, and full scale IQs on both tests. For example, on the WAIS the point scores required to maintain a constant IQ decrease beginning at ages 45-54 for verbal IQ, at 25-34 for performance IQ, and at 35-44 for full scale IQ. Thus age corrections will be similar for GS and BGS but different for OGS.

Such complexities of age scoring and the difference in difficulty between the W-B and WAIS require adjustments to IQs for age comparisons within our samples and between our samples and those of others (e.g., Kangas & Bradway, 1971). Therefore, we report both unadjusted and adjusted WAIS IQs (see Table 4.1). The adjustments were accomplished by first adding 4 points to the weighted point scores for the performance scale of the WAIS; Rabourn (1957, see preceding) found a significant difference of this size and direction between average performance scores on the W-B and WAIS. Then the full scale point scores were recomputed. Finally, these two sets of adjusted point scores and the unadjusted verbal point score (verbal scores have not been found to differ significantly between the W-B and WAIS) were referred to the test norms for ages 17 (OGS) and 18 (GS and BGS) to obtain IQs with no age correction. These IQs can then be compared to those earned by our samples in late adolescence to assess whether any changes have occurred that are not attributable either to changes in age norms or to differences in difficulty between the W-B and WAIS.

To assess the legitimacy of combining groups we did an analysis of variance with six subgroups (two sexes in each of three samples) at each age period. With two exceptions, no significant differences emerged. At both ages, OGS women had significantly lower IQs than all other subgroups, although their scores, too, are above the average of the general population. Despite similar procedures for selecting male and female participants within any given study (Chapter 2), the OGS women came from homes of lower than average socioeconomic status than did any of the other subgroups (see Table 4.2). This is the only difference to which their lower scores can be traced. An IQ difference appears at their first testing (about age 10½) and remains through middle age. Combining them with the other women creates a significant difference between the average scores of males and females at each age period, but does not significantly influence age-to-age correlations or associations with other variables, such as personality or socioeconomic status.

INTERAGE CORRELATIONS

Combining all three samples yields a correlation between IQs at late adolescence (17–18) and middle age (36–48) of .83 for males and .77 for females, with no significant difference between the sexes. These correlations are very similar to those found by Owens (1966) for college-educated males tested with the Army Alpha at 19 and 50 (.79) and 19 and 60 (.78); by Tuddenham et al. (1968) for soldiers of average ability tested with the Army General Classification Test in their twenties and forties (.79), and by Kangas and Bradway (1971) for part of the standardization sample for the 1937 S-B later tested between ages 27 and 32 and ages 39 and 44 on the WAIS (.73) and the 1937 S-B (.77). As did Kangas and Bradway, we found the cross-age correlation to be lower for performance IQs (.69 for males and .63 for females) than for verbal IQs (.84 and .81, respectively). For each sex, the difference between the correlations for the two scales is significant ($p < .001$).

The similarity of all these results, despite differences in test, average IQ, birth cohort, age range, and sex, suggests considerable stability of individual differences (rank order of individuals) across the age range from late adolescence or early adulthood to late middle age. Even correlations of this level permit sizeable IQ changes across age for some individuals and, of course, have no bearing on a group's average IQ at any age and, hence, on average change.

AVERAGE UNADJUSTED SCORES ACROSS AGE

For the three samples combined the unadjusted mean IQs are 120.4 [standard deviation (SD)=12.6] for males and 116.0 (SD = 11.5) for females at late adolescence and 124.4 (SD = 11.7) for males and 119.7

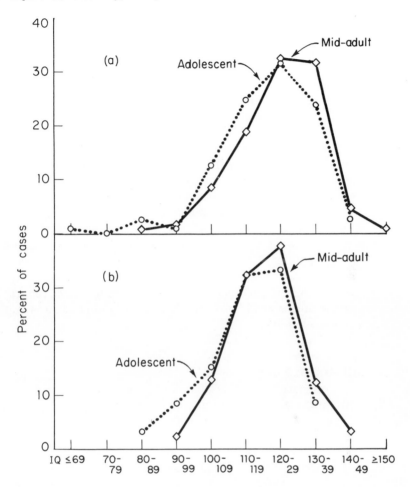

Fig. 4.1 Distribution of IQ at adolescent and mid-adult testing for combined study samples of (a) 117 men and (b) 133 women tested at both ages.

(SD = 10.1) for females at middle age. At each age period the sex differences in average IQ is significant, but only because of the lower scores of the OGS women. For GS and BGS combined the averages are 120.5 at 18 and 123.6 at 36–40 years for males and 118.7 and 123.2, respectively, for females; the sex difference is not significant at either age when OGS is omitted.

These mean scores are definitely above the average (100) for the general population and the standard deviations are lower (SD = 15 for standardization groups), indicating some restriction of range. Except for the narrower range, the shape of the IQ distributions for our samples (see Fig. 4.1) are similar to the general population, especially at late adolescence, when the scores range from mentally deficient (below 69) to very superior, as they did in childhood. A long "tail" in the lowest IQ range is also typical in random samples of the general population. By adulthood the lower range in our samples extends only to low normal, not because of drop-outs (we include only persons tested at both ages), but because the previously very low scorers had increased in IQ.

The average IQs probably somewhat overestimate the extent of the superiority of our samples to the general population. Data from the standardization samples for the revisions of both the Wechsler (Sattler, 1974; Wechsler, 1955), and the Binet (Kangas & Bradway, 1971; Sattler, 1974), as well as cross-sectional data for the Primary Mental Abilities test (Schaie, LaBouvie, & Beuch, 1973), indicate increasing IQs at most age levels during the historical period encompassed by the testings of our samples. The standardization samples for the tests used with our participants were from earlier birth cohorts than our samples. Had the standardization samples been drawn from the same cohorts as our groups, the norms would probably have been higher so our samples would not be as deviant.

IQ CHANGE ACROSS AGE

Adjusted gains among subgroups for the verbal, performance, and full scales are shown at the bottom of Table 4.1. For the reasons stated earlier (see section on Samples and Procedures), the best estimate of change in the full scale as well as the verbal Scale for OGS members is the difference between their age-adjusted verbal IQs on the WAIS at 48 and their derived standard deviation IQs from the S-B at 17. (Performance scale gains cannot, of course, be calcualted for OGS.) Combining the GS and BGS samples for each sex yields mean gains of 6.0 for men and 7.2 for women on the full scale, 5.8 and 9.8, respectively, on the verbal scale, and 8.3 and 6.3, respectively, on the performance scale. Pooling sexes for GS and BGS yields mean gains of 6.7 for the full scale, 8.0 for the verbal, and 7.2 for the performance. Pooling all groups (OGS verbal IQ, GS and BGS full scale IQ) gives a mean gain of 6.2 points for the entire sample of 250 persons. Gains for all subgroups and combined groups are highly significant.

Within both GS and BGS, men tend to show greater gains in performance IQ than verbal IQ, whereas the inverse is characteristic of women. Of perhaps greater interest is the fact that for the combined

GS–BGS the average gains in performance and verbal IQs are essentially the same. Most of the literature to date suggests larger gains during adulthood on such verbal tests as vocabulary, information and similarities (all included on the WAIS verbal scale) than on performance tests, particularly when speed affects score, as is true of the WAIS. However, our finding is supported in part by the results of Kangas and Bradway (1971), whose sample was tested at about 27–32 years and again at 39–44 years with both the 1937 S-B and the WAIS. Corrections for age differences in the WAIS norms were not used, but average point scores are presented, so an adjustment can be approximated. For the full scale of WAIS, the mean change in age-adjusted IQs is 6 points (the same as the change on the S-B in their group and close to the 6.7 adjusted change in our samples). For the verbal scale their adjusted mean change is 5 IQ points (ours is 8.0 for GS–BGS or 7.0 if OGS is included); for the performance scale their adjusted change is 5–7 points, depending on whether the adjustment is made at the younger or older age; our adjusted change is 7.2.

The results of these studies not only contradict cross-sectional data showing declines in IQ by middle adulthood but also raise questions about the verbal-performance dichotomy in age changes during adulthood. Part of the answer may lie in the factor structure of the WAIS, because both the verbal and performance scales probably contain subtests loading not only on both "crystallized" and "fluid" factors, but also on a third factor (Horn & McCardle, 1980). Another issue is the age at which declines in performance subtests begin. Bayley's (1966) analysis of adjusted performance scale subtests suggests differences among subtests, but in the main gains occur to age 26, with a plateau or decline to 36, depending upon the subtest. In the present study, the 48-year-old OGS men score as high or higher on the adjusted verbal scale as the 36- to 40-year-old GS or BGS members, who score lower on the adjusted performance scale.

ARTIFACTS IN IQ CHANGE

At any age an individual's intellectual functioning may be affected by other personal characteristics, such as physical or mental health, as well as by life experiences, for example, education. Before examining such potential influences, however, we must ask whether the average IQ gain of our sample could be an artifact of practice effects, regression to the mean, or bias from selective attrition.

Three sources of evidence indicate that the mean gain is not attributable to practice effects. First is a comparison of 184 pairs of longitudinal study members with their spouses. Study members had been tested repeatedly, but their spouses only once. The mean uncorrected IQ at middle adulthood was 120.9 (SD = 10.8) for participants and 119.7 (SD = 11.0) for their spouses. This difference is not significant, nor was the difference between male participants (mean = 123.6) and male spouses (mean = 121.3) or female participants (mean = 118.2) and female spouses (mean = 118.1). Second, no significant differences in IQ level or gain occur among samples, although they differ markedly in the number of previous testings—a maximum of 7 in OGS, 16 in GS, and 41 in BGS. Finally, Bayley (1968) found no significant differences at age 36 between a group of BGS participants who had all 41 previous tests and a group matched for childhood IQ, socioeconomic level of the parents, and other relevant variables who had not been tested since age 8. Although the absence of any evidence for practice effects was unexpected, it is confirmed by Schaie and Gribbin (1979) for repeated testing during adulthood. These results are not necessarily inconsistent with clear evidence in the literature for practice effects when the same test is repeated over short intervals. In our groups alternate forms of one test or different tests were used at adjacent ages, and the testing interval was at least 1 year for all tests administered after age 5. In Schaie's study the same test was used at each age but the intervals were about 10 years.

To some extent the changes observed are consistent with regression to the mean. All 8 persons with IQs below 89 at adolescence increased their score by middle adulthood, 7 of them by 10 or more full scale IQ points before upward correction of performance scores. Only 2 of the 42 persons with adolescent IQs of 130 or above had increases of this magnitude, a finding that suggests "ceiling" effects, as well as regression to the mean. However, a wide range of IQ level at age 17–18 characterizes both the approximately upper and lower quartiles of the IQ change distribution, as well as the middle group. For the 56 persons (22.4% of the sample) who increased 10 or more uncorrected IQ points, the IQ range at 17–18 years was 69–139; the 56 persons who decreased 2 or more points had an adolescence IQ range of 90–139; and the "typical" change group (N = 138; 55.2%) ranged from 80 to 149. Further, although the correlations between IQ change and adolescent IQ level (−.33 for men; −.43 for women) are significant ($p < .001$), they are far below the correlation of −.71 expected from regression to the mean (Honzik, Hunt, & Eichorn, 1976). Opportunity remains for other factors to influence IQ change.

In cross-sectional as well as longitudinal samples, greater attrition is expected—whether from death, severe illness, or refusal to participate—among persons with lower IQs. We compared the IQs at ages 17–18 of the 82 persons tested at that age but not at middle age with the 250 tested at both ages. The correlation ratio (eta) between presence or absence at middle age testing and IQ at late adolescence is low: .18 (probable error, .03). However, an analysis of variance with six subgroups (2 sexes × 3 studies) yields, as predicted, a significant difference ($p < .002$), with the retested group having a higher average IQ (mean difference, 5.2 points) at late adolescence. Posttests, however, reveal that of the six subgroups only one, the GS males, shows a significant difference ($p < .001$). GS and BGS females conform to the overall trend, but the differences do not approach significance. For both males and females in OGS, the mean difference is negligible (about 1 point); for BGS males the direction of the difference is reversed, with the retested having an insignificantly lower adolescent IQ (3 points).

The data on regression to the mean presented in the preceeding indicate a tendency for our participants with lower IQs to show greater gains than those with higher IQs. To the extent, then, that attrition in our samples has been greater among those with lower IQs, the average gain we observe is an *under*estimate of what would have been found had all participants tested at ages 17–18 been retested in middle age.

In summary, the evidence indicates that the average gain we observe in full-scale IQ does not result from practice effects nor entirely from regression to the mean. Insofar as selective attrition has occurred in our samples, the net effect expected is an underestimate of gain. We can now examine other potential influences on IQ level and change, especially those that are the topics of other substantive chapters in this volume, that is, personality characteristics.

ASSESSING CORRELATES OF IQ LEVEL AND CHANGE

IQ level and gain and factors associated with them often interact in ways that make clear causal inferences difficult. For example, having a well-educated spouse may contribute to the maintenance or improvement of cognitive abilities. However, opportunity to marry such a person is greater among those who are themselves well educated, and educational level in turn is associated with IQ. Sometimes the causal direction of association can be assessed by new statistical techniques (e.g., LISREL, Jöreskog & Sörbom, 1977) or can be deduced more simply, as we do here, by comparing reciprocal pairs of partial correlation or sets of correlations.

Several other psychometric problems also obscure correlates of IQ change. First, gain in our sample was only moderate on the average, that is, about half the standard deviation of the IQ distribution (cf. Cohen, 1977). Second, adolescent and adult IQ are so highly correlated (about .8) that only about 36% of the variance in IQ at middle age remains to be explained by other variables. In contrast, IQ *gain* is *negatively* correlated with adolescent IQ. This regression to the mean is sufficiently strong ($r = -.43$ for women and $-.33$ for men), particularly in conjunction with only moderate gains and a relatively small amount of unaccounted variance, to mask gains associated with variables that correlate positively with IQ level. Hence, potential influences on IQ change cannot be satisfactorily assessed by correlating scores on each independent variable with adult IQ and then statistically partialling out adolescent IQ. Instead, we use gain scores to compute the first-order correlations and then partial out the regression of IQ change on IQ level. Fortunately, IQs from the Binet and Wechsler tests are sufficiently robust (e.g., reliable) to meet major criticisms of change scores (Cronbach & Furby, 1970).

A problem with the direct correlational approach arises, however, when an association is not linear; for example, variation within the normal range of the independent variable may have no effect, but values outside the normal range in one or both directions may be associated with marked change in the dependent variable. When such "threshold" effects were suspected, average change scores of subgroups were compared (e.g., heavy and "problem" drinkers versus social drinkers and abstainers; see Chapter 9).

To assess factors that required review of, and tabulation from, individual case records (e.g., qualitative aspects of physical health), two extreme groups were contrasted: Extreme Increasers (14 men and 14 women, 11% of the sample), who gained 13 or more IQ points (before upward correction of performance score), and Extreme Decreasers (12 men and 16 women, 11% of the sample), who lost 6 or more uncorrected points. (Recall that the average increase in uncorrected IQ was essentially 4 points; thus the remainder of the sample—77.6%—had a range of IQ change from -5 to $+12$ points.) All tabulations from case histories were done "blind," that is, by staff who did not know the person's IQ or change score.

EDUCATION AND OCCUPATION

Education was assessed on a scale from 1 (completed less than eighth grade) to 10 (doctoral degree) for participants and their mothers, fathers, and spouses and occupation on the Hollingshead Scale from 1

Table 4.2

Education and Occupation Data for Samples
Used in IQ Analyses

Education and occupation	OGS		GS		BGS	
	Men (N=45)	Women (N=49)	Men (N=51)	Women (N=64)	Men (N=21)	Women (N=20)
Education (1 = low)						
Father	4.6	3.4	4.9	4.5	6.0	7.0
Mother	3.9	3.4	4.5	4.7	4.0	6.7
Spouse	5.5	5.6	6.1	6.7	6.1	7.7
Subjects	7.0	5.1	7.0	6.0	7.0	6.9
Occupation-Hollingshead rating (1 = high)						
Men/male spouses	2.0	3.0	2.5	2.5	2.5	1.8

(professional) to 7 (unskilled labor) for fathers, male participants, and the husbands of female participants (few female study members were regularly employed). Group averages for these measures are presented in Table 4.2. The correlations among these measures, as well as their correlations with IQ level of participants at both adolescence and middle age (see Tables 4.3 and 4.4), range from about .3 to .6, values consistent with those from more representative samples of the general population. The only exception is the insignificant correlation of .18 between father's occupation and son's IQ at ages 17–18. Also, father's occupational status adds little to the prediction of daughter's IQ at

Table 4.3

Correlations with IQ for Samples
Used in IQ Analyses

Education and occupation		Men			Women	
	N	17–18 years r	36–48 years r	N	17–18 years r	36–48 years r
Education						
Father	117	.35****	.45****	129	.43****	.44****
Mother	116	.35****	.40****	130	.35****	.37****
Spouse	108	.49****	.45****	122	.42****	.39****
Subject	117	.60****	.57****	132	.48****	.57****
Occupation[a]						
Father	90	.18	.41****	100	.33****	.41****
Men/male spouses	117	.46****	.42****	122	.32****	.31****

[a]Signs reversed to indicate that higher occupation is associated with higher IQ.
****$p < .001$.

Table 4.4

Intercorrelations of Socioeconomic Measures
(N = 94–132)

	Men				Women			
Education	Mother r	Spouse r	Subject r	Occupation[a] (subject) r	Mother r	Spouse r	Subject r	Occupation[a] (spouse) r
Father	.54****	.40****	.42****	.26****	.66****	.45****	.51****	.35****
Mother		.35****	.43****	.30***		.48****	.55****	.36****
Spouse			.50****	.40****			.40****	.62****
Subject				.64****				.40****

[a] Signs reversed to indicate that higher occupation is associated with higher IQ.
***p < .01.
****p < .001.

ages 17–18 beyond the prediction from father's education (partial r = .08), whereas the inverse is not true (partial r = .30). Note that the signs of all correlations of occupation with IQ or education have been reversed; high levels of one tend to be associated with high levels of the other, but the scoring system for occupation is inverse (1 = high, 7 = low).

In our predominantly middle-class sample, adolescent IQ appears to be a better predictor of boys' educational attainment than is father's education (partial rs of .53 and .28), whereas for girls IQ is not more effective (partial rs are .34 and .38). Although inclusion of the OGS women means that more of our women than men came from working-class homes, this apparent sex difference probably is representative of differential expectations and treatment of the sexes rather than a sample peculiarity. More effort was made to send boys to college even if financial resources were limited, and men with military service also had the advantage of federal education funds (the "GI Bill").

None of these variables is significantly associated with IQ level or IQ gain before partialling out the negative correlation between adolescent IQ and IQ gain. However, a number of the partial correlations are significant. Their own education is equally predictive of gain for both sexes (rs of .27, p < .01). Father's and mother's education are correlated with gain in men (rs of .30, p < .001 and .25, p < .01, respectively), and father's occupation is a significant correlate for both sexes (−.43 for men, p < .001; −.22 for women, p < .05). However, the relationships among the data suggest that parental education and father's occupation are not directly influential but instead increase the likelihood that offspring will attain higher educational levels, which are directly associated with IQ gain.

Quality of the participant's advanced education (assessed by relative prestige of the institution) did not appear to contribute anything further to IQ gain. However, another kind of "enriching" experience was significantly associated with gain in the extreme groups. Almost half (13 of 28) of the Extreme Increasers had traveled outside the United States, whereas only 3 (12%) of the 28 Extreme Decreasers had done so. The meaning of this association is not clear. Such travel may contribute to IQ increase, but individuals who choose to travel may in general be more highly motivated to explore and learn. The difference between extreme groups is not a function of education nor occupation, because their mean years of education are almost identical, as are their occupational levels at middle age and the occupations of their fathers when they were adolescents.

Men's own occupational level is correlated with their IQ gain (r = .18, p < .05), but like parental education and father's occupation, this association seems to derive from educational level rather than from occupational experiences directly. Increasers and Decreasers do not differ in mean occupational level at middle age. Further, an analysis of variance of the social mobility groups described by Clausen (Chapter 13) shows equal gains among men in middle class occupations whether or not they had moved up or down or stayed at the same occupational level as their fathers (adjusted gains of about 6 points in each group). However, men in middle-class occupations who had moved up from workingclass homes gained significantly less than the other three groups (mean about .3 points).

Even economic deprivation during adolscence did not seem to influence either IQ level or gain, although OGS members classified by Elder (1974) as having been economically deprived in adolescence (family income reduced more than 35% during the Great Depression, when the cost of living declined 18%) had lower mean IQs at both late adolescence and middle adulthood than those who had not been so deprived. This trend was consistent for both men and women but not statistically significant for either sex or for the sexes combined.

MARITAL EXPERIENCES

Similarity of spouses in both socioeconomic level and IQ has been observed in many samples (Watkins, 1979) and is evident in ours. The spouse correlations for education (see Table 4.3) and for IQ are identical—.50 for male study members and .40 for female members. However, instances of considerable difference in IQ were noted. We hypothesized that living with a spouse whose IQ was markedly different would influence the study member's IQ, a prediction that was supported for females by both correlational and extreme group analyses but only by the latter for males. Partialling out the negative correlation between IQ gain and adolescent IQ yielded a partial correlation of .25 ($p < .05$) between women's gain in IQ and their husbands' IQ level. The partial correlation for men was positive (.15) but not significant.

Because data plots suggested greater effects when spouses differed markedly in IQ, the number of marriages in which the spouse's adult IQ was 10 or more points higher or lower than the subject's IQ at 18 was tabulated. Twelve of the 20 (60%) marrieds among the Extreme Increasers but only 1 of the 23 (4%) marrieds among the Extreme Decreasers had spouses whose adult IQs were at least 10 points higher than their own had been at late adolescence. Conversely, 11 of the 23 (48%) Decreasers but only 3 of the 20 (15%) Increasers had spouses with IQs 10 or more points lower than their own at age 18 ($p < .001$). Like foreign travel, living with a spouse who is brighter than oneself may be intellectually stimulating. Unfortunately, the inverse influence also occurs (although apparently less frequently); that is, instead of the lower IQ spouse being stimulated the brighter may be depressed.

The effect of spouse IQ on participant's IQ gain does not seem to be mediated by educational level—the correlations of gain with spouse's education are essentially zero for both sexes, even after partialling out the regression of IQ gain on adolescent IQ. Restriction of range in education also does not account for the lack of association with education, because, as noted in the preceding the educational levels of spouses are significantly correlated at about the moderate levels reported for more representative samples.

Correlations were computed between IQ at late adolescence and IQ at middle age and with information about length of current marriage, number of marriages, age at marriage, and number of children. The first two of these variables are not completely independent, but neither do they reflect identical aspects of marriage.

None of these variables is significantly associated with IQ level or gain in men. For women, however, the correlations are significant at middle adulthood for number of marriages ($-.25$, $p < .01$) and at late adolescence for number of children (.18, $p < .05$). In each instance the correlations at the other age are in the same direction and of almost equal magnitude but only approach significance ($p < .10$). However, there is no evidence that any of these factors contributed to IQ change in adulthood. Again, the most straightforward interpretation is that the better-educated women have had stable marriages and more children. In this wartime generation, having larger families was not associated with low socioeconomic status as it had been in other generations. Also, within the socioeconomic range of this sample, age at marriage is not associated with IQ in either sex. In the general population of their generations early marriage was somewhat more frequent among the less well educated.

PERSONALITY CHARACTERISTICS

Associations between personality characteristics and IQ level and change were examined using data from two very different assessments—the California Psychological Inventory (CPI) and the Q sort. As described in Chapters 2 and 10, the CPI is a questionnaire of 480 items, each of which the subject checks as true or false with respect to himself or herself. The test yields scores on 18 scales that are not independent; indeed, the author's conceptualization of personality assumes that many personality characteristics are intercorrelated.

In contrast to the self-report data of the CPI, the Q-sort ratings of personality were made by experienced clinicians who based their judgments on lengthy personal interviews or comprehensive case records and did not take the person's self-description at face value (Chapters 2 and 5). The Q-sort methodology makes no particular assumptions about the intercorrelations of personality characteristics, but the PARAFAC technique by which the Q sorts were factor-analyzed yielded six independent factors (Chapter 5) common to each of the four age periods included in the analysis (early and late adolescence and early and middle adulthood).

CALIFORNIA PSYCHOLOGICAL INVENTORY

Of the 250 persons tested for IQ at both late adolescence and middle adulthood, 164 (72 men and 92 women) also completed the CPI at the older age. This subsample does not differ from the total sample on any of the other measures examined here (e.g., IQ levels and gain, socioeconomic and marital status, Q-sort personality) so any significant findings should not be a result of selective bias. Twelve of the 18 scales are significantly correlated with the concurrently measured middle adult IQ in both sexes (see Table 4.5). Because IQ at adolescence and middle adulthood are highly correlated, correlations of CPI scores at the older age with IQ at the younger age would be anticipated. In fact, the correlations are of the same order at both ages.

Table 4.5

Correlations of Middle Adult CPI Scale Scores
with Concurrent and Adolescent IQ

CPI scales	Men (N = 72)		Women (N = 92)	
	17–18 years	36–48 years	17–18 years	36–48 years
Self-Acceptance	.46****	.41****	.23**	.21**
Sociability	.42****	.39****	.34****	.32***
Dominance	.27**	.18	.27***	.25***
Social Presence	.40****	.40****	.35****	.33****
Capacity for Status	.48****	.49****	.37****	.38****
Self-Control	.04	.05	-.01	.05
Good Impression	.07	.09	-.05	.02
Well-being	.08	.08	.04	.14
Achievement via Conformity	.32***	.29***	.25**	.30***
Socialization	.15	.18	-.02	.12
Tolerance for Ambiguity	.33***	.41****	.43****	.48****
Responsibility	.27**	.31***	.32***	.38****
Flexibility	.40****	.42****	.58****	.51****
Achievement via Independence	.54****	.59****	.49****	.55****
Communality	-.23**	-.21	-.11	-.06
Psychological Mindedness	.38****	.43****	.39****	.42****
Intellectual Efficiency	.43****	.48****	.40****	.52****
Femininity	-.12	-.12	-.11	-.14

**p < .05.
***p < .01.
****p < .001.

Of the six scales uncorrelated with IQ level, three are "control scales" used to assess attitudes toward test-taking (Sense of Well-Being, Good Impression, and Communality). Seven of the 12 scales correlated with IQ level are also significantly associated with IQ gain. Significant for each sex are Intellectual Efficiency (.43 for women, .40 for men, p < .001); Achievement via Independence (.30, p < .01; .43); Tolerance for Ambiguity (.28 and .32, p < .01); Responsibility (.23 and .28, p < .05); and Capacity for Status (.20 and .31). Achievement via Conformity and Psychological-mindedness are significant only when the sexes are combined (rs of .22 and .17, p < .05).

Factor analyses in other samples (Crites, Bechtoldt, Goodstein, & Heilbrun, 1961; Mitchell & Pierce-Jones, 1960) suggest that the 18 scales of the CPI represent about four or five dimensions. Omitting the "control" scales, a representative grouping is (1) "Ascendancy and Self-Assurance" (Dominance, Capacity for Status, Sociability, Social Presence, and Self-Acceptance); (2) "Socialization" (Responsibility, Socialization, Self-control, Tolerance of Ambiguity, and Achievement via Conformity); (3) "Achievement Potential" (Achievement via Independence and Intellectual Efficiency); and (4) "Intellectual and Interest Modes" (Psychological-mindedness, Flexibility, and Femininity). In general, this description fits the factor structure in our sample. However, as can be seen in Table 4.5, where the scales are grouped according to the factor structure for men and women combined, Flexibility and Psychological-mindedness fall in Factor 3 and femininity constitutes essentially a single-scale factor. This is the only factor having no associations with IQ level or gain.

Correlates of IQ level and gain come from all three other dimensions, although not necessarily from their primary definers. In particular, Self-Control and the two control scales with which it is highly correlated are not associated with IQ level or gain. Extreme scores on this scale seem to reflect overcontrol and a superficial concern with making a good impression that does not characterize either those with high IQs or those who gain in IQ. A characteristic of most of the scales that correlate highly with IQ gain (especially Intellectual Efficiency, Tolerance for Ambiguity, and Psychological-mindedness) is that they are not primary definers of any scale but instead load moderately on at least two dimensions and are highly intercorrelated among themselves. The picture that emerges is of the IQ gainer as a balanced person, well- but not over-socialized, and highly but not extremely independent, adaptable, and self-confident.

Q-SORT PERSONALITY FACTORS

Not all study members who had IQ tests at both late adolescence and middle age also had Q-sort personality factor scores at all four ages because the latter were computed only for participants meeting the criteria for inclusion in the analyses done for Chapter 5. Therefore, we did two sets of correlations between IQ level and change and Q-sort personality factors, one for a constant sample of 63 who had all of the measures being considered in this chapter (including personality factor scores at all four age periods) and one for all participants who had factor scores at any of the age periods. The numbers available for the second set of analyses were sufficient (125 to 172) to permit computing the correlations for each sex separately. In all respects, the results for the constant and total samples were consistent.

As Table 4.6 shows, four of the six personality factors are significantly associated with IQ level at middle age, late adolescence, or both. Factor 1, Cognitively Invested, is the most pervasive, with significant and generally moderate correlations for both sexes at all ages. The Q-sort items with the highest positive loadings on this factor are the following: Values Intellectual Matters, High Aspirations, and Verbally Fluent. Scores on this factor at younger ages are, in general, as highly correlated with IQ at middle adulthood as with concurrent assessments (i.e., with IQs at the younger ages). Similarly, Factor 1 assessed at middle adulthood is at least as highly correlated with IQ at late adolescence as with the concurrent measure of IQ (i.e., at 40–48). Because IQs are highly correlated across time, and scores on Factor 1 are also correlated across age periods, some intercorrelations would be expected. However, a similar statement can be made for other factors that do not show such strong intercorrelations.

If the negative correlation between IQ gain and adolescent IQ is partialled out, Cognitive Investment at late adolescence is also significantly correlated with IQ gain in men ($r = .44$; $p < .001$), and the correlation between IQ gain and this factor approaches significance at early adolescence for men and at early adulthood for both sexes. By middle adulthood, when gain as we measured it is complete, the association has disappeared, although, as already noted, IQ level at middle age is still significantly correlated with Cognitive Investment.

Two factors associated with self-control, Factor 5 (Under/ Overcontrolled, Heterosexual) and Factor 2 (Emotionally Under/ Overcontrolled) when measured in early or late adolescence have negative correlations with IQ at middle adulthood as well as with adolescent IQ. In contrast, these self-control measures at either early or middle adulthood are not associated with IQ at middle age. The items with the highest negative loadings on Factor 5 are the characteristics of overcontrolled, aloof, and dependable; the major positive definers are interested in the opposite sex, undercontrolled, eroticizes, and talkative. The major definers for Factor 2 are calm, bland, overcontrolled, and dependable. Thus, adolescents who were highly controlled (perhaps especially in sexual expression), dependable, calm, and somewhat aloof from their peers were those who in middle adulthood, as well as at adolescence, had the higher IQs. However, by adulthood (even young adulthood) persons with high IQs were no longer distinguished by these characteristics.

The implication in these findings that self-control at the younger

Table 4.6

Correlations of Q-sort Personality Factors with IQ
(Sample: GS and OGS only)

		Men			Women	
Q-sort factors	N	17-18 years	40-48 years	N	17-18 years	40-48 years
Junior High	61			66		
Cognitively Invested		.60****	.53****		.41****	.30***
Emotional Under/Over control		-.19	-.21		-.23**	-.29**
Open/Closed to Self		-.09	-.00		-.06	-.11
Nurturant/Hostile		.05	.13		.19	.17
Under/Overcontrol, Heterosexual		-.28***	-.33***		-.20	.37***
Self-Confident		-.14	.05		-.14	-.05
Senior High	59			66		
Cognitively Invested		.58****	.59****		.36***	.39****
Emotional Under/Over control		-.27**	-.34***		-.14	-.13
Open/Closed to Self		.00	-.04		-.07	-.09
Nurturant/Hostile		-.07	.06		.18	.13
Under/Overcontrol, Heterosexual		-.21	-.25		-.14	-.32***
Self-Confident		-.22	.00		.02	.01
Young Adult	76			96		
Cognitively Invested		.36***	.34***		.32****	.41****
Emotional Under/Over control		.06	-.06		-.04	-.10
Open/Closed to Self		-.27**	-.29**		-.18	-.14
Nurturant/Hostile		.07	.14		.14	.16
Under/Overcontrol, Heterosexual		.02	-.08		.02	-.12
Self-Confident		-.05	.14		-.14	-.19
Middle Adult	75			94		
Cognitively Invested		.47****	.33****		.21**	.31***
Emotional Under/Over control		.09	-.03		-.09	-.07
Open/Closed to Self		-.21	-.31***		-.21**	-.17
Nurturant/Hostile		.11	.12		.10	.11
Under/Overcontrol, Heterosexual		.19	.17		-.02	-.08
Self-Confident		.05	.07		.08	.13

**$p < .05$.
***$p < .01$.
****$p < .001$.

ages is predictive of subsequent IQ gain as well as of concurrent IQ level is supported primarily through Factor 5. For the total sample, scores on this factor at both early adolescence and early adulthood are negatively and significantly correlated ($-.18$; $p < .02$ and $-.14$; $p < .04$, respectively) with IQ gain between late adolescence and middle adulthood. For men, Factor 5 at late adolescence is also significantly predictive of IQ gain ($r = -.25$; $p < .03$), and the correlations for women ($-.19$; $p < .06$) and for the total group ($-.14$; $p < .06$) approach significance. Correlations of Factor 2 at younger ages with IQ gain are also negative but are significant only for two subgroups at one age each.

Because both extremes of Factor 2 represent ineffective responses to conflict or stress (see Chapter 5), it is not surprising that by adulthood this factor is correlated neither with IQ level nor gain. However, at all ages the mean scores on Factor 2 of persons in the lower quartile in IQ gain indicate that they are significantly more likely than either the top quartile or the middle group to be seen as undercontrolled and self-dramatizing.

By young adult ages, Factor 3, Open/Closed to Self, has significant correlations with IQ for men. This factor is reflected, so the direction of the correlation means that men with higher IQs are more likely to be characterized as insightful, introspective, unconventional, comfortable with uncertainty, and less repressive and self-defensive. Both sexes tend to become more open by adulthood (see Chapter 5), and this trend is significantly stronger among the IQ increasers than among either decreasers or the middle half of the sample.

Although Factor 6, Self-Confident, is not correlated with IQ level at any age, by middle adulthood the correlation of IQ gain and self-confidence is significantly negative ($-.29$; $p < .001$). Because this factor is reflected, the direction of the correlation means that those who decrease in IQ are less confident at middle age. Comparison of means shows that both Increasers and the middle group tend to become more self-confident with age, whereas the Decreasers show the reverse trend.

Only Factor 4, Nurturant/Hostile, has no significant associations with either IQ level or IQ change at any age.

PSYCHOLOGICAL HEALTH

As described in Chapters 2 and 6, an individual's Psychological Health Index (PH) is the correlation between the person's Q-sort profile and that of an "ideal" psychologically healthy person, as judged by experienced clinicians. For men, PH at both late adolescence and middle adulthood are significantly ($p < .001$) correlated with IQ level at ages 17–18 (.34 and .33, respectively). However, IQ at middle age is only tenuously associated with either concurrent PH (.14, not significant) or adolescent PH (.15; $p < .06$). IQ gain in men is not associated with PH at either age.

For women, IQ level and PH are significantly associated only at middle age. PH measured at this time is significantly correlated with both concurrent IQ ($r = .24$; $p < .004$) and with IQ gain since adolescence ($-.20$; $p < .018$).

PHYSICAL HEALTH

As described in Chapters 2 and 3, physical health was rated on a 5-point scale from 1 (excellent) to 5 (very poor). It is only weakly associated with IQ level. The correlations tend to be higher in middle age than at adolescence, and, for GS and OGS women, but not BGS women nor the total sample of women, are significant by the older age. At ages 40–48 (GS and OGS combined), the correlation between IQ and health rating is .21 for men (not significant) and .27 ($p < .01$) for women.

Although physical health ratings are not associated with IQ change, qualitative analysis of health records indicates a higher incidence among Extreme Decreasers of disabilities likely to have adverse effects on mental test performance. Among the 28 Extreme Decreasers, two had had shock therapy; one had a serious traffic accident resulting in head injury; one had very poor eyesight ("cannot read"; "depressed"); another reported anxiety states and colitis; and a sixth had (and subsequently died of) emphysema. None of the Extreme Increasers reported health problems of these kinds.

CONSUMPTION OF ALCOHOL

Problem drinking may be associated with impairment of both psychological and physical health. We compared the proportion of Extreme Increasers and Decreasers classified by M. C. Jones (see Chapter 9) as "heavy" or "problem" drinkers. Sixty-eight percent of the Extreme Decreasers but only 12% of the Extreme Increasers were in these categories, a significant difference ($p < .01$). In the total sample, however, the correlations between IQ and drinking classification (5-point scale, abstainer through problem drinker) are essentially zero for each sex at both age periods, suggesting that alcohol consumption belongs to that group of variables in which associations with IQ are nonlinear. Here effects are observable only at one extreme. Whether the declines in IQ are a manifestation of depression, with which alcoholism is thought to be associated, or are symptoms of organic changes resulting from excessive consumption, or both, cannot be determined from these data.

SUMMARY

IQs derived from the 1937 Stanford-Binet or Wechsler-Bellevue at 17 or 18 years and from the Wechsler Adult Intelligence Scale at middle age (36–48 years) were analyzed for individual consistency across age, age trends, and correlates of IQ level and change. In all three samples (two cohorts) individual consistency, as judged by the cross-age correlations, was high in each sex (about .8).

Despite overall findings of individual consistency across intervals, varying with sample, of 18 to 31 years and of a modest increase in IQ level, our longitudinal data also show that many individuals did not conform to the group trends. As earlier publications from these studies demonstrated the reality of intraindividual IQ variability (changes as great as ±20 points) during childhood and adolescence, so the present data show such variability continuing into middle age.

Contrary to trends inferred from cross-sectional data, decrease in IQ by mid-life was not the norm; in fact, modest to moderate increases (average of 6.2 points) were characteristic. For both sexes in all three samples gains in verbal IQ were observed, and for the two samples in which it was measured at both ages, the average gain in corrected performance IQ was about equal to that in verbal IQ (8.0). However, contrasts between the performance IQs of the older and younger cohorts at middle age and tests of the BGS between 18 and 36 suggest not only that the gain in performance IQ was made earlier in adulthood but also that a modest decline occurred sometime between the mid-30s and 50.

Comparisons between frequently tested persons and groups tested only as adults (i.e., spouses) or less frequently between adolescence and middle age showed that the gains observed cannot be attributed to practice. Significant evidence for selective attrition was found for only one subgroup (GS males), with drop-outs more frequent among those who had lower IQs at adolescence. Because *larger* gains were more characteristic of those with lower IQs, the mean gain in our sample does not result from attrition. However, the regression effect was sufficient to mask correlates of IQ gain that were also positively correlated with IQ level. Therefore, change scores, with the regression partialled out, were used to examine correlates of IQ change.

In general, IQ level had the same correlates at both late adolescence and middle age. Moderate associations with education and occupation of self (about .6), parents (about .4), and spouse (about .4–.5) were expected and are consistent with the cross-sectional literature. The sequence of influence was for adolescent IQ and education of the parents to be positively associated with attainment of advanced education. Education, in turn, was positively associated with IQ gain and seemed to account for associations of IQ gain with parental education, father's occupation, and, for men, their own occupational level. However, an association of IQ change with spouse's IQ, particularly when the spouses differed substantially in IQ level, was not an indirect effect of spouse's education, which was not correlated with IQ gain in the study members.

Numerous correlations of both IQ level and gain were found for personality characteristics, as measured by scales of the CPI and by factors derived from the Q sort. Some of these associations are equal to, or of greater magnitude than, those between IQ and socioeconomic status. Correlations between IQ at middle age and personality characteristics during early and late adolescence were sometimes larger than those between concurrently measured IQ and personality characteristics and, indeed, of cross-age correlations for the personality variables themselves. Noteworthy in these respects are the correlations of IQ with the factor from the Q sort labelled Cognitively Invested and with 10 CPI scales. The CPI correlates of IQ level suggest important associations between IQ and modes of thinking, socialization, and self-confidence; correlates of IQ gain suggest a healthy balance of independence, socialization, and self-confidence.

Correlations between IQ and personality factors from the Q sort indicate that adolescents who were highly controlled, dependable, calm, and somewhat aloof from their peers were those who in middle life as well as at adolescence had the higher IQs. But by middle age these personality characteristics were no longer correlated with IQ level. However, new correlates emerged for men. In middle age those with high IQs were more likely to be seen as insightful, rebellious, interesting, and having unusual thoughts (Open/Closed to Self).

Ratings of physical health were uncorrelated with IQ at late adolescence but showed association by ages 40–48, at least for women. An index of psychological health derived from the Q sort had low positive correlations (.20–.34) with IQ at both ages in both sexes, reaching significance for men at late adolescence and women at middle age. For women, psychological health was correlated at a comparable level with IQ gain.

Finally, several qualitative comparisons were made between groups with the most extreme gains and losses in IQ (top and bottom 11%). Extreme Decreasers had a disproportionate incidence of heavy alcohol consumption and of debilitative illness. Those with marked increases were more likely to be married to a spouse whose adult IQ was at least 10 points higher than that of the study member at adolescence.

Quality of education did not distinguish Extreme Increasers and Decreasers, but travel outside the United States during their early adult years was more characteristic of the Extreme Increasers.

Our findings of individual consistency in adult IQ, average gains, some marked individual differences in IQ change, and significant correlates of IQ level and change (particularly for personality characteristics), should be of practical as well as scientific interest. The robustness of the results is attested by marked similarity among three different samples and, in general, both sexes. They encourage us to believe that means can be found to promote intellectual growth among adults, as they have for young children.

5

Common Dimensions of Personality Development: Early Adolescence to Middle Life

NORMA HAAN

INTRODUCTION

Agreement on a definition of personality and its basic dimensions would improve research and enhance understanding of personality development. Since the influence of psychoanalysis has diminished, no model of personality development over the life span guides research. Some researchers deal with a single theme, such as creativity (Kogan, 1973) or moral development (Kohlberg, 1973). Others focus on factors that may influence development, such as the effects of societal age grading on personality changes (Atchley, 1975; Nardi, 1973; Neugarten & Datan, 1973). Others essentially extend general theories to encompass the life span, for example, Erikson's elaboration of psychoanalysis to include eight "stages of man." Brim (1976a) proposes a life-span theory of "oneself"; van den Daele (1975) and Loevinger, Wessler, and Redmore (1970), a stage theory of ego development; and Haan (1977), a theory of coping and defensive processes that is tied to "structural" developments. A more empirical strategy, which this study represents, takes personality variables commonly used in cross-sectional studies and traces their fate developmentally. Similarly, Lowenthal, Thurnher, and Chiriboga (1975) and their associates chose to investiage goals, morals, anxiety, and modes of adaptation, first with separate age groups and then longitudinally.

Disagreements about research goals are not unique to life-span re-

117

search. However, life-span research may eventually lead to greater consensus about the basic elements of personality because the nature of the task highlights our confusions. No conceptualization can satisfactorily encompass the life course unless it is relatively abstract and general, rising above the concrete details of ever-changing individual lives and situations. The kinds of description and explanation required by life-span research lead investigators to search for "basic" variables because they can neither control nor systematize the complex, intimate details or the sociohistorical contexts of persons' lives.

Until consensus about the definition of personality is achieved, we may benefit from modest, empirical descriptions. A common framework for observations on the personalities of our study members from early adolescence to the middle years was generated in this study. The common dimensions I identify probably do not represent the ultimate themes, but they may suggest ways to work toward them. The data were reduced to manageable proportions with a new methodology PARAFAC (see Appendix A)—a three-way, principal-component factor analysis that yields a unified descriptive model of people and variables over several occasions.

The findings bracket a substantial portion of the life cycle—from 12 to about 40 years for GS and from 12 to 47 years for OGS. The intent is to produce the most general description of these persons over the course of these years and then to bring this development picture to bear on the most recent observations of the participants in their middle years. Unlike several chapters in this book, this one reports analyses only for study members with Q sorts for all four time periods. No moderator variables, such as psychological health, marital status, or social maturity, are used.

The psychological implications of the measures and methodology must be discussed first. Several aspects of the Q-sort and the particular gains, sacrifices, and biases that PARAFAC imposes on the actualities of development need to be examined. No statistical model fully represents life.

Equivalent scaling of measures made at different ages is a particularly thorny problem in longitudinal studies. We cannot assume that the same score for a personality variable is equivalent for child and adult nor that the adult's characteristic is a transformed version of the child's. If age-graded stages of personality were known to exist, they could constitute one kind of age-related measurement that would permit descriptive statements of ordinality—younger or older than. Efforts to identify stages of personality are underway (Loevinger *et al.*, 1970; van den Daele, 1975). But without verification that stage sequences exist, measurement of personality across age usually has no mooring. Because of difficulties in equating scores across ages, our staff some years ago turned to measuring personality within the ipsative framework of the Q sort (Block in collaboration with Haan, 1971). This form of scaling involves an intra-individual rank ordering of attributes (rather than an attempt to measure variables in terms of absolute quantities). A difference in a person's characteristic between two time periods represents a change in the relative salience of this characteristic within the person's profile. (As noted in Chapter 2, the wordings of items were designed to be age-relevant, and judges were not required to make age-normative evaluations.) Each person is his or her own frame of reference; no claim is made, explicitly or implicitly, that absolute differences are being measured.

The relational framework of the Q sort is illustrated by the following example. The amount of a person's aggression during adolescence may be, in absolute terms, greater than at adulthood. But it could be given a lower Q score at adolescence if some other characteristics were judged then to be comparatively more salient. From some points of view it is doubtful that any personality attribute will ever be measured absolutely. In any event, there seems to be no better approach at present than the Q sort for longitudinal personality research.

Another feature of the Q-sort that must be kept in mind is the forced distribution and its effect on analyses of normal samples. Approximately 40% of the Q-sort items represent "healthy" qualities and another 40% pathological qualities. Because our study members are generally well-functioning persons, pathological items more often have low values and "healthy" items, high values. This phenomenon produces positive correlations within both the pathological set and healthy set of items and negative correlations between the two sets. Hence, the general levels of intercorrelation among items in our samples are higher than they would be in samples representing the full range of psychological well-being in the population (see Chapter 12). Because a modest level of item intercorrelation over the entire Q sort exists within the present sample, we can expect that the various factors identified by PARAFAC reflect more bipolarity between pathology and adequacy—as well as more cohesiveness among healthy items and among pathological items—than probably exists in the population at large.

The statistically sophisticated reader may read Harshman and Berenbaum's detailed description of the PARAFAC method in Appendix A. Here I am concerned with the psychological implications of this method. In using PARAFAC one chooses the number of factors to be derived (six in our evaluation) and then proceeds to a simultaneous solution of this predetermined number of factors for several samples (here four) across several time periods (also four). The solution is based on the assumption that the derived factors can be meaningfully understood in terms of linear combinations of the original variables. Although this assumption is the practical basis of much research, it may not always represent the personality development of real people for several reasons.

If important personality variations occur within one time period, they may not be included in PARAFAC's general solution for all four time periods, particularly when data are not perfectly reliable and the number of factors is limited. For these reasons, the total variance accounted for in the final solution will be less than investigators normally consider. This effect of the procedures is no sacrifice for life-span research because period-specific variables can be regarded as reflecting concurrent statuses and not historical descriptions, to use Baltes and Schaie's (1973) terminology. Nor is this effect a disadvantage here, because my purpose is to identify and describe common *developmental* themes. Because the PARAFAC solution is based on a simultaneous consideration of all periods, neither a child-centric nor adult-centric model of development (Baltes & Schaie, 1973) determines the results. All time periods have equal opportunity to affect the general solution.

PARAFAC locates factors that exist for all occasions, producing a solution common to all time periods, but different factors vary in their importance for different time periods. Thus, systematic variations in the relative strength of a factor's variance can occur. In developmental study such variations are expected.

The substantive implications of these methodological features are several. Persons are assumed to possess constellations of traits that are stably patterned across time periods. These constellations are expected to assume greater or lesser importance in the overall personality organizations of persons because the original context of measurement is an ipsative one. Moreover, a theory of personality that describes development as a series of "structural" reorganizations based on qualitative transformations of variables evident early in life (e.g., as concrete cognitive operations are reworked and incorporated into formal operations in Piaget's theory) could not readily be represented by this methodology. In other words, PARAFAC finds and capitalizes on the sameness of configurational patterns in personality attributes across time periods. Change (but not developmental reorganization) can be observed as the variances of the factor scores fluctuate and their mean levels rise and fall.

Finally, the factorial solution used here is orthogonal (i.e., factors are independent of each other), again a decision of convenience that is consistent with the idea that personality is composed of independent faculties or dimensions. This effect does not represent personalities as unitary in nature, a view held by some theorists.

No factor-analytic procedure can generate a developmental model if the input variables are not relevant to development; results are circumscribed by the pool of variables available. The California Q sort (Block, 1961) and its adolescent-relevant version (Block in collaboration with Haan, 1971) represent attributes commonly used by clinicians to describe personality. However, this Q sort does not include some qualities that may be important in describing the life span from adolescence to the middle years. For instance, some tender, noninstrumental characteristics, such as empathy and depression, are not well represented. Particularly lacking are structural-developmental variables, such as the personality manifestations of concrete or hypothetical-deductive thinking or interpersonal reciprocity, which some investigators think may be critical in developmental study.

METHOD

Participants

Four subsamples (total $N = 136$) with Q-sort descriptions for all four time periods—early and late adolescence and young and middle adulthood—are used: OGS females ($N = 41$) and males ($N = 37$); GS females ($N = 32$) and males ($N = 26$). To minimize the risk of capitalizing on chance, I consider a finding meaningful only if it is replicated in at least two of the four samples with significance levels of at least .05. This requirement is stringent because participants in all longitudinal samples have vastly different life experiences. Further, more than a 7-year age difference separates OGS and GS, and the four sub-samples have other personal-demographic differences, which will be discussed. Given such variations among samples and the requirement that findings be replicated at least once, results suggesting similar developmental trends should be reliable.

To give the reader a better "clinical" understanding of the nature of these samples, some demographic differences are summarized in Table 1. Compared to the other samples, the OGS females had the least education, the lowest socioeconomic status (SES) during childhood, and

Norma Haan

Table 5.1

Social and Personal Characteristics of OGS and GS Participants

	$\bar{X}$s					
	Females		Males			
	OGS	GS	OGS	GS		Significant
Item	1	2	3	4	F ratio	post hoc comparisons
Subject's education[a]	3.42	2.81	2.40	2.35	10.30***	1/2** 1/3*** 1/4**
Subject's SES[b]	31.32	26.50	24.27	26.46	1.50	
Father's SES[b]	36.52	32.06	35.32	18.35	4.69**	1/4*** 2/4* 3/4**
Number of siblings	.41	.31	.37	.26	.50	
Number of offspring	2.63	3.55	2.86	3.00	2.03	
IQ[c]	114.87	121.73	125.27	122.48	6.69***	1/2* 1/3* 1/4*
Divorces (%)[d]	34	16	14	31		
Political position (self-checked)						
Conservative (%)	50	21	49	24		
Moderate (%)	24	25	34	47		
Liberal (%)	18	36	11	18		
Independent (%)[e]	8	18	6	12		

[a] Education: 1 = professional training; 4 = high school graduate; 7 = under 7 years.
[b] Class I (highest) = 11.17; Class III = 32.47; Class V = 64–77 (Hollingshead).
[c] IQ is Wechsler Adult Intelligence Scale, full scale, administered in 1968.
[d] Chi square = 6.49, $p < .10$.
[e] Chi square = 15.12, $p < .10$.
* $p < .10$.
** $p < .05$.
*** $p < .01$.

the lowest mid-life IQ scores (although still high relative to the general population), are the most often divorced, and the most conservative politically. GS females are better educated, infrequently divorced, and most liberal politically, and have higher IQs. OGS males show marked upward socioeconomic mobility, had the highest adult SES and IQ (at approximately age 50), and are politically conservative. GS males have the most education and came from the most advantaged homes, but they themselves have actually been downwardly mobile in SES (some had nowhere to move but down).

The high divorce rates for OGS females (34%) and GS males (31%) contrast with those of the OGS males (16%) and GS females (14%). The latter two were near the national averages for people of these ages (50 and 40, respectively), reported at about the time of the most recent followup: 10% for college graduates and 25% for high-school graduates (*San Francisco Chronicle*, 1972). Moreover, considering their age, a disproportionate number of the divorced OGS females and GS males made this decision between the first and second adult follow-up: of those divorced, 36% and a surprising 75%, respectively. Approximately one-half of all divorces, according to current national figures, occur within the first 7 years of marriage. GS marriages had lasted for approximately 10–20 years and the OGS marriages for 20–30 years. Finally, we cannot assume that these subsamples are representative of their age groups or locale, although demographically they do not seem different from the original samples (Chapter 2).

Data

The main data were derived from the original Q sort, described in Chapter 2, using the 90 items with equivalent meanings for all four time periods. Only 86 items were actually used, however, because four items had insufficient reliability ($r < .45$) for more than one time period and for each of the sexes. The PARAFAC procedures produced an orthogonal solution that fitted non-normalized covariance matrices for the samples at each time period and provided four sets of factor scores for each person (six factors per set), one set for each time period. These scores are used in all analyses.

RESULTS

After the particular factors that were identified are described, stabilities and changes in factor scores and their trends toward heterogeneity or homogeneity within samples are considered. The associations of factor scores to socioeconomic status and mobility are also described, and the distinctive characteristics of the samples at their middle years, both in terms of PARAFAC scores and scores for the scales of the California Psychological Inventory (CPI), are summarized.

Description of Factors

Table 5.2 shows the items with factor loadings at least 1.5 standard deviations from the mean which give each factor its flavor. These sets of descriptive items must be understood as integrated constellations; shorthand labels cannot reflect all facets of each dimension. Titles with slashes indicate bipolar factors,—both extremes define clear constellations; the negative and is not clearly a diminished version of the positive end.

Table 5.2

Distinctive Item Loadings of Common Dimensions
(1½ Standard Deviations from the $\bar{X}$)

High positive loadings	score$^{\sigma}$	High negative loadings	score$^{\sigma}$
Factor 1: Cognitively Invested			
Values Intellectual Matters	2.6	Self-Defensive	1.9
		Undercontrolled	1.8
Ambitious	2.1	Withdraws When Frustrated	1.7
Verbally Fluent	2.0	Uncomfortable with Uncertainty	1.6
Wide Interests	1.6		
Productive	1.6	Pushes Limits	1.5
Introspective	1.6		
Philosophically Concerned	1.6		
Appears Intelligent	1.6		
Dependable	1.5		
Factor 2: Emotionally Under/Overcontrolled			
Self-Dramatizing	2.1	Calm	2.4
Talkative	1.9	Emotionally Bland	2.1
Undercontrolled	1.7	Overcontrolled	1.9
Pushes Limits	1.5	Dependable	1.8
Assertive	1.5	Sympathetic	1.6
Rebellious	1.5	Submissive	1.5
Unpredictable	1.5		
Factor 3: Open/Closed to Self			
Insightful	2.5	Conventional	2.5
Introspective	2.3	Uncomfortable with Uncertainty	2.3
Thinks Unconventionally	1.8		
Rebellious	1.7	Repressive	2.1
Interesting	1.7	Self-Defensive	2.1
		Fastidious	1.5
		Power-Oriented	1.5
Factor 4: Nurturant/Hostile			
Giving	2.1	Aloof	2.4
Sympathetic	2.0	Negativistic	2.0
Warm	1.9	Rebellious	1.8
Gregarious	1.7	Condescending	1.8
Arouses Liking	1.7	Distrustful	1.7
Cheerful	1.6	Skeptical	1.7
Protective	1.5	Deceitful	1.6
Dependable	1.5	Pushes Limits	1.5

Table 5.2 *(continued)*

High positive loadings	score	High negative loadings	score
Factor 5: Under/Overcontrolled, Heterosexual			
Interested in the Opposite Sex	2.1	Overcontrolled	2.5
		Aloof	1.8
Undercontrolled	1.9	Dependable	1.7
Eroticizes Situations	1.8	Ruminative	1.6
Talkative	1.8	Fearful	1.6
Gregarious	1.7	Values Intellectual	
Self-Indulgent	1.7	Matters	1.5
Self-Dramatizing	1.6		
Factor 6: Self-Confident			
Assertive	2.2	Fearful	2.0
Satisfied with Self	2.1	Self-Defensive	1.9
Poised	2.0	Withdraws When Frustrated	1.8
Values Independence	1.8	Feels Victimized	1.8
Productive	1.5	Brittle Ego Defenses	1.7
		Feels Life Lacks Meaning	1.7
		Reluctant to Act	1.5
		Ruminative	1.5

Factor 1, Cognitively Invested, is positively defined by a pattern of items that indicates ease and skill in dealing with intellectual matters, deliberate reflectiveness, and concomitantly, interest in personal achievement. Persons with high scores value thinking; they are verbally fluent, introspective, philosophically concerned, and appear intelligent. They are also unusually ambitious, productive, and dependable. Persons with low scores are apparently defensive, diversely and disjointedly, because they are not only undercontrolled and push limits, but they are simultaneously self-defensive, uncomfortable with uncertainty, and withdraw when frustrated. Together, these items define a dimension that represents on the high end, successful adaptation, achievement, and use of abilities, whereas the low end includes various defenses that probably hinder adaptation, achievement, and efficient use of abilities.

Factor 2, Emotionally Under/Overcontrolled, is positively defined by items that represent a pressured, dramatic, and aggressive approach to interpersonal exchanges (self-dramatizing, talkative, undercontrolled, pushes limits, assertive, rebellious, and unpredictable) and at the other end, a calm, dependable, and sympathetic approach that is, nevertheless, clearly restricted. Emotionally bland ("flattened affect"), overcontrolled, and submissive are also important aspects of the negative end. Both extremes represent ineffective approaches to conflict. Two different ways that some people react when they are stressed—erratically flaying out or guardedly pulling in—are indicated. Because this dimension is clearly bipolar, both extremes are indicated in the title.

Factor 3, Open/Closed to Self, is also bipolar. It is positively defined by items that suggest an openness to one's own thoughts and experiences along with an easy self-expressiveness. In contrast, the negatively weighted items suggest need for certainty and a reliance on external, conventional standards as well as a striking lack of self-awareness. High scorers are insightful about themselves, introspective, rebellious, interesting, and think unconventionally, whereas low scorers are conventional, uncomfortable with uncertainty, repressive, self-defensive, fastidious, and power-oriented. This dimension reflects the self-reflexive ways persons think about and deal with their own psychological beings, either as objects of interest and resource or, defensively, as unpredictable entities that need the security of external guidance.

Factor 4, Nurturant/Hostile, is positively defined by consideration, warmth, and responsiveness to other people, whereas the negatively weighted items indicate hostility, suspiciousness, and wariness toward others. High scorers are giving, sympathetic, warm, gregarious, arousing of liking, cheerful, protective, and dependable; low scorers are aloof, negativistic, rebellious, condescending, distrustful, skeptical, deceitful, and pushing of limits. This bipolar dimension reflects a manner of relating to other people, whether fully, intimately, and generously; or hostilely, suspiciously, and deceitfully.

Factor 5, Under/Overcontrolled, Heterosexual, is positively defined by items that again suggest undercontrol, but unlike Factor 2, Emotionally Under/Overcontrolled, impulsiveness here is sexualized, gregarious, and self-indulgent instead of aggressive and rule-violating. Three positive items are shared by the two "control" factors—undercontrolled, talkative, and self-dramatizing—as are two negative items—overcontrolled and dependable. However, the low items for Factor 5 define an obsessive-compulsive constellation that includes affective vulnerability, compensatory investment in thinking, and asexuality. High scorers are interested in the opposite sex, undercontrolled, eroticizing of situations, talkative, gregarious, self-indulgent, and self-dramatizing; whereas low scorers are overcontrolled, aloof, dependable, ruminative, fearful, and valuing of intellectual matters. The underlying dimension is not entirely clear. As for Emotionally Under/Overcontrolled, neither extreme can be said to represent effective ways of relating to others. In fact, the positive items suggest the classic hysteric, whereas the negative items suggest the classic obsessive-compulsive. Clinicians do not usually regard hysteria and obsessive-compulsive neuroses as lying on the same dimension.

Factor 6, Self-Confident, is positively defined by items indicating great effectiveness in interpersonal relations, and concomitantly, self-confidence. In sharp contrast, the negative items suggest a tentative, uncertain sense of the self as being vulnerable in interpersonal exchanges. High scorers are assertive, satisfied with self, poised, productive, and they value independence. In contrast, low scorers are fearful, self-defensive, ruminative; they withdraw when frustrated, feel victimized, feel life lacks meaning, are reluctant to act and are judged to have brittle ego defenses. This factor appears to represent the social characteristics of the person as confident or vulnerable and fearful.

In summary, the various factors seem to reflect several important aspects of personality: Cognitively Invested, effective or ineffective use of cognitive abilities; Emotionally Under/Overcontrolled, reacting to stress by attacking or withdrawing; Open/Closed To Self, views of the self as self-guided or as regulated by external rules and standards; Nurturant/Hostile, ways of relating to other persons—generously and openly or hostilely and closed; Under/Overcontrolled, Heterosexual, ways of openly expressing and indulging the self and sexual interests or guarding against interpersonal involvements; Self-Confident, ways of regarding one's self in social contexts as competent or vulnerable. We cannot know whether these constellations approximate the basic dimensions of the life span, but perhaps we shall be able to move closer to making such evaluations after the course of their development from early adolescence to the middle years is reported.

Stabilities of the Common Dimensions across Age

Inter-correlations of the factor scores among age periods are shown in Table 5.3.[1] Only findings significant at the .05 level or better in at least two samples will be discussed. The total number of significant correlations in Table 5.3, irrespective of time interval, serves as a

[1]These correlations were also corrected for attenuation to estimate the levels they would achieve if each factor were measured with complete reliability. Reliabilities were calculated by generating factor scores for each judge (for each time period) and estimating the agreements for each factor by intraclass correlations (Haggard, 1958). The resulting reliabilities were uniformly high, that is, for the entire sample and all time periods the results ranged from .59 to .93, with a median of .85. Medians and ranges were almost identical for both sexes. Given (a) initial construction of a "floor" under case reliabilities by adding extra judges when agreement was low (see Chapter 2); (b) exclusion of the four least reliable items from analyses for this chapter; and (c) increased reliability achieved from factoring procedures themselves, the corrections for attenua-

Table 5.3

Correlations between Time Periods for the Common Dimensions

Q-sort factor	Age span for OGS				Age span for GS			
	14-17	17-37	37-47	14-47	14-17	17-30	30-40	14-40
Females								
Cognitively Invested	.70****	.54****	.66****	.49***	.52***	.42**	.38**	.03
Emotionally Under/Over controlled	.58****	.30	.44***	.48***	.72****	.54***	.45***	.30
Open/Closed to Self	.43***	.39**	.49***	.37**	.75****	.57****	.62****	.46***
Nurturant/Hostile	.57****	.49***	.48***	.13	.54***	.27	.40**	.20
Under/Overcontrolled, Heterosexual	.64****	.46***	.69****	.42**	.54***	.62****	.19	.11
Self-Confident	.48***	.44***	.65****	.30	.54***	.36**	.38**	.41**
Males								
Cognitively Invested	.63****	.58****	.78****	.62****	.73****	.40**	.59***	.34
Emotionally Under/Over controlled	.52****	.26	.56****	.32**	.67****	.21	.53***	.36
Open/Closed to Self	.30	-.08	.37**	.16	.35	.36	.45**	-.06
Nurturant/Hostile	.55****	.30	.29	.16	.65****	.24	.16	.37
Under/Overcontrolled, Heterosexual	.65****	.21	.33**	.03	.62****	.29	.21	-.05
Self-Confident	.61****	.24	.43***	.01	.66****	.27	.50***	.57***

$**p < .05.$
$***p < .01.$
$****p < .001.$

rough indication of overall stability: 63 (66%) were significant at the .05 level or better. Whether one concludes that the dimensions are impressively, moderately, or mildly stable over time, depends on one's theoretical expectations and what one accepts as evidence.

Table 5.3 shows, not unexpectedly, a larger number of significant correlations over the shorter intervals than the longer ones: of the 63 significant correlations, 35% are for the adolescent interval, 32% for the adult interval, 19% from late adolescent to young adult years, and 14% for the entire span from early adolescence to the middle years. The implication seems to be that people change slowly, while maintaining some continuity. The evidence does not suggest—even when these dimensions are corrected for imperfect reliabilities—that the personalities of these study members were immutable.

The two study groups have approximately the same overall number of significant correlations—54% of the total are for OGS and 46% for

---

tion could not be expected to have marked effects on the cross-time correlations. The median increase from the uncorrected to the corrected calculations was .08 with a range from −.03 to .31. In only six instances was the increase greater than .20, and these substantial gains were not systematic, that is, did not occur for any one factor, sex, or sample (OGS or GS). As a consequence, discussion is most economically focused on the results shown in Table 5.3.

GS—and do not differ markedly in the number significant for any one time interval.

Several sex differences in periods of stability are noteworthy: women are markedly more stable between late adolescence and young adulthood (10 significant correlations of 12) and between early adolescence and the middle years (6 significant correlations of 12) compared to men (2 and 3 significant correlations, respectively, of 12). Differences in the reliability of measure between the sexes do not account for this trend. Therefore the period from adolescence to young adulthood appears to be a time of special change for individual males (whatever the group mean levels). However males were also less predictable than women over the entire span studied.

The dimensions vary somewhat in the extent of stability: 22% of the significant correlations are for Cognitively Invested, 19% for Self-Confident, 17% for Emotionally Under/Overcontrolled, 16% for Open/Closed to Self, 14% for Under/Overcontrolled, Heterosexual, and 11% for Nurturant/Hostile. Although this range is not remarkable, it suggests that ways of using cognitive abilities and attitudes toward personal strengths or vulnerabilities are more durable than patterns of nurturance or sexuality.

Consideration of specific age intervals shows that from early to late adolescence all samples were stable for all dimensions with one exception: neither of the male groups was stable during this period for Open/Closed to Self. As a group they became more open, but the correlations indicate that one cannot predict which boys will become more open.

Stabilities are considerably less impressive from adolescence to young adulthood. All samples are stable for Cognitively Invested and the female samples are also stable for Open/Closed to Self; Under/Overcontrolled, Heterosexual; and Self-Confident. Between the two adult follow-ups, all samples have significant correlations for Cognitively Invested, Emotionally Under/Overcontrolled, Open/Closed to Self, and Self-Confident. Nurturant/Hostile is also stable for the two female samples, and Under/Overcontrolled, Heterosexual for the OGS samples. Finally, the number of significant correlations over the entire span (early adolescence to middle age) is not great: the two OGS samples are stable for Cognitively Invested and Emotionally Under/Overcontrolled; the two women's samples for Open/Closed to Self, and the two GS samples for Self-Confident.[2]

---

[2]The correlations just discussed are based on four samples of small size, a consequence of the replicate design used to examine cohort and sex differences in developmental trends. When the same calculations are done for all participants combined, making a

Altogether, these observations suggest a middle ground between change and the maintenance of sameness in personality functioning within these samples. None of the dimensions persists in immutable form. Again, persons change, but they change slowly. Women's personalities are generally more stable than men's. Men shift most radically between adolescence and adulthood when they take on the responsibilities of a career and financial independence. Dimensions most directly concerned with the self—Cognitively Invested, Self-Confident, and Open/Closed to Self (the latter, particularly for women)—are more stable. Dimensions that more directly reflect the quality of interpersonal relations—Nurturant/Hostile and Under/Overcontrolled, Heterosexual—are less stable. I suggest that the participants' standings on these interpersonal dimensions were affected, from one time to another, by actual changes in their interpersonal relationships that may have resulted from such events as deaths, divorces, illness, births, and work successes and failures. (See Datan & Ginsberg, 1975, and Dohrenwend & Dohrenwend, 1974, for discussions of stressful life events.) The stability of the self variables, compared to interpersonal, needs to be borne in mind as we consider the systematic developmental changes across time.

Effects of Time, Sex, and Sample

To assess the effects of time, sex, and sample on the factor scores, multivariate analyses of variance were done separately for each factor score. Orthogonal polynomial decomposition was used so no assumptions about the homogeneity of covariance were necessary (Bock, 1975; McCall & Appelbaum, 1973). The modal chronological ages for each sample at each time period defined the points in time. The aims were to identify (a) sample differences for each dimension, with sex and time controlled, (b) sex differences for each dimension, with sample and time controlled, (c) changes in mean levels of each dimension across time (the developmental trends), with sex and sample controlled, and (d) two-way interactions between sex, sample, or time for each dimension. (No three-way interactions were significant.) Time changes can be regarded as developmental, whereas sample effects presumably re-

---

sample of 136, all the correlations become significant at the .05 level or better, compared to 66% of all correlations for the four separate samples. Although calculations based on the total sample produce greater reliability, the overall substantive implications of the results are not changed because the magnitudes do not shift markedly. The medians of the two sets of correlations—for particular dimensions or for all dimensions across a particular time period—all lie within a $-.04$ to $+.04$ of each other.

flect either cohort differences or initial sampling differences between GS and OGS. Note again that the ipsative framework of Q-sort measurement means that the results reported below represent differences or changes in the importance of a dimension *within* individuals.

Main Effects for Sample and Sex Differences

The first noteworthy finding is the absence of significant differences between GS and OGS (see Table 5.4). However, three strong sex differences emerged. With time and sample effects controlled, females are strikingly higher for Nurturant/Hostile and Under/Overcontrolled, Heterosexual, but are considerably lower for Self-Confident. Plots of the mean factor scores for each sample and time (see Figs. 5.1–5.6) show that these differences generally hold for all time periods. Interpretively, these differences seem to suggest that although these women apparently extended themselves toward others, nurturantly and sexually, these behaviors were not particularly rewarded within their sociohistorical context. A consequence may be their comparatively lower self-confidence.

Developmental Trends and Two-way Interactions

The most striking results in Table 5.4 are the time trends; these findings break new ground. All dimensions except Emotionally

Table 5.4

Multivariate Analyses of Variance
for Effects of Sex, Sample, and Time Periods

	F ratios					
	Main effects			Interactions		
Q-sort factor	Sex	Sample	Time	Sex × sample	Time × sex	Time × sample
Cognitively Invested	.19	1.75	15.92****	.00	1.54	1.26
Emotionally Under/Over controlled	1.14	1.11	1.28	3.78**	1.70	1.01
Open/Closed to Self	.40	.02	17.07a****	.08	6.92****	2.99**
Nurturant/Hostile	16.12****	3.57	5.69****	.00	1.46	4.46***
Under/Overcontrolled, Heterosexual	15.54****	.00	10.21****	3.26	4.80***	1.58
Self-Confident	7.22***	.04	4.91***	.32	1.13	.55

Note: Three-way F ratios are not shown; none were significant.

[a]This finding is significant at $p < .0001$.

**$p < .05$.

***$p < .01$.

****$p < .001$.

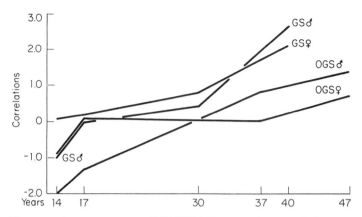

Fig. 5.1. Average scores on PARAFAC Factor 1, Cognitively Invested.

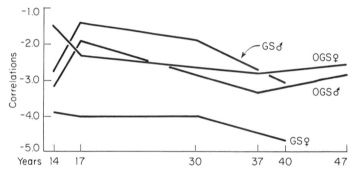

Fig. 5.2. Average scores on PARAFAC Factor 2, Emotionally Under/
OverControlled.

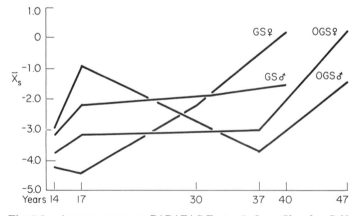

Fig. 5.3. Average scores on PARAFAC Factor 3, Open/Closed to Self.

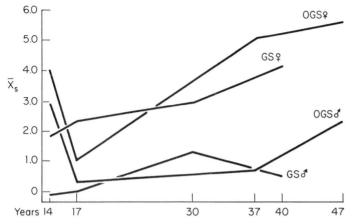

Fig. 5.4.   Average scores on PARAFAC Factor 4, Nurturant/Hostile.

Under/Overcontrolled showed strong and significant developmental trends with sex and sample controlled.

Cognitively Invested generally rises for all four samples from age 14 to the middle years. Apparently, intellectuality and interest in achievement came to occupy an increasingly important role in the participants' personalities from adolescence to the middle years. The intervals of marked gains are during adolescence and adulthood, with very little change *between* adolescence and adulthood. The reasons for

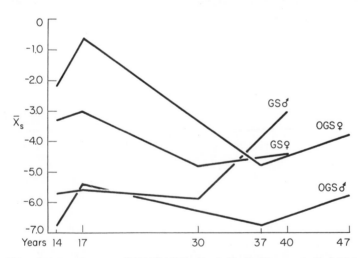

Fig. 5.5.   Average scores on PARAFAC Factor 5, Under/Overcontrolled, Heterosexual.

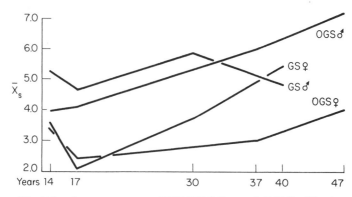

Fig. 5.6.   Average scores on PARAFAC Factor 6, Self-Confident.

these two different periods of gain are undoubtedly different. The adolescents' burgeoning abilities to use "formal" cognitive operations probably account for the early gain, because their increased cognitive abilities affect all aspects of dealing with the world and with themselves (Inhelder & Piaget, 1958). However, the increase from early to middle adulthood may be attributed to the diminution of earlier pressures for career choices and achievements, marital commitments, and early parenting, followed by greater reflectiveness and deliberation. In a word, perhaps middle-aged adults become "wise."

The time trend for Emotionally Under/Overcontrolled is not significant, indicating that this dimension is not relevant to development despite its importance in accounting for variations in the data at four time periods. Consequently, I suggest that this dimension is reactive to shifing personal situations instead of developmentally related influences. Recall that both extremes represent ineffective, defensive ways of dealing with stress, at one extreme attacking and at the other, withdrawing from pressure. Given this dimension's lack of developmental significance, we may conclude that these two different approaches probably represent ways that people can react to stress at almost *any* age. Moreover, these defenses are apparently not set for life. Recall from Table 5.3 that Emotionally Under/Overcontrolled was significantly stable only for the two shorter intervals—during adolescence and adulthood—but not stable between adolescence and adulthood. This pattern indicates that some persons change their general strategies for dealing with stress during the transition; for example, over-reactive, emotional boys can become stoic men. The relative instability of this dimension is consistent with Haan's (1977) finding that people's preferences in defensive processes are less stable over time than are their preferences in coping processes.

Finally, this dimension has a significant interaction between sex and sample when time is controlled. Examination of each sample mean for all periods combined, reveals that OGS men and GS women were more overcontrolled and OGS women and GS men were more undercontrolled. This interaction probably reflects the same enduring personal differences between the groups that were briefly described in the section on participants. OGS men and GS women share several gross characteristics compared to their sex or sample counterparts; for instance, they have higher IQs and are less often divorced. Finding that they are more overcontrolled further elaborates these personal differences. OGS men and GS women tend to react to stress by internalizing their difficulties and withdrawing, whereas OGS women and GS men are more likely to externalize their difficulties and attack.

Open/Closed to Self has the most significant developmental trend. Its curves are complex, but the essential general movement for all samples is toward greater openness. However, two samples—OGS males and GS females—take roundabout courses. OGS males become strikingly open at late adolescence but are closed by 37—a time when many of these men, who were highly mobile socioeconomically, were deeply engrossed in furthering their careers; they became more open again by the middle years, when questions of achievement were more settled. GS females were comparatively closed during adolescence but became markedly more open by adulthood.

Both of these exceptions are reflected in significant two-way interactions. The means for the first interaction—sex by time (with sample controlled)—indicate that the sexes shift their relative positions over time. During adolescence, both male samples were more open than the females, but by the middle years they became less open than the females. This pattern suggests that adolescence is the more difficult period for females, whereas adulthood is more difficult for males.

The second significant interaction is for time by sample (with sex controlled). Examination of these means suggests that the critical difference occurs at the time of the first adult follow-up, when the 37-year-old OGS samples were less open than the 30-year-old GS samples. However, both groups are almost equally open by the middle years.

The general, long-term movement toward greater openness is similar to the trend for Cognitively Invested. From adolescence to middle age, these people became increasingly aware of themselves as well as more cognitively invested.

Nurturant/Hostile also has a significant time trend, but it is of smaller magnitude than that for either Cognitively Invested or Open/Closed to Self. The highly significant sex difference, previously discussed, indicating that women were consistently more nurturant, is clearly seen in Fig. 5.4. Still, the general movement for all samples is toward greater nurturance after comparatively low scores at late adolescence, typically a time of greater concern with self than with others. A significant time by sample interaction (with sex controlled) occurs that seems primarily to arise from the OGS samples' high level of nurturance at early adolescence and its decrease at late adolescence. GS males have a consistently low level across the four time periods. The general substance of findings for Nurturant/Hostile is consistent with those for Cognitively Invested and Open/Closed to Self. With increasing maturity, these study members become not only more cognitively invested and more open to their own personal experience, but also better able and more willing to interact with others generously and dependably.

Under/Overcontrolled, Heterosexual has a substantial time trend with similar curves for all samples. The mean scores increase to high levels—especially for females—at late adolescence, decrease at the first adult follow-up, and then increase moderately by the middle years. The significant interaction between time and sex must be primarily a function of the early sex differenes, given near convergence by middle adulthood. Clearly the late adolescent peak is compatible with our understanding of adolescent sexual interest and activity. Resurgence of this dimension at mid-life reveals renewed sexual- and self-expressiveness at a time when such a trend is not commonly anticipated. (The recently and frequently divorced GS males are higher than other samples at the time of the last follow-up). Whether this is a phenomenon of liberation, compulsion, nostalgia, or compensation is not certain. In view of the participants' increased cognitive investment, awareness of self, and nurturance, their sexual- and self-expressiveness seems adaptive.

Finally, Self-Confident, along with its moderately significant sex differences indicating greater self-confidence in men, generally increases over time. Both female samples become markedly less self-confident at late adolescence but then steadily improve, as do the OGS males through the middle years. Only the GS males' relatively flat curve is exceptional.

SUMMARY OF THE EFFECTS OF TIME, SEX, AND SAMPLE

Before considering the main implications of these results, I reiterate that no consistent differences were found between the OGS and GS that reasonably could be attributed to their age difference (over 7 years) or to the different historical contexts of their lives (e.g., for the OGS, the Depression during their adolescence and World War II during their young adulthood, and for the GS, World War II during their adolescence and the Korean War during their young adulthood). Presumably those who argue that cohort effects explain much of developmental variance (e.g., Schaie, 1965) would expect opposite results. Personality data of the complexity of these Q sorts, and based on as rich material as these were, may not be as reactive to cohort differences as are data based on questionnaires or personality inventories. However, two moderately significant time-by-sample interactions did occur for Open/Closed to Self and Nurturant/Hostile. The critical sample differences for Open/Closed to Self were during the young adult years. At 37 the OGS members were less open than the GS were at 30. This contrast may simply reflect somewhat different timing in achieving career security and completing parenting. The critical differences for Nurturant/Hostile were during early adolescence, when the OGS samples were the more nurturant. This contrast could be attributed to historical trends: perhaps no generation was more concerned about popularity than the one that was adolescent during the depressed 1930s.

Clear sex differences were found. Irrespective of sample or time, men almost always had higher scores for Self-Confident, whereas women almost always had higher scores for Nurturant/Hostile and Under/ Overcontrolled, Heterosexual. These differences seem to mirror typical consequences of sex differences in socialization experiences. Developmental differences between the sexes were also found. Males were more open than females at adolescence but became more closed by adulthood; females were more obviously sexually oriented until the middle years, when some convergence between the sexes took place.

More extensive than sex differences were the time trends that represent developmental functions from early adolescence to the middle years. Stated simply, during this segment of the life span, the participants typically progressed in (a) using their cognitive capabilities in more differentiated and effective ways; (b) viewing themselves as self-guided psychological beings; (c) regarding themselves with self-confidence and acting accordingly; (d) becoming more nurturant of others; and (e) expressing themselves sexually—strongly during adolescence, mildly during young adulthood, and comparatively strongly during the middle years. This late recrudescence of interest in the self as a sexual being was not expected. Because this trend occurs within a general context of well-functioning middle-aged adults, I conclude that it represents personal liberation instead of sexual preoccupation that compensates for personal uncertainties. Finally, Emotionally Under/Overcontrolled proved not to be a developmental dimension. Instead, it seems to be situationally reactive, representing two different ways people react to stress at any age. Lack of stability in this dimension from adolescence to young adulthood suggests that ways of dealing with stress are not unalterable. At least some study members switched from attack to avoidance, or vice versa, during this time interval, while the means for the samples remained relatively constant over all periods.

Trends Toward Heterogeneity or Homogeneity

The last indices of development considered here are trends toward greater homogeneity or heterogeneity across time *within* each sample. The analyses were accomplished by examining the changes in the variances of factor scores across time. When a sample becomes more heterogeneous at a particular age than it was before, I hypothesize that new, age-specific, situational opportunities or tasks are being met and that initial reactions are diverse and individuated in character. When a sample becomes more homogeneous at any specific period, I infer that the group as a whole has generally accommodated to common social experiences with similar, age-specific solutions. The method of testing the convergence and divergence within samples between time periods, is the *t* test between variances (McNemar, 1969). Table 5.5 shows the results. Again before a difference was considered meaningful, it was required to be significant for two samples but now both results had to be significant at the .01 level or better because multiple *t* tests were done between two periods at a time.

Two dimensions have noteworthy convergences and divergences: Open/Closed to Self and Under/Overcontrolled, Heterosexual. Both samples of females become more heterogeneous on Open/Closed to Self from early to late adolescence, suggesting that the social-psychological event of adolescence is initially handled in diverse ways by females. Some appear to use the experience to achieve greater liberation and more differentiated understandings of themselves, whereas others apparently conservatively foreclose on their new experiences and possibilities. During adolescence, males apparently handle their reactions to themselves in rather similar ways. (OGS men's point of marked diversity in Open/Closed to Self occurred between adolescence and adulthood, but this trend was not replicated by the GS men, nor was it characteristic of the women.) Three samples move toward greater heterogeneity for Open/Closed to Self over the entire span studied.

Table 5.5

Samples' Trends Toward Homogeneity or Heterogeneity
(t Tests between Variances)

	Age span for OGS				Age span for GS			
Q-sort factor	14-17	17-37	37-47	14-47	14-17	17-30	30-40	14-40
Females								
Cognitively Invested	3.12^{c***}					3.28^{b***}	3.28^{b***}	
Emotionally Under/Over controlled								2.35^{b**}
Open/Closed to Self	4.71^{ac***}			4.23^{c***}	4.31^{c***}			4.38^{ac***}
Nurturant/Hostile	2.99^{c***}							
Under/Overcontrolled, Heterosexual		3.81^{ab***}	3.01^{b***}	5.39^{b***}		2.78^{***}		3.47^{ab***}
Self-Confident								
Males								
Cognitively Invested								
Emotionally Under/Over controlled								
Open/Closed to Self		3.17^{c***}		3.62^{ac***}			2.24^{c**}	
Nurturant/Hostile							3.00^{b***}	
Under/Overcontrolled, Heterosexual	2.85^{c***}	5.76^{ab***}		2.52^{b**}				
Self-Confident								

[a] This finding is significant at $p < .002$.
[b] Variances become smaller at the later time period during each age span.
[c] Variances become larger at the later time period during each age span.
**p < .05.
***p < .01.

(Results for the fourth sample—GS males—had a probability of .05.) Evidently successive experiences in dealing with life events—whether salubrious or deleterious in their meanings—are accompanied by increases or decreases in freedom to be intraceptive. This finding may describe an important and not infrequent divergence that occurs with aging—some people become increasingly liberated; others, increasingly closed and rigid.

Three samples—OGS men and women and GS women—become more homogeneous on the dimension Under/Overcontrolled, Heterosexual between late adolescence and adulthood; the same three samples also converge over the entire period. These findings suggest that adolescents' new opportunities for sexual self-expressiveness—legitimated by society's expectancies and empowered by their own biological maturations—were initially experienced and reacted to in diverse ways by different persons. But by early and middle adulthood the study members had generally moved to a common solution, so this dimension occupies a position of similar importance within the participants' overall personality organizations.

In sum, these observations indicate that over time people become more highly individualized in their degree of openness to their psychological experience, but they become more alike in the extent of their sexual self-expressiveness.

Integration of Developmental Findings for Each Dimension

As the main replicated findings are drawn together, the reader needs to keep in mind that the various procedures performed on these data (placing a floor on the reliability of ratings, compositing ratings, and subsequent factoring) produced higher levels of reliability than are usually achieved for personality measurements. In addition, the requirement that a significant result occur in two samples before it is accepted should make the findings dependable.

An account of the dimension Cognitively Invested can be simply given: it was generally stable across all intervals; it markedly increased in importance in the hierarchies of the participants' personality attributes across time, without variation as to sex or sample; and the degree of its heterogeneity within samples remained constant. This pattern suggests that Cognitively Invested is an important, omnipresent dimension of development that comes systematically to play a more important role in personalities over the life span.

Emotionally Under/Overcontrolled was stable only during adolescence and the 10-year interval between the two adult follow-ups. It did not show developmental gains or losses, variability within samples did not change; and no sex differnces were found. Evidently, Emotionally Under/Overcontrolled is not a developmental dimension; it probably fluctuates with specific, non-age-related changes in life situations. Both extremes of this dimension represent maladaptive, defensive ways of dealing with stress that can probably be observed in persons of all ages. These results suggest two specific understandings with respect to life span research: (a) although these defenses were not age associated, probably defensive patterns need to be taken into account to understand the error variance that attenuates the observation of developmental trends; (b) people's styles of defensiveness are apparently not stable, that is, once adopted, they are not necessarily maintained for life.

Open/Closed to Self was stable for women for all intervals and for men during adulthood but was no more prominent in females' personality hierarchies than in males'. It generally increased throughout the entire span studied, especially during adulthood; participants steadily became more heterogeneous across the entire span, females especially so during adolescence. Thus, Open/Closed to Self, as a self-reflexive way of thinking and dealing with one's self, is a strong developmental dimension. But over time some individuals became increasingly more open and others more closed to their psychological experience. The clear sex difference in stability indicates that females are more likely to adopt a basic position of being open or closed, at least by early adolescence, which they then maintain over the years. In contrast, the men did not become stable on this dimension until the adult interval (even then the correlations between time periods are not high). Men's openness is evidently more situationally responsive and may have been, on occasion, inconsistent with successful career performance and with the responsibilities of being the sole breadwinner for the family.

Nurturant/Hostile was stable for all samples during the short adolescent interval and for women during the longer adult interval. Scores generally increased after a temporary decrease during late adolescence; sample variations remained relatively constant across time. Males and females were sharply distinguished, with the women being considerably more nurturant than the men. Thus, Nurturant/Hostile is a developmental dimension that steadily gains across this portion of the life span but it is differentially organized within men and women, having greater importance in the women's personalities, particularly by the middle years.

Under/Overcontrolled, Heterosexual was stable for all samples during the short adolescent interval but only for women between adolescence and adulthood and only for OGS samples during the adult interval. Scores for this dimension changed in complex ways—the curves had high points at late adolescence and middle age. Samples generally became more homogeneous over the entire time, particularly between adolescence and adulthood. This dimension was more important in females' than in males' personality organizations. Both extremes define maladaptive ways of relating to other people—hypersexualized and externalizing or asexual and rigidly internalizing. Apparently different persons chose one or another of these routes during their adolescence, but the samples generally moved toward more temperate, homogeneous solutions by the later years. Under/Overcontrolled, Heterosexual also appears to be a developmental dimension, but it registered neither positive nor negative linear changes across the life span studied. Instead, sexual interests are most salient at adolescence when both society and biological maturity first make sexual expressiveness a possibility. When marriages permit accommodation and when careers and parenting absorb energies, this dimension becomes less salient for a time. But it again becomes more important in the participants' personalities by the middle years. This late resurgence needs to be understood within the context of the other dimensions, for the middle-aged adult's general stance is clearly more integrated than is the adolescent's.

Finally, Self-Confident was generally stable only for the adolescent and adult intervals; as a developmental dimension it registered moderate gains across the years. Samples maintained approximately equal variations within themselves across time, and men were generally more confident than women. Consequently, I conclude that a sense of social competence gradually accrues as people successfully deal with experience.

Associations of Basic Dimensions with Socioeconomic Status and Mobility

The associations of the dimensions with both concurrent and achieved SES need to be considered. If the correlations between factor scores and concurrent SES at the various time periods were high, it could not clearly be said that the dimensions represent common *developmental* trends. Instead, their levels and trends might reflect the advantages or disadvantages of the participants' socioeconomic circumstances. Additional analyses were done to predict adult SES from the level of each dimension at adolescence. Here the focus is not on external social advantage but on early personality characteristics that may predict later social mobility.

Table 5.6 shows the results of these analyses. When the rule of replication is applied, three dimensions—Emotionally Under/Overcontrolled, Open/Closed to Self, and Self-Confident—are independent of concurrent socioeconomic indices and are unrelated to social mobility. Thus, ways of responding to stress (attacking or withdrawing), ways of dealing with one's self (intraceptively or extraceptively), and ways of regarding one's self in interpersonal contexts (as strong or vulnerable) are independent of SES or socioeconomic mobility. This result is *not* because the Ns in each subsample are small; the findings hold for the two female and two male samples combined.

Nurturant/Hostile has one replicated correlation—negative associations with concurrent SES in three samples at late adolescence. This finding suggests that study members of higher SES were more hostile during adolescence than were those of lower SES. The difference may arise because middle-class youngsters are subject to greater parental control and have more difficulty achieving independence (Coleman, 1963).

Under/Overcontrolled, Heterosexual at early and/or late adolescence is significantly and negatively associated with adult SES in six of eight

Significant Correlations between SES Indices and the PARAFAC Dimensions

	OGS						GS					
	Concurrent associations				Mobility to adult SES		Concurrent associations				Mobility to adult SES	
Q-sort factor	Early adoles.	Late adoles.	Adult 1	Adult 2	Early adoles.	Late adoles.	Early adoles.	Late adoles.	Adult 1	Adult 2	Early adoles.	Late adoles.
Females												
Cognitively Invested		-.32**	-.29**	-.49****		-.39***	-.29**	-.34**				-.38**
Emotionally Under/Over controlled												
Open/Closed to Self		.32**	.39***			.27**				-.30**		
Nurturant/Hostile		.43***			.28**	.30**		.32**				
Under/Over controlled, Heterosexual					.36***				.44***			
Self-Confident								-.44***				
Males												
Cognitively Invested	.32**		.53****	.65****	.50****	.41***	.33**	.56****	.61****	.71****	.48**	.68****
Emotionally Under/Over controlled							.37**	.58****				
Open/Closed to Self												
Nurturant/Hostile							.47***	.55***	.35**			
Under/Over controlled, Heterosexual		.35**				.36**			.45***		.40**	.46***
Self-Confident												

*p < .10.
**p < .05.
***p < .01.
****p < .001.

analyses. These results suggest that strong sexualization at adolescence is associated with downward socioeconomic mobility. Under/ Overcontrolled, Heterosexual also has one concurrent negative association with SES at the first adult follow-up for both GS samples, suggesting that the lower SES participants had not muted their sexual expressiveness by age 30 to the extent that the middle-class study members had.

Unlike the other dimensions, Cognitively Invested is consistently and positively associated with all but one concurrent measure of SES for the two male samples. These correlations become stronger with each successive time period and are substantial by the time of the second adult follow-up, moving from approximately .30 to .70. Moreover, scores on this dimension at adolescence predict upward social mobility. In fact, scores at adolescence are more strongly associated with adult SES than they are with adolescent SES. Thus, we may infer that although the males' early socioeconomic advantage was modestly associated with their early cognitive investment, this early cognitive investment also facilitated their later socioeconomic mobility. The females' pattern is similar, but much weaker. Their scores for Cognitively Invested at late adolescence are related to both concurrent and achieved SES.

Altogether these analyses indicate that socioeconomic advantage was not a major determinant of the levels nor the developmental paths of these dimensions, with the exception of Cognitively Invested for the males. Thus, we may regard these dimensions, with some qualification for Cognitively Invested, as being "class fair" in describing the development of the various SES groups represented in these samples.

Distinctive Characteristics of the Middle Years

Two sets of comparisons were made between the participants' PARAFAC scores and their scores on the scales of the California Personality Interview (CPI) for the first and second adult follow-up (using multivariate analyses with orthogonal polynomials). The Q descriptions indicate that with sex and sample controlled, the study members are significantly higher at the second adult follow-up in Cognitively Invested ($p < .001$), Open/Closed to Self ($p < .0001$), and Under/ Overcontrolled, Heterosexual ($p < .0001$). Thus, these results suggest that the participants had generally developed more cognitive breadth at the same time that they became more intraceptive, self-guided and self-expressive (socially and sexually).

The reality of this move toward greater self-reflexiveness, if not self-liberation, at middle age is supported by the CPI, which presents the mirror image of the Q results by indicating the study members had become proportionately less commitment to social achievements by their middle years than they had had at the early adult years. The CPI results with sex and sample controlled show that the study members had come to have lower scores on 7 of Gough's 18 (1957) scales. These include Sense of Well Being ($p < .001$), Intellectual Efficiency ($p < .01$), and 5 scales concerned with social reactions and social accountability— Sociability ($p < .05$), Social Presence ($p < .01$), Tolerance ($p < .01$), Responsibility ($p < .001$) and Socialization ($p < .05$). The analysis of the Femininity scale also revealed a move away from adherence to the socially conventional, with a significant sex by time interaction ($p < .05$). The women had become less feminine and the men more feminine between early and middle adult years.

This constellation of Q and CPI findings is consistent with the thrust of observations from a previous study (Haan, 1976) wherein well-functioning young and geriatric samples were compared. In that study, younger people's self-views and modes of interaction were well suited for supporting the socioeconomic and personal achievement required of them, whereas the older people's did not reflect these kinds of structural pressures and tensions but instead were well suited to deepening and conserving their individual integrity.

DISCUSSION

What do the results contribute to the conceptualization and study of personality over the life span? What do they suggest about the nature of personality during the middle years?

Conceptualizing the Life Span

Basic Personality Dimensions

Initially I commented, with some optimism, that the results might suggest the nature of the "basic" variables of personality development over the life span. If this goal was even minimally achieved, we must now consider what class of conceptualizations these dimensions represent. Varying ways that the active self operates seem to be represented: cognitively invested or impoverished, defensively externalizing or internalizing when stressed, open or closed to own experience, nurturing or hostile to others, sexually expressive or asexually aloof, and regarding self as strong or vulnerable. Brim (1976a), considering the same problem of identifying the critical dimensions of the life span, proposed that a "theory of oneself" might be the keystone. As examples of potentially fruitful areas of study, he suggested research on the self's theories of personal control, on future career achievements, and on changes in one's self. The results of the present study, which suggest that self-views and ways of acting do parsimoniously describe the life span, seem not far removed from Brim's proposals.

In hindsight, the enterprise of studying the self as the center of developmental activity makes good sense. Life-span and longitudinal research must always deal with a large mass of ever-shifting detail in people's lives, but persons' self-views and their ways of processing life must continue even as change and transformation occur. Although the variables used in my analyses represent a potpourri of personality contents, their organization by PARAFAC into personality dimensions seems to have produced something like "quasi-structures" that reflect meaningful organizations of the participants' self-views and their ways of acting. The 10 variables "excluded" from the overall solution because they did not serve to define any dimension in a distinctive way (neither one standard deviation above or below the mean) are states of being more than ways of acting: satisfied with physical appearance, physically attractive, masculine (or feminine) style, esthetically reactive, aware of impression created, has bodily concern, expressive, responds to humor, and proffers advice.

Stage Theories of the Life Span

These findings contrast with widely cited descriptions of the life span (e.g., Gould, 1978; Levinson, Darrow, Klein, Levinson, & McKee, 1974; Sheehy, 1976) constructed from self-reports of life periods and transitions that investigators later organized into "stages." Indeed, so many different segmentations of the life span by stages are now proposed that it is difficult to keep their differences and similarities in mind. I question the "reality" of these ad hoc formulations of stages, if not on empirical grounds, at least on logical grounds.

If conceptualizations of stages are to follow Piaget's definition, then the proposed stages should have the structural properties of wholeness, relatedness of parts, qualitative differences, and hierarchical integration. As far as we now know, there are no structural changes in later life. If they occur, they are not likely to be purely cognitive in nature, yet little is known about other possible kinds of intrapsychic structures, such as might represent self-formulations or social meanings. Brim's proposal for developing a "theory of oneself" and increasing interest in social cognition (e.g., Haan, 1977, 1978; Kohlberg, 1973;

Selman, 1971; Swanson, 1974) are examples of work that acknowledge the possibility of other kinds of intrapsychic structures. Moreover, according to many present views, personality is fluid and situationally adaptable. Such characteristics are not consistent with views that personality develops by stages. Consequently, the most fruitful questions about personality development over the life span may not concern self-described life stages or transitions, such as "leaving the family" (Levinson *et al.*, 1974) or "pulling up roots" (Sheehy, 1976). Strictly speaking, most writers are not positing formal stages of personality development. Instead, they are describing circumstances arising from social or biological events that require the person to re-accommodate, for example, an "empty nest" or menopause. Because we have no knowledge of adult structural changes, our best questions may concern the possibly more pervasive and invariant *ways* that people negotiate inevitable changes in their milieu during their lifetimes.

The results of my study also lead to some doubts about recent formulations of life stages. Most curves do change over time from early adolescence to the middle adult years (Fig. 5.1–5.6), but in general their forms do not show the abrupt shifts consistent with a stage sequence. Three dimensions do show abrupt shifts between early and late adolescence: Nurturant/Hostile and Self-Confident drop sharply at late adolescence, and Under/Overcontrolled, Heterosexual rises abruptly at late adolescence and mildly at middle age. The late adolescent changes may signal the development of a new personality stage. But they coincide with a known structural transformation—the shift from thinking concretely to using formal hypothetical-deductive operations.

Two important qualifications of these observations must be made. First, these study members were not observed continuously during their adulthood; they may have undergone dramatic states of disequilibrium and changes that we did not observe, although our clinical impression from their interviews is that many did not. Second, the PARAFAC methodology imposes more continuity on the data than may exist in real life.

Investigators' Preconceptions and Life-Span Description

Different ways of viewing "subjects" and, in consequence, different designs and procedures of data collection importantly predetermine the nature of results. Important differences exist between the procedures used at IHD and those used by investigators such as Gould and Levinson. These contrasts may account for the different views of the life span. The Q sorts are not derived directly from self-reports by the persons being studied, but on clinicians' observations and evaluations of the participants, self-presentations and processes of self-reporting, a fine but critical distinction. Self-reports and descriptions influence evaluations, but clinicians do not translate them directly and naively into item scores. Instead they consider the meaning and context of statements in such ways that a manifestly depressed woman who declares that she is cheerful is not given a high score for cheerful. This is not the usual concern of whether observations represent the genotype or the phenotype. Instead, it is a recognition that self-descriptions cannot be taken at face value, given subjects' readiness to cooperate and be led by investigators' questions and their own needs to deceive themselves. (For a discussion of artifacts in data collection see Rosenthal & Rosnow, 1969).

Moreover, the Q sorts for each time period were independent of all other periods, so neither the clinicians' preconceptions about development nor the participants' opinions about their own life course could determine the nature of the results. No clinician evaluated the same study member at two different time periods nor had access to information about the study members' past histories and evaluations. Had the clinicians expected to characterize the life span in a certain way, there was no way this result could be achieved prior to interpretation.[3]

A related and important difference between our procedures and those of several other investigators concerns the nature of the interviews and other materials that provided the basis for the clinicians' sorts. These source materials were not "patho-centric" in the sense that they were designed to find or highlight pathology. All times in life undoubtedly have their ups and down, so it is reasonble to assume cooperative participants (and most are) will be willing and even eager to relate their recent crises to attentive, permissive interviewers who expect to hear about traumas. Gould's (1978) study seems particularly flawed in this regard because he developed his prime variables from observations of age-homogeneous persons in group psychotherapy. Psychotherapeutic clients are more likely to dwell on their problems than on their strengths.

Another difference in design between this study and others, which is twice ensured by PARAFAC's age-impartial solution and by the judges' ignorance of the participants' childhood status, is that the frequent supposition of infantile determinism (discussed by Brim, 1976a) is avoided. Child-centric models are based on expectancies that early

---

[3]Block in collaboration with Haan (1971) had judges sort their own stereotypic formulations of early and late adolescence. Almost without exception the judges evaluated study members as individuals and not stereotypically. We may reasonably infer that clinicians do not have sterotypes about adults aged 30–47.

effects are permanent. When these suppositions are built into designs, the dynamic meanings of later changes and developments are not easily captured and understood.

Nevertheless, the present research does not address the most fundamental question of development, that is, the nature of the dialectical interplay between self-conservation and the person's wishes and needs to change and transform within the context of new assimilations. So far, the essence of this dialectic can be satisfactorily approached only with more clinical analyses, such as those in Chapter 8.

Summary Recommendations for Studying Personality across the Life Span

(1) The "basic" variables must be abstract and age-impartial, that is, potentially observable at all ages.

(2) Methods of reducing and analyzing observations should also be age-impartial.

(3) No compelling reasons now exist for expecting structural stages during the adult years.

(4) Nevertheless, adults can be expected to undergo impressive changes as they interact with the progression of life events.

(5) Self-reports about portions of, or transitions within, the life span probably are not a reliable base for a general developmental theory, given each person's interest in his or her own life drama and the irreducible and inevitable stresses and strains of all lives.

(6) Developmental changes must be "found" empirically between independent, time-separated observations; they probably are not reliable when built into the measuring instrument.

(7) The most interesting observations probably concern the ways people view themselves and cope with the inevitable changes that their milieux demand and that they expect of themselves as they age.

(8) A search for life-span variables that are either patho-centric or child-centric will not yield sufficient understanding of the accruing strengths that typify development from early adolescence to the middle years, judging by the present study.

The Middle Years

With minor exceptions, OGS members at 47 and GS members at 40 were more cognitively invested, nurturant, self-confident, open and intraceptive than at younger ages. They were more self- and sexually-expressive than in earlier adulthood and had also become more like each other with respect to the importance of sexual self-expressiveness within their overall personality organizations. But they had diverged from one another on the dimension of Open/Closed to Self. Only one dimension failed to show some kind of systematic change over the span studied—at middle age the groups are neither more nor less Emotionally Under/Overcontrolled than they were earlier.

The twin observation of developmental movement toward a revived saliency and greater homogeneity in sexual self-expressiveness is especially interesting. Apparently the general well-being and skill in self-expression characteristic of middle-aged adults, means that they can be self-expressive without serious consequences. The observed developmental movement of increasing divergence among study members for Open/Closed to Self well reflects contradictory commonsense views that people become rigid or liberated as they age. Empirically, both trends were found. Some persons do become less self-aware and more closed to themselves, but others become more acquainted with themselves and open to their own possibilities. I assume, but have not shown, that a concatenation of life events, interacting with particular kinds of personal resources and deficiencies, accounts for this divergence. Yet the general movement for all samples is toward greater openness.

As groups, these study members gave no evidence (with the possible but unreplicated exception of GS men) of undergoing a mid-life crises. Instead, adaptation at mid-life appears to reflect the accrued wisdom of people who have grown tolerant and become instructed, socially and psychologically. These findings have precedent. In cross-sectional data, Neugarten and Gutmann (1968) note that middle-aged men and women are tolerant of their own impulses. This observation is consistent with the steady rise of the dimension Open/Closed to Self and the upswing of Under/Overcontrolled, Heterosexual by the middle years. Neugarten (1968) further observes, from the perspective of her various studies, that middle-aged persons consciously and deliberately process new information, integrate it with past knowledge, and then use these understandings to achieve desired ends. This pattern is corroborated here by the middle-aged participants' high scores for Cognitively Invested. Further, Neugarten describes the middle-aged as belonging to the "command" generation, people who are of an age to be in charge of themselves and of others, younger or older. The parallel in my findings is represented by high scores at middle age on the dimension Self-Confident. Vaillant's (1977) longitudinal analysis of Harvard men is also consistent with these trends.

Two other general findings from this study seem not to be presaged in Neugarten's observations. Our middle-aged had also become considerably more giving and self-extending (as the changes in Nurturant/ Hostile and Self-Confident suggest), as well as interpersonally predictable and accountable to others—or generative, to use Erikson's term.

All of these dimensions show systematic gains for entire samples, but the destiny of individuals—despite the unusually strong reliability of these measures—is only modestly predicted. Undoubtedly, personal fluctuations in response to unexpected life events, fortunate and unfortunate—deaths, births, illnesses, divorces, marriages and remarriages, promotions and bankruptcies—attenuate estimates of stability and become reflected in individuals' changes, up and down, in the omnipresent, bipolar, defensive dimension of Emotional, Under/ Overcontrolled. Few persons have unceasing good or poor fortune and few cope or defend unremittingly.

Despite the unpredictable traumas and dramas visited on some person's lives, the "generalized" middle-aged persons described here appear to be equipped by reason of past experiences both to savor and deal with themselves effectively and comfortably. This interpretative framework focuses on persons' views of themselves and ways of handling themselves in interaction with life experiences. I argue that conceptualization of processes rather than "states" is necessary if we are to match theories with the movement of life itself. Many of our middle-aged study members have not yet begun to deal with the facts of death and biological inadequacy that must figure strongly in later adult development. However, some persons seem to manage these irreversible events with grace and wisdom, and many of these study members will undoubtedly do as well.

6

Uses of the Past in Adult Psychological Health

HARVEY PESKIN AND NORMAN LIVSON

The growing discipline of adult development disputes axioms of much child-centered personality theory: that what is past is *cause,* and what is present, *outcome;* that the child constructs experience, and the adult repeats or reconstructs it; that childhood years are formative, and adult years formed. Without formative properties of its own, adulthood is conceptualized as fully constructed and changeless—the "mythical plateau of adulthood" (Brim, 1976a). To borrow Piaget's (1962) ironic critique of psychoanalysis, such child-centric propositions are "too much a science of the permanent." Freud (1898, 1905) etched a child-centric view of memory into psychoanalytic thinking in warning about the older patient who needs inordinate time to recover significant early cognitions buried by passing years. This notion of continuous decline in the availability of the past, part of the folk wisdom about aging, has not been disproved, perhaps because of the dearth of work with older age persons.

When not simply or strategically ignored, adolescence enters adult-developmental theory not as "formative" but, contrariwise, as formed and re-formed for the continuously active development of the self. Such prominent theorists as Piaget, Erikson, and Jung have tried to separate *past/present* from *cause/effect* and assert that what is prior can be constructed by what comes after. In their separate ways, they offer conceptual bridges between the segregated camps of child and adult development. Piaget (1962), ostensibly least adult-centered among them, implicitly formulates the idea that the past is reorganized by the

153

evolving tasks of adulthood in holding that the "living aspects of the past" are preserved by continual accommodation "to the manifold and irreducible present."

Erikson (1975), on psychohistorical evidence, states that memories "intrinsically belong to" the adult stage in which they are recalled and heighten the sense and opportunity of present actuality, rather than belonging to a static past, recovered with declining reliability. Memories are not only delivered to a changeless, receiving ego; they are recruited and changed by a coping ego. Memories are useful resources for coping with the present; old modes of responding may be recovered and used appropriately.

Jung (1933), the most adult-centered of early psychoanalysts, suggests that in their "second half of life" adults can bypass the recent for the more distant past to recover long-suppressed potentialities that are again congruent with life goals and tasks. In Chapter 8, F. Livson makes an excellent case for such time-arching recovery. *Discontinuous* recoveries make up a central theme, albeit often implicit and metaphoric, in life-span theory—the recognition that adults selectively reactivate certain traits that can serve as resources for a sought-after life structure (Brim, 1976a; Gutmann, 1975; Levinson *et al.*, 1974; Livson & Peskin, 1979; Neugarten, 1968). This view allows for the possibility of disparate goals and tasks at adjacent stages, but similar ones at widely separated ones.

STUDY I: DISCONTINUITY AND CONTINUITY
IN PAST/PRESENT RELATIONSHIPS

An adult-centered view means that selection of past modes of responding is determined by relevance, not recency. Past modes are as likely to (a) serve later as earlier adulthood, and (b) draw from the remote as from the recent past. In both cases past/present relationships may be discontinuous. First, behaviors from a given time are as likely (or more likely) to be correlated with psychological adaptation in later adulthood as in earlier adulthood. Second, more remote behaviors are as likely (or more likely) as more recent ones to be correlated with current adult adaptation. This second discontinuity has been called the *sleeper effect* (Kagan & Moss, 1962), but we also include a subtype of *reversal* in which the adult outcome predicted from the more recent period is opposite to that predicted from the more distant period (Peskin, 1972). Conversely, a preponderance of continuous relationships in both cases, with recency producing a larger yield of correlations, supports the child-centric position of declining influence of the past with the passage of time.

To study either type of past/present relationships, assessments must be done at least twice during youth and during adulthood to distinguish earlier versus later phases of each age period. Q-sort assessments during early and late adolescence and adulthood (30 and 40 for the GS, 37 and 47 for the OGS) provide our data for comparing the number of discontinuous and continuous relationships. (The hiatus in data collection between late adolescence and adulthood adds a qualification to our second case: we call a characteristic continuous if ratings of that characteristic at late adolescence and adulthood are highly correlated. This interpretation implies that the quality is maintained continuously during the hiatus. If the correlation actually had vanished during the gap, it would in fact be a discontinuous sleeper effect. Hence, in our tally of continuous relationships, evidence for the child-centric model will be inflated, whereas evidence for the adult-centric model is probably underestimated.)

Prediction of adult adaptation is made by the multiple correlation of the same behavior over early and late adolescence (from Q-sort ratings) with a measure of psychological health at each adult age. For each adult age, 104 multiple correlations were computed, one for each Q-sort item over junior-high and senior-high assessments. Discontinuity of the first case is indicated when the number of significant ($p < .05$) multiple correlations for the later adult age exceeds the number for the earlier adult age. For discontinuity of the second case, a sleeper effect in a significant multiple correlation is indicated when only the beta for early adolescence is significant; a *reversal* is indicated when both betas are significant, but have opposite signs. Continuity is indicated when beta weights are significant for late adolescence only, or for both early and late adolescence.

Adult Psychological Health

Adult assessments that reach to broad dimensions of psychosocial competence, purpose and self-consistency are highly appropriate for demonstrating an adult-centric view of the past because they are pertinent to specific adaptive requirements of different adult eras yet are unlikely to be set by an unchanging repertoire of youthful behaviors and motives. We expect assessment of such dimensions will, therefore, also capture adaptation to the tasks of different adult eras pertaining to work, affiliation, and child-rearing.

Our method for broadly assessing psychosocial adaptation or psychological health at each adult age has been described (Livson & Peskin, 1967; Peskin & Livson, 1972) and is used in Chapters 7 and 8. This index of psychological health (PH) *is* the correlation between each participant's adult personality profile on the 100-item California Q sort (Block, 1961) and an "ideal" sort of a "psychologically healthy" person. The latter represents a composite of independent Q sorts of a hypothetical psychologically healthy person made by four clinical psychologists. The most salient items in the PH Q sort are very much in line with current broad concepts of psychological health and adaptation. In addition to excluding explicit psychopathology, the PH Q sort encompasses many generally accepted indicators of effective functioning in a variety of areas: capacity for work and for satisfying interpersonal relationships, a sense of moral purpose, and a realistic perception of self and society. Agreement between judges on the hypothetical PH Q sort is high (average inter-rater reliability of, .82).

The PH index has been shown to be related to satisfaction and effectiveness in marriage, family, and occupation. For each sex of the GS and OGS cohorts at each adult age, PH is positively correlated with multiple indices, independent of the Q sort, of emotional adjustment and of closeness and affection in the marriage. For GS and OGS women and GS men at both adult ages, PH is positively related to ratings of competent parenting and satisfaction in child-rearing. For men of both cohorts at both adult ages and OGS women at 47, PH is positively correlated with satisfaction, involvement, and skillful performance on the job.

Correlations of PH between adult follow-ups show marked variation as a function of age, cohort, original differences between samples (Chapter 2), or some combination of these. Such variation alone is sufficient reason to doubt the "plateau" notion of adulthood. For GS males ($N = 31$), the correlation of PH indices between 30 and 40 is only .17; for GS women ($N = 36$), only .29. Neither correlation is significant. However, for OGS men ($N = 40$), PH at 37 and 47 correlate .54 ($p < .01$); for OGS women ($N = 42$), .75 ($p < .01$). These correlations are not differentially attenuated by subsample differences in the variance of PH scores. The correlation over the 10-year period is significantly larger for OGS women than GS women ($p < .01$), less so for OGS men than GS men ($p < .10$). Follow-up of the GS at 50 is needed to separate effects of age, cohort, and sample. We can then determine whether this apparent substantial and surprising difference between the stability of adult PH during the fourth decade (30–40) and approximately the fifth decade (37–47) is a reliable phenomenon associated with age or, is instead, associated with cohort or sampling differences.

Table 6.1

Number of Multiple Correlations ($p < .05$)
Predicting Adult Psychological Health
from Early and Late Adolescent
Q-sort Items

Sample	Predicted adult age	Number of significant items for males	Number of significant items for females
GS	30	7	19
GS	40	28	7
OGS	37	20	14
OGS	47	32	20

Results

In Tables 6.1 and 6.2, tallies of correlations between adolescent Q-sort items and adult PH are reported that indicate discontinuous and continuous past/present relationships for both cases. Sample sizes are given in Table 6.3. Discontinuous relationships favor the adult-centered model of lack of decline (or even increase) in the use of past modes of responding for present (adult) adaptation. Continuous relationships support the child-centric position in which uses of past modes are inversely related to the passage of time; that is, the more distant, the less "used." Table 6.1 lists the number of significant Q-sort items that multiply predict, from early and late adolescence, adult PH for each of four subsamples (GS males and females, OGS males and

Table 6.2

Q-sort Item Classification of Multiple Correlations
by Discontinuous and Continuous Types

		Males		Females	
Sample	Predicted adult age	Discont.[a]	Contin.[b]	Discont.[a]	Contin.[b]
GS	30	3	4	12	7
GS	40	19	9	2	5
OGS	37	3	17	8	6
OGS	47	28	4	10	10

[a]Discontinuous denotes (a) significant beta for early adolescence only (sleeper effect) or (b) significant beta for both early and late adolescence with opposite sign (reversal).

[b]Continuous denotes (a) significant beta for late adolescence, (b) significant beta for both early and late adolescence (same sign), or (c) no significant beta for either period, but joint-effect term accounts for > 25% of variance.

females) at two adult periods. Declining incidence of past/present correlations over time is clearly *not* the rule. In three of the four subsamples, the number of Q-sort items in adolescence that significantly predicts adult PH actually increases from early to later adulthood. Discontinuity, which the adult-centric model requires, is thus strongly supported.

In Table 6.2, the significant multiple correlations of Table 6.1 are categorized by whether their beta weights for early and late adolescence indicate continuity or discontinuity (sleeper effects and reversals) between past and present. There are more discontinuous than continuous correlations in four of the eight comparisons, whereas continuous correlations are more common in three of the comparisons. In one comparison, frequencies are the same. Again the findings do not indicate a decrease in past/present relationships across time. This support for adult-centered effects, independent of the supportive findings in Table 6.1 is, as noted earlier, probably conservative because we have not data for the period between late adolescence and early adulthood.

Such discontinuous patterns are consistent with a model of selective access to the past but hardly confirm it. Rather, they legitimize the next research step, forecasting the *content* of significant adolescent predictors in such adult-centric terms as the changing uses of learned modes of responding for changing life-span adaptations. This language is our construction. Although the findings of Tables 6.1 and 6.2 lend substantive underpinning to it, more evidence is needed.

STUDY II: USES OF THE PAST BY ADULT AGE AND FAMILY STAGE

If adolescence provides resources for adulthood, life-span theory suggests which specific modes of early behavior may help accommodate the changing purposes of adult eras. Thus, for younger adults whose individuation and autonomy must be constructed in the contexts of becoming established in the outside world, adolescence should provide the instrumental and expressive modes connected with familial and occupational achievements. Such prior learnings, we expect, will be associated with traditional sex and age-role expectations pertaining to parenting and occupation. For later adulthood, resources from the past should consist of behaviors that are less constrained by sex- and age-appropriate roles and functions (Gutmann, 1975). The increasingly earlier age for retiring from parenting (Hareven, 1977; Neugarten & Moore, 1968) places OGS women at 47 within this "second half of life"; their oldest children are over 25, the youngest, over 18; among

OGS men at 47 the oldest child has turned 21, the youngest, 13 (see Table 6.3).

Uses of the Past for Women

A primary task of women's adolescent socialization is to prepare resources of reliable nurturance and empathy for mothering. The need for such resources declines with the offspring's developing individuation and separation from the close mother–child attachment. When the last-born enters school, the maternal function itself is on the wane and with it, the use of adolescent resources for parenting.

If socialization for parenting is a strong suit of female adolescence, preparation for the decline of mothering is a weak one (Pearlin, 1975). Therefore we expect few adolescent resources for adaptation during the waning of the parental function. Findings of Chapter 8 suggest that disengagement from parenting at about 40 temporarily left some OGS women with fewer resources. We predict decline in the uses of the past between 30 and 40, as the oldest child of the GS women grows from early school age to the junior year of high school and the youngest from preschool to middle elementary school (see Table 6.3).

The decline for GS women is seen in Table 6.1; this is the only subsample with a drop in past/present correlations over the two adult ages. Such a decline is, of course, also compatible with the child-centric

Table 6.3

Family Size and Age of Last- and First-born

Age	Total N	Zero children	No. of Children $\bar{X}$	σ	Age of Last-born $\bar{X}$	σ	Age of First-born $\bar{X}$	σ
GS Women								
30	35	5	2.2	1.4	2.5	1.9	5.7	2.8
40	32	3	3.2	1.8	8.9	4.2	16.6	3.7
GS Men								
30	30	7	1.9	1.4	2.1	1.6	5.0	2.8
40	26	0	3.0	1.4	9.2	4.6	14.4	5.8
OGS Women								
37	48	4	2.5	1.3	7.7	4.2	13.6	3.2
47	41	3	2.6	1.3	18.6	4.8	25.3	2.9
OGS Men								
37	46	4	2.4	1.6	4.9	3.4	9.7	3.9
47	37	3	2.9	1.9	13.2	5.0	21.0	3.9

proposition of fading effects with passing time. If, however, it is not time but parental function that mainly determines the past/present association, then the association should stay strong if age is held constant and the parental function varies. We should then expect women who are mothering young children at 40 to (a) make considerably more use of the past and show higher correlations with their adolescent characteristics than those at 40 who are mothering only older children, and (b) make use of the same early modes of responding as had the full GS sample at 30 when almost all had a preschool child.

In the post-parental period a new clarity of separateness from the child can be expected to replace the equivocal and declining role of later parenting. Modes of response pertaining to personal identity in adolescence that had been kept in abeyance by parenting should become more accessible for adaptation in the post-parental period. This access, we expect, should be apparent for OGS women at 47, especially for those whose last-born was over 18. In the thinking of Jung (1933) and Gutmann (1975), resources for the woman's post-parental period should consist of early ways of responding congruent with autonomy and achievement, the so-called "masculine" aspects of the self.

Uses of the Past for Men

Men are socialized in youth to reach for long-term goals in the adult world considerably beyond marriage and early parenting. Indeed, adolescent males plan their lives less tentatively over significantly longer periods than do females (Brim & Forer, 1956; Douvan & Adelson, 1966; Ezekiel, 1968; Lessing, 1968). For many men, being settled in the adult world is expected by 40 (Levinson et al., 1974). Even when vocational permanence is evident as early as 30—the situation for many men in the Intergenerational Studies (IGS) samples—the young adult's sense of exploring choices may prevail in his need to review and re-affirm the steady occupation. Accordingly, we expect that men by 40, drawing close to or already adaptively settled in the adult world, will also draw amply from the adolescent past when such long-term goals were constructed.

Although research in time-perspective has not yet reported whether adolescent males envision age 30 with as much clarity and detail as females, one can imagine that adolescent males' longer view of their own development presupposes a certain ambiguity about the nearer age of 30. Adult models for "being thirty" are not abundant for the adolescent male, whose father is older, and siblings and friends younger, than 30.

It may be that for young manhood the resources established in the past can be usefully reclaimed only when one feels irrevocably established as an adult, as at 40. These resources may mean a surge ahead in individuation rather than a step backward to a less self-possessed time. Indeed, drawing from the non-autonomous past of adolescence might seem to close off options and endanger the forward motion, the pressing ahead of a man of 30. If the man at 40 is a finder, than at 30 he is a seeker, whose search for linkage between the self and the wider world is usually shifting away from the family of his youth and adolescence (Levinson *et al.*, 1974). Accordingly, we expect the adapted man at 30 to be further from his own adolescence than he will be at 40, and, as Table 6.1 shows, there are more past/present correlations involving PH at 40 than at 30.

For fatherhood too, the past may be more safely and usefully drawn upon in later than earlier adulthood. Certainly for IGS cohorts, socialization for parenting was less focused for the male than female adolescent, notwithstanding the reality of fatherhood for more than 75% of the GS males at 30. Fatherhood, rather than being a specific task to learn and master, seems more to be regulated by and subordinated to the distant and global anticipations of being in the adult world, and of becoming established and autonomous, tasks accomplished later rather than earlier. If this is so, then the better father is likely to be the older father, and indeed, older fathers (regardless of parental experience) are described (Nydegger, 1975) as able to communicate, express warmth to their child, encourage the child's independence and individuality, and promote intellectual achievement; younger fathers are less permissive, more rejecting and in general more concerned with "demanding socialization"—as perhaps these young men play out their own socialization of impulse control. These polar differences suggest what Erikson has identified as the generativity of the older man, beginning at around age 40. The male's past resources for parenting may then indeed exist but stay dormant until he becomes a self-sufficient adult. Are yet different resources drawn upon by the older OGS father at 47, who is within "the second half of life" with the purported emergence of the inward-looking, "feminine" aspect of the self (Gutmann, 1975; Jung, 1933; Neugarten, 1964)? These issues may perhaps be effectively explored by assessing the degree and nature of the early modes of behaving used by healthy men at different ages and in different stages of the family.

Method

This second study deals with the major content of the significant correlations in Table 6.1 and 6.2 based on adult age and, from our discussion, adds a new analysis of adolescent prediction of adult PH by stage of family development. The age of the last-born at the time of each adult follow-up is taken as an approximate marker for several developmental steps in the family, starting with the priority of the parental function and ending with the family as fully established. This family-stage analysis seeks to determine uses of the past for parenting of younger and of older children, including the post-parenting era for OGS women at 47.

The large yields of Q-sort findings (Tables 6.1 and 6.2) can be managed more conveniently for content analysis if reduced by cluster analysis. A common solution for the early- and late-adolescent Q sorts yielded 11 oblique clusters accounting for all the reliable covariance among the items and defining important and identifiable dimensions that also run through Q-sort personality characterizations (Livson & Day, 1977). These clusters have also been successfully tested for fit within each of the "component" groups (two sexes × two samples × two adult age periods). In addition to the clusters, eight single items qualify as separate "dimensions" in that they (a) neither define a cluster nor have their variance "explained" by any combination of the 11 clusters and (b) show sufficiently high interjudge reliability. (See Chapter 2 for the clustering procedure.)

These 19 Q-sort *dimensions*—11 clusters and 8 single items—are encountered throughout this second study and where significant, listed in the following tables. Not surprisingly, redoing the multiple correlations of our first study with the Q-sort dimensions maintains the essential pattern of the analysis involving the 104 items of the Q sort. Table 6.4 lists the 19 Q-sort dimensions and, for the clusters, the defining Q-sort items.

In Tables 6.5 and 6.6, Q-sort dimensions with significant multiple correlations are listed under either early or late adolescence according to the significance of their beta weights for the periods. A Q-sort dimension in parentheses indicates a joint effect, namely the effect of a variable when its statistical value is maintained over both adolescent periods, that is, when at least 25% of the variance is accounted for by the combination of periods. (The joint effect is that component of the explained variance that is a function of the amount of correlation between the two predicting periods; see McNemar, 1969). A joint effect can occur with or without separate effects from either adolescent period.

Significant Q-sort items, summarized in Table 6.1, are not tabled further. But items that are not definers of the Q-sort dimensions are presented in the text to support the primary analysis of the Q-sort

Table 6.4

Q-sort Dimensions in Early and Late Adolescence

Dimensions	Item definers
Cluster	
Responsible	dependable, does not push limits, not rebellious, not negativistic, not deceitful, productive, not unpredictable
Nurturant	sympathetic, giving, protective
Emotive	talkative, expressive, rapid tempo
Intellectually Competent	values intellectual matters, wide interests, appears intelligent, verbally fluent, interesting
Sociable	not aloof, gregarious, not distrustful
Decisive	assertive, not reluctant to act, does not withdraw when frustrated
Self-Insightful	not extrapunitive, not self-defensive, insightful, socially perceptive, not projective, aware of impression created
Somatizing	somatizes, has bodily concern
Eroticizing	eroticizes situations, interested in opposite sex
Physically Attractive	physically attractive, not concerned with appearance, fastidious
Defensive	thin-skinned, bothered by demands
Single-item	
Moralistic	
Fantasizing	
Feels Guilty	
Esthetically Reactive	
Repressive	
Power-Oriented	
Masculine/Feminine Style (Sex-appropriate)	
Emotionally Involved with Same Sex	

dimensions. Finally, at times it is useful to proceed beyond our summary measure of adult PH to specific adult adaptations (measured by Q-sort items at the adult age) linked to the adolescent predictors. Such instances occur when adolescent traits seem to contradict our predictions or are patently opposed to popular intuitions about antecedents of adult psychological health, namely, "good leads to good." These intuitions are violated in a reversal effect, that is, when the same behavior predicts good psychological health at one time and poor health at another. Knowing the specific adult traits that show this pattern helps

Table 6.5

Relationship of Adolescent Q-sort Cluster
Dimensions to Adult Psychological Health
(Females)

Age	Sample	N	R^a	Early adolescence	Late adolescence
30	GS	35	.41**	Responsible	
			.40**		Self-Insightful
			.38**	Intellectually Competent	
			.38**		not Power-Oriented
			.35**		not Repressive
			.32*		not Moralistic
			.29*	Fantasizing	
			.29*	(Nurturant)^b	(Nurturant)
40	GS	32	.51***	not Esthetically Reactive	Esthetically Reactive
			.43**		not Moralistic
			.40**		Self-Insightful
			.33*		not Power-Oriented
			.30*	not Physically Attractive	
			.30*	(Nurturant)	(Nurturant)
37	OGS	48	.35**		does not Feel Guilty
			.33**	not Somatizing	
			.32**		Power-Oriented
			.26*		not Nurturant
			.24*		not Responsible
47	OGS	41	.39***	(Intellectually Competent)	(Intellectually Competent)
			.36**		does not Feel Guilty
			.30**		Esthetically Reactive
			.27*	Emotive	
			.26*		not Defensive
			.25*	(Decisive)	(Decisive)

^{a}corrected R.
^{b}Q-sort dimension in parentheses indicates a joint effect only.
*$p < .10$.
**$p < .05$.
***$p < .01$.

in understanding the accommodation of the predictive adolescent traits to adult developmental tasks. Note that "past resources" are essential elements from which new adult constructions are made, but not necessarily the adult outcome itself. In general, knowing the specific adult traits linked to an adolescent response enables us to distinguish between past traits and the transformations they must undergo to serve their adult tasks. Q-sort items correlating with PH at $p < .05$ or better are reported.

Study of adult development from 30 to near 50 (or from early parent-

Table 6.6

Relationship of Adolescent Q-sort Cluster
Dimensions to Adult Psychological Health
(Males)

Age	Sample	N	R^a	Early adolescence	Late adolescence
30	GS	30	.36*	not Responsible	Responsible
40	GS	26	.53***	Sociable	
			.52***		not Defensive
			.51***	Sex-Appropriate	
			.46**		Power-Oriented
			.45**	(Decisive)^b	(Decisive)
			.44**	Responsible	
			.40**	Nurturant	
			.39**		Emotionally In-volved with Same Sex
			.38**	not Fantasizing	
37	OGS	46	.41***		Intellectually Competent
			.31**	(Responsible)	(Responsible)
			.26*	Esthetically Reactive	
			.25*		Moralistic
47	OGS	37	.61****	Responsible	
			.52****	Intellectually Competent	
			.42***	Nurturant	
			.39***	Esthetically Reactive	
			.39***	not Power-Oriented	
			.37***	Self-Insightful	
			.28*	not Somatizing	
			.26*		not Sex-Appropriate

^{a}corrected R.
^{b}Q-sort dimension in parentheses indicates a joint effect only.
*$p < .10$.
**$p < .05$.
***$p < .01$.
****$p < .001$.

ing to post-parenting) is best served by following well-matched longitudinal cohorts over this full span, observing each in timely succession to separate effects of cultural change from indigenous processes of
age or stage (Nesselroade & Baltes, 1974; Schaie, 1965). This design
cannot be fully achieved when GS and OGS cohorts were not assessed
at exactly the same ages. New uncertainties arise when initial selection
resulted in sample differences on such dimensions as socioeconomic
status and intelligence (Chapter 2). Our cross-sectional analysis of
family-stage groupings requires a similar caveat, that is, sample dif-

ferences irrelevant to the family-stage notion may exist (although we do not detect substantive personality differences between these groupings on adolescent Q-sorts). Such realities necessarily intrude upon our conceptual discussion of development from 30 to 50 and, although they promote confidence in predicted results, they make unexpected outcomes more difficult to interpret.

Results from Guidance Cohort

It is useful first to recast the findings of Table 6.1 according to their fit with the adult-centered perspective toward uses of the past in early and middle adulthood. GS men and women show contrasting access to the past between age 30 and 40. Men at 30 and women at 40 draw relatively little from the adolescent past for psychological health, whereas women at 30 and men at 40 draw abundantly on adolescent modes of responding. This reversal supports our expectation that adolescent socialization will be of diminishing usefulness over this adult period for women as maternal functions decline but of increasing utility for men as they become further established outside the home.

Guidance Women at Age 30

As Table 6.5 indicates, psychologically healthy GS women had shown capacities in adolescence for cognitive (Self-Insightful, Intellectually Competent) and affective (not Repressive, Nurturant, Fantasizing) mastery, as well as productive purpose and commitment (Responsible). Ingredients for an interpersonal morality (Haan, 1978), informed by reciprocity and concern for others' integrity (not Power-Oriented, not Moralistic), are also evident.

These adolescent behaviors transcend narrow role prescriptions for marriage and early parenting. The availability of an earlier rich inner life, insight into one's own motivations, interpersonal morality and generosity seem to be components of empathic relatedness, whether for adult intimacy or parenting. One also readily discerns resources for the adaptation to reality that is required by early motherhood (Deutsch, 1944).

Further adolescent supports for women's PH at 30 are indicated by significant correlations for the following adolescent Q-sort items. In early adolescence these women were regarded as philosophically concerned, not affected, not self-indulgent, not concerned with appearance, and not irritable. In late adolescence these women were rated as not conventional, responding to humor, and comfortable with uncertainty.

Only one Q-sort item, does not Vary Roles, reveals a reversal, that is, women's PH at 30 draws on restriction of role-playing capacity in early adolescence and then on increased role-playing capacity in late adolescence. This sequence suggests that women's adaptation at 30 actually gains from an initial rigidity or, conversely, loses from early flexibility in role-playing. Role variability in early adolescence may be too early, as indicated further by its Q-sort correlates at 30 that point to a lack of authenticity and integrity, namely, not straight-forward, not insightful, deceitful, fearful, not evaluating others' motivations, and not warm. An early role rigidity may then actually express a budding selfhood able to resist pretense.

The reversal draws attention to other qualitative differences between behaviors drawn from early and late adolescence and to the temporal order in which they are recruited. As indicated in Table 6.5, resources for a firmly autonomous and competent self (responsible, intellectually competent) precede affective and reflective resources (self-insightful, and not power-oriented, repressive, or moralistic). These results introduce the issue of the effect on adult function of timing and sequencing in the earlier development of instrumental and expressive characteristics. As we report subsequently, the order in which GS men recruit traits for PH tends to reverse the order observed in GS women, that is the men draw on expressive traits before instrumental ones.

Guidance Women at Age 40

As Table 6.5 shows, adolescent predictors of PH at 40, though fewer in number, include several of the Q-sort dimensions predictive to age 30 (not Moralistic, not Self-Insightful, not Power-Oriented, Nurturant) as well as two new predictors: not Physically Attractive and a reversal effect on Esthetically Reactive. The new early-adolescent predictors (not Physically Attractive and not Esthetically Reactive) suggest again (as did lack of early role-playing for PH at 30) the salutory contribution of an earlier "thick-skin." This suggestion of earlier toughness is supported by another reversal effect on the Q-sort item, Arouses Liking, where the health-predictive sequence is from arousing dislike in early adolescence to arousing liking in late adolescence. Again one may hypothesize that an earlier unyielding stance establishes a basic sense of autonomy that allows subsequent sociability to be sensed as self-controlled rather than responsive to social pressures. Adult Q-sort items at 40 that are correlated with not arousing liking in early adolescence and arousing liking in late adolescence yield a picture of a woman whose sociability and social presence at

40 are in a larger context of both basic trust and personal control, a woman who does not feel victimized, does not feel life lacks meaning, is not distrustful or self-pitying, and is cheerful, poised, and has feminine style.

The decline by 40 of the adolescent predictors for 30 leads to the question of differential access to the past for GS women who gave birth over the preceding 10 years and those who did not. At 30 almost all GS women had a preschool child; 10 years later maternal roles were more diverse, a change reflected in a significantly larger variance of the age of the last-born at 40 ($p < .01$; see Table 6.3). As one might expect for the 1950s and 1960s, women who gave birth in their mid- or late thirties had larger families than those who had not given birth by this age period. Using a median split of age of the last-born, we find that women with younger last-borns (8 years and below) at 40 had an average of 4.3 children; those with older last-borns (9 years and above) averaged 2.6 children. The striking difference in paid employment between these groups further points to their divergent paths with respect to caretaking and homemaking; of the mothers with younger last-borns, 71% had not worked for pay in the prior decade, whereas only 18% of the mothers of older last-borns had not been employed. Having young children at 40 is associated with a more prolonged and less work-interrupted history of parenting, adding to our expectation that these women will show greater access to their adolescent past and draw on resources similar in content to those used by all of the women in this sample at 30.

Table 6.7 lists the Q-sort dimensions in early and late adolescence that significantly predict PH for each subgroup (mothers of the younger family, $N = 16$, and mothers of the older family, $N = 13$) at 40. The specific contributions of early and late adolescence are omitted because this question does not require such analysis.

As expected, the greater access to the past by the mothers of younger families is strikingly evident: nine Q-sort dimensions predict their PH, whereas none do so for mothers of older families. Moreover, mothers of younger families, again as expected, show many of the same adolescent traits drawn upon by all women in this sample at 30. Six of the nine predictors in Table 6.7 overlap with the age 30 predictors (not Moralistic, Intellectually Competent, Fantasizing, Self-Insightful, Nurturant, not Power-Oriented). Such similarity in findings supports the priority of the parental task over chronological age and contradicts child-centric hypotheses that rely heavily on the effect of time. Nevertheless an age-specific aspect interacts with maternal function, as indicated by the non-overlapping predictors of Esthetically Reactive, Feels Guilty

Table 6.7

Relationships of Adolescent Q sorts to Age–40
Psychological Health for Guidance Sample by Age of Last-Born

Women			Men		
Q-sort dimensions	N	R	Q-sort dimensions	N	R
Younger ($\leqslant$ 8 years)	16		Younger ($\leqslant$ 9 years)	12	
Esthetically Reactive		.80****	Responsible		.70**
not Moralistic		.66**	not Somatizing		.59*
Intellectually Competent		.62**	Moralistic		.57*
Feels Guilty		.57*	Nurturant		.56*
Fantasizing		.56*	Intellectually Competent		.52*
Self-Insightful		.55*			
Nurturant		.55*			
not Power-Oriented		.55*			
not Eroticizing		.54*			
Older ($\geqslant$ 9 years)	13		Older ($\geqslant$ 10 years)	14	
none			not Defensive		.74***
			Decisive		.65**
			Sex-Appropriate		.64**
			Power-Oriented		.59**
			Sociable		.58**
			does not Feel Guilty		.53*

*p < .10.
**p < .05.
***p < .01.
****p < .001.

and not Eroticizing. In parenting young children as late as 40, the psychologically healthy woman may draw on resources that involve tolerance of delay, even subordination of self-interest, yet permit sublimated ego satisfactions.

Guidance Men at Age 30

Among all subgroups, GS men at 30 draw least from adolescence for adult PH. The little that is drawn upon seems congruent with an orientation to the present and with the exploratory and hopeful thrust of this early-adult stage. The ambivalent aspect of role demands at 30, for example, making and unmaking provisional occupational choices and decisions (Levinson *et al.*, 1974), is suggested in the mild reversal effect on one Q-sort dimension, Responsible (see Table 6.6). PH at 30 tends to be associated with being less responsible in early adolescence and more responsible in late adolescence. This sequence from rebelliousness and testing limits to dependability highlights the self-determined quality of socialized action rather than the docile acceptance of socially prescribed roles. This reversal correlates with such Q-sort items at 30 as Thinks Unconventionally, not Conventional, not Deceitful, and not Distrustful. From willful to willing suggests an emergent capability that confers self-possession rather than external necessity on one's socially desirable behavior. Further resources for this effort to establish the personal will, perhaps including activating a personal dream or vision of the future (Levinson *et al.*, 1974), are evident in the few adolescent Q-sort characteristics that predict PH at 30. In early adolescence these men were seen as romanticizing individuals and causes and were cheerful; in late adolescence, they were not reluctant to act, self-pitying, or self-defeating.

Guidance Men at Age 40

Nowhere in our study is the adolescent past drawn upon so richly as by GS men at 40. The nine predictors of PH (see Table 6.6) comprise many of the essential ingredients of stability and striving in the stereotypic established male—worker, achiever, provider, friend, and parental model. The individualistic surge at 30 seems to have "settled down" to recovering focused and manageable goals in a social fabric of expectable tasks and obligations. Proven performance, earned achievement, and straightforward action and interaction are drawn from adolescence for PH at 40, rather than inner processes of imagining, reflecting, or deliberating. In the former resources is a sense of rapprochement with the hopes of masculine socialization during adolescence that individuation at 30 seemed to ignore. Single Q-sort items correlated with PH at 40, all with significant early-adolescent weights, support this impression that the adolescent past is drawn upon in becoming an invested, loyal, and productive member of the social order. These men were turned to for advice, not self-defeating, proffed advice, did not feel life lacked meaning, poised, straightforward, did not have brittle ego defenses, aroused liking, thought conventionally, were comfortable with decisions, did not complicate simple situations, and were aware of the impression they created. Such adolescent behaviors are consonant with the overriding tasks of the "grown-up" man at 40, that is, being self-reliant and a provider to others.

The impression of a simple continuity between adolescent and adult efficacy is interrupted, however, by the reversal effect in the Q-sort item, Seeks Reassurance, where the health-promoting order is from seeking reassurance in early adolescence to relinquishing reassurance in late adolescence. This recovery *and* relinquishment of early dependency as a resource for adult adaptation suggest that age 40 is more than a time of simple control and mobility, and adolescence, in turn, more than a repository of role prescriptions to appear self-assured and "self-made." Rather, this order suggests that self-reliance, when preceded by reliance upon others, promotes caring and dependability in adulthood. The health-promoting sequence from seeks reassurance to relinquishes reassurance is correlated with the following Q-sort items at 40 that indeed indicate a highly humane adult disposition, an adult that does not have brittle ego defenses, is calm, straightforward, giving, sympathetic, arouses liking, is turned to for advice, is not self-indulgent, not negativistic, productive, aware of impression created, and not bothered by demands.

Note from Table 6.6 that the behaviors related to caring and dependability (sociable, responsible, nurturant) in men at 40 come from early adolescence, whereas those associated with striving (power-oriented, sex-appropriate, not defensive) are drawn from late adolescence. A trend toward the inverse order was noted among psychologically healthy GS women at 30 and 40, that is, instrumental, ego-controlling modes of behavior preceded the expressive. For men, initial receptivity (seeking reassurance) may be critical for a basic social attachment that later sex-appropriate autonomy cannot invalidate, whereas for women, prior autonomy assures a basic ego mastery that will endure even after the onset of sex-appropriate receptivity (Livson & Peskin, 1979; Peskin, 1972).

The influence of current family stage for men at 40 is indicated by the adolescent Q-sort dimensions (Table 6.7) that predict adult PH for men with younger (9 years or less) and older (10 years or more) last-born children. Although the groups do not differ in average number of children, men with younger families seem less established by virtue of their older age at marriage (means of 26.0 versus 22.6 years). The larger yield of significant Q-sort dimensions for those with older families supports our general prediction that the past is more accessible to the established man. Moreover, the decline of mothering with children's increasing age may promote more significant fathering roles, and in turn, stimulate the search for past resources to parent the older child.

The differential content of the significant Q-sort dimensions for men with older and younger families suggests that personal power and confident ascendency in adolescence (characterized by not being defensive, acting in a sex-appropriate manner, being decisive, and not feeling

Table 6.8

Relationship of Adolescent Q sorts to Adult Psychological Health
for Oakland Sample by Age of Last-Born

Women age 37			Women age 47			Men age 47		
Q-sort dimensions	N	R	Q-sort dimensions	N	R	Q-sort dimensions	N	R
Younger (≤ 8 years)	21		Younger (≤ 18 years)	15		Younger (≤ 13 years)	17	
Power-Oriented		.48*	Self-Insightful		.65**	Responsible		.86****
			Intellectually Competent		.59*	Nurturant		.71***
						Esthetically Reactive		.65***
						Intellectually Competent		.62***
						Self-Insightful		.57**
						not Power-Oriented		.57**
Older (≥ 9 years)	23		Older (≥ 19 years)	23		Older (≥ 14 years)	17	
does not Feel Guilty		.59***	Intellectually Competent		.54**	not Somatizing		.51**
not Responsible		.46*	Emotive		.53**			
not Nurturant		.46*	not Responsible		.53**			
Intellectually Competent		.46*	does not Feel Guilty		.51**			
			not Nurturant		.50**			

*p < .10.
**p < .05.
***p < .01.
****p < .001.

guilty) are drawn upon by the healthy father of the older family, whereas personal caring and dependability (seen in the attributes responsibility, nurturance, and being moralistic) in adolescence are resources for the healthy father of the younger family. Resources for guiding the next generation are more evident for fathers of younger families. However, one might argue that the older last-born is as much guided to age-appropriate instrumental goals when a father draws on the past for self-assertion and personal striving. All of these generalizations are tentative because, as noted earlier, the analyses here are only cross-sectional.

Results from Oakland Cohort

For both sexes, the results suggest increased access to adolescent achievements between 37 and 47, the periods of late-parenting and post-parenting. Far from being strained further, the association between adolescent modes of response and those in the "second half of life" actually is strengthened.

Oakland Women at Age 37

By 37, most OGS women had completed their families, and the last-born child was beyond preschool (7.7 years). As shown in Table 6.5, the predominantly late-adolescent predictors of PH (does not Feel Guilty,

Power-Oriented, not Nurturant, not Responsible) at this juncture seem, however, better suited for adaptation at an even older age, that is, closer to the post-parental period, for which we predicted a need for resources to regain personal autonomy. As early as 37, which is transitional for women with no more young (preschool) to mother, the psychological health of the OGS women seems associated with past ways of responding that reflect almost opportunistic behavior and an intrepid, individualistic striving. The Q-sort items significantly correlated with PH come predominantly from early adolescence. These women in early adolescence were ambitious, did not complicate simple situations, were interesting, not dependent, and skilled in imaginative play; in late adolescence they were self-dramatizing. These resources contrast with those of GS women at 40, whose uses of the past were congruent with the maternal function. Indeed, these two female cohorts draw on opposite poles of two Q-sort dimensions: Power-Oriented and Nurturant.

That the same dispositions are so differently drawn upon for later health necessarily suggests initial sample differences between the GS and OGS, such as socioeconomic status, and/or cohort differences in parenting careers and valuation of the parental function. Either or both of these sorts of disparity might be reflected in number of children, outside employment, history of single parenting, and the like. If the parental functions of the two cohorts did unfold in different social-psychological contexts, then different resources from the past would be needed to maintain good parenting or to create alternate life satisfactions.

In terms of family size and employment, a stronger familial and parental orientation characterizes the GS women. The GS cohort at 40 averages 3.2 children, the OGS at 37, 2.5 children. (Ten years later, at 47, family size is virtually unchanged for OGS women.) OGS women had more full-time or part-time employment between 27 and 37 (70%) than did the GS women (57%) between 30 and 40. OGS women with older children may already have begun the transition to post-parenthood by 37 rather than simply accepting role decline. Indeed, OGS mothers of older families (last-born 9 years or older) show more of the predicted post-parental self-centeredness (do not feel guilty or responsible, and are not nurturant) than do those with younger families (Table 6.8). Elder's (1974) findings, however, dispute the overall characterization of the OGS women in these terms. For a large subsample (those economically deprived during adolescence by the Depression), preference for family roles, Elder reports, is especially prominent.

For many OGS women, the realities of mothering are embedded in the context of World War II. Single parenting of preschool children was more than twice as prevalent for OGS as GS mothers (36% versus 15%) and came entirely during the war years, primarily because the husband was in military service. For most of these women, single parenting came shortly after the birth of the first child, a stress hardly anticipated in early socialization for marriage and family and, coming so soon in family formation, may have set a pattern for later mothering as well. Lacking the support in their own autonomous marital or family unit that was available to GS women, OGS women may have had to find resources for autonomy elsewhere—for example, from their past—to mobilize energy for mothering. What appear to be self-centered uses of the past may reflect recovery of instumental strengths to carry the parental task alone, including provisions for the expressive side of mothering. Such behaviors from adolescence may actually serve to release nurturance by strengthening the woman's sense of being in charge of herself in an otherwise deprived reality. Strengths developed in early adolescence may then be called upon to help the woman cope with the affective demands of mothering without "burn-out." The adolescent Q-sort dimension, does not Feel Guilty (the best predictor of PH at 37), predicts just such adaptations in relevant Q-sort items specific to 37. At age 37 the women were turned to for advice, not bothered by demands, did not feel victimized, were not moody, cheerful, did not seek reassurance, did not arouse nurturance, and were not negativistic.

Not only because of single parenting but also as a result of assumption of household responsibilities during adolescence because of losses suffered by their parents during the Depression (Chapter 1), OGS women in mid-parenthood may have accepted great responsibility for family maintenance that placed instrumental and seemingly self-centered resources in the forefront of their uses of the past. Where such disadvantaged conditions in the family do not prevail, the past can perhaps be searched more freely and directly for expressive resources, as in the case of the GS. We have here a broad hypothesis for further study, namely, that the uses of the past by the GS and OGS are shaped by different histories surrounding issues of family and personal security, as well as by similar adult tasks.

What exigencies of past or present may account for low access to the adolescent past by OGS mothers with younger last-borns? Such low access is clearly contrary to predictions well supported in the GS (Table 6.7), when early mothering was particularly apt to make use of affective adolescent resources. This unexpected break between present and past calls for a fuller description of the contemporary situations of the study members to find clues about the adult goals toward which past resources are aimed. The most apparent differences between and within cohorts pertain to work-history and family size. Fewer GS mothers with younger last-borns had entered the labor market (71% unemployed for the prior 10 years) compared to a comparable OGS group (38% unemployed). The implied difference in child-centeredness is further supported by the larger family size among GS mothers of younger children (4.3 children) than OGS mothers of younger children (3.3).

Oakland Women at Age 47

PH at 47 for OGS women draws anew from adolescent behavior, notwithstanding the relatively high correlation ($r = .75$) between the indices of PH at 37 and 47. The following Q-sort dimensions in adolescence (Table 6.5) are multiply correlated with PH at 47: Intellectually Competent, does not Feel Guilty, Esthetically Reactive, Emotive, not Defensive, and Decisive. Of these dimensions, only does not Feel Guilty is common to correlations with PH at 37 and 47.

The bold antecedents of PH at 37 appear to shift to more lenient and sublimated modes of response by 47, when the average age of the last-born (18.6) places OGS women at the threshold of the post-parental period. Their resources are less abrasive, perhaps less daring than 10 years earlier, as if individuation had been confirmed during the ensuing late-parenting decade, so less vigilence is required. The Q-sort items predictive of PH at 47 include, as at 37, not Dependent (from both early and late adolescence) and Ambitious and Skilled in Imaginative Play (from early adolescence). Signs of greater security and declining self-consciousness in current individuation are indicated by the new adolescent Q-sort correlates that indicated the women were not fearful (from late adolescence) and did not favor status quo, were poised, did not compare self to others, initiated humor, and responded to humor (from early adolescence.) Overall, the sense of selfhood seems to have expanded rather than—as at 37—only been successfully defended.

A closer look at the components of adult health for women supports the renewal of the personal self in the "second half of life." The changing adult correlates of the adolescent Q-sort dimension, does not Feel Guilty, between 37 and 47 gives a sense of the new individualistic and incisive face of adulthood in the post-parental period. Does not Feel Guilty now predicts characteristics specific to 47: ambitious, self-dramatizing, physically attractive, verbally fluent, insightful, appears intelligent, values intellectual matters. The adolescent resources used at 47 are clearly for the self, not for the cooperative social unit as they seemed at 37. Use of the same adolescent response over adult eras, then, need not mean that the adult task remains the same over time, but rather that even the "same" early mode of responding can be drawn upon for different purposes.

When this cohort is partitioned by family stage at 47, the post-parental women, as predicted, draw more from adolescence than those still in the late-parenting era. Table 6.8 lists the adolescent correlates of PH for OGS women whose last-born child is 18 years or younger, and for those whose last-born is 19 or older. Again, as expected, women who have been freed of the role ambiguity inherent in declining parental function have greater access to resources that pertain to personal autonomy and striving—in adolescence they were intellectually competent, emotive, not responsible, did not feel guilty, and were not nurturant.

Oakland Men at Age 37

At 37 OGS men make relatively modest use—less than at 47—of adolescent resources for PH (intellectual competence, sense of responsibility, esthetically reactive, and moralistic; see Table 6.6). Where uses of the past are limited, we infer that personal security is less established, consistent with our view that the youthful past can safely be drawn upon only as a sense of self is affirmed. For GS men, we therefore predicted and confirmed a growing access to the past between earlier (30) and middle (40) adulthood, as the goals of male maturity were reached. Can this view apply to the increasing access of OGS men between ages 37 and 47?

In addition to age differences and possible initial sample differences between the OGS and GS groups, both their adolescent and adult experiences occurred in different psychosocial eras. Any or all of these differences between the groups may underlie the greater access to the adolescent past of the GS men at age 40 than the OGS men at 37. Although the effects of psychosocial eras cannot readily be separated from other group differences, several considerations suggest that the former may play a particular role. Compared to the GS men at 40, OGS men at 37 established their families later than expectable from the 3-year average age difference. World War II postponed parenthood for the OGS males but not age at marriage. Nearly all OGS men were on active duty, but few started families, so only about 10% were absent fathers during the war. Family size had not reached its final level when they were 37; mean age of the last-born was 4.9 years, and mean age of the first-born was 9.7 years (Table 6.3). (Because more than 65% of OGS men were fathers of preschool children, a subgroup analysis of younger/older fathers was not undertaken.)

To the psychosocial delays brought about by military service may be added the effect of being an adolescent in the Great Depression on the nature of adult goals. OGS men at 37 were willing to be turned from the culturally normative male preoccupation with power and other symbols of "success" to attain, in the words of one of them, "the serenity that has eluded the lives of our parents" (Elder, 1974). The psychologically healthy OGS men at 37, unlike the healthy GS men at 40, draw little from the past that would promote personal power and control over the outside world. The Q-sort items, all from late adolescence, predictive of PH at 37 further support Elder's evidence for their pursuit of serenity, with an added aspect of reflective judgment and cognitive coping: OGS men tended to be calm, not have a rapid tempo, philosophically concerned, not irritable or moody, prided themselves on objectivity, were not uncomfortable with uncertainty, and not self-dramatizing. The predictive item from early adolescence, Ambitious, a trait not obviously related to the reflective tone of the other adolescent Q-sort items, is correlated with PH at 37. Yet early-adolescent aspiration turns out to be just such a resource; at 37 the following Q-sort items correlate significantly with Ambitious in early adolescence: Calm, not Irritable, Cheerful, Has Wide Interests, Values Intellectual Matters, Incisive.

Oakland Men at Age 47

At 47, psychologically healthy OGS men draw much more than at 37 on affectively softer, generative, inward-seeking and cognitive dimensions: Responsible, Intellectually Competent, Nurturant, Esthetically Reactive, not Power-Oriented, Self-Insightful, and not Sex-Appropriate (Table 6.6). These findings support the Jungian-Gutmann formulation of men's changing relationship to the self in the "second half of life." Several relevant Q-sort items, all from early adolescence, predict PH at both 47 and 37: not Moody, Philosophically Concerned, not Self-Dramatizing, not Irritable, Ambitious. Behaviors newly drawn on for PH at 47 include these early-adolescent items: not Under-controlled, not Affected, and not Self-Indulgent.

For both Q-sort dimensions and items, the major locus of past resources shifts from late adolescence at 37 to early adolescence at 47. This result suggests that the OGS man at 47 is freer than he was at 37 to recover seemingly less mature aspects of the self. Consistent with this freedom in mid-life to revalue socially unsanctioned aspects of selfhood is the late-adolescent resource of not Sex-Appropriate. Behaviors deemed unmasculine by the standards of late adolescence are recovered by the psychologically healthy men at 47. One is reminded of

Levinson's *et al.* comment (1974) that the man at mid-life learns "to love formerly devalued aspects of the self."

Healthy men at 47 again draw upon late adolescence in reversing the direction of correlation for the Q-sort item, Self-Indulgent. The health-predictive sequence from lack of self-indulgence in early adolescence to self-indulgence in late adolescence correlates with a considerable number of Q-sort items at 47, pointing to an emergent effect from opposite behavioral components. The most significant (*p* < .001) of these items are: not Distrustful, Esthetically Reactive, Sensuous, Satisfied with Self, not Bothered by Demands, Sympathetic, Giving. These correlates suggest movement from narcissistic (denied or indulged) components toward the mid-life tasks of men (Jung, 1933, Levinson *et al.*, 1974)—deepening emotional relatedness, caring, and generosity to the self and to others. Managing such significant mid-life tasks is not then to be attributed to the simple continuity of highly stable and circumscribed behaviors, but to seeming contradictory changes over time that may really reveal the complex developmental makeup of the task. Behavioral reversals offer compelling cases for discontinuity and for the developmental complexity of integrating the caring for others with caring for oneself at adult mid-life.

As Table 6.8 shows, only OGS fathers with younger children (13 and younger) at 47 draw abundantly from the past, suggesting (as Gutmann contends) that nearness to the post-parental period may not be essential for the males' inward turn at mid-life. (An adequate test of this idea requires the study of parents who have actually reached the post-parenting time. Unlike mothers in the OGS cohort, few fathers have last-borns who are already 18). Perhaps the inward turn at mid-life is more "seeded" by the playfulness of younger children than we are accustomed to think.

A final note concerns the Q-sort item, Ambitious, which holds the distinction of being the only adolescent item or dimension that predicts psychological health at both adult ages and for both sexes in the OGS. (No Q-sort item or dimension does so for any GS subgroup.) Resources for PH that cut across age and sex are rare. Moreover, the fact that this item predicts only in the OGS suggests an historical, cohort-specific effect, such as the enduring usefulness of adolescent aspiration that had originally served well in coping with the psychosocial stress of the Depression years. Among OGS subgroups, the largest yield of adult Q-sort correlates with adolescent ambition appears for the men at 47—33% of the adult Q-sort items correlate significantly with ambition in adolescence. Males rated high on aspiration level in early adolescence rate high at 47 on a wide range of affective, intellectual, and moral characteristics consistent with the deepening inner goals of the second half of life. One suspects that the capacities to delay, sustain, and persist which shape personal aspirations in youth and adolescence are conducive to the development of more internal, less acquisitive aspects of selfhood in the later years.

THE ADULT-CENTRIC ONCE AGAIN

How well does the adult-centric view that underlies the uses-of-the-past model stand up empirically as an alternative to the child-centric position? For the GS samples, the initial conceptualization requires no important modifications to account for the findings: the extent and content of their access to the past reflects our predictions about the resources needed for adult development according to sex, age, and family stage. Briefly, family stage for women and chronological age for men seem to organize the degree and kind of access to the past.

Results for OGS men and women at 37 could not be organized so simply. We then examined several aspects of their past (e.g., work histories, military service, and occurrence of single parenting) to assess possible cohort-specific meanings of the parental role that could explain the unexpected resources drawn upon from adolescence. But resort to this cohort's "case history" could be interpreted as accepting the child-centric view that the present is indeed assimilated to the past. In our view, however, use of such case history material does not defeat the adult-centric model but instead challenges us to construct a "psychodynamic" for it. We refer especially to the chain of reasoning and evidence that led us to infer that the disadvantaged parental history (e.g., single parenting) of the OGS mothers disposed them at 37 to find past resources for parenting in ostensibly unmaternal adolescent traits. At 47, however, the same adolescent dimension (namely, does not Feel Guilty) was associated with essentially new, more self-centered adaptations, in keeping with the post-parental position of many women at this later age. Discrimination between the child-centric and adult-centric is contingent not on whether case history material is used to define the current adult stage, but on whether the adult task dominates the organization of past resources.

The concept of "regression in the service of the ego" (Kris, 1952) and "control-mastery" (Weiss, 1971), which are significant attempts to recognize the transformative processes by which both impulses and defenses can be safely experienced and used by a strong ego, prepare the way for formulating a theory of the recovery of the past in adult-centric terms—and perhaps the eventual rapprochement of adult development and reconstruction in psychoanalysis (Cohler, 1980). Such psychodynamic constructs as manifest and latent levels of meaning, unconscious motivation, multiple determination, and so on may be as germane and demonstrable for the adult-centric as for the child-centric points of view and especially applicable to our findings of the relative inaccessibility of earlier modes of responding at certain *younger* adult ages.

More work is needed to show the transformations that past resources undergo to become fully useful for the present. Herein lies a major task in formulating a psychodynamics of the adult-centric model: to identify the processes by which adult stages give new motion to fragments of the past. Specific adult dimensions, rather than simply global states (such as psychological health) must be included as criteria and analyzed by appropriately complex multivariate techniques. The several instances, such as adolescent reversals, where specific adult correlates of past resources could be demonstrated, led us to a better sense of how such adult-centric processes might be described. Beyond this, adult-centered models of the past will inevitably blossom with multiple adult follow-ups of longitudinal cohorts, as conceived for the IGS. Lacking repeated follow-ups necessarily reduces evidence of developmental discontinuities and withholds support for adult-centered models of the past perhaps as surely as avoiding the older patient has prevented psychodynamic theory of memory and recollection from being informed by middle age and aging.

In this chapter we recovered the past statistically, as it were, and submitted it to an adult-centered interpretation. Self-report methods for the recovery of the past are more or less tuned to child-centric or adult-centric phenomenologies. Respondents in interview can be invited to assume an adult-centric focus toward personal recollection and reminiscence by being helped to review what in the past has (or, more therapeutically, might be) proven useful for present functioning. The work of Progoff (1975) and Butler (1963) are noteworthy examples of this neglected approach.

Changing uses of the past may be gleaned also by examining the altered contents of open-ended, free-associative recall at different points along the life span. The life-evaluation interview and self-ratings of life satisfaction constructed at IHD are suitable for such an approach, as are graphic self-rating methods (Back, 1976). If change in the recall of the "same" past can be linked to adult transitions such as marriage or childbirth (Peskin & Gigy, 1977), robust evidence becomes available for additional levels of adult-centric psychodynamics. Comparison of our findings with those from self-report or phenomenological methods for assessing uses of the past, and these to each other, are also important to establish whether different realms of the useful past exist within and outside of awareness and reflection. Reminiscence, recollection, nostalgia, review, and usefulness suggest common as well as distinct states of mind that longitudinal research efforts can help to separate and to integrate.

7

Psychological Health at Age 40: Prediction from Adolescent Personality

NORMAN LIVSON AND HARVEY PESKIN

Complementing Chapter 6, this chapter provides an independent view of associations between adolescent personality and adult psychological health. The psychological health index (PH) at 40 is predicted from the 19 personality dimensions, whose derivation is detailed in Chapter 6 for the *combined* OGS and GS samples. The predictive power of these dimensions is assessed separately for early and late adolescence and for men and women. Our approach is intentionally a summary and global one, in contrast to the detailed analyses necessary for the very different sorts of questions asked in Chapter 6. However, our adult-centric orientation is maintained and directs interpretation of the additional results.

Age 40 is our "outcome" point because we have identical data for both samples at approximately this age only. Because psychological health, as we measure it, is not a particularly stable characteristic between 30 and 50 (Chapter 6), the results for 40 are not necessarily applicable to other ages. We stress, therefore, that prediction of health *specifically at 40* is our concern here and not something called "*adult* psychological health," which data in Chapter 6 suggest is not a legitimate construct. This "instability" of the PH index over the middle years is not a matter of concern here because, as demonstrated in Chapter 6, the notion that psychological health may be something different at different adult ages has promising implications for under-

183

standing personality development. (Chapter 8 explores one important source of such differences.) Neither should this "instability" raise questions as to the validity of the PH measure at 40. We have much evidence for its construct validity. For example, the measure has very substantial positive correlations with another index of healthy functioning at 40—Haan's Total Coping Score. The values are, for men and women respectively, .62 and .63 ($p < .001$).

In combining OGS and GS we hypothesize that some predictive patterns are common to both samples. If our assumption is incorrect, the results will be incoherent and trivial. However, if a reasonable and comprehensible yield of predictors is obtained, then we shall have generated some more broadly useful hypotheses about more general antecedents of PH at 40. This approach in no way contradicts cohort differences in patterns of prediction reported in Chapter 6; the sharpness of the analytic focus is deliberately different. In Chapter 6 we paid close heed to the different sociohistorical contexts within which the two cohorts matured. Here, we seek only what is *general* across samples: specifically, those adolescent personality dimensions that are predictive of PH at 40, having survived (and possibly even having been strengthened by) the comingling of cohorts.

Our design is straightforward: we use the zero-order correlations of each of the 19 personality dimensions at each of the two adolescent periods with the PH measure at 40. In addition, separate stepwise multiple regression analyses, using these same predictors, are done for early and late adolescence. The samples are identical to those in Chapter 6 for the age 40 outcome. Combining OGS and GS yields sample sizes of 72 men and 80 women.

MULTIPLE REGRESSION PREDICTIONS OF PSYCHOLOGICAL HEALTH AT AGE 40

Stepwise multiple regression analysis determines the maximum predictability possible from the 19 adolescent personality dimensions. Beginning with the dimension with the highest zero-order correlation with PH at 40, a second dimension is added to the regression equation, selected on the criterion of producing the greatest predictive increment. Dimensions continue to be added on this criterion until additional predictors do not significantly increase the multiple correlation.

The PH index at 40 is predictable from early adolescent personality for both men and women; the multiple correlations, are, respectively, .47 and .46 ($p < .001$). Significant prediction is also possible from late adolescence. For men, the multiple correlation is .45 ($p < .001$); for women, only one dimension, Intellectually Competent, is necessary for maximum predictability ($r = .29$; $p < .01$).

The specific weights of the dimensions in each multiple regression equation are not given here because the particular dimensions recruited by the stepwise procedure can be, in an important sense, rather arbitrary. When the variables in a predictor pool are not fully independent, and especially—as is the case here—when they are substantially intercorrelated, the specific predictors picked up by the stepwise procedure typically are determined by trivial differences in degree of association with the criterion. In men's early adolescence, for example, Self-Insightful does not enter the predictive equation despite its highly significant (and second highest) correlation with PH ($r = .30$, $p < .01$) because it correlates .63 with the strongest and first-entered predictor, Responsible ($r = .36$; $p < .01$). In effect, the stepwise procedure partials out the variance accounted for by earlier predictors before assessing the predictive power of later ones. In the instance just mentioned, if the slight difference in zero-order correlation with PH between the two highest predictors had been reversed, the interpretive emphasis (had we chosen to make such interpretation) would have been placed upon Self-Insightful rather than on Responsible.

This example should suffice to support our decision to use the multiple correlations only to establish that, taken together, the adolescent dimensions can predict PH at 40, and do so from both periods of adolescence and for both sexes. To get at the qualitative nature of the dimensions of adolescent personality that are predictive, we do better to focus upon the zero-order correlations. These tell the predictive story in a more direct manner. Because we demonstrate that the overall predictive associations are clearly significant, this approach is legitimate.

MEN'S PSYCHOLOGICAL HEALTH AT AGE 40

The PH index of men at 40, as we have just seen, can be reliably forecast from personality characteristics during both early and late adolescence. Table 7.1 presents the product-moment correlations of the 19 adolescent personality dimensions with PH at 40, for both sexes and both adolescent phases.

The most striking result is that being responsible and intellectually competent during either early or late adolescence significantly predicts PH at 40. Furthermore, these two dimensions are moderately indepen-

Table 7.1

Adolescent Personality Dimensions Predicting
Age-40 Psychological Health

Personality dimensions	Men		Women	
	Early	Late	Early	Late
Responsible	.36***	.29**	.04	-.02
Nurturant	.26**	.17	-.04	-.04
Emotive	-.04	-.17	.14	.11
Intellectually Competent	.30***	.27**	.32***	.29***
Sociable	.23**	.16	.01	.14
Decisive	.19	.24**	.04	.03
Self-Insightful	.30***	.05	-.01	.10
Somatizing	-.21	-.21	-.27**	-.02
Eroticizing	-.16	.04	-.03	-.04
Physically Attractive	.20	.18	.01	.08
Defensive	-.10	-.27**	-.01	-.06
Moralistic	.12	.28**	-.03	-.06
Fantasizing	-.15	.04	.24**	.10
Feels Guilty	.12	.06	.05	-.09
Esthetically Reactive	.17	.05	.06	.21
Repressive	.06	.04	-.05	-.05
Power-Oriented	.15	.19	.06	.15
Masculine/Feminine Style (Sex-Appropriate)	.13	.08	-.25**	-.14
Emotionally Involved with Same Sex	.07	.06	.05	-.07

Note: Entries are product-moment correlations. Sample sizes
are 72 men and 80 women.

**p < .05.

***p < .01.

dent within both adolescent periods—(intercorrelations of .37 in early
adolescence and .50 in late adolescence). Thus, in the parlance of Chapter 6, males at 40 draw on their adolescent past directly for dependability and responsibility, both integral features of PH, suggesting the
long-term persistence and usefulness of these facets of socialization. In
addition, however, the psychologically healthy male at 40 makes use of
a different and clearly more cognitive characteristic of his adolescence,
intellectual competence. Although undoubtedly an adaptive asset at
any age, intellectual competence is not a salient feature of the Q sort
that provides our yardstick for psychological health (see p. 191).

Several other dimensions predict significantly from either early or
late adolescence—but not from both—PH at 40. Patternings of these

characteristics at early and late adolescence suggest somewhat different "syndromes" of adolescent precursors of adult PH. At early adolescence the predictive dimensions that join with Responsible and Intellectually Competent, most notably, Nurturant, Sociable, and Self-Insightful, seem, viewed as defining a personality profile, almost obvious, that is, they can be read as an instance of the "good" continuing to be "good."

This is not the case—or, at least, not so clearly—at late adolescence. The three dimensions specifically predictive from the earlier period (Nurturant, Sociable, Self-Insightful), are not predictive from later adolescence. Instead, characteristics predictive from late adolescence rather dramatically refocus the image. Psychologically healthy males at 40 were moralistic, decisive, and not defensive during late adolescence. Combining Responsible and Intellectually Competent with these specific predictive features of late adolescence produces a characterological blend that seems "strong" to the point of toughness. Among males who are likely to be psychologically healthy at 40, the mellow mask of the younger adolescent has, just a few years later, hardened into an almost stern visage.

Why this stylistic change in the adolescent faces of the psychologically healthy male at 40? Perhaps these two faces represent better adaptations to the different tasks of the two periods. "Getting along" and being supportive to others—but not to the point of distorting one's perception of self—seem a fair characterization of the predictive personality profile at early adolescence. In a developmental period in which the biological and social transition to adulthood is just beginning, these characteristics can be regarded as indicating a sensible, even cautious tack taken at the start of the journey through adolescence. To be sociable and nurturant at this time of lesser urgency appear to be adaptive interpersonal tactics, especially so when combined with intrapersonal integrity (implied by self-insightfulness). Later, a developmental course correction seems necessary if the "about-to-be" man is to become inner-directed as he moves into adulthood. Those who evolve a reasonably firm sense of self during the late adolescent period of hormonal and competitive pressures and do not founder on the shoals "identity diffusion" (Erikson, 1968) should be able to steer with some certainty. The traits specifically predictive of PH at 40—being decisive, not defensive, and even moralistic—convey a sense of sureness of purpose that seems adaptive to the different demands of this later development period.

When these traits combine with competence and responsibility, the portrait that emerges closely resembles the "continuous growth" subgroup in Offer and Offer's (1975) longitudinal study (at age 22) of boys carefully selected on the criterion of their "normality" in late adolescent years. This subgroup (23% of their total sample) followed one of the three "developmental routes" derived by factor analysis from their data. The Offers clearly regard this route as the most promising for maintaining psychological health into later adulthood. Not a single member of this subgroup ever required psychotherapy.

In any event, the particular traits at early and late adolescence that we find predictive of PH at 40 for males appear congruent with generally accepted images of adaptive behavior during adolescence generally. Being moralistic (in late adolescence) is perhaps the single exception; it is also not a salient characteristic of adult PH. Being moralistic during this period may be transient "over-steering" to control newly emerged sexual stirrings until more flexible and appropriately modulated modes for handling such impulses evolve.

Our interpretations are hypotheses generated by the data and certainly are not "proved" by them. Other longitudinally studied samples could test these hypotheses. Some within-sample analyses of our data do permit internal tests of such hypotheses, although not direct validation. We next present evidence on associations *between* personality dimensions at early and late adolescence that is consistent with our developmental hypotheses.

The basis for examining these associations is the concept of "genotypic continuity" (Livson, 1973), which posits associations across time between phenotypically dissimilar personality variables, a step beyond the traditional restrictive concern with simple persistence of the same characteristics across of the life span. This approach permits the assumption that personality development is a continuous "causative" chain at a level underlying directly manifest behavior if, *and only if,* such development is conceptualized as involving *qualitative* transformations in the expression of underlying themes and traits throughout development. The time span here is quite short—from early to late adolescence—so such developmental transformations may be minimal. However, to the extent that these two phases of adolescence present different tasks (as we have suggested), some transformations may be triggered by changing adaptive challenges.

We find some of these transformations in male adolescents, and they seem in line with our hypotheses. As one example, having been self-insightful in early adolescence is predictive of PH at 40, but is apparently irrelevant in late adolescence; the correlation with PH drops from .30 to .05. Furthermore, Self-Insightful is one of the least persistent dimensions between the two adolescent periods for boys ($r = .35$). In early adolescence, however, it is at least as predictive of Not Defensive in late adolescence ($r = .40$)—a predictor of adult health—as it is of itself at that later period. Also, it predicts Responsible ($r = .47$) and Intellectually Competent ($r = .30$) in late adolescence, the two dimensions generally predictive of PH at 40. Thus, early adolescent self-insight does not disappear from the predictive picture; rather it seems to change form toward a more self-protective toughness.

Nurturance shows a similar pattern, predicting PH at 40 from early (but not late) adolescence and predicting Not Defensive in late adolescence ($r = .39$), which in turn predicts PH at 40. Only Sociable seems to be "lost." Although it is quite persistent during adolescence ($r = .52$), by late adolescence it no longer predicts PH at 40, nor does it show a transformation to any of the late-adolescent predictors. As a resource to be drawn on for adult psychological health, sociability is apparently phase-specific to early adolescence.

All this is admittedly ad hoc, but seems a worthwhile excursion beneath the surface of the raw predictive correlations between adolescent personality and PH at 40. At the more manifest level, one may be content with the generalization that, for males, a set of positively regarded characteristics in adolescence forecast effective adult functioning. This is certainly the more parsimonious interpretation. Our results could easily suggest a perhaps even less interesting conclusion—that the psychologically healthy adolescent male develops into a healthy adult, at least at 40. As we show in our final section, there is some truth in this interpretation, but it must be qualified. For now we conclude that the men's PH at 40 draws on antecedents in adolescent personality, and on somewhat different ones from its early and late phases.

WOMEN'S AGE 40 PSYCHOLOGICAL HEALTH

The PH index of a woman of 40 is reliably predictable from aspects of both her early and late adolescent personality, although only a single dimension—Intellectually Competent—is a significant predictor from the later period. This dimension is also the most powerful influence from the earlier period (see Table 7.1). Again, and even more strongly, the predictive burden is carried primarily by a dimension that is substantially cognitive in nature, one not obviously embedded in our Q-sort measure of psychological health. This result is even more unexpected for women because, for them, Responsible (which shared equally with Intellectually Competence in predicting psychological health at 40 in men) shows essentially zero correlations from both adolescent periods.

Focusing first on early adolescence, we read from Table 7.1 that, in addition to the dimensions Intellectually Competent, Fantasizing, being less prone to Somatizing, and not having a Feminine Style join the predictive pattern. Competence and femininity tend to be incompatible characteristics in early adolescence (intercorrelation, $-.33$; $p < .01$). Consider that these data are for girls whose adolescent development took place in the 1930s and early 1940s—an era well before the emergence of major emphasis on women's effectiveness and achievement potential. Thus, women who are psychologically healthy at 40 had characteristics in early adolescence that suggest a certain attitudinal "deviance" from then-acceptable patterns of female behavior, and perhaps also the courage to express this deviance in behavior. Somatizing and Fantasizing, although quite independent dimensions (intercorrelation of .07 at early adolescence), can be interpreted as tapping different facets of openness to one's emotional life. *Not* to express psychic conflict in bodily symptoms and being able to transcend in imagination the strict bounds of reality may be seen as expressing trust in, rather than a defensive posture toward, one's emotions and feelings. If there is a message in this predictive early adolescent syndrome, it is that girls who (at this developmental period) are able *directly* to express characteristics that either they or their culture consider somewhat unacceptable have a better prognosis for psychological health at 40 than those who suppress such characteristics.

Only Intellectually Competent survives as a predictor at late adolescence; the other three more "emotional" early adolescent dimensions are no longer predictive. Yet, a curious transformation occurs with respect to Feminine Style. This dimension has the same correlations with Intellectually Competent at both early and late adolescent ($-.33$ and $-.34$, respectively). It also shows substantial stability across these periods ($r = .52$). However, Feminine Style behavior in *early* adolescence is strongly associated with *late* adolescent intellectual competence ($r = -.51$). This association between not being conventionally feminine in early adolescence and being competent in late adolescence is essentially independent of the correlations of these two measures with early competence, that is, partialling out early Intellectually Competent reduces the correlation between late Intellectually Competent and early Feminine Style only slightly (from $-.51$ to $-.42$). Put another way, two early adolescent characteristics—Intellectual Competence and not having a feminine style—are positively, and essentially independently, associated with late adolescent competence. Together, these two predictors account for over half of the variance in late adolescent competence (multiple $R = .72$). We suggest that "tomboyish" behavior in early adolescence is *transformed* into an increment in competence in late adolescence. How can we account for this? Our hypothesis is that sex-inappropriate behavior in early adolescence is an expression of protest against the incompetency "demands" of the conventional feminine role; a few years later it is channeled into more effective, coping behavior.

Once again we speculate—although the suggestion is more tentative for women than for men—that adolescent dimensions predictive of PH at 40 are generally positively valued ones. There is one obvious exception: when our cohorts were adolescents in the 1930s or early 1940s, lack of conventional femininity was not regarded "positively." However, by the 1960s (when these women reached 40), failing to conform to conventional femininity may well have been regarded as an asset, and the healthy woman could then draw upon her earlier "defect" to enhance her functioning.

In any event, becoming a psychologically healthy woman by 40 arose, in our cohorts, from a background of adolescent characteristics that convey an image of personal effectiveness. We must ask, as we did with men, whether being a healthy adult reflects simply maintenance of psychological health already manifest in adolescence. We next consider this possibility for both sexes. In doing so we encounter what is perhaps the most provocative finding from these analyses.

HAVE WE FOUND ONLY THAT ADOLESCENT PSYCHOLOGICAL HEALTH PREDICTS HEALTH AT 40?

Probably the best way to answer this question is to examine more closely our most general finding—highly significant prediction from Intellectually Competent at both adolescent periods to PH at 40 for both sexes. Intellectually Competent is a cluster of 5 Q-sort items: values intellectual matters, wide interests, appears intelligent, verbally fluent, interesting. None of these items immediately calls to mind the construct of psychological health, but none is inconsistent with it. Empirically, we can determine whether, as a cluster, they "go with" health in adolescence. We did so by first computing PH scores for early and later adolescence in precisely the same way we obtained PH scores at 40, that is, by correlating each adolescent Q sort with the hypothetical, "ideal" PH Q sort (Chapter 6). We then correlated PH and intellectual competence at each adolescent period for each sex. The two constructs show substantial positive correlations in all four instances—.48 and .55 for boys and .33 and .47 for girls, respectively, for early and late adolescence. But do these associations account for the ability of adolescent competence to predict PH at 40? Yes and no.

For men the answer is yes. Partialling adolescent PH from the males' predictive correlations between adolescent competence and PH at 40 reduces the early adolescent value (.30) to .15 and the late adolescent correlation (.27) to .14. Neither partial correlation approaches statistical significance although, as we have seen, the zero-order correlations are reliable in their "uncorrected" form. This attenuation may be directly attributed to the fact that, for males, PH in adolescence *does* predict PH at 40 (r of .40, $p < .001$, at early adolescence and .31, $p < .01$, at late adolescence). By the same procedure, of course, we can demonstrate that adolescent PH is nonpredictive when we partial out adolescent competence. Hence the data *per se* provide no reason to assign higher explanatory priority to the health-predicts-health interpretation for males. What we have found is that adolescent competence and PH are of about equal importance in predicting PH of men at 40.

The story for women is quite different. Partialling out adolescent PH does not significantly reduce the correlations between adolescent competence and PH at 40 (.32 to .30 in early adolescence, .29 to .25 in late adolescence). Why does adolescent competence in girls continue significantly to predict PH at 40 when the contribution of adolescent PH is eliminated? Because in women, PH in adolescence and at 40 are *essentially unrelated*. The predictive correlation to PH at 40 from adolescent PH is identical from the two adolescent periods ($r = .12$), requiring the surprising conclusion that, for women, psychological health during adolescence has practically nothing to do with health at 40.

Why should this be? Again, from the data available here, we can only speculate, drawing somewhat on the "uses of the past" orientation. We showed in Chapter 6 that the adolescent antecedents of adult PH differ substantially for ages 30, 40, and 50, and argued that these differences demonstrate that the developmental phases of adolescence provide repositories of experiences from which the individual can draw selectively and adaptively to meet the particular and different requirements of each adult phase of development. We therefore suggest that the fact that women's PH at 40 does not seem to draw upon their having been healthy during adolescence—and does draw upon their having been intellectually competent in both early and late adolescence—is a phenomenon phase-specific to age 40.

F. Livson (Chapter 8) shows that of OGS women who were above the median on PH at 50, only 7 were also so at 40. The other 17 (her "nontraditional" women) were relatively unhealthy at 40, in part because at that age they apparently suppressed certain "positive" but "sex-inappropriate" characteristics they had in adolescence. Among these are characteristics closely related to our Intellectually Competent cluster, and some (such as showing ambition) that might have been regarded as sex-inappropriate. By 50, however, this suppression no longer seemed required to meet the role prescriptions and proscriptions for older women, and they experienced an upsurge in psychological health through again having access to such "masculine"—and now adaptive—resources available from their adolescence.

We suspect that the paucity of adolescent predictors of PH in women at 40—and their particular flavor—indicates that, for women in our cohorts, age 40 is a phase in some sense aberrant, and apparently transitory. A woman was not easily permitted to "be herself" in the cohorts we studied, particularly at that point (about 40) in her development. Those who did manage to be, and hence were psychologically healthy at 40, drew then upon the resource of their adolescent competence. This resource perhaps enabled them to cope effectively with the social reality confronting the typical woman of 40 at that time. Thus, it was not the healthy adolescent girl who later flourished psychologically at 40, but rather the one who showed a combination of competence and "masculinity."

If we are correct that 40 was a time of discontinuity in the psychological health of these women, then adolescent PH should better predict adult PH at the other two ages, 30 and 50. The correlations of early and late adolescent PH with PH at 30 for GS are, respectively, .23 and .38. With PH at 50 for OGS these correlations are .36 and .13. These results tend to support our expectation; three of the four values indicate a significant predictive increment over the correlation of .12 between PH at 40 and PH at each adolescent period.

However the reader may evaluate our interpretations, one general finding is remarkably solid. Intellectual competence, as defined here, is a substantial predictor of PH for both sexes and from both early and late adolescence. It is an empirically derived construct, representing an admixture of personality and cognitive characteristics (see p. 191) and is something more than, and different from, tested IQ, although the two measures are not independent. Because one item in the Intellectually Competent cluster is an assessor's *impression* of "degree of intellectual capacity," we would expect this rating to be positively related to IQ scores. Indeed, we would hope so, because such a result supports the validity of the assessment. Stanford-Binet Full Scale IQ at age 13 is significantly correlated with intellectual competence in early and late adolescence for both sexes. This is an encouraging result, but we must not lose sight of the multifaceted nature of intellectual competence; it is, as we have seen, a sensible (though neither obvious nor necessary) blend of being intellectually capable *and* valuing and using one's intellectual capacity.

Because this tantalizing lead toward an understanding of the evolution of psychological health is as unexpected as it is robust in our cohorts, replication in other longitudinal samples should be attempted. Although primary data vary from study to study, we are optimistic that valid indices of the constructs of "intellectual competence" and "psychological health" can be derived from any comprehensive data base. Replication holds the promise of a deeper insight into *why* being intellectually competent in adolescence forecasts effective psychological functioning in both men and women at 40.

8

Paths to Psychological Health in the Middle Years: Sex Differences

FLORINE B. LIVSON

The decade between ages 40 and 50 is a time of change and re-evaluation, heightened for men as well as women by the departure of children, endocrine changes, shifting role expectations, and narrowed time perspective. Do the challenges of change in these middle years allow some individuals to grow and expand their psychological horizons? Are there different paths to psychological health, and different ways of being healthy, as individuals enter the second half of life?

This chapter explores such questions for a subgroup of OGS women and men who were psychologically healthy at 50. The focus on the interface between personality and life structure at different stages of the life cycle assumes that age-related tasks and roles—especially sex roles—shape the expression of personality at different ages and that personality in turn influences how the individual responds to role changes.

THE MIDLIFE TRANSITION

Most investigators agree that the decade of the forties brackets a major transition in the life span often punctuated by stress (Brim, 1976b; Frenkel-Brunswik, 1968; Gould, 1978; Levinson with Darrow, Klein, Levinson, & McKee, 1978). At 40 most individuals are still engaged in tasks belonging to young adulthood. By 50 a person is middle-aged. Confronted with this shift, most individuals share certain experiences. Perhaps the most universal is a growing awareness of death as a personal reality (Neugarten, 1970). The sense of timelessness and infinite possibility, common in youth, gives way to a realization that one's life span is finite and one's options limited. Denial and procrastination (e.g., "Someday I'll do it"; "When the kids grow up") become less convincing. Both men and women also have to cope with narcissistic losses: youthful attractiveness for women, sexual vigor for men, signs of physical decline for both sexes. Awareness of aging can shake one's sense of control over destiny and undermine youthful fantasies of omnipotence (Brim, 1976b). This shift in time perspective may give rise to a new sense of urgency—or to relief in settling for what is. Either way there may be an increased need to take responsibility for one's future before time runs out—a heightened consciousness of self that may be comparable to the adolescent years.

Changes in life situations may also lead to a re-evaluation of self and goals. Issues of identity—of who one is and where one is going and whether either is gratifying—may become more salient. Traditional sex roles, if taken for granted in early adulthood, may change or demand redefinition. Women who organized their identities around mothering may now be motivated to find new roles and sources of satisfaction. The major mid-life transition for most women occurs at the termination of the family cycle, whereas for men it occurs at the termination of their occupational careers (Thurnher, 1974). Long before retirement, however, mid-life men may become aware of narrowing career opportunities or disappointment in their achievements or life-style.

As goals and role expectations change, the individual may, to an extent, shape a "new self" that fits her or his current life structure and calls upon qualities that were dormant earlier. Conflicts postponed during the child-rearing or career-building years may be revived to allow new solutions. Parts of the personality that were suppressed because they were not congruent with nurturance in the mothering role or achievement in occupational roles may surface to add new dimensions to the person.

How does the transition into middle age affect psychological well-being? Although much has been written in recent years about the "mid-life crisis," and although most researchers agree that the middle years mark an important transition, we have little hard evidence that this transition invariably reaches crisis proportions (see Brim, 1976b).

Psychiatric literature focuses on the emotional stresses of the middle years—particularly depression in women at menopause (Deutsch, 1945). Bart (1971), a social scientist, stresses loss of the mothering role, rather than menopause, as a source of depression in middle-aged women. She found depressive disorders in women hospitalized for mental illness to be associated with the departure of their children. Field studies of healthy women in the community, however, question the generality of these observations. Instead they suggest improved psychological functioning for many women in late middle age *after* they move through a stressful period prior to the departure of their children (Lowenthal *et al.,* 1975; Neugarten, 1970).

Similarly, studies of nonclinical samples suggest that menopause is less stressful than commonly believed and that women even report emotional gains once menopause is past (Lowenthal *et al.,* 1975; Neugarten, Wood, Kraines, & Loomis, 1968). In cultures in which women's social status rises in the middle years, menopause is not seen as stressful (Bart, 1971). Neugarten (1970) observes that major role changes in middle life may indeed be experienced as losses; but when role changes are expected and occur "on schedule" in the normal life course, they can be anticipated and worked through without disrupting the sense of self.

Not all persons, of course, respond the same way to becoming middle-aged. How particular women or men experience themselves at this time of life and how they adapt to the many social and psychological forces impinging on them will depend, to a large degree, on how their personalities—strengths, sensitivities, and adaptive skills— mesh with the unique circumstances of their lives. A key factor may be the "fit" between an individual's personality and his or her social roles.

This study examines personality patterns of women and men from adolescence to middle age that lead to *successful* functioning by age 50. Special attention is given to the *timing* of personal growth and to how differences in timing correspond to differences in personality.

THE SAMPLE

The group studied here is drawn from OGS members with data at all four age periods: early and late adolescence (ages 12–14 and 15–18, respectively), early maturity and maturity (approximately ages 40 and 50). To observe *successful* patterns of development in the middle years, those members of this core sample who were functioning best at 50 were selected, that is, 24 women and 21 men who scored above the mean for their sex on the index of psychological health (see Chapter 6) developed by Livson and Peskin (1967).

Like the OGS sample as a whole, this subgroup of relatively well-functioning 50-year-olds is predominantly urban, middle class, and Protestant. The male study members and the husbands of the women are generally employed in business or industry. (Current socioeconomic status for women is assessed by spouse's occupation and education.)

The majority (16 of 24) of women in this "healthier" group are upper middle class (Classes I or II on the Hollingshead Scale) as compared with 7 of 16 women in the less healthy group. Of the healthier group, 15 are married to men at the top two occupational levels on the Hollingshead Scale (major executive, professional, or business manager) as compared with 5 of the less healthy group. Although the selected subgroup of healthier women thus appears somewhat more advantaged in social position at 50 than less healthy women in the core OGS sample, the differences are not statistically significant. Further, spouses' occupations in *both* groups range over the full occupational scale and include some blue-collar workers. Their average level of education is also similar; roughly half of both groups continued their education beyond high school. However, the average IQ (118) of the healthier group, as measured by the WAIS at 50, is significantly higher than that of the less healthy (111; $p < .05$). In adolescence the two groups did not differ in IQ.

Despite some indication of higher current socioeconomic status, healthier women clearly do not differ from the less healthy in social class origin, as measured by father's occupation and education. The majority of both groups (15 of 24 healthier women and 10 of 16 less healthy) grew up in middle- and lower-middle-class families. Thus, healthier women may have been somewhat more socially mobile in their marriages than the less healthy.

With the exception of one of the healthier women who never married and another who remained childless, all members of both groups married and have children. Neither family size (averaging between two and three children) nor the proportion of both groups who are *currently* married (about 80%) differentiates the more and less psychologically healthy. The remainder—5 healthier women and 2 less healthy—are widowed or divorced. At some time in their lives, 15 women (9 healthier women and 6 of the less healthy) were divorced but all except 3 remarried. Half (12 of 24) of the healthier women are currently employed full or part time as compared with 6 of 16 women in the less healthy group.

In sum, the healthier women selected for study here may have been more mobile socially and thus may be at a somewhat higher socioeconomic level, as defined by the husband's status, than the remainder of the core sample of OGS women. They do have somewhat higher IQs by age 50, and more work outside the home. However, in their status as primarily wives and mothers, in marital histories, and in socioeconomic origins the two groups of women do not differ.

The healthier men are more successful in their careers and at a higher socioeconomic level than all other members of the OGS core sample. Of the 21 healthier men, 15 hold positions at the highest occupational level on the Hollingshead Scale (major executive or professional) as compared with 6 of the 19 less healthy men ($p < .05$). Correspondingly, 13 are at the highest socioeconomic class level on the Hollingshead Scale as compared with 4 of the less healthy men ($p < .01$). At 50 the average WAIS IQ (129) of healthier men is significantly higher than the average of the less healthy men (120; $p < .01$) and of the healthier women (118; $p < .001$). Note, however, that the average IQ of OGS men is higher than that of OGS women at all ages (see Chapter 4). And unlike the female contrast groups, healthier men also had consistently higher IQs than less healthy men at all earlier ages ($p < .05$). Not surprisingly healthier men came from more advantaged backgrounds than less healthy men ($p < .10$) and are somewhat better educated. A larger proportion are college graduates or have postgraduate training, but the difference is not significant.

With the exception of one bachelor in the healthier group, all men in the core sample are currently married and have relatively stable marital histories. Only 3 of the healthier and 2 of the less healthy were ever divorced. (As noted, 9 of the 24 healthier women and 6 of the 16 less healthy have a history of divorce.) Healthier men have larger families than the less healthy: roughly half (10) have four or more children, whereas roughly half (10) of the less healthy group have two children ($p < .01$). (Most of the healthier women have two or three children.) The majority of healthier men and women still have some children living at home (17 of the 21 men and 13 of the 24 women). However, healthier men began their families at an older age than did the women (on the average at 27 as compared with 24) so their oldest child is somewhat younger ($p < .01$).

To summarize: subgroups of OGS women and men functioning relatively well psychologically at 50 were selected for study. On the whole, they are advantaged socially and economically. Their political values tend to be conservative and their life-styles traditional. The women are predominantly wives and mothers. Though half are employed part or full time, their primary values center on home rather than career. The men are particularly high-achieving and bright, with a strong family orientation. They have long-term, stable marriages and relatively large families.

PROCEDURES

The primary data are derived from the 100-item California Q sort (Block, 1961; Block in collaboration with Haan, 1971; Chapter 2 in this volume). Among the psychologically healthier women and men at 50, two patterns emerged (see Fig. 8.1): (a) Seven women and 7 men had remained relatively *stable* in psychological health since age 40; that is, they were relatively healthy psychologically at *both* 40 and 50 and below the median level of improvement for all members of their sex in the OGS. (b) At age 40, 17 women and 14 men were in relatively poor psychological health but *improved* substantially between 40 and 50 (above the median of improvement for all members of their sex in the total sample).

To assess whether the stable group was more consistent over time in overall personality, apart from psychological health, Q sorts at adja-

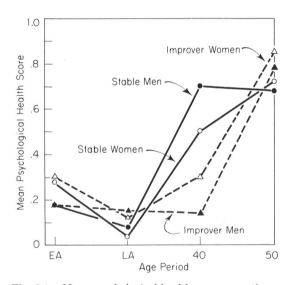

Fig. 8.1. Mean psychological health scores over time.

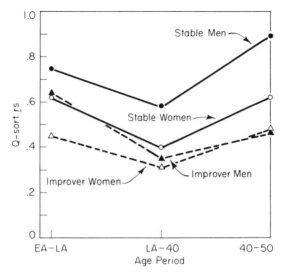

Fig. 8.2. Q-sort correlations between adjacent age periods.

cent age periods were correlated for each participant. The average correlation between age periods for each group gives a measure of the stability of personality in that group over time (see Fig. 8.2). Although personality stability was consistently greater in the stable than the improver groups of both sexes, particularly for the periods between early and late adolescence and between 40 and 50, differences were not statistically significant. (Not surprisingly, personality characteristics were least stable between adolescence and age 40 for all groups.) These comparisons, if only suggestive, point to greater consistency over time in the stable group than among improvers, not only in psychological health but also in overall personality structure.

Are these two groups of men and women, both psychologically healthy by 50, made up of distinct kinds of people? And if so, do stable men and women differ from improvers in their paths of development toward this healthy "end product" over the four age periods?

These questions are approached by examining personality differences between stable and improver groups at each age period. For ease of exposition, each group is described as a distinct personality type. However, the reader should note that these descriptions are relative: they refer to significant differences *between* groups in Q-sort characteristics at each age period.

TRADITIONAL AND NONTRADITIONAL WOMEN

Differences at Age 50

At 50 the stable women are relatively gregarious and nurturant, placing high value on closeness with others (see Table 8.1). They are pleased with their appearance and conventional in their outlook. These qualities fit traditional role expectations for women in our culture. For this reason, the stable group is labeled Traditional. They seem to attach more importance to friendships than do improvers (ratings: $p <$ .10),[1] and affiliative needs are expressed in trusting, protective relations with others.

These are not introspective women: they handle conflicts by repression, turn their attention outward rather than on their inner life and tend to express concern about bodily functions. At 40, for example, Traditionals expressed more anxiety about their health than improvers, ($p < .05$) and at 50 they assessed their health as poorer than did improvers ($p < .02$). However, the groups did not differ in health as assessed by physician's examinations at age 34, suggesting a tendency for the traditional group to convert emotional stress into concerns about health. (Medical examinations were not completed for most of these women at 50. The same proportion of both groups—slightly over half—were in menopause at this age.)

Overall, these traditional individuals are well-functioning, conforming women whose defenses tend to be of an hysterical type, but not to a pathological degree. They are extroverted in that they turn outward for satisfaction. They rely on ego functions that further interpersonal skills. These qualities are well suited to traditional roles of wife and mother, and these roles in turn satisfy basic personality needs in this group.

Improvers present a different picture. At 50 they are more ambitious, intellectual, and unconventional in their thinking than Traditionals. They rely on their intellect to cope with the world and to deal with themselves. This group is labeled Nontraditional. Insightful and psychologically minded, Nontraditionals are more individualistic and skeptical in their outlook than traditional women. Verbal and expressive, with a good sense of humor, they impress others as interesting people with high intellectual ability. (They do not in fact differ

---

[1]Findings for ratings and measures other than Q sorts do not appear in tables and are reported in the text with p values.

Table 8.1

Personality Differences between Traditional and Nontraditional Women
at Maturity (47-50)

Traditionals higher ($N = 7$)			Nontraditionals higher ($N = 17$)		
Characteristics	Mean scores T	NT	Characteristics	Mean scores T	NT
Adaptive style			Adaptive style		
Gregarious	8.0***	5.9	Values Intellectual Matters	5.1	6.2**
not Aloof	7.3*	6.1	Appears Intelligent	5.9	6.8**
Protective	6.7*	5.9	Verbally Fluent	5.3	6.4***
Turned To for Advice	6.5*	5.8	Skeptical	4.6	5.7**
not Distrustful	6.2*	5.4	Thinks Unconventionally	3.6	5.4***
Conventional	5.6*	4.5	Ambitious	5.1	6.1*
Feminine Style	7.3^a	6.4	Interesting	5.3	6.5***
Defenses			Defenses		
Repressive	5.3**	3.8	Insightful	5.5	6.8***
not Introspective	4.6**	3.1	Evaluates Others' Motivations	5.9	7.2***
Somatizes	6.6***	4.6	not Self-Defensive	4.6	6.3***
Affect			Affect		
Satisfied with Physical Appearance	6.0**	5.1	Expressive	5.4	6.5**
Has Bodily Concern	6.4**	5.0	Expresses Hostility Directly	3.9	5.3*
			Responds to Humor	5.8	6.6***
			Initiates Humor	5.9	6.8*

Note: Q-sort characteristics are on a 9-point scale, representing a forced normal distribution of nine steps. Higher scores indicate traits *more* characteristic of a person; lower scores are *less* characteristic. Symbols for significance of a group difference always accompany the higher (more characteristic) group mean.
^{a}Though not significant, this item was included because Traditionals were consistently higher at all four age periods.
*$p < .10$.
**$p < .05$.
***$p < .01$.

from Traditionals in tested IQ at this or at earlier ages.)[2] As compared with Traditionals, they express feelings, particularly anger, openly and directly, and are not defensive.

Nontraditional women, in short, are more autonomous than traditional women and more in touch with their inner life. They cope with conflicting feelings by insight and direct expression, rather than by conformity and repression. They are "doers," with interests in activities that are intellectual or skill-oriented rather than primarily social. They spend more time than traditional women participating in musical activities ($p < .05$), reading ($p < .10$), and sports ($p < .05$). Their main satisfactions come from developing their "selves" rather than

[2] IQ at 50 (WAIS): Traditionals, 116; Nontraditionals, 118. *IQ in Late Adolescence* (Stanford-Binet): Traditionals, 115; Nontraditionals, 118. *IQ in Early Adolescence* (Stanford-Binet): Traditionals, 104; Nontraditionals, 107. None of these differences approaches significance.

from affiliation with others. In this sense, they are self-oriented rather than people-oriented.

The two groups do not differ significantly in socioeconomic status (current or in childhood), education, or the occupational level of their husbands. They are primarily upper middle class. In life-styles, however, traditional women are more family oriented. All traditional women are currently married whereas almost one-third ($N = 5$) of nontraditional women are widowed or divorced. However, the proportion who divorced at some time in their lives is the same (about 33%), indicating higher remarriage rates among Traditionals. Overall ratings of marital adjustment at 50 are also higher for Traditionals ($p < .05$). One-third of nontraditional women ($N = 6$) have full-time jobs; no traditional women work full time. However, the proportion (about half) of both groups working outside the home at least part time does not differ.

Average family size (two or three children) is similar and average ages of children are comparable, ranging from preadolescent to over 25. Nearly half ($N = 8$) of the nontraditional group are in the postparental stage of family life as compared with two traditional women, but the difference is not significant. The groups do not differ in their relationships with children (ratings of closeness and critical attitudes).

Traditional women, in sum, tend to be more family- and home-oriented. All are living with their husbands and they tend to have happier marriages; none has a full-time career.

Differences Over Time: Adolescence to Age 50

To trace development since adolescence, personality characteristics of the two groups were compared in early and late adolescence and at ages 40 and 50 (see Table 8.2). Both groups by early adolescence reveal a ground plan—a core personality style—that evolves and differentiates into a more complex form by 50. Each, however, evolves along a different path with different timing.

Traditionals

From early adolescence on, Traditionals are more gregarious. This is their most prominent characteristic at all age periods. However, in early adolescence their gregariousness has not yet differentiated into the more sophisticated social skills observed later. Their tendency at 50 to turn outward rather than inward—to avoid introspection and to rely on repressive defenses to cope with conflict—is also evident in early adolescence. At the younger age, however, they show signs of

Table 8.2

Personality Differences between Traditional and Nontraditional Women
in Early and Late Adolescence and Early Maturity

Age period	Traditionals higher (N = 7)			Nontraditionals higher (N = 17)		
	Characteristics	Mean scores T	NT	Characteristics	Mean scores T	NT
Early adolescence (12-14)	Adaptive style			Adaptive style		
	Gregarious	8.4*	7.5	Values Intellectual Matters	3.0	4.7***
				Thinks Unconventionally	3.0	4.5*
				Ambitious	4.5	5.2*
	Defenses			Defenses		
	Repressive	7.1*	6.1	Moralistic	4.8	5.9*
	not Introspective	5.7**	4.2			
	Withdraws When Frustrated	5.6***	4.0	Affect		
				Compares Self to Others	5.3	6.2*
				Has Bodily Concern	5.1	6.3**
Late adolescence (15-18)	Adaptive style			Adaptive style		
	Gregarious	7.5*	6.2	Appears Intelligent	5.6	6.7*
	Clear-cut, Consistent Personality	5.5*	4.2	Verbally Fluent	4.6	5.8**
	Conventional	6.8*	5.6	Thinks Unconventionally	2.9	4.5**
	Feminine Style	7.7*	6.0	Interesting	4.6	6.1**
	Affect					
	Satisfied with Self	5.0*	3.9			
Early maturity (37-40)	Adaptive style					
	Gregarious	8.1***	5.4			
	not Aloof	6.2*	4.5			
	Sympathetic	6.9*	6.0			
	Giving	7.3*	6.3			
	Arouses Liking	8.0**	6.2			
	Straightforward	7.3**	5.9			
	Aware of Impression Created	5.9**	4.9			
	not Negativistic	6.8**	5.5			
	not Distrustful	6.2*	4.8			
	Defenses			Defenses		
	Submissive	6.0*	4.4	Fantasizing	3.4	4.4**
	Somatizes	7.2*	5.6	Complicates Simple Situations	2.5	3.6**
	Affect			Affect		
	Cheerful	7.5*	6.2	Unpredictable	3.1	3.9**
	Calm	5.6**	3.9	Thin-Skinned	4.1	5.2*
	Poised	7.6*	6.2	Bothered by Demands	3.3	4.5**

Note: Q-sort characteristics are on a 9-point scale, representing a forced normal distribution of nine steps. Higher scores indicate traits more characteristic of a person; lower scores are less characteristic. Symbols for significance of a group difference always accompany the higher (more characteristic) group mean.
*p < .10.
**p < .05.
***p < .01.

insecurity, responding to frustration and interpersonal conflict by withdrawal.

By late adolescence, signs of anxiety have abated. Traditionals have elaborated their gregariousness into a clear, consistent personality style, conventional and clearly feminine. These are popular, sociable young women in high school, developing personalities that conform to feminine role expectations. They are satisfied with themselves and seem to be establishing, in Erikson's (1959) terms, a firm sense of ego identity.

In adulthood, gregariousness continues to organize their sense of self and orientation to life, but this quality has now matured beyond the sociability of adolescence. Traditionals, by 40, have become close, trusting, sympathetic, and giving in their relations with others. Their popularity has deepened into intimacy. Poised and aware of the impression they create. Traditionals arouse liking. They do not complicate situations. Though their cooperativeness has a submissive tone, they show little open anxiety, possibly because distress is channeled into concern about health. As noted earlier, traditional individuals tend to consider themselves in poorer health than do nontraditional persons. Yet physicians' ratings of overall health, based on comprehensive medical examinations at age 34, reveal no significant differences between the groups at this earlier age. (See Chapter 3 for description of health ratings.) Thus, we have some reason to believe that Traditionals pay a price for their other-directedness in concern about bodily functions.

To summarize, by age 40 Traditionals have evolved a repertoire of skills that serves their core needs for sociability—and these needs themselves have matured, in the sense of becoming less narcissistic. Their psychological health scores are relatively high. No "crisis of the early forties" is evident. Their development is congruent with traditional role expectations for women in our culture. They seem to be on a steady course of growth that continues to 50, when their gregariousness takes on a more protective, giving quality. By 50, their sociability, while remaining high, evolves beyond intimacy and trust into nurturance.

Nontraditionals

The nontraditional group, like the traditional, reveal key personality traits in early adolescence that persist to age 50 and organize their adult development. From early adolescence Nontraditionals value intellectual matters more than do Traditionals, are more ambitious, and more unconventional in their thinking. They do not, as noted, differ from Traditionals in IQ. Their intellectual orientation, like Traditionals' gregariousness, has emerged at least by junior high-school. As with Traditionals, however, this basic orientation is less fully differentiated than at later periods and there are signs of insecurity: comparing self to others, bodily concern, a moralistic attitude.

By late adolescence, the nontraditional group, like the traditional, achieve a more integrated level of functioning. The anxiety apparent earlier has abated; they are no longer concerned with the adequacy of their bodily functions or with comparing themselves to others. Their intellectuality continues to be expressed in originality of thought but is now enriched by greater verbal fluency and an interesting style. In all these characteristics they surpass Traditionals, and they now appear brighter. Again, measured IQ at this age period (Standford-Binet) does not differ significantly (see footnote 2). Like Traditionals, they have elaborated ego functions congruent with their preferred adaptive style, their intellectual orientation. Both groups seem to move toward a more consistent, integrated identity during late adolescence.

By age 40 the picture changes. Nontraditionals show signs of conflict. They are relatively thin-skinned, bothered by demands, and unpredictable. They no longer use their intellectuality in an adaptive way. They complicate simple situations. Their originality has turned to fantasy and daydreams. The cognitive skills they were developing in adolescence—verbal fluency, originality, and brightness—are no longer prominent. There are signs of irritability (possibly reflecting depression). And, of course, their overall psychological health score is relatively low. These women, who seemed to be progressing toward a firm identity in adolescence, appear to have regressed.

Whether this regression represents a temporary crisis at or about 40 or an ongoing constriction emerging some time after later adolescence is uncertain because data are not available for the intervening years. Possibly these nontraditional women functioned more successfully during the early years of mothering when the care of young children challenges practical resources and calls on managerial skills.[3] Unlike traditional women, whose affiliative needs meshed with the mothering role, nontraditional women may have used child-rearing to *substitute for* (or defend against) their achievement needs. By 40, when caretaking

---

[3]The mean age selected by Nontraditionals, when asked at 50 to indicate their most satisfying period of life, falls in the late twenties when children, on the whole, are still young enough to require extensive care. The mean age selected by Traditionals falls in the late thirties when children are less dependent. However, this difference does not reach statistical significance and is at most suggestive ($p < .13$).

functions were disappearing, these nontraditional women may have experienced an identity crisis as they faced the unfulfilled potential of achievement drives denied since adolescence. Having suppressed opposite-sex characteristics to conform to conventional feminine sex roles, these women seem to have paid a price in stress and personality constriction.

This crisis is resolved by 50 with a dramatic rebound in intellectuality and a general freeing of emotional life (see Table 8.1). Intellectual skills that had declined by 40—verbal fluency, unconventional thinking, brightness—again rise to prominence. Additional intellectual functions become salient: insight, psychological-mindedness, skepticism ($p < .05$).[4] Nontraditional women are now more spontaneous than Traditionals: humorous, expressive, direct about anger. The general picture is an opening up and flowering of potential, emotionally and intellectually. Impulses and feelings are expressed more freely and intellectual interests expand. Nontraditionals seem to revive the identities they were forming in their youth—with renewed energy and flourish.

TRADITIONAL AND NONTRADITIONAL MEN

Psychologically healthy men at 50 were also separated into two groups: 7 whose psychological health was relatively stable from 40 to 50 and 14 whose health improved. Do these groups of men, like stable and improver women, reveal different personality styles and follow different paths of development from adolescence to middle age?

Differences at Age 50

Stable men at 50 are less emotional than improvers and more controlled. Like stable women, Traditional seems the proper label for this group (see Table 8.3). Although traditional men and women have very different personality styles, each conforms to traditional gender roles. Traditional men impress others as more intelligent than improvers although they too do not, in fact, differ from improvers in tested IQ at this or earlier ages.[5] This impression of intelligence seems to arise

---

[4]Mean scores on these Q-sort items increase significantly from 40 to 50 in the nontraditional group ($p < .05$). Changes between age periods in mean scores of Q-sort characteristics do not appear in the tables. Significance levels are given in the text.

[5]IQ at 50 (WAIS): Traditionals, 130; Nontraditionals, 129. IQ in Late Adolescence (Stanford-Binet): Traditionals, 132; Nontraditionals, 128. IQ in Early Adolescence (Stanford-Binet): Traditionals, 116; Nontraditionals, 111. None of these differences approaches significance.

Table 8.3

Personality Differences between Traditional and
Nontraditional Men at Maturity (47-50)

Traditionals higher (N = 7)			Nontraditionals higher (N = 14)		
Characteristics	Mean scores T	NT	Characteristics	Mean scores T	NT
Adaptive style			Adaptive style		
Appears Intelligent	7.9**	6.9	Gregarious	4.1	5.6*
Aware of Impression Created	6.3*	5.8	Arouses Liking	6.5	7.0*
			Talkative	4.9	6.3**
Defenses			Defenses		
Overcontrolled	6.0**	4.6	Projective	3.3	3.9*
Affect			Affect		
Emotionally Bland	4.1**	2.8	Feels Life Has Meaning	6.0	6.9**
			Expressive	5.0	6.0**
			Sensuous	4.5	5.5**

Note: Q-sort characteristics are on a 9-point scale, representing a forced normal distribution of nine steps. Higher scores
indicate traits *more* characteristic of a person; lower scores are
less characteristic. Symbols for significance of a group difference always accompany the higher (more characteristic) group mean.
*p < .10.
**p < .05.

from a difference in style; they are rated as placing high value on
rationality, and their intelligence has an analytic, logical, objective
quality. Traditional men not only value objectivity, but they are also
more realistic than improvers in their perception of themselves and
their effects on others and less likely to project their feelings outward.
Like improvers, they are highly ambitious and productive, qualities in
keeping with the occupational success of both groups.

In short, traditional men value intellectual mastery, rationality,
self-discipline, and achievement. Two fundamental themes of the traditional male role in our society stress instrumental skills and suppression of affect (Pleck, 1976; Sawyer, 1970). Traditional male personalities are suited to the performance of instrumental, masculine
roles in middle-class American society.

Improvers at 50, by contrast, are emotionally expressive, sensuous
men—talkative, gregarious, and outgoing (see Table 8.3). These are
characteristics commonly linked to feminine stereotypes. This group,
labeled Nontraditional, is more extroverted than the Traditionals—
more other-directed and less controlled. Possibly because their expressiveness leads to rewarding relationships (they arouse liking more
than do traditional men) they have a strong sense of personal meaning

in their lives. But at the same time they are less realistic in their views of other people, more apt to distort their perceptions by projection.

With the exception of educational level—more traditional men have postgraduate training ($p < .05$)—the two groups of men do not differ significantly in demographic characteristics, either at 50 or in adolescence. As noted, the majority of both groups have highly successful careers; their occupations, on the average, are at major or lesser executive and professional level. Both were highly mobile in the occupational structure as compared with their fathers. Marital histories of both groups are stable: only two men in each have been divorced, and they remarried. Both groups rate high on marital happiness. Traditional men have slightly (but not significantly) larger families, averaging from four to five children as compared with three to four for nontraditional men. Over 80% of both groups still have some children at home. Though medical examinations were not completed for the majority of these men at age 50, both groups view their health as satisfactory.

In sum, both groups are high-achieving men with strong family ties and conventional life-styles. They grew up in the Depression years and both have strong commitments to occupational success, financial stability, and conservative, middle-class values. But they differ in the ways their personalities mesh with these values.

Differences Over Time: Adolescence to Age 50

Traditional and nontraditional men, like women in the comparable groups, reveal a central personality style by early adolescence that evolves through age 50, moving toward or away from conventional sex-typing.

Traditionals

From early adolescence on, traditional men are overcontrolled and value thinking rather than feeling (see Table 8.4). Perhaps because of their early (possibly premature) concern with impulse control, they show signs of insecurity in early adolescence, tending to be submissive and to complicate simple situations. However, social conformity is balanced by a straightforward, direct manner, and their intellectuality has a freewheeling tone: they are philosophically concerned, searching for meaning, and tend to romanticize causes and ideas. In sum, these are conforming, nonrebellious boys who suppress feelings and turn their energies to intellectual interests. By early adolescence their tendencies toward introversion, impulse control, and intellectuality are clearly evident.

Table 8.4

Personality Differences between Traditional
and Nontraditional Men in Early and Late Adolescence

	Traditionals higher ($N = 7$)			Nontraditionals higher ($N = 14$)		
	Characteristics	Mean scores		Characteristics	Mean scores	
		T	NT		T	NT
Early adolescence (12-14)	Adaptive style			Adaptive style		
	Straightforward	6.4*	5.4	Is Affected	2.0	3.0**
	Philosophically Concerned	4.4*	3.4	Self-Dramatizing	2.6	4.0*
	Questing for Meaning	4.9*	3.8	Negativistic	2.6	4.2*
	Romanticizes Individuals and Causes	5.9*	4.9	Deceitful	1.9	2.8**
	Defenses					
	Overcontrolled	6.9**	5.4			
	Submissive	5.8*	4.3			
	Complicates Simple Situations	5.1**	3.8			
	Affect			Affect		
	Emotionally Bland	5.8*	4.4	Responds to Humor	5.4	6.4**
				Initiates Humor	4.1	5.7**
Late adolescence (15-18)	Adaptive style			Adaptive style		
	Ambitious	8.1**	6.2	Is Affected	2.6	4.1*
	Productive	7.2**	5.4	Self-Dramatizing	3.1	4.7**
	Prides Self on Objectivity	7.1***	5.5			
	Skeptical	6.7**	4.8			
	Distrustful	5.8*	4.4			
	Thinks Unconventionally	6.4*	5.0			
	Defenses			Defenses		
	Overcontrolled	6.7*	5.0	Undercontrolled	2.8	4.6**
	Affect			Affect		
	Comfortable with Decisions	6.2**	4.9	Expressive	4.3	5.5*
				Initiates Humor	4.8	6.6**
				Has Bodily Concern	4.8	6.2*

Note: Q-sort characteristics are on a 9-point scale, representing a forced normal distribution
nine steps. Higher scores indicate traits *more* characteristic of a person; lower scores are *less*
characteristic. Symbols for significance of a group difference always accompany the higher (more
characteristic) group mean.
$*p < .10.$
$**p < .05.$
$***p < .01.$

In late adolescence, traditional men continue to be overcontrolled
but are less insecure. They now shape their intellectuality into an
analytic, rational attitude, less romantic than before and more geared
toward coping with the outside world. They are skeptical, question
ideas and motives, pride themselves on their objectivity and are unconventional and innovative in their thinking. These are ambitious,
productive young men, comfortable with decisions, trusting of their
judgment. Intellectual competence has become a dominant ego function, and achievement a dominant goal. They seem to be developing

the masculine side of their personalities into an adaptive style focused on achievement and effective control of their lives. Their personalities prepare them for middle-class masculine role expectations—but at the price of emotional spontaneity.

By 40 their masculinity evolves further in a socially adaptive direction (see Table 8.5). Traditionals are productive, dependable men, ethical and straightforward in their dealings with others, incisive in their thinking. However, their intellectuality is less one-sided than before. Traditional men by 40 are introspective, insightful, psychologically minded, and aware of their impact on others. Correspondingly, their masculinity is now tempered by softer, more affiliative qualities. They have become more perceptive than nontraditional men in their reactions to other people and more spontaneous: warm, sympathetic, likeable, and esthetically reactive. By 40, Traditionals develop a more balanced personality—expressive as well as instrumental.

Like traditional women, traditional men experience little conflict between their personalities and conventional gender roles. Having established an effective masculine identity by 40, they allow more expressive parts of themselves to emerge. They express feelings, particularly warm feelings, more freely than before and, like traditional women, seem to move into what Erikson (1950, 1959) calls the stage of intimacy. And, of course, their psychological health scores are relatively high at this age. However, they continue to value intellectual competence, rationality, self-control, and achievement. Though they are more balanced than before, their dominant mode remains consistently masculine and instrumental to 50.

Traditional men change little between 40 and 50. Having achieved their main gains by 40, they continue to express both sides of their personalities—objectivity and self-discipline as well as sensitivity—and their psychological health remains high at 50 (see Table 8.3).

Nontraditionals

Nontraditional men in adolescence reveal qualities less suited to middle-class masculine roles and more signs of inner conflict. In early adolescence they are emotionally expressive, as they are at 50 (see Table 8.4). But their early expressiveness, like their assertive drive, seems poorly integrated. They tend to be affected, self-dramatizing, attention seeking at this age. More rebellious than traditional men, they assert themselves indirectly through negativism and subterfuge. In early adolescence they are more spontaneous and humorous than Traditionals but also seem less secure.

By late adolescence, their emotionality, while continuing to be ex-

Table 8.5

Personality Differences between Traditional and
Nontraditional Men in Early Maturity (37-40)

Traditionals higher (N = 7)			Nontraditionals higher (N = 14)		
Characteristics	Mean scores T	NT	Characteristics	Mean scores T	NT
Adaptive style			Adaptive style		
Productive	8.2**	7.0	Power-Oriented	4.9	6.9***
Values Intellectual Matters	7.3*	5.5	Condescending	3.2	4.7***
Incisive	6.6***	4.9	Creates Dependency	3.0	4.4***
Socially Perceptive	6.2***	3.7	Self-Dramatizing	2.4	4.5**
Aware of Impression Created	5.5*	4.7	Eroticizes Situations	3.0	4.0*
Straightforward	7.1***	4.6	Distrustful	3.4	4.8**
Ethically Consistent	7.7**	5.9	Negativistic	2.8	4.6***
Dependable	8.7***	6.7	Deceitful	2.1	3.5**
Sympathetic	7.0**	5.5			
Arouses Liking	7.2**	5.6			
Physically Attractive	6.1*	5.3			
Defenses			Defenses		
Insightful	6.4***	4.0	Brittle Ego Defenses	2.2	4.4***
Evaluates Others Motivations	6.1**	4.5	Projective	3.0	4.7***
Introspective	6.2*	4.5	Extrapunitive	3.2	5.2***
Overcontrolled	6.5^a	6.0	Self-Defensive	3.2	6.2***
			Ruminative	4.1	5.4*
			Complicates Simple Situations	3.0	4.7***
Affect			Affect		
Calm	7.2***	4.1	Basically Anxious	4.5	6.2***
Warm	6.5**	4.6	Thin-Skinned	4.0	4.9*
Poised	6.9*	5.7	Irritable	3.3	4.4*
Esthetically Reactive	5.7**	4.7	Basic Hostility	4.3	6.5***
			Has Bodily Concern	4.2	5.9**

Note: Q-sort characteristics are on a 9-point scale, representing a forced normal distribution of nine steps. Higher scores indicate traits more characteristic of a person; lower scores are less characteristic. Symbols for significance of a group difference always accompany the higher (more characteristic) group mean.
[a] Though not significant, this item was included because Traditionals were consistently higher at all four age periods.

*$p < .10$.
**$p < .05$.
***$p < .01$.

pressed in humor and dramatic behavior, takes on an impulsive quality. (Undercontrol increases slightly from early to late adolescence in this group while it decreases for traditional men.) They now also show *inner* signs of anxiety expressed in bodily concern. In their teens, nontraditional men seem unable to integrate either their expressive or assertive sides. They do not foreclose on either a masculine or a feminine mode in adolescence.

Mussen (1961), in an earlier study of OGS boys in late adolescence, reports a similar association between sex typing in adolescence, adjustment, and an independent measure of gender identification. Boys who scored relatively high in feminine interests on the Strong Vocational Interest Blank were rated higher in expressive behavior (sociable, attention seeking, talkative, humorous) than those with masculine interests. Those with more feminine interests also showed more signs of tension and emotional instability in adolescence than did boys with masculine interests. (Mussen's sample was limited to OGS boys with extreme scores on the masculinity-feminity scale of the Strong and so does not entirely overlap with the present sample.)

By 40, nontraditional men seem to have made a choice. They suppress their emotionality in favor of conventionally masculine, assertive behavior (see Table 8.5). Emotional expressiveness and impulsivity decrease significantly ($p < .05$).[6] Overcontrol rises almost to the level of traditional men (Traditionals: 6.5; Nontraditionals: 6.0; difference not significant). Nontraditional men become more self-disciplined and more openly assertive. However, their assertiveness at 40 is power-oriented, exploitative, and condescending—colored by a compensatory, "macho" quality. They emphasize sexuality and seem to engage in a kind of masculine protest—exaggerating stereotyped masculine behavior—but uneasily and at a high cost. Although they are high achievers like Traditionals, they are less productive. At 40 these men are angry and defensive, tending to project their anger outward in a blaming, punitive fashion. Their adolescent tendencies to manipulate are now colored by distrust and hostility. At the same time, their defenses are brittle, easily punctured. They are generally anxious, defensive, ruminative, concerned about their bodily functions. Yet, like the women, nontraditional and traditional men do not differ on physicians' ratings of actual health based on medical examinations at 34.

Nontraditional men are under considerable stress as they approach middle age. I suggest that their stress results from suppressing their emotionality to fulfill the instrumental roles expected of high-

---

[6]Mean scores on these Q-sort items decrease significantly from adolescence to age 40.

achieving men. Like Traditionals, these are men with successful careers and high social mobility. But like nontraditional women, their temperaments and personalities do not conform easily to conventional gender role norms. To perform such roles effectively in early adulthood, nontraditional men and women suppress cross-sex characteristics. Both assume an identity that for them is somewhat artificial and leaves important needs unsatisfied. Both pay a price for this suppression in emotional stress and poor psychological health at 40.

But by 50, nontraditional men give up their exaggerated masculine posture. They integrate their expressive (more conventionally feminine) side and show a corresponding rise in psychological health (see Table 8.3). Between 40 and 50, they become significantly more expressive and sensuous ($p < .01$).[7] Overcontrol and reliance on projective defenses decline ($p < .05$), although these men still rely more heavily on projective defenses than do Traditionals. Their power orientation drops off ($p < .05$), and their anger and anxiety subside ($p < .01$). Nontraditional men are now more gregarious, talkative, and likeable than traditional men; their sociability is less histrionic and more adaptive. Like nontraditional women, nontraditional men by 50 repossess the cross-sex characteristics suppressed in early adulthood, but at a more differentiated and integrated level of functioning. Having resolved their identity conflict, they are now able to move toward intimacy with others and a sense of personal meaning in life.

ROADS TO HEALTH

In tracing the development of these men and women, we see not only how personality articulates and evolves with age, but also how it remains the same. Each group reveals a "ground plan" (Erikson, 1959)—a core characterological style—by early adolescence that is consistent to middle age. Their styles develop, differentiate, and become more complex in the ongoing process of growth, but also remain coherent over at least this much of the life span. Traditional women are consistently gregarious, feminine, conventional, and lean toward repressive defenses. Nontraditional women value intellectuality and achievement. Traditional men are consistently rational, self-disciplined, and value intellectual competence. Nontraditional men are closer to their emotions and impulses. By 50, both traditional and nontraditional groups have evolved a "self" consistent with earlier

[7]Mean scores on these Q-sort items increase significantly from ages 40 to 50.

positions but more differentiated and complex—and at a higher level of psychological health. An ultimately integrated personality develops, more articulated than before and appropriate to the age level and life-style of the individual.

Traditional women and men show relatively uninterrupted personality growth from adolescence to 50. Traditional women steadily develop their affiliative side, with a gradual conversion of sociability into intimacy and nurturance. Men develop their instrumental, rational side, ultimately balancing self-control with more affiliative qualities.

Nontraditional women and men interrupt their development in early adulthood but recover by 50, reviving and expanding ego functions they were developing in adolescence. Nontraditional women repossess their intellectuality, elaborating it into originality of thought, insight, and psychological sensitivity. Their achievement orientation leads them to sharpen verbal and critical skills. Nontraditional men rediscover their expressiveness and develop it into sociability and charm. Their emotionality and impulsivity evolve into sensuousness and an integrated capacity for pleasure.

Each group follows its own path to psychological health by 50, drawing on personality characteristics outlined in broad strokes by adolescence. Each proceeds to this goal with different timing. The key factor, I suggest, is the fit between an individual's cultural roles and her or his personality.

Women

Women with traditional personalities fit conventional roles for women socialized to value domesticity and a middle-class, feminine life-style. Deriving their basic satisfaction from affiliation with others, they elaborate their interpersonal skills in the mothering role and develop their nurturant side. As wives and mothers, they are able to live out valued aspects of their personalities. They continue to find satisfaction in relationships with others, even as their children grow older and begin to leave home. They are not motivated to change as they move into middle age.

Most traditional women in this study, however, still have some children at home. One can only speculate whether they will function as well in the postparental stage. However, Maas and Kuypers (1974), in their longitudinal study of parents of the BGS and GS from ages 30 to 70, find that women who are gregarious at 30 are still active socially at 70 and continue to have high morale.

The preferred adaptive skills of nontraditional women—intellectuality and ambition—make them less suited to traditional roles, particularly in a generation socialized to value domesticity and the "feminine mystique." I suggest that their expectations of themselves in these roles induce conflict in these individualistic, achievement-oriented women, requiring them to suppress their "natural" adaptive style. Nevertheless, there is little to indicate that nontraditional women directly reject or even resent their domestic life-style while children are at home. Most had been conscientious parents who internalized their roles as wives, mothers, and homemakers. By 40, however, when children are growing up, they seem to be confronted with an identity conflict. Having suppressed their intellectual competence, yet moving away from child-care demands, they seem unable for a time to connect with a valued sense of self. I suggest that it is disengaging from the mothering role that stimulates these women to revive their more intellectual, goal-oriented skills. Nontraditional women make dramatic gains when changes in role expectations free them to reach into their past and develop this more traditionally masculine side of their personality.

In considering the fit between cultural role and individual personality, one cannot ignore the debate in the literature on the fate of "feminine" and "masculine" women at middle age. Psychoanalytic writers, such as Benedek and Rubenstein (1942) and Deutsch (1945), assert that menopause is more difficult for masculine women. Benedek and Rubenstein describe the masculine woman as one dominated by strivings of the ego rather than gratifications of motherliness. Bart (1971) finds—to the contrary—that women exclusively committed to the mothering role may respond with depression when children depart. But all of these authors draw their conclusions from clinical populations. The present study looks at the other end of the spectrum—women selected because they were psychologically healthy by 50. In this group, neither a feminine nor a masculine orientation is a better prescription for successful adaptation at middle age.

Men

Men with traditional personalities fit conventional roles for high-achieving men in middle-class, urban society. Deriving their self-esteem from a sense of competence and intellectual mastery, they elaborate their coping skills in their careers—judgment, insight, self-discipline, productivity—and develop the instrumental side of their personalities. As successful businessmen and professionals as well as responsible family men, they, like traditional women, are able to live out valued aspects of themselves.

But unlike traditional women, who maintain an exclusively feminine orientation to 50, traditional men allow cross-sex qualities to emerge by early middle age. Having established an effective masculine identity earlier in life, they temper their "masculinity"—their instrumental orientation—with softer, more affiliative qualities and interpersonal skills: poise, perceptiveness, and warmth. By 40 they are more androgynous than traditional women. Traditionally feminine women seem less flexible—or less inspired to change—than traditional men.

I suggest, however, that this inflexibility reflects a cultural difference in gender *roles* rather than a fundamental difference between men and women. As Pleck (1976) points out, skill in interpersonal relationships is a valued part of male competence in occupational roles in contemporary middle-class, industrial society, particularly at the management level. Domestic roles, by contrast, do not encourage women to develop cross-sex characteristics such as assertiveness, independence, or ambition. Indeed, self-assertion—useful in the occupational system—is apt to introduce role strain in women whose primary identities are organized around satisfying affiliative needs within the family. Conventional male roles—at least in their "modern" middle-class version (Pleck, 1976)—may allow a man greater range in personal style.

Nontraditional men and women, on the other hand, follow parallel life patterns. Like women, the nontraditional men have personalities that do not fit conventional roles particularly in a generation of men socialized to value work, success, and the Protestant ethic. Their preferred adaptive style—expressiveness and emotionality—does not blend comfortably with the impulse control and delay of gratification required for occupational achievement. Similarly, the personalities of nontraditional women do not easily fit the domestic values to which this generation of women was socialized. At 40, nontraditional men and women are suppressing cross-sex characteristics. Men deny their emotionality and impulsivity, women their intellectuality and achievement drives. Both put aside cross-sex characteristics and exaggerate same-sex characteristics in order, I suggest, to function successfully in traditional gender roles—achievement for the men, mothering for the women. Both deny essential parts of their identities and pay a price in emotional stress.

But by 50, nontraditional men and women resolve this identity conflict. Men give up their exaggerated, masculine posture—their emphasis on power and control—and revive their expressive, emotional side, but at a more adaptive and integrated level than earlier. Both sexes give up rigid conformity to traditional sex-typed behavior and come to terms with parts of their personalities suppressed in early adulthood (probably since adolescence). Both, to borrow Peskin and Livson's metaphor (Chapter 6), reach into their past to revive an adaptive mode that fits their current age and life structure, as well as their fundamental personality style. They become more balanced or psychologically androgynous by 50 and experience an upsurge in psychological health. Having resolved the identity conflict evident in early adulthood, nontraditional men and women now move into the stage of intimacy achieved earlier by traditional men and women (Erikson, 1950).

Whether this resolution becomes possible because women begin to disengage from mothering in the middle years and men come to terms with their occupational goals, or whether it reflects shifts in time perspective or other age-related changes, are open questions. Probably all of these play a part. Most investigators agree that stress in early middle age (around 40) is followed by a period of resolution and stability later (Frenkel-Brunswik, 1968; Gould, 1978; Levinson with Darrow et al., 1978). Some studies find that functioning improves for women in late middle age after children depart and menopause is past (Neugarten, 1970; Neugarten et al., 1968). Advantaged, high-achieving men and women at middle age describe an increased sense of freedom, the "beginning of a period in which latent talents . . . can be put to use in new directions" (Neugarten, 1968, p. 96).

Jung (1933, p. 108) speaks of a psychic revolution in the middle years of life in which, "[the man] discovers his tender feelings, and [the woman] her sharpness of mind." Evidence from a number of studies suggests that sex-role conformity does indeed become less rigid in the second half of life (Gutmann, 1977; Lowenthal et al., 1975). Women become more accepting of their aggressive impulses in their later years and men of their nurturant impulses (Neugarten & Gutmann, 1968).

Gutmann (1977) proposes that men and women suppress cross-sex characteristics in early adulthood to provide optimal conditions for care of the young: men deny their passivity to provide protection, food, and shelter, and women suppress their aggressiveness to provide nurturance. He suggests that sex roles become less distinct when parenting is completed in the second half of life.

I would add more generally that the tasks of young adulthood—mating, parenting, career-building—tend to specialize and, hence, polarize sex roles. To perform these external roles efficiently, individuals tend to polarize their inner roles (values and behavior). The present study suggests that men and women whose personalities fit culturally prescribed sex roles follow a smoother course over the first half of life than those whose personalities fit cross-sex roles. But changes in life tasks and time perspective at middle age shake up old patterns and allow new ones to form. Individuals may now give themselves permission to change their self-image and live out unused parts of themselves. The personalities of nontraditional men and women expand by 50 when changing role demands free them to allow cross-sex characteristics to surface.

This interpretation is consistent with the view of Peskin and Livson (Chapter 6): namely, individuals at any life stage *actively select* from the repertoire of their past (skills, experience, and ego functions) to construct their present selves, rather than blindly following earlier conditionings or current environmental forces. The present study supports the view that persons guide or shape *what* they select from the past to create a self that fits their current life structure and allows them to cope with current life tasks. When an individual's life-style is congruent with her or his basic personality and continues to be so in the middle years, she or he has little need to call on suppressed parts of the self. But when role expectations in early adulthood require denial of incongruent parts of the self, at least some persons take advantage of changing role demands at middle age or changing time perspective or age itself to shape a new self out of the past.

To summarize, the findings from this exploratory study of small subsamples support the view that psychological health can and sometimes does improve in the adult years. The path of this development, however, may not be smooth, and conflicts unresolved at an earlier stage may become an issue at a later one. Patterns of growth in traditional and nontraditional men and women have in common the evolution and differentiation of personality traits that appear by early adolescence (perhaps earlier). Within each pattern, these traits evolve or regress in ways that mesh with shifts in age and role expectations. Yet both groups by 50 arrive at a unified, integrated personality style, more complex than before and appropriate to the developmental level and life style of the individual.

The patterns described here do not, of course, exhaust all possible routes to psychological health at middle age, even among housewives and businessmen of this generation and social class. Nor do they reveal how prevalent these patterns are in the general population. They do illustrate two different, and in the end successful, paths women or men can take from adolescence to middle age when born at a time and place in which gender roles are culturally distinct.

Thus, for women and men with a conventional sex-role orientation, traditional roles are not necessarily restricting. These individuals may move smoothly through adulthood with little change in sex-typed behavior. But for men and women whose personalities are less conventional—who prefer to deal with life in modes usually defined as appropriate to the opposite sex—traditional roles *can* be restricting. Such individuals may pay a serious price when they internalize traditional role expectations and experience a discontinuity in their "natural" development. With changing social norms, new generations may be able to select more flexibly from available gender roles prior to their middle years. For the generation now reaching their fifties, however, role expectations in early adulthood allowed less freedom. For that generation, middle age can open fresh options to diversify roles and expand the boundaries of the self.

9

Midlife Drinking Patterns: Correlates and Antecedents

MARY COVER JONES

Despite many studies of problem drinkers (Cahalan, 1970; Gomberg, 1974; Lisansky, 1958; Plaut, 1967), no "alcoholic personality" has been delineated (Armstrong, 1958; Gomberg, 1968; Sutherland, Schroeder, & Tardella, 1950; Syme, 1957) nor evidence produced that psychological disorders are preconditions for alcoholism (Blum & Blum, 1971). Early antecedents have usually been examined through retrospective reports. Our longitudinal groups afford a unique opportunity to study personality, social, and sociological characteristics associated with patterns of alcohol use (as well as the developmental antecedents of these characteristics) in a nonclinical sample that includes problem and nonproblem drinkers.

DRINKING PATTERNS IN ADULTHOOD

The Sample

The 193 study members who responded to questions about drinking in the most recent (IGS) study constitute my sample. OGS members answered questions about drinking habits in the IGS and three previous follow-ups (approximately ages 49, 43, 37, and 33); the GS members answered these questions twice (average ages of 42 and 30). Supplementary findings are presented for a smaller number (108) of OGS participants who were also interviewed in 1964–1965 (Jones, 1968, 1971).

223

Classification of Drinking Patterns

Participants were classified into five categories—problem drinkers, heavy drinkers, moderate drinkers, light drinkers, and abstainers—on the basis of an amount-frequency index used in a number of studies (Cahalan, Cisin, & Crossley, 1969; Knupfer & Room, 1964; Straus & Bacon, 1953). Abstainers seldom or never drink and tend to have scruples: "I don't drink at all; I think it is stupid." Light drinkers drink small amounts, infrequently; moderate drinkers fall between heavy and light. Heavy drinkers typically have two or more drinks daily and more on occasions.

Our attention here is largely on problem drinkers, a category based on quantity drunk (about as much as heavy drinkers) *plus* a *social* criterion—either complaint about drinking by the participant, his or her spouse or children or evidence that the person has had difficulties attributable to drinking (e.g., losing a job). As expected in a middle-aged, middle-class group, the numbers in this category are small, six men and eight women still participating and five OGS members, two men and three women, with drinking problems who have died, four of them since interviews at age 43.

Over a period of more than 15 years, changes occurred in the drinking behavior of our cohorts. New recruits joined the ranks of excessive drinkers, while some who had been excessive drinkers now drink normally or abstain. Consumption patterns of some nonproblem drinkers also changed. At age 43, 26% of OGS males said they drank more than they had at earlier ages, 24% said less; percentages for OGS women were the same (24%). This question was not routinely asked at the last follow-up, but more of those to whom the question was put indicated less drinking—62% of the men, 55% of the women. In their fifties, OGS members drank a little less than formerly. This trend has been noted in other studies (Abelson, Fishburn, & Cisin, 1977; Cahalan, 1972).

Time, Place, and Amount of Drinking: General Findings

Here are answers of our predominantly middle-class sample to questions about their drinking habits at middle age.

When do you drink? For these participants, as for persons interviewed in the Berkeley State Survey (Knupfer, Fink, Clark, & Goffman, 1963), the preferred places and times for a drink are at home before dinner.

How much do you drink?   The median number of drinks during the last week, for those who had not abstained completely, was five for men and three for women. However, the percentage of men and women who exceeded two drinks per day during this period was the same—12%. The range of drinks of distilled liquor consumed in the past week was 0–27 for the men, 0–26 for the women. More men (nearly 50%) than women (33%) say they drink nearly every day.

What do you drink?   Our samples use more wine with meals than 12 years ago and less distilled liquor, especially in mixed drinks. However, "hard" spirits are still the most popular with both sexes. Beer has lost none of its previous popularity as a hot weather thirst quencher and an accompaniment to watching television and spectator sports. More women than men drink wine, more men than women drink beer. Some women who drink wine (including champagne and sherry) do not drink distilled beverages, but beer drinkers, both men and women, also drink liquor. In general, according to Cannon (1977) and McCarthy (1964), more Americans are using alcohol than formerly, but, except for young people (Cahalan & Treiman, 1976; Johnston, Bachman, & O'Malley, 1977; Smart, 1976; Wechsler & McFadden, 1976), they are using less.

Why do you, or do you not, drink?   The most common responses refer to sociability, relaxation, and relief of tension. Men who drink heavily also indicate a personal need for this form of relief and give more reasons for drinking (see also Nuttall & Costa, 1975). Women and men in their forties say they drink more than they did as young marrieds because they can afford to and find it expected in their social and business circles. Executives drink more at lunch, often resenting the custom of providing drinks to clients. In their fifties some respondents have developed ulcers, high blood pressure, or hypertension requiring medication, sometimes with alcohol counter-indicated. Others now look on alcohol as medicinal.

Sex Differences

As in other studies (Cahalan, 1972, Cahalan *et al.*, 1969; Knupfer & Room, 1964), fewer women than men report problems with drinking. More women than men report they had their first drink in approved circumstances, usually in the family (Ullman, 1962). Typically, they also had their first drink at a younger age, perhaps because girls mature earlier than boys and are more likely to have older friends (Jessor & Jessor, 1977).

More women than men drink sparingly and only in social situations and more abstain. This may be related to the way in which drinking behavior was learned as well as to social expectations that women will drink decorously. As in other studies (Gomberg, 1974), women report more use of medicine, evidence more health concerns (see Chapter 3), and value the therapeutic qualities of alcohol. Some take alcohol on a doctor's prescription to improve appetite or relieve tensions. Slightly more women than men drink for "personal" reasons, but they are not necessarily heavy drinkers.

These sex differences are not as great as reported in most national surveys, probably because our study members are preponderantly urban, middle class, and middle-aged. Drinking is more common among women of this status (Cahalan *et al.*, 1969; Knupfer & Room, 1964; Room, 1972). In addition, my 1964–1965 interview with OGS members was intensive, and I have long acquaintance with the respondents. This encouraged frank discussion and admissions, especially among women who might otherwise have been "hidden" drinkers (Keller & Efron, 1955).

PERSONALITY AND DRINKING IN THE MATURE YEARS

We now turn to the small group of problem drinkers—six men and eight women—whom I compare with participants in all other categories (i.e., heavy, moderate, light, and abstainers combined). Men and women are treated separately. Because the numbers of participants in the probelm drinker category are so small, findings must be interpreted very cautiously.

Some Composite Pictures from Interviewers' Notes

Ned presents a mixed picture—sense of humor, liking people, and yet an undercurrent of anxiety and depression; a lot of self-abasement along with bragging. He seems pretty realistic in talking about his life experiences and yet there is a rigidity, a confusion, and disrupted thought processes that alcohol probably does not help. He "barks" a lot and sounds aggressive but at the same time gives the impression of being very vulnerable and probably an "old softie."

He refers to participation in "good" drinking affairs in the service and service-connected reunions and recounts his drinking adventures with boyish pride. "I can put 'em all down at a party."

Rob explained: "I can't see this social drinking. Can't see mixed drinks, two martinis before dinner . . . that's 'fool around' drinking. I drink because I like the taste and the effect. After a few you can't think. You take a glass and you are floating again."

Some of these men exhibit the usual ambivalence and concern of heavy drinkers about the effects of over-imbibing. Floyd says, "I've had trouble once in a while. The doc told me, 'if you lay it down there with no lining, it is too much for your stomach' . . . When I drink too heavy, my heart goes pounding like crazy, it sounds loud enough for the neighbors to hear and goin' a mile a minute. Boy, that's scary. It doesn't do it 'til you lie down, when you're plastered. Then you pass out. Now I drink my fifth a day slowly, otherwise you lose the effect."

No women talked as candidly and as vividly about their drinking as the men did. The swagger with which some of the men related their escapades was entirely lacking in the women, who tended to express more quiet distress: "I'm kind of hooked on alcohol. Maybe I need it emotionally. It blocks things out. I escape. There are times when I don't know what happens." "I have an occasional bout with booze. Then I get so ashamed I worry about it." "I asked God to forgive me for my drinking. I don't drink at all anymore. I wouldn't want to meet Him with a glass of liquor in my hand."

Marital and Family Adjustments of Problem Drinkers

As might be anticipated, problem drinkers have more difficult and unsatisfactory marital and family relationships than their peers. According to ratings by the interviewers, all of the male problem drinkers and five of the seven married females were below average on an overall scale of marital adjustment; all other categories had higher than average scores. For women problem drinkers, only four (57%) of their marriages were rated as "more satisfactory than average marriages," while 83% of the women nonproblem drinkers' marriages were given the same rating. The divorce rates for problem drinkers (men, 38%; women, 33%) are higher than for the total IGS sample (24%).

On ratings of hostile–friendly relations between husband and wife all problem drinkers except one man and two women were rated in the hostile direction, whereas persons in all other categories had high scores in the friendly direction. On a rating scale of somber–spontaneous, problem drinkers' families tended to have a serious tone.

Families of four of the six problem drinker men and five of the seven married problem drinking women were rated low (somber); families in other categories averaged above the mean (spontaneous).

ADULT PERSONALITY OF PROBLEM DRINKERS

Q Sort

Tables 9.1 and 9.2 summarize comparisons between the adult Q-sort ratings assigned to problem drinkers of each sex and to other participants.

Given the large number of significant differences, we may reasonably conclude that problem drinkers have many distinctive characteristics. A core of traits characterize the problem drinkers' affective dispositions, interpersonal relationships, self-concepts, and coping and adjustment devices. Furthermore, although men and women problem drinkers differ from each other in some aspects of personality, they resemble each other in many attributes that distinguish them from the other study participants. Compared to other participants, problem drinkers of both sexes are more undercontrolled, self-indulgent, irritable, moody, unpredictable, and fearful. They tend to fantasize more, have more brittle ego defenses, and feel their lives lack meaning (Table 9.1). Problem drinkers were also rated as less ethically consistent, less dependable, less warm, less aware of the impression they create and less productive (Table 9.2). Chapter 4 reports a significant relationship between decline in IQ and problem drinking in our samples. Problem drinkers are also seen as more rebellious, negativistic, and self-defeating, and at the same time less independent, less giving, less considerate, less sympathetic, and less charming. The problem drinkers' negative attitudes toward themselves are reflected in their higher ratings on such characteristics as anxious, self-pitying, self-dramatizing.

In brief, the Q-sort ratings for problem drinkers of both sexes show them to be poorly adjusted, generally lacking in self-esteem, uncomfortable with themselves, and dependent. Not surprisingly, their relationships with others are unsatisfactory.

Additional characteristics distinguishing male problem drinkers from other men, and female problem drinkers from other women, lend further support to this general conclusion. As Tables 9.1 and 9.2 indicate, compared to other men, male problem drinkers are submissive, basically hostile, moody, concerned with adequacy and seek reassur-

Table 9.1

Q-sort Items on Which Problem Drinkers Score Higher
than Nonproblem Drinkers

Q-sort items	Men[a] Mean ratings		Q-sort items	Women[b] Mean ratings	
	PD	NPD		PD	NPD
Thin-skinned	6.2	4.7***	Thin-skinned	5.7	4.8*
Feels Life Lacks Meaning	5.8	3.7**	Feels Life Lacks Meaning	4.8	3.4**
Extrapunitive	6.0	4.1**	Extrapunitive	4.7	3.6**
Irritable	5.5	4.2**	Irritable	5.2	4.1*
Negativistic	4.8[c]	3.4**	Negativistic	4.4	3.3**
Fearful	5.3	3.7**	Fearful	5.6	4.3*
Brittle Ego Defenses	5.9	3.7*	Brittle Ego Defenses	5.3	4.3***
Fantasizing	5.8	4.4*	Fantasizing	6.1	4.3***
Unpredictable	4.5	3.5*	Unpredictable	4.8[c]	3.7***
Undercontrolled	6.3[c,d]	3.8***	Undercontrolled	5.9	3.8***
Self-Defeating	5.3	3.8*	Self-Defeating	5.8	3.5***
Rebellious	5.1[c,d]	3.3**	Rebellious	4.5	3.1**
Self-Indulgent	7.9	5.0***	Self-Indulgent	6.9	4.7***
Basically Anxious	6.8	5.1**	Basically Anxious	7.1	5.1***
Bothered by Demands	5.4	4.1**	Bothered by Demands	5.0	3.9**
Self-Pitying	4.6	3.1**	Self-Pitying	5.3	2.8***
Self-Dramatizing	6.1	4.1**	Self-Dramatizing	6.4	4.6***
Submissive	4.3	3.3*	Introspective	7.0	5.5*
Seeks Reassurance	6.3	4.7**	Withdraws When Frustrated	5.8	2.8***
Deceitful	4.0[c]	3.0*	Thinks Unconventionally	5.9	4.6**
Basic Hostility	6.4	5.2*	Reluctant to Act	5.2	3.3***
Distrustful	5.4	4.5*	Aloof	4.4	3.3*
Pushes Limits	5.1[c]	3.4**	Feels Victimized	5.3	3.3***
Concerned with Adequacy	7.6	5.7**	Ruminative	6.4	4.6***
Projective	5.3	4.1**	Complicates Simple Situations	5.2	3.9***
Moody	5.9	4.7**			
Repressive	6.6	5.2*			

[a]Problem Drinkers $N = 6$; Others $N = 84$.
[b]Problem Drinkers $N = 8$; Others $N = 95$.
[c]Also significant in early adolescence.
[d]Also significant in late adolescence.
*$p < .10$.
**$p < .05$.
***$p < .01$.

Table 9.2

Adult Q-sort Items on Which Problem Drinkers
Score Lower than Nonproblem Drinkers

Men[a] Mean ratings			Women[b] Mean ratings		
Q-sort items	PD	NPD	Q-sort items	PD	NPD
Dependable	4.6	$7.4^{c,d}$*	Dependable	5.4	7.6***
Giving	3.8	6.0^{c}***	Giving	5.5	6.8**
Protective	3.0	5.9^{c}***	Protective	4.8	6.5**
Light Touch	3.5	4.8**	Light Touch	4.3	5.4**
Sympathetic	3.6	$5.9^{c,d}$*	Sympathetic	5.5	6.6**
Overcontrolled	3.1	5.2^{c}**	Overcontrolled	3.4	4.9***
Productive	5.8	7.2**	Productive	4.1	7.2***
Aware of Impression Created	4.3	5.5**	Aware of Impression Created	4.9	5.8**
Ethically Consistent	4.6	6.9***	Ethically Consistent	5.9	6.9**
Clear-cut, Consistent Personality	3.5	4.8**	Clear-cut, Consistent Personality	3.5	4.9***
Charming	4.3	5.2*	Charming	4.9	5.8***
Values Independence	4.8	6.6**	Values Independence	3.6	5.6***
Skeptical	4.4	5.9**	Wide Interests	3.7	5.8***
Initiates Humor	4.7	5.7*	Conservative	4.2	5.4*
Prides Self on Objectivity	5.0	6.5***	Appears Intelligent	5.3	6.3**
Turned To for Advice	3.5	5.3***	Rapid Tempo	3.7	6.1***
Warm	4.1	5.4*	Arouses Liking	5.6	6.5**
Responds to Humor	4.6	5.4**	Gregarious	4.6	5.8*
Socially Perceptive	3.4	5.3***	Creates Dependency	3.1	4.2*
Esthetically Reactive	3.5	5.1**	Ambitious	3.7	5.9***
Incisive	2.8	5.1***	Satisfied with Self	5.6	6.7***
Masculine Style	5.1	6.4**	Candid	4.5	6.3*
Does Not Vary Role	3.6	4.5^{c}*	Cheerful	4.9	5.8***
			Power-Oriented	3.6	4.7*
			Poised	5.4	6.4**
			Verbally Fluent	4.8	5.7*

[a]Problem Drinkers N = 6; Others N = 84.
[b]Problem Drinkers N = 8; Others N = 95.
[c]Also significant in early adolescence.
[d]Also significant in late adolescence.

*$p < .10$.
**$p < .05$.
***$p < .01$.

ance. They are rated low in prides self on objectivity, masculine style, incisive, socially perceptive, and esthetically reactive; they are not turned to for advice and they seldom initiate or respond to humor.

Compared to other women, female problem drinkers think unconventionally, are ruminative, aloof, do not have wide interests, are reluctant to act and do not have a rapid tempo. They are generally not satisfied with self, not ambitious, and not poised; they are not cheerful and do not arouse liking. They feel victimized and complicate simple situations.

Many of the characteristics ascribed to problem drinkers have also been found to be associated with downward occupational mobility (Elder, 1974), heavy smoking (Clausen, 1968; Stewart & Livson, 1966), and social immaturity (Chapter 10).

On the index of psychological health (Chapter 6), problem drinkers score lower than other participants although the difference is statistically significant only for women. Male problem drinkers score lower on all 16 Q-sort items indicative of good psychological health, while they have higher scores on the 16 items considered to be least characteristic of good psychological health.

Thematic Apperception Test and California Psychological Inventory

Independent corroboration of some of the Q-sort findings comes from the TAT and the CPI. Skolnick (1966a,b) scored the TAT protocols on four motives: achievement, affiliation, power (using the McClelland-Atkinson approach; Atkinson, 1958) and aggression (scored according to a system that Skolnick devised). Male problem drinkers differ significantly from the other men on three of these four motives. Their rebelliousness, hostility, and self-defeating qualities, evident in their Q-sort ratings, are also reflected in their TAT stories. Specifically, they scored significantly higher ($p < .01$) than nonproblem drinkers on Aggression, expressing fantasies involving direct aggression and also defending against aggression (McClelland, Davis, Kalin, & Wanner, 1972). The relatively large number of stories of suicide or self-injury ($p < .05$), and victimization ($p < .01$) also suggest that much of their aggression is turned against themselves. Consistent with the Q-sort ratings indicating that these problem drinkers are unsuccessful in social relationships, anxious, and suffering from feelings of inadequacy, their TAT stories include less achievement ($p < .10$) and affiliation motivation ($p < .01$) than the stories told by other men.

In contrast with this last finding for men, stories of women problem drinkers reveal significantly greater needs ($p < .01$) for affiliation than those of the other women. However, as in the case of the male problem drinkers, women who were problem drinkers tend to score higher than their peers in Aggression ($p < .10$), a finding congruent with their Q-sort ratings on Extrapunitive, Negativistic and Rebellious.

The CPI findings yield further impressive evidence reinforcing the Q-sort differences. Compared with other male participants, the problem drinkers had significantly lower scores on the following: Sense of Well-being (productivity, versatility), Socialization (responsibility, sincerity), Self-Control (freedom from impulsivity and self-centeredness) (see Fig. 9.1), and on Block's Ego Control Scale (Block in collaboration with Haan, 1971).

Women with drinking problems describe themselves on the CPI as lacking in many qualities that would enable them to cope with life's demands. On 8 of the 18 scales they score significantly less favorably than all other female study members. For example, like the male problem drinkers, they score lower on Well-being ($p < .05$), Socialization ($p < .01$), Self-Control ($p < .05$) and Ego-Control ($p < .05$). In addition, they are less responsible ($p < .01$); less capable of creating a good impression ($p < .05$), for example, less warm, concerned, outgoing; more undercontrolled ($p < .10$) and less achieving by conformity ($p < .10$) (see Fig. 9.1).

DEVELOPMENTAL CHARACTERISTICS
OF PROBLEM DRINKERS

Are the personal characteristics of adult problem drinkers the consequents of heavy drinking, or are they antecedents, factors associated with the development of problem drinking? Adolescent data—particularly Q-sort ratings, ratings based on observations of social behavior, personal documents, and projective tests—permit us to examine this question in some depth.

Essentially, our concerns here are with two interrelated issues: (a) are the personal characteristics of problem drinkers long-standing ones and (b) can one predict future drinking problems on the basis of early psychological characteristics? Results of the data analyses lead me to conclude that the answer to both is a qualified yes. Many of the distinctive personal qualities of the male problem drinkers as adults are clearly discernible during their early adolescence, long before their adult drinking patterns were established. Fewer adolescent personal

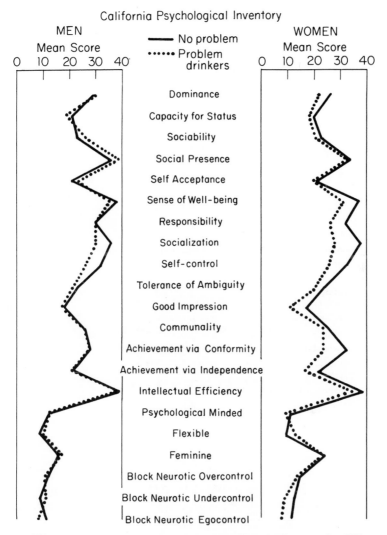

California Psychological Inventory

MEN
Mean Score

—— No problem
•••••• Problem
          drinkers

WOMEN
Mean Score

Dominance
Capacity for Status
Sociability
Social Presence
Self Acceptance
Sense of Well-being
Responsibility
Socialization
Self-control
Tolerance of Ambiguity
Good Impression
Communality
Achievement via Conformity
Achievement via Independence
Intellectual Efficiency
Psychological Minded
Flexible
Feminine
Block Neurotic Overcontrol
Block Neurotic Undercontrol
Block Neurotic Egocontrol

Fig. 9.1. Ratings for problem and nonproblem drinkers on the CPI.

characteristics distinguish between women who later became problem drinkers and those who did not.

Compared with the other men during adolescence, problem drinkers were more undercontrolled (impulsive and self-indulged), rebellious, negativistic and deceitful, and less dependable, giving, and sympathetic (see Table 9.3). These early attributes continue to characterize them in maturity and, thus, seem to constitute important antecedents

Table 9.3

Comparison of Future Problem and Nonproblem
Drinkers on Adolescent Q-sort Items

Q-sort items	Early adolescence Mean ratings[a]		Late adolescence Mean ratings[b]	
	PD	NPD	PD	NPD
Items on which male problem drinkers have high scores				
Talkative	6.9	5.0**		
Rapid Tempo	6.6	5.0***	6.6	4.7**
Negativistic	6.4	4.2**		
Deceitful	5.3	3.0***		
Assertive	7.1	4.8**		
Undercontrolled	5.0	3.6***	6.5	3.9**
Rebellious	7.2	4.1***	6.1	4.4*
Pushes Limits	6.9	3.6***		
Eroticizes Situations	4.0	3.2**		
Interested in Opposite Sex			5.9	4.1*
Romanticizes			5.7	4.6*
Items on which male problem drinkers have low scores				
Dependable	3.8	6.4**	3.9	6.1**
Giving	3.6	5.0*		
Status Quo	3.9	5.6**	3.9	5.3*
Protective	3.7	5.2**		
Thin-skinned	4.4	6.0**		
Sympathetic	3.5	5.3**	4.2	5.5*
Submissive	2.6	4.8**		
Dependent	3.3	5.3**		
Seeks Reassurance	3.6	5.0**		
Overcontrolled	2.9	5.7***		
Reluctant to Act	2.9	4.3*		
Concerned with Appearance			5.1	6.3**
Repressive			5.1	6.4*
Emotionally Bland			3.4	5.0*
Does Not Vary Roles	3.9	5.4**	3.7	5.4**
Accepts Dependency	2.4	5.6***	2.9	5.4**
Items on which female problem drinkers have high scores				
Evaluates Situations in Motivational Terms			5.2	4.6*
Unpredictable	4.6	3.5*		
Views Self as Causative			5.3	4.3*
Socially Perceptive			5.9	4.7**
Initiates Humor			5.7	4.3**
Items on which female problem drinkers have low scores				
Uncomfortable with Uncertainty			4.9	6.1**
Compares Self with Others			5.6	6.4*

[a]Problem Drinkers $N = 4$; Others $N = 58$.
[b]Problem Drinkers $N = 7$; Others $N = 67$.

$*p < .10.$
$**p < .05.$
$***p < .01.$

of later problem drinking in men. Recall, however, that as adults, male problem drinkers are also seen as relatively hostile, submissive, socially unsuccessful, and anxious. Q-sort ratings provide no evidence that these were distinguishing qualities during their adolescence, although, according to data from a self-report inventory, they had significantly poorer self-concepts (greater feelings of inferiority and self-damaging feelings) than the others. They also pictured themselves as having less satisfactory social relationships as early as the ninth grade (Tryon, 1939a). In general, according to the Q sorts, they appeared to be rather extroverted at that time—talkative, assertive, and had rapid tempo. They were not thin-skinned, submissive, dependent, seeking reassurance, repressive or emotionally bland; on the average, they rated lower than the other boys in these characteristics and in accepting dependency. As adults they seem to be submissive and dependent, findings consistent with other studies (Gomberg, 1968; McCord & McCord, 1960). Hence, we may infer that as adolescents, those who will become problem-drinking men were immature, negativistic, impulsive, and self-centered but rather extroverted and assertive. We may hypothesize that as adolescents these boys were generally insecure and therefore had strong needs to form relationships with peers. They acquired some techniques that were effective in establishing superficial social relationships and thus appeared to be extroverted. But these same techniques may be unsuccessful, or even counterproductive, in forming the deeper, more intimate friendships necessary for maintaining gratifying social relationships in adulthood.

Women who became problem drinkers could not be so readily identified from their girlhood personalities. During early adolescence particularly, few Q-sort ratings significantly differentiate those who later became problem drinkers from those who did not. Some of the differentiating characteristics (Table 9.3) are identical with those that differentiate male future problem drinkers from other men and persist into adulthood. Thus, female problem drinkers as adolescents were regarded as significantly more unpredictable ($p < .05$) than those who became normal drinkers or abstainers. Although they also had higher ratings than the others on Undercontrolled, Rebellious, Pushes Limits, Anxious, and Concerned with Adequacy, these differences were not statistically significant.

Information about adolescent personality and social relationships from other sources in our archives reinforce and supplement the picture constructed from the adolescent Core Q sorts. Consider, for example, the Interpersonal Q sort designed to describe the participants' behavior with their peers, as well as their attitudes towards parents (see Chapter 2). The marked adolescent social orientation of the boys who were future problem drinkers, evident in their adolescent Core Q-sort ratings, is also reflected in their high ratings on the Interpersonal Q sort on Claims the Privileges of Adolescence, Needs Association with Peers, Seeking Attention of Peers, Oriented Toward Going Steady, Talkativeness in Social Situations, Assertiveness and Humor with Peers. Although socially oriented, these boys do not seem socially sensitive or sympathetic, because, according to other ratings, they also feel superior and condescending toward peers (Table 9.4). (See also Blane, 1970.)

Although some of the interpersonal Q-sort items differentiating women problem drinkers from the others are similar to those that distinguish the comparable men's groups, the differences are not as sharp or as significant. Again, the evidence suggests more difficulty in predicting from early characteristics to later drinking patterns of women.

Responses to TATs during adolescence also yield information consistent with that derived from the adolescent Core Q sort. Compared with other adolescent boys, those who became problem drinkers received higher TAT scores on aggression and lower scores on achievement motivation ($p < .05$). Similarly, the imagery produced by adolescent girls who later drank excessively contained less emphasis on achievement and more concern with aggression ($p < .10$) than that of the other girls. As we have seen, high scores for aggression recur in the problem drinkers' adulthood.

Another source of data on adolescent personality and social behavior is observational ratings of the OGS participants made when small like-sexed adolescent groups came to the Institute of Human Development (IHD) semiannually for a day of physical and psychological assessment. During the noon hour, six or eight boys on one day and girls another, with some friendships represented, ate lunch and engaged in activities in a yard equipped with appropriate play materials for the age group. Three staff members, usually one man and two women, participated in these free-play situations, subsequently rating each participant and writing descriptive comments supporting the ratings (Newman, 1946). These measures are independent of those included in the Q sets for the adolescent period.

The scores represent the combined judgments of three raters at each 6-month period, averaged over the 3-year junior high-school period and over 2 years of senior high school. Because some students graduated early or transferred to technical high schools in the senior year, scores for the last year are less complete and have not been included.

These observational ratings amplify the picture of the adolescent

Table 9.4

Comparison of Problem and Nonproblem Drinkers on the
Interpersonal Q sort during Adolescence

Q-sort items	Boys[a] Mean ratings				Girls[b] Mean ratings			
	Early adoles. PD	NPD	Late adoles. PD	NPD	Early adoles. PD	NPD	Late adoles. PD	NPD
Items on which problem drinkers have high scores								
Privileges of Adolescence	5.8	4.0**						
Rebellious with Adults	7.0	4.0***			6.3	4.3*		
Seeks Attention of Peers	6.4	4.0**						
Talkative	7.0	4.9**						
Assertive with Peers	7.1	4.7**						
Feels Superior to Peers	5.4	3.9**						
Humorous with Peers	6.7	5.3***					5.5	4.4*
Condescending to Peers	5.3	4.0***						
Knowledgeable of Peer Culture					6.9	5.8**		
Needs Association with Group			6.6	5.1**				
Fantasizes about Opposite Sex	5.8	4.4*						
Oriented Toward "Going Steady"			5.6	3.2**				
Items on which problem drinkers have low scores								
Closer to Mother							4.4	5.8*
Sees Parents as Happy	3.6	4.6*	3.2	4.5*				
Affectionate Family			3.4	4.7*				
Respects Parents	4.9	6.6**						
Sees Parents as Reasonable	4.1	5.5*	3.4	5.0*				
Mother Respected in Community	5.1	5.8*					4.7	5.7**
Sees Father as Attractive	5.3	6.3*						
Sees Mother as Attractive							4.4	5.3**
Passive and Nonreactive with Adults	2.5	4.3*						
Parents Accepting His Growth			3.9	5.5*				
Is Protective of Friends	3.6	5.0**						
Is Sympathetic to Peers	3.1	5.3***						
Age-Appropriate Behavior	3.9	5.4**						

[a]Problem Drinkers $N = 5$; Others $N = 65$.
[b]Problem Drinkers $N = 7$; Others $N = 67$.
*$p < .10$.
**$p < .05$.
***$p < .01$.

behavior of future problem drinkers derived from other rating techniques. During junior high-school, boys in this category seemed to have
a glorious time in social situations with other boys of their acquaintance, being rated significantly higher than the others on items describing social engagement. Specifically, they were more outgoing, expressive (differences significant at the .01 level) and acceptable, and
received higher ratings on leadership ($p <$. 05); popularity ($p < .01$),
assurance ($p < .01$), self-acceptance ($p < .01$) and good spirits ($p < .01$),
as well as on masculine behavior ($p < .05$) and uninhibitedness ($p
< .01$). In contrast, boys who did not become problem drinkers were
well-groomed ($p < .10$), matter-of-fact ($p < .05$), and submissive (as
contrasted with bossy) ($p < .10$). The social activities of those who were
later to have drinking problems were of an extroverted, childish type
that flourished in same-sex friendship groups.

Analysis of the sociometric Reputation Measure (Tryon, 1939b; see
Chapter 2) indicated that their junior high-school classmates concurred with adult raters in their assessments of boys who later became
problem drinkers. Compared with other boys, they were considered
more restless ($p < .01$), talkative ($p < .01$), friendly ($p < .05$), leaders
($p < .05$), unkempt ($p < .10$), liking a fight ($p < .05$), and childish ($p
< .05$).

When these boys moved into senior high-school, they were still expressive and socially oriented, but they were no longer accorded the
social acceptance they received earlier. "A rather significant change"
was the tenor of notes entered by observers toward the end of the junior
high-school years. Ratings at that time show their standings on prestige, confidence, and buoyancy to be down sharply. Figure 9.2 presents
the ratings for one member of this group (Jones, 1965). I infer that the
latency (childhood) and early adolescent periods were the heyday of
sociability and superficial social success for these boys; transitions to
later adolescence, manhood, and heterosexual orientation brought
them into situations with which they could not cope adequately.

As staff observed OGS girls interacting with their peers during
junior and senior high-school, they recorded little that was predictive
of later drinking behavior. Girls who were to drink more than most of
their classmates, but without signs of alcohol dependency—that is,
heavy drinkers, *not* problem drinkers—were clearly defined in the
adolescent period as more *expressive* ($p < .05$), attractive ($p < .05$),
confident ($p < .05$), and assured ($p < .01$). According to observational
ratings made in larger, mixed-group social situations, the future problem drinkers tended to be less popular with boys ($p < .10$), less socially
self-confident ($p < .10$), and less self-assertive ($p < .10$) than the others.

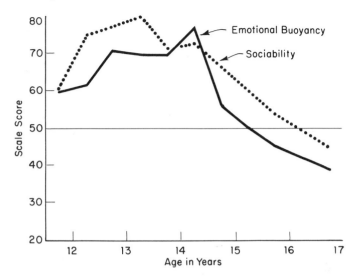

Fig. 9.2. Observational ratings in adolescence of one future problem drinker.

Again, classmates' ratings (Reputation Measure, Tryon, 1939b) generally agree with those of staff observers. Girls who became alcohol
dependent were seen by the classmates as less talkative ($p < .10$), less
friendly ($p < .10$), less humorous ($p < .10$), less enthusiastic $p < .10$),
but more attention-seeking ($p < .10$), and more bossy ($p < .10$) than
comparison groups. In brief, adolescent girls who will become problem
drinkers seemed not to share their male counterparts' outgoingness
and social orientation during the early high-school years. On the contrary, females in this group tended to have unsatisfactory peer relationships.

Youthful Sketches

Excerpts from observers' and interviewers' notes add some "real life"
flavor to the statistical analyses. Here is the introductory description
of Ned, later a problem drinker, at his first visit to IHD when he was 10
years old: "Ned is a small, energetic youngster. With these new companions he is completely unafraid, interested and energetic." (When
Ned was asked at 38, "What were you like as a child?" he unhesitat-
ingly answered, "Call me active. I didn't pass up many dares.")

Some of the OGS boys were concerned about growing up and facing
manhood. Each time he was measured, "Shorty" would inquire ea-
gerly: "How much have I grown?"; he was always disappointed by the

answer. As an adult, looking back upon his youth, he again emphasized this worry over his size: "I was afraid I would never grow." And about drinking he commented, "You grow taller with every drink. You drink and drink and grow and grow. You think you're nine feet tall. Some little guys use it for courage like that."

Jed's periods of greatest social success and personal satisfaction were childhood and preadolescence. In the ninth grade observers noted: "On the playground today he was destructive, insolent, rebellious, selfish." (Thirty years later he was to tell us that it was during this period of upheaval that he and a group of friends, no longer attuned to the social activities of their classmates, established a retreat in the hills where through alcohol they relived some of the glorious fun of their earlier childhood days.)

Another problem drinker equated heavy drinking with manliness. "This (bar) was a place where I was accepted as an adult—in an adults' world. Here is a guy of your father's generation, your school principal's generation, the policemen's generation" (see McClelland *et al.*, 1972).

Sadie describes her adolescence: "I felt like a heel for quitting Girl Scouts. I didn't like anything decent. I began to go bad in the eighth grade. I couldn't be trusted at all at thirteen; getting drunk in the hills with boys."

Naomi confided: "When I was out with boys I felt very assured but I was very uneasy with anyone in authority. I always felt that I was bad and that they could always tell that I was bad." A staff interviewer commented: "Naomi's delinquency is within the context of a primitive and punitive superego so that the demands she makes on herself are so stringent they could not possibly be lived up to."

Family Adjustments of Future Problem Drinkers during Adolescence

Because the personality structures of future problem drinkers, particularly males, can be distinguished clearly in adolescence, we might predict that their relationships with their parents differed from those of peers who did not become problem drinkers. At least partial confirmation of this hypothesis is derived from the Interpersonal Q-sort (see Table 9.4).

Compared with their adolescent peers, future problem drinkers, especially males, had more negative attitudes toward their parents and perceived them in less favorable ways. They regarded their families as less happy, less close and affectionate, less reasonable, less accepting of growth and independence. They showed less admiration and respect for their parents, and felt that they were relatively unattractive people who were not well respected in the community.

Corroborative evidence of less satisfactory parent–child relationships in the future problem drinkers' families comes from ratings by home visitors who observed family interactions during the participants' adolescence. These observers rated the mothers of boys who later became problem drinkers as less interested in their children ($p < .05$), less alert ($p < .05$), less satisfied with their lives as family members ($p < .10$), and less energetic ($p < .01$) (Jones, 1971).

These data are not as rich nor as detailed as we might wish, and the number of significant relationships is not large. Nevertheless, the findings are consistent with the hypothesis that problem drinking in middle life stems from unsatisfactory social, including familial, experiences during adolescence, or perhaps earlier.

SUMMARY

My findings, derived from a variety of assessment techniques, generally confirm the results of cross-sectional studies demonstrating that problem drinkers are clearly distinguishable from nonproblem drinkers and abstainers in adult personality and social adjustment. The former generally have more unsatisfactory and conflictful marital and family relationships, are more poorly adjusted, dependent, and lacking in self-esteem. Most prominent among their personality characteristics are rebelliousness, hostility, and self-defeating tendencies. Compared to other adults, problem drinkers are *more* undercontrolled, irritable, moody, unpredictable, rebellious, negativistic, self-defeating, and brittle in their defenses. At the same time, they are *less* consistent, dependable, cheerful, productive, independent, considerate, sympathetic, and charming.

The longitudinal data reveal at least some of the problem drinkers' distinctive characteristics to be stable ones, already apparent in adolescence. Evidence of stability, and hence predictability, was found for male problem drinkers. In adolescence these men were already significantly differentiated from their peers in being *more* undercontrolled, impulsive, self-indulged, rebellious, negativistic, and harbor deeper feelings of inferiority. They were *less* dependable, giving, and sympathetic. At early adolescence, they were also highly extroverted (albeit in a somewhat immature way), a characteristic they did not manifest as adults. On the other hand, hostility, submissiveness, and anxiety—distinctive characteristics in adulthood—were not highly salient during adolescence. In fact, according to observational ratings made at that period, they were more outgoing, expressive, popular, and uninhibited than others and were given high ratings on leadership and self-acceptance. Problem drinkers among middle-aged women showed few of their distinctive adult characteristics during adolescence.

Our data give some support to the hypothesis that problems of alcohol abuse have roots in early socialization experiences, particularly in the family. During adolescence, future problem drinkers, especially males, regarded their families as less happy, less affectionate, and less accepting of the child's growth and independence than other families. Compared with their peers, they expressed less affection, admiration, and respect for their parents.

10

Social Maturity in Middle Age and Its Developmental Antecedents

JANE B. BROOKS

Social skills and a basic enjoyment of people contribute to effective functioning throughout the life span. In early and middle adulthood these qualities play an important role in such developmental tasks as establishing intimate personal ties in marriage, nurturing children, and producing work. Chapters 11 and 13 describe specific types of social interaction, for example, marriage and work. This chapter assesses (a) the behavioral significance of a general quality of social maturity in the everyday lives of a well-functioning sample of persons in middle age, and (b) the adolescent antecedents of adult social maturity.

Gough's Social Maturity Index (SMI), derived from his California Psychological Inventory (CPI), is the measure used here. Gough uses "socially mature" to refer to people "who can live comfortably with others, ... respond to both ordinary and extraordinary stress, and ... when appropriate, rise above or depart from the mores and institutional givens of social control" (Gough, 1971). Thus, he distinguishes between socialization—the internalization of societal rules, attitudes, and values laid down in childhood and rarely relinquished later, and social maturity—the ability to function well in ordered situations without losing one's critical abilities, for example, early behaviors can be relinquished when no longer adaptive. "Social maturity" includes an emphasis on flexibility, resilience under stress, and an ability to enjoy people. In this emphasis it resembles the concept of psychological health. However, psychological health goes beyond social maturity in implying freedom from disruptive levels of affect, accuracy of perceptions, and satisfaction in life circumstances.

Gough developed the SMI empirically, selecting a combination of six CPI scales that, when weighted appropriately, provided maximum discrimination between nondelinquent males (considered more mature) and institutionalized delinquents and adult male inmates (who represented lower levels of maturity). The resulting regression equation, yielded by analysis of 3000 CPIs, was SMI = 28.062 + .148 Dominance + .334 Responsibility + .512 Socialization − .317 Good Impression − .174 Communality + .174 Flexibility. The SMI includes scales measuring the internalization of social norms and responsible behaviors along with the capacity for flexible self-direction. In a cross-validation sample of almost 3000 men, the SMI discriminated significantly between "mature" men and incarcerated men, correctly classifying 92.3% of these individuals. In other studies this index discriminated between (a) Italian (Gough, 1966), Japanese (Gough, De Vos, & Mizushima, 1968), and French (Gough & Quintard, 1974) samples of delinquents and nondelinquents with accuracies ranging from 83.2% to 90.3%; (b) cheaters and noncheaters in college examinations (Hetherington & Feldman, 1964); and (c) students nominated as high or low on responsibility by high-school principals (Gough, 1966).

The SMI was originally standardized on men. Subsequently, Gough (1966) reported personality correlates for samples of men and women (students and adults) rated by peers or psychologists. In this second approach to construct validity, high scorers of both sexes were described as dependable, reliable, mature, responsible, and capable; low scorers were described as impulsive, defensive, intolerant, and temperamental. In view of the developmental tasks of adulthood, I expect the SMI to be associated with satisfaction in the marital and family setting and effectiveness at work and in the community.

Because this chapter emphasizes the developmental antecedents of SMI, only those members of the GS and OGS who had Q sorts at early adolescence, late adolescence, and early adulthood (ages 30–38) as well as CPIs at time of middle (40–48) adulthood are included. Of these 125 persons, 36 were OGS men, 38 were OGS women, 21 were GS men, and 30 were GS women, for a total of 57 men and 68 women. Most analyses combine the OGS and GS, but data were analyzed by subsample as well. Any significant subsample differences are reported.

CHARACTERISTICS OF SOCIAL MATURITY SCORES

Table 10.1 presents the means and standard deviations for SMI at the two adult periods and, for comparison, the means and standard deviations of Gough's normative sample of mature men and a sub-

Table 10.1
Means and Standard Deviation of Social Maturity Index

Means and standard deviations	Men	Women
Mean, 30–38 years	49.82	52.54[****]
Standard deviation, 30–38 years	3.73	3.27
Mean, 40–48 years	50.47	51.44[a]
Standard deviation, 40–48 years	3.45	3.26
Mean of Gough socially mature sample	50.76	54.74
Standard deviation	3.52	2.88

[a]Sex difference not significant.
****$p < .001$.

sequent sample of mature college women. The means for our men are similar to that of Gough's male sample, but means for our women are below that for his college women. Educational level is probably the influential factor. OGS and GS women were not, on the average, college graduates, although most had some college.

In his sample of mature men, Gough found that a cutting score of 44 (all those above this number classified as mature and all those below, considered immature) correctly identified 96% of the sample. The same percentage of longitudinal study members (96%) was above the cutting score of 44. The similarity of the longitudinal samples to the normative sample is noteworthy because these study members are above-average in socioeconomic status, IQ, and psychological health (see Chapters 4, 6–8, and 12). Nevertheless, it should be emphasized that these study members, like Gough's mature men, are a well-functioning sample, none of whom is known to have had serious trouble with the law.

In their thirties, women scored significantly higher (.001 level) on the SMI than the men. By the forties, the men's scores had increased slightly (though not significantly) and the women's scores had dropped ($p < .001$). Although the women's scores are still higher than the men's in the forties, the difference is no longer significant.

The correlations between early and middle adult SMI scores were .59 for men and .76 for women, suggesting considerable stability during these adult years. Cross-time correlations (range = .59–.79) for the subsamples are similar. Whatever cultural changes or mid-life crises may have occurred did not result in marked changes in individual variation in this molar variable.

Descriptive comments by clinicians who interviewed the study members in the last follow-up illustrate some of the personal qualities of individuals identified as being high and low on the SMI. To minimize the effects of stylistic differences in interviewers, the comments about men are taken from the same interviewer, and the comments about women are taken from a second interviewer. Identifying information has been deleted.

High-Scoring Man (Interviewer A)

He is a competent, complex man who values both involvement in activities and people, and his own independence. He is an assertive, honest man who does not try to hide his shortcomings or play down the shortcomings of others.... He is undoubtedly highly socially skilled and perceptive. His work revolves about his skill in understanding... others. He is very involved with his family, yet somehow I would not describe him as warm.... In brief, he seems very perceptive and socially effective but somewhat independent and slightly distant from others except his family.

Low-Scoring Man (Interviewer A)

I enjoyed talking to this man and he is likeable, despite his immaturity and intolerance, mainly because of his interpersonal honesty. He is very critical of others, but he sees and describes his own faults as well. In many ways he is more immature and self-centered than many of the subjects I have seen. He rarely has contact with his family and most of his money goes for his own pleasures of wine, women, and song. Nevertheless, he is candid in talking about this. Despite his self-indulgence, he does appear a lonely man who... seems to have few satisfactions that give him lasting pleasure, and he roams around, spending money and looking for fun in a desperate way.... He is an unusual person in the sample.

High-Scoring Woman (Interviewer B)

She is an active, enthusiastic, assertive woman, has meaningful relationships with her family and friends. Her humor is excellent. Needs and impulses seem to be monitored in a healthy way, her outlets for expression are genuinely satisfying and meaningful.

Low-Scoring Woman (Interviewer B)

She strikes me as a woman who... has lived for many years with poor impulse controls. She seems to have achieved more stability in her current stage of life, partly by restricting her environment, repressing painful experiences, and focusing her emotional needs almost exclusively on children.... Her self-destructive tendencies seem to have diminished with age.

SOCIAL MATURITY IN THE ADULT YEARS

To assess the association between SMI and personal and social functioning in everyday life, the SMI at 40–48 was correlated with measures of happiness and satisfaction at home and effectiveness at work and in the community at large. Table 10.2 presents the correlations with demographic variables, for example, intelligence and social status. Table 10.3 presents the associations with clinicians' assessments of both work effectiveness and patterns of family interaction. Table 10.4 presents for men the association with self-ratings of areas of work satisfaction.

These data show SMI to be associated with competence in a variety of areas, assessed by diverse measures, for example, tests (WAIS, Kohlberg moral judgment), clinicians' ratings from interviews, and self-ratings from the IGS questionnaire. For both sexes, SMI is positively correlated with social status achieved in adulthood, but not the social status of the family of origin, with IQ at three ages and with ethical and moral judgment (available for OGS only). SMI is also associated with an absence of problem drinking ($F < .02$ for men and $< .07$ for women), marital satisfaction and adjustment, happy emotional tone of the family, and agreement between parents on child-rearing techniques. No significant correlations exist between SMI at 40–48 and concurrent measures of political preference (see Chapter 15), overall self-rating of job satisfaction, or marital status (single, married, divorced).

Table 10.2

Correlations Between Adult Social Maturity Index and
Indices of Social and Personal Functioning

Variable	Men		Women	
	1958 SMI	1970 SMI	1958 SMI	1970 SMI
Psychological health, 30–38 years	.45****	.35****	.01	.11
Psychological health, 40–48 years	.43****	.42****	.02	.10
Hollingshead SES in childhood (1 = high)	-.10	-.16	-.19**	-.15
Hollingshead SES, 40–48 years (1 = high)	-.49****	-.56****	-.44****	-.48****
IQ at 12	.11	.26**	.27**	.36****
IQ at 18	.26**	.36****	.34****	.41****
IQ at 40–48 years	.32****	.35****	.26**	.41****
Physical health, 30–38 years	.05	.10	-.04	.08
Physical health, 40–48 years (1 = high)	.02	-.28**	.00	-.08
Kohlberg levels of moral judgment, 1968 OGS only, 48 years	.43****	.43****	.26	.28

**$p < .05$.
****$p < .001$.

Table 10.3

Correlations Between Social Maturity Index and Clinicians'
Ratings of Family and Personality

1970 Family and personality ratings	Males 1970 SMI	Females 1970 SMI
Values friendships	.29***	
Job involvement		
High job involvement	.35****	
Job effectiveness	.26***	
Marriage and the family		
Marital adjustment	.38****	.22***
Emotional tone of the family	.30****	.23***
Closeness of bond: subject and spouse	.38****	
Friendliness: subject to spouse	.35****	.21***
Marital satisfaction	.40****	.22***
Marital happiness	.27***	
Congruence of parents on child-rearing	.44****	.23**
Self-satisfaction as parent	.24***	
Satisfaction with spouse as parent	.34****	
Closeness of family	.36****	

**p < .05.
***p < .01.
****p < .001.

The greater number of correlates between SMI and men's functioning suggests that social maturity represents a more influential variable for men. Mid-life SMI is related to psychological health, physical
health, clinicians' assessments of occupational involvement and effectiveness as well as self-assessed areas of satisfaction at work. For men,
then, social maturity as measured here is related to competence as a
worker, a husband, and an individual. It involves an ethical commitment reflected in moral judgment, and it is accompanied by involvement and enjoyment in church activities. Clinicians rate friends as
very important to socially mature men, but the men do not report
greater frequency of seeing friends.

SMI is not associated with as many aspects of women's behavior. It is
correlated with IQ, social status achieved in adulthood, absence of
problem drinking, and satisfaction as a wife and family member. However, it does not have the wide-ranging correlates indicative of
psychological competence in many areas that it does for men. Speculation about the reason for this difference is reserved for a later section
when all the correlates of SMI have been presented.

Table 10.4

Correlations Between Social Maturity Index and
Self-Descriptions of Leisure and Occupational Activities

Activities	Males
Frequency visit friends	$-.24^{**}$
Frequency seeing close friends	$.30^{**}$
Frequency church activities	$.40^{****}$
Enjoyment church activities	$.33^{***}$
Rated satisfaction with:	
Job choice	.22
Level of tension	.19
Degree work involves interests	$.37^{***}$
Opportunity for advancement	.20
Meeting and being with people	$.28^{**}$
Use of abilities	$.28^{**}$
Respect others give job	$.27^{**}$
Freedom to develop ideas	$.38^{***}$
Security of job	.19

(Note: Those with no asterisk are significant at
the .10 level.)
$^{**}p < .05.$
$^{***}p < .01.$
$^{****}p < .001.$

Social Maturity and Adult Q-Sort Descriptions

Examining significant associations with Q-sort data at two adult periods adds to our understanding of the behavioral significance of social maturity (see Table 10.5). For men, SMI in the thirties is correlated (p < .05 level or better) with 41% of concurrent Q-sort items; SMI in the forties is correlated with 43% of concurrent Q-sort items. The corresponding percentages for women are 8% and 10%.

The socially mature man in both early and middle adulthood has many positive qualities: he is dependable, sympathetic, turned to for advice, insightful, ethically consistent, incisive, philsosphically concerned and prides self on objectivity. In addition, he is free of many negative qualities such as irritability, fearfulness, moodiness, basic anxiety, undercontrol, brittle ego defenses. Comparison of the highest correlates at 30–38 years with the highest correlates at 40–48 years suggests that in early adulthood SMI is most closely associated with control of impulses, productivity, and the expression of social concern in warm, nurturant relationships. In middle adulthood social maturity seems to reflect a cognitive approach to life, with an emphasis on advising rather than nurturing others. The change in salience of SMI

Table 10.5

Q-sort Items Predictive of Social Maturity Index
at Two Adult Periods

	Males		Females	
	30–38 Q sorts and SMI	40–48 Q sorts and SMI	30–38 Q sorts and SMI	40–48 Q sorts and SMI
Q-sort items	($N = 49$)	($N = 57$)	($N = 60$)	($N = 68$)
Skeptical		.28**		
Dependable	.51****	.35***		
Giving	.39***			
Appears Intelligent	.29**	.52****		
Uncomfortable with Uncertainty		−.31**		
Somatizes		−.31**		
Protective	.36***			
Thin-skinned	−.33**	−.39***		
Sympathetic	.37***	.34***		
Seeks Reassurance		−.26**		
Feels Life Lacks Meaning		−.30**		
Extrapunitive		−.39***		
Prides Self on Objectivity	.32**	.45****		
Overcontrolled	.33**		.37***	
Productive	.48****			
Arouses Liking	.48****			
Turned To for Advice	.34**	.38***		
Withdraws When Frustrated		−.35***		
Satisfied with Physical Appearance	.42***			
Aware of Impression Created		.34***		
Irritable	−.39***	−.40****		
Warm	.35***			
Negativistic	−.34**			
Deceitful	−.49****			
Thinks Unconventionally			−.29**	
Fearful	−.34**	−.26**		
Moralistic		−.42****		
Evaluates Others' Motivations		.41****		
Brittle Ego Defenses	−.36***	−.43****		
Distrustful	−.36***			
Unpredictable	−.38***	−.37***		
Values Intellectual Matters	.44****	.48****		.28***
Undercontrolled	−.44****	−.35***		

Table 10.5 (*continued*)

Q-sort items	Males 30-38 Q sorts and SMI (N = 49)	Males 40-48 Q sorts and SMI (N = 57)	Females 30-38 Q sorts and SMI (N = 60)	Females 40-48 Q sorts and SMI (N = 68)
Self-Defeating	-.30**	-.45****		
Interesting		.27**		
Insightful	.34**	.30**		
Creates Dependency	-.33**			
Rebellious		-.42****	-.29**	
Socially Perceptive		.51****		
Pushes Limits	-.34**			-.36***
Self-Indulgent	-.50****			
Basically Anxious	-.36***	-.31**		
Bothered by Demands		-.26**		
Ethically Consistent	.43****	.29**		
Ambitious	.32**	.36***	.34***	
Concerned with Adequacy		-.38***		
Eroticizes Situations	-.54****		-.30**	
Satisfied with Self		.35***		
Clear-cut, Consistent Personality	.32**			
Projective	-.43****	-.44****		
Straightforward	.31**			
Feels Victimized	-.29**	-.36***		
Ruminative				-.26**
Interested in Opposite Sex			-.34***	
Physically Attractive	.39***	.29**		
Moody	-.39***	-.45****		
Incisive	.40***	.41****		
Self-Pitying	-.33**			
Repressive		-.30**		
Charming		.28**		
Compares Self to Others		.26**		.27**
Philosophically Concerned	.40***	.45****		
Poised			.27**	.28***
Masculine/Feminine Style				.30***
Expresses Hostility Directly			-.33***	
Verbally Fluent		.33***		
Self-Dramatizing	-.32**			
Does Not Vary Roles				-.38****

**p < .05.
***p < .01.
****p < .001.

correlates suggests that a warm, nurturant orientation is followed by a philosophical, advising attitude. This change conforms to Erikson's speculation that wisdom develops after the capacity to care for and provide for others.

SMI is associated with a smaller number of women's behaviors. The significant correlates do reflect the capacity to control impulses, a central concept of social maturity. The Q-sort descriptions of the socially mature women in their thirties emphasize conventionality. When the women are in their forties and the SMI scores have dropped significantly, conventionality is not a salient aspect of the significant correlates. At both ages the Q-sort correlates suggest that socially mature women are self-assertive; in their thirties, they are ambitious, and in their forties intellectually oriented, assuming a variety of roles.

Changes in Social Maturity Scores in the Adult Years

We have seen that from the thirties to the forties, men's SMI scores increase slightly and women's scores decrease. The change is not significant for men but is for women ($p < .001$), although cross-time correlations of SMI scores (.59 for men and .76 for women) indicate greater individual variability for men. What can we say about the factors producing changes in scores from the mid-thirties to mid-forties? Examination of case materials is helpful.

For men who increased or decreased in SMI by more than a standard deviation, two factors seem salient. First, but perhaps less important, are business improvements (associated with increases in SMI) or difficulties (associated with decreases). For example, one study member reported in his mid-forties follow-up that a business failure at the time of the previous follow-up had colored all his responses in a pessimistic direction. His SMI changed from well below to well above the mean in the 10-year interval.

A second, and more important, factor is experience in the marriage and family setting, as illustrated in case materials on two men who share common characteristics of interest. Each lost a parent in childhood, did well in school, went into a profession, married after a war, and had three children. In their thirties both were involved in their work and had young children. Despite many characteristics in common, they were almost four standard deviations apart on the SMI—both equidistant from the mean. Joe, the man below the mean, spent much time traveling as part of his job, so he had less contact with spouse and children. Jim, the man above the mean, was actively involved with his family despite long working hours. In their forties the two men's scores were within a point of each other, both at about the mean. What happened?

Joe, whose SMI increased, advanced in his profession and ceased traveling. Contact with his family was more extensive, producing some conflicts and requiring adjustments on his part. In response to an interview question about factors making for personal change in the 10-year interval, he cited increased contact with his wife, who was a more social person, and increasing social ease and enjoyment of social situations. Jim, the man whose SMI decreased to a mean level, also advanced in his profession and had a major supervisory role. The rebellion of his teenage children in the late 1960s appeared an important factor in the drop in his score. His sons argued with him, not about the goals of society but about the means to achieve these goals. He had always enjoyed excellent relationships with his wife and was highly emotionally involved with his children. As the children became independent and argued with his world views, he maintained good relationships with them and seemed influenced by their critical social attitudes. "I am in sympathy with their goals, but we argue a lot. I am interested in what they say." This man did not attribute any change in his social attitudes to his children. Nevertheless, I suspect their arguments caused him to become more critical and less accepting of social norms with a consequent decrease in SMI to an average level.

Men's scores also changed with specific family problems. A dramatic drop in score occurred in a man whose teenager was having acute difficulties at the time of the mid-40 follow-up. He reported he was completely stymied and demoralized by the problem. Cases of dramatic change were not numerous, but they serve to highlight the importance of familial factors assessed as significant by statistical analyses as well.

Examination of women's scores reveals increases in SMI in the very few women who had children in the years between 1958 and 1970. If increases in scores are related to the addition of children, then perhaps the decreases in scores of the vast majority of our sample of women are associated with children's growing up and leaving home. Statistical analysis reveals a low but significant correlation ($-.24$, $p < .03$ level) between SMI and age of youngest child. The younger the child, the higher the mother's SMI. As the pressures of child-rearing decrease, women's commitment to social norms and goals appears to decrease. Note, however, that their scores are still above the standardization mean. The comparable correlation between SMI and age of youngest child was not significant for men, although it was in the same direction.

Table 10.6

Prediction of Social Maturity Index at 40-48 from Q-sort
Items by Multiple Regression

Males

Q-sort items	Beta weight	r
Early adolescent core items[a]		
Appears Intelligent	.62****	.39
Pushes Limits	-.52****	-.38
Introspective	-.51****	-.17
Productive	.36***	.48
Fastidious	-.29**	.08
Verbally Fluent	-.28**	.20
Expresses Hostility Directly	.25**	-.08
Moralistic	.22**	.15
Early adolescent interpersonal items[c]		
Changeability of Peer Attachments	-.28**	-.39
Claims Privileges of Adolescence	-.27**	-.38
Late adolescent core items[e]		
Values Intellectual Matters	.71****	.43
Complicates Simple Situations	.47***	.14
Giving	.40***	.15
Concerned with Appearance	.33***	.08
Self-Defensive	.31***	-.03
Aloof	-.29**	-.10
Expresses Hostility Directly	.28**	.01
Compares Self to Others	-.26**	.26
Late adolescent interpersonal items[g]		
Protective of Friends	.43***	.16
Protected by Peers	-.39***	-.17
Competitive with Peers	.35***	.34
Oriented toward Going Steady	.33***	-.30
Compares Self to Others	.35***	.26
Rebellious	-.31***	-.42
Giving	.27***	.21
Self-Indulgent	-.23**	-.26
Productive	-.23**	.09
30-38 items[i]		
Values Intellectual Matters	.84****	.60
Undercontrolled	-.48****	-.33
Deceitful	.45****	-.10
Verbally Fluent	-.40***	.28
Repressive	-.38***	-.32
Gregarious	.23***	.06

Females

Q-sort items	Beta weight	r
Early adolescent core items[b]		
Appears Intelligent	.33***	.4
Values Intellectual Matters	.32***	.4
Accepts Dependency	.28**	.2
Views Self as Causative	-.22**	-.2
Proffers Advice	.22**	.1
Clear-cut, Consistent Personality	.21**	.3
Power-Oriented	.20**	.3
Fastidious	-.17	.2
Early adolescent interpersonal items[d]		
Father Attractive	.41***	.3
Rebellious with Adults	-.35***	-.3
Protected by Peers	-.32***	-.0
Closer to Mother	.25	.4
Selective in Friends	.20	.2
Late adolescent core items[f]		
Appears Intelligent	.56****	.4
Self-Indulgent	.41****	.0
Accepts Dependency	.28**	.3
Favors Status Quo	.26**	.3
Ambitious	.25**	.3
Power-Oriented	.23**	.1
Arouses Nurturance	.23**	.2
Skeptical	-.22**	-.3
Late adolescent interpersonal items[h]		
Covertly Hostile to Adults	-.70****	-.3
Assertive with Peers	.53****	-.0
Family Affectionate	.49****	.4
Considerate of Peers	-.45***	.0
Attention-Getting with Peers	-.44***	-.1
Knowledgeable of Peer Culture	.40***	.2
Condescending with Peers	.12	.1
Concerned with Adequacy	-.30***	-.1
Feels Victimized	-.29***	-.2
Feminine Style	.28***	.3
Productive	-.28***	-.2
Arouses Liking	-.28***	-.0
30-38 items[j]		
Feels Victimized	-.65****	-.3
Values Intellectual Matters	.60****	.3
Moody	.31***	.0
Prides Self on Objectivity	-.29***	-.1
Interested in Opposite Sex	-.28***	-.2
Self-Pitying	.27	-.0
Conventional	.25	.1

Table 10.6 (continued)

Males			Females		
Q-sort items	Beta weight	r	Q-sort items	Beta weight	r
40-48 items[k]			40-48 items[l]		
Appears Intelligent	.47****	.52	Pushes Limits	-.42****	-.36
Satisfied with Self	.38****	.35	Does Not Vary Roles	-.42****	-.38
Protective	-.37***	.06	Compares Self to Others	.35***	.27

[a] $R = .79$****; $R^2 = 62\%$.   [g] $R = .60$****; $R^2 = 36\%$.
[b] $R = .74$****; $R^2 = 55\%$.   [h] $R = .79$****; $R^2 = 62\%$.
[c] $R = .45$***; $R^2 = 20\%$.   [i] $R = .80$****; $R^2 = 64\%$.
[d] $R = .58$****; $R^2 = 34\%$.   [j] $R = .76$****; $R^2 = 58\%$.
[e] $R = .74$****; $R^2 = 55\%$.   [k] $R = .82$****; $R^2 = 67\%$.
[f] $R = .83$****; $R^2 = 69\%$.   [l] $R = .81$****; $R^2 = 66\%$.

**$p < .05$.
***$p < .01$.
****$p < .001$.

The greatest decreases in SMI were seen when teenage offspring had been rebellious and critical of the existing social order. The mothers did not attribute change in themselves to the children, but it did appear that in attempting to adapt to their maturing children, they themselves were changed. These were families in whom, by and large, affectional ties were strong between parents and offspring despite differences of opinion.

In brief, changes in SMI in both men and women appear closely tied to affectional relations and events in the marriage and family. Men's scores may be more variable because occupational experiences, an additional source of change, are a more influential factor. Although SMI predicts a wider array of behaviors and suggests greater changes in social behavior for men in the adult years, it is associated with many aspects of women's behavior as well.

BEHAVIORS PREDICTIVE OF SOCIAL MATURITY

Because the Q-sort items are intercorrelated, precise levels of significance cannot be known. To obtain a more precise assessment of the predictive power of the Q-sort items, prediction of SMI from the Q sort was done by multiple regression. Table 10.6 presents the Q-sort items (at four time periods) that predict SMI at 40-48 in the multiple regression. Predictions from the two adolescent periods were made from both the Core Q sorts and the Interpersonal Q sorts (see Chapter 2 and Appendix A).

SMI in middle age is well predicted by the Core Q-sort items at four time periods, with from 55% to 69% of the variance in SMI accounted for by the relevant items. Of equal importance is the finding that early adolescent assessments of behavior predict SMI at 40–48 as well as concurrent assessments.

In Table 10.6 the correlations of each item with mid-life SMI are presented in the column next to the beta weights to clarify the meaning of each item. Note that some items function as moderator or suppressor variables. For example, in the equation predicting SMI for men at 40–48 from Q items at 30–38, the item Deceitful has a beta weight of .45. Yet the zero-order correlation for this item is −.10.

Also keep in mind the correlations between IQ and SMI at 40–48 (Table 10.2). These range from .26 to .41 and are approximately the same for both sexes. They are not as high as the beta weights of the Q-sort items reflecting intellectual capacity and interest.

Note that the multiple correlations using adult Q-sort items to predict SMI at 40–48 are as high for women as for men. This is of particular interest because the number of significant individual item correlates is smaller for women. Thus, though small in number, the significant correlates are important predictors. The main function of the multiple correlations is to demonstrate that SMI is well predicted by clinicians' assessments of personal and social behavior as early as the junior high-school period.

Adolescent Behaviors Predictive of Social Maturity at 40—48

The early and late adolescent Q-sort items significantly correlated with mid-life SMI are presented in Table 10.7. Men scoring high on SMI in middle age were already socially and psychologically integrated in early adolescence. They were productive, dependable, self-assertive, intellectually able boys with good impulse control and a capacity for nurturance and consideration in interpersonal relations. During late adolescence the predictive items reflect primarily productivity, intellectual competence, and impulse control.

Women who scored high on SMI in their forties were described in early adolescence much as boys were. They were intellectually able and productive persons who could assert themselves in social situations, at the same time respecting the rights of others. They were ambitious and effective. In late adolescence, these women were seen as intellectually competent, psychologically confident persons who accepted themselves and a dependent situation. They set goals for themselves, refused to give up if frustrated, yet accepted the restrictions of the feminine role without undue irritation.

For both sexes at both adolescent periods, intellectual effectiveness, impulse control, and broad interests are significantly predictive of

Table 10.7

Adolescent Q-sort Items Predictive of
Social Maturity Index at 40-48

Q-sort items	Men Early adoles. (N=57)	Men Late adoles. (N=50)	Women Early adoles. (N=68)	Women Late adoles. (N=67)
Skeptical				-.32***
Dependable	.41****	.35**	.30***	
Has Wide Interests	.26**	.36***	.25**	.38****
Giving	.29**			
Fastidious			.26**	.36***
Favors Status Quo	.24*		.33***	
Appears Intelligent	.39***		.41****	.48****
Uncomfortable with Uncertainty		-.24*		
Protective			.21*	
Skilled in Imaginative Play			.21*	
Sympathetic	.24*			
Dependent				.20*
Feels Life Lacks Meaning			-.27**	
Extrapunitive			-.27**	
Prides Self on Objectivity	.28**	.36***	.24**	
Overcontrolled		.23*	.24**	
Productive	.48****	.35**	.36***	
Arouses Liking	.28**			.23*
Turned To for Advice	.24*			
Withdraws When Frustrated		-.31**		-.31***
Aware of Impression Created				.21*
Irritable		-.25*	-.24**	-.35***
Negativistic	-.34***		-.32***	-.40****
Deceitful	-.30**			
Basic Hostility	-.27**			-.33***
Thinks Unconventionally		.24*		
Fearful	-.22*			
Brittle Ego Defenses	-.23*	-.39***	-.22*	-.28**
Distrustful				-.32***
Unpredictable	-.33***		-.24**	-.31***
Values Intellectual Matters	.38***	.43****	.43****	.26**
Assertive	-.28**			
Undercontrolled		-.30**	-.28**	
Self-Defeating	-.33***	-.36***	-.25**	-.28**
Interesting			.23*	
Sensuous			-.33***	
Insightful	.26**			

Table 10.7 (*continued*)

Q-sort items	Men		Women	
	Early adoles. (*N*=57)	Late adoles. (*N*=50)	Early adoles. (*N*=68)	Late adoles. (*N*=67)
Views Self as Causative			$-.27$**	$.20$*
Rebellious	$-.31$**		$-.38$****	$-.39$****
Pushes Limits	$-.37$***		$-.35$***	$-.25$**
Self-Indulgent	$-.25$*	$-.30$**	$-.24$**	
Other Directed	$-.28$**		$-.33$***	
Ambitious			$.30$***	$.33$***
Is Affected	$-.22$*			
Eroticizes Situations	$-.47$****			
Satisfied with Self	$.24$*		$.23$*	
Projective	$-.23$*		$-.22$*	
Straightforward	$.44$****			
Feels Victimized	$-.23$*			$-.41$****
Moody	$-.33$***		$-.26$**	
Comfortable with Decisions	$.29$**			
Cheerful				$.24$**
Communicates Through Nonverbal Behavior			$-.28$**	
Compares Self to Others		$-.26$*		
Philosophically Concerned			$.25$**	
Expresses Hostility Directly				$-.37$***
Values Independence				$-.26$**
Verbally Fluent		$.24$*		$.35$***
Accepting of Self-Dependency			$.23$*	$.32$***

*$p < .10.$
**$p < .05.$
***$p < .01.$
****$p < .001.$

adult SMI. In addition, for both sexes, behavioral qualities often attributed to the opposite sex emerge as predictive. For example, boys who are nurturant and warm in early adolescence and girls who are ambitious, goal-oriented, and confident in late adolescence tend to be socially mature in their forties.

Looking at differences in predictors, one can say that in early adolescence boys who will score high on adult SMI display sympathy, warmth, and general consideration of others. In later adolescence these boys seem characterized by breadth and depth in cognitive development, that is, they accept uncertainty, think unconventionally, and possess objectivity. One can speculate that after boys have gained competence in interpersonal relations, they can turn to an intellectual inquiry of the world about them. The shift in the content of predictive items during adolescence suggests that in the earlier period girls who will be socially mature adults are less bound than other girls by conventional notions of femininity, that is, they are productive, interesting, objective and philosophically concerned. In late adolescence, they become more stereotypically feminine—dependent, more indirectly hostile, uncritical, and conservative—yet they retain their ambition and good humor. The freedom to behave in a nonstereotypic fashion for at least a period in early adolescence appears an important feature in the development of adult social maturity for both men and women.

Correlations of Q sorts at each adolescent period with SMI at 40-48 were computed separately for OGS men, GS men, OGS women, and GS women to assess cohort effects. On variables such as IQ, SES of origin and achieved SES, the two samples of men are very similar, so any differences in results can be attributed largely to cohort. A complicating factor, however, is the small number of GS men. Items may fail to achieve significance solely because of a smaller N. Only the general trend of the differences can be summarized here. The predictive items referring to dependability, productivity, and goal-orientation tend to appear at an earlier time period for OGS than GS men, that is, these items tended to be more salient in early adolescence for OGS men and late adolescence for GS men. One can speculate with Elder (1974) that one of the effects of the Depression on OGS men was to stimulate an earlier assumption of adult behavior. GS men were too young during the Depression to assume adult roles. In general, GS girls tend to be older than OGS girls when they manifest the predictive characteristics. Because these results are similar to those found in the male groups, we can have more confidence in them, but comparisons of OGS and GS women are inconclusive because differences existed in the initial samples. Difference may reflect sample, age, and/or cohort differences. Age seems the more likely source of the difference in mean SMI ($p < .06$) between GS women at 40 and OGS at 48 because the mean of GS women at 40 (52.29) is very close to that of OGS women at 38 (52.09).

To describe familial backgrounds and to focus on peer relationships, Block formulated the Interpersonal Q sort. Three clinicians independently and reliably described study members at early and late adolescence with this instrument. Table 10.8 lists for men and women the items correlated with SMI at 40-48.

The content of the predictive items suggests that socially mature men had as adolescents experienced satisfying relations with both

Table 10.8

Interpersonal Q-sort Items Predictive of
Adult Social Maturity Index

Q-sort items	Men Early adoles. (N=57)	Men Late adoles. (N=50)	Women Early adoles. (N=68)	Women Late adoles. (N=67)
Life Pattern Laid Down by Parent			.32***	
Sees Parents as Happy	.28**		.25**	.25**
Sees Family as Affectionate			.31***	.44****
Sees Family as Interesting	.22*		.22**	.33***
Sees Family as Conflicted	-.22*			-.40****
Respects Parents	.33***		.29**	.38****
Sees Parents as Fair			.31***	.31***
Sees Mother as Respected Woman	.27**			.22**
Has Crush on Adults		.26*	.25**	
Has Appropriate Relations with Adults	.24*		.26**	
Claims Privileges of Adolescence	-.36***		-.30***	
Covertly Hostile to Adults				-.38****
Sees Father as Attractive Person			.33***	.26**
Sees Father as Respected Person				.31***
Rebellious with Adults	-.26**		-.37***	-.35***
Sees Mother as Attractive Person	.28**			.40****
Is Passive with Adults				-.33***
Cool with Adults				-.33***
Thinks Parents Restrained Him/Her				-.26**
Sees Parents as Old-Fashioned			-.28**	-.24**
Thinks Parents Uninterested in Him/Her				-.43****
Sees Parents as Consistent			.26**	.25**
Thinks Parents Single Him/Her Out	-.24*			
Candid with Peers	.31**			
Poised with Peers	.21*			
Competitive with Peers		.34**		
Seeks Attention of Peers	-.24*		-.30***	
Adult Oriented			.30***	
Accepts Peer Value System			-.22**	
Judgmental of Peers			-.29**	
Liked by Peers	.27**			
Expresses Hostility Directly			-.24**	-.36***
Is a Fall-Guy	-.27**			-.34***
Knows Peer Culture Well				.22**
Fantasizes about Opposite Sex	-.30**			
Changeable Peer Attachments	-.36***			-.22**

$*p < .10.$
$**p < .05.$
$***p < .01.$
$****p < .001.$

260

adults and peers. They viewed their parents as happy, interesting persons whom they could respect, and they had continuing relations with peers who liked them. Socially mature women had regarded their families as happy, affectionate, and interesting, particularly in late adolescence when alienation and distance are often characteristic of parent–offspring relations. They saw their parents as warm individuals who were consistent and fair with them. They were drawn to positive relationships with adults; in fact, all but four of the correlated items for late adolescence refer to interactions with adults. Girls who developed into socially mature women were knowledgeable about the peer culture and attached to friends, but they maintained their own values. In general, boys and girls who later were described as socially mature adults appeared to develop in families where parents and children regarded each other positively. These positive modes of interaction generalized to interactions with other adults among girls and to peer relationships among boys. Salient dimensions here appear to be respect and self-esteem. Parents were happy, presumably satisfied persons who stimulated the same qualities in their children, who respected them. For girls, parental affection was predictive, particularly in late adolescence, but the more salient theme was a parent–offspring relationship characterized by respect and trust in both parties. There is some suggestion that the parent of the opposite sex was particularly important.

SUMMARY

Adult social maturity, as defined here, has important behavioral antecedents in adolescence. Boys and girls who develop into socially mature adults are described as productive, dependable persons with self-esteem and good self-control. Those persons especially skilled and perceptive in interpersonal relations may be particularly mature in the mid-thirties, whereas those with heightened intellectual awareness and sensitivity may express greater maturity in their mid-forties. For both men and women, social maturity seems enhanced by early freedom to develop qualities often associated with the opposite sex. Events that encourage early independence may stimulate the development of social maturity. The capacity for adult social maturity appears to be facilitated by familial relationships in which parents and children regard themselves and each other positively; the parent of the opposite sex may be a more salient influence in the development of social maturity. Such maturity, however, appears to be a more dynamic force in the functioning of men than of women.

Summary of Sex Differences

Here I summarize sex differences that have emerged in the antecedents and correlates of the SMI and speculate about them. Sex differences do not occur in the long-term predictability of SMI nor in the kinds of early experiences that predict adult SMI. Differences emerge primarily in the number of significant correlations between SMI and personal-social effectiveness in adulthood. For men, SMI is highly correlated with effectiveness in many areas—effectiveness as an individual, husband, family man, and worker. For women, SMI is correlated with effectiveness as an individual, wife, and mother, but not to such a high degree.

The salient role of social maturity in understanding men's general effectiveness in middle age draws attention to cultural prescriptions that may be a source of difficulty for them. Males in this sample matured in an era when achievement and striving were highly encouraged. For some men these qualities were encouraged early because of the Depression. In the cultural context of an emphasis on independence and assertiveness, men who were able to harmonize both instrumental productivity and adaptability to others' needs were effective as adult workers, family members, and individuals. The capacity to integrate diverse behaviors of assertiveness and adaptability is associated with physical as well as psychological well-being. Because optimal functioning for men appears to require a synthesis of behaviors, some of which are not culturally prescribed, we perhaps need to socialize boys more strongly than we do to get along with others and to harmonize assertive drives. Far from decreasing effectiveness, a union of the assertive with the adaptive elements of personality leads to greater capacity for achievement.

Social norms strongly encourage women to orient their behavior to other people's needs and wishes. Because the average woman is well socialized, perhaps too conforming to social norms (Bronfenbrenner, 1961; Block in collaboration with Haan, 1971), SMI does not relate to as many facets of women's behavior.

As noted earlier, the adolescent personality characteristics predicting adult SMI are similar for boys and girls. However, there is a suggestion in the data that girls are socialized in adult–child relationships and boys in peer-group relations.

The results also suggest a different life trajectory for men and women with respect to social maturity. We have no test of social maturity during adolescence. However, socially mature men and women are described by adolescent Q-sorts as manifesting good impulse control, competence, self-direction, and enjoyment of others. In the thirties, the childbearing and child-rearing years, women's SMI scores were significantly higher than men's. Men's scores increase between the thirties and forties, perhaps because of close relationships with their families of procreation. By the forties, when their children are leaving home and women face an "empty nest," SMI scores of women drop significantly, although their mean is still higher than that for men. By the forties, men score similarly because both stress individual goals when the children are grown.

Gutmann (1975) speculates that the task of parenting in young and middle adulthood intensifies sex differences in personality. Before marriage, both sexes are allowed some freedom in expressing characteristics of the opposite sex. Girls can be tomboys, and boys can escape at times to lazy, carefree behavior. With marriage and parenthood, sex differences are heightened to meet the needs of young children. According to Gutmann, society has evolved so that men's role is to provide physical sustenance and women's role is to provide emotional sustenance. Freed from parenting roles, both men and women can express aspects of their personalities they suppressed in the parenting period. Thus, they become more similar in personality.

Data on SMI support these speculations. Women's scores are correlated with the age of the youngest child, and they score significantly higher than men while they are rearing children. As children grow up and leave home, men and women become more similar with respect to SMI. One may speculate that in their fifties, both men and women will score at the mid-point, and that as women in their late fifties and sixties take responsibility for heading households, their scores may decline to the level of men's scores when in their thirties. As men withdraw energy from the competitive world of work, their scores may increase.

DISCUSSION

Socially mature men and women have established ways of life that are valued in contemporary society. They achieved high social status in adulthood, marriages are happy, family life is congenial, and alcohol abuse is not a problem. The men are satisfied at work and enjoy good physical health.

This study indicates that social maturity in adulthood is preceded by self-control, responsibility, and self-direction in adolescence. The continuity in these behaviors over a 30- to 40-year period is impressive and relevant to current controversy about the rules of traits and situations in personality (Mischel, 1968, 1969; Block, 1977).

How do we account for stability of behavior over a long period that includes change in role from child to adult and the experience of many important social and personal events? We can speculate that childhood experiences with other persons, particularly parents, result in the development of modes of interpersonal behavior, ways of responding to people (both adults and peers), that are stable despite changes in the specific behaviors. That is, interpersonal behavior in childhood can be characterized, in part, as reflecting trust, mutual respect, and self-esteem regardless of whether one is interacting with adults on whom one is dependent or with peers in a cooperative venture. In adulthood, such dimensions as respect, trust, and enjoyment are still important in interpersonal relations, although the individual is now a self-sustaining adult and nurturing parent. It is the mode of interpersonal behavior or the process that is stable over time, regardless of the actual role occupied.

An alternative explanation for behavioral stability draws on Erikson's theory of developmental stages. By early adolescence, boys and girls have met the early tasks of consolidating trust, autonomy, initiative, and industry and are well along in fashioning a sense of identity. How one resolves these early dilemmas appears predictive of how one will resolve the problems of intimacy and generativity in adulthood. If the balance of experiences is on the positive side in the early years, then individuals seem able to establish intimate personal ties and engage in generative activity in adulthood.

Longitudinal data on the patterns of familial interaction that characterize the socially mature adult are reminiscent of Mead's interpretations of the development of the self. Mead (1934) emphasized the social origin of the self; the individual learns to regard himself as others have responded to him. Children who will be socially mature adults, and appear to have a strong sense of self, perceive their parents as self-confident persons who foster trust and respect in their children, who, in turn, are self-confident, trusting, and respecting persons.

Not only are family experiences in childhood important in establishing the qualities associated with social maturity, but also family experiences and close affectional ties in adulthood are important influences on social maturity. Although men's work experiences are significant factors as well, impressions from the case material suggest family experiences are more salient.

In a critical examination of trends in personality theory and research, Sampson (1977) develops the position that psychologists have emphasized individualism and independence as admirable qualities to be achieved by individuals and understood by scientists. He suggests that such an emphasis may have to change if we are to live successfully in a world where limits and constraints abound and cooperation is necessary for survival. He believes psychology should help refocus society on the value of interdependence and the ties that bind people together. On the theoretical level he looks for conceptualizations that touch on the work of such earlier theorists as Lewin and Mead. At the methodological level he looks for research techniques that permit observation of behaviors important in interdependence. The concept of social maturity and the CPI technique of measurement provide one response to Sampson's suggestions.

Sampson cites research suggesting that self-esteem and morale are associated with independence and self-assertiveness, and he relinquishes these positive benefits reluctantly. Research on social maturity suggests we need not give up these benefits. Self-esteem, good morale, and effective functioning accompany the capacity to adapt to limitations.

Part III
INTERPERSONAL DIMENSIONS: FAMILY AND SOCIETY

11

Married Lives: Longitudinal Perspectives on Marriage

ARLENE SKOLNICK

Despite rising divorce rates and changing attitudes, marriage continues to occupy a central place in the lives of most persons. The vast majority of Americans—over 95%—marry at least once, and most who divorce eventually remarry. Both the popularity of marriage and its fragility reflect the peculiar place of marriage in American culture. As Goode (1977) observes, "No other society has asked so much of marriage as ours"—no other culture has entertained the "peculiar faith" that the purpose of marriage is to make a couple happy.

Marriage may not guarantee happiness, but intimate relationships seem the key to overall morale. Large-scale surveys find married people, especially men, higher in psychological well-being than the unmarried (Bradburn, 1969; Campbell, Converse, & Rogers, 1976; Freedman, 1978). A study of links between marital status, life stress, and depression concluded that marriage protects people from the full impact of external strains; in the absence of alternative relations providing similar functions, it remains a surprisingly stable institution (Pearlin & Johnson, 1977).

Rapid changes in sexual behavior, sex roles, and family life have awakened new interest in marriage and couple relationships for both social scientists and the general public. A growing interest in the bonds that hold people together is shown by the recent proliferation of studies of attraction and love.

Our longitudinal samples permit study of marriages in a "normal" population in greater depth and over a wider span of time than is

269

usually possible. Using both quantiative and qualitative approaches, I examine in this chapter the kinds of personal and social characteristics associated with differing degrees of satisfaction in marriage. The chapter also asks what are the specific ways in which emotionally satisfying marriages differ from less satisfactory ones. Finally, it examines how the marriages of the study participants changed over a decade. Does time take an inevitable toll on couple relationships as some studies (Blood & Wolfe, 1960; Pineo, 1961) seem to show? Or do marriages, like fine wine, improve with age, as other studies (Rollins & Feldman, 1970) suggest?

ISSUES IN THE STUDY OF MARITAL SATISFACTION

Emotional quality—variously defined as "adjustment," "satisfaction," or "happiness"—is the most common dependent variable in the large literature on marriage. Nevertheless, we know little about why marriage leads to emotional satisfaction for some couples and for others difficulty and dissolution. The best established correlates of marital satisfaction are demographic: occupational status, income and educational level, religious participation, and age at marriage. Yet even such well-established associations are not supported by some well-controlled studies (Glenn & Weaver, 1978). Similarly, certain aspects of childhood experience are reported to have important consequences for marital relationships: growing up in a broken home, or in an urban rather than a rural community, and the father's education. In a recent national survey, however, none of these factors was significantly correlated with satisfaction in marriage (Campbell et al., 1976).

Further, concepts and methods used in studies of marital adjustment have received persistent and widespread criticism (Glenn & Weaver, 1978; Hicks & Platt, 1970). Some researchers argue that the concepts of marital adjustment, happiness, success, and satisfaction are hopelessly vague, undefinable and value-laden and, therefore, should be abandoned (Lively, 1969). Even a study with the best measures, samples, and controls may fail to capture what actually goes on in that elusive scene, the psychological interior of the family. Nevertheless, marital satisfaction is too significant in real life to be ignored by researchers, so studies of marital adjustment continue, augmented by studies of unmarried couples living together. To avoid conceptual confusion, many recent studies have simply used subjective satisfaction as the measure of marital adjustment. However, self-report data present problems. People may be unwilling to admit dissatisfaction with their marriages, even to themselves. Surveys of self-reported marital dis-satisfaction find that most people rate themselves as happy, with few at the extreme negative end of the distribution. Self-reports are almost never validated against other criteria (Hicks & Platt, 1970).

Our longitudinal data offer an opportunity to explore marriage in ways not usually possible. For example, although interviews with the participants are a form of self-report, they are not so limited or one-dimensional as the paper and pencil questionnaire items usually employed. Our trained clinical interviewers did not translate self-reports directly into scores, but instead considered the context of a person's statements. For example, if an obviously depressed and angry person reported being perfectly delighted with the spouse and marriage, the interviewer's rating modified that self-assessment.

Social scientists who study marriage rarely can examine the early lives of their respondents. Our data permit exploration of the associa-tion among marital outcomes, early experience, and personality. In addition, interviews with each spouse avoid the problem of studying marriage from only wives' reports (Safilios-Rothschild, 1969).

THE SOCIAL CONTEXT

Let us look first at the historical context in which the study members prepared for and entered marriage. The economic crisis of the 1930s had a sharp impact on marriage and fertility (Chapter 1). Average age at marriage rose, as did the proportion of the population who never married. Birthrates were low during this period, and lifetime childlessness approached 20% (Glick, 1975). During the post-World War II economic boom, the United States entered the period of greatest domesticity in its history. Age at marriage reached an historic low, and the birth rate an all-time high. Only 4% of the marriageable popula-tion remained single. Both our cohorts came of marital age during the post-war era of "togetherness" and the "feminine mystique." In their middle years they encountered marked changes in ideas and behavior associated with women's liberation, sexual revolution, and the youth counterculture.

Many social scientists now regard family life after World War II as a historical oddity brought about by a particular set of economic, de-mographic, and historical circumstances (Ryder, 1974). Our longitudi-nal subjects, however, are products of the post-war era of "together-ness." Both adult interviews reveal a profound commitment to family life. Whereas many of today's young marrieds see the focus of marriage as the relationship between spouses, our study members see marriage as part of a larger family picture. For both men and women, the enjoyment of parenthood ranks as the most salient aspect of the marital relationship.

Central tendencies, however, do not do justice to the great variation in marital relationships among our participants. In any cohort or any historical era some persons follow the dominant life-style; others continue patterns of a previous era; and others adopt unusual life-styles that may later become widespread.

DATA BASE

The major sources of information about the study members' marriages are interviews conducted during the two adult follow-ups (Chapter 2) and factual information in the files. Study members and their spouses were interviewed separately, usually by different interviewers. The 1958 interview lasted approximately 12 hours, whereas the IGS interviews averaged about 3 hours. After the interviews were completed, the interviewers rated each participant on a number of variables using a 5-point scale. Five variables related to marriage: marital adjustment, closeness, hostility, satisfaction, and congruence in child-rearing. Transcripts of the interviews were rated by additional judges (average correlation between raters, .79). In addition, participants rated their own marital satisfaction on IGS I questionnaires and in a 1964 mailing.

Because the interviews had to cover many issues besides marriage, the nature of marital relationships was not probed as deeply as would have been possible had more time been available. Furthermore, in the interests of keeping the participants comfortable with the interview and thus encouraging their future cooperation, sexual relationships were treated more gingerly and, hence, more superficially, than other aspects of marriage. Finally, the data do not include observations of the spouses in face-to-face interactions.

Overview of Marital Careers of Study Members

In 1979, information about current marital status was available for 232 members of GS and OGS (see Table 11.1). Six women and five men never married. Of the rest, 164 (75%) were married to their original spouses; 43 (19%) had been divorced. Of these, 28 had remarried. Mean age at marriage was 21.7 for women and 24 for men. Hence, at the time

Table 11.1

Marital Histories of Longitudinal Study Members
As of Spring 1979

Marital status	OGS		GS		Total
	Male	Female	Male	Female	
Never married	0	1	5	5	11
Still in first marriage	36	29	41	58	164
Total divorced	6	11	13	13	43
Divorced with one remarriage	(5)	(5)	(8)	(7)	(25)
2 or more remarriages	(0)	(2)	(2)	(0)	(4)
Widowed	1	9	1	3	14
Total	43	50	60	79	232
Divorced (%)	14	22	22	16	
Median number of children	2.84	2.47	2.63	3.03	

of the IGS follow-up, GS men and women had been married an average of 16 and 18 years, respectively, and OGS men and women, 24 and 27 years, respectively. Divorce rates varied somewhat. OGS men and GS women had lower rates (14% and 16%) than OGS women and GS men (each 22%). All these are lower than the national rate—about 25% for 15 years of marriage (McCarthy, 1978). This rather high degree of marital stability may reflect our study members' relatively high socioeconomic status and their tendency to social conservatism—two traits often found to be correlated with marital stability.

Assessing Marital Satisfaction

As described previously, the marital satisfaction scores used here are based on ratings made by the interviewer and at least one other rater. As also noted, these ratings differ from those in other studies in that they are the assessments of trained observers rather than simple self-ratings. One unusual feature of the data is the possibility of comparing expert ratings with self-reports. In addition, evaluations by husbands and wives can be compared. Table 11.2 presents correlations between staff ratings and self-ratings of marital satisfaction for the same follow-up. Agreement is fairly strong; indeed, these levels would be considered acceptable agreement between two expert raters.

Table 11.2 also reveals that for men, all five aspects of marriage, as judged by the raters, are significantly correlated with self-ratings of marital satisfaction, whereas for women the different aspects of marriage are more loosely linked. Thus, women's satisfaction with their marriages does not seem to depend on emotional closeness, nor on

Table 11.2

Correlations between Self and Expert
Ratings of Marital Satisfaction

Factors used for evaluating	Female	Male
Marital adjustment	.52****	.59****
Closeness	.14	.34***
Hostility	.48****	.63****
Satisfaction	.63****	.58****
Congruence in reference to child-rearing	.43****	.52****

***p < .01.
****p < .001.

whether the spouses agree in child-rearing matters. This finding is in accord with other work suggesting that women, because of economic dependence on their husbands, do more of the adapting or "emotional work" in marriage (Bernard, 1973; Tharp, 1963).

How well did the spouses agree? Although the correlations are statistically significant—.36 for the marital adjustment rating and .31 for marital satisfaction—these are lower than the agreement between raters and each of the spouses. The relatively low level of agreement between spouses lends support to Bernard's (1973) notion that every marriage is two different marriages—the husband's and the wife's.

ANTECEDENTS AND CORRELATES
OF MARITAL SATISFACTION

Marital satisfaction is approached in three different ways. First, the effects of some variables previously found to correlate with marital satisfaction are examined. Then the contribution of personality factors to marital satisfaction among the currently married study members is discussed. Finally comes the issue of what personality factors, at what time periods, differentiate three groups: (a) those still in their first marriages who have high marital satisfaction, (b) those still in their first marriage who have low marital satisfaction and (c) those who have been divorced.

Demographic and Social Correlates of Marital Satisfaction

The sample includes all GS and OGS members with marital satisfaction ratings at the IGS follow-up (1969-1970), namely, 88 women and

83 men. Marital satisfaction scores did not differ significantly among the four subgroups (two sexes × two samples), so GS and OGS were pooled. However, the sexes were analyzed separately because associations between satisfaction and other variables do differ between the sexes.

Table 11.3 presents Pearsonian correlations between marital satisfaction and a number of social and demographic variables that have often been found to correlate with self-reported marital satisfaction, for

Table 11.3

Correlations between Socioeconomic Variables
and Marital Satisfaction

Socioeconomic variables	Men	Women
Age at first marriage	.22**	.30****
Age at current marriage	.01	.07
Adult church attendance[a]	.20**	.08
Childhood church attendance	.13	.00
Number of marriages	.18**	-.18**
Wife's employment[b]	.18*	.01
Life course stage[c]	.02	.05
Father's education[d]	.18**	.06
Father's occupation[e]	.13	.24***
Father's SES[f]	.19**	.20**
Member's current occupation	.33****	.15
Spouse's current occupation	.23**	.12
Education - self	.21**	.18**
Spouse's education	.20**	.21**
Member's current SES[g]	.32****	.23***
Spouse's current SES	.27****	.16

[a]Church attendance was reported on a scale of 1-4: 1 = never; 4 = regular.
[b]Wife's employment was treated as a dummy variable: 1 = not currently employed; 2 = currently employed.
[c]Age of youngest child in the home determined life course stage: (1) 1-5, (2) 6-12, (3) 13-17, (4) 18-21, (5) 22 or over, (6) "empty nest" - all children away from home.
[d]Education was scored on a 7-point scale: 1 = under 7 years; 7 = post and college professional training. Correlations based on reflected scores.
[e]Occupation was scored on a 7-point scale: 1 = unskilled laborer; 7 = high executives and major professionals. Correlations are based on reflected scores.
[f]Father's SES (socioeconomic status) measured by the Hollingshead index based on both education and occupation. On both dimensions, scores range from 1-7 (see footnotes d and e). Occupational rank is weighted by a factor of 7; education by a factor of 4. The range of total scores is divided into five status categories.
[g]Current SES for study members and their spouses is based on the two Hollingshead factor index scores before conversion into five categories. The range of scores is from 11-77.
*p < .10.
**p < .05.
***p < .01.
****p < .001.

example, occupational and educational status, age at marriage and length of marriage, and stage of the family life cycle. Although 11 of the 22 variables are significant ($p < .05$ or better) for men and 7 for women, the coefficients are modest.

The strongest correlate of marital satisfaction in men is current occupational status ($r = .33$). Other variables reaching significance, but with lower rs, are: age at first marriage, adult church attendance, wife's education and occupation. For women the strongest correlate of current marital satisfaction is age at marriage. Both fathers' and husbands' occupational and social status are also correlated with marital satisfaction. (All the associations just cited are positive, e.g., later marriage is associated with higher marital satisfaction.) Note that neither length of marriage—as indicated by age at current marriage—nor stage of the family life cycle is significantly associated with marital satisfaction.

Many of the variables in Table 11.3 are correlated. A multiple-regression analysis shows the independent contribution of each variable to marital satisfaction. For men, current occupation is the most influential variable, accounting for 20% of the variance in marital satisfaction. Age at marriage emerges as the most influential variable for women, accounting for 8% of the variance. Father's socioeconomic status accounts for an additional 4%.

The fairly strong association of male occupational status with marital satisfaction, also noted in other studies, may arise because the higher standard of living at upper income levels promotes contentment, whereas economic problems at the lower income levels produce tensions. Another related reason is that men with higher incomes are more likely to enjoy their work than the poorly paid.

Two other points are noteworthy. First, the husband's occupation is more highly correlated with his own satisfaction than with his wife's. Second, male occupational status is not correlated with self-reports of marital satisfaction for either husbands or wives (see also Chapter 13). Perhaps interviewers are better able to discriminate among levels of satisfaction than are the study members themselves. On the other hand, interviewers may tend to view higher-status men as more satisfied with their marriages than they actually are.

The finding that age at marriage is a strong correlate of marital satisfaction in women also agrees with most previous research. Early marriage is associated with growing up in lower-class families; within the middle class it is associated with emotional difficulties in the home. Early marriage is likely to interfere with a woman's education, and women who marry early are also less likely than women who go to college to meet and marry occupationally successful men.

One puzzling finding in Table 11.3 concerns the correlation between the number of marriages and current marital satisfaction: it is positive for men, negative for women. Although there is little evidence of such a sex difference in the literature on remarriage, it does appear that women are at a greater disadvantage relative to men in the remarriage market than in the first marriage market (Glick, 1980), and therefore women may derive less satisfaction from remarriage than men.

Marital Satisfaction and Personality: The Issue of Complementarity

Surprisingly few firmly established findings exist about the influence of psychological factors on the quality of the marital relationship. Some studies (e.g., Dean, 1966, 1968; Murstein & Glaudin, 1966) support the commonsense notion that "good" personality traits such as stability, adaptability, and flexibility correlate with marital happiness. One difficulty with these studies is that both the personality and the marital factors were assessed at the same time, leaving the direction of causality unclear: were the personality traits the forerunners or the outcome of the marital relationship?

The greatest interest in personality as a variable in marriage has centered around the concept of complementarity, that is, is the basis of mate selection and marital satisfaction that "opposites attract?" Most research has found either no relationship or similarity, rather than complementarity (Barry, 1970; Meyer & Pepper, 1977; Tharp, 1963).

The rich data on the personalities of our study members make it possible to look at the patterns of spouses' traits as well as the association between individual personality and marital satisfaction. The principle measures of personality are items from the Q sorts and the six dimensions yielded by PARAFAC analysis of Q sorts at four age periods (Chapter 5).

Let us begin our look at the evidence for complementarity in the patterning of husbands' and wives' personalities by comparing spouses' scores on the 100 items on the Q sort at IGS (at about 40 for GS and 48 for OGS).The results yield little support for the concept of complementarity but a good deal for similarity. On 17 of the 100 items, spouse correlations were significantly positive ($p < .05$ or better). The items seem to fall into several categories: cognitive capacity and style (Appears Intelligent, Has Wide Interests, Is Skeptical, Thinks Unconventionally); social character (Is Gregarious, Dependable, Giving, Calm); adaptive or coping style (Is Self-defensive, Feels Victimized); and hedonism (Is Self-indulgent, Sensuous, Eroticizes).

Only two items are significant in a negative direction (and with a low r). These are: Warmth ($r = -.14$; $p < .04$) and Deceitful ($r = -.16$; $p < .02$). Given the size and number of correlations indicating similarity between husbands and wives, this study must be added to those failing to support an hypothesis of complementarity.

The effects of degree of overall similarity on marital adjustment were also explored. Q-sort profiles of 163 husbands and wives were correlated. These within-couple profile correlations yield r values ranging from $-.42$ to $+.80$. Marital satisfaction scores for the 20 couples most highly correlated in a positive direction were compared with the 20 least similar couples via t-tests. The difference in satisfaction, in favor of the similar couples, was significant at better than the .001 level (one-tailed test). Thus, the hypothesis that personality likeness is associated with greater marital satisfaction is strongly supported.

Marital Satisfaction and Individual Personality

The main data for this analysis are scores on the six independent PARAFAC components (Chapter 5). Because only members with Q sorts for all time periods were included in PARAFAC procedures, N here is somewhat smaller (overall $N = 136$, 73 women and 63 men) than in the other analyses reported in this chapter. Several relevant findings about PARAFAC scores should be kept in mind. First, the GS and OGS do not differ significantly in PARAFAC scores. Second, the PARAFAC dimensions, with one exception, appear to be "class fair"— that is, socioeconomic status is not strongly associated with either the absolute levels or the developmental paths of these dimensions. The one exception is Cognitively Invested, which is consistently and positively associated with socioeconomic status (SES) measures.

Are these personality dimensions associated with marital satisfaction? The first step was to determine one time period at which the PARAFAC scores, taken together, had the greatest impact on marital satisfaction. A step-wise multiple regression, in which current SES for men was entered into the equation first, was done to control for the effects of social class. Women's current and childhood SES and men's childhood SES were not used because each explained less than 1% of the variance in marital satisfaction. PARAFAC variables were entered in a reverse temporal order, beginning with middle adulthood, concurrent with the marital satisfaction scores, and followed by early adult-hood, senior high-school, and junior high-school scores.

As shown in Table 11.4, concurrent PARAFAC scores had the strongest association with marital satisfaction scores for both men and women (overall F, $p < .001$ for both). For men, current social class accounted for 20% of the variance in marital satisfaction and the PARAFAC variables an additional 24%. For the women concurrent PARAFAC scores accounted for 37% of the variance.

Controlling for PARAFAC scores in middle adulthood (and SES in men), the later adolescent PARAFAC scores were predictive of later marital satisfaction in women, accounting for 16% of the variance. None of the earlier male scores was strongly associated with marital satisfaction in middle adulthood.

A similar step-wise multiple regression was used to examine the contribution made by each of the particular PARAFAC dimensions, summed across the four time periods. For males, with social class controlled, Self-Confidence has the strongest association with marital satisfaction, accounting for 14% of the variance, with Nurturant/Hostile the next strongest, accounting for 10% of the variation. Other PARAFAC dimensions make no significant contributions to the regression equation. For women, Nurturant/Hostile (r^2 change = 23%) is the variable most strongly associated with marital satisfaction, followed by Self-Confident (r^2 change = 15%), and Under/Overcontrolled,

Table 11.4

Stepwise Regression of PARAFAC Scores on Marital Satisfaction

Variable	Males ($N = 58$)[a] R^2 change	Variable	Females ($N = 60$)[b] R^2 change
Time period		Time period	
SES	.196		
Middle adulthood	.243	Middle adulthood	.365
Early adulthood	.041	Early adulthood	.052
Later adolescence	.041	Later adolescence	.155
Early adolescence	.087	Early adolescence	.038
PARAFAC factors		PARAFAC factors	
Self-Confident	.196	Nurturant/Hostile	.228
Nurturant/Hostile	.144	Self-Confident	.148
Under/Overcontrolled, Heterosexual	.104	Under/Overcontrolled, Heterosexual	.124
Cognitively Invested	.046	Emotionally Under/Overcontrolled	.040
Open/Closed to Self	.034	Open/Closed to Self	.047
Emotionally Under/Overcontrolled	.017	Cognitively Invested	.023

[a] Overall $F = 1.99$, $p < .05$; multiple $R = .78$; $R^2 = .61$
[b] Overall $F = 2.28$, $p < .05$; multiple $R = .78$; $R^2 = .61$

Heterosexual (r^2 change = 12%). Other dimensions do not contribute significantly to the equation.

In summary, there is a substantial association between personality and marital satisfaction, especially when measured concurrently. Note that the strongest associations within each sex are for dimensions stereotypically associated with that sex: Self-Confident in men and Nurturant in women; on the other hand, the cross-sex characteristic was for both sexes the next most strongly related to marital satisfaction. This finding seems in line with traditional views of sex roles within marriage—men being the instrumental partners, women the expressive (Parsons & Bales, 1955). It suggests that marital satisfaction is greatest when the demands of marital roles are in harmony with one's personality traits. Association between self-confidence and marital satisfaction in men is also in accord with Barry's (1970) suggestion that secure self-identity in the husband is the key to marital satisfaction. Such a finding, however, might not be replicated in cohorts who came of age in an era of less stereotyped sex roles.

The fact that concurrent marriage and personality scores are most strongly correlated raises certain questions about these findings, however. On the one hand, because these personality dimensions do show change as well as continuity over time (Chapter 5), it is not surprising that marital satisfaction at a particular time is most closely linked with personality at that time. On the other hand, because both the personality ratings and the marital satisfaction scores are based on ratings of the same interviews, it is possible that the correlations represent raters' preconceptions about what kinds of personality factors go with what levels of marital satisfaction. Although this explanation cannot be entirely ruled out, there are reasons to doubt it. First, the women's adolescent personality scores are predictive of adult marital satisfaction. If halo effects were operating, they were doing so only for men. Second, if halo affected the judging process, why were some dimensions affected and not others, that is, self-confidence and nurturance but not openness to self or emotional under and overcontrol? Nevertheless, the issue cannot be decisively answered unless marital satisfaction is assessed by raters with no knowledge of the participants' personalities—a rather difficult situation to imagine.

California Personality Inventory Results

An independent source of information on the personalities of study members is the CPI administered at early and middle adulthood (Chapter 10). Although CPI scores also offer an opportunity to check

Q-sort findings, they do not directly correspond to Q-sort items or PARAFAC dimensions.

For women, marital satisfaction at middle adulthood correlates (p < .05 or better) with 4 of the 18 regular scales: Socialization (r = .29), Self-Control (r = .20), Achievement via Conformity (r = .17) and Achievement via Independence (r = .22). Note that the femininity scale and marital satisfaction are not correlated.

For men, 13 of the 18 scale scores correlate significantly with marital satisfaction: Dominance (r = .32), Capacity for Status (r = .27), Sociability (r = .40), Social Presence (r = .21), Sense of Well-being (r = .43), Responsibility (r = .29), Socialization (r = .57), Self-Control (r = .39), Tolerance of Ambiguity (r = .35), Good Impression (r = .50), Achievement via Conformity (r = .32), Psychological Minded (r = .33), Flexible (r = .24).

These results are consistent with the PARAFAC findings concerning the link between marital satisfaction and nurturance in women and self-confidence in men. In addition, they suggest that social maturity and achievement orientation are associated with satisfaction in marriage. Note, however, that although both types of achievement are related to marital satisfaction in women, only achievement via conformity is related in men.

Stability versus Satisfaction

Many researchers have used stability as an index of marital satisfaction, but marriages may be stable without being satisfactory. A family may live together, each member fulfilling instrumental obligations to the others but not emotional ones (Goode, 1976). Why such marriages persist is a major question in need of research attention. One approach is to ask whether the divorced, the satisfactorily married and the unhappily married differ in personality.

The sample for the following analysis consists of all GS and OGS members who had ever been divorced, regardless of current marital status (N = 13 men, 18 women) and all those who were still married to the original spouses. The latter group was divided at the mean on scores of marital satisfaction at middle adulthood into a high satisfaction group (30 men, 22 women) and a low to moderate satisfaction group (18 men, 21 women).

PARAFAC scores for the three groups were compared using analysis of variance for repeated measures. This method enables us to examine (*a*) whether the three groups differ on the six PARAFAC dimensions when all four periods of measurement are considered as one, (*b*) whether the three groups show different developmental trends for the PARAFAC components, and (c) whether sex differences exist in the relations between personality dimensions and marital experience. In addition, t tests are used to examine the contrasts between the high satisfaction and low satisfaction groups, and between the low satisfaction and the divorced groups.

Table 11.5 summarizes the results. Accepting significance levels greater than .05 but less than .10, we find that four of the six PARAFAC dimensions show significant main effects, and one other shows a significant interaction between marital group and sex.

For the first PARAFAC dimension, Cognitively Invested, the main effect for marital group was significant at the .06 level; there was also a three-way interaction between marital group, sex, and time of rating. Figure 11.1 presents the means over time for the three marital groups within each sex. At all four times, divorced women were less cognitively invested than the other two groups. Further, they showed a drop in cognitive investment at senior high school, which did not appear in the other two groups of women or among the divorced men. Divorced men did not differ from the low satisfaction group of men on this dimension, but both were lower than the high satisfaction group of men. Because Cognitive Investment is the one PARAFAC dimension that correlates with SES, these findings may reflect the socioeconomic contrast between the high satisfaction group of men and the other groups. Only the contrast between high and low satisfaction men approaches significance ($p < .10$) when averaged over time, however. Also, SES could account for the difference between the divorced and low satisfaction groups of women.

Table 11.5

Summary of Repeated Measures Analysis of Variance:
PARAFAC Scores of Three Marital Groups
(p values)

PARAFAC factor	Main effect marital group	Marital group × sex	Marital group × time	Marital group × time × sex	T-test marital groups over time Men	Women
Cognitively Invested	.06			.09	HiSat vs. LoSat .08	
Emotionally Under/ Overcontrolled, Aggressive	.08					HiSat vs. LoSat .03 LoSat vs. Divorced .0
Open/Closed to Self						HiSat vs. LoSat .03
Nurturant/Hostile	.06	.001		.04		
Under/Overcontrolled, Heterosexual	.008			.001	LoSat vs. Divorced .04	LoSat vs. Divorced .0
Self-Confident		.01			LoSat vs. HiSat .08	

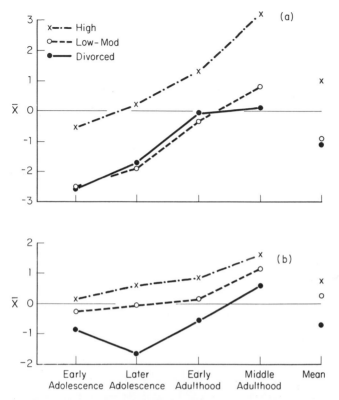

Fig. 11.1. Means of three marital outcome groups on PARAFAC factor 1, Cognitively Invested, for (a) males and (b) females.

For the second PARAFAC dimension, Emotionally Under/Overcontrolled (aggressive), the main effect for marital groups approaches significance ($p < .08$). As seen in Figure 11.2, the low satisfaction groups of men and women are more aggressively undercontrolled than the other two groups. The low satisfaction group of women are markedly more aggressive than the other two groups at all four time periods. This is reflected in the t-tests contrasting low and high satisfaction groups of women, and low satisfaction and divorced women, with PARAFAC scores averaged over time. The low satisfaction group of women are significantly different from both other marital groups ($p < .03$) for both contrasts).

The third PARAFAC dimension, Open/Closed to Self, does not differentiate among the marital groups. Evidently being insightful and somewhat unconventional in one's thinking is consistent with greater or lesser degrees of marital satisfaction.

284   Arlene Skolnick

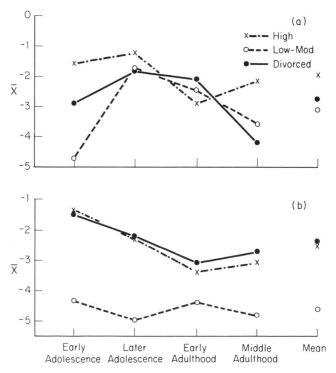

Fig. 11.2.   Means of three marital outcome groups on PARAFAC factor 2, Emotionally Under/Overcontrolled: Aggressive, for (a) males and (b) females.

The fourth PARAFAC dimension, Nurturant/Hostile, reveals a main effect for marital groups at the $p < .06$ level of significance (see Fig. 11.3). When scores are averaged across time, and for both sexes, the high satisfaction group is the most nurturant, the low satisfaction group the least. There is also a strong interaction between sex and marital group and a three-way interaction between marital group, sex, and time. Divorced and high satisfaction women start out with identical scores in early adolescence and follow a similar developmental course, dropping sharply in later adolescence and rising sharply in adulthood. The low satisfaction group of men fluctuate in relation to the other two groups. They are markedly lower in nurturance at late adolescence, but slightly higher in early adulthood.

The fifth variable, Under/Overcontrolled, Heterosexual, shows a strong main effect ($p < .008$) and a significant three-way interaction. Also, it distinguishes between divorced and the low satisfaction group of women and men when scores are averaged across time. In sum, in both

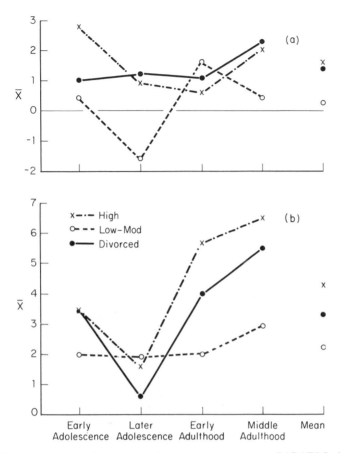

Fig. 11.3. Means of three marital outcome groups on PARAFAC factor 4, Nurturant/Hostile, for (a) males and (b) females.

sexes, and at all four time periods, participants who were divorced at some point in their lives are more erotically inclined than the stably married, regardless of their level of satisfaction. This eroticism is strongly evident in both early and late adolescence, long before the first marriage took place.

The three-way interaction indicates a sex difference in developmental trends in this factor. The women's scores converge at middle adulthood, whereas the three groups of men are more widely separated. Also, the men rise rather sharply between the two adult ages. During early adolescence the future satisfied husbands are the least erotic.

For the sixth dimension, Self-Confidence, there is a significant in-

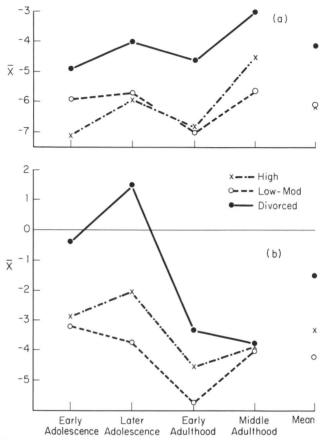

Fig. 11.4. Means of three marital outcome groups on PARAFAC factor 5, Under/ Overcontrolled, Heterosexual, for (a) males and (b) females.

teraction between marital group and sex but no main effect (Figure 11.5). Low satisfaction men are at all times lower in self-confidence than the other two groups. Among women, the divorced are lowest in this factor, particularly at late adolescence and early adulthood. The high satisfaction groups of men and women are higher in self-confidence at both early and middle adulthood.

Summing up, the findings suggest personality differences among people with differing levels of marital satisfaction and stability, including contrasts between the divorced and the married but dissatisfied. These personality traits cannot be attributed to the influence of

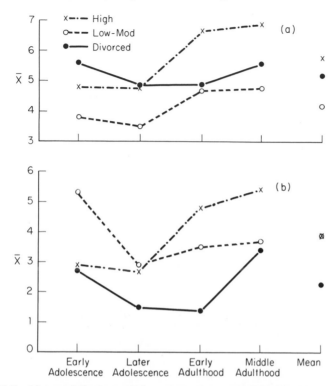

Fig. 11.5. Means of three marital outcome groups on PARAFAC factor 6, Self-Confident, for (a) males and (b) females.

the marital relationship itself on personality, because they also appear in adolescence. For the same reason, they probably are not raters' halo effects.

Eroticism is the characteristic most clearly distinguishing divorced men and women from the more stably married, regardless of degree of marital satisfaction. By early adolescence, the divorced were more interested in the opposite sex, undercontrolled, eroticizing, talkative, gregarious, self-indulgent, and self-dramatizing. The process by which this sexualized gregariousness influenced marital experience is not clear; for example, we do not know whether it affected mate selection or marital interaction.

The low satisfaction groups of men and women differ in other ways from the divorced and the maritally satisfied. The low satisfaction group of men tend to be lower in self-confidence than the more satisfied men. The low satisfaction group of women tend to be more aggressive and less nurturant than the high satisfaction and divorced groups of women. As noted earlier, these are traits that in the sample as a whole show significant sex differences.

Certain cautions should be observed in generalizing from these findings. The categorization of study members, particularly the divorced, was quite crude. Because the N was so small, the divorced group could not be divided into those who had successfully remarried and those who had not, nor could those who divorced after few or many years of marriage be contrasted.

In younger cohorts, eroticism may have lost its association with instability, and the increased acceptability of divorce may have restricted the range of satisfaction levels within marriage. In other words, the propensity to have an unsatisfactory marriage, and the propensity to divorce, may no longer be as distinctive as they were.

THE QUALITY OF MARRIAGE

Subjective evaluation of marital satisfaction by spouses is a useful but limited variable. It is limited because couples with the same levels of satisfaction or dissatisfaction can have different kinds of relationships and different patterns of interaction. In this section we explore qualitative differences between marriages rated high and low in satisfaction, as well as differences over time in marital quality.

A 100-item Marital Relations Q sort was devised by the author to assess expectations and assumptions about marriage, satisfactions and dissatisfactions with the spouse's performance of marital roles, the depth and quality of the personal relationship between the spouses, sex role ideology, the division of labor within the household, patterns of conflict and dominance, leisure time activities, and relationships with kin, friends, and community groups. Raters for this Q sort were not those who had originally rated the interviews on marital adjustment, nor were they aware of the previous ratings. The average agreement between the two marital Q-sort raters was .76.

First I use this Q sort to understand differences between the marriages previously rated in global terms as satisfactory or unsatisfactory. Scores for the 100 individual items were summed and ranked for the high and low satisfaction study members separately; the five highest and lowest ranking items within each group were compared.

The most salient quality in the highly satisfactory marriages is a strong affective commitment to the spouse, that is, an affectionate and enjoyable personal relationship between husband and wife. For example, these items rank as *most characteristic*.

1. Person likes spouse.
2. Person admires and respects spouse.
3. Person and spouse enjoy each other's company.
4. Person would marry spouse again.
5. Marriage has improved over time.

The items *least characteristic* of the satisfied marriages are:

1. Marriage is a utilitarian living arrangement (as opposed to a close personal relationship).
2. Person has seriously considered leaving spouse.
3. Serious conflicts and disagreements between the spouses.
4. Person and spouse have discordant personality traits.
5. Sexual adjustment is or has been a source of tension.

Although the spouses rated as satisfied did not have serious conflicts, they did not avoid conflict. Thus, the item "tries to avoid conflict with the spouse" does not appear as highly characteristic of happy marriages, whereas the item "sees conflict as a normal part of married life" does appear as a salient item in many of the Q-sorts of individual happy marriages. In an observational study of marital interaction, Rausch, Barry, Hentel, and Swain (1974) identified two types of "harmonious" marital relationships—(*a*) the couple avoids dealing with conflictful issues, or (*b*) the couple is able to deal with conflict openly and constructively. In my study, only marriages of the latter kind were rated as very happy or adjusted.

Unsatisfactory marriages, by contrast, are marked either by conflict avoidance or serious conflicts resulting in hostility and tension. The following items are *most characteristic* of the unhappy marriages.

1. Person is critical of spouse.
2. Serious conflicts and disagreements between the spouses.
3. Spouses have discordant personalities.
4. Person tries to avoid conflict with the spouse.
5. Marriage is a utilitarian living arrangement (rather than a close personal relationship).

In addition, for a large number of low satisfaction marriages the item "drinking problems cause conflicts between the spouses" appears as highly characteristic.

These items are *most uncharacteristic* of the *low satisfaction* marriages.

1. Marital relationship has improved over time.
2. Person sees spouse very much like self in temperament.
3. Spouses basically agree on child-rearing.
4. Person is pleased with spouse's performance of daily tasks.
5. Person feels loved by spouse.

In addition, for many of the dissatisfied men and women, the item "marriage of own parents seen as happy" appears as highly salient. This may have more to do with the perceptions of the participants or of the raters than with the reality of the parents' marriages. The marriages of GS members' parents were rated during the members' early childhood; the contrasting marital outcome groups do not differ significantly on this variable. Case histories show some of the most happily married come from homes marked by instability or great parental discord (see also Mueller & Pope, 1977).

The perception of dissatisfied spouses that they are unlike each other in temperament and personality has more basis in reality. As noted earlier, there is a significant association between marital satisfaction and husband-wife Q-sort similarity in Q-sort personality profiles.

Returning to the issue of the quality of marriage, we find from the Marital Relations Q sort that, apart from degree of emotional attachment and commitment, both the satisfied and unsatisfied vary a great deal among themselves. In other words, the affective component seems relatively independent of other aspects of marriage. Affectionate spouses may do many things together, or each may go his or her own way; they may have an egalitarian relationship, or follow traditional sex-role patterns; they may have an active social life, or keep to themselves; they may have close contacts with kin, or may be isolated from kin; they may be religious, or shun religious observances. Comparable variability prevails at the opposite end of the scale in unhappy, discordant marriages. Furthermore, factors that have sometimes been thought to be associated with marital adjustment, such as conventionality, religious participation, and lack of conflict, do not necessarily affect the quality of the emotional commitment between husband and wife. These findings support the hypothesis that the relational *processes* in marriage are the key to marital adjustment, and that the *content* of the relationship—the specific kinds of behaviors the spouses engage in—is less important (Quick & Jacob, 1973).

Individual case materials also show that although happy marriages may vary greatly from one another, these variations occur around a common core of a close, even romantic, personal relationship. One man remarked after almost 30 years of marriage, "I still have stars in my eyes." A woman said, "I just can't wait for him to get home every night; just having him around is terrific." This woman's husband said, "I think I love my wife more than I did when we were first married but in a different way."

However, "togetherness" is not an essential ingredient in happy marriages. For example, one of the happiest marriages combines both affection and distance. The husband and wife enjoy different things, but each one "gets a kick" out of what the other is doing. If she's not in the mood, he may go off to a party by himself. She may go off to play tennis for several days. Their friends "get uptight" about their arrangement, but she feels their separate activities keep things interesting because they can come home and describe their activities to one another. There is little conflict between them.

Another happily married woman, in contrast, described a very close relationship with her husband, which is particularly striking because she had a difficult relationship with her father. She grew up "hating men" and planned never to marry. Her husband was also the child of a very unhappy marriage that ended in divorce. This couple are more involved with one another than most couples because they work together, lunch together every day, and are together in the evening.

Few of the happy marriages seem to be completely smooth and without dissatisfaction and irritations. One highly rated couple reported having major "silent arguments," which last for about a week. The wife observed, "People always say you should talk over your differences, but it doesn't work in our family." As has sometimes been found in research on individual happiness, positive and negative feelings in marriage may represent two independent dimensions (Bradburn & Caplovitz, 1965). In the happy marriages, dissatisfactions seem to be treated with a grain of salt rather than being defined as serious grievances; the positive aspects of the relationship clearly outweigh the negative. In short, the satisfied spouses did not expect perfection.

As satisfactory marriages were not problem-free, so satisfied spouses were not necessarily free of problems in other areas of their lives. Happy marriage, at least on the basis of the present data, does not cure all ills. Nor is it necessary to be a problem-free or even un-neurotic person to enjoy a good marital relationship.

Unsatisfactory Marriages

We approach the case materials on the low satisfaction marriages with two questions: what are the sources of the dissatisfaction, and what keeps the marriage together in spite of it? The first question is harder to answer than might appear at first glance. For only a relatively small proportion of cases does a clear-cut problem seem to be the source of the trouble. In about 25% of the cases, the spouse's drinking seems to be the source of major marital difficulties. In a small group of marriages, discussed in more detail in the following, severe personality conflicts dominate the relationship and become the central preoccupation of the couple's daily life. Finally, many of the marriages rated as unsatisfactory have problems that seem no more severe than those of the satisfactory marriages. In fact, in reading the descriptions of such specific difficulties—clashes of temperament, dissatisfactions with personal habits, leisure time preferences—it is hard to know whether one is reading the case history of a happy or unhappy marriage. As noted above, highly satisfactory marriages are not problem-free. The difference between the two kinds of marriages emerges when the general nature of the marital relationship is discussed—for satisfied spouses, the problems are minor annoyances overshadowed by the enjoyment of emotional attachment and communication; in many of the unsatisfactory marriages, these compensating pleasures are lacking.

The fact that dissatisfied couples stay together is also not as surprising as it may at first seem. We noted earlier that stable marriages are not necessarily "happy" marriages according to anyone's definition (Hicks & Platt, 1970). The "instrumental" commitment and utilitaritan value of many stable marriages seems to compensate for the lack of emotional commitment (Cuber & Harroff, 1965).

Marriages with many minor problems and little emotional closeness resemble utilitarian marriages. Some of our unsatisfactory marriages, however, seem to differ in two ways from such utilitarian arrangements: (a) they seem to involve more profound and disturbing conflicts, and (b) the spouses seem to be held together not merely by convenience or concern for the children, but also by affective commitments to one another. These affective commitments seem an ambivalent mixture of positive and negative feelings—a kind of negative attachment. In some cases it almost seems as if the person is attached to the spouse not in spite of the problems and conflicts, but because of them.

A clear example of negative attachment is a woman described as a bright, immature person totally wrapped up in her dissatisfaction with her husband. Yet the interviewer felt that her annoyance with her spouse did not depress her and that she would complain even if her husband were the way she wanted him to be. The woman reported that the problems in the marriage had been there from the beginning and that their adjustment had never improved. She holds no hope for change in the future. The primary clash seems to be in temperament and needs—she describes herself as expressive and outgoing; he is more withdrawn and private. She would like to do more things as a couple; he prefers male friends. They also have conflicts over decision-making—his mother and her father were decision makers, and each of them expects the other to assume this role.

In his interview, the husband seemed pleasant, relaxed, and calm—almost too calm, with no sign of enthusiasm about anything. He reported chronic difficulties with his wife, describing her as demanding, domineering, and dissatisfied. He describes himself as dealing with these conflicts by "folding his tent and stealing away," which makes her even more angry. He hopes their marriage will improve after the children leave home, but he thinks that it may break up.

Negative attachment need not prevail on both sides of a marriage. In some marriages, one of the spouses may be embroiled in a painful, "negative attachment," while the other maintains an instrumental or even positive affective commitment to the relationship. For example, one woman complained that her husband was a "married bachelor." When asked for satisfying things about her marriage, she said her husband is a "good provider" and their sexual adjustment has always been good. She has considered divorce, but feels too dependent on her husband.

In his interview, the husband seemed content with both his work life and his marriage, although he acknowledged difficulties in his relationship with his wife. He is secure in the knowledge that she loves him, and is a good mother to the children; "My heart flutters when I see them together."

MARRIAGES IN THE MIDDLE YEARS

This section examines two issues: (a) changes in marital satisfaction for the sample as a whole from early to middle adulthood and (b) factors associated with increases and decreases in marital happiness.

It has been argued that the quality of marriage declines as couples reach their forties and fifties. Terms such as disenchantment, disengagement, and corrosion are used to describe the process. Decline in satisfaction may be associated with reductions in the number of things the spouses do with and for one another (Blood & Wolfe, 1960; Pineo, 1961).

Other studies, however, indicate that the later stages of marriage are as satisfactory as earlier ones. Many couples reach a new high in marital happiness after their children leave home. Freed from the social and economic burdens of raising children, the spouses can renew their relationship with increased intensity (Deutscher, 1964; Feldman, 1976; Maas & Kuypers, 1974).

Our longitudinal data offer the opportunity to examine the course of marital satisfaction over a decade in the same couples. Is there evidence of corrosion, or of a U-shaped curve—a rise in marital satisfaction in the later stages of the relationship? For the 47 women and 35 men with data at both follow-ups (only GS had marital ratings at the earlier follow-up) there is no evidence of decline in marital satisfaction. In fact, means for marital satisfaction and adjustment are higher at the later period, although the difference is not significant. Recall also that despite the differences in age and length of marriage, there are no differences in marital satisfaction scores between the GS and OGS.

Thus, the data provide no support for the notion that the mere passage of time corrodes marital relations. Although they also provide little support for the notion of a U-shaped curve, our data may include only the middle part of the U. We do not have direct information on the earliest stage of the family life cycle—the period from marriage to the birth of the first child. Also, at the most recent follow-up, the GS members were not yet in the post-parental phase of the life course. Future follow-ups will reveal the course of marital satisfaction over the next decade of life.

Despite little mean change, many marriages changed either positively or negatively. Of the 82 men and women who had marital ratings at both times, 38 changed markedly. Twenty-four study members (63%)—16 women and 8 men—had marriages that improved over the decade. Fourteen (37%)—6 women and 8 men—declined in marital satisfaction over the decade. [Improvement and decline were defined as a change of 10 points or more (one standard deviation) in marital adjustment rating standardized to a mean of 50.] Case histories of these marital "uppers" and "downers" were examined in an attempt to identify factors associated with the changes in marital satisfaction.

Note that changes did not always mean a marriage went from good to bad or bad to good; some marriages went from good to better, some declined from very good to good, some went from bad to worse, some from bad to bearable. Also, in a few cases, an apparent improvement or decline seemed to result from a change in self-disclosure from one interview to the next—a person presented a rosy picture of the marriage at one time, but in the other interview detailed irritations and problems. The interviews give the overwhelming impression that situational factors have a great deal to do with increases or declines in marital satisfaction. (By definition, persons who divorced in the interim were excluded.) Money starts coming in after hard times or becomes more of a problem; difficulties in the years of diapers and bottles smooth out as the child grows older, or an easy parental career runs into difficulties when the children become teenagers; health problems go and come; in-law problems ease as the couple grows into middle age, or grandparents become a problem as they advance into old age. Such situational strains may create tension and unhappiness in one or both spouses which affects the emotional climate of the marriage, or they may create conflicts between the spouses, or they may set off personality "disturbances" in one or another of the spouses. One question that could be raised about such a finding is whether some personality factor was causing both the stressful events and the marital difficulties. Our longitudinal data suggest that because the marital relationships changed when the external situation changed, life stress can have an independent effect, apart from personality.

Let us examine a typical example of a marriage that improved. At 30, the husband was a graduate student and lived with his wife and two children in a cramped apartment. He worried about finals, his wife's health (she was pregnant), and his chances of getting a good job after graduation. He was upset by lack of money because it meant a lot to him to be a good provider. He felt his wife was too reserved and did not easily discuss problems. He also reported a strained relationship with his father.

A decade later the husband is very successful and is proud of it. The children are doing well, and the family enjoys many activities together. His wife is involved in community affairs and seems more outgoing, more willing to share feelings with him. They enjoy each other's company a great deal. His father is dead.

In many of the marriages that improved, the wives at the time of the early adult interview were overwhelmed mothers, struggling to cope with several young children. The husbands were perceived as uncommunicative, preoccupied with work or other concerns and not often available to help. One woman was seen as "schizogenic" in her ambivalence towards her children. In the later interview she was functioning very well. Another "overwhelmed mother" with an aloof husband had numerous physical ailments and was on tranquilizers for her tensions and worries. Ten years later she had developed a tremendous sense of humor and had no physical complaints. Her husband had become "a good friend."

Situational stresses are also implicated in several marriages that declined in satisfaction. For example, in 1960, one woman and her husband were happily fixing up the house they had just bought. They owned a boat and did many recreational activities together and with other couples. She described her husband as easygoing and considerate. He was then on the verge of quitting his job to go into business partnership with another man. The 1970 interview, however, was dominated by her concern with her husband's drinking. She attributed his drinking to difficulties with his business partner. She recently gave him an "ultimatum" to quit the partnership, which he did. Nevertheless, he still had occasional binges. She believed his drinking problem had disrupted their entire marital relationship. Since he began to drink he has had no interest in sex or their former recreational activities. Drinking problems appear as a factor in many of the marriages that declined in satisfaction whether or not they were associated with specific life stresses. In few cases is there evidence of a mid-life crisis, in the sense of a sudden emergence of identity and sexual concerns comparable to those of adolescence. Two of the marriages that declined do seem to fit that image, however. One involved vague dissatisfactions and sexual longings; the other, a dramatic upheaval—the husband left to try out a homosexual identity.

In conclusion, this study offers no support for the hypothesis that marriages inevitably corrode, with spouses becoming disengaged or disenchanted. Despite more support for the contrary hypothesis (marriages improve as the burdens of child-rearing lessen), there are many exceptions.

Perhaps the most striking impression from the case histories is the great potential for change in intimate relationships. The other impression concerns the impact of situational factors on marriage, especially work pressures on the husband and early child-rearing responsibilities of women. In reading some of the early adult interviews, it occurred to me that if the same marital problems arose today, a couple might conclude that they were incompatible and seek a divorce. As divorce becomes more frequent and more acceptable, commitment to marriage and to working through its problems inevitably lessens. Certainly the increased acceptability of divorce has released many people from deeply unhappy relationships. But it may also encourage too many people to discard relationships that have the potential for change and growth.

SUMMARY

The findings here substantiate some previous studies on marriage and challenge others. Some new findings are also reported concerning personality correlates and antecedents of different kinds of marital outcomes, particularly differences between the divorced and the unhappily married.

The data confirm the importance of socioeconomic status for marital satisfaction, particularly the impact of the husband's occupational level on his own marital satisfaction. SES indicators play a lesser, but still significant, role for women.

This research demonstrates that when the contributions of SES are controlled, personality factors also contribute significantly to marital satisfaction and stability. Husbands and wives tend to be similar in personality, rather than opposite, and the greater the degree of similarity, the higher the level of satisfaction. In currently married couples, level of satisfaction correlates most strongly with self-confidence in men and nurturance in women.

Study members who have been divorced clearly differ from those who are dissatisfied but still married to their original spouses. We may therefore infer that marital dissatisfaction and instability are not simply different stages of the same process but rather responses of different personality types to marriage and/or marital difficulties. The most striking difference is that divorced men and women are more erotically expressive, gregarious, and self-indulgent than either long-married group (high or low satisfaction) and have been so since early adolescence. Other personality dimensions differentiating among the three marital groups are nurturance, aggressiveness, self-confidence, and cognitive investment.

Case histories of marriages high and low in satisfaction reveal that the emotional aspects of a relationship do not seem to depend on particular patterns of behavior. A variety of different life-styles seems to be compatible with a satisfying emotional relationship between husband and wife. Highly satisfactory marriages are not free of conflict and dissatisfactions, but these negative qualities are offset by the positive feelings of the spouses toward one another. Many of the unsatisfactory marriages have no more problems than the satisfactory marriages do, but the emotional bonds between the spouses do not seem strong enough to offset them. Other unsatisfactory marriages are marked by severe personal or interpersonal problems, such as alcoholism or "negative attachment"—a strong bond to a relationship that is full of discord.

Marriages rated at two adult periods approximately a decade apart yielded little evidence of systematic or developmental change. Thus, the findings support neither the corrosion hypothesis—marriages inevitably decline in satisfaction over time—nor the U-shaped hypothesis—decline in marital satisfaction while children are in the home and improvement thereafter. However, individual marriages did change over time, more in a positive than a negative direction, and external life circumstances seemed to be an important influence on such changes in marital satisfaction.

12

Involvement, Warmth, and Parent–Child Resemblances in Three Generations

JOHN A. CLAUSEN, PAUL H. MUSSEN, and JOSEPH KUYPERS[1]

For many reasons we expect children to resemble their parents in a variety of personal characteristics. Aspects of temperament appear to have genetic components, as do intellectual abilities, physical capacities, and appearance. Also, because parents and children share a sociocultural milieu, we expect intergenerational similarity in traits and response tendencies. A behavioral influence hypothesized to influence parent–child resemblance is the child's identification with his or her parents—the child's tendency to emulate the parents' ideals, attitudes, behavior, and characteristics. Finally, as a consequence of interacting with their children, parents may change and become more like their offspring.

Although all these factors are, in theory, powerful in promoting similarities between parents and children, we have little systematic empirical evidence about the nature and degree of intergenerational resemblance in personality and social behavior. However, some data suggest that overall resemblance in attitudes and values between generations is substantially higher than resemblance between matched pairs of parents and children (see, e.g., Kandel & Lesser, 1972). Could this be true of other features of personality?

[1]The authors are indebted to Norma Haan for a number of the ideas and indices incorporated in this chapter as well as for substantial portions of the data analysis.

299

Complete similarity is not expected on either a genetic or environmental basis. Generations are subject to somewhat different patterns of early experience, fashions of child-rearing and developmental demands; zeitgeists change. Furthermore, not all children identify strongly with their parents. Especially in adolescence, orientations may at times clash and lead to familial conflicts. With increasing maturity, children usually undergo greater individuation, separating themselves psychologically from their parents. Relationships with people outside the family increase in number and become more intense. As a result, children may develop characteristics that differ from those they acquired in the family circle.

One widely held hypothesis is that the motivation to identify with a parent is rooted in satisfactions derived from interactions with that parent. Thus, parents who are highly involved with their children, warm, attractive, rewarding, powerful, and nurturant, are more likely to evoke strong identification than parents lacking these characteristics. In this chapter, data from the longitudinal studies are used to test this hypothesis directly in three generations. The "intermediate" generation is the study members, the individuals on whom this book is focused. We look at them first as the middle-aged children of elderly parents, examining similarities in these two generations. Then we shift our attention to these study members as parents, and assess the resemblances between them and their adolescent children. These data enable us to examine whether warmth and involvement play a greater role in the determination of parent–child resemblances at one period of life than at another.

Data on involvement and warmth of relationships between the generations are available from the perspectives of all three generations, but, for each parent–child combination, we focus on the reports of the younger generation in assessing parental involvement and warmth. This vantage point was selected because in each generational pairing the younger generation appears to play a greater role in determining the degree and kinds of relationships. In contrast, parents are enjoined by tradition and strong moral constraints to maintain relationships with their offspring. Moreover, parental reports of interactions with their children are likely to be tinged by a personal need to appear competent in the parental role. Perhaps this is the explanation of the fact that, when both generations were asked about parent–child relationships in the family, the adolescent children of the original study members report far more disagreement with their middle-aged parents than their parents report.

THE STUDY

Participants

Elderly Parents and their Middle-Aged Offspring

The middle-aged parents are members of the Guidance and Control groups of the Guidance Study (GCS) who were interviewed, and whose elderly mothers and/or fathers were also interviewed, in the last follow-up. The interviews formed the basis for clinicians' Q sorts of personality characteristics of each generation (Chapter 2). Because of differential death rates, only 20 pairs of elderly fathers and middle-aged offspring exist, so subanalyses that further segment this small sample are not feasible. However, the 50 elderly mother/middle-aged offspring pairs permit examination of all the questions of interest. Initial analyses of the mothers' and of the fathers' sample indicated no gross differences between the middle-aged sons and daughters in their involvement with, and warmth toward, parents, so the middle-aged of both sexes were merged for the analyses of these generational dyads. In some instances the total sample was divided into four parent–offspring combinations: mother/daughter, mother/son, father/daughter, and father/son.

The modal age of the members of the GCS was 40 (Chapter 2); the modal age of the elderly fathers, 71, and of the elderly mothers, 69 (Maas & Kuypers, 1974). All of the fathers but only 65% of the mothers were living with their spouses; most other mothers were widows living alone. Overall, the elderly were somewhat advantaged socioeconomically. However, 41% of the mothers and 20% of the fathers reported some economic strain, and many of these elderly people (22% of the mothers and 30% of the fathers) were engaged in part-time or full-time work. The elderly mothers seemed to encounter greater strains (were more likely to be widows and worried about money) than the fathers. However, about 70% of both the mothers and fathers reported good health, whereas 17% indicated that their health was average and only 10% considered their health "poor."

Parents and Adolescent Offspring

The samples for this cross-generational analysis consist of those middle-aged parents (study members) who were interviewed and whose adolescent offspring, aged 14–18 and still living at home, were also interviewed. Considerably larger numbers of these parent–adolescent combinations are available (198 adolescents). However, several substantive and methodological considerations substantially reduce the numbers used in analyses.

First, the kind of involvement—and possibly warmth—between parents and adolescents may be affected by the adolescent's age and sex. Because older adolescents may have more intense relations with persons outside the family, we divided the adolescents into sex and age groups—one group of 14 and 15 year olds, the other of those 16-18 years. Second, only one adolescent in a family was included; whenever siblings were in the same sex and age group, the oldest child was arbitrarily chosen as the "subject." Finally, some adolescents did not complete all questionnaire items used to assess warmth and involvement with parents. The numbers available for most analyses were: younger adolescents: 20 boys and their mothers, 22 girls and their mothers, 18 boys and their fathers, 18 girls and their fathers; older adolescents: 53 boys and their mothers, 63 girls and their mothers, 48 boys and their fathers, 57 girls and their fathers.

Data Sources

The data come from several sources, including a Q-sort evaluation based on interviews in the 1968-1972 follow-up (Chapter 2), and a questionnaire answered by the adolescents. Indices of warmth toward, and involvement with, parents were derived from responses to this questionnaire.

Involvement and Warmth: The Variables and Their Characteristics

Dyads of Elderly Parents and Middle-Aged Offspring

During their interviews the middle-aged adults were asked five general questions about their relations with their elderly parents, for example, "Describe your father [and then mother] as persons" and were probed about the nature of their present relationships with each parent and changes in this relationship. Typed transcripts of these responses were coded and rated for involvement and for warmth. For all adults with living parents, involvement was rated on a 5-point scale—no involvement, slight, medium, strong, and strongest involvement. The last step implies high dependency; it was anchored with the statement "no decision undertaken without parental advice." The reliability of this rating for involvement, based on independent evaluations by two raters and a subsample of 34 interviews, was .82.

Warmth of the participants' relationship to their elderly mothers and fathers was rated separately on a five-point scale ranging from extreme strain, for example, a conflictual, difficult relationship (rated 1) through average and above average warmth, to great friendliness and closeness (rated 5). The reliability estimates, determined in the same way as the reliabilities of the involvement ratings, were .86 for warmth toward mother and .93 for warmth toward father. Socioeconomic status for both generations was assessed from the Hollingshead Index of Social Position (weighted score).

Contrary to what one might expect intuitively, the two central variables, involvement with parents and warmth toward parents, were independent in all sets of middle-aged participant/parent dyads (mother/daughter, mother/son, father/son, father/daughter). Apparently, high levels of involvement with parents and dependence on them is not a function of strong warmth toward these parents. Involvement may be strongly influenced by many other factors, such as felt obligation, guilt, desire to set an example for one's own children. On the other hand, low levels of involvement may not stem from lack of warmth but rather from preoccupation with one's children or other activities, intergenerational differences in life-style, or the belief that the parents are well looked after by others or ought to maintain their independence from their children.

Most of the middle-aged participants visited their parents several times a year but less than several times a month. However, neither warmth toward, nor involvement with, these parents was associated with the distance between the residences of the two generations (median, approximately 200 miles; range, less than 10 to more than 1,000 miles). One exception to this generalization was found; among the middle-aged participants lesser involvement with fathers was associated with greater distance between residence ($r = -.49$, $p < .01$). Neither warmth nor involvement with elderly parents was associated with the socioeconomic status of these parents, but study members of lower socioeconomic status tended to be more friendly toward their elderly fathers ($r = .38$, $p < .05$).

Evaluating the Adolescents' Warmth and Involvement with Their Middle-Aged Parents

Assessment of these two central variables was made in ways comparable to—but not identical with—those used to evaluate the relationship between the middle-aged participants and their elderly parents. Quality of the adolescents' warmth and affection toward their parents was indexed by summing the ratings of warmth toward each.

Ratings were made by the interviewer of the adolescent offspring and by another rater, who read a transcript of the interview. The rater reliabilities, calculated for the entire sample of adolescents interviewed, as well as for boys and girls separately, ranged from .69 to .75. In general, these adolescents felt warm toward their parents, the average ratings for all dyads being above the midpoint of the scale.

Two measures, both derived from questionnaire responses, were combined to assess the adolescents' involvement with their parents. One was the extent of perceived parental influence on ideas and opinions; the other was sharing social activities with parents. Among the items in the questionnaire completed by the adolescent children were their (a) ratings of the degree to which they felt their ideas and opinions were influenced by each of parents, and (b) responses about whether parents or friends were their usual companions in six social activities (e.g., movies, picnics, and vacations). Younger adolescents reported an average of approximately three out of six activities shared with parents; the older adolescents' average was about 1.5. Girls of both age groups were slightly less involved with, and warm toward, their parents. For each subgroup, the average "influence" score was above the midpoint of the scale indicating that these adolescents generally felt involved with their parents.

The score for involvement was calculated by summing influence ratings for mother and father to achieve a general parental influence score; then the number of activities the adolescent indicated (s)he shared with the parents was added to the influence score. Because the absolute ranges of the influence and shared activity scores were identical, the summation represents a 50% contribution from each component. The influence and sharing components of the involvement measure were independent of each other.

Involvement with parents and warmth toward them are positively but not significantly correlated in three of the four subsamples; the correlation between the two variables is substantial in the older boys' sample ($r = .59$, $p < .001$). Both factors are independent of socioeconomic status except, again, in the case of the subsample of older boys. Among them, lower socioeconomic status is associated with greater warmth toward parents ($r = .44$, $p < .01$).

General Personality Similarities between Parents and Children

The same Q-sort items—or, in a few cases, items with equivalent meanings—were used to assess the personalities of the three generations, enabling us to calculate Q correlations between all generational pairs. That is, the 90 Q-sort ratings of each middle-aged father or mother who participated in the study could be correlated with (*a*) those of his elderly father and mother and (*b*) those of his or her son and/or daughter. The resulting correlations of Q-sort profiles provided indices of *general*, rather than specific, parent–child resemblances in personality.

Several cautions must be heeded in interpreting such correlations between sets of Q-sort ratings because the nature of the samples and the particular pools of items affect the distribution of correlations obtained. Specifically, ours was a nonclinical population; by and large, the participants functioned normally and well. Because this Q sort was originally developed for use in clinical settings (Block, 1961), 40% of its items represent pathological characteristics (e.g., deceitful, somatizes, fearful, feels victimized) while another 40% are "healthy" characteristics (e.g., dependable, poised, insightful, cheerful). In a sample such as ours, we would expect most individuals to be rated relatively high on the "healthy" items and relatively low on the pathological. Consequently, the average correlations between pairs of individuals— whether they are kin or chosen at random—will be positive.

To distinguish between "true" and "artifactual" Q-profile correlations, we calculated correlations between randomly chosen pairs of fathers and sons, fathers and daughters, mothers and sons, mothers and daughters as well as between actual family dyads. By comparing the distributions and average levels of correlations between actual kin pairs with those of random pairs, we can ascertain whether resemblances between parent–child pairs are greater than would be expected by chance. All possible random pairings were done between the two older generations (the number of comparisons ranged from 1888 for mother/daughter dyads to 768 for father/son). Because of the larger number of middle-aged parent/adolescent child dyads, we took the less expensive course of calculating Q correlations for only 20% of all possible random pairings (for example, 2553 for the older girls and their mothers; 703 for the younger girls and fathers).

Figure 12.1 presents the comparisons between the average correlations for the kin and random pairs. The range and distribution of the correlations generated by the two types of pairings are approximately the same (range of −.60 to +.80 for random pairings and −.50 to +.80 for kin pairs; standard deviations ranged from .28 to .30 for random pairs and .27 to .31 for kin pairs).

As is apparent from Fig. 12.1, the means for all the kin pairings involving older adolescents are significantly greater than those gener-

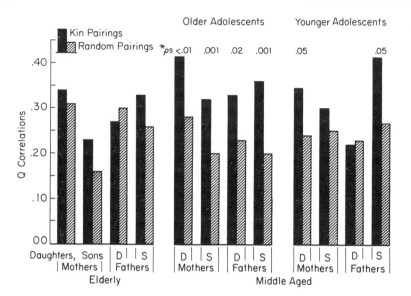

Fig. 12.1.   Comparisons between average correlations for kin and random pairs. * *p*
levels are for significance of differences between kin and random pairings.

ated by using randomly-paired counterparts. Younger adolescents also
show significant nonartifactual resemblances to their like-sexed parents in two of four comparisons (mother/daughter and father/son).
Among middle-aged participants and their elderly parents, however,
the tendency for parents and children to show closer resemblance than
random pairings is negligible. None of the means of these correlations
of the dyads of kin pairing differs significantly from its random coun-
terpart.

The significant correlations between the kin pairings cannot be attributed simply to similarities in socioeconomic status of parents and
their children. Analyses of variance comparing the parent–child Q correlations for different social classes within the elderly parent/middle-
aged offspring dyads as well as the middle-aged parent/adolescent
child dyads yield no significant differences.

The comparisons shown in Fig. 12.1 suggest far less similarity in
personality structure between parents and children—that is, smaller
correlations between Q profiles—than we expected. The combined effects of genetic linkage, similar sociocultural milieu, and identification
processes, at least as they appear in these data, are modest. Although
modest, parent–child personality resemblance appears greater be-

tween adolescents and their middle-aged study member parents than between the latter and their aged parents. Only for pairs of adolescents and parents is statistical significance achieved. In addition, resemblance is somewhat greater for all age combinations within same-sex pairs (mother/daughter, father/son) than within opposite sex pairs.

Adolescents and parents who live together (the case with these participants) share a socioeconomic milieu. A greater degree of resemblance would therefore be expected than among parents and children who have been living apart for a substantial period of time, as is the case with the elderly parents and their middle-aged children. Other research suggests, for example, the important influences of spouse's personality and of occupational experience on personality change in the middle years (Kohn & Schooler, 1978; Vincent, 1964).

Only for daughter/mother and daughter/father dyads do the correlations for older adolescents substantially exceed those for younger adolescents. However, the mean level of resemblance between younger adolescent sons and their fathers is greater than that for older adolescent sons and their fathers. Thus we cannot say with any conviction that the older adolescents are more similar to their parents.

The younger adolescents, age 14 or 15, are dealing with many developmental tasks and crises characteristic of this period and far different from those their parents face. Consequently, the two generations are likely to manifest quite different patterns of response and characteristics. Among the critical problems of adolescence is the adoption of behaviors appropriate to one's own sex role. In most cases the most readily available model is one's own same-sex parent; thus it is not surprising that at this age sons resemble their fathers more than they resemble their mothers and daughters are more like their mothers.

Obviously, many other factors serve to attenuate the degree of parent–child similarities. Each member of the family has his or her unique genetically determined predispositions and each has special experiences not shared with other members of the family that influence personality development. Moreover, the nature of the structure of the nuclear family, including assignment of different tasks to different members, tends to some extent to generate distinctive—complementary or reciprocal—personalities. In addition, the striking shifts in personality during the adult years described in Chapter 5 show that the middle-aged participants in this study changed considerably after they left their parental homes and adopted new roles in the families they established. This fact in itself would tend to attenuate similarity with parents.

INVOLVEMENT AND WARMTH IN RELATION TO OVERALL
PARENT—CHILD SIMILARITIES IN PERSONALITY

One can speculate about many possible sources of parent-child similarities and differences; fortunately, our data permit us to examine directly certain potentially influential variables. Underlying the present study is the hypothesis that greater involvement with parents and strong feelings of warmth toward them foster the child's development of personality characteristics that are similar to those of his or her parents. To test this hypothesis, we use a straightforward method. The Q correlation for each dyad—that is, for each father/son, mother/daughter, father/daughter, mother/son combination—is used as the index of intergenerational similarity. We then determine whether individuals high in involvement and warmth are more like their parents than are individuals low on the warmth and involvement variables.

The scale used to assess the middle-aged participants' involvement with their elderly parents is probably not a true continuum because of the extreme statement of overinvolvement at the end of it. Therefore, we trichotomized the group on this variable, and, for consistency, also trichotomized on the basis of scores on the warmth variable. Then one-way analyses of variances were performed to determine whether the three groups (high, medium, and low involvement—and, analogously, high, low, and medium warmth) differed from each other on the measure of similarity to parents. The scales for adolescents' involvement and for warmth do constitute meaningful continua, so the younger and older adolescent groups were dichotomized into high and low (rated above or below the mean) warmth and high and low involvement groups. We use t-tests to evaluate the differences between the average similarity scores of those high and low on the two central variables.

Tables 12.1 and 12.2 present the results of the 22 analyses testing the hypothesis. The hypothesis receives considerable support: in 12 (55%) of the 22 analyses the differences are significant and in the predicted direction. Specifically, high levels of involvement and warmth are associated with parent-child similarities between the elderly mothers and their middle-aged offspring and between the middle-aged participants and their adolescent children. Six analyses yield no support for the hypothesis: among the younger adolescent boys neither warmth nor involvement is associated with similarity to the father or the mother and, among the older adolescents of both sexes, involvement is unrelated to similarity to the mother.

Almost all the average levels of parent-child similarity (the mean Q

Table 12.1

Personality Similarities of Family Dyads in Relation
to Middle-Aged Offsprings' Involvement
and Warmth with Elderly Mothers
(Q Correlations)

Involvement	$\bar{x}$'s	F ratio[a]	Warmth	$\bar{x}$'s	F ratio[b]
Dependent/mother	.47	7.22****	Friendly	.45	4.07**
Medium/mother	.22		Average	.23	
Aloof/mother	.13		Strain	.23	

Note: Highest $\bar{x}$'s are in italic. *p* levels are one-tailed
tests because an explicit hypothesis is being tested.
[a]df = 2/58.
[b]df = 2/49.
**p < .05.   ****p < .001.

correlations of the dyads) for those high in involvement and warmth
are considerably above the averages based on all father/son dyads and
those derived from random pairs (in Fig. 12.1). The highest level in
Fig. 12.1 is .41, whereas the highest in Table 12.1 is .61. Warmth appears more closely associated with parent–child similarities in the
dyads involving adolescents and their parents, whereas involvement is
the more important correlate in the elderly parent/middle-aged offspring dyads.

Table 12.2

Personality Similarities of Family Dyads in Relation to Offsprings'
Involvement and Warmth with Middle-Aged Parents
(Q Correlations)

	Involvement					Warmth			
	$\bar{x}$'s					$\bar{x}$'s			
Relationship	High	Low	df	t ratio	Relationship	High	Low	df	t ratio
Middle-aged parent/older adolescent offspring					Middle-aged parent/older adolescent offspring				
Girls									
Mother	.47	.49	34	ns	Mother	.58	.34	36	3.02***
Father	.50	.26	34	2.89***	Father	.46	.31	35	1.69**
Boys									
Mother	.34	.24	27	ns	Mother	.41	.17	28	2.16**
Father	.53	.29	27	1.95**	Father	.51	.23	35	2.40**
Middle-aged parent/younger adolescent offspring					Middle-aged parent/younger adolescent offspring				
Girls									
Mother	.50	.23	27	2.02**	Mother	.61	.17	30	4.61****
Father	.38	.11	24	1.83**	Father	.40	.08	26	2.39***
Boys									
Mother	.40	.41	19	ns	Mother	.33	.47	19	ns
Father	.54	.40	19	ns	Father	.49	.44	19	ns

Note: Highest $\bar{x}$'s are in italic. *p* levels are one-tailed tests because an explicit hypothesis
is being tested.
**p < .05.
***p < .01.
****p < .001.

Our data do not provide answers to questions about why one variable, warmth, critically affects the degree of parent-child similarities in personality at one stage of development while another, involvement, is more influential at another. However, one tenable explanation is that among families living together (as in the case of the parent/ adolescent offspring dyads) warmth toward parents promotes identification and thus the assumption of parental characteristics and behavior, whereas absence of warmth may imply "negative identification," that is, resistance to adopting parental traits. After families have ceased to live together, as in the case of the elderly parent/ middle-aged offspring dyads, warmth towards parents appears to be unrelated to parent-child resemblance but involvement is related to resemblance. Perhaps those who resemble their parents continue to be involved with them; those who do not see themselves as similar to their parents are less involved with them.

FURTHER EXAMINATION OF GENERAL
CROSS-GENERATIONAL PERSONALITY SIMILARITIES

Note that even for dyads of highly involved and warm parents and children, the dyads in which we found the closest overall similarities, the average Q correlations are generally moderate rather than high. The degree of association may be attenuated either because (a) parents and children strongly resemble each other in some aspects of their personality, but not in others, or (b) because the parent-child dyads are generally, but weakly, similar in many or all of the descriptive Q-sort items. Analysis of parent-child similarities in individual items clarifies this ambiguity and provides more information about the specific nature of similarities between parents and their children.

Our strategy, then, was to examine the correlations between the scores of the members of each dyad (father/son, father/daughter, mother/son, mother/daughter) for each of the 90 Q-sort items. First, however, it was necessary to determine whether or not the kind of artifactual positive relationships that exist between random pairs for the entire 90 items are also present at the level of individual items. To do this, we generated thousands of random pairs of cross-generational dyads and calculated correlations for each of the 90 Q items. The range of the obtained correlations was $+.02$ to $-.02$. Clearly, the two-person correlations for single items were not affected, as the overall correlations were, by artifacts of the nature of the population or of the items in the Q sort. We can, therefore, turn our attention directly to the correlations among the kinship dyads. Parent–child resemblances for a characteristic are considered significant or real if (*a*) the correlation between the ratings of the members of one dyad is significant at the .05 level or better, and (*b*) the significant correlation is replicated in at least one other dyad. Of the total of 90 items, 24 (27%) show significant parent–child similarities as judged by this double criterion: Appears Intelligent, Values Intellectual Matters, Insightful, Verbally Fluent, Ethically Consistent, Philosophically Concerned, Sympathetic, Interested in the Opposite Sex, Productive, Fastidious, Masculine/ Feminine Style, Satisfied with Self, Uncomfortable with Uncertainty, Ruminative, Brittle Ego Defenses, Self-Defensive, Repressive, Negativistic, Conventional, Bothered by Demands, Withdraws when Frustrated, Feels Victimized, Under-Controlled, Power-Oriented.

Of these cross-generational similarities, 66% are found in same-sex dyads, whereas only 37% are found in opposite-sex dyads. This result is fully consistent with theory and with research evidence pertaining to identification and sex-typing that indicates that children are more likely to identify with the parent of their own sex.

Of the 24 significant items that show generational similarities, 12 are indicative of high levels of psychological health (the first 12 listed) and 12 of low levels (the second group of 12) (see Chapters 6 and 7). Apparently, children are as likely to resemble their parents in psychologically unhealthy characteristics as in attributes associated with good psychological health.

We further analyzed the content of the Q-sort items with significant parent–child correlations, using the classification scheme of Haan and Day (1974), which subdivides the 90 Q-sort items into four major categories. In this system, 13 Q-sorts items pertain to socially appropriate/inappropriate behavior, that is, they refer to characteristics that are the focus of socialization pressures. Children are like their parents in 6 (46%) of these items, specifically Productive, Fastidious, Masculine/Feminine Style, Withdraws When Frustrated, Feels Victimized, and Undercontrolled.

These traits may be acquired through identification with, and imitation of, parents, for parents clearly, frequently, and relatively consistently exhibit (model) behaviors that reflect these characteristics directly. However, the effects of these basic processes on parent–child resemblances, apparently do not persist over very long periods; the correlations involving the middle-aged parents and their adolescent children are not replicated in the dyads of elderly parents and their middle-aged offspring.

There are significant, replicated cross-generation similarities in 10

(42%) of the 24 Q-sort items classified as information processing: Appears Intelligent, Values Intellectual Matters, Insighful, Verbally Fluent, Ethically Consistent, Philosophically Concerned, Uncomfortable with Uncertainty, Ruminative, Brittle Ego Defenses, Self-Defensive, Repressive. Similarity in estimated intelligence may not be entirely a function of familial interaction; genetic factors may also be involved. However, placing high value on intellectual matters and being insightful and fluent are also clear and compelling characteristics that many of the participants share with their parents. These study members observe their parents at home and are likely to emulate behaviors expressing these characteristics and be rewarded for displaying them.

Although adolescents resemble their parents in information-processing variables associated with low psychological health (Uncomfortable with Uncertainty, Ruminative, Brittle Ego Defenses, Self-Defensive, Repressive), these correlations are not replicated in the elderly parent/middle-aged offspring dyads. This finding may be interpreted to mean that children adopt aspects of their parents' cognitive styles— even those that are psychologically unhealthy—and maintain them while they are living at home, but learn new adjustment techniques, approaches to problems, and ways of thinking and processing information after they leave their parents' home. The data also suggest that effective ways of reacting to problems and coping with personal crises—are established early, manifested in many situations, and endure over long periods of time (Haan, 1977).

Significant and replicated cross-generational resemblances are found in only 5 (20%) of the 25 items classified as interpersonal reaction—Sympathetic, Interested in Opposite Sex, Negativistic, Conventional, Bothered by Demands. Again, while they are still living at home, adolescents are likely to adopt their parents' explicit reactions, expressing sympathy, interest in opposite sex, negativism, and conventionality. These similarities are not apparent in the dyads consisting of elderly parent and middle-aged offspring, perhaps because new patterns of relating to others, different from those acquired at home, develop after the individual leaves the parental home, establishes new relationships and roles.

Of the 24 self-presentation Q-sort items, only two (8%)—Satisfied with Self and Power-Oriented—show cross-generational similarities. These aspects of personality may be more strongly influenced than others by experiences outside the home, for example, with peers in and outside of school. It is also possible that the structure of the nuclear family is conducive to the development of reciprocal or complementary roles with respect to self-presentation. For example, if parents are rated high in the variable Reluctant to Act (another self-presentation item), their children may have to be willing to act (low in Reluctant to Act); otherwise, the family could not function effectively.

The findings on intergenerational similarities in individual Q-sort items aid in interpreting the rather low level of overall personality similarity across generations previously discussed. Parents and children tend to resemble each other in some personality and social characteristics—particularly those involving information processing and appropriate social behavior, but the members of the parent–child dyads do not generally resemble each other in characteristics that reflect modes of self-presentation and interpersonal reactions. Consequently, correlations between parent and child overall measures personality of yield an incomplete picture of generational resemblances. Apparently, the degree of this resemblance varies with the characteristic, as well as with the sex and age of members of the dyad and the degrees of their warmth and involvement.

PARENT–CHILD RESEMBLANCE IN VALUED PERSONAL ATTRIBUTES

In addition to many measures of personality and social behavior, our data base included the responses of the study members and their adolescent children to questions about values (Clausen, 1974). These data permit us to analyze the resemblances of the middle-aged parent/ adolescent child dyads in ways that parallel our analysis of parent–child similarities in personality described previously. Findings from this analysis may aid in interpreting the findings on resemblance in personality.

The questionnaires administered to adolescents and those completed by the parents contained comparable questions asking about the personal attributes or qualities most desired in an adolescent. Parents were asked to report the three qualities they regarded as most important and the one they regarded as most important of all from a list of 16 attributes, for example, honesty, considerateness, self-control, obedience, ambitions, independence, being a good student (Kohn, 1959). Adolescent offspring were asked to indicate both the qualities that their parents regarded as most important and those to which they themselves gave highest priority.

The top three choices of fathers and mothers for both sons and daughters included honesty, dependability, and considerateness, but the mothers ranked them in different order for sons and daughters, while the fathers did not. In reporting their perceptions of the values held by their parents, adolescents agreed in assigning first rank to honesty and relatively high priorities for dependability and considerateness. However, there were several respects in which the youth of both sexes gave strikingly different rankings than did their parents. Both sons and daughters perceived their parents as attaching very great importance to their being good students and ranked this quality second only to honesty. Adolescents also ascribed to their parents greater concerns with obedience and good manners than was indicated by the parents. On the other hand, they thought their parents accorded very low rankings to their being independent, self-controlled and "curious about things." Thus it appears that many adolescents received from their parents messages about the most valued personal qualities that were somewhat different from the ones parents thought they were transmitting.

Yet the value rankings of the adolescents themselves are much closer to the parents' actual choices than to the adolescents' perceptions of those choices. For the total group of adolescent children and parents, the rank-order correlation for the 16 values is above .70. It is highest among upper middle-class adolescents and their parents and lowest among working-class children and their parents (again taken as groups rather than as matched pairs).

When matched pairs of adolescents and parents are compared on the value rankings, the correlations (tau beta) are generally positive but below .30 and seldom statistically significant. To assess the association between closeness to parents and degree of parent–child similarities in values, we use an index of closeness that somewhat resembles the index of involvement used for the analysis of personality resemblance. However, in the present analysis, we combine the adolescent's perception of parental influence and understanding with his or her perceived agreement with each parent on a number of issues. Then we again compare close and more distant pairs. Close pairs of parents and children show only marginally greater resemblance in their rankings of values than pairs whose relationship is more distant or conflicted. On the other hand, where the parent–child relationship is close, adolescents are somewhat more likely to assign high rankings to values they *think* their parents ranked high.

We conclude that value resemblance between parents and adolescent offspring appears to be less closely linked to parental transmission of a particular set of priorities than to the existence of a substantial consensus in the general milieu as to the most important personal qualities a young person should possess. Other researchers have reported similar findings for matched pairs of parents and offspring, though there is a suggestion that for younger children—around age 10—there is higher resemblance in value priorities than for children under 10 or over 12 (Perron, 1971). Once the child participates more fully in the larger community, parent–child value resemblance may well decline.

Two additional facets of the analysis of value resemblance are highly relevant. First, values expressed are in general modestly correlated with Q-sort items which might reflect such values, with one striking exception. For example, fathers who chose "dependable" as one of the three most important qualities for a son were rated on the Q sort as predictable, consistent, and moralistic to a significantly greater degree than fathers who did not assign a high rank to "dependable." (They were also seen as uncomfortable with uncertainty, self-defensive, and repressive.) Fathers who chose "considerateness" as an important value for a son tended to be classified as warm and considerate persons, although the correlations were modest (between .20 and .30). On the other hand, fathers who chose "self-control" as one of the three most important values for their sons or daughters (but especially for their sons) were seen as undercontrolled, unpredicatable, and rebellious, and these correlations, while again modest, were significant. In general, then, parents appear to be telling their children, "Be somewhat like me," but in at least one respect (and probably in several) they appear to be saying, "Don't have the problem that I have."

Another finding deriving from the values analysis supports our hypothesis that closeness or involvement with the parent fosters identification and the acquisition of that parent's characteristics. Those adolescents who report themselves as feeling close to the same-sex parent (i.e., who report that the parent has strong influence and is understanding and that in general parent and offspring tend to agree on a number of issues relating to values) are more likely to view that parent as a happy, competent person. These adolescents also report that this parent is easier to talk with than the opposite-sex parent and they believe that they resemble that parent most. Thus closeness or involvement, as measured here, does indeed connote identification with a positively valued model. Moreover, closeness is more often characteristic of children from middle-class families than of those from families of lower socioeconomic status, which may help to explain the greater resemblance overall of the value rankings of children and parents among those in the middle class.

Implications of Close and Nonclose Relationships among Adolescents and Their Parents

As might be expected, a substantial number of personal attributes of parents are significantly related to the children's feelings of closeness to their parents. Thus, according to the Q-sort data, mothers of daughters who feel close to them are rated significantly more dependable, sympathetic, productive, poised and warm than mothers of nonclose daughters. The latter mothers are more often rated as negativistic, lacking meaning in their lives, aloof, unpredictable, undercontrolled and rebellious. Similar relationships hold for fathers who are close and not close to their sons, and, for the most part, for cross-sex closeness as well.

Although parent–child resemblance in overall personality profile is greatest when the child identifies with or feels close to the parent, the influences of parental personality upon the child's personality are actually more potent in those instances where the child is *not* close. Thus in a separate, unpublished analysis by Clausen, nearly twice as many highly significant relationships are found between attributes of parents and attributes (not necessarily the same ones) of children in nonclose relationships than in close families. For example, father's negativism is significantly related ($p < .01$) to son's rebelliousness, negativism, lack of warmth and lack of insight where sons are *not* close but is not related significantly to any of these attributes when the relationship is a close one. Where the relationship between father and son is close (and the mean score and range of father's scores on negativism are less) resemblance on negativism is an insignificant .14 (as against .78 where it is not close), but father's negativism is associated with undercontrol (.41), sensuousness (.41) and self-indulgence (.45) in the son.

For daughters who are not close to their mothers, negativism as a maternal attribute predicts negativism, undercontrol, self-defensiveness, lack of productiveness, lack of personal meaning, feelings of victimization, repression and not being cheerful (all $p < .01$). Here again, in close relationships, negativism of the mother is not significantly related to negativism in the daughter, and its only significant personality correlates ($p < .05$) are daughter's lack of interest in the opposite sex and not proffering advice to others, quite probably chance correlates.

Thus certain parental attributes not only tend to preclude closeness but have important negative implications for the personality development of the children. Apparently negative attributes of the same-sex parent carry somewhat more potent socialization effects on personality than those of the opposite-sex parent, but cross-sex effects are nevertheless substantial. For example, a number of fathers' attributes—extrapunitive, ruminative, basic hostility—have many significant correlates in daughters' personalities, most of them negative or maladaptive. Likewise, rebellious mothers tend to have sons who are repressive, dissociative, and lack personal meaning.

We have not yet fully analyzed the complex relationships entailed in the joint effect of the personalities of both parents. Parents may be similar in a number of salient positive or negative personal attributes that affect degree of closeness of children to both. Thus, the exceptional strength of some of the relationships found thus far with negative attributes may be a product of interactions with both parents. In some instances, however, one parent's positive attributes may offset the other's negative ones.

We may conclude, then, that although overall personality resemblance is found most often in same-sex parent–child pairs in which the child feels close to the parent, the effects of parental personality problems (which appear to be more prevalent among parents whose children do not feel close to them) may be even greater, sometimes producing similar problems for the child.

Adolescents who feel close to a parent who is rated as moderately to extremely high on a trait that generally has negative effects on parent–child relationships are not likely to resemble the parent on that particular trait. Nor do these adolescents' characteristics show significant negative correlations with those of the parent. On the other hand, in nonclose pairs one finds both significant positive correlations (resemblances) on certain types of attributes and significant negative correlations on others. For example, among nonclose father/son pairs there is resemblance on such items as Negativistic, Aloof, Self-Defeating, Repressive (all connoting defensive maneuvers). Significant *negative* correlations, suggesting conscious or unconscious efforts to be different from the parent, are found on such items as Fearful, Rebellious, Overcontrolled, Self-Indulgent and Unpredictable, most of which are suggestive of interpersonal behaviors that a boy would readily recognize in his father and react against.

The foregoing analysis indicates that the delineation of parent–child resemblances cannot be reduced simply to an examination of identification and modeling. The configurations of parental attributes and patterns of relationship in the family appear to have major and demonstrable effects upon the child's personality, but an adequate delineation of those effects requires careful analysis of both personalities and interpersonal relations. Further, it is probable that sociocultural dimensions of systems of relationships may limit the generalizability of results from any given study. We hope, however, that the strength of the relationships found in this sample will lead to further research of broader scope.

SUMMARY

In this study of the nature and extent of parent–child similarities in three generations, study members are both *children*—that is, the middle-aged children of elderly parents—and *parents* of adolescents. The measures of parent–child similarities are correlations of Q-sort profiles. Resemblances between the middle-aged participants and their own parents in personality are not significantly greater than the Q-sort correlates between random pairs of middle-aged participants and elderly parents. However, the personality resemblances between adolescents and their parents are significant, although modest, and same-sex dyads (mother/daughter, father/son) are more alike than opposite sex parent–child pairs.

Greater warmth toward parents and involvement with them are found to be conducive to the child's acquisition of personality characteristics similar to those of the parents. Warmth appears to be more closely associated with adolescent–parent resemblances whereas involvement is the more important factor underlying similarities in elderly parents/middle-aged offspring dyads.

Parents and children resemble each other significantly in 24 of the 90 Q-sort items, similarities being twice as frequent in same-sex pairs (father/son, mother/daughter) as in opposite-sex dyads. Cross-generational resemblances are apparent in the following cognitive and personality characteristics: Productive, Fastidious, Masculine/Feminine Style, Withdraws When Frustrated, Undercontrolled, Appears Intelligent, Insightful, Verbally Fluent, Ethically Consistent, Uncomfortable with Uncertainty, Self-Defensive, Repressive, Sympathetic, Interested in Opposite Sex, Conventional, Satisfied with Self, and Power-Oriented.

Both the study members and their adolescent children had ranked, in order of importance, 16 attributes or qualities such as honesty, considerateness, obedience, and self-control. The rank order correlation between the two generations *as a whole* is above .70, the relationships being higher for the upper-class adolescent/parent groups and lower for working-class participants. However, correlations between the value rankings of matched pairs of adolescents and parents are generally low although positive, regardless of degree of closeness between them. Other analyses indicate that parents who are *not* close to their children have a more potent influence on some aspects of their children's personality development than parents who are close. For example, girls who are not close to their negativistic mothers tend to become negativistic, undercontrolled, self-defensive, unproductive, and depressed.

13

Men's Occupational Careers in the Middle Years

JOHN A. CLAUSEN

No social role approaches occupation in salience and pervasiveness of influence on the life course of the average American male. In general, a family's life-style is dependent on the husband's occupational level and success; so are the life chances of the children.

ISSUES IN THE STUDY OF OCCUPATIONAL CAREERS

Studies of occupational attainment in the United States show that blue-collar workers tend to achieve their highest occupational status, if not their highest pay, by the time they are 40 (Blau and Duncan, 1967). Male white-collar workers tend to advance occupationally into their forties and fifties, either because they become technical specialists or because they assume greater supervisory responsibilities. In general, blue-collar workers have less education, start their occupational careers earlier and marry earlier than do men who will later occupy high-prestige white-collar positions. Throughout their occupational careers, blue-collar workers are likely to be less emotionally invested in their jobs. In the years when income is lowest and family needs are great, the blue-collar worker is far more likely to take a second job, whereas white-collar workers are likely to invest themselves more heavily in their primary jobs, hoping for promotion at the earliest possible time (Wilensky, 1963).

Although white-collar workers can expect to continue advancing occupationally longer, ultimately almost everyone reaches a ceiling. In a

321

society where occupational success has long been a prime value, there has been much speculation and limited research on how men adapt to the knowledge that they have gone about as far as they can go (Faulkner, 1974; Sofer, 1970). Some scholars posit a midlife crisis when the aspiring businessman realizes that he is unlikely to make it to the top. But that is not the only source of occupational reevaluation. The psychiatric literature is replete with examples of men whose crises came when they found success empty of satisfaction.

Systematic research on men holding middle management jobs in their late thirties and early forties does not support the notion that most men expect to make it to the top or that they experience great psychological stress when they do not. For example, in a study of middle managers in several large British firms, Sofer (1970) noted that many men concluded that the psychological cost of occupying senior positions outweighted the rewards. Tausky and Dubin (1965), in a survey of management personnel of all ages, discovered that older men were likely to view their careers in terms of how far they had come from their origins, while younger workers more often focused on the distance to the top.

Almost all studies of workers in their middle years have simply compared responses of men in different age groups at a given time. Such age groups are members of different cohorts; they differ in background, in the historical contexts within which they developed, and in life experience. Their different orientations toward their occupations and their striving at any given point may be a product of something other than aging. Our longitudinal data permit us to examine changes associated with aging, at least for a subgroup of study members, and to relate career orientations to other facets of the men's lives.

Many blue-collar and clerical jobs are routine and repetitive. Workers in such jobs are more likely to be alienated and dissatisfied than are upper-level white-collar workers. But Blauner (1964) and others have documented great differences in job satisfaction within the ranks of blue-collar workers, depending on industry, organization of the work and the work group, skill level and other features of the job and its setting. In a group of men who were classmates in the early adolescent years, to what extent are differences in general life satisfaction and in satisfaction with job related to level of occupational attainment?

Yet another issue relates to involvement in work in the middle years. When do most men begin to retract from heavy investment in the job? Do men who occupy middle-level positions reduce hours and efforts sooner than those who occupy higher-level professional and managerial jobs? By their mid-forties men who have not achieved as much as they had anticipated tend to participate less than more successful men in community organizations and to turn more to family and recreation, "checking their job concerns at the work place" (Wilensky, 1961).

How is job involvement related to past mobility experience? Elder's (1969b) examination of work investment by OGS males at 38 revealed that men who had climbed higher than their fathers on the occupational ladder gave higher priority to the job than to family or leisure. Does this tendency persist into the later years? Does job involvement affect marital happiness and the perception of the man by his wife and children?

Studies of personality correlates of occupational achievement and of particular features of occupations have only recently begun to appear (Elder, 1969; Kohn, 1969, 1977; Kohn & Schooler, 1973, 1978). Elder's analysis of the personality correlates of upward mobility of OGS males revealed that those who became most successful occupationally tended to be distinguishable from their peers early in adolescence. The men who were upwardly mobile had been seen as more productive, responsible, controlled, and better integrated than less successful men even in junior high school. On the other hand, Kohn and Schooler (1973) demonstrate that features of the job, especially the complexity of the tasks entailed, appear to have appreciable effects on intellectual flexibility, self-esteem, anxiety, and authoritarian conservatism even when social class, education, and a number of other background variables are controlled.

DATA AND APPROACH OF THIS CHAPTER

For the most part, the OGS and GS men have been highly successful. Although roughly 40% had working-class origins—that is, their fathers held blue-collar jobs—less than 10% of the active participants now hold blue-collar jobs. This chapter deals with occupational histories, job satisfaction, and general career orientations of these men (often in combination with data on the husbands of female study members). For some purposes, I ignore the age differential; for others, I must examine the two groups separately, for they have had somewhat different experiences, achieved occupational mobility differentially, and are at slightly different points in their careers.

Data on current occupational involvement, job and career satisfaction, and aspirations for future advancement came from both interviews and questionnaires. The questionnaire contained many specific and factual questions on job history and features of the current job, while the interviews permitted a more global assessment of satisfaction, involvement in work, and aspirations. I also compare, for a subsample of OGS members, responses to questions about work life in the interviews at 48–50 with their responses to similar questions 10 years earlier. Some developmental data are used in seeking to ascertain whether occupational experience has markedly modified the men's personal and social orientations or whether personality attributes were major determinants of occupational performance.

Occupational careers are, on the one hand, a reflection of abilities and opportunities and, on the other, a pervasive set of influences on the further development of the person. The demands of the job, the nature of supervision received and the characteristics of job settings can influence personal values, cognitive skills, and a host of social attitudes (Kohn, 1977). We have only meager data on actual job demands and characteristics, but we know a good deal about the study members' occupational careers overall, the occupational levels attained by their fathers at various ages, and, in some detail, the members' attitudes toward various features of the current job and the career as a whole. I examine the ways in which current occupational level and occupational mobility (change in occupational status from that of one's father) influence the work orientations and satisfactions of our study members and the perceptions of their wives. Finally, the associations between personal attributes and both occupational level and mobility are examined in developmental perspective.

FEATURES OF CURRENT OCCUPATIONAL CAREERS

At 50, most of the OGS men feel they have reached the peak of their occupational attainment if not of income. At 42, on the other hand, many GS men have aspirations for further advancement. Few members of either cohort anticipate retirement in the near future, though a few OGS males have already partially retired. For the most part, the members of both cohorts find their current jobs satisfying and their careers rewarding. As we shall see, there is substantial evidence that the decade of the forties is one in which men tend to come to terms with their jobs and with their careers, if they had not already done so.

Current Occupational Distribution

The current occupational distributions differ appreciably; OGS men have achieved higher occupational status than have GS men. Moreover, the older group had already achieved higher status when they were the same age as the GS members are now. At the time of the most recent follow-up, nearly half of the OGS were high-level executives or major professionals, while this was true of less than 33% of GS males. Husbands of female OGS members were somewhat less successful than were the male members of the study, while the opposite was true for the GS. Table 13.1 shows the occupational distribution (Hollingshead's categories) of the several segments of our population.

The differences in occupational attainment by OGS men and husbands of female members appear to derive, in part at least, from initial sampling differences. The OGS men were substantially higher in IQ and in parental socioeconomic status than were OGS women (Chapter 4), whereas GS men and women differed little. In both samples spouses tend to be similar in IQ. As a consequence, the mean IQ and socioeconomic status of husbands of female OGS members were lower than those of male OGS members. Because both IQ and parental social status are significantly related to occupational achievement, difference in mid-life occupational attainments of OGS men and husbands of OGS women seem most likely to derive from marital selection.

Because the samples vary in age and achievement, and because the numbers involved are relatively small, I examine intergroup differences on numerous occasions but combine groups whenever possi-

Table 13.1

Occupational Distribution of Male Study Members and Husbands of
Female Members by Study Groups, and Distribution by Broad
Age Groups and Occupational Groups Used in Analysis
(%)

Occupation level	GS and Control		OGS		Age group	
	Study Members	Sps.	Study Members	Sps.	45 and under	46 and over
Higher executives, major professionals	27	33	48	31	32	39
Managers and lesser professionals	27	31	16	21	26	21
Lower administrative, small business	21	16	25	28	21	24
Clerical and sales	20	7	7	5	12	7
Skilled workers and foremen	5	9	5	13	7	9
Semi-skilled		4		3	2	
Total	100 (56)[a]	100 (53)	101 (44)	100 (39)	100 (91)	100 (101)

[a]Numbers in parentheses are sample sizes on which percentages are based.

ble. The most recent follow-up secured data on the job histories and work-related attitudes of husbands of female study members; these data are drawn upon to increase the sample size when current correlates of occupational status and mobility are examined. Almost all husbands of OGS women are at least as old as the study members, and most of the husbands of GS women are not more than 3 or 4 years older than their wives. Nevertheless, enough husbands of GS women are closer in age to OGS men so that it seemed desirable to use age (with the forty-sixth birthday as the dividing line) rather than study membership as the criterion for examining differences between the groups when husbands of female members are included in the data analysis. Table 13.1 permits a comparison of the occupational distribution of this age grouping with that of study membership.

A substantial proportion of men in both groups occupy positions that are of higher prestige than those occupied by their fathers at roughly the same age—that is, they have been upwardly mobile. Both the antecedents and current correlates of occupational mobility are of interest. The sample falls into six groups, based upon the categorization of occupational levels used in Table 13.1:

1. Men who moved up from the middle-class occupations of their fathers (MC Up),

2. Men with middle-class positions of roughly the same level as their fathers (MC Stable),

3. Men with middle-class positions at lower levels than those of their fathers (Down in MC),

4. Men with middle-class positions whose fathers had working-class occupations (MC, Up from WC),

5. Men in working class jobs although their fathers had middle-class positions (WC, MC Origins), and

6. Men who, like their fathers, occupy working-class jobs, though often at higher skill levels than those of their fathers (WC, WC Origins).

The last two groups are far smaller than the first four for two reasons: (a) relatively few men are downwardly mobile to, or remain in, working-class jobs because the number of such jobs has been decreasing, while clerical, sales, and service occupations in the lower-middle-class range have expanded; and (b) men who have been least successful occupationally more often ended participation in the research (see Chapter 2). Men who have done well occupationally seem to find it easier to talk in some detail about their current life situations than those who have not achieved as much as they had hoped. Because the number of men in working-class jobs is small, I am unable to compare those who have always held such jobs with those who have moved down from middle-class backgrounds.

Table 13.2 shows the distribution of mobility for male study members and the younger and older groups of members and spouses. In both age groups, nearly 60% of male study members and the husbands of female study members exceed their fathers' occupational levels. The older group more often moved up within the middle class while the younger group contains somewhat more men who made the transition from working-class family origins to middle-class occupational status. In both age groups, more than 60% of the men who were upwardly mobile within the middle class are in professional or executive positions, the top occupational category.

Those who were upwardly mobile from working-class backgrounds are less likely than the MC Up group to be in professional or upper level executive positions; in the younger group half of these men are in lower-level white-collar jobs or have small businesses, as are a third of the older men who have middle-class jobs but whose fathers were blue-collar workers.

Because of the small numbers in several of the mobility groups, groups must be combined in certain analyses. In general, middle-class men who are at the same occupational level as their fathers resemble the downwardly mobile group more than they do those who have moved up, so the former two groups are combined, except for one subgroup. Those men whose fathers were professionals or high-level executives cannot move up in categories used here, so sons who attained top occupational status are combined with the MC Up group rather than the MC Stable or Down group. And men who now hold working-class jobs, regardless of their origins, are combined for contrast with those who moved from working-class origins into middle-class jobs.

A measure of intergenerational mobility is expected in any Ameri-

Table 13.2

Mobility Groupings by Age of Male Study Member
or Spouse

Class	Under 46		46 and over	
	N	%	*N*	%
Middle class – up within class	26	31	35	38
Middle class – stable or down	28	33	31	34
Middle class – up from working class	24	28	16	18
Working class – all	7	8	9	10
Total	85	100	91	100

can sample in recent decades by virtue of the increasing proportion of professional, managerial, and clerical positions relative to blue-collar jobs (Blau & Duncan, 1967). The exceptionally high occupational achievements of our groups probably also reflect selective factors such as the decision of some families with high aspirations for their children to live near a major university and the effects of the GI Bill, which afforded veterans of World War II and the Korean War an opportunity for higher education.

Many of these men prepared for professional careers and moved at the start of their careers into positions that had higher prestige than those of their fathers. Others—nearly half—started in lower-level jobs and worked their way up. Very few top executives started in blue-collar jobs, but a number began their careers in low-level administrative jobs. Of men now in sales and clerical jobs, roughly a third started in blue-collar jobs. Thus the study men and the husbands of women in the study have shown substantial job mobility within their own careers.

Satisfaction with Career and Job

In their middle years most study men are satisfied both with the jobs they now hold and with their general career development. On the follow-up questionnaire, 30% report that their career "truly represents what I have wanted to do." For another 45% the career "approximately represents what I have wanted to do." Thus 75% seem generally pleased with what they are doing. Of the remainder, less than 5% express dislike for their occupations; most express a measure of acceptance but indicate that if circumstances had been different they would have preferred some other career.

Discussion of jobs in the interview affords another basis for classification of satisfaction. Viewed in the context of family relations and more general life situations, feelings about the current job appear somewhat less positive, with qualifications noted by many who on the questionnaire reported they were doing what they truly wanted to do. Nevertheless, 67% of men were judged to be very well satisfied with their work. At the other end of the continuum, less than 10% appeared dissatisfied; the remainder reported both satisfying and unsatisfactory features of the job which appeared roughly to balance each other.

Both occupational level and mobility patterns are associated with satisfaction with job and career, whether the data source is interview ratings or questionnaire. The small group of men in working-class occupations does not differ markedly in reported satisfaction from men in middle-class occupations, but among men in middle-class occupations, those in top-level jobs report significantly higher satisfaction than those in lower status jobs, especially in the older cohort. The interview ratings for the younger cohort reveal no difference by occupational level, but the greater satisfaction of men in high-status jobs is significant ($p < .01$) for the older cohort on both indices; it is also significant ($p < .05$) when the questionnaire responses are used for the younger cohort.

Men who have been upwardly mobile relative to their fathers are also more likely to be well satisfied with job and career than those who have not. Of particular interest is the comparison between men who moved up from working-class backgrounds to middle-class jobs and those who had middle-class backgrounds but hold jobs at the same or a lower level than those their fathers held at approximately the same age. The distribution of current occupations within these two groups is very similar, yet in three of four comparisons a substantial difference in satisfaction is reported, with men who moved up more pleased with both current job and career than those who were stable or downwardly mobile within the middle class. Although only the difference in interview reports for the older cohort reaches significance ($p < .01$), the pattern is clearly consistent for all except the questionnaire reports of the younger cohort. As we shall see, this mobility group, which overlaps considerably with the lower level of middle-class occupations, shows a number of divergences from what we might expect in terms of aspirations, job investment, and satisfaction with particular job features.

Table 13.3 suggests a marked decline in job and career satisfaction from the early to the late forties for men in lower middle-class occupations and those who have not been upwardly mobile. Because we are comparing different cohorts, we cannot be sure this decline reflects a true age difference, but the lack of an appreciable decline in satisfaction for other occupational levels and mobility groups suggests that the forties may indeed be a critical period for men who have not yet made their mark occupationally.

Elements of Job Satisfaction

What makes a job satisfactory? We have two ways of trying to answer this question. First, all men were asked to rate their satisfaction with various features of the job, both intrinsic (e.g., degree to which the work involves interests and use of skills and abilities) and extrinsic (e.g., hours and pay) and to indicate which features of the job were most important in making the job satisfactory to them. A second index is to

Table 13.3

Interview and Questionnaire Responses Indicating High
Occupational Satisfaction by Occupational Level and
by Mobility Grouping, by Age (% Well Satisfied)

	Interview		Questionnaire	
Occupation and mobility	Under 46	46 and over	Under 46	46 and over
Occupational level				
Professional, executive	67 (27)	79[b](31)	95[a](21)	91[a](35)
Managerial	65 (23)	60 (16)	75 (21)	67 (18)
Clerical, sales	67 (28)	41 (24)	67 (21)	50 (22)
Blue collar	50 (6)	67 (9)	75 (4)	75 (8)
Mobility group				
Middle class - up	71 (31)	74[c](42)	75 (20)	80 (35)
Middle class - stable or down	52 (23)	30 (23)	79 (24)	58 (26)
Working class to middle class	74 (23)	82[c](17)	81 (21)	84 (13)

Note: Numbers in parentheses are sample sizes on which percentages are based.

[a]Professional, executive significantly different from clerical, sales at $p < .05$.

[b]Professional, executive significantly different from clerical, sales at $p < .01$.

[c]MC-up and WC-MC significantly different from MC-stable and down at $p < .01$.

compare ratings of the importance of job features by men who are highly satisfied, and men who have major reservations about their jobs and careers.

For both the older and the younger cohorts, and for all levels of occupation, there is substantial agreement as to the features most important in making a job satisfactory. Three intrinsic features—the extent to which the job reflects personal interests, the extent to which it permits utilization of abilities, and freedom to develop one's ideas—and one extrinsic feature—income—each tend to be selected by approximately half the men as among the three most important features. Job security is chosen by more than half the blue-collar workers, whereas less than 20% of white-collar workers select security as of major importance, perhaps because they take it for granted.

Much the same picture emerges from the association between rating of job features and overall satisfaction with career (Table 13.4). Men who feel most positive about their careers overall rate their jobs as highly satisfying in the extent to which the work involves their inter-

Table 13.4

Mean Satisfaction Scores Relating to Features of the Job,
by Overall Career Satisfaction, by Age Group

Job satisfaction variables	Total			Under 46			46 and over		
	High	Med	Low	High	Med	Low	High	Med	Low
Hours	4.7****	4.0	3.3	4.6***	4.3	3.3	4.8****	3.6	3.3
Tension	3.9***	3.0	2.9	3.7	3.4	2.7	4.1**	2.5	3.0
Income	4.4***	4.0	3.6	4.3	4.0	3.9	4.6****	4.0	3.4
Involves interests	4.9****	4.5	3.6	4.9****	4.4	3.6	4.9****	4.5	3.6
Convenience	4.3	3.7	3.7	4.1	3.9	4.1	4.7**	3.4	3.5
Use of skills	4.8****	4.4	3.6	4.7***	4.3	3.7	4.9****	3.4	3.4
Respect	4.6****	3.9	3.3	4.6****	4.0	3.1	4.5***	3.7	3.4
Freedom to develop ideas	4.7****	4.2	3.4	4.7***	4.4	3.4	4.8***	3.9	3.4
Security	4.6***	4.0	3.8	4.6	4.1	3.9	4.7**	3.7	3.7

**$p < .05$.
***$p < .01$.
****$p < .001$.

ests, gives them an opportunity to use their skills and abilities, and gives them freedom to develop their own ideas. In each respect they differ sharply ($p < .001$) from men who indicate that their careers did not take the direction they might now choose.

Several extrinsic features of the job, especially hours and the respect given to the job by others, are significantly related to career satisfaction even though not mentioned as often as the intrinsic features cited as most important. Income, on the other hand, differentiates the highly satisfied from the less satisfied only in the older cohort. Among men under 46, overall career satisfaction is not significantly related to satisfaction with income. Nor do assessments of tensions on the job, convenience of the job, or job security relate to overall career satisfaction for the younger group. For the older group, on the other hand, all these features are significantly related to job satisfaction. The very substantial associations between ratings of almost all features of the current job and career satisfaction in the older cohort suggest that for these men the current job is viewed as the final embodiment of the career.

Although strong positive associations exist between career satisfaction and most features of the current job for the younger cohort, smaller differences are found in satisfaction with the extrinsic features noted above—hours, income, convenience of hours worked and job security. Even those most satisfied with their careers, taken as a whole, are in general slightly less satisfied with most aspects of the current job.

Occupational level is little associated with satisfaction with either intrinsic or extrinsic features of the job except for the lowest level white-collar workers (clerical and sales), who tend to report lowest levels of satisfaction with most features of the job. In both age groups, men in blue-collar jobs express very positive feelings about most aspects of their work, and in the younger cohort they significantly exceed expectation in the number of respects in which they rate their jobs as more satisfactory than do men in the three groups of white-collar workers. Blue-collar workers are especially happy with lack of tension and the convenience of work schedules.

Most of our blue-collar workers are skilled craftsmen or foremen and enjoy good incomes. There is reason, even so, to be somewhat skeptical of these high ratings. As we shall see when data from personality assessments are presented, men who remained in, or were downwardly mobile to, blue-collar jobs were rated as more self-defensive and less insightful than were middle-class men. It is possible that in their ratings of the features of their jobs they have been less candid than men at higher occupational levels.

Job Changes in the Past Decade

Most men change jobs more frequently in the early stages of their careers than later, especially if they have not prepared for a particular occupation. A succession of jobs may be tried out for "fit" until one is found that is sufficiently rewarding to invest oneself in. Once an investment has been made in acquiring the skills and knowledge required in a particular occupation, the individual is likely to stay with that occupation, though he may change employers or move into an administrative position that changes his occupational classification.

GS and OGS men are at career stages that entail substantial investments in their occupations. Most are well satisfied with the occupational choices they made. Yet in both age groups we find a substantial amount of job change in the decade prior to the most recent interviews (Table 13.5). Moreover, in each group the men who occupy higher status positions are most likely to have changed jobs in the past decade and those who are in the lowest level jobs are least likely to move. At every occupational level, the group 45 and under had made more changes than the group 46 and over. Greatest job stability was found among the blue-collar workers. In neither age group did any of the blue-collar workers who returned questionnaires change jobs in the previous decade (though several who had been in blue-collar jobs a decade before had shifted into lower middle-class jobs).

As indicated earlier, a majority of the men in professional and higher executive positions were upwardly mobile. It is, then, not surprising to

Table 13.5

Mean Number of Job Changes in the Past Decade by Age
Group and by Occupational Group (Male Study
Members and Husbands of Female Members)

Occupation and mobility	Under 46	46 and over
Occupational group		
Top executives, professionals	2.0 (20)	1.4 (35)
Managers, lesser professionals	1.6 (24)	.8 (18)
Lower administrators, clerical, sales	1.5 (20)	1.0 (22)
Blue-collar jobs	.0 (4)	.0 (8)
Mobility group		
Middle class - up	1.9 (20)	1.4 (35)
Middle class - stable or down	1.7 (24)	.8 (26)
Working class to middle class	1.4 (19)	.9 (13)

Note: Numbers in parentheses are sample sizes on which means
are based.

find that upward job mobility is associated with more frequent job changes than is failure to advance beyond one's father's occupational level.

The older group of middle-class workers who were not upwardly mobile had few promotions and fewer changes of employers in the previous decade. This group as a whole placed a high valuation on job security—substantially more than any of the other middle-class groups—and exhibited job stability second only to that of working-class men. The younger men who occupied jobs comparable to or of lower status than those of their fathers averaged 1.7 job changes in the previous decade. During their thirties these men often made job changes even when the change did not represent an appreciable advance. Their older nonmobile counterparts, on the other hand, appear to have resigned themselves to their jobs and careers—they stuck with the jobs they had a decade earlier. Recall that these older MC Stables were much less satisfied with their careers than the younger group.

Current Job Plans and Aspirations

Most men at all job levels in both age groups say they will probably remain in their present type of work and with their present employer for at least the next 5 years. Surprisingly, men under 46 and those 46 and over differ little in this respect. But when asked about their aspirations for advancement, the age groups differ substantially: nearly half the men in their early forties but only 20% of men 46 and over say they aspire to advance and expect to advance beyond the level of their current job.

Among the older cohort, occupational level is not related to aspirations for advancement, but among the younger men, those with middle-class jobs are substantially more likely to expect advancement than are those with blue-collar jobs (Table 13.6). Indeed, GS blue-collar workers, at an average age of 40, expect no greater advancement than do OGS members at an average age of 48. Equally impressive, however, is the inverse relationship between occupational status and aspirations among the younger middle-class workers, though it does not quite attain statistical significance.

A substantial proportion of men in lower level middle-class jobs have not exceeded the occupational levels attained by their fathers and are thus in the mobility category MC, Stable or Down in MC. When aspirations for advancement are examined by mobility group, those middle-class men who have not exceeded the occupational levels of their fathers prove to report substantially higher aspirations than either of the groups of middle-class men who exceeded their fathers in occupational attainment. Again, the difference is not quite significant statistically, but it is consistent with the general pattern of our findings and accords with theoretical expectations. Men who have moved up from the working class to the middle class have already validated themselves; they and upwardly mobile middle-class men more frequently

Table 13.6

Percentage of Men Aspiring to Advancement by Age Group, Present Occupational Status, and Mobility Status

Occupation and mobility	Younger group	Older group
Occupational status		
Major professionals and higher executives	38 (24)	23 (28)
Managers and lesser professionals	53 (19)	24 (17)
Other white collar	64 (25)	17 (23)
Blue collar (largely skilled)	14 (7)	**22** (9)
Total	47 (75)	21 (77)
Mobility status		
Middle class – up	43 (21)	16 (26)
Middle class – stable or down	63 (27)	26 (27)
Working class to middle class	42 (19)	20 (15)

Note: Numbers in parentheses are sample sizes on which percentages are based.

express expectations of advancement than do men who remain in the working class, but it is the middle-class stables, especially in the younger age group, who most seek to advance.

Hours Worked—Investment in the Job

Our men report working a very full week—an average of more than 48 hours, including time worked at home for their jobs. In both age groups men in white-collar jobs work longer hours than those in blue-collar jobs, but the difference is significant only for the older group. On the average, men in the younger group report that they work 1.2 hours a week more than those in the older group, suggesting that the latter are tapering off slightly in their work investment. When the several occupational levels are examined separately, all but professional and higher executives among the older men show a substantial decrease in hours worked—nearly 4 hours a week—but the older professionals and higher executives report working three hours a week *more* than their younger counterparts—51 versus 48 hours. The latter difference is not statistically significant, but for all other occupational levels the difference between age groups in hours worked is significant ($p < .05$). Thus it appears that all but the most successful men tend to cut down their working time in the decade of the forties; higher-level professionals and top executives seem, if anything, to increase their investment in work.

A number of questions asked in the interviews afforded a basis for coding the degree of commitment or investment in the job and the effect of work on family life. In general, higher-status workers are more heavily invested in their work, but within the younger age group, the lower-status white-collar workers are rated as showing the highest investment in work. This group has the highest aspiration for future advancement, nearly 67% indicating that they aspire to greater authority and responsibility and expect to secure it.

Overall, blue-collar workers are significantly ($p < .01$) less likely to be heavily invested in their work, and the job is less often seen as resulting in diminished time for family life. Thus the picture derived from interviews supports that given by questionnaire responses in terms of time spent on the job and satisfaction deriving from convenient job schedules and lack of tension.

Changes from age 38 to Age 49

Several studies comparing occupational attitudes and social participation of men by age group have found the forties to be a decade in which considerable shifts in occupational orientation appear to take place. For example, Tausky and Dubin (1965) found that while only 40% of middle level managers ages 41–45 were "anchored downward" in their occupational orientations, nearly 75% of those 45–50 were anchored downward. Downward anchorage meant that the men were inclined to look back to how far they had come occupationally rather than focusing on how far they might yet go. Men aged 31–40 differed little from those 41–45 and those 51–60 differed little from those 46–50. Thus the forties appear to be a turning point. Cohort differences may, however, account for at least a part of the shift in orientation, because the several age cohorts in the Tausky and Dubin study varied in educational level and early work history.

A segment of our data permits us to address the question of shifts during the decade of the forties. Forty of the men in OGS who were interviewed about their job plans and aspirations in 1958 or 1959 and again in 1969 or 1970 provide a basis for examining changing career orientations during the middle years. Nearly 75% reported in the earlier interviews that they hoped for advancement (including most who were in administrative jobs), though some indicated they did not really expect advancement; roughly 25% expressed no special aspirations. A little more than a decade later half the men had moved into higher status jobs, either by promotion or by changing employers, exactly 25% going each route. Of that half who did not advance, 67% stayed in essentially the same job with the same employer; a few went on their own. Over the decade, 54% of the men had a single employer, 34% had two employers and 12% had three or four.

With reference to specific goals they expressed earlier, a little more than a third were judged to have realized or exceeded their expectations. Only one man said he still hoped to achieve the position he had aspired to a decade previously. Of the remainder, some had lowered their sights and expressed themselves as reconciled to no further advance, but nearly as many had changed either employer or field of work (usually to something they had done earlier) and their aspirations. In general, the men who occupied high-status positions—higher executives and professionals—were most likely to have realized their aspirations (44% versus 22% of men at lower levels of status) and least likely to have lowered their sights (9% versus 29%), though neither difference is statistically significant because of the small numbers.

Even among men who realized their earlier aspirations, few expect further advance at age 48. As one vice-president of a manufacturing company commented: "I think it would be a disaster for me to be president. . . . I couldn't give this corporation what they want in that job."

Very few people can. We've got a remarkable man as president and when he leaves it will take another remarkable man."

In general, those who had achieved or exceeded their aspirations were satisfied with their current situations except for the tensions and/or the amount of administrative detail they had to handle. Men who had to lower their sights were somewhat less satisfied, but most of them expressed generally positive feelings about their jobs and were reconciled to having reached their ceilings.

FAMILY BUSINESSES

Several study members had worked with their fathers in businesses owned by the father. Although our sample is too small to report any quantitative data, the availability of periodic soundings of the sons' occupational satisfaction reveals that such arrangements are often fraught with great tension. Indeed, most of those who at some time had worked with their fathers had ceased to do so well before their middle years. Some had worked during adolescence and cut loose when they entered military service or when an alternative job prospect was available. In most instances, they look back on those early work years as demanding and unpleasant. As one study member whose parents operated a store noted: "My parents became more somebody that I worked with than my parents during most of the hours of the day." Paternal supervision was generally felt to be close and overly critical. In a number of instances, bitter resentment came pouring forth even though 20–30 years had elapsed.

Some men persisted in the family business, usually with the expectation that they would eventually become partners or would take over the business when the father retired. The timing of the fathers' yielding a measure of control frequently became a matter of recurrent wrangling, with much tension on both sides. Sons almost always felt they were ready for major responsibility well before their fathers granted it. In several instances it was only after the son's threat to leave and find a position elsewhere that the father yielded control. Even here, when a son's ultimatum to the father resulted in apparent capitulation of the latter, the father subsequently reversed himself and refused to give over control in one instance and ostensibly yielded but kept interfering in another.

Where sons were kept in the position of employees, having no firm commitment as to when they might be taken into the business as partners, the son's dissatisfactions and failure to cope effectively with the father's authority often led to tensions in the marital relationship. A husband who frequently complains to his wife about the unfairness of his father's treatment of him is likely in time to be told to assert himself. If he fails to do so, he may lose the respect of his wife and his children. In one family, husband and wife were at the point of separation after more than a decade of conflict over the husband's inability to break away from his father; both adolescent children had become alienated and one had been seriously delinquent. In another instance in which the study member worked for a father who expressed little confidence in the son's ability, the break with the father came after his wife had left him. This man has drifted for some time, unable to find a position that satisfies him.

Yet another type of problem not infrequently occurs in those families in which the husband is an independent professional or has his own small business, most often a retail store, an insurance agency or other small venture. Here husbands often expect their wives to work with them or at least keep the books for the business. Again this seems to be a source of considerable tension except in instances where the wife is a full, willing participant or partner. Some wives helped their husbands for a time but then decided to take a paid position elsewhere. They felt they derived more satisfaction and self-respect from jobs that they had obtained themselves. In other instances, wives continue to help their husbands but with a certain amount of resentment; most do not feel that their contributions are fully appreciated.

There are, of course, more harmonious arrangements in some family businesses, whether they entail the father-son or the husband-wife relationship. In general, however, the descriptions given by our study members suggest that a son's involvement in a family business is likely to precipitate a battle of the generations, and a wife's participation in her husband's business is likely to precipitate a battle of the sexes.

OCCUPATIONAL ATTAINMENT AND PERSONALITY

Personal abilities and motivations underlie occupational choice and occupational success. At the same time, attributes of a job help to shape further development, cognitive and social. The longitudinal data permit us to gauge, at least roughly, the relative importance of selection and subsequent experience, by comparing adolescent personality assessments with assessments in the middle years for study members having data of both periods.

Twenty items from the Block personality Q sort were selected as especially relevant for this analysis—items dealing with intellectual skills and interests, dependability, aspiration level, interpersonal style, and personal effectiveness. Table 13.7 summarizes differences among men at the four occupational levels when they were still in junior high school and at ages 40–50. Of the 20 items, 9 show significant variation ($p < .05$) among groups of junior high students classified by occupational level in the middle years, and 11 (most overlapping the 7) show significant variations at middle-age. Only 7 show no signficant association for either period.

The items that most sharply differentiated in early adolescence those who would later occupy top-level jobs were intellectual capacities and interests on the one hand and items that may be said to index the "Protestant Ethic" on the other (Ambitious, Productive, Dependable, not Self-Indulgent). More successful men were rated higher on personal productiveness and lower on self-indulgence early in adolescence but not in the middle years. Their superiority in ratings of cognitive skills, on the other hand, was greater in the middle years than in adolescence. Professionals and higher-level executives showed the greatest gains in ratings of intellectual capacity and in verbal fluency. Men at higher occupational levels were also rated as much less uncomfortable with uncertainty, as taking pride in their ability to be objective, and as less hostile.

Rather surprisingly, the groups did not differ significantly in assertiveness, self-defensiveness, power orientations, or conventionality, when analysis is limited to men for whom we have data from both the junior high and the middle years. If the whole sample available for the middle years (study members and male spouses) is used, however, the higher status workers are seen as significantly more assertive and less defensive than are blue-collar workers. Greater freedom from close supervision and greater occupational responsibility apparently influenced the interpersonal functioning of men in higher status positions.

Use of the whole battery of Q-sort items for men in the middle years—where we have a markedly larger sample by virtue of being able to include both male spouses and control subjects of GS (for whom adolescent Q sorts were not feasible)—permits us to examine associations with a finer classification of occupational levels (four middle-class groups plus men in working-class jobs). For many items relating to cognitive skills and styles, there is a steady progression from high values at the top echelons of occupational status to low values among men who occupy working-class positions in the middle years. All of the following items, for example, show F probabilities less than .001 and

Table 13.7

Mean Q-sort Ratings on Selected Personality Attributes by
Occupational Group and by Period (Junior High
School and Middle Years)

Q-sort ratings	F Probability (ANOVA)	Male study members (constant sample) Occupational group-middle years[a]			
		PE	M	C	BC
Dependable					
Junior high years	(.01)	7.2	6.7	5.4	5.5
Middle years	(.01)	8.0	7.6	6.6	6.0
Appears Intelligent					
Junior high years	(.01)	7.1	6.2	5.7	4.9
Middle years	(.001)	7.6	6.6	5.9	4.6
Uncomfortable with Uncertainty					
Junior high years	(NS)	6.0	6.2	6.3	6.8
Middle years	(.01)	4.2	5.7	5.4	7.6
Prides Self on Objectivity					
Junior high years	(.05)	5.4	5.7	4.7	4.7
Middle years	(.001)	7.3	6.7	5.5	4.1
Productive					
Junior high years	(.001)	6.9	6.1	5.0	3.9
Middle years	(NS)	7.6	7.1	7.1	7.0
Basic Hostility					
Junior high years	(.10)	5.4	5.9	6.1	7.1
Middle years	(.04)	4.6	5.1	5.8	6.1
Values Intellectual Matters					
Junior high years	(.001)	6.1	5.3	3.8	2.7
Middle years	(.001)	7.0	5.5	4.6	3.5
Self-Defeating					
Junior high years	(.04)	3.9	4.4	5.0	6.1
Middle years	(.001)	2.6	3.7	4.9	6.3
Self-Indulgent					
Junior high years	(.02)	4.0	4.1	5.1	5.5
Middle years	(NS)	4.6	4.8	5.8	5.8
Ambitious					
Junior high years	(.001)	6.6	6.2	4.9	3.8
Middle years	(.001)	7.2	6.7	5.8	4.0
Verbally Fluent					
Junior high years	(.06)	5.7	5.1	4.5	3.7
Middle years	(.001)	6.6	5.2	5.1	3.4
Does Not Vary Roles					
Junior high years	(NS)	5.5	5.2	5.2	5.9
Middle years	(.03)	4.0	4.8	4.1	5.6
Incisive					
Junior high years	(------------not available------------)				
Middle years	(.001)	5.7	5.4	4.1	3.3

Note: No significant relations in either period: Sympathetic,
Feels Satisfied with Self, Self-Defensive, Power-Oriented, Assertive, Values Independence, Conventional

[a]PE = professional, executive; M = managerial; C = clerical;
BC = blue collar.

not more than one slight variation from a consistent relationship, step by step, with the five levels of occupational status: Skeptical, Appears Intelligent, Uncomfortable with Uncertainly, Introspective, Prides Self on Objectivity, Values Intellectual Matters, Insightful, Ambitious, Philosophically Concerned, and Verbally Fluent.

There are also substantial differences on a number of items that relate to psychological impairment of personal effectiveness. Again listing only items that are significant at less than .001, we find a negative association between occupational level and Extrapunitive, Withdraws When Frustrated, Fearful, Basically Anxious, Projective, Feels Victimized, and Complicates Simple Situations. The one occasional deviation from a linear relationship involves the lowest level of white-collar workers (sales, clerical, and non-industrial technicians), who are rated most extrapunitive, anxious, projective, and most likely to feel victimized. This lower middle-class group is also seen as most concerned with own adequacy, most extreme in basic hostility and lowest in valuing their own independence, though not significantly different from the working-class group.

Q-sort scores for the middle years may, of course, be influenced by the rater's knowledge of the study member's occupational status, while those for the early years are not likely to have been appreciably influenced by knowledge of the family's social status. But since current occupational status is itself influenced by status of the family in the developmental years, an examination of the personality correlates of mobility is called for.

Occupational Mobility and Personality

Associations between occupational mobility and personality attributes (interpersonal skills, capacities, modes of coping) in the early years reflect two countervailing types of influence. On the one hand, boys who came from families in which the parents were less well educated and provided fewer cultural and economic resources should appear at some disadvantage relative to peers who came from families of higher socioeconomic status. On the other hand, those who subsequently were most successful in their occupations might be expected to show certain attributes (personal effectiveness, responsibility, high achievement aspirations, etc.) that set them off from peers of comparable background.

Study members who were upwardly mobile within the middle class came from families in which the father's occupational status was slightly lower than that of fathers of stable or downwardly mobile study members. Differences between these two groups in the junior high-school years favoring the upwardly mobile are, therefore, not attributable to initial family status. Both groups originating in the middle class did have a substantial initial advantage over men who were upwardly mobile from the working class and over men who remain in the working class in the middle years. These latter two groups, however, had comparable origins, insofar as the father's occupation was concerned.

Although there are fewer statistically significant differences in individual scores on the selected Q-sort items when study members are classified by mobility rather than by occupational level, the pattern of differences is highly significant. Men who moved up occupationally within the middle class and those who moved from working-class backgrounds into middle-class occupations both exceeded their nonmobile peers from comparable backgrounds in dependability, productivity, personal effectiveness, aspiration level, and intellectual capacities and interests in every one of the 16 comparisons for the junior high-school years shown in the top segment of Table 13.8 ($p < .001$).

Early differences in ratings of dependability and productivity (and several other items, not shown, that index the "Protestant ethic"), which in adolescence approached statistical significance, diminish slightly in the later years. However, early differences in cognitive functioning and intellectual interests were markedly accentuated as men moved up the occupational ladder. In their forties the MC Up group exceeds all others in various measures of effectiveness, but it is only in intellectual capacity and values that they stand out as markedly superior at a high level of statistical significance.

Men from working-class origins who moved into middle-class positions occupy slightly higher average occupational status than middle-class stables. In adolescence, the middle-class stable and down group received appreciably higher ratings of intellectual capacity, but at middle age the two groups receive almost identical ratings as a consequence of a very substantial increase in the ratings of the men who moved up from the working class.

As adolescents the working-class mobiles were seen as more dependable, considerate, likeable, and warm than were the middle-class stables, though none of these differences achieved statistical significance. The picture that emerges from a comparison of these two groups is of pleasant, dependable, conventional working-class boys who worked productively to get ahead, contrasted with more rebellious, self-defensive, less conventional, middle-class boys who were seen as less pleasant and less dependable.

Table 13.8

Mean Q-sort Ratings on Selected Personality Attributes, by Period,
for Occupational Mobility Groups Within the Middle Class,
and for Men Now in Working-Class Occupations

Q-sort items	F Probability (MC only)	Mobility groups[a]			
		MC up	MC stable and down	Up from WC	All WC
Dependable					
Junior high years	(NS)	7.0	5.9	6.3	5.5
Middle years	(NS)	7.8	6.9	7.3	6.0
Appears Intelligent					
Junior high years	(.01)	7.0	6.2	5.2	4.9
Middle years	(.001)	7.4	6.3	6.2	4.6
Prides Self on Objectivity					
Junior high years	(NS)	5.4	5.2	4.8	4.7
Middle years	(.02)	7.2	6.1	6.0	4.1
Productive					
Junior high years	(NS)	6.5	5.6	5.8	3.9
Middle years	(NS)	7.5	7.0	7.3	7.0
Values Intellectual Matters					
Junior high years	(.04)	5.8	4.9	4.1	2.7
Middle years	(.001)	6.7	5.2	4.7	3.5
Self-Defeating					
Junior high years	(NS)	4.2	4.6	4.6	6.1
Middle years	(.05)	3.0	4.4	3.7	6.3
Ambitious					
Junior high years	(NS)	6.3	5.8	5.2	3.8
Middle years	(.02)	7.2	6.2	5.9	4.0
Verbally Fluent					
Junior high years	(NS)	5.5	5.1	4.4	4.0
Middle years	(.02)	6.3	5.4	4.9	3.4
Number of cases		(26)	(25)	(13)	(4)
Adolescent cluster scores					
Arouses Nurturance					
Junior high years	(.04)	5.3	4.8	6.0	
Senior high years	(.02)	5.4	4.8	6.1	
Socially Perceptive					
Junior high years	(.03)	5.3	5.0	6.5	
Senior high years	(NS)	4.9	4.8	5.4	
Emotionally Involved with Same Sex					
Junior high years	(.005)	5.7	5.6	6.8	
Senior high years	(NS)	6.0	5.6	6.3	

[a]MC = middle class; WC = working class. Sample is constant.

For the adolescent years, we can also compare groups on cluster scores developed by Peskin and Livson (Chapter 6) for the junior high and senior high Q sorts (shown in the bottom segment of Table 13.8). Three additional dimensions emerge that set off those boys who were subsequently upwardly mobile from the working-class to the middle-class. In comparison both with their working-class peers and with middle-class boys (especially the nonmobile), the MC, Up from WC group were seen as more nurturant (sympathetic, giving, protective). Differences are significant for both the junior high and senior high years. The upwardly mobile working-class boys were also seen as more sociable and as more oriented to other boys; in both these respects, differences in the junior high years were much more substantial than in the senior high years.

The upwardly mobile group from the working class secured more education than their peers who remained in the working class and markedly increased their intellectual skills and interests as they moved up the ladder. In their forties they remain warm, sympathetic individuals. Of our several mobility groups, they are seen as the most conventional and least likely to push limits. In general, they now more closely resemble men who came from middle-class families than they do their former working-class peers who are employed in blue-collar jobs. Indeed, on a majority of the Q-sort items, men upwardly mobile from working-class families to middle-class occupations are inter- mediate between upwardly mobile middle-class men and middle-class stables. Thus a combination of personal characteristics, the socializing effects of higher education, and the requirements of white-collar jobs have served increasingly to differentiate these men from their early peers.

The Downwardly Mobile

The larger number of men in the combined total of male study mem- bers and spouses permits us to compare those who were downwardly mobile into the working class with those men who came from working-class families and remain in working-class positions. Al- though only a few differences attain statistical significance, a clear pat- tern again emerges. The men downwardly mobile from the middle class are seen in middle age as more talkative, fluent, submissive, introspec- tive, undercontrolled, self-defeating, anxious, and concerned with ade- quacy than other working-class men. They feel victimized and are less incisive and autonomous. On the other hand, those men whose fathers held blue-collar jobs and who themselves occupy such jobs were rated lowest in intellectual capacity, most uncomfortable with uncertainty, most defensive, least introspective, and least likely to evaluate motivations.

Although these characterizations are fairly typical of other descriptions of personality tendencies among working-class men (e.g., Kohn & Schooler, 1973), a caution is necessary. Our interviewers and raters were largely upper middle-class intellectuals. They knew the occupational attainments of the study members, so it is quite possible that the adult ratings were influenced both by the apparent occupational success (or lack thereof) of the study members and by expectations based largely on experience with middle-class persons. Although our small sample of working-class men precludes a high level of statistical significance for the findings, the differences between the downwardly mobile and the men who have always inhabited a working-class milieu are sufficiently large and consistent to warrant consideration in larger-scale research.

Occupational Attainment and IQ

Professional and executive positions require high intelligence and long, complex training. One would in general expect a direct and moderately strong relationship between intelligence and occupational attainment, and this is reflected in associations with Q-sort data already discussed. Data from intelligence tests administered in the adolescent and middle years partially sustain the Q-sort findings but not entirely so. Whether one examines IQ at age 18 or in the middle years, there is a general gradation from men in top-level white-collar jobs to those in lower-level white-collar jobs. Tested IQs at both times are available for only three men in blue-collar or working-class jobs, and they are probably a select subsample. In any event, their somewhat higher mean IQ when compared with men in low-level white-collar positions may be a chance fluctuation.

We had anticipated that occupational experience would have an influence on IQ, with men in top-level jobs gaining in IQ and those in lower-level jobs holding steady or decreasing in IQ, as suggested by the Q-sort findings reported. This was not the case. In the middle years there is a consistent progression in IQ level as one moves from the lowest to the highest occupational levels within white-collar occupations, but gains do not vary appreciably by occupational level.

As expected, occupational mobility is clearly related to IQ. In the middle class, men who moved up had higher IQs than peers who did not; the working-class sample is too small to permit inferences. In adolescence, those working-class boys who were to achieve middle-

Table 13.9

Adolescent and Adult IQ by Occupational
and Mobility Group

Occupation and mobility	Adolescence	Middle years	Sample N
Occupational group			
Professional, higher executives	126	129	33
Managerial, lesser professional	118	123	20
Administrative, small businessmen	120	122	19
Clerical, sales, technicians	109	115	10
Skilled manual workers	114	119	3
Mobility group			
Middle class - up	125	129	34
Middle class - stable	118	123	14
Middle class - down in MC	118	124	16
Working class to middle class	117	116	18

Note: Sample is constant.

class jobs had an average IQ almost exactly the same as that of non-mobile middle-class boys (though their Q-sort ratings suggest that the latter group was more favored, perhaps as a consequence of differences in the salience of other attributes rated in the Q sorts). The highest IQs in adolescence were those of middle-class boys who would be upwardly mobile or who duplicated the top-level occupational classifications of their fathers.

The IQ differences among mobility groups are not as great as had been anticipated, and a major surprise is the failure of upwardly mobile working-class men—MC, Up from WC—to show a gain in IQ despite occupying demanding positions. These data suggest that the intellectual functioning measured by intelligence tests probably does not adequately reflect the cognitive flexibility and use of social intelligence in day-to-day activities that is tapped by the ratings made from the sources on which the Q sorts were based. The latter probably include a greater component of social skills, while IQ is a better measure of potential intellectual power.

HUSBANDS' OCCUPATIONS AND WIVES' ATTRIBUTES

In general, the higher a man's job level, the less likely was his wife to be working at the time of the follow-up or to have worked in the past 10 years. This was true of both age groups, though the wives' employment status was significantly related to husbands' job level only in the older group. Wives of men in higher status positions were not only more likely to remain at home but also to indicate that they had not seriously considered taking a job (see Chapter 14).

One would expect wives of men who occupy higher-level positions to express, on the average, greater satisfaction with their husbands' jobs and careers than wives of men at lower occupational levels. This expectation is borne out, albeit modestly, by the data. In general, the higher the husband's occupational level, the more pleased the wife is with the prestige of the job (but not income, security, or hours), the more influence the husband is reported to have on his wife's political and social views, and, according to the wife's report, the more influence he has on his children.

On the other hand, husband's occupational level is not significantly related to either the wife's or the husband's rating of marital happiness. There is, however, a significant difference in the importance accorded by both husband and wife to mutual understanding in marriage. Particularly among professionals and higher executives, mutual understanding is named as the most important feature of marriage, whereas at lower occupational levels companionship and children are more often seen as having greater salience.

Husbands' Occupational Level and Wives' Personality

Because men and women tend to seek mates with social backgrounds, intellectual abilities, and value orientations similar to their own, we might expect that wives' personalities would also be somewhat influenced by their husbands' occupations. We do not have data on the early adolescent personalities of the wives of our male study members, but we can classify our female members according to their husbands' occupational levels and mobility. In general, the higher their husbands' occupational status, the higher the study wives score on items relating to intellectual abilities and interests, although differences between the top two groups are slight. Differences in Appears Intelligent and Values Intellectual Matters were already significant in adolescence ($p < .02$), but those in the middle years are much more striking ($p < .001$ for both items). In addition to the very substantial differences in wives' scores on intellective items, we find a significant tendency for wives of higher status men to be seen as less self-defensive, more ambitious, and valuing independence. None of these characteristics except ambition differentiated the groups at even the .10 level of significance in adolescence. On the other hand, in adolescence the girls who later married men with high occupational achievements were rated somewhat more power-oriented, a difference not sustained in the middle years.

Husbands' Occupational Mobility and Wives' Personality

Thus, the level of occupational attainment of their husbands was clearly associated with ratings of the personalities of our female study members and with greater differentiation of wives' personalities in the adult years than in the adolescent years. One might have expected this to be true of husbands' mobility experience as well, except for the fact that the three major mobility groups—middle class up, middle-class stable or down, and working class to middle class—differed far more in their origins than in ultimate occupational level. Recall that the MC Stables came from childhood families in which the fathers had the highest mean occupational status, the MC Up groups was slightly lower, and the MC, Up from WC group was far lower in fathers' occupational level. In the middle years, the MC Up group had achieved highest status, followed by the MC, Up from WC men and by the MC Stable and Down in MC groups. Nevertheless, the three groups differ only modestly in occupational status in the middle years, so that one might expect to find greater differences in the adolescent personalities of the women than would be manifest later.

As earlier noted, men upwardly mobile from the working class were seen in adolescence as more dependable and productive than either their working-class peers or boys of middle-class origins who would subsequently remain at or below the level of their fathers' occupation. Men who moved up from the working to the middle class were also seen as more sympathetic and protective and as less rebellious than the middle-class stables. Their wives show very similar patterns. Many, but by no means all, of the wives of men who moved up from the working class were themselves from working-class families. In comparison with girls who would later marry men from middle-class family backgrounds, those who would marry men upwardly mobile from the working class were seen as more dependable, protective, submissive, sympathetic, overcontrolled, aloof, and distrustful in their junior high years. On all these items they differed significantly from peers who married men who were not upwardly mobile in the middle class, and in a few they also differed significantly from peers who married men in the MC Up group. Women who married men upwardly mobile from the working class also were rated lowest on Satisfied with Self, Has Wide Interests, Rebellious, Pushes Limits, Interested in Opposite Sex, Expresses Hostility Directly, Emotionally Involved with Same

Sex. On all these items, girls who would marry middle-class men who did not exceed their fathers' occupational attainments were at the other extreme.

In general, girls who would marry men upwardly mobile within the middle class were intermediate between the middle-class stables and the working-class up groups, though more similar to the latter except for such items as Submissive, Overcontrolled, Aloof, Distrustful, and Satisfied with Self, on which they resembled the wives of middle-class stables. Both groups of women who married upwardly mobile men were seen in adolescence as significantly more productive, more dependable, and less rebellious than those who married middle-class stables.

Thus, it appears that girls who were rated as dependable, productive, and relatively conforming subsequently chose and were chosen in marriage by men who had been dependable, productive, and conforming in adolescence and who, partly by virtue of these attributes, achieved higher occupational status than their fathers had. But when we compare the three groups of wives in the middle years, there are relatively few significant differences in their personalities. Perhaps the most striking is the change in ratings for submissiveness. In junior high, it was the girls who would marry men upwardly mobile from the working class who were most submissive; by their forties, these women were seen as significantly *less* submissive than those who married men in the middle-class stable and the downwardly mobile category. Each group moved two full scale points in the salience of submissiveness between adolescence and the middle years, but in opposite directions. In general, women who married men upwardly mobile from the working class became more assertive, markedly broadened their interests, became less overcontrolled, decreased in bodily concern, became much more satisfied with themselves, and increased their ability to express hostility directly. They remained significantly more distrustful and more aloof than the other groups, but to a lesser extent than in adolescence. Women who married men who were upwardly mobile within the middle class showed relatively few differences as a group from adolescence to the middle years. In most cases, these women came from middle-class backgrounds and on the whole appear to have been effective persons, comfortable with themselves both in adolescence and in adulthood.

Greater shifts between adolescence and the middle years are found for women who married men who were occupationally stable or downwardly mobile within the middle class. Not only did these women move toward being more submissive, but they markedly increased their ratings on Protective, Sympathetic, and Productive, and decreased their ratings on Undercontrol and Rebelliousness. They remained relatively satisfied with themselves, and, as of the middle years, were seen as the most gregarious of any of the groups of wives.

Surprisingly, except for the finding that in adolescence the future wives of men upwardly mobile from the working class were rated significantly lower on the salience of wide interests, the three groups of wives did not differ significantly in cognitive or intellective functioning at either period. Such differences as were found in adolescence were related to the social status of their parental homes, but to a lesser degree than was found in the case of the male study members.

There are of course considerable differences *within* these groups, despite the significant differences *between* them. Some women had achieved mobility from their own parental family backgrounds by virtue of working productively in settings where they were in contact with higher-status males (see Elder, 1969b, 1970). Others continued their education beyond the level of their peers, again thereby having an opportunity for establishing contacts with males who would move up the occupational ladder. It is of interest that women who married men upwardly mobile from the working class were less involved both with the opposite sex and with their own sex in the junior high years; thus they appear to have been much more oriented to more remote goals than were their peers. But undoubtedly there were also some upper-status girls who married men upwardly mobile from the working class and one might anticipate rather different patterns of personality and of adolescent activities for such girls. Unfortunately, the limited samples available from adolescence do not permit analyzing in detail the different paths followed. Suffice it to say that the convergence of the personalities of these women in the middle years attests to the marked impact upon wives of the occupational attainments of their husbands.

DISCUSSION

This chapter examined the general career trajectories and current job situations of our study members in the middle years. Overwhelmingly, they have been successful occupationally. Roughly 60% of the men came to occupy positions of higher status than those their fathers had occupied, while less than 20% moved in the other direction. Current occupational status and mobility can be explained in part by the backgrounds from which the men came and by their personalities and attitudes. Their occupations have also helped to shape their personalities and current attitudes.

Our data permitted assessment of some of the characteristics of wives that are influenced by their husbands' occupational status, but this analysis did not fully examine the implications of a man's position for the other members of his family. A reading of our interviews with wives and adolescent children yields insights that are not dealt with in this chapter. We did not initially think of coding interview responses that dealt with the meaning of the husband and father's occupation for his family, either in the past or at present, but we hope that such coding will be possible in the future. In the future, too, we hope to study more closely the effect of attributes of the husband's job upon the wife's occupational and social activities and her attitudes. Although relatively few of the women in our study may be considered ardent feminists, many have been influenced by the women's movement. Many were beginning, at the time of the last follow-up, to formulate plans that will entail greater autonomy, especially after their children have left home.

In our next contact with the study members we hope to be able to explore in greater depth orientations of husbands and wives both to their own and to their partner's job involvement. For our older cohort, as they approach retirement, will occupational identities become less important to the men? Will husbands and wives tend to spend more time together in leisure pursuits or nonoccupational activities that are self-fulfilling, or will the occupational role continue to take the major part of the men's energies and an increasing part of the energies of their wives? These are questions to be addressed in a future analysis; the combination of longitudinal data with the current assessments of both spouses should yield much more insight into the relationships between work life and family life in the later years.

14

Women's Careers: Work, Family, and Personality

JANICE G. STROUD

The central issue of this chapter is the association between women's roles in work and family and their personality differentiation from adolescence to middle age. On the one hand, I explore associations between women's psychological functioning in mid-life and their involvement in work and family; on the other, I examine associations between adolescent personality characteristics, educational and marital outcomes, and adult careers.

Recent ferment over changing sex roles centers around the relative contributions of work and familial roles to the quality of women's lives; the traditional view that most women find personal fulfillment as wives and mothers has been challenged. Some scholars look upon the postparental stage of family life as a crisis of role loss for women similar to retirement for men, a high risk period for personal disorganization and pathology. By implication, women who do not invest themselves exclusively in motherhood are likely to enter this period with a more adaptive stance.

From a broader developmental standpoint, some analysts (Rossi, 1968) suggest that the traditional housewife–mother role is insufficiently challenging to promote full adult personality development, particularly a sense of self-worth and personal autonomy. Discrepancies between men and women in rates of mental illness and psychosomatic symptoms are attributed to the social role of housewife (Bernard, 1973; Gove & Tudor, 1973). In contrast, paid employment is viewed as liberating and self-enhancing, providing a basis for self-esteem in personal achievement.

353

Explicitly or implicitly, the college-educated woman serves as the paradigmatic case for the thesis that the housewife role is destructive to women's emotional health. Educated housewives are thought to experience marked discontinuity between their training for competence and the skills required for the housewife role. Higher education raises women's expectations for an interesting public life and renders them particularly vulnerable to the presumed lack of challenge and prestige of domestic roles. If employed, college women have access to better jobs than women with less education. The potential psychological benefits of work outside the home are more apparent for professionals than for assembly-line workers, although feminists argue that work would benefit the latter groups as well (Feree, 1976).

Moderating this rosy view of the role of employment in women's self-development is the realization that employed wives and mothers have two demanding jobs, worker and housewife–mother, which may result in role conflict, role overload, and personal strain. Working women also face barriers to success in work because of discrimination in the occupational system. (See Kreps, 1971, for an overview; Epstein, 1971, for the professions; and Suter & Miller, 1973 for income differences between men and career women.)

Empirical research on women's roles and psychological well-being yields results that sometimes contradict and sometimes support conventional wisdom. For example, studies of postparental women consistently find little dissatisfaction or pathology (Deutscher, 1964; Lowenthal & Chiriboga, 1972). Morale and marital satisfaction are generally higher in this stage than in the immediately preceding one, when teenage children are living at home. Maas and Kuypers' (1974) study of aging parents suggests, however, that a husband- or family-centered life-style persisting into old age may be less adaptive at the later period than involvement in work or community activities. Similarly, when Sears and Barbee (1976) questioned women over 60 who had been selected for their high IQs in childhood, those who had worked felt more satisfied with their careers than those who were homemakers.

The morale or mental health of housewives and working women has been directly compared in several studies. For women in the middle years, the results do not consistently favor either role. Data from a national sample in the 1950s (Feld, 1963) showed middle-aged working mothers to be more positive about themselves and their health than housewives, but work was negatively related to marital happiness. However, in a small-scale study conducted in the same decade (Wood, 1963), middle-aged women with a work-oriented life-style were judged lower in life satisfaction than housewives active in community and family roles.

Another small study (Birnbaum, 1975) found that university faculty, both married and single, felt more competent and mentally healthy during their middle years than did bright, college-graduate housewives, and professional work was positively related to marital happiness. Finally, a recent national survey (Campbell *et al.*, 1976) found role-related differences in morale only among college graduates—these working wives reported more satisfaction with life and with marriage than did housewives. No differences in morale existed between workers and housewives with less education.

In sum, results of previous research are most consistent for highly educated women. Among them, working women are more positive about themselves and their lives than housewives. For women in the middle years, the results are more equivocal. Inconsistent results may be found in broadly based samples of working women and housewives because the employed category includes women of diverse social position who have diverse motives for, and commitment to, work. Women who want to work are combined with those who have to work, women in high-status jobs with those in low-status jobs, continuously employed women with those who have recently re-entered the labor force. These distinctions have important implications for the personal satisfactions derived from work and familial roles. For example, Orden and Bradburn (1969) found the marriages of women working only because of financial need to be unhappier than those of housewives or of women who were working by choice.

Whatever the nature of the psychological differences between working women and housewives, the results of these studies raise the same interpretive issue. Do the relationships result from *selection* of different kinds of people into different roles or from *reaction* to the roles? For example, do happier and more confident women seek employment, or does work make them happy and confident?

My research uses longitudinal data to compare the influence of selective and reactive processes on adult career and personality, particularly the morale of middle-aged housewives and working women. The study also differs from previous research in other important respects: (*a*) a multifaceted conception of psychological functioning, and (*b*) a focus on sequential career lines and the meaning of work. Comprehensive assessments of personality are analyzed in relation to women's career patterns, a typology based on the timing and salience of employment over the life course. Four career patterns are identified: (*a*) a normative pattern of homemakers with limited early employment, (b) former workers not currently employed, (c) dual roles of family-oriented working women, and (d) work commitment by women who may or may not have families. By distinguishing two types of careers among working women and two types among housewives, I hope to capture the differences between women whose work is just a job and those whose work is part of their identity, and the differences between housewives who followed the normative work-family role sequence and those who worked "off-time," that is, were employed while children were young but left the labor force when family responsibilities diminished. These variations in commitment to work and family should prove important in understanding associations between women's multiple roles and their personality development from adolescence to the middle years.

SAMPLE

The sample consists of 65 GS women who participated in early maturity ratings (age 40–43) and for whom Q-sort ratings of personality in young adulthood (age 30–33) and pre-adulthood are on file. At the time of the last follow-up, 67% of this sample had attended college, and 50% of these had graduated; 83% were middle class on Hollingshead's Index of Social Position; 66% were middle-middle class or higher (Class I or II). Half lived in suburbs in the San Francisco Bay Area; 15% lived outside of California. More than 80% were living with their husbands, and family size was relatively large: 45% had four or more children. Median age of the youngest child was 9 years; most families had both preadolescent and adolescent children living at home.

Forty-six percent of the sample were currently employed, almost all in white-collar jobs. Two-thirds of the working women were married. One-quarter of the employed held professional positions, 23% were in administrative posts or self-employed, 37% were clerical or sales workers, and 13% were service workers. Half of the working women (70% of the working wives) worked part time.

MEASURES

Ratings of adult personality, marriage, parenthood, and involvement with work are based on the adult interviews described in Chapter 2. Q sorts and other personality ratings are available at 30 and 40; involvement with work was rated only at 40. The questionnaires at 40 provide self-evaluations of life satisfaction and of satisfaction with husband's income at 40. Demographic data, for example, work history and education, were collected from all sources in the adult records.

Personality

The primary method for assessing adult personality was the Q sort (see Chapters 2 and 5). In addition to these ipsative ratings, normative ratings made for GS participants from the interviews at 30 and 40 were used. Items for the normative scales were drawn mainly from those used with the GS members or their parents during the first 18 years of the participants' lives (Macfarlane, 1938). At 30 the scale consisted of 20 personality characteristics (e.g., demonstrative, confident, emotionally dependent), two items on marriage (adjustment, and closeness of bond between spouses), and one on the emotional tone of the family. There were rated independently by a clinical psychologist and a developmental social psychologist. At 40 the normative ratings came from two scales. The Tryon Rating Scale (Macfarlane, 1938), consisting of 31 items assessing personality and cognitive characteristics, was also used with GS parents when the participants were between 21 months and 17 years old (Maas & Kuypers, 1974). The Personality and Family Ratings, 33-item scale, repeats items used with GS members at 30, and adds items about marital satisfaction, occupation (involvement, effectiveness, and degree to which job draws on person's abilities), and parenting (e.g., satisfaction with self as a parent and spouse's congruence on a number of areas of child-rearing). Independent ratings were made by the interviewer and one other rater from the group of professionals who did the Q sorts and then composited. Mean reliability of the composite normative ratings of personality is .70, of marriage, .83, and of parenting, .60. Each of the adult personality evaluations was obtained independently of characterzations of the respondent at any other period. Judges making each adult evaluation had no knowledge of the respondent's earlier history.

Although all of the adult data were available for both Guidance and Control groups of the GS, only the Guidance group had the early and late adolescent personality Q sorts described in Chapter 2 and used elsewhere in this book. Data on participants in the Control group were not extensive enough to warrant sorts for separate periods during the pre-adult years. Therefore, to increase the number of cases for this study, Katten Q sorts of pre-adult personality, which had been done for both groups, were used instead. Using items from Block's (1961)

California Q sort (see Chapter 2), one rater (E. Katten) who knew the comprehensive case histories well, did sorts based on the entire period from infancy through 17 years. Because her sorts were done at about the time of the 30-year follow-up, they are not necessarily independent of the participants' status at 30. They are, however, independent of the data at 40. One-third of the cases were also rated independently by another psychologist to estimate reliability; Q correlations between the two raters for these cases averaged .72.

Although the pre-adult Katten Q sorts are based on data from infancy to late adolescence, I speak of them as characterizing the respondents as adolescents. It seems likely that adolescent data weighed more heavily in personality ratings than data obtained in childhood, particularly because interviews in adolescence were far more extensive and probing than those in childhood.

Work Life

Work History

Work in the labor force is defined as paid employment or unpaid regular work in a family business. Descriptive data on the respondents' work lives were collected from adult interviews, questionnaires, and records of informal contacts. These data were used to construct chronological records of employment, listed concurrently with familial events such as marriage and childbirth. From the work history records, the sequencing of work and familial roles could be readily determined, and this information was used to code career patterns (see section on Career Pattern).

Job Involvement

Clinical psychologists who evaluated the IGS interviews rated each employed person on a 7-point Likert-type scale of job involvement, defined as the respondent's "cathexis of work, the importance of job in overall life pattern." Ratings made by two judges independently were composited; reliability of the composite was .86. Ratings ranged from 1 to 7, with a mean of 4.4 and a standard deviation of 1.9. As was the case for other ratings of this nonclinical sample, the job involvement scale was skewed toward the positive end: one-third of the working women received ratings of 6 or higher, whereas only one-sixth were rated at 2 or lower.

To find the job involvement scale skewed to this extent was surprising, because sex role norms in our society prescribe a higher priority in women's lives for family than for work (Coser & Rokoff, 1971). Although women rated high in job involvement (6 or higher) had a strong intrinsic interest in, and identification with, their work, analysis of their interviews showed that their lives do not revolve around their jobs to the extent that would be expected for men described as highly involved with work. Two of the never-married respondents do invest most of their time and energy in work-related activities, but the majority of the highly involved lead a more balanced life, with a high cathexis of both work and family or other activities.

On the whole, these highly involved women have not had "orderly" work careers. More than half worked throughout most of their adult lives, but only a few had careers involving an orderly progression through a sequence of related positions (the common pattern for male study members). The highly involved differ from the less involved mainly in that their work, along with their family life, is currently a major domain of emotional investment and intrinsic satisfaction.

For women rated as average or lower in job involvement, family is much more salient in their lives and identities than work. Compared to the highly involved, they receive less intrinsic satisfaction from their work. Work is valued more as a means of contributing to family income or keeping busy. Many of these women enjoy working (only one-third would stop if they did not need the money), but their primary emotional investment is in family life. This lower level of job involvement is normative for working wives in our society. In the 1976 study of Campbell *et al.,* only 25% of working wives claimed that their paid work was more important to them personally than their housework.

Career Pattern

Women's work histories and current job involvements were combined to construct a typology of careers in work and family. Women who were working in 1970 were divided into two groups on the basis of involvement with work. Working women who scored 6 or higher on job involvement are designated *work-committed* women, while those with scores of less than 6 are called *double-track* workers. Women who were not employed in 1970 were divided into two types on the basis of work history. *Homemakers* had never been employed or had left employment at marriage or the birth of their first child and had not returned to the labor force by age 40. Other nonemployed women are termed *unstable* workers; they had been intermittently employed or had once been working mothers but by age 40 were no longer in the labor force. Definitions of career patterns and their frequencies are shown in Table 14.1.

Table 14.1

Career Patterns: Definition and Frequency in the Sample

Career pattern	Definition of career pattern by work history/job involvement	Frequency N	%
	Not currently employed		
Homemaker (H)	Not employed after first birth or never employed	27	42
Unstable (U)	Employed after first birth or intermittently employed	8	12
	Total not currently employed	35	54
	Currently employed		
Double-track (DT)	Medium or low job involvement	20	31
Work-committed (WC)	High job involvement	10	15
	Total currently employed	30	46
	Total	65	100

Two polar types of commitment to work and to family are represented in this typology, together with two intermediate types. Homemaking represents exclusive commitment to familial roles, whereas a work-committed career reflects strong but not exclusive commitment to work. Double-track and unstable careers involve simultaneous participation in work and familial roles.

These career patterns should be distinguished from those analyzed by Elder (1974), two of whose types have the same names but are defined differently. Elder's conceptualization is based on work history alone; mine includes work history, current employment status, and involvement with work (see Table 14.1).

By definition, job involvement is not high among double-track workers; the level of involvement of unstable workers is not known. The latter may be work-oriented women who are temporarily frustrated in their search for a rewarding job or family-oriented women who work temporarily under economic or other pressure. Elder found that OGS women with unstable work histories were not less domestically inclined than homemakers but were less fortunate economically.

Women's careers are studied here only until approximately age 40, a relatively early point when most of the sample still had children in elementary school. As the women and their children age, some women doubtless will be recruited into one of the working groups (possibly the double-track), and some current workers will leave employment to become unstable workers. Indeed, as working women approach retirement age, many will enter the category I designate as unstable, and the non-normative connotation of this career pattern will no longer be appropriate. Although the careers of older women may be classified according to the patterns defined here, the social and psychological entailments of careers of women in the "full house" stage of family life (see Lopata, 1971) are likely to be quite different from those of women in the postparental stage.

The effect of cohort and family stage on career is illustrated by the differences between OGS women and the GS sample studied here (see Chapter 2). OGS women are older; fewer attended college; they had fewer offspring. At the IGS follow-up, many OGS women had no children living at home. Nevertheless, fewer were employed, and only two OGS women were viewed as committed to work (compared to ten GS women). Because of these differences, I limit my analysis to GS. By including the Control Group, a full range of career types could be studied within a single cohort.

METHODS OF ANALYSIS

Separate orthogonal factor analyses with varimax rotation yielded 17 Q-sort factors and 5 factors from selected normative ratings (see Stroud, 1977, for procedures). The first four factors from the Q sort and the first three from the normative ratings, each of which explained more than 10% of the total variance in the item pools, are analyzed in the following. These factors and their item loadings are shown in Table 14.2.

Factor scores, Q-sort items, and demographic data were analyzed in relation to career pattern primarily by one-way analyses of variance. *Chi*-square tests and *t*-tests were also used to compare a career pattern group with the remainder of the sample and to analyze demographic data. (Where the significant results yielded by analyses of variance and *t*-tests overlap, only the analyses of variance are reported.) Although multivariate analyses that partition variance would have facilitated the testing of hypotheses, they were inadvisable because of small sample size, multicolinearity of variables, and interactions. Significance tests are used here not to make generalizations to a population but to provide an objective criterion for discriminating group differences large enough to merit attention. The .10 level was adopted as an appropriate criterion for this exploratory study.

The analysis has three main parts. First, the social and familial antecedents and concomitants of career patterns are examined. Next, personality data are analyzed. Career is viewed (*a*) as an independent variable in relation to adult personality and (*b*) as dependent in rela-

Table 14.2
Item Loadings $\geq \pm$ 50 on Selected Factors from
Q-sort (Q) and Normative (N) Ratings

Factor	Item	Loadings
Cognitive[a]		
Flexibility (Q)	Conventional	-85
	Conservative	-85
	Thinks Unconventionally	78
	Moralistic	-15
	Repressive	-15
	Insightful	70
	Evaluates Others' Motivations	69
	Rebellious	69
	Uncomfortable with Uncertainty	-68
	Introspective	67
	Appears Intelligent	60
	Interesting	58
	Values Intellectual Matters	53
Effectiveness (N)	Intelligence	87
	Use of Language	81
	Open-Mindedness	77
	Accuracy in Thinking	77
	Mental Alertness	74
	Speed of Mental Processes	64
Interpersonal	Frankness in Discussion	52
Hostility (Q)	Extrapunitive	79
	Sympathetic	-75
	Giving	-75
	Negativistic	74
	Warm	-73
	Basic Hostility	72
	Dependable	-70
	Distrustful	60
	Brittle Ego Defenses	56
	Bothered by Demands	56
	Turned To for Advice	-53
	Protective	-53
	Aware of Impression Created	-51
Submissiveness (Q)	Submissive	78
	Assertive	-64
	Values Independence	-61
	Power-Oriented	-61
	Withdraws When Frustrated	60
	Feminine Style	55
	Seeks Reassurance	54

Table 14.2 (continued)

Factor	Item	Loadings
Intrapersonal[b]		
Morale (N)	Satisfaction with Lot	87
	Morale	87
	Worry	-83
	Cheerfulness	67
	Tendency to Criticize (general)	-63
	Self-Centeredness	-53
Self-Deprecation (Q)	Concerned with Adequacy	81
	Feels Guilty	78
	Satisfied with Self	-73
	Basically Anxious	73
	Self-Defeating	65
	Cheerful	-65
	Fearful	60
	Moody	57
	Feels Victimized	56
	Self-Pitying	55
Reactivity (N)	Excitability	82
	Restlessness	71
	Energy Output	70
	Talkativeness	58

Note: Factors explaining less than 10% of the total variance
are not shown. Scores on the normative Tryon scale were reversed.

[a]Pearson r = .74 between Q-sort and Normative factors.
[b]Pearson r = -.70 between Morale (from Tryon scale) and Self-
Deprecation (from the Q sort).

tion to adolescent personality. These two analyses reflect, respectively, the *selective* and *reactive* approaches to career-personality relationships. Finally, continuity and change in personality is considered in relation to career, and the role of selective and reactive processes in linking career pattern and personality in middle age is discussed in the light of the findings.

RESULTS AND DISCUSSION

Social and Familial Correlates of Career

Among the working women, education and marital status were critically important factors in occupational attainment and involvement with work. Although most of the respondents were married and living with their husbands at 40, those who were single but had at least some college education were particularly likely to be employed in relatively high-status occupations, to have advanced in occupational status and to be highly involved with work (see Table 14.3). Married college women were the next highest in occupational status; married or single women who did not attend college had comparatively low-status jobs. Nearly half of the noncollege women declined in occupational status from their first to their current jobs. Although wives with a high-school education were more likely to be employed than their college-educated counterparts (50% versus 26%), none of the former were rated as highly involved with work.

Involvement with work was directly related to education ($r = .44$). Work is much more likely to become an important part of a woman's identity among those who have attended college, have relatively high occupational attainments and are not currently married. In view of the apparently different role of work in the lives of college- and high-school-educated women, I analyzed career-personality associations separately for the two groups. Controlling marital status as well would have been ideal, but single women were too few. Had the analyses been

Table 14.3

Occupational Status, Mobility from First to Current Job, and
Job Involvement of Currently Employed Women
by Marital Status and Education

Occupational variables	Single college		Married college		Married and single high school[a]	
	N	%	N	%	N	%
Occupational status						
Professional	4	44	4	44	0	0
Administrative or self-employed	4	44	1	11	2	17
Clerical or less	1	11	4	44	10	83
Total	9	99	9	99	12	100
Occupational mobility						
Up	6	67	3	33	2	17
Stable	2	22	5	55	5	42
Down	1	11	1	11	5	42
Total	9	100	9	99	12	101
Job involvement						
High	8	88	2	22	0	0
Medium or low	1	11	7	77	12	100
Total	9	99	9	99	12	100

[a]Seventeen percent are single.

restricted to married women, linkages between personality and work commitment could not have been explored. Similarly, sample size was too small to permit separate analyses of women with college degrees and those who attended college but did not graduate.

The distributions of career patterns of high school and college women are markedly different. Working women who have attended college are divided between work-committed careers (with high job involvement) and double-track careers (with medium or low job involvement), whereas all of the employed who had only a high school education are double-track workers. Because the full complement of career patterns is found only among college-educated women, the analysis of career-personality associations is reported first for this group. Next high school women are considered to determine whether the concomitants of a homemaking career found among college women are replicated among those with less formal education.

COLLEGE-EDUCATED WOMEN

Social Background, Current Status, and Family Life

Major differences in social background, current status, and adult family life among college-educated women with different career patterns are summarized in Table 14.4. Both original and current social class is higher for homemakers and work-committed women than for double-track and unstable workers. Most of the homemakers and work-committed women come from middle-middle- or upper-middle-class families of origin. Almost all are middle or upper-middle class in adulthood (classifed according to own or husband's occupational status). On other variables, the two groups differ.

The work-committed are highly educated. Half had postgraduate training, and education enabled them to advance occupationally. Six (60%) work as professionals, compared to 25% of the double-track group.

Eight (80%) of the work-committed are currently unmarried, and the ever-married have few children (mean of about 2). Every form of non-marriage is represented among the work-committed. Four are divorced or separated, three never married, and one is widowed. None has permanently remarried. With one exception, all other college-educated women have intact first marriages. The two work-committed women who are married are happily married.

In this sample, then, commitment to work and to marriage are al-

Table 14.4

Social and Familial Characteristics by Career
Pattern of College-Educated Women
(in Group Means and Percentages)

Social and familial characteristics	Career pattern[a]					F (df)
	H	WC	DT	U	Total	
All respondents						
Years of education (mean)	15.0	17.0	15.4	14.7	15.5	3.55**
% Postgraduate	10	50	25	0	21	
Adult social class[b] (mean)	1.6	1.9	2.1	2.3	1.9	1.27
%, I and II	90	80	75	50	79	
Childhood class[b] (mean)	2.2	1.9	2.9	3.5	2.4	3.73**
%, I and II	58	80	37	17	53	
Marital status (% married)	100	20	88	100	80	
Adult IQ[c] (mean)						
Total	125.0	124.5	124.2	124.7	124.7	.021
Verbal	125.2	125.5	120.8	121.3	123.9	.847
Performance	121.3	119.6	126.0	125.8	122.4	.741
Number of cases	19	10	8	6	43	(3,39)
Adolescent IQ[d] (mean)	120.0	114.2	118.1	119.8	118.3	.821
Number of cases	17	9	8	6	40	(3,36)
Currently married						
% Second marriages	0	0	0	0	0	
Marital adjustment at 40[e] (mean)	3.7	4.0	2.9	2.8	3.4	2.65*
% Above mean	79	100	29	33	49	
Occupational status of husband[f] (mean)	1.7	1.5	2.4	2.8	2.1	1.53
%, 1 and 2	85	100	57	50	73	
Number of cases	19	2	7	6	34	(3,30)
Ever married						
Marital adjustment at 30[e] (mean)	3.4	2.7	2.4	2.9	3.0	3.05**
% Above mean	63	0	14	33	43	
Number of cases	19	3	7	6	35	(3,31)
Number of children	4.3	2.1	3.2	2.8	3.5	4.02**
%, 4 or more	63	14	38	33	45	
Number of cases	19	7	8	6		(3,36)

Table 14.4 (*continued*)

Social and familial characteristics	Career pattern[a]					F (*df*)
	H	WC	DT	U	Total	
Currently employed						
Occupational status and type of job[f] (%)						
1-2 Professional	60	25			44	
3-4 Administrative, self-employed	30	25			28	
4 Technical, aide	10	0			6	
4 Clerical, sales	0	50			22	
6-7 Service	0	0			0	
Total percent	100	100			100	
Number of cases	10	8			18	

[a]H = Homemaker, WC = Work-committed, DT = Double-track, U = Unstable.

[b]Hollingshead 5-point scale, I = high. Social class is based on husband's occupation and education or on own if single.

[c]WAIS at age 40.

[d]Stanford-Binet at age 16.

[e]5-point scale.

[f]Hollingshead 7-point scale, 1 = high.

*p < .10.

**p < .05.

most mutually exclusive. This is not the case with parenthood, for although most of the work-committed are currently unmarried, the majority of them are mothers. That marriage appears to be a greater obstacle to work commitment than motherhood is a suggestion to be explored further when personality data are analyzed. Feldman (1973) made a similar observation about the relationship of divorce to professional success in graduate school, and Havens (1973) showed the proportion of unmarried women to rise with women's income.

In marked contrast to the work-committed, homemakers have stable marriages and the largest families in the sample (mean number of children, 4.3; 53% have five or more children). Most are happily married, in contrast to double-track and unstable workers, whose marriages are stable but less happy. Double-track and unstable workers have families intermediate in size between those of homemakers and work-committed women.

Although not statistically significant, two indicators suggest that homemakers have the most affluent households. Their husbands are highest in occupational status, and 75% of homemakers versus 46% of wives with other career patterns are very satisfied with husband's income [$\chi^2(1) = 2.53$, n.s.]. Homemakers feel committed to, and secure in, their role: 70% expect never to work; only 10% have definite work plans.

Personality in Relation to Career Pattern

Comparison of Middle Age and Adolescence

The psychological functioning of these college women at 40 is clearly associated with career pattern. Analyses of variance indicate that 33% of the Q-sort items are associated with career pattern at the .10 level or better; if items were uncorrelated the chance expectation would, of course, be only 10%. The percentage of variance in the factor scores explained by career pattern ranges from 15% to 42%. The most important results, shown in Table 14.5, indicate that both homemakers and work-committed women are functioning well. For middle-aged women with other career patterns the picture is less positive.

However, only a weak association of adolescent personality with adult career is found, that is, analyses of variance of adolescent Q-sort items yield results of marginal statistical significance. (See Table 14.6; 8 items significant at the .10 level, 2 at .05, and 1 at .01.) The content of the significant items suggests definite psychological patterns, however, so further analyses were conducted by t-tests to determine how each career group differed from the remainder of the sample. In combination these analyses present a clear picture of the adolescent personalities of three of the four career pattern groups.

Homemaking and Work-Committed Careers

Homemakers

Homemakers have the highest morale and self-esteem of any career group at 40. Descriptions most characteristic of homemakers reflect an optimistic approach to life: they do not feel life lacks meaning, are cheerful and not self-defeating. Consistent with their traditional roles and nurturant orientation, they have conventional feminine style, are giving and warm, and are the most submissive of the four groups.

During adolescence homemakers also had personalities congruent with traditional sex-roles. They were conventional, conservative, submissive, and dependent young women with good social skills. Aware of the impression they created, they apparently received positive feedback from others, for they felt satisfied with their physical appearance.

Table 14.5

Psychological Functioning of College-Educated Women
in Middle Age by Career Pattern
(in Group Means)

Psychological functioning	Career pattern[a]				F (3,39)	η^2	Pairwise contrasts $p < .10$
	H	WC	DT	U			
Cognitive							
Flexibility (Q)	.17	*.68*	(.02)	.05	.89		
Values Intellectual Matters	6.3	*7.9*	(6.0)	(6.0)	3.41**		W-H, D
Appears Intelligent	6.8	7.6	6.6	(6.2)	2.73*		W-U
Insightful	6.1	7.0	6.1	(4.8)	2.36*		W-U
Effectiveness (N)	.31	*.91*	.00	(-.20)	2.31*	.15	
Other (Q)							
Incisive	5.2	*7.0*	5.2	(4.1)	5.40***		W-U, H
Prides Self on Objectivity	5.2	*6.9*	(4.9)	5.7	2.60*		
Ambitious	6.0	*7.1*	6.4	(5.4)	2.60*		
Interpersonal							
Submissiveness (Q)	*.46*	-.44	(-.72)	.01	3.70**	.22	H-D
Feminine Style	*6.9*	(5.3)	6.4	6.3	3.47**		H-W
(Values Independence)	(5.1)	*7.0*	6.9	5.3	3.05**		
Hostility (Q)	-.24	(-.63)	.04	*1.53*	9.52****	.42	U-all
Extrapunitive	3.8	(2.6)	3.6	*5.7*	6.02***		U-all
Negativistic	3.0	(2.0)	3.1	*5.0*	5.55***		U-W, H
Basic Hostility	4.5	(4.4)	5.5	*6.8*	5.23***		U-W, H
(Giving)	*7.0*	6.8	5.8	(5.1)	4.41***		U-W, H
(Sympathetic)	6.5	*6.7*	6.2	(4.8)	3.72**		U-W, H
(Warm)	6.7	*6.8*	6.3	(4.9)	2.70*		U-H
Brittle Ego Defenses	3.2	(2.6)	3.2	*4.3*	2.40*		U-W
Other							
Socially Perceptive	*6.4*	*6.4*	6.0	(4.7)	5.39***		U-all
Ethically Consistent	7.0	*7.6*	6.4	(5.4)	4.65***		U-W, H
Irritable	4.1	(3.3)	4.8	*5.0*	3.28**		U-W
Expresses Hostility Directly	4.7	(3.6)	4.6	*6.2*	3.12**		U-W
Intrapersonal							
Self-Deprecation (Q)	(-.47)	.06	*.33*	.32	2.22*	.15	
Self-Defeating	(2.9)	3.4	3.6	*5.6*	5.27***		U-all
(Cheerful)	*7.1*	5.9	(5.2)	5.5	4.18**		H-D
(Satisfied with Self)	*5.4*	5.2	4.7	(3.3)	2.19*		
Morale (N)	*.60*	.08	-.68	(-1.14)	9.21****	.41	W-U
Reactivity (N)	.19	-.76	-.16	*.23*	3.32**	.20	W-H
Other							
Feels Life Lacks Meaning	(2.6)	3.6	3.9	*4.9*	6.02***		U-H
Number of cases	19	10	8	6			

Note: Factor scores ($\overline{X} = 0$, s.d. = 1) derived from Q sorts or normative ratings are indicated by Q or N, respectively. Q-sort items are on a 9-point scale ranging from those most characteristic of a person (9) to those least characteristic (1). Q-sort items with high factor loadings ($\geq +$ .50) are shown only if any group mean is ≥ 6.7 or ≥ 3.3, indicating that the item is or is not highly character-istic of the group. Items with high negative loadings are in parentheses. For each variable, the highest group mean is italicized; the lowest is enclosed in parentheses.

[a] H = Homemaker, WC = Work-committed, DT = Double-track, U = Unstable.
  *$p < .10$.
  **$p < .05$.
  ***$p < .01$.
  ****$p < .001$.

369

Janice G. Stroud

Table 14.6

Psychological Functioning of College-Educated Women
in Adolescence by Career Pattern
(in Group Means)

Psychological functioning	Career pattern[a]					F (3,39)	Pairwise contrasts $p < .10$	t (41)
	H	WC	DT	U	Re			
Cognitive								
Flexibility								
(Conservative)	*7.0*				5.8			2.37*
(Conventional)	*6.4*				5.0			2.10*
Interpersonal								
Submissiveness								
Feminine Style	*7.1*	(5.2)	6.9	7.0		3.02**	H–W	
(Values Independence)	(4.7)				5.9			1.90*
(Power-Oriented)	4.9				3.9			1.79*
Seeks Reassurance			(4.5)		5.9			1.71*
Submissive	5.4				4.2			1.67*
Hostility								
(Aware of Impression Created)	6.2	5.6	*6.2*	(4.8)		2.72*	H–U	
Brittle Ego Defenses			(3.1)		4.3			2.00*
Basic Hostility		6.7			5.8			1.81*
Other								
Straightforward	5.7	5.0	*6.8*	(4.7)		2.20*		
Creates Dependency	6.4				5.0			2.10**
Irritable	(3.7)				4.7			1.73*
Intrapersonal								
Self-Deprecation								
Basically Anxious		*7.1*			5.7			1.90*
Self-Pitying		*4.4*			3.1			1.73*
Feels Victimized		*4.5*			3.2			1.67*
Other								
Unpredictable	(2.9)	*4.1*	(2.9)	3.7		6.67***	W–H, D	
Physically Attractive	6.2	(5.0)	*7.0*	6.2		2.69*	D–W	
Satisfied with Physical Appearance	5.4	(4.0)	5.2	4.2		2.58*		
Self-Defensive	5.6	*7.5*	(5.4)	5.5		2.64*		
Ruminative	4.2	*5.2*	5.0	(4.0)		2.36*		
Has Bodily Concern		*7.1*			6.0			2.14**
Clear-cut, Consistent Personality	5.4				4.6			1.74*
Number of cases	19	10	8	6	varies			

Note: Q-sort items are organized according to their loadings on adult factors. The highest group mean is italicized; the lowest is enclosed in parentheses. Items with high negative loadings are enclosed in parentheses.

[a]H = Homemaker, WC = Work-committed, DT = Double-track, U = Unstable. The heading "Re" refers to the complement of a career pattern group, i.e., the remainder of the sample. Its composition varies depending on which one of the career pattern groups is analyzed by *t*-test.

*$p < .10$.
**$p < .05$.
***$p < .01$.

Less irritable than their peers, homemakers were oriented towards pleasing others in conventionally feminine ways. Not surprisingly, they were considered to have clear-cut, consistent personalities with no sign of disequilibrium or inner conflict.

Although career groups were not distinguished by the Q-sort rating of aspiration level in adolescence, independent evidence shows the occupational aspirations of future homemakers to be the most conventional. Responding to a checklist of occupations at age 15, adolescents who became homemakers were least likely to say they wanted to be a major professional, such as a physician, when they grew up (71% of homemakers versus 35% of the others checked none of the major professions listed; χ^2 [1] = 4.66, $p < .05$).

Altogether then, girls who became college-educated homemakers seem to have had an early affinity for this conventional female role. They were particularly suited to become the supportive wives that high-status husbands often have (Bardwick, 1974). More submissive in adulthood than women with any other career pattern, homemakers have grown more nurturant in their adult roles. Success in their socially sanctioned career has expanded their sense of personal well-being. Perhaps homemakers are functioning very well at 40 because their personality style has been adaptive in the context of their family-oriented career. Whether it will be as adaptive to role changes that come with advancing age remains to be seen.

Work-Committed Women

Career-committed women are not polar opposites of homemakers in personality at mid-life. Like homemakers, they are functioning well at this period. Although their marital and familial situations are vastly different, work-committed women are equal to homemakers in their capacity for warm interpersonal relationships (giving, warm, and sympathetic). They are the least negativistic, irritable, or likely to project blame onto others (not extrapunitive). Work-committed women are lower than homemakers in morale, self-esteem and submissiveness (although not significantly so), but women with other career patterns are even lower. The two groups differ most in valuing independence and in sex-typed feminine style, and only the latter comparison is statistically significant.

The distinctive resources of work-committed women are intellectual. Although career groups do not differ in tested IQ (Table 14.4), the work-committed seem especially intelligent and incisive during interviews. They value intellectual matters highly and pride themselves on objectivity. Their intellectual orientation is consistent with their education and employment: half are college teachers, writers, or graduate students. Other distinctive characteristics are ambitiousness and their insightfulness. In sum, middle-aged work-committed women maintain a complex personality organization in which stereotypically feminine characteristics such as warmth and insight are integrated with stereotypically masculine ones such as rationality, independence, and ambition.

Whereas homemakers seemed firmly launched in adolescence on a path leading to adult domestic roles, the distinctive characteristics of adolescent girls who became work-committed women reflect primarily their *exclusion* from these traditional pathways. Only slight evidence exists that they were *attracted* to a different life-style. During adolescence many of the girls who grew up to become work-committed women did not conform to conventional standards of feminine attractiveness and behavior. Viewed as the least physically attractive and the least sex-typed in feminine style and behavior, they were self-conscious, basically anxious, self-defensive, and had bodily concern. Their interpersonal relationships tended to be hostile (Basic Hostility) and self-evaluations were negative (not Satisfied with Their Physical Appearance, Self-pitying, and Feel Victimized). Not surprisingly, they were viewed in adolescence as the most unpredictable of the four groups.

These characteristics suggest a period of identity crisis rooted in a sense of failure to live up to traditional expectations of adolescent femininity. The future work-committed did not yet entertain alternative self-definitions and did not differ from their college-bound peers in intellectual orientation or aspiration level. Nor were they particularly assertive or independent. Indeed, the only early personality characteristic that points to an adult career of work-commitment is sextyping. A range of differences bearing on future roles may stand behind the rating of the work-committed during adolescence as less sextyped than others. Among the most important are interests and aspirations.

By late adolescence more than half of the work-committed women had intellectual interests that are commonly considered "masculine" (e.g., science), or they pursued "feminine" interests with unusual intensity (e.g., creative writing). They were more likely than homemakers to favor high-level professional occupations, although they were not unique in this regard. These early interests and aspirations can be construed as resources for later life patterns, opening up a world of achievement outside the home.

But unconventional or "masculine" interests may function as a two-edged sword: resources for adulthood but deficits in adolescence. In a peer culture oriented to adolescent social success and popularity, girls with unusual interests may have been defined as different and somehow undesirable. Sex-typing was related to social success with peers in junior high school. Popular girls were rated as more sex-typed than the less popular. [Q-sort means were 7.3 and 5.9, respectively, for girls scoring above and below the median on sociometric ratings of popularity; t (22) = 2.04, $p < .10$.] Without cultural sanction or social support, unconventional interests were not likely to lead to a positive self-identity during the adolescent period. The talents and ambitions of these adolescents may have been submerged in ambivalence and self-rejection.

During adolescence the work-committed women were not only rated as less sex-typed than others, they were also viewed as less attractive. The negative consequences for self-identity are obvious from the group's other distinctive characteristics: bodily concern and dissatisfaction with appearance. Q-sort ratings of sex-typing and attractiveness are correlated ($r = .57$), perhaps because many of the less attractive girls are tall and heavy-set, characteristics that did not fit the cultural ideal of feminine appearance. Although sex-typing and physical appearance may have had similar consequences for adolescent self-esteem, the two factors seem to affect adult career pattern differently.

Adolescent attractiveness is associated with permanence of marriage in adulthood. College women who were viewed as less attractive than average in adolescence were more likely to remain single or to divorce than were their more attractive peers [42% versus 10%; χ^2 (1) = 5.85, $p < .05$]. Marital outcome, then, is a crucial intervening link between adolescent characteristics and adult career in this sample. Youthful aspirations and interests that were not stereotypically feminine did not guarantee development of commitment to work in adulthood, although they probably set the stage, especially by motivating young women to continue with higher education. For aspirations and interests to be expressed in work commitment rather than in the more usual channels of volunteer or intermittent work, conventional solutions to the problem of women's multiple roles had to be exhausted.

Broadly speaking, sex-typing seems to affect values and preferences, what women *want*. The most feminine want traditionally feminine roles. The least feminine envision more options and may find it more difficult to settle for traditional solutions. Peer ratings of femininity ("acts like a little lady") in elementary school were related to occupational aspirations at age 15. Only 17% of the girls who scored above the median on femininity wanted to be a major professional, compared to

57% of those below the median [χ^2 (1) = 4.47, $p < .05$]. Although not statistically significant, the same trend was observed in junior high school. Attractiveness, on the other hand, affects opportunities, what women *get*. The less attractive have less opportunity to make a career of traditional domestic roles. The conjunction of values and opportunities seems crucial to the differentiation of career patterns in this sample.

The adolescent antecedents of work commitment among these college-educated women appear to function more to select women *out of* conventional female roles than directly *into* work careers. For most, commitment to work crystallized in the decade between 30 and 40, especially as actual or anticipated marital roles became less salient. Developing such commitment seems to have been more a process of capitalizing on areas of interest and success than one of following an inner drive for achievement from an early age. Birnbaum (1975) made a similar observation about the professional women in her study who were single. They differed markedly from married professionals, who reported holding high aspirations unambivalently from an early age.

Although the development of work commitment in this sample was associated with adaptive psychological functioning at age 40, this process clearly took a personal toll in adolescence and young adulthood. At age 30, work-committed women were already viewed as outstanding in intellectual functioning, but they were also seen as self-defeating and extremely self-critical. As Rossi (1965) predicted for career-committed women, their self-esteem was at a low point in young adulthood, when they saw other women establishing homes and families. By age 40, the work-committed were much more self-accepting. They were, however, less buoyant than homemakers, whose traditional path through adulthood is accompanied by a smoother course of personal development. These results for college-educated homemakers and work-committed women parallel those reported by F. Livson in Chapter 8 for psychologically healthy women with traditional and nontraditional personality styles. In each study, development was smoother for the group whose personality style in adolescence was more congruent with conventional sex-role expectations.

Double-Track and Unstable Careers

Compared to homemakers and work-committed women, college-educated, double-track and unstable workers share some social and familial characteristics (Table 14.4). Fewer were reared in upper middle-class families, and fewer are married to men in professional or managerial occupations. These wives are less satisfied with their husbands' incomes than are homemakers, and only 33% are above the mean in marital happiness compared to 79% of the homemakers. In both emotional and economic terms, then, these women's marriages have been less successful than the homemakers'.

At age 40, Q-sort ratings show that neither group is functioning as well as the homemakers or the work-committed (Table 14.5) and self-reports reveal that they find mid-life much less satisfying. Eighty percent of both homemakers and work-committed women describe the period from age 30 to 40 as bringing them the most satisfaction, compared to 36% of women with double-track or unstable career patterns [$\chi^2 (2) = 6.12$, $p < .05$]. Conversely, 45% of double-track and unstable workers consider this period the least satisfying, compared to 7% of homemakers and none of the work-committed.

Despite these similarities in social background, marital situation, and life satisfaction, double-track and unstable workers differ from each other in psychological functioning in adulthood and adolescence. Unstable workers have more distinctive personalities in middle age; double-track workers were more distinctive in adolescence (Table 14.6).

Double-Track Workers

Double-track workers are the most assertive of the four groups at 40. In most other respects their psychological functioning is less distinctive than that of any college-educated subgroup. Pairwise comparisons show double-track workers to be more forceful than homemakers but less cheerful and lower in morale (unstable workers are still lower). Compared to the unstable group, they have better social skills and are less self-defeating. As do work-committed women, double-track workers value independence, but thought and rationality are less important to them. Neither intellective processes nor interpersonal warmth are particularly salient in their personalities. Aside from assertiveness and independence, relatively low morale and self-esteem are the most notable characteristics of the double-track group.

In adolescence, the independence of double-track workers was linked with self-confidence and emotional stability (Table 14.6). Viewed as the most physically attractive group, double-track adolescents, like future homemakers, were satisfied with their physical appearance, aware of the impression they created, and were not unpredictable. Unlike homemakers, however, they were not oriented towards dependency and social approval in interpersonal relationships. Anticipating their adult assertiveness, double-track adolescents were quite straightforward and forthright in their dealings with others. They were the least likely to seek reassurance from others. The ego defenses of double-track adolescents were considered resilient, not brittle; they were viewed as functioning adaptively under stress.

Although the psychological functioning of double-track workers in adolescence suggests that these girls had the potential to become strong, individuated, emotionally resilient adults, only the potential for assertiveness has been fulfilled. As was the case with work-committed women, the personality style of double-track workers seems to have come into conflict with conventional sex-role expectations. Thus, although double-track workers' attractiveness may have facilitated their marital opportunities, their assertiveness may have made a comfortable adjustment to traditional domestic roles unlikely.

Unlike the work-committed, most double-track workers remain married, even if the relationship is relatively unrewarding. They work outside the home but remain primarily identified with familial roles and invest little of themselves in work (in which they are underemployed) or in education that would enable them to move out of relatively routine jobs. With marriages less happy than homemakers and jobs less rewarding than the work-committed, double-track workers seem to have the worst of both worlds. Indeed, this group seems personally unfulfilled compared with either homemakers or work-committed women. But the dual roles of double-track working women are more personally sustaining at mid-life than is the familial role of women with unstable work careers—those who have tried dual roles but no longer choose to work.

Unstable Workers

College-educated housewives with unstable work careers are by far the most distinctive group in psychological functioning at 40. They are the most hostile, angry, and depressed. Morale is very low. The most characteristic descriptors of this group, Basic Hostility and not Satisfied with Self, reflect problematic functioning in interpersonal relationships and in self-evaluation. Other functional deficits are in intellectual effectiveness and social and self-awareness. Individual members of the group have various psychological strengths, but none appears to be held in common.

Adolescent personality is not much implicated in either the career pattern or adult psychological functioning of the unstable group. At adolescence, they could hardly be distinguished from their peers. They were neither particularly socially skilled (not Aware of Impression Created) nor straightforward in communication and were considered somewhat unpredictable. Although fairly attractive they tended not to be satisfied with their physical appearance. A relative lack of social awareness has been a personality constant, but otherwise the array of deficits observed at 40 differs considerably from adolescent characteristics.

Experiences during adulthood may help to explain the relatively troubled psychological functioning of the unstable group in mid-life. By definition, women with unstable careers have at least one adult experience in common—a history of employment that is "off-time" in terms of normative role sequences. These women worked while still rearing children but left the labor force before age 40, a period when many other women go back to work. Although in theory an unstable work history can be associated with either positive or negative attitudes towards work and familial roles, in this sample college-educated women with unstable careers tend to be dissatisfied with both work and familial roles.

Satisfaction with previous jobs cannot be measured directly with our data, but interviews and questionnaires suggest that at 40 most women with unstable careers do not view employment favorably. One formerly ambitious woman writes about her future work plans, "I haven't the energy or motivation to absorb the responsibilities of two jobs."

College-educated unstable workers are less happily married than homemakers. In this respect, they are like the double-track group. But the domestic dissatisfactions of unstable workers extend to parental as well as marital roles. Of all college-educated career groups, unstable workers are rated as most dissatisfied with themselves as parents and most critical of their children (Table 14.7). The generalized hostility that is such a salient feature of their personalities may prevent unstable workers from establishing any kind of rewarding interpersonal relationships. Where the interpersonally competent double-track workers are disappointed with life at 40, the unstable are in despair.

Role attitudes, then, appear to link an unstable work history with poor psychological functioning in this relatively affluent and well-educated sample. In less affluent samples, however, the same kind of work history may reflect economic pressures or labor market opportunities rather than role dissatisfactions and may not have the strong associations with psychological deficits found here.

Immobilization seems as important as role dissatisfaction in understanding the situation of women with unstable careers. Campbell *et al.*, (1976) suggest that in general, "[wives] who choose to work outside the home are motivated in some degree at least by a failure to find

Table 14.7

Attitudes Toward Parental Role by Career
Pattern of College-Educated Women
(in Group Means)

Parental attitudes	Career pattern[a]					F
	H	WC	DT	U	Total	(df)
Satisfied with Self as Parent[b]	4.1	*4.2*	3.9	(3.2)	3.9	3.73^{**}
Not Critical of child[c]	4.4	*5.2*	4.0	(3.3)	4.3	6.26^{***}
Number of cases	19	6	8	6	39	(3,35)

Note: The highest group mean is italicized; the lowest is enclosed in parentheses.
[a]H = Homemaker, WC = Work-committed, DT = Double-track, U = Unstable.
[b]5-point scale.
[c]7-point scale.
$**p < .05.$
$***p < .01.$

homemaking totally satisfying, and those who choose to remain at home do because they find it rewarding." In our sample homemakers (56% of the college-educated wives) are those who find the most fulfillment in the housewife–mother role. The other 44%, who may find domestic roles less satisfying, have for the most part developed alternative sources of satisfaction in work. But women with unstable careers have not. Although most of them find homemaking unrewarding, they remain in the role and experience high levels of psychological distress.

Other studies have identified similarly distressed housewives with similar role attitudes. Housewives who are dissatisfied with their role (would prefer to be working) have been found to have the following characteristics: lack of confidence in themselves as mothers and many problems in child-rearing (Yarrow, Scott, de Leeuw, & Heinig, 1962); poor marital adjustment (Nye, 1963); dissatisfaction with their lives and themselves (Fidell and Prather, cited in Tavris, 1976); and use of psychoactive drugs (Prather, 1977). Radloff (1975) found marital happiness and employment to have an additive effect on women's scores on a depression scale. Housewives with unhappy marriages were the most depressed group (compare our unstable workers), more depressed than unhappily married working women (compare our double-track group), and, of course, more depressed than happily married housewives (compare our homemakers) or working women.

Diminished activity level and social isolation have also been found to be related to poor mental health among housewives. Housewives who were inactive in home and community activities were rated lower on life satisfaction than working wives and active housewives (Wood, 1963), and working-class housewives who were socially isolated were highly dissatisfied with their lives, compared to those who were employed or who had many social contacts (Ferree, 1976).

Our data provide no direct answer to the questions of how unstable workers came to be dissatisfied with familial roles and relatively immobilized. At 30 their psychological functioning was not very different from the double-track group. Both unstable and double-track women were already involved in relatively unhappy marriages at 30, and both groups were viewed as more hostile (scored high on Basic Hostility and Extrapunitive) than homemakers or work-committed women. Unstable workers expressed hostility more directly than did double-track workers, who were rated as more distrustful.

From these unpromising young adult beginnings, the group with more extensive psychological resources in adolescence, that is, double-track workers, went on to develop relatively satisfying relationships with their children. Their work lives provide them with regular social contacts and a means of contributing to valued family goals, even if work is not intrinsically rewarding. Unstable workers, who had fewer adolescent resources, became even more hostile. By middle age, few have found satisfaction in any of the major arenas of adult life— marriage, parenthood, or work.

Summary

At mid-life the college-educated women who have been most successful in their roles, traditional or nontraditional, have more extensive psychological resources than do the less successful. Successful participation in different social domains is associated with specialized psychological resources in adulthood: a sense of personal well-being for homemakers and intellectual effectiveness for the work-committed.

College women who by mid-life had had different careers in work and family seem to have been more alike as adolescents than they are as adults. Nevertheless, some personality antecedents of career patterns were found. From adolescence onward, the personalities of homemakers were remarkably congruent with traditional sex-role expectations. The adolescent personalities of girls who developed other career patterns were much less congruent with traditional expectations. Personality antecedents appeared to affect career primarily through their impact on the possibilities for, and the outcome of, marriage. Thus, both selective and reactive processes are at work in the development of career patterns and their personality concomitants among these college-educated women.

WOMEN WITH A HIGH-SCHOOL EDUCATION

Because career patterns are distributed differently among high-school and college women, only part of the analysis of the college group can be replicated among women with a high-school education. The analysis of social and personal concomitants and antecedents of career among those with a high-school education proceeds by comparing homemakers with others, termed the "employed." The employed group includes women with both double-track and unstable careers, who constitute 86% and 14% of this group, respectively.

Social Background, Current Status, and Family Life

In this sample, working-class status is more prominent among high school than among college women: 68% of the high-school group came from families of working-class origin; 41% are working class at age 40. Homemakers came from families of lower-status origin than did the employed, but the two groups do not differ significantly in current social class (see Table 14.8). The only familial factor on which the two groups are significantly different is marital history. All but one of the homemakers have intact first marriages, compared to only 33% of those with double-track or unstable careers [χ^2 (1), corrected for continuity, = 3.71, $p < .10$]. The other 67% have remarried after being divorced or, in one case, widowed. Two double-track workers never married, so that, altogether, only 29% of the employed have intact first marriages [χ^2 (1), corrected for continuity, = 4.91, $p < .05$].

High-school-educated career groups differ significantly on only two social-familial characteristics, whereas college-educated homemakers were characterized by numerous social and familial advantages in comparison to double-track and unstable workers who attended college. Less educated homemakers do resemble their college counterparts in their feelings of satisfaction with their husbands' incomes (67% of the homemakers with high-school educations are very satisfied, compared to 33% of their employed peers).

Thus, the contrast between homemakers and the employed in commitment to, and success in, familial roles is less clear-cut among noncollege than among college women. Among noncollege women,

Table 14.8

Social and Familial Characteristics by Career Pattern
of Women with a High School Education
(in Group Means and Percentages)

Social and Familial Characteristics	Career pattern[a]			
	H	DT,U	Total	t (df)
All respondents				
Adult social class[b] (mean)	2.6	3.9	3.4	.68
% I and II	50	29	36	
Childhood social class[b] (mean)	4.2	3.6	3.8	1.92*
% I, II, and III	12	43	32	
Marital status (% married)	100	86	91	
Number of cases	8	14	22	(20)
Currently married				
% Second marriages	12	67	45	
Marital adjustment at 40[c] (mean)	3.2	3.0	3.1	.57
% Above mean	50	42	45	
Occupational status of husband[d] (mean)	2.9	3.8	3.4	1.25
% 1 and 2	62	33	45	
Number of children (mean)	2.8	3.8	3.4	1.55
% 4 or more	50	42	45	
Number of cases	8	12	20	(18)
Ever married				
Marital adjustment at 30[c] (mean)	3.1	2.7	2.9	.80
% Above mean	50	18	32	
Number of cases	8	11	19	(17)

[a]H = Homemaker, WC = Work-committed, DT = Double-track,
U = Unstable. The non-homemaking group is composed of 86%
double-track, 14% unstable workers.
[b]Hollingshead 5-point scale, I = high. Social class is based
on husband's education and occupation or on own if single.
[c]5-point scale.
[d]Hollingshead 7-point scale, 1 = high.
*$p < .10$.

homemakers have experienced less marital instability than the employed, but the current marriages of the two groups are equally rewarding. Neither number of offspring nor satisfaction with parenthood significantly differentiate the noncollege career groups.

Altogether then, commitment to, and satisfaction with, the housewife-mother role may influence the career patterns of these women with high-school educations less than those of the college-educated. Homemakers with high-school educations feel themselves to be in a better position economically than their counterparts with other career patterns, and they have not had the experience of divorce in which their husbands' financial support is withdrawn or attenuated. If economic security rather than role attitudes and satisfactions is the main factor separating homemakers from non-homemakers among noncollege women, the relation between career pattern and personality may be weaker here than in the college group.

Personality in Relation to Career Pattern

Comparison of Middle Age and Adolescence

Extensive associations between career pattern and adult personality were found among the college women, but the data provide no evidence that adult personality is related to career pattern among those with a high school-education. The t-tests between less educated homemakers and employed on Q-sort items at ages 30 and 40 yield only four items that are significant at the .10 level at each time period, well within the chance expectation. At 40, the factor scores of the two groups were not significantly different, and only one of the 18 scales of the California Psychological Inventory (CPI) was statistically significant at the .10 level, again not exceeding chance expectations. Finally, their own reports on periods of greatest and least life satisfaction do not consistently distinguish between the career groups, whereas they did for college women. More of the less-educated employed than homemakers describe the decade from 30 to 40 as the most satisfying period of their life (81% versus 60%), but (in a separate question) more also find the same period least satisfying (27% versus 0%). I conclude, then, that adult psychological functioning is not associated with career pattern among these women with a high-school education.

Pre-adult personality, however, is more predictive of adult careers among women with high-school educations. When the pre-adult Q sorts of future homemakers were compared to those of girls who became double-track or unstable workers, 18 items significantly differentiated the groups at the .10 level (Table 14.9).[1] In general, homemakers functioned better during adolescence than others in the noncollege group in cognitive and interpersonal skills.

---

[1]Because only significant items are shown, the entries in Table 14.9 may not parallel those in Table 14.6.

Table 14.9

Psychological Functioning in Adolescence by Career
Pattern of Women with a High School Education
(in Group Means)

Psychological functioning	Career pattern[a]		
	H	DT,U	$t(20)$
Cognitive			
Flexibility			
Insightful	5.5	3.9	3.06***
Values Intellectual Matters	3.0	1.7	2.34**
Rebellious	2.2	3.6	2.06**
Other			
Ambitious	5.7	3.7	2.89***
Skeptical	4.9	3.9	1.86*
Wide Interests	4.0	2.7	1.78*
Interpersonal			
Submissiveness			
Feminine Style	8.0	6.6	1.88*
(Power-Oriented)	2.8	4.1	1.74*
Hostility			
(Warm)	7.5	5.5	2.56**
Turned To for Advice	4.5	3.2	2.35**
Bothered by Demands	3.6	5.1	1.87*
Other			
Pushes Limits	3.1	4.9	2.02*
Creates Dependency	3.6	4.9	1.84*
Intrapersonal			
Self-Deprecation			
(Satisfied with Self)	3.8	5.4	1.99*
Other			
Esthetically Reactive	7.0	5.4	3.14***
Projective	4.6	5.6	2.48**
Expressive	4.8	6.4	2.08**
Sensuous	6.2	4.6	1.93*
Number of cases	8	14	

Note: Q-sort items are organized according to their loadings
on adult factors. The highest group mean is italicized. Items
with high negative loadings are enclosed in parentheses.

[a] H = Homemaker, WC = Work-committed, DT = Double-track,
U = Unstable. The non-homemaking group is composed of 86%
double-track, 14% unstable workers.

    $*p < .10.$
   $**p < .05.$
  $***p < .01.$

Homemakers

The Q-sort items viewed as most characteristic of youngsters who became homemakers described them as sex-typed (Feminine Style), warm, and not at all rebellious. Although homemakers did not rebel against, nor test the limits of, authority, they were not inhibited in their internal impulse life: they enjoyed both sensuous and esthetic experiences (Esthetically Reactive). More ambitious than their peers, they valued intellectual matters more and had wider interests. Perhaps their high aspirations for themselves (Ambitious), coupled with greater insight or self-awareness (Insightful), made them more self-critical (not Satisfied with Self) than girls who developed other career patterns.

As was the case for college-educated women, some of the characteristics of future homemakers in the high-school group anticipate this role: sex-typing, nurturance, and lack of rebelliousness. However, their ambition and cognitive investment do not seem congruent with avoidance of work roles. Homemakers were even more ambitious occupationally in adolescence than other noncollege youth. Three-fifths of the homemakers but only 33% of the others who did not go to college indicated any liking for a high-status profession, reversing the relationship found among college-bound adolescents.

These characteristics are all the more striking when the relative class position of homemakers and employed in adolescence is considered (homemakers were lower). Among these women who did not attend college, youthful ambition seems to have been successfully channeled into conventional roles, perhaps accounting for the homemakers' social mobility through marriage. These working-class girls may have achieved their definition of success in adult roles by attaining the relative luxury of a homemaking career—not having to combine child-rearing with a routine job outside of the home.

Double-Track and Unstable Workers

The most striking adolescent characteristic of noncollege girls who became double track or unstable workers is the low salience of intellective processes in their overall psychological functioning. Compared to future homemakers, these girls were more rebellious, pushing of limits, power-oriented and likely to create (or exploit) dependency in others. They were also less nurturant: more bothered by demands, less warm and less likely to be turned to for advice. In addition to the outward thrust of their rebelliousness, these girls tended to use the externalizing defense of projection. Perhaps such externalizing strategies enabled them to feel relatively well-satisfied with self, in comparison to homemakers.

Unlike homemakers, adolescents who became double-track and unstable workers did not have personal resources that would predict success in either traditional marriage or work roles. The impermanence of their marriages is not surprising in view of their youthful rebelliousness and non-nurturant orientation. Their limited cognitive investment may have rendered work an unlikely source of satisfaction, although their economic position both in and outside of marriage may have made employment a necessity. Indeed, taking both social class and personal resources into account, it is hard to avoid the impression that the "cream of the crop" of the less educated young women became homemakers, while the others ended up with double-track or unstable work careers.

Summary

Although college women with different career patterns were more alike in adolescence than in adulthood, the reverse was true of the high-school group. Here, homemakers and women with other career patterns have become more homogeneous in personality in adulthood. The psychological differences between homemakers and the employed during adolescence seem to have served as selective factors to exclude the latter from homemaking careers. However, double-track and unstable workers' subsequent experiences with marital disruption and work appear to have stimulated the development of better coping skills.; by mid-life they had caught up with homemakers in cognitive and interpersonal functioning.[2] (In contrast, Clausen finds that differences in cognitive skills between men in higher- and lower-level occupations, or between men with different patterns of occupational mobility, persist from early adolescence to the middle years; see Chapter 13.)

Earlier I suggested that in this sample, career pattern was more independent of current role attitudes and satisfactions among women

---

[2]Another possible interpretation of these results is that the psychological functioning of homemakers deteriorated in adulthood. This interpretation is less consistent with the data than the one advanced in this chapter. The data show sharp increments in the cognitive and social skills of the employed between adolescence and early adulthood, while changes over time are less consistent for homemakers.

with a high-school education than among college-educated women. High-school-educated homemakers and the employed may be equal in commitment to, and satisfaction with, the housewife–mother role, with career pattern being determined mainly by pragmatic economic or situational factors. If this is the case, adult psychological functioning seems to be associated with careers in work and family only when role attitudes and satisfactions also vary with career. When women with different careers do not differ greatly either in commitment to work or to family, or in their satisfaction with marriage or family life, personality concomitants of career are likely to be few.

Finally, we should note that for most of the psychological variables associated with the careers of college women, the scores of unstable workers were more negative than those of any other career group. The unstable career pattern is relatively infrequent in the sample as a whole. Among noncollege women (33% of the sample), only two had this type of career. They were grouped together with double-track workers for statistical analysis. If in this middle-class sample an unstable career pattern reflects profound ambivalence about both familial and work roles (or if unstable workers differ from other women in some other unexplained way), the fact that no association was found between adult personality and career among high-school women may be accounted for by the low frequency of unstable careers in the high-school group.

CONCLUSION

This study focused on an array of women's careers that was more extensive than the usual dichotomy of working and nonworking women. Although analytical costs were imposed by a typology, substantive returns were great. The most extensive personality differences in mid-life were found, not between working and nonworking women, but rather between college-educated housewives with different types of careers. Housewives with a conventional work history (homemakers) were the happiest women in the sample, while housewives with unstable work careers were the most depressed. I suggest that role attitudes and satisfactions associated with these two career patterns are more important concomitants of psychological functioning than the work history itself, but this idea needs to be examined in other, larger samples.

Similarly, our two types of college-educated working women, those who were highly involved (work-committed) and less involved (double-track) with work, differed in psychological functioning, al-though less extensively than the two types of college-educated house-wives. In mid-life, work-committed women were functioning well both interpersonally and intellectually, but their morale (and that of double-track workers) was lower than that of homemakers. Again, the psychological implications of involvement with work need to be exam-ined in a larger sample, one in which marital status and education (closely associated with job involvement here) can be controlled.

In contrast to such differences for the college educated, I found no mid-life personality contrasts between homemakers and working women who did not attend college. The marital disruption and em-ployment that typified the life course of high school-educated double-track and unstable workers may have served as maturing experiences for them, for personality deficits apparent in adolescence had been overcome by age 40. Here, career differentiation in the adult life course was related to movement towards greater personality homogeneity in adulthood rather than greater personality differentiation.

Selection versus Reaction

Interpreting these career–personality relationships in terms of selec-tive or reactive processes was more complicated than anticipated. The selective hypothesis postulates that career is associated with adult personality primarily because people tend to be recruited into the careers for which they are best suited. The reactive hypothesis posits that experience within a career affects personality directly, indepen-dently of the initial characteristics of the recruits.

Under a simple selective theory, antecedent personal characteristics would be expected to "fit" role requirements. Thus, girls who are pas-sive and dependent would be likely to become housewives, whereas more active and independent youngsters may seek challenging jobs. This hypothesis predicts considerable personality continuity between adolescence and adulthood, and adult experiences in different roles should maintain the personal characteristics which made the roles attractive in the first place.

If selective factors serve to allocate individuals to careers indepen-dently of the fit between youthful personality and role, the picture is more complicated. Adolescent-adult personality associations are then mediated not by career per se but by those aspects of the life course that are associated with career—in the present sample, marital per-manence and marital happiness in interaction with education.

College-educated homemakers, who seemed to be well socialized to traditional female roles even in adolescence, showed the strongest evidence of personality continuity. Rather than affecting career directly, adolescent personality antecedents seemed to affect career indirectly through their impact on martial "success." Likewise, the impact of career on psychological functioning in mid-life (predicted by the reactive hypothesis) could not be adequately understood without taking into account the marital contexts in which career decisions were made. In this sample, then, marital experiences (stability and/or marital happiness) intervene between adolescent personality, career, and psychological functioning in mid-life. This is true for well-educated women as well as for those whose formal education ended with high school. To understand these results, the life course of our respondents should be viewed in its specific historical context.

Cohort Characteristics and Historical Context

Women in our sample attended high school during World War II and graduated at the close of the war. They married at the median age of 21 (22 for college women) and had their first child 2 years later. By the end of the next decade, they had an average of 3.4 children, with the last birth occurring at the median age of 31, in 1960. Thus, the major years of family formation and childbearing for this cohort coincided with the postwar baby boom. The baby boom culminated in 1958 when the national birth rate reached its peak.

The women of this cohort were subject to intense socialization toward family-centeredness. If young women who attended college in the late 1940s were being prepared along with men for competence in the public world of work, other socialization influences were telling them that women's fulfillment lay in the family. Thus, although the women in our sample may seem to have been well prepared for work in the sense of obtaining educational qualifications, they were socialized to devote their lives to their families.

Apart from socialization, the life course of this cohort was affected by the expanding economy of the 1950s and 1960s. Raising their families in an economy characterized by neither stagnation nor severe inflation, full-time motherhood was not the luxury it is fast becoming. Also, because of the size of their families, maternal responsibilities lasted for a long time. At 40, most of these mothers were still busy with children in elementary school. One-quarter of the sample still had preschool children.

These special ideological, economic, and demographic conditions could profoundly influence the relative contributions of work and familial roles to the quality of life experienced by women in this study. Under these conditions, it is not surprising that married women who work are those who have been comparatively less successful in marriage, economically and/or emotionally. Nor is it surprising that when a homemaking career is associated with perceived success and satisfaction in marriage, homemakers have higher morale than working wives. Domestic roles did not restrict the adult development of college-educated homemakers, who by adolescence had already developed personal qualities that would enhance their future performance and satisfaction in traditional female roles. But the association found here between exclusively domestic roles and sense of personal well-being may not be found in other birth cohorts, especially more recent ones.

Serious involvement with work is found in this sample mainly among well-educated women who are single in mid-life. Marked discontinuity in personality between adolescence and adulthood characterizes this group. At 40, work-committed women are functioning better than ever before. Their psychological resources seem to have been liberated by the ending of unhappy marriages and the resolution of identity issues around singlehood and involvement with work.

The cohort in this study came of age at the height of the feminine mystique, whereas young women today are entering adulthood in an era characterized demographically by declining birth rates, later marriages and rising rates of divorce, and ideologically by changing conceptions of sex roles. Under these conditions, the social pressures that influenced "well-adjusted" young college women to become homemakers with large families may now be influencing them in the opposite direction.[3] Changes in women's socialization, education, and occupational opportunities may also influence the relationships found here between commitment to work, socially defined "deviance" in marital experience, and morale. Rising rates of divorce and age at first marriage may make a substantial period of singlehood in adult life more the norm than the exception. Talented women may experience fewer internal and external barriers. to launching a serious work career in their twenties. If the personal and social cost of nontraditional careers is reduced, the extensive psychological resources found among work-

---

[3]Luria (1974) suggests that the association between psychological adjustment and future career may now be reversed in direction. Seniors graduating from a New England college in the late 1960s who preferred traditional or nontraditional work careers were more optimistic, striving, extroverted, and better adjusted than those who preferred not to work.

committed women in the present sample may come to be associated with a greater sense of personal well-being.

Although critics of the housewife role have emphasized the personal cost of the role to women, I found that the role did not restrict the development of women with certain personal inclinations at a certain historical period. Social changes, however, will influence the relationship between women's careers and personalities in the future. One hopes that the congruence between personal affinities and social roles will increase while the personal cost of nontraditional career lines will decrease. Changes in the definition of sex roles both in and outside of marriage will be essential if women are to realize their full human potential for love and for work.

15

A Longitudinal Study of Patterns of Personality and Political Ideologies

PAUL H. MUSSEN and NORMA HAAN

The *Authoritarian Personality* (Adorno, Frenkel-Brunswik, Levinson, & Sanford, 1950), and a number of subsequent studies confirming these findings, showed fascist social and political attitudes to reflect the authoritarian's deep-seated personality and motivational structures. Authoritarians were characterized as rigid, power-oriented, stereotyped in thinking, conventional, lacking in intraceptiveness, unable to introspect, cynical about the motives of others, and preoccupied with virility, strength, and toughness.

Because individuals with less extreme political orientations—for example, liberal democrats, left-wing radicals, democratic socialists—have not been studied intensively, we cannot make broad generalizations about the relationship between personality structure and political attitudes and/or behavior. In fact, many students of political socialization doubt that meaningful relationships exist between these two kinds of variables (see, e.g., Greenstein, 1965). After a critical review of relevant empirical studies, Sears (1969) concluded that the role of personality variables in political behavior is minimal, and Rossi (1966) maintained that no one has demonstrated any strong relationships between personality and "partisan choice."

As psychologists concerned with personality development, we find such conclusions intuitively unreasonable. Deep-seated personality characteristics are influential mediators of individuals' perceptions, conceptualizations, and interpretations of others' behavior. Because fundamental personality characteristics and attitudes toward others

391

and toward society are likely to be shaped during childhood as consequents of particular socialization experiences, they tend to be relatively stable and enduring. For these reasons, we hypothesize adults' political opinions to be associated with their contemporary personality structures which, in turn, develop from—and are continuous with— early established, deep-seated expectancies about self and interpersonal relationships.

A critical test of these hypotheses depends on systematic data on the *developmental course* of personality characteristics associated with different sociopolitical orientations—that is, evidence derived from the longitudinal study of these characteristics from childhood through adulthood. With few exceptions, associations between personality and sociopolitical attitudes have been studied in adults only. The study reported here is designed to fill this gap, using longitudinal data to determine whether personality characteristics that differentiate adults of varying political orientations emerge early and consistently differentiate liberals and conservatives over long developmental periods.

Our attention focuses on 62 of the 90 personality and social variables for which we have Q-sort ratings at four time periods. More than half of these (32) were selected because we judged them to be directly related to characteristics of authoritarians or nonauthoritarians. Although our sample probably includes very few authoritarians in the full sense of the term, we hypothesize that conservatives are more likely than liberals to manifest characteristics associated with authoritarianism. Specifically, studies of authoritarians leads us to hypothesize that conservatives will be rated higher, on the average, than liberals on the following 17 variables: Uncomfortable with Uncertainty, Skeptical, Somatizes, Self-Defensive, Fastidious, Submissive, Seeks Reassurance, Repressive, Extrapunitive, Overcontrolled, Condescending, Basic Hostility, Moralistic, Conventional, Power-Oriented, Distrustful; for males, Masculine Style and, for females, Feminine.

We also hypothesize that characteristics typical of those low in authoritarianism will be more characteristic of liberals than of conservatives. That is, we predict that liberals will have higher mean ratings than conservatives on these 15 characteristics: Introspective, Thinks Unconventionally, Expressive, Values Intellectual Matters, Insightful, Socially Perceptive, Fantasizing, Esthetically Reactive, Sensuous, Philosophically Concerned, Values Independence, Evaluates Others' Motivations, Rebellious, Wide Interests, Prides Self on Objectivity.

Because this study is in part exploratory, we consider the possibility that 30 other characteristics that have no obvious relationship to authoritarianism or democratic attitudes may also be related to political orientation. If we find relationships between those characteristics and liberalism or conservatism, we have a more comprehensive description of the personality structures underlying these orientations. However, we formulate no specific predictions about the nature of the relationships.

To determine whether political orientations are associated with each of the personality characteristics, we use the technique of multivariate analyses of repeated measures for (a) three political orientations—liberal, middle-of-the-road, and conservative, (b) sex, and (c) time (period of testing). This procedure enables us to discern whether each of the 62 characteristics (a) distinguishes the three political groups when all four periods of measurement are considered as one (sex and time controlled); or (b) shows differential developmental trends for the three political groups (time × politics interaction with sex controlled); or (c) differentiates males and females of different political orientations (sex × politics interaction with time period controlled). These analyses address three different kinds of personality contrasts: (a) those persisting among the political groups for all four time periods combined, (b) those arising from developmental differences among the political groups (i.e., differences among political groups that are apparent at some, but not all, time periods), and (c) those specific to the interactions between sex and politics that also persist across the years (i.e., differences among political groups of either males or females, but not both).

METHODS

Participants

The participants are a subsample of the 196 members of the OGS and GS interviewed at the most recent follow-up (1968–1970). During the 4-hour interview, they were asked about political issues on which American opinion appeared to be polarized at that time—specifically the Vietnam war and demands of Blacks. Responses were coded by trained professionals. In addition, questionnaires included a 7-point scale of political position on which individuals rated themselves on a continuum from "strongly conservative" to "radical." None chose "radical."

Study members were categorized as liberals or conservatives only when their classification on all three criteria—the war, Black demands, and self-rating on political position—were consistent. The conservatives were those who rated themselves as strongly or moderately conservative, believed the United States must win the war and were thoroughly unsympathetic with Black demands, expressing the view that the socioeconomic position of most Blacks was "their own fault." Liberals rated themselves as liberal or liberal-radical, felt the war was wrong from the beginning, favored rapid withdrawal from Vietnam, supported Black demands, and felt Black militancy was justified. Those who rated themselves as "middle-of-the-road," said they "didn't know what to think" about ending the war although they had approved of it in the beginning, and claimed they were not prejudiced against Blacks but disapproved of Black militancy.

Using these criteria we were able to classify 74% of the 196 study members: 31 (21 females and 10 males) were liberal, 71 (33 females and 38 males) were conservative, and 43 (18 males and 25 females) were middle-of-the-road. Of the unclassified 26%, 7% had insufficient information; the other 19% were inconsistent in their ideological positions. The fact that about 75% of the participants could readily be categorized strongly suggests that, in this predominantly middle-class group, consistent political orientations are the rule rather than the exception. Contrary to what many political scientists believe, political beliefs do not generally vary from issue to issue.

The results reported here are for those 100 of the 196 participants for whom we have Q-sort data for all four time periods. These include 46 males (24 conservatives, 15 middle-of-the-roaders, and 7 liberals) and 54 females (21 conservatives, 18 middle-of-the-roaders, and 7 liberals) and 54 females (21 conservatives, 18 middle-of-the-roaders, and 15 liberals).

The participants are generally politically active. According to questionnaire responses, 90% of each group voted in the last three presidential elections and 50% regarded themselves as "active in political organizations." More of the conservatives voted, but more of the liberals considered themselves politically active. However, these differences are not statistically significant. As a group, middle-of-the-roaders were least active and voted least. Compared with the other two groups, more liberals did precinct work, donated to political causes, signed petitions, marched, and demonstrated. Middle-of-the-roaders were least likely to participate in these activities.

The participants were also asked to compare, by ratings, their present (middle-age) position with their orientations at 21 and with their parents', children's, and spouses' current views. Their ratings indicate that both liberals and conservatives perceive themselves as having become more firm and self-consistent in their political orientations. Liberals rated themselves as more liberal than they had been when they were younger and more liberal than their parents and spouses, but not more liberal than their children. The conservatives regarded themselves as more conservative than they had been at 21 and more conservative than their children and spouses, but more liberal than their parents.

The political groups were compared on a number of demographic variables, such as size of family of origin, birth order, education, and occupation, as well as the occupation, education, and combined socioeconomic status (SES) rating of father and spouse. Only one difference is significant: liberal women have more education that women in the other two groups ($p < .05$) and their fathers and husbands also tend to have more education than the fathers and husbands of other groups ($p < .10$); the male participants do not differ significantly in occupational and SES levels. Analyses of the IQ scores of the three political groups, for males and females separately, at three time periods (early and late adolescence and middle age) yield only one significant difference; liberal women scored higher on the Stanford-Binet, Form M, in late adolescence. No other IQ comparisons approach significance.

RESULTS

Continuity of Sociopolitical Attitudes

We are able to make some assessment of the association between sociopolitical beliefs during adolescence and later political orientation because the F (Fascism), PEC (Political-Economic-Conservatism), and E (Ethnocentrism) scales were administered to 32 girls and 15 boys of the present sample in the early 1940s. Spearman rank order correlations between liberalism in middle age (ages 40–47) and scores on each of the scales are given in Table 15.1.

For females, liberalism in middle age is significantly and negatively correlated with both ethnocentrism and authoritarianism during adolescence. For males the correlations are also negative, significantly in the case of ethnocentrism and nearly significantly in the case of authoritarianism. The ordering of means on all three scales was the same for both sexes: the adult conservatives had been the most ethnocentric, authoritarian, and politically and economically conservative; the middle-of-the-roaders were next; and the liberals had scored

Paul H. Mussen and Norma Haan

Table 15.1

Relationships between Adolescent Political-Social
Attitudes and Middle-Age Adult Liberalism

Adolescence	Adult liberalism		
	Total Rho	Male Rho	Female Rho
Ethnocentrism (E)	-.65***	-.65***	-.62***
Authoritarianism (F)	-.48***	-.39	-.51***
Political-economic conservatism (PEC)	-.15	-.31	-.17
Number of persons	47	15	32

Note: Only GS subjects (N = 47) are included.
***p < .01.

lowest on all three scales. We therefore infer an appreciable degree of continuity or consistency in political orientations and attitudes from adolescence to middle adulthood, a period of approximately 35 years.

Testing the Hypotheses

We now turn to the 32 variables that, according to our hypotheses, should differentiate the political groups for all time periods taken together and developmentally, that is, across the four time periods. Multivariate analyses of variance, using orthogonal polynomials with chronological age defining the points in time (Bock, 1975; McCall & Appelbaum, 1973), show significant main effects for political orientation on eight of these variables with time of testing (or age of subject) and sex controlled. Persistent differences across time occur for: Submissive, Seeks Reassurance, Prides Self on Objectivity, Moralistic, Rebellious, Conventional, Philosophically Concerned, and Values Independence (see Table 15.2).

In addition, significant interactions between time period and political orientation indicate differential developmental trends in four other personality variables for which we hypothesized group differences: Uncomfortable with Uncertainty, Extrapunitive, Fantasizing, and Sensuous. Further, Moralistic and Conventional, both of which have significant main effects, also have significantly different developmental trends.

Having established that political orientation itself and the interaction between time and political orientation significantly affect ratings on a number of personality variables, we turn to the group means to determine whether the differences are in the predicted directions. Al-

Table 15.2

Significant Effects for Political Differences
(Multivariate Analyses)

| | F ratios[a] | | |
| | | Interactions | |
Variable	Main effects politics (time and sex controlled)	Sex × politics (time controlled)	Time × politics (sex controlled)
Hypotheses tests			
Submissive	4.14**	ns	ns
Seeks Reassurance	5.32**	ns	ns
Prides Self on Objectivity	3.94**	ns	ns
Moralistic	4.02**	ns	4.71*
Rebellious	5.96***	ns	ns
Conventional	11.59****	ns	4.91***
Philosophically Concerned	5.37**	ns	ns
Values Independence	4.42**	ns	ns
Uncomfortable with Uncertainty	ns	ns	2.72**
Extrapunitive	ns	ns	4.70***
Fantasizing	ns	ns	3.83***
Sensuous	ns	ns	2.84**
Other variables			
Giving	5.83***	ns	ns
Sympathetic	4.58**	ns	ns
Cheerful	4.11**	ns	ns
Responds to Humor	ns	ns	3.03**
Moody	ns	ns	2.94**
Proffers Advice	ns	ns	3.33**
Satisfied with Self	ns	6.09***	ns

Note: No three-way interactions were significant.
[a] ns indicates "no significance."
    *$p < .10$.
   **$p < .05$.
  ***$p < .01$.
 ****$p < .001$.

most all confirm the hypotheses. Table 15.2 shows the variables having significant overall F tests. The mean ratings assigned at each time period, which describe political positions of the groups, are also shown graphically in Figs. 15.1-15.6. For clarity of discussion we focus primarily on the differences between the liberals and conservatives. The interested reader will find the means for the middle group on the graphs.

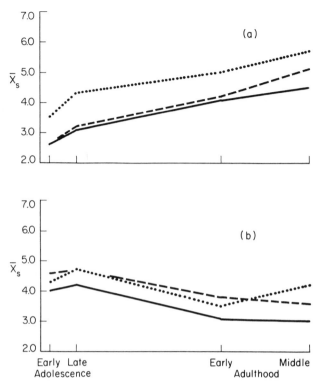

Fig. 15.1 Political groups' average scores on (a) Philosophical Concern and (b) Rebellious. In Figs. 15.1 through 15.6, three groups are presented: ——conservative; ---middle of the road; . . . . . liberal.

Personality Differences between Political Groups (Time and Sex Controlled)

Table 15.2 and the graphs in Figs. 15.1–15.6 clearly demonstrate that from early adolescence on, liberals and conservatives evidence distinctive cores of personal attributes. Throughout the long period from early adolescence through middle age (about 35 years) liberals were, according to the ratings, more philosophically concerned and rebellious than conservatives, valued independence more, and prided themselves more on objectivity. On the other hand, for these same long periods, conservatives were consistently rated higher than liberals on Submissiveness and Seeks Reassurance.

Political orientations show significant main effects for two other personality characteristics, Conventional and Moralistic. Both these characteristics also show significant developmental trends. As pre-

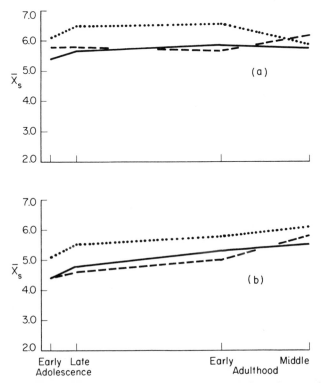

Fig. 15.2.   Political groups' average scores on (a) Values Independence and (b) Prides Self on Objectivity.

dicted, liberals are significantly less conventional than conservatives at three of the four time periods (see Fig. 15.4), the differences being particularly large during early and middle adulthood. In late adolescence liberals and conservatives are undifferentiated with respect to ratings on this variable, but after that time, liberals become relatively less conventional. Middle-of-the-roaders, originally highly conventional, also show a decrease in conventionality, although their decrease is not as sharp as that of the liberals. In this, as in several other characteristics we discuss later, incipient group differences are discernible during early adolescence, but clearer, more distinctive patterns related to political orientation emerge fully only in the later years.

Mean ratings of the three groups on Moralistic at the four time periods (see Fig. 15.4) indicate that as adolescents liberals tended to be more moralistic than the other two groups, but became substantially less moralistic in adulthood. Perhaps the liberals' relatively high

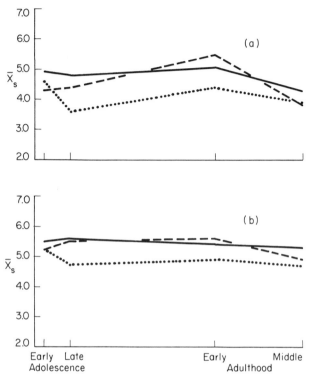

Fig. 15.3. Political groups' average scores on (a) Submissive and (b) Seeks Reassurance.

ratings on Moralistic during adolescence represent an aspect of their philosophical concerns. Philosophically concerned adolescents are likely to have strong, and perhaps absolutistic, interests in abstractions, moral principles, justice, and values. With increasing age, however, the liberals become less moralistic, more aware of the relativity of moral values. Conservatives maintain their relatively high standings in this characteristic. Thus, the predicted difference between the groups in tendency to be moralistic obtained only in the adult years.

We conclude from these findings that liberals and conservatives differ significantly from each other in the hypothesized ways, and the differences are consistently manifested in repeated independent ratings beginning in early adolescence. From that period onward, conservatives (like authoritarians) appear to be insecure, submissive to

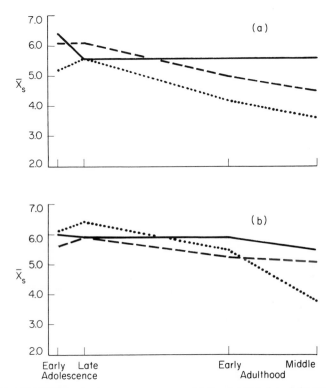

Fig. 15.4. Political groups' average scores on (a) Conventional and (b) Moralistic.

authority, and highly sensitive to "external agencies"—and, hence, to have strong needs for reassurance. In contrast, liberals manifest opposite characteristics that are similar to those of nonauthoritarians: They are more concerned with subjective matters and "tenderminded"— that is, they show more philosophical concern, rebelliousness and independence, willingness to acknowledge their feelings and to regard their own and others' problems and feelings with detachment (high rating on Prides Self on Objectivity), and relatively little adherence to conventional values.

These findings contradict the broad thesis that political orientation is "acquired haphazardly." Rather, they strongly support the argument that political orientations are associated with—and, perhaps, reflect—early established, deep-seated, and enduring personality characteristics.

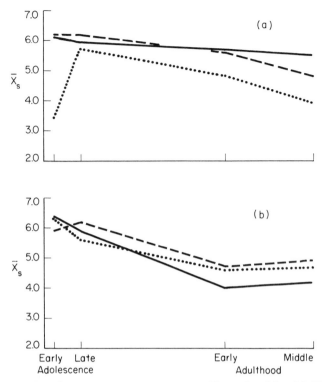

Fig. 15.5. Political groups' average scores on (a) Uncomfortable with Uncertainity and (b) Fantasizing.

Developmental Trends

In addition to the eight Q-sort variables showing main effects of political orientation and generally confirming our predictions, four Q-sort ratings have significant time × political orientation interactions that support predicted differences in developmental trends, although these differences are marked only at certain time periods (see Figs. 15.5 and 15.6). For example, we predicted that conservatives would be consistently more uncomfortable with uncertainty than liberals, and clear-cut group differences are found at three periods: late adolescence, early adulthood, and middle adulthood, but *not* during early adolescence. Thus the hypothesis is partially confirmed. Apparently the liberals' tolerance of uncertainty is a characteristic that gradually and steadily evolves with increasing maturity.

Authoritarians have been found to be more rigid and stereotyped in

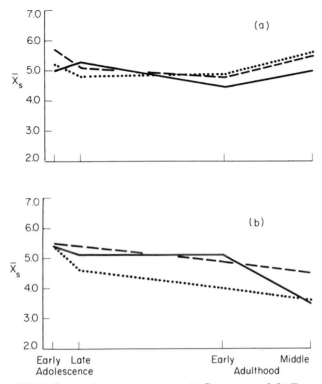

Fig. 15.6. Political groups' average scores on (a) Sensuous and (b) Extrapunitive.

thinking, more sensitive to external pressures, and unable to intro-spect or acknowledge their own feelings and fantasies. Therefore, we hypothesized that liberals would manifest more fantasizing than con-servatives and be rated as more sensuous and less extrapunitive. These predictions are confirmed, for parts of the developmental curves, by significant interactions between time and political orientation on these variables (see Table 15.2 and Figs. 15.5 and 15.6). As adolescents, the liberals were not markedly different from conservatives on Fantasiz-ing, but they shifted in the direction of the predicted difference, becom-ing strikingly more likely to fantasize in early and middle adulthood. As early adolescents, liberals and conservatives did not differ in Sen-suousness and, in late adolescence, liberals were rated lower than con-servatives in this characteristic. However, in adulthood, the liberals are clearly regarded as more sensuous individuals, as we predicted.

The mean rating for liberals on Extrapunitive is lower than for con-

Paul H. Mussen and Norma Haan

servatives in late adolescence and early adulthood, partially confirming another hypothesis. However, the two groups do not differ on this variable in either early adolescence or middle adulthood.

Summary of Hypothesized Differences

In brief, Q-sort ratings, made completely independently at four widely separated periods, yield findings that fully or partially confirm 12 (38%) of the 32 hypothesized personality differences between groups of different political orientations. For six of these characteristics the differences are clear-cut and consistent—that is, liberals and conservatives differ significantly from each other in the predicted direction at all four time periods. The individual's relative standing in these characteristics, linked with either liberal or conservative positions, was established by early adolescence and maintained through the period of middle adulthood. The other six group differences in personality characteristics are also in the direction predicted from the hypotheses, but they are not apparent at all age periods studied. Therefore we cannot conclude that the individual's relative standing in these characteristics is established early and remains relatively stable.

Developmental trends in some of the variables indicate that, as they matured, the liberals became less constricted, more aware of their own and others' feelings and emotions, more flexible, less stereotyped and less rigid in their thinking and judgments of others. For example, although they valued independence highly and were rebellious even as young adolescents, the liberals, like the conservatives, were rated as highly moralistic, conventional, and uncomfortable with uncertainty at that time. But whereas conservatives maintained high standings in these traits, the liberals' ratings declined considerably. As adolescents, liberals and conservatives also were not differentiated in characteristics indicative of expressiveness or contact with their own feelings and emotions, specifically in tendency to fantasize or in sensuousness. Over the years, however, the conservatives' tendency to fantasize decreased sharply while liberals changed relatively little in this respect. In early adolescence, conservatives appeared to be somewhat more sensuous than liberals. Perhaps the strong independence of the liberals and their philosophical concern inhibited their sensousness at this period. During adulthood, however, liberals apparently became more sensuous as conservatives became appreciably less so.

A synthesis of these signifcant findings yields reasonable and coherent general pictures of liberals' and conservatives' personality structures. The enduring qualities associated with a liberal sociopolitical

orientation are independence, unconventionality in thinking and behavior, rebelliousness, orientation toward philosophical matters, objectivity, willingness to accept one's own motivations and desires as
well as responsibility for one's own actions. In contrast, conservatives
are, over prolonged periods of time, lacking in independence, submissive, in need of reassurance, moralistic, little given to introspection,
and uncomfortable with uncertainty (that is, intolerant of ambiguity).

These data strongly suggest that contrary to what some students of
political socialization have said, political orientations *are* associated
with distinctive deep-seated and enduring personality characteristics
that are acquired early in life. Furthermore, the consistency over time
of some of the group differences indicate that an individual's relative
standing on these characteristics, compared with the peer group, is not
transient, but rather is persistent over long periods of time.

Other Characteristics Related to Political Orientation

The relative standings of the three political groups on 30 other personality variables were also examined. Significant effects of political
orientation, with sex controlled, were found for six of these variables,
and with time controlled, for one variable (totaling 23%). Examination
of the means for specific time periods shows conservatives had the
highest ratings, and liberals the lowest, on Giving at every time
period. The conservatives were also regarded as significantly more
sympathetic and more cheerful than the liberals during both periods of
adolescence, but not during the adult years; conservatives surpassed
middle-of-the-roaders in these characteristics at all time periods. As
adults, the liberal and conservative groups are not strikingly differentiated with respect to these variables.

These differences between liberals and conservatives may be interpreted in the context of other findings already summarized. The conservatives' high standings on Giving, Sympathetic, and Cheerful may
reflect the conventionality of their thinking and behavior—their concepts of socially acceptable behavior, their needs for reassurance and
for social approval. The liberals' relatively low rating on cheerfulness
and sympathy during adolescence was perhaps a reflection of their
high levels of independence, rebelliousness, and unconventionality—
characteristics that may lead to conflicts with parents, poor relationships with peers, and a sense of alienation from others. If this is true,
adolescence is more likely to be a period of maladjustment and conflict
for liberals than for the more submissive, conventional conservatives.

In addition, significant effects of the interaction between political orientation and time indicate different developmental trends on three variables—Moody, Responds to Humor, and Proffers Advice. In early adulthood, liberals were rated higher than conservatives on Responds to Humor and lower in Proffers Advice, but the two groups did not markedly differ from each other in moodiness at any time. The significant interaction effects noted are attributable largely to the contrasts between middle-of-the-roaders and liberals, the latter being rated as less moody, more responsive to humor, and less likely to proffer advice than the middle-of-the-road group at all time periods.

Finally, the multivariate analyses yielded only one significant effect of the interaction between sex and political orientation (with time held constant). Among the male subjects, liberals were rated highest on Satisfied with Self and conservatives lowest, whereas among the females, the liberals were least satisfied with themselves and conservatives the most.

California Personality Inventory

The CPI was administered to the study members during early and middle adulthood (Chapter 10). One-way analyses of variance were applied to each of the subscale scores for the two separate time periods.

Only a few findings are significant, but these are generally congruent with—and thus reinforce—the results from the Q-sort assessments, particularly for women. For women, significant main effects of political orientation in middle adulthood are found on 4 of the 26 CPI scores [18 regular (Gough, 1957) and 8 coping scales (Haan, 1965)]. Conservative women score highest of the three groups on the Communality scale, indicating that "their reactions and responses correspond to the modal (common) pattern of this inventory" (Gough, 1957). This finding is consistent with the conservatives' characteristically conventional thinking, noted in their Q-sort assessments. During middle adulthood, liberal women score significantly higher than the others on the scales that measure independence, flexibility, and intraceptiveness, that is, Flexibility, Logical Analysis, and Regression in the Service of the Ego. The scores on Logical Analysis indicate that the liberal women are more interested than the others in "analyzing thoughtfully, carefully and cogently the aspects of situations personal and otherwise," while their high scores on Regression in the Service of the Ego show their willingness and ability to "utilize past feelings and ideas ... in an imaginative way in order to enrich the solution of problems, the handling of situations and the enjoyment of life" (Haan, 1963).

Only two CPI scales differentiate the political groups of men during middle adulthood. Like their female counterparts, the conservative men score highest of the three groups on the Communality scale and the liberals score highest on Flexibility.

None of the CPI scales significantly differentiate the three men's political groups in early adulthood, but seven significant F ratios are derived from the women's early adult CPI scores. Liberal women score highest of the three groups on scales measuring adaptability, high ego strength, independence of thought, responsibility, and intellectuality: Flexibility, Psychological Mindedness ["interest in, and responsiveness to, the inner needs, motives, and experience of others" (Gough, 1957)], Intellectuality (capable of detachment, impartial analysis, and awareness), Logical Analysis, Concentration (ability to set aside disturbing or attractive feelings or thought in order to concentrate on the task at hand), Suppression ["holding infeasible and inappropriate impulses in abeyance ... until an appropriate time or place presents itself" (Haan, 1965)], and Total Coping (general use of coping mechanisms to handle problems).

To summarize, the yield of significant findings from the CPI is not as rich as that of the Q sort, but all the group differences—particularly those pertaining to the women—corroborate the Q-sort results. Conservatives again reveal conventionality, and liberals manifest flexibility, independence, intellectuality, psychological mindedness, and willingness to probe their own and others' motives and emotions.

DISCUSSION

We conclude that, contrary to what several social psychologists and political scientists suggest, sociopolitical beliefs and orientations are not inconsistent or acquired haphazardly. Adolescents who are antiauthoritarian and nonethnocentric are likely to develop into liberal adults. Moreover, since differences in the personalities and social orientations of conservatives and liberals are already clear during adolescence and are stable over prolonged periods of time, the influence of personality on the choice of political ideology cannot be ignored. The evidence from this study demonstrates that individuals of contrasting sociopolitical orientations are characterized by distinctive constellations of psychological traits, interpersonal attitudes, and styles of processing information, thinking, and responding to the world and to their own feelings.

The enduring liberal personality constellation is composed of independence, rebelliousness, unconventional thinking, concern with philosophical and intellectual matters, pride in objectivity, and greater acceptance of one's own and others' feelings, emotions, and motivations. In contrast, those with conservative sociopolitical orientation present a longstanding pattern of characteristics that includes submissiveness, dependence on others, strong needs for reassurance, moralism, little inclination toward introspection, and being uncomfortable with uncertainty (intolerant of ambiguity). Political views appear to be congruent with, and perhaps extensions of, certain early-established personal characteristics.

Although the sources of these contrasting distinctive constellations of personality characteristics are not fully understood, it is reasonable to suggest that they are the consequents of different kinds of socialization experiences. We hypothesize that authoritative (Baumrind, 1967) or democratic (Baldwin, 1949) child-rearing practices—which foster the development of independence, unconventionality, curiosity, initiative, expressiveness, social responsibility, and self-acceptance—are conducive to the development of liberal political thinking. Conservatives, by contrast, may be the products of authoritarian homes in which the parents exercise high degrees of control, encourage submissive behavior, and discourage or punish expressiveness and independence.

Once established, these personal attributes may predispose the individual to acquire particular political or social orientations. Simply stated, our view is that broad general qualities, such as independence, intellectual curiosity, unconventionality in thinking, and awareness of one's own and others' feelings, may be the foundations of a proclivity to examine and challenge the sociopolitical and economic status quo, and perhaps to advocate changes in existing institutions—that is, to uphold liberal points of view on sociopolitical matters. In contrast, the individual who is submissive, conventional, uncomfortable with uncertainty, and in need of reassurance is more likely to accept the status quo without question or challenge, to advocate maintaining the existing sociopolitical system, and to oppose social change—in short, to adhere to conservative sociopolitical philosophy.

The need for caution in generalizing from these findings must be emphasized. The conservatives of our sample should not be considered authoritarians. Although many of the traits and characteristics associated with political conservatism are also linked with authoritarianism, there are some notable differences. For example, we have no evidence that the conservatives studied here share the authoritarian traits of basic hostility, domination, superstitiousness, and preoccupation with virility, toughness, and aggression.

Nor is their substantial support for the suggestion that liberals are fundamentally more stable or better adjusted than conservatives. Although the group difference tends in this direction during the adult years, during adolescence liberals were described as moralistic, relatively unsympathetic, and not cheerful—hardly models of good personal adjustment. Perhaps at times of great personal change and turbulence, such as adolescence, those who readily accept conventional values and follow socially prescribed norms without question—that is, those who are conservative—make the most comfortable social adjustments. The adolescent rebelliousness, independence, and unconventionality of the liberals, on the other hand, are probably sources of conflicts with parents and peers, and consequently of some disturbance and maladjustment at this period. These same adolescent characteristics, however, may be the precursors of later good adjustment and more effective handling of personal problems and tensions.

Finally, personality structure and cognitive styles, although highly influential in the determination of sociopolitical opinions and beliefs, account for only part of the variance in political behavior. Clearly, individuals' political views may be strongly affected by their social and economic fortunes, and by social, historical, and economic events. The role of personality factors in political behavior must be assessed within the broad context of such factors.

16

Overview

DOROTHY H. EICHORN, PAUL H. MUSSEN, JOHN CLAUSEN, NORMA HAAN, AND MARJORIE P. HONZIK

The life course from adolescence to middle age, a period that encompasses most of the major role changes in industrialized societies, is the focus of this volume. During the earlier phases—late adolescence and early adulthood—the pace of role change is swift. Most persons leave their parental homes, become economically independent, marry, produce children, and both directly, and indirectly through taxes, undertake the care of the young, the old, and the handicapped of all ages. They go on to guide their children through successive developmental steps, assume roles in community organizations, and change jobs, typically to positions of greater complexity and responsibility. Toward the end of the middle years they make the transition to the "empty nest" and the grandparental role. Later, as both physical and role changes draw attention to the approach of old age, they begin to anticipate other shifts in life's balance of loss and gain. With retirement from work roles and, perhaps, from many roles in the wider community, loss of friends and spouse, and physical deterioration will also come greater freedom from responsibilities for earning a living and full-time child-rearing, opportunities to explore new and old interests, and time to enjoy relatives, friends, and the world around them.

SAMPLES

All of these transitions occur in a changing historical context, so the experiences of one cohort may be an imperfect guide for later generations. The lives studied here are those of three groups born in the San

411

Francisco Bay Area, one in the early 1920s and the other two at the end of that decade. These have been "beset" generations. The Great Depression and the greatest war the world has yet seen were their lot in childhood and youth (Chapter 1). Reared on the "work ethic," patriotism, and other traditional values, they became generations of parents with a large investment in the nuclear family. Yet they lived to see many of their children and, indeed, many adults, militantly reject traditional values while their nation declined in economic and political prestige. As have other generations, they had to cope simultaneously with rebellious teenage offspring and the unmistakable signs of their own aging, but they were the first generation in which a majority also had to be concerned about their aging parents. Now they can anticipate a long life span, but in a time of rampant inflation.

We must remain aware not only of the sociohistorical context in which our samples lived but also of ways in which they resemble or differ from the general United States population. Although our groups include a wide range of talents and socioeconomic backgrounds, they were, on the average, advantaged intellectually and economically both as children and as adults. Their IQs in adolescence were above average, and most showed at least small increases in IQ by middle age (Chapter 4). Nationwide, the cohorts born during the early and late 1920s attained socioeconomic status above that of their parents, in part because the number of jobs for unskilled labor decreased while professional and technical positions increased. Even so, our samples exceed the average of their birth cohorts in educational and occupational level, with a majority of those from working-class backgrounds moving into the middle class (Chapter 13).

Despite this upward socioeconomic bias, the intercorrelations of education and occupation in our samples and the correlations of these socioeconomic indicators with IQ are similar to those in more representative populations (Chapter 4; Featherman, 1980). Further, the personality characteristics of our study members, as assessed by the California Psychological Inventory (CPI), are not remarkably different at either early or middle adulthood (the two periods for which we have these data) from those of the cross-sectional samples on which this inventory was standardized (Chapter 10). Similarly, their physical health, and age trends in health status, also approximate norms from surveys of the United States population in these age ranges (Chapter 3).

Most of our participants married, and they produced an average number of children for their birth cohorts. As a group their marriages have been more stable than the national average, although probably not different from persons of comparable educational and occupational level. During middle age, however, the divorce rate among two subgroups (GS men and OGS women) has come to approximate the national average (Chapter 11). In judging the extent to which our findings are applicable to other groups, all these similarities to, and differences from, national norms must be considered.

METHODS

We addressed the three basic concerns of developmental research—age trends, individual consistency (stability in rankings of individuals across age) and factors associated with group and individual stability or change. Most current information on these issues comes from cross-sectional studies. Yet only repeated measures on the same persons can speak to the issue of individual consistency or change across age or reveal what have been termed "heterotypic continuities" (Kagan, 1980) or "sleeper effects" (Kagan and Moss, 1962), that is, instances in which a trait at one age predicts an apparently different trait at a subsequent age. For example, assertiveness and IQ may not be correlated at age 3, but assertiveness at 3 may be associated with IQ in adolescence. Such apparent inconsistencies may not represent true discontinuity but may instead become understandable when we have sufficient longitudinal data on intervening developmental linkages (see Chapters 6 and 8 for illustrations).

Longitudinal data also provide an essential check on the accuracy of the developmental picture provided by cross-sectional studies, for they often yield age curves that differ from cross-sectional ones. Cross-sectional data "smooth" the more abrupt transitions seen in individuals. For example, cross-sectional curves of growth in height show continuous gradual increases, although longitudinal data (Stolz & Stolz, 1951) make it clear that many individuals display irregular spurts. Furthermore, differences between age groups may result from cohort differences (Schaie, 1970) rather than from changes in individuals across time. Sixty-year-olds may have scored lower than, say, 40-year-olds, on tests of verbal intelligence given in 1978, not because the former had actually declined in ability but because persons of that age had on the average fewer years of schooling than those who were 40.

Researchers from various disciplines are aware of the myriad complexities involved in the study of constancy and change (Brim & Kagan, 1980). Among these are the several kinds of change that may occur: (*a*) in amount or degree of a characteristic (including its disappearance) with no change in its form, (*b*) in form (transformation) of the characteristic, such as differentiation or more complex organization, for example, infants may express affect quite simply and directly, whereas adolescent expression is more complex and more subtle, (c) ipsative change, that is, change in the hierarchical organization of characteristics within individuals, with some characteristics dominant at one age and others at another, and (d) shifts in the hierarchy or standings of individuals with respect to some characteristics. Studies of the last kind are the most common in the literature, although very few involve the wide age span we examine. Ipsative studies are rare (Moss & Susman, 1980; Wohlwill, 1980).

All four types of change have been examined in our longitudinal data, although the third is not directly represented in this volume. However, the Q-sort personality data reported here are derived ipsatively and then used to examine other kinds of change. Because it is very difficult to find measures, particularly of personality and cognition, that are appropriate across a wide age span, the Q-sort approach has special appeal.

Some developmental scientists stress the need for study of individuals instead of groups (Wohlwill, 1980). Carried to its extreme, such an emphasis precludes scientific generalization. An alternative used in a number of chapters in this volume is to examine selected subgroups.

AGE TRENDS

Because the years between adolescence and old age have only recently become a focus of developmental research, the empirical and theoretical bases for predictions about this period are limited. Certainly no general theory exists to account for continuity or change, either within or across the major domains—behavioral, social, and physical—that we examine. Nonetheless, theorists with diverse viewpoints have been essentially unanimous in regarding early and middle adulthood as a period of stability following rapid changes during childhood and adolescence (Brim & Kagan, 1980). For most of the characteristics we assess, however, a "steady state" during adulthood is not characteristic.

Intelligence

Although the cross-sectional literature indicates declines in IQ during adulthood on general tests of intelligence, longitudinal data already published from our own and other samples suggest qualifications in this conclusion. Horn and Donaldson (1980) argue cogently that "crystallized" intelligence, represented in tests highly dependent on acculturated learning, (e.g., information and vocabulary), increases into old age, whereas "fluid" intelligence, which is largely independent of such learning, begins to decrease in early adulthood. Subtests of the performance scale of the Wechsler tests are considered to assess primarily fluid intelligence, whereas the verbal scale contains subtests primarily dependent on crystallized intelligence, so trends in full scale IQ will reflect a balance between the two. However, the analyses reported in Chapter 4, show increases of about 6 to 8 points in Wechsler performance IQ, as well as increases in verbal (and, of course, full scale) IQ between late adolescence and middle age. These findings, supported by the work of Kangas and Bradway (1971), contradict Horn's predictions of different age trends for the two subscales.

Health

Considerable cross-sectional data are available on a number of the indices of physical health examined in Chapter 3. Therefore, the increases within our samples in obesity, blood pressure, and blood levels of cholesterol and the declines in pulse rate and in visual and auditory acuity all were expected. Also, as expected, accidents, casualties of war, and suicides, rather than disease, are the major causes of mortality through age 50. Among the major disease categories, only cardiovascular disorders yield any evidence of predictability from past medical history.

The decline in general health (as rated by physicians) from early to middle adulthood and a trend from acute to chronic illness also were anticipated. However, we expected general health to improve between early adolescence and early adulthood because many authorities consider adolescence to be a period of physiologic instability, as well as one in which accidents and infections are frequent, whereas early adulthood is viewed as the "prime of life." But contrary to prediction, we find a decline in ratings of general health between adolescence and early adulthood and an early adult onset of chronic disorders. These trends are especially surprising in our economically advantaged samples. Only a few reversals of the general downward trend in health occur; respiratory and infectious complaints of men decrease through age 50, and the incidence of hematological complaints does not change systematically.

Psychological Adjustment

Adolescence has also been viewed as a time of emotional turmoil, and previous research with these samples yields some support for this inference particularly among girls: an index of psychological adjustment derived from the personality Q sort declines from early adolescence to late adolescence and then increases to early adulthood (Block, in collaboration with Haan, 1971). The psychological health index (PH), a similar measure used in the present study, shows some continuing improvement from early adulthood to middle age for the group as a whole (Chapters 6, 7, and 8). However, much of this period was stressful for persons whose personalities differed from traditional gender stereotypes (Chapter 8). Other sources of stress, often interacting with each other, were child-rearing (Chapter 6), work pressures (Chapters 13 and 14), conflicts over the husband's work (Chapters 11 and 13), and other marital problems (Chapter 11). Nonetheless, "mid-life crises," a phenomenon of current scientific and popular concern, were rare. Instead, by middle age, those whose personalities did not conform to sex-role stereotypes had achieved a level of "psychological health" equal to that of the more conventional men and women.

Marital satisfaction (Chapter 11) improved slightly but not significantly instead of declining, as predicted by some cross-sectional studies. This finding may be consistent with the results of other investigators who report marital satisfaction to decrease after the "first flush of happiness," particularly as children arrive, and then to increase as children leave the home (Deutscher, 1964; Feldman, 1976).

Half of the men advanced in their careers between early and middle adulthood; most of the others had by 40 or 50 come to terms with less occupational success than they had aspired to (Chapter 13). Although men changed jobs less frequently during middle age than earlier, a substantial amount of job change did occur in their thirties and forties, particularly among those in high-status positions. Blue-collar workers had the highest job stability. By middle age all but professional men are working fewer hours per week than they had previously.

The rich personality data on the study members, transformed into Q-sort measures and factor scores derived from these measures, yield complex trends (Chapter 5; Haan, 1976; Haan & Day, 1974). Strong and significant trends are apparent between early adolescence and middle age in five of the six derived factors. In general, the participants in our studies became more cognitively invested (more concerned with intellectual and philosophical matters), more self-confident, more nurturant, more open to themselves and their experiences, and more intraceptive. Expression of sexual interest was high in adolescence, lower in early adulthood, and then high again by middle age. Only one dimension shows no systematic change between early adolescence and middle age—our groups are neither more nor less emotionally overcontrolled or undercontrolled at 40 or 50 than they were earlier.

Our evidence for personality change continuing into middle adulthood challenges the notion that personality is fixed by early adulthood (or even younger) and is inconsistent with the hypothesis that experiences during infancy and early childhood are the primary determinants of adult personality. Together with the findings for cross-age correlations (see the following), these longitudinal data suggest that personality evolves continuously at least to middle age, although abrupt changes could have occurred between our observations.

Political Attitudes

Contrary to assertions by political scientists, our data indicate that liberals and conservatives manifest distinctive clusters of personality characteristics that endure from early adolescence to middle adulthood (see Chapter 15). Over the long period and changing sociopolitical contexts from the 1930s to the 1970s, liberals are characterized by independence, rebelliousness, unconventional thinking, concern with philosophical and intellectual matters, pride in objectivity, and greater acceptance of their own and others' feelings, emotions, and motivations. In contrast, conservatives are more submissive, dependent on others, strongly in need of reassurance, moralistic, little inclined toward introspection, and uncomfortable with uncertainty (intolerant of ambiguity).

Some age changes in other personality correlates of political orientations suggest interesting shifts in the personal and social accommodations of liberals and conservatives across the years from adolescence to middle age. For example, Q-sort data on the liberals describe them as moralistic, relatively unsympathetic and not cheerful during adolescence, although during adulthood they were as well adjusted psychologically as the conservatives. Holding different opinions from one's peer group may be more stressful during adolescence than it is when one has become more secure in his or her identity.

CONSISTENCY AND STABILITY OVER TIME

Although terms such as consistency, stability, discontinuity, and change are variously defined (Brim & Kagan, 1980), we use the phrase individual consistency to refer to individuals' maintaining the same rankings within a group on a characteristic across age or situations even though the group as a whole may increase or decrease in average level of the characteristic. For example, a person may be high in energy, relative to the group, at both 20 years and 70 years, although the average energy level of all members of the group decreases between 20 and 70.

For decades scientists and laymen alike assumed considerable individual consistency in most human characteristics, particularly during the adult years. More recently this assumption has been questioned, especially with respect to personality characteristics (Mischel, 1969, 1973). This contrary position holds that behavior is to a great extent a function of the situation, with little individual consistency across time or circumstances. Our results do not support either extreme in this controversy, although they offer some comfort to both. In all the domains assessed, some evidence for individual consistency was found, but, as would be expected, some characteristics are more stable across time than others, and some individuals change markedly even on characteristics for which the group as a whole is consistent.

IQ

Despite correlations of about .8 (the highest observed for any behavioral or social measure) between late adolescence and middle age for both full scale and verbal Wechsler IQs, about 50% of our participants increased or decreased by at least 10 points in IQ. Consistency across age is higher for the verbal scale than for the performance scale, but the subtests of the latter generally have lower reliabilities than the subtests of the verbal scale.

Physical Health

In a commonsense way most of us predict consistency across age in physical health—we expect the healthy to remain healthy and poor health to predict poor health. Yet because physical health has traditionally been the domain of greatest deliberate intervention for human welfare, one might predict little consistency. Although physicians' overall ratings of health from medical examinations and laboratory tests show low levels of year-to-year consistency, the correlations for health ratings rise to moderate levels when computed between age periods, for example, adolescence and adulthood, a procedure that increases reliability. Even these correlations, however, are lower than the interperiod correlations for specific health-related measures, such as blood pressure and obesity. Our findings of only low to moderate cross-age consistency in general health and other health related indices are consistent with results of longitudinal studies covering the period from childhood to late adolescence (Starfield & Pless, 1980). The fact that most childhood illnesses are acute while chronicity is increasingly characteristic of adult disorders is an additional factor in influencing correlations across the wide age span (childhood to middle age) assessed in our medical data.

Psychological Health

Scientific and lay expectations about mental health are like those for physical health; "good" is expected to lead to "good" and "poor" to "poor," although deliberate intervention to promote mental health is frequently undertaken. In both the GS and OGS, women are more consistent than men between early adulthood and middle age on the psychological health index (PH). For the GS between ages 30 and 40 the correlations are, however, low in both sexes, whereas for the OGS between 38 and 50, the correlations are moderate. Whether this difference in consistency arises from age, cohort or sample differences cannot be determined until data at age 50 become available for the GS. Certainly prediction of PH at early and middle adulthood from early and late adolescent personality dimensions and individual Q-sort items presents one of the most complex patterns observed. In general, personality characteristics measured in adolescence better predict PH during middle adulthood than during early adulthood, but some sample and sex differences occur. At least some of these differences seem to be interpretable in terms of the different experiences of the two sexes or two cohorts during their adolescent and adult years. For example, adolescent personality dimensions are less predictive of PH for OGS men at 37 than for GS men at age 40 perhaps because more of the OGS still had young children in the home. Service in World War II postponed parenthood for them, although not age at marriage.

Personality Characteristics

Scores for social maturity, assessed by a weighted combination of several scales of the CPI, are available only for the early and middle adult years. Consistency between these two periods is moderate for men (r about .6) and high (r about .8) for women.

Both individual Q-sort items (Haan, 1976; Haan & Day, 1974) and factor scores derived from the Q-sort measures of personality (Chapter 5) show considerable individual consistency across age, although with variation associated with the kind of characteristic, the ages and time interval examined, and sex; no sample (cohort) differences are found. Dimensions more directly concerned with the self (Cognitively Invested, Self-Confident, and Open/Closed to Self—the latter particularly for women) show greater consistency than dimensions more reflective of the quality of interpersonal interactions (Nurturant/Hostile and Under/Overcontrolled, Heterosexual). Perhaps the latter are more influenced by actual changes and demands of interpersonal relationships. Although the total number of significant cross-age correlations is greater when the interval between evaluations was relatively short (for example, early to middle adulthood)—a finding that suggests persons do change in adulthood, but slowly—the effects of age or time interval are not marked (except in GS males). Indeed, in many instances the correlations for personality variables between early adolescence and age 40 are as high as those between 17 and 30, a finding like that summarized above for PH.

Social Mobility

Consistency of socioeconomic status is usually judged with reference to that of the childhood home, either by correlations between offspring and parental education and/or occupation or by social mobility, as reflected in a difference in educational or occupational level between child and parent. In our samples the offspring–parent correlations for occupation and education are moderate, about .4–.5 (see Chapter 4), a magnitude consistent with data from more representative samples. As judged by occupational mobility, about 60% of the men in our samples exceeded the occupational status of their fathers by middle age; the remainder are at the father's level or downwardly mobile.

Marriage

As noted under age changes, average marital satisfaction increased slightly but not significantly from early to middle adulthood. Within this general trend, however, almost half the marriages rated at both age periods changed by one standard deviation or more on the scale of marital adjustment (Chapter 11). Many shifts in marital satisfaction seem to be associated with situational changes—increased satisfaction with relief from economic strain or the burdens of tending small children and decreased satisfaction with alcohol abuse or middle-age emergence of concerns about sexual or other aspects of personal identity. Contrary to expectation based on some studies in the literature, the participants' marital happiness could not be predicted from that of their parents. For example, unhappy marriage is no more common among participants whose parents' marriages had been unhappy.

Sociopolitical Attitudes

Individual consistency in sociopolitical attitudes was assessed by correlating scores on liberalism at middle age with three scales used to assess authoritarianism during adolescence. An hypothesis of consistency would predict negative correlations between degree of liberalism in adulthood and ethnocentrism and authoritarianism in adolescence. This prediction is well supported by correlations of $-.40$ to $-.65$. Correlations with political–economic conservatism are also in the direction predicted by individual consistency, but are low and not statistically significant ($-.15$ to $-.31$).

SOURCES OF DIFFERENCES AND CHANGE

Although a trend toward study of more discrete experiential variables and personal variables is evident in all disciplines concerned with human development, to date sex, age, cohort, and socioeconomic status have been among the sources of group and individual differences most frequently examined in the sociological, medical, and behavioral literature. These attributes are often called "surrogate" variables because each represents a number of possible sources of variation (e.g., differences in education, medical care, and social norms among cohorts).

Sex Differences

Within our samples, who have lived most of their lives in cultural contexts in which gender roles were polarized, sex differences are prominent. For example, women are more nurturant, less self-confident, and less inhibited in the expression of sexual interests than are men at all ages studied, although by middle age the sex difference is no longer statistically significant (Chapter 5). A trend toward convergence is also observed in the index of social maturity (Chapter 10). Women scored higher than men on this index at both early and middle adulthood, but between these periods men's scores increased while women's decreased, so at the older ages the sex difference is no longer significant. Women are also generally more consistent, in the sense of cross-age correlations, from early adolescence to middle age in Q-sort personality dimensions (Chapter 5), Social Maturity (Chapter 10), and in both psychological and physical health (Chapters 6 and 3, respectively). On the other hand, predictability of adult psychological (Chapter 7) and physical health (Chapter 3; Bayer, Whissell-Buechy, & Honzik, 1980), drinking patterns (Chapter 9), and career patterns (Chapters 13 and 14) from adolescent personality characteristics is better for men than for women. Also, in adulthood social maturity is more closely associated with personal-social effectiveness among men than among women (Chapter 10).

As these examples illustrate, sex differences are observed not only in the average level of characteristics at various ages but also in age trends (i.e., an interaction with age) and in concurrent and predictive correlates. Sex differences in socialization experiences and social demands are probably an important source of the behavioral differences described, a point discussed at greater length in Chapters 5, 6, 7, 8, 10, and 14. Gutmann (1975) suggests that parental roles intensify sex differences in personality during early and middle adulthood and that cessation of these role demands is the source of decline in the sexual polarization of traits in middle and old age. We may also speculate that recent cultural trends toward lesser polarization of sex roles at all ages may have contributed to the decline in sex differences among our study members by middle age. However, the fact that such a trend was noted by Jung (1933) at least 50 years ago and by Gutmann in more sexually polarized societies than our own indicates that sociohistorical change is not the only influence. Perhaps the increasing self-confidence reflected in our Q-sort analysis (Chapter 5) is also a factor. By middle age most men and women may feel secure enough in their identities and their social milieux to permit them to reveal less conventional aspects of themselves more fully and directly. Jung (1933) hypothesized that persons anticipating the latter part of their lives feel a need to develop previously latent aspects of their "selves."

Cohort

In the current developmental literature, particularly on aging, many differences previously attributed to age are being interpreted as cohort differences, that is, as associated with differential life experiences of successive generations. Most of the age trends we observe are essentially identical in both our cohorts, so we infer that they are associated with age changes rather than cohort differences, although the source of change may be biological or social (e.g., changes in role demands with age). One cannot, however, assume that groups differing markedly from ours in characteristics or circumstances would show similar trends.

Although their 8-year separation in birth dates is not large, our cohorts differed sufficiently in life experiences to lead us to expect differences, particularly in health and personality. Improvements in medical care between the early and late 1920s were sufficient to achieve marked reductions in infant mortality and in the incidence of serious diseases of infants and children (Nelson, 1950). The GS had the benefit of immunizations and antibiotics at an earlier age and for a longer period than the OGS. OGS members were adolescents during the Great Depression and many made real contributions to the family economy—boys held part-time jobs and girls assumed household chores to substitute for their working mothers or for household help that could no longer be afforded (Elder, 1974). GS members were children during this period, imposing a strain on family funds but unable to contribute significantly. Almost all OGS men served in World War II and some were recalled for the Korean conflict whereas World War II ended before most of the GS were old enough to fight, and only a small portion of them went to Korea. At about age 40 more OGS than GS men still had young children in the home—military service delayed parenthood for OGS men. For many OGS women, World War II imposed the strain of single parenting of their first-born child during its infancy and early childhood.

Despite these contrasting social histories, differences that can with confidence be attributed to cohort are less frequent and less marked than we predicted, and much less common than sex and age differences. Nevertheless, they occur in relevant domains. Both self-reports and physicians' ratings show poorer adult health in OGS than the GS. During adolescence OGS boys also had poorer health, but the direction of the cohort difference was reversed for girls. Therefore, the poorer adult health of the older cohort seems more likely to be a function of adult experiences (such as greater exposure to the hazards of war for OGS men) than of "carry-over" from health problems in childhood or adolescence.

Predictability of adult social maturity (Chapter 10) from adolescent traits of dependability, productivity, and goal orientation was established by early adolescence in the OGS boys but not until late adolescence in the younger cohort. The older group also showed increases in responsibility earlier in adolescence (Haan & Day, 1974). Their work and family responsibilities in adolescence may underlie their earlier maturity in these characteristics. Also, at 40 the OGS men held positions of higher occupational status than did the GS men. However, the difference was in the opposite direction for spouses of OGS and GS women, so a cohort difference cannot reasonably be inferred.

Except where the nature of the differences is similar for the two sexes we cannot be reasonably confident that contrasts for women are a function of cohort experience, because the GS women have been more advantaged socioeconomically throughout their lives. In both sexes the later born cohort is more liberal politically, a finding consistent with decreased conservatism in successive generations (Glenn, 1980). OGS members of both sexes were also more nurturant in early adolescence than the GS and less open in their thirties. The former difference may be attributable to their adolescent responsibilities and the latter to the differences in their parenting careers. Surprisingly no other cohort differences in marital circumstances, occupation, or personality were found, nor were there differences in education or IQ other than those expected from original socioeconomic differences in the two female cohorts.

Socioeconomic Status

In our analyses socioeconomic status (SES) was indexed by education, occupation, or a combination of the two. In addition, occupational achievement was a subject of study as well as a "surrogate" variable for predicting status or change in other measures.

Examination of the correlates of SES reveals some expected associations and some surprises. Moderate positive correlations between occupational attainment and education, IQ, and parental SES have been well documented, although the reasons for these associations are not completely understood. Such interrelationships were well established by adolescence, for adolescent IQ is as highly correlated with occupational status at middle age as is IQ at middle age. This finding is consistent with two others: (a) as expected, the kinds of intelligence assessed by standardized tests contributed to adult achievement— among boys from homes of comparable middle-class status those with higher adolescent IQ achieved higher occupational status, and (b) contrary to expectation, neither experience in intellectually demanding positions nor advantaged home background is associated with IQ gain between adolescence and middle age, except as an indirect function of the positive association between IQ gain and advanced education.

Of particular interest are the similarities and differences in the correlational patterns for IQ and the Cognitive Investment factor derived from the personality Q sort. Both measures predict occupational attainment, but Cognitive Investment is a better predictor of social mobility (advancement beyond the level of the father). Further, Cognitive Investment becomes more strongly correlated with occupational status across age, particularly in males (from .3 with parental SES in early adolescence to .7 with achieved status in middle age), whereas the IQ-occupation correlations remain about .6. Other evidence that the association of occupational attainment with Cognitive Investment is not simply a function of IQ is the fact that the correlations between adolescent Cognitive Investment and middle-age IQ are as strong or stronger than *concurrent* associations of Cognitive Investment with IQ at either adolescence or middle age. These findings are consistent with those from the adult longitudinal study of Kohn and Schooler (1978) in indicating that occupational experiences, such as the complexity of intellectual demands, influence cognitive and personality styles. They also suggest one way in which the association of parental SES with education, occupation and IQ of offspring is mediated, that is, the modeling and encouragement by advantaged parents of the traits that define this factor—valuing of intellectual matters, ambition, verbal influency, wide interests, productivity, introspection, philosophical concern, and dependability. As we have seen, the associations of occupational achievement with IQ, Cognitive Investment, and social origins are clearly presaged in early adolescence. However, education and work experiences on white-collar jobs can provide socialization to similar attitudes, values, and skills for those less socially advantaged in childhood as well as maintain a consistent socialization process for those from advantaged homes.

Social maturity at early and middle adulthood is not associated with social class origins in either sex, but is correlated at both adult periods with *achieved* social status. Apparently, this composite of personality characteristics, whose early predictors resemble Cognitive Investment, facilitates achievement of advanced education and higher occupational status. Neither parental nor achieved SES is correlated with Q-sort factors reflecting emotional control, self-acceptance, or self-confidence. However, lack of control of sexual expression during adolescence is associated with decrease in IQ and with downward social mobility in adulthood. This finding is consistent with other studies showing that those who marry or become parents during adolescence are less likely to complete their educations and advance in the occupational hierarchy.

Other adolescent predictors of adult social mobility are clusters of Q-sort items indicative of nurturance (sympathetic, giving, and protective) and, for working-class boys, sociability. During late adolescence, boys of lower SES also expressed greater warmth toward their parents, and as adults both sexes in the working class are more friendly toward their elderly fathers. Otherwise, the classes are not different in their warmth or involvement with parents, and the personality similarities of parent–child pairs does not vary with SES.

In other ways, however, men's jobs influence their relationships with their families. In general, the higher the man's occupational level, the more influence he is reported to have on his wife's political and social views, and the more she sees him as having influence on their children. Professional men and higher executives and their wives consider mutual understanding the most important aspect of their marriages, whereas those at lower occupational levels give more weight to companionship and children. Men's occupations also had complex associations with changes in their wives' personalities. One of the most expectable findings was that being married to an occupationally successful husband seem to increase the wife's self-confidence. Work pressures are a common source of marital problems (Chapter 11), and a family business, whether the partners are father and son or husband and wife, is a special source of conflict (Chapter 13).

Our findings, like others in the literature, indicate positive associations of SES with marital satisfaction (Chapter 11), political liberalism (Chapter 15), and physical health (Chapter 3), and a negative association with alcohol abuse (Chapter 9). In our groups, however, the correlations of parental and achieved SES with health (.2–.4) are probably lower than would be found in a more representative sample. Further, the association with health obtains only for education, not occupation, suggesting that among persons who can afford good medical care, factors such as knowledge and motivation are more influential determinants of health-related behaviors than is occupation.

Studies such as the Manhattan project (Srole, Langner, Michael, Kirkpatrick, Opler, & Rennie, 1962) lead one to expect poorer mental health in the economically disadvantaged. For OGS men this expectation is confirmed, both for their achieved status and that of their original home (Chapter 8). Social class origins do not, however, differentiate OGS women in terms of psychological health, although there is a tendency for an association with their current status, as judged by husband's occupation.

IQ

Expected associations with parental and achieved SES have already been mentioned, as have the associations with Cognitive Investment, which predicts IQ level at adolescence and middle age as well as IQ change. In general, the personality correlates of IQ are of equal or greater magnitude than those between IQ and SES. Correlations between IQ at middle age and personality characteristics during early and late adolescence are sometimes larger than those between IQ and those traits in adulthood, or, indeed, the cross-age correlations for the personality variables themselves.

The association of IQ level and gain with traits represented in Cognitive Investment is supported by correlations with such CPI scales as Intellectual Efficiency, Achievement via Independence, and Tolerance. Correlations of other Q-sort factors with IQ level and/or gain or loss echo some of the attributes associated with occupational achievement and mobility. For example, those who decrease in IQ are less self-controlled at adolescence. For the most part the correlates of IQ level are the same at both adolescence and middle age, but a few characteristics show differential age trends. In particular, persons who were highly controlled, dependable, calm, and somewhat aloof from peers as adolescents have higher IQs at both adolescence and middle age, although by middle age these traits are no longer associated with IQs. In middle age, new Q-sort correlates emerge for men—those with high IQs are rated as more insightful, unconventional, comfortable with uncertainty, and less repressive and self-defensive. Our understanding of the personality correlates of IQ level and change is extended by the associations with such CPI dimensions of Independence and Adaptability, Flexibility, Sociability, Socialization, and Self-confidence.

Finally, qualitative comparisons of persons who show the most extreme gains and losses in IQ between adolescence and middle age reveal a disproportionate incidence of alcohol abuse and debilitating illness among the Decreasers. Extreme Increasers are more likely to be married to spouses whose IQs are at least 10 points higher than was of the study member's in late adolescence. They were also more likely to have traveled outside the United States during their adult years, although they are not better educated in a formal sense nor of superior occupational status.

Health

Of all the domains examined, physical health has the fewest associations with other characteristics. We already commented on the low positive association with parental and own education. To our surprise, restraint in smoking and drinking bore only a very slight, although increasing, relation to good health. This low association may be explained by rather marked changes in drinking (Chapter 9) and smoking (Clausen, 1968) patterns during adulthood. For example, between early and middle adulthood about 25% of study members began to drink less while an equal proportion began to drink more heavily. The only strong correlate of health at middle age is a calm, self-controlled, and responsible personality, manifest at least by early adolescence. This picture of the physically healthy person from the Q-sort is supported in adulthood by correlations with a number of congruent CPI scales.

Personality

The pervasive influence of personality is evident in every domain examined. Illustrations from previous sections include strong and predictive associations with physical health, IQ, and occupational attainment in men. Adolescent and adult personality characteristics also differentiate persons with contrasting marital histories—divorced, stable and happy, stable and unhappy (Chapter 11), and different political attitudes (Chapter 15), paths to psychological health in middle age (Chapter 8), drinking habits (Chapter 9), and career patterns. Prediction from adolescent personality is better for men (Chapter 13) than for women (Chapter 14).

Two of the most influential dimensions are cognitive investment and emotional control, as reflected in both Q-sort and CPI measures. Emotional control, for example, appears to influence the overall course of lives, for it is predictive of adult health status, early death, problem drinking, marital career, and even IQ. Persons with poor impulse control may take more risks in their activities, such as driving or sports, and in smoking, drinking, and eating to excess and find it difficult to "break" maladaptive habits. Several studies (Starfield & Pless, 1980) suggest considerable individual consistency in risk-taking behavior, and in analyses of the GS sample, Bronson (1966, 1967, 1968) found continuity in impulse control and expression of affect across the period from infancy to adolescence or early adulthood. However, impulse control seems to become differentiated in the sense of being expressed differently in home and school environments (Bronson, 1966, 1967). Research with both the GS and OGS indicates that parental example and child-rearing practices influence the development of ego-control in offspring (Block, in collaboration with Haan, 1971; Block, von der Lippe, & Block, 1973).

Our analyses also reveal some other sources of group differences and age changes in personality characteristics. Among these are leaving the parental home (Chapter 12), the intellectual and interpersonal demands of executive and professional careers (see above and Chapter 13), deviance from cultural expectations, for example, sex-role stereotypes (Chapter 8), spouse's characteristics (Chapters 4 and 13), marital problems (Chapter 10), and stage of parenthood (Chapter 7).

Implications for Theory and Research

Several aspects of continuity and change across the life course are issues of high interest and great controversy in the developmental literature. One is whether differences observed among cross-sectional age groups reflect simply secular trends, that is, cohort differences resulting from differential experiences in different sociohistorical contexts, or whether they are "true" age changes, for example, changes characterizing all cohorts. "True" age changes have typically been interpreted as having a biological basis. However, changes systematically linked with age may occur because certain experiences regularly occur at certain ages in successive cohorts of our society or because the cumulative effects of positive or noxious experiences typically become manifest at about the same point in the life course. Such considerations point to the necessity for cross-cultural cohort research.

To date, most studies, particularly of behavioral phenomena, have been directed simply toward demonstrating differences among cohorts. Relatively little attention is given to assessing reasons for these differences. Among the exceptions to this generalization is the parallel reported between age decrements in primary mental abilities and average level of education (Schaie et al., 1973) and analyses of the effects of experiencing the Great Depression at different ages (Elder & Rockwell, 1978a). Our finding of an association between educational level and change in IQ within cohorts supports the inference that cohort differences in IQ have at least one of their sources in educational differences.

Reviews of the literature (Glenn, 1980, Moss & Susman, 1980) suggest that attitudes are more responsive to cultural changes than are "deeper" personality characteristics. It may also be that the age difference between our cohorts is not large enough to expect major differences in personality. However, personality differences during adolescence have been reported for cohorts separated by only 1 or 2 years (Nesselroade & Baltes, 1974). Moss and Susman (1980) suggest that response sets on the questionnaires used in that study may have influenced these results. The severe and selective sample attrition with respect to both age and sex evident in other reports from the same sample (Baltes & Nesselroade, 1972) may also be a factor. Nevertheless, such contrasts in results indicate the need for cohort studies that carefully examine different kinds of characteristics measured in different ways, together with assessment of the kind and extent of cohort differences in specific experiences. As methodology and theory become more sophisticated, it should be possible to test hypotheses about expected cohort differences from known experiential differences and to select assessment devices best suited to revealing associated cohort differences if they exist.

Regardless of the characteristic assessed or instrument used, group (e.g., cohort) differences and individual change should be examined separately. The sources of group differences are not necessarily those most closely associated with age change among individuals within the group, as illustrated by the contrast cited above between positive association of IQ and education among cohorts (Schaie, *et al.*, 1973) and a lack of association between education and IQ change in our samples. Further, Elder's (1974) contrasts between youngsters whose families were or were not deprived during the Great Depression makes clear that sociohistorical events do not have equal impact on all members of a cohort. Both his results and ours suggest that sources of individual change are more likely to be found in specific aspects of the environment than in general measures of sociohistorical and socioeconomic context. Note, for example, that alcohol abuse and spouse's IQ were among the few variables we found to be associated with adult IQ change.

Finally, some secular trends may reach an asymptote either permanently or temporarily. For example, the worldwide trend toward increasing height in successive generations apparently came to an end in the United States by the 1960s (Hamill *et al.*, 1976). An analogous phenomenon may now be occurring with the effects of education on IQ (Chapter 4; Schaie, *et al.*, 1973).

A second major controversy concerns what we have called individual consistency, that is, whether persons retain their ranks within a group under different circumstances. Results summarized in previous sections of this chapter provide evidence of both consistency and change during adulthood and about some of the sources of change. In addition, sufficient data have been reported from our own and other longitudinal studies covering the life course from early childhood to adolescence or early adulthood for certain communalities to emerge (Block, 1977; Moss & Susman, 1980). Our results for the period from adolescence to middle adulthood are in accord with inferences drawn from younger age periods, that is, that cognitive style, impulse control, and introversion–extroversion are characteristics that most consistently differentiate among individuals across time.

Some of the findings reported here also suggest a rapprochement between the conflicting results of short- and long-term studies of individual consistency that is congruent with Block's (1977) analyses of individual variation found in data based on observers' ratings (R data), self-reports (S data), such as questionnaires and personality inventories, and standardized behavioral situations (T data). T data, which represent quite specific behaviors, show great situational variation, that is, little individual consistency, whereas both R and S data reveal considerable long-term individual consistency. In Chapter 8 two groups with very different personality styles are identified in each sex. Throughout the period from adolescence through middle adulthood the basic personality characteristics of these groups as judged by R data (personality Q sorts) are distinct. Yet within each sex the behavior (T data) of the traditional and nontraditional groups in prescribed social roles—spouse, parent, and worker—is very similar. Individual inconsistencies occur in responses to situational variation, but not in basic personality characteristics nor in role behaviors. Inconsistency is observed in the kinds of behaviors and attitudes incorporated in the index of psychological health. During the periods of greatest polarization of sex role demands, that is, adolescence and, particularly, early adulthood, those whose personalities were not congruent with traditional sex stereotypes were rated as less well adjusted psychologically than their more conventional peers. When circumstances— probably both diminished sex role demands and less cultural pressure toward gender polarization—changed, the psychological health of the unconventional improved to the point of equaling that of the traditional group. These results suggest the hypothesis that persons may inhibit preferred behaviors and, hence, if measured by T data, will appear to be inconsistent from situation to situation, although their "deeper" personality characteristics show much less and probably more gradual change. However, change may occur simultaneously in such characteristics as self-esteem, self-confidence, and other aspects of intrapersonal morale. Changes of this sort were detected here with R data, but might well have appeared also in T data had these been obtained.

A third controversy among developmental researchers is about models of change in personality (Perun & Bielby, 1979). In one paradigm, crisis is considered a modal experience, and change occurs only through experiencing a crisis. A second model assumes crisis to occur only when major "expectable life events," such as the "empty nest," occur at ages when they are *not* expected (Neugarten, 1970); personality change is not necessarily linked to crisis. Within our samples instances of mid-life crisis were rare. Instead, some of our data (Chapters 8 & 14) indicate, as described previously, that a lack of "fit" between preferred "styles" and cultural expectations, for example, stereotypic sex roles, may inhibit expression of the "inappropriate" characteristics but at the cost of psychological disequilibrium. This observation leads one to ask if this discrepancy is only one, albeit thus far culturally prominent, source of individual differences in both level and change in personality and cognitive variables, and perhaps also in physical health. That is, deviance from cultural norms of other sorts may also be accompanied by evidence of psychological or physical distress, if not real crisis. Under certain circumstances the psychological strain imposed by the person's perception of his or her deviance from peers and/or by inhibiting preferred responses and instead conforming to prescribed behaviors may be severe enough to precipitate a "crisis."

Changes in personality, cognition, or health, whether or not accompanied by symptoms of psychological or physical distress, may be more likely to occur at periods in the life course characterized by a "density" or concentration of "life events." Browning (1968) singles out early adulthood as such a period because of the number of role changes, for example, job entry, marriage, and parenthood. School entry and puberty are other examples. The developmental literature suggests that both of these periods are associated with discontinuities in cognition and, less clearly, personality. For adults, retirement can be another time of concentrated changes in status, roles, and social interactions.

An important task for developmentalists may be to assess the communalities and differences among phases of the life course in the demands they impose on individuals and the kinds of responses appropriate to these demands. For example, the period of career establishment and consolidation and the traditional Freudian "latency" period may both demand strong task orientation, whereas school entry, job entry, marriage, parenthood, and retirement may have in common the demands of adjustment to major role change and require flexibility and tolerance of ambiguity. If certain periods resemble one another in the kinds of characteristics required for successful response, then we might expect stronger cross-age correlations of these characteristics for those periods than for periods in which the required demands and appropriate responses differ. Such a phenomenon would account for numerous instances in our data (e.g., "uses of the past" in Chapters 6 and 8), as well as a few other studies (Moss & Sussman, 1980) in which correlations are stronger for longer age intervals than shorter ones.

The constructs of "life events" and "support systems" offer means for integrating developmental research with the burdgeoning general literature on stress and coping (Dohrenwend & Dohrenwend, 1974). To assess stress, researchers are developing inventories of life events and differentiating between positive and negative events, expected and adventitious events, and between major events and minor but continued daily "hassles." They are also studying the role of "support systems," such as emotional and financial help from relatives and friends, in ameliorating the deleterious effects of stress. Personal resources, such as intelligence, personality characteristics, education, past experience in coping with stress, and financial resources also constitute supports in dealing with stress.

Thus far most studies of stress and coping have been cross-sectional. Longitudinal studies will permit us to assess, for example, whether the striving (Type A) personality, reported to be associated with cardiac disorders, is the antecedent or result of the physical symptoms. At the same time, the techniques being developed in cross-sectional studies for the assessment of stress, support systems, and coping styles should contribute to longitudinal research through better specification of the nature of environmental changes and of cohort and individual differences in the nature, extent, and timings of such changes. A tripartite approach to the issues of human constancy and change, combining refined measures of stress, environmental support systems, and individual characteristics should be productive.

Another methodology that holds promise for longitudinal research is the ipsative technique. Developmentalists who have analyzed various ways of assessing change (e.g., Kagan, 1980; Moss & Susman, 1980; Wohlwill, 1980) emphasize the value of ipsative data for examining changes in the hierarchical organization of personality characteristics across age. Haan (1976) used Q-sort measures in this fashion in a cross-sectional comparison of our middle-aged participants with elderly parents. Both groups are characterized by such traits as dependability and productivity, but striving is more salient in the personality organization of the middle-aged and "savoring" of interpersonal experiences in the personalities of the elderly. In the present volume, as well as in other publications from our Q-sort data (e.g., Haan & Day, 1974), ipsative data are used in another way, that is, to examine age trends, individual consistency, and sources of group and individual differences in single characteristics or dimensions. The ipsative technique makes it possible to assess at least some characteristics and behaviors across a wide span of ages for which appropriate and comparable normative measures are not available and, hence, increases the likelihood of developing a life-span conceptualization of personality. As described in more detail in Chapter 5, the conceptualization suggested by our longitudinal factor analysis argues against true "stages" of adult personality, but does support Brim's (1976) suggestion that a theory of the self may identify the critical dimensions of personality across the life course.

Despite frustrations over the many opportunities in our data archives that we have yet to explore, the fruitful yield of longitudinal research and the prospect of a greater yield through improved methodologies and longer time spans of study make us eager to be on with the task. We trust that our generous and loyal band of study members will also find this exploration a worthy investment of their "future selves."

Appendix A

Basic Concepts Underlying the PARAFAC-CANDECOMP Three-Way Factor Analysis Model and Its Application to Longitudinal Data[1,2]

Richard A. Harshman and Sheri A. Berenbaum

In the following pages we present the basic concepts and assumptions underlying the PARAFAC-CANDECOMP factor analysis model and consider possible benefits and disadvantages of this approach to analyzing longitudinal data.

MULTIMODAL RELATIONSHIPS

Two-Way versus Three-Way Data

To understand three-way factor analysis, it is important first to understand the difference between two-way and three-way data. A

[1]The authors appreciate the opportunity to work with the IHD staff on possible applications of PARAFAC. In particular we would like to thank Dr. Dorothy Eichorn, Norma Haan, and Marjorie Honzik for their contribution and support throughout this study. During the preparation of this appendix, S.A.B. was supported by NIMH Grant # MH 14647.

[2]PARAFAC and CANDECOMP are two procedures for three-way analysis that were developed independently but are essentially equivalent. PARAFAC stands for *PARA*llel *FAC*tors factor analysis and is described in Harshman, 1970, 1972b, 1976. CAN-

435

multivariate data set usually consists of a rectangular array of observations. Such sets are organized according to two intersecting "modes" or "ways" of classification. For example, in a set of personality measurements, the data point x_{ij} might correspond to the score on the ith personality variable which was obtained by the jth individual and thus the two modes of classification would be "variables" and "persons." Frequently, factor analysis deals with a matrix of correlations between variables; in this case the data point r_{ij} would represent the correlation between variables i and j. Here, both "ways" correspond to the same basis of classification—"variables." (This case is considered two-way because it takes two intersecting classifications—the row variable and the column variable—to locate a single datum.)

It is becoming more common to collect three-way data. For example, a two-way array might be collected for each of several experimental conditions, producing a three-way set where "conditions" represents the third mode. Most relevant here is the fact that longitudinal multivariate data usually have a three-way form of organization. For example, in a set of longitudinal personality measurements, x_{ijk} might correspond to the score of the ith personality variable, as measured on the jth individual, on the kth occasion. Or, the data might consist of correlations, so that the data point r_{ijk} corresponds to the correlation between variables i and j, computed from their values on the kth occasion. (If the data are correlations, it is not necessary that the same individuals be measured on the different occasions; a cross-sectional approach is also possible.) (For useful discussion of these and related distinctions among types of data see Carroll & Arabie, 1980.)

Two-Way versus Three-Way Factor Analysis

Traditional forms of factor analysis can only be applied to a two-way array. For this reason, longitudinal researchers have had to factor their three-way data by indirect means, e.g., "collapsing" the three-way array into a two-way summary matrix, by averaging over one of the three modes. However, such a procedure entails considerable loss of information. In particular, it does not allow the analysis to incorporate any of the three-way structural relationships among the observations. To reduce loss of information, longitudinal analyses are often done by dividing the data set into a series of two-way "slices" and then perform-

---

DECOMP stands for *CAN*onical *DECOMP*osition and is described in Carroll and Chang, 1970. We sometimes refer to the basic model as the "PARAFAC-CANDECOMP model," but often call it simply the "PARAFAC model" for short.

ing a separate factor analysis on each slice. However, it is then necessary to compare the factors across slices in order to recover three-way information. Here again, any systematic three-way relationships are not available to the factor analysis procedure itself. Another limitation of such piecewise approaches is that there are several different ways to "slice" a three-way longitudinal array. The most obvious, perhaps, is to produce a two-way slice for each occasion, but one might instead want to make a slice for each person, so that each slice would be a two-way longitudinal matrix of variables by occasions. Alternatively, it is sometimes useful to consider a slice for every variable, so that each slice is a longitudinal matrix of persons by occasions. With each method, different aspects of the three-way structure of covariation are revealed (see, e.g., Cattell, 1952).

In the last 10–15 years several new types of factor and principal component analysis have been developed which can *directly* analyze three-way data sets (e.g., Bentler & Weeks, 1979; Carroll & Chang, 1970; Corballis, 1970; Harshman, 1970, 1972a, 1976; Jöreskog, 1971; Kroonenberg & de Leeuw, 1980; Sands & Young, 1980; Tucker, 1963, 1966). Yet, surprisingly, few attempts have been made to apply these methods to longitudinal data. The potential benefits of such application seem considerable: several of these three-way methods should be able to extract common factors that describe the covariation of variables *both* across persons and across time, without losing the distinctness of the two aspects of variation. Some of these models promise uniquely determined factors—potentially resolving the ambiguities of rotation that have hampered two-way factor analyses. Although the three-way methods vary in their assumptions, generality, and in the complexity of the resulting solutions, many of them should prove valuable for studying longitudinal multivariate patterns. We have concentrated on exploring applications of one of these techniques, PARAFAC.

THE PARAFAC-CANDECOMP MODEL

PARAFAC provides what is probably the simplest three-way generalization of traditional factor analysis, yet it is also one of the most powerful—when its particular assumptions are appropriate to the data. But these assumptions are somewhat restrictive. PARAFAC is not a completely general model appropriate for any type of three-way data. For example, some data may need to be transformed before they are suitable. Therefore, a clear understanding of the model is important not only for correct interpretation of PARAFAC solutions, but also for determining its correct application to various types of three-way data. We consider first a formulation of the model for analysis of raw data (or centered and rescaled data). Then we develop the equivalent model for analysis of covariances computed from the raw data.

Recall that the traditional *two-way factor model* for a raw data point can be written (for q factors) as follows:

$$x_{ij} = a_{i1}f_{j1} + a_{i2}f_{j2} + \cdots + a_{is}f_{js} + \cdots + a_{iq}f_{jq} + e_{ij} \tag{1}$$

Consider an interpretation of this equation in terms of personality factors. For such data, x_{ij} would represent the score obtained by the jth person on the ith personality variable or item. In the model, a_{i1} represents the loading of the ith variable on the first factor, that is, the amount that the ith variable is affected by (or measures) the first factor, while f_{j1} represents the loading of the jth person on the first factor, that is, the amount that the first factor is expressed in that individual—how much of that factor the individual has. (This person loading is traditionally known as the individual's "factor score" on that factor.) By multiplying these two loadings together, the term $a_{i1}f_{j1}$ represents the contribution of the first factor to the data point x_{ij}. (It is apparent, for example, that if either the jth person's loading or the ith variable's loading on that factor is very small, the factor will not contribute appreciably to the observed data point x_{ij}.) In like manner, the term $a_{i2}f_{j2}$ refers to the contribution of the second factor, $a_{is}f_{js}$ represents the contribution of factor s, and so on for the rest of the q factors. The term e_{ij} is an error term and represents the unique or unsystematic part of the data point that cannot be fit by the q common factors. (For further details on e_{ij}, see section on assumptions about error terms.)

The PARAFAC-CANDECOMP Model Applied to Score Matrices

To continue our example using personality item scores, suppose we are dealing with a *longitudinal* array of such scores, where a given set of items was administered to the same individuals on several different occasions. If we applied the PARAFAC model directly to such data, the underlying structure of a personality item score would be represented as follows:

$$x_{ijk} = a_{i1}f_{j1}w_{k1} + a_{i2}f_{j2}w_{k2} + \cdots + a_{is}f_{js}w_{ks} +$$
$$\cdots + a_{iq}f_{jq}w_{kq} + e_{ijk} \tag{2}$$

this equation, x_{ijk} represents the score on the ith personality item, obtained by the jth person, on the kth occasion. On the right-hand le of the equation are $q + 1$ terms. The first q of these terms repre-nts the contributions of the q common factors to the observed score; e last term is an error component. In this three-way model data int, the a and f coefficients have the same meaning as in the two-y model: they are variable loadings and person loadings. However, each term there is an extra coefficient, the w_{ks} coefficient (e.g., w_{k1} r factor 1, w_{k2} for factor 2, etc.). These w_{ks} coefficients are occasion adings, and are perfectly analogous to the a_{is} and f_{js} coefficients ken from the two-way model. For example, w_{k1} is the loading of the st factor on the kth occasion, that is, the amount that the first factor nds to be expressed on the kth occasion, the size or importance of the ctor on that occasion. (In more precise terms, w_{k1} is proportional to e standard deviation of the contributions of the first factor on the kth casion, provided these contributions have zero mean; otherwise, w_{k1} proportional to the root-mean-square average of the contributions of ctor 1 on the kth occasion.)

In terms of the *algebra* of the model, Eq. 2 represents perhaps the nplest and most mathematically straightforward three-way neralization of factor analysis possible. Conceptually, however, it volves more than might at first be apparent. PARAFAC was not veloped simply because it seemed a natural extension of the two-way odel. Rather, it is a formalization and extension of Cattell's (1944) sightful theoretical approach to solving the problem of factor rota-on. This approach postulates that any "real" factor present on two casions will maintain, across the two occasions, a simple proportion-ity of factor loadings or factor scores. In PARAFAC, the w_{ks} values e the proportionality coefficients which relate the loadings of a given ctor across occasions. When this proportionality assumption is ap-opriate, the factor axes which reveal this proportionality are *iquely* located in the factor space, the "real" factors are determined a way not possible with two-way factor analysis. (This point is dis-ssed in more detail in the section on uniqueness.)

Such proportionality is not, however, always a reasonable assump-on. Consider, for example, the problem that arises when we try to ply the PARAFAC model in a simpleminded way to longitudinal rsonality data. The model implies an exceptional orderliness in the y that individuals change their personalities across time.

When interpreting the model, we can imagine that the w coefficient ultiplies either the person loading (factor score) or the item

loading—the results are mathematically equivalent. With the perso
ality data example, it is perhaps more appropriate to consider the ite
loadings as fixed and the individuals' factor scores as changing acro
occasions. Under this interpretation, an individual's loading (fact
score) at time k for factor s can be written $f_{js} w_{ks}$. This implies that
occasion k, everyone's loading on factor s goes up or down in proporti
to the occasion loading w_{ks}. For example, if $w_{3s} = 1.0$ and $w_{4s} = 1.3$,
that factor s increases 30% from occasion 3 to occasion 4, th
everyone's factor score is increased by exactly 30% between these tv
occasions. If factor s were Extroversion, then everyone would becor
30% more extroverted during this period. Such an orderly pattern
change seems unlikely when one is dealing with individual pe
sonalities. It seems more reasonable to expect that the circumstances
each person's life will produce a change in any given personality fact
that is specific to the individual. Each person may change by a d
ferent amount, and some may even change in the opposite directi
from others.

The pattern of variation in which every data source shows the sar
percentage increase in the expression of a given factor across a partic
lar time period may be more appropriate for the description of da
drawn from points in some causally interconnected system. For exa
ple, if the data sources were points in an individual's brain, and tl
variables were measurements of different kinds of brain activity,
might be reasonable to expect all points of observation to show a coo
dinated proportional increase in the amount of a certain brain activi
from one time to the next. For such reasons, the type of orderly vari
tion implied by Eq. 2 has been called "system variation" (see Ha
shman, 1970, pp. 19–21 for further discussion). In contrast, when tl
sources of variation across time are thought to reside independent
inside each data source (e.g., persons), the resulting variation
termed "object variation" (Harshman, 1970, pp. 22–25). In the obje
variation case, one might write the expression for person j's fact
score for occasion k as follows: $f_{jsk} = (f_{js} + v_{jsk})$, where v_{jsk} represen
the idiosyncratic shift or variation in the factor score for person j (
occasion k.

Some longitudinal data sets may display a mixture of object vari
tion and system variation. Even with personality data, there may be
the life span of most persons certain common experiences that cause
trend toward increases or decreases in particular factors at particul
times (e.g., a factor of "responsibility" might generally tend to increa
as individuals age). By applying the PARAFAC system variatio
model directly to the raw score or deviation score matrices for suc

a, one would obtain w_{ks} values that would represent the systematic
t of the cross-time variation. Such an approach may be more appro-
ate with longitudinal growth data, for example, than with personal-
data. However, it is possible to factor analyze both the system
iation and object variation parts of the temporal variation by treat-
the data in a slightly less direct fashion, that is, by taking
ariances or deviation cross-products of the variables on each occa-
n and then analyzing the resulting three-way set of covariance or
ss-product matrices according to the PARAFAC model. Both system
d object variation will contribute to the covariances. Furthermore,
ugh the distinction between system and objection variation disap-
rs in covariance analysis, it can be recovered. If desired, the two
es of variation can be reconstructed *after* the factor analysis, and
died separately or in combination. This is the approach that was
en in our work at IHD.

e PARAFAC-CANDECOMP Model Applied
Covariance Matrices

Before we discuss the PARAFAC model for covariances, let us first
all, for comparison, the traditional two-way factor model for cross-
ducts or covariances:

$$c_{ij} = a_{i1}a_{j1} + a_{i2}a_{j2} + \cdots + a_{is}a_{js} + \cdots + a_{iq}a_{jq} + e_{ij} \qquad (3)$$

re, a_{is} and a_{js} represent the loadings of personality variables i and j
factor s, as before. The observed covariance c_{ij} is simply the sum of
cross-products of the factor loadings for the two variables, plus
or. (For simplicity, discussion here is restricted to the formulation
orthogonal factors.) We discuss covariances, rather than correla-
ns, because the covariances properly reflect changes in variance
oss occasions: computation of correlations on each occasion would
pose a standardization within each occasion that would disturb the
sired proportional relationships between factors across different oc-
sions.

The three-way generalization of this covariance model can be de-
ed from Eq. 2 (Harshman, 1972a). It has the following simple form:

$$c_{ijk} = a_{i1}a_{j1}w^2_{k1} + a_{i2}a_{j2}w^2_{k2} + \cdots + a_{is}a_{js}w^2_{ks} +$$
$$\cdots + a_{iq}a_{jq}w^2_{kq} + e_{ijk} \qquad (4)$$

re c_{ijk} is the covariance between variables i and j, computed across
rsons, on occasion k. (Alternatively, it can be the sum rather than

the average of deviation cross-products, the covariance "uncorrect for sample size," as in Chapter 5.) The a_{is} and a_{js} represent the loading of variables i and j on factor s, as before. The w^2_{ks} coefficients are t occasion loadings, indicating the size or importance of factor s on occ sion k. These occasion loadings correspond to those of Eq. 2, with o difference: whereas the raw-score formulation (Eq. 2) was in terms w_{ks} coefficients that are proportional to the *standard deviation* of fa tor s on occasion k, the covariance or cross-product formulation of Eq involves w^2_{ks} coefficients that are proportional to the *variances* of t factors, that is, these loadings are exactly the squares of the w_{ks} loa ings of Eq. 2. (The occasion loadings are squared in Eq. 4 because t cross-product of two variables contains a w_{ks} coefficient for each va able.)

Note that any reference to an individual's factor score has disa peared from Eq. 4. As a result, it can be shown (Harshman, 1972a) th fitting Eq. 4 to a three-way set of covariances does not entail the stro assumption of system variation that is entailed by Eq. 2. Although E 4 allows the overall factor score variance to change from one occasi to the next, it does not require that the percentage change in fact score size be the same for each person; only the average change factor size appears in the equation. Thus it does not matter wheth individual shifts are coordinated or not. Because the weaker assum tions of Eq. 4 are consistent with data showing object variation, th model may provide an appropriate means of analyzing longitudin personality score data.

It may seem that going from Eqs. 2 to 4 results in the loss of valuak information about the factor scores of individuals. In fact, howev this loss is only temporary. We show below that factor scores for in viduals can be recovered, once the common factor loadings are c tained.

UNIQUENESS OF SOLUTION

Significance of Uniqueness

We now consider what is perhaps the most important property of t PARAFAC-CANDECOMP model: its ability to determine facto uniquely, without "rotation." The potential significance of such capability is apparent to anyone familiar with the history of fact analysis and the controversy that has surrounded the issue of fact rotation. In the personality domain, for example, Cattell has advocat

lique simple structure; Eysenck and Guilford have preferred ortho-
nal solutions while differing on how to bring additional empirical
formation to bear on the rotation process. As a result, differences in
tational procedure have repeatedly led to debates about the correct
scription and interpretation of dimensions underlying the variables
a given domain (Eysenck, 1977, versus Guilford, 1977, provides a
cent example of such a dispute). As Comrey (1967) has said, "The
tation process has been the target of much criticism, and continues to
the weakest link in the entire [factor analysis] process."
Because of the variety of rotations possible with any set of factors,
me psychometricians suggest that there is no such thing as a "real"
"correct" set of factors for describing the patterns of covariation in a
rticular data set. They interpret the different possible rotations of a
ven set of factors as representing alternative, equally valid, ways of
scribing the same set of relationships.
Indeed, when factors are used only for convenient description of a
ven two-way data set and not for inference beyond that data set, this
lativistic attitude may be justified. For some investigators, however,
ctor analysis provides one of the main sources of empirical informa-
m on which to build new explanatory constructs; such constructs are
tended to have broad application beyond the limits of a particular set
data. For these researchers, the attempt to identify "real" or "expla-
tory" factors is simply another expression of the time-honored scien-
ic endeavor of attempting to identify the underlying causes of ob-
rved regularities. Certainly, theorists such as Cattell and Eysenck
nsider their factors to have such causal implications (Cattell, 1952;
senck, 1970, Chapter 12), and thus, for them, the dispute over alter-
tive sets of factors is both meaningful and important.
Differently rotated factors will often give rise to different scientific
potheses about underlying causes in a given data domain and thus
ill lead to different predictions about the outcome of possible experi-
ents in that domain. (For example, different factor theories of in-
llectual abilities give rise to different predictions about patterns of
tellectual change due to drugs, brain damage, etc.) Clearly, in such
ses those factors that lead to the most accurate predictions should be
nsidered the most accurate descriptions of "reality" in that domain.
f course, any scientific construct is only an approximation to "real-
," and the constructs derived from factors are probably rougher ap-
oximations than many. Yet there seems no reason why factor-
rived constructs should not be granted the same empirical status as
her scientific constructs, as long as they play the same sort of role in
nerating scientific hypotheses that are empirically testable.

One real objection to using factors as starting points for the d
velopment of explanatory constructs is that they are often depende
on relatively arbitrary decisions concerning rotation. The choice of
"simple structure" rotation, for example, is often fairly hard to defei
on empirical grounds, and when this is so, any claim of explanato
validity for the particular factors that result from such rotation h
little internal support. If it is claimed that such factors have great
empirical validity, this claim usually needs to be supported by a seri
of external verifications of their distinctive predictions (i.e., predi
tions that would be implied by those factors, but not by factors obtain
through alternative rotations; see Harshman, 1970 or 1976, for furth
discussion). Certainly the extensive series of investigations and inte
locking experiments conducted by researchers such as Eysenck, Ca
tell, and Guilford give their findings much greater weight than tl
results of any one or two factor analyses in isolation. Nonetheless, t
differences in rotational philosophy of these investigators has appa
ently led them down different paths, and their conclusions, therefoi
represent somewhat different perspectives on the nature of persona
ity.

PARAFAC was developed to help overcome the problems of rotati
by strengthening the factor model itself. PARAFAC incorporates in
the three-way extension of the factor model an important princip
first conceived by Cattell (1944), which takes advantage of the ext:
information about factors present in three-way data to obtain a uniqi
set of factors without rotation.

Unlike two-way data, where factors produced by many alternati
rotations will fit the data equally well (forcing one to go outside tl
data to test the implications of a given factor rotation), with tl
PARAFAC model for three-way data, differently rotated factors w
not, in general, fit the data equally well. Thus one can empirically te
different potential factor rotations *within the same data set* from whi
the factors are being extracted. (Of course, further confirmation fro
experiments that go beyond the data would also be important.) Wi
longitudinal data, for example, different rotations of the possible fa
tors underlying a set of variables will give rise to different predictio:
concerning patterns of change in covariances among the variabl
across time. If the data are adequate, there will be one "rotation" (i.
one set of a, f, and w values) that fits the data *across time* better tha
any other. By seeking and finding this unique set of factors, PARAFA
provides an empirically grounded basis for selecting the best "rot
tion," that is, the best candidates for "real" or "explanatory" facto
underlying a given domain.

e Basis for Uniqueness: The Principle
Proportional Profiles

In 1944 Cattell proposed what he called "the principle of parallel
oportional profiles" as an alternative to the simple structure crite-
on for selecting a preferred rotation of factor axes (Cattell, 1944). His
ea was simple, yet powerful: by comparing the factors extracted
parately from two different but related data sets, it should be possi-
e to discover the "real" orientation of axes in the two solutions by
ading that orientation that brings their factor loadings (or factor
ores) into parallel, proportional correspondence across solutions. As
ag as the two data sets are not equivalent, but instead possess the
me common factors in different relative proportions, there is only
e rotational position that will reveal this correspondence. It can be
own that such a correspondence of proportional (rather than identi-
l) loading patterns or factor scores would be very unlikely to arise in
o data sets by chance or as a mathematical artifact. Hence, its dis-
very in real data would indicate some common empirical influences
ting to organize both data sets, but in different degrees in each.
us, Cattell argued that factors determined by rotation to parallel
oportional profiles would have stronger empirical meaning than
ose given by other rotations of the same axes (Cattell, 1944; Cattell
Cattell, 1955).
Because of mathematical and computational difficulties, the propor-
nal profiles criterion was not successfully implemented as a rotation
chnique (Cattell & Cattell, 1955), and so was subsequently ne-
ected. The mathematical difficulties have more recently been over-
me, however, by noting that the principle of proportional profiles
plies a particular three-way generalization of factor analysis,
mely the PARAFAC models already discussed (Harshman, 1970,
76). (Interestingly, the equivalent CANDECOMP model was de-
loped without reference to Cattell's idea. It is based instead mainly
a rationale growing out of a consideration of individual differences
multidimensional scaling; see Carroll and Chang, 1970.)
There is a sense in which the discovery of substantial proportional
anges in loadings across occasions can be taken to constitute confir-
atory evidence both for the empirical "reality" of the factors defined
a particular rotation of axes and for the incorrectness of other rota-
nal positions. To see this, imagine the following oversimplified case.
researcher is comparing covariances among a set of variables on
casion 1 with the corresponding covariances on occasion 2. If the
vestigator finds only small, random differences between the

covariances on the two occasions, the comparison will provide no rea son to choose a particular rotation of the factors. Appeal must be mad instead to "simple structure" or other principles invoked to determir rotations in two-way factor analysis. If, on the other hand, changes i covariances across time showed certain systematic patterns, these pa terns could strongly imply a particular rotation of the factor axe Suppose, for example, that the covariances could be divided into thre sets: one set that consists of covariances showing no real chang across the two occasions, only small random fluctuations; a second s of covariances, all of which increase by approximately 20% (with ra dom fluctuations around this value); and a third set of covariances, a of which decrease by approximately 35%. Suppose further, that th three sets of covariances are, in fact, covariances among three distin sets of variables. What could an investigator conclude?

First, one would be compelled to acknowledge that the pattern changes is far too systematic and coordinated to have happened k chance. Second, to explain all the covariances that shifted by the san proportion, one would infer that the variables involved must shar some common influence, that is, the variance of a common facto Third, one would justifiably prefer a rotation of three underlying fa tors that assigned each factor to one of the three groups of variable that show different shifts in covariances across time. With such a rota tion, the pattern of changes across time could be simply explained i terms of changes in the variances of the factors. Other rotations wou not provide an explanation of the changes across time, and, in fac would be inconsistent with them. It would not be possible to have th *same* factors on all three occasions unless they were rotated to k consistent with the patterns of shift across occasions. Normally th situation will be more complicated, because factors will probably ove lap in influence and affect some of the same variables. Furthermore, given factor will affect different variables to different degrees. Yet th mathematical idea is still applicable (though the resulting patterns ar harder to describe verbally) and the conclusion is still the same: ce tain coordinated patterns of change in covariances across time (or acro experimental conditions, or whatever else is represented by the thi mode) can help to identify the underlying factors that are changin Further, such coordinated patterns of change provide *confirmator evidence* for the particular rotation of factors that they help to identify

Reliability Check

But how does one distinguish patterns of covariance-change acro time that are only random sampling fluctuations from those system c enough to establish unambiguously a preferred rotation for the ictors? One method is to compare factors obtained in random split alves of the data. The degree of similarity of factors found in two ibsets of a given data set can provide an impression of the stability of ie factors obtained and of the likelihood that they would be found by »meone analyzing a new sample of similar data. If approximately the ime set of factors and orientation of factors is determined in two alves of one's subject sample, the characteristic patterns are evidently :liable enough to be repeatable, even with half as many subjects in ich sample. Features of the solution that do not replicate across split alves should be interpreted with caution. (For examples of the use of)lit-half validation of PARAFAC factors, see Gandour & Harshman,)78; Meyer, 1980).

Precautions in addition to checking for the replicability of particular :atures of one's solution are advisable. The factor model represents a articular type of linear additive approximation to the patterns pre- :nt in the data. Such a simple approximation is often quite useful and dequate for empirical investigations, but this will not always be the ise. One must be aware of the limitations of the model one is fitting to ie data and sensitive to any indications that a more complex model iay be required. (For example, certain types of violations of the model's nearity assumptions can be recognized and interpreted by looking for onlinear relationships between PARAFAC factors, an approach less kely to be feasible with two-way factor analysis; see Harshman, 1970, hapter 7.)

ecessary Conditions for Uniqueness

As is apparent from the foregoing discussion, PARAFAC depends on istinctive patterns of variation of factors across the third mode (e.g., me) to separate the influences of the different factors and thus deter- iine the best orientation of factor axes, that is, to identify the unique ictors. If, however, the factors do not change in distinct ways, but istead certain factors always change their sizes together, and to the ame degree, across the third mode, then PARAFAC will not be able to :solve the influence of these factors into unique components.

Consider the following algebraic analogy (borrowed from Harshman, adefoged, & Goldstein, 1977). In the simple equation $x + y = 20$, iere is no unique solution because an infinite number of x, y pairs ·ill satisfy the weak constraints imposed by this specified relation- iip. This example corresponds to the kind of nonuniqueness of load- igs that occurs in two-way factor analysis. However, if we consider dditional information about the unknown parameters, for example, if we consider several related equations in parallel, such as $x + y = 2$ and $2x + 3y = 55$, and if we require the same values of x and y t satisfy both equations, we obtain a unique solution. Similarly, parallel analysis of several data sets in terms of a common set of factors (ur known parameters) can provide a unique solution for the factors. But is essential that the coefficients of x and y do not have the same rati to one another in the two simultaneous equations. If the second equa tion were $2x + 2y = 40$ it would not provide any new constraints on th solution, and so would not provide a unique solution. The ratio of th factor sizes for two factors must differ across at least some of the occa sions in order for the three-way data set to determine a unique solutio for those factors. (If most of the factors vary in independent fashio across occasions, but two factors always change size together, then a factors except those two will be uniquely determined.) For more de tailed discussion of uniqueness, and mathematical proofs, see Ha shman, 1970, 1972b, 1976; Kruskal, 1976, 1977.

Before a factor analysis is performed, distinct patterns of variation for each factor might be *expected* but one could not be *certain* that the would be present. After performing the analysis, however, one ca partially verify the presence or lack of distinct patterns of factor varia tion across time by examining the table of occasion loadings (the w_f coefficients). If the patterns of variation of these loadings across tim are distinct for each factor, then the interpretation of the solution ca proceed with greater confidence. However, if several columns hav very similar patterns of loadings, then those factors may not b uniquely determined. One must proceed with caution in interpretin those factors and certainly test the solution for uniqueness and relia bility by methods described above and elsewhere (e.g., Harshman al., 1977).

IMPLEMENTING THE MODEL: COMPUTATIONAL
CHARACTERISTICS OF PARAFAC-CONDECOMP

To properly evaluate any application of PARAFAC, one must ap preciate not only the differences between the two-way and three-wa factor *model,* but also the resulting basic differences in computationa procedures. Even with two-way factor analysis, one cannot simply "ir put the data and output the results." It is important to test variou alternatives, select the most appropriate options, and make informe decisions at various stages of the analysis. With PARAFAC, an ir telligent understanding of the basic stages of the computational proce dure is even more important. There is a specific series of steps fc

etermining the correct number of factors and ensuring that the opti-
al solution has been obtained for any given number of factors.
nderstanding these steps and evaluating how well the results sup-
ort the conclusions drawn by the investigator is an important part of
valuating any PARAFAC analysis.

The computational characteristics of PARAFAC differ from those of
onventional factor analysis in two basic respects: (a) the factors must
e extracted simultaneously rather than successively, and thus a sepa-
ate analysis must be performed each time a solution with a different
umber of factors is to be examined; (b) each solution is obtained
eratively, rather than by a "closed form" direct computation; con-
quently checks must be made to ensure that the iterative procedure
as reached an optimal solution and that the same optimal solution
ill be obtained consistently.

Finally, for longitudinal applications of PARAFAC involving
alysis of covariance, we propose a modified method of computing
ctor scores. This could be considered a third computational difference
tween our approach and conventional two-way factor analysis. It is
seful to consider all three of these differences more carefully.

multaneous Extraction of Factors: Testing Effects
Different Numbers of Factors

Conventional two-way factor analysis normally proceeds by extract-
g factors stepwise, that is, first extracting one factor, then extracting
second factor from the variance that is left over after removing the
rst factor, and in this way removing succeeding factors from a given
ta set. In this conventional procedure, the first factor will be the
rgest, explaining as much variance as is possible with one factor,
ith the next factor explaining as much residual variance as possible,
d so on. Such an approach imposes certain arbitrary restrictions on
e form of the factors. First, it causes the factors to be orthogonal to
e another in all modes. Further, because it maximizes the variance
tracted by each successive factor, it forces the early factors to repre-
nt a combination of influences whenever such a combination can
plain more variance than can a factor that represents a single under-
ing pattern of influence. Such "raw" unrotated factors are not nor-
ally interpretable.

In two-way factor analysis, the stepwise approach causes no prob-
ms because a subsequent rotation is used to "untangle" the combina-
ns of influences in the unrotated factors. However, for PARAFAC
e incorrectly rotated (sequentially extracted) factors would actually

capture less of the data variance than the same number of factors i
the correct orientation. To take advantage of the important uniquenes
of PARAFAC in determining the best factor orientations, it is neces
sary to extract all the desired factors *simultaneously*. This procedur
provides the best estimate of each factor, given the presence of other
and removes the arbitrary restrictions imposed by sequential extrac
tion. Because of the requirement of simultaneous extraction, one mus
perform a separate analysis at each dimensionality to be examine
Thus, for example, one must perform a four-dimensional analysis, an
then a separate five-dimensional analysis, to compare the form of th
factors in four- and five-dimensional solutions. Generally, it will not k
the case that the factors in the five-dimensional solution are identic:
to those found in the four-dimensional solution plus one addition:
factor.

Iterative Computation: Checking for Convergence, Optimality, and Uniqueness

To perform a PARAFAC analysis at a given dimensionality, a
iterative procedure is used. Unlike two-way factor analysis, there is r
direct "closed form" procedure for obtaining the optimal factor loa
ings. Instead, each solution starts with a random set of values for th
variable loadings, person loadings, and occasion loadings (the a, f, an
w coefficients). PARAFAC then improves this random first guess i
crementally in small steps, increasing the fit of the solution to the dat
at each step, until a final optimal solution is reached. Stepwise chang
are comparatively large at first, but gradually become smaller as th
solution approaches its final form. When these steps become vanisl
ingly small, the process is said to have converged. Obviously it is ui
reasonable to try to interpret a solution that is far from convergenc
because additional iterations may change the loadings enough to alt
the interpretation. Therefore it is necessary to establish, for each sol
tion, that it is close enough to convergence to provide accurate est
mates of the final loadings.

Because PARFAC proceeds by successive iterations, different sets
initial random loadings will cause the program to pass through a di
ferent series of intermediate stages on the way to the final converge
solution. It is important to determine, therefore, whether the fin:
solution obtained is completely determined by the data or is instee
partially a function of the random initial loadings. With data that ha
the necessary independent variations of the underlying factors acro:
all three modes (as explained previously in the discussion of uniqu

ss), different starting points should converge to the same final solu-
on, as long as the number of factors being extracted does not exceed
1e number underlying the data. If too many factors are extracted, the
·lution may be nonunique and differ with different starting points. (In
·rtain circumstances nonuniqueness may also occur when too few
·ctors are extracted, but this is less common. If, e.g., the "true"
1mber of factors is 5, there can be a unique 5-dimensional solution
1t also sometimes two competing 4-dimensional solutions, each with
factors that resemble a different subset of the full 5 factors.) Local
·tima can also cause problems by "trapping" the iterative procedure
. an invalid partial solution before it reaches the overall best fitting
·lution for a given dimensionality.

To check that an obtained solution is the desired global optimum for
1at dimensionality and that it is in fact unique and independent of
·arting position, several analyses are conducted from different ran-
·m starting positions and the resulting solutions and fit values are
·mpared. The obtained factors are also compared with factors ex-
·acted at lower and higher dimensionalities to gain further informa-
·n on their stability. (For more detailed discussion of these, and re-
.ted checking procedures, see Harshman *et al.,* 1977.)

·ethod of Computing Factor Scores

Given item loadings for q PARAFAC dimensions, factor scores can
· computed by the same regression technique often used in two-way
·ctor analysis. To obtain an individual's q factor scores for a given
·casion, that person's column of all item *ratings* (his/her column of
.w data for that occasion) is approximated by a weighted combination
· the q columns of all item *loadings* (the PARAFAC dimensions ob-
.ined from the covariance analysis). The q multiple regression
·eights that yield the best-predicting combination of factor loadings
·come the factor score estimates. They represent the amounts of the q
·ctors which, in combination, would produce a set of ratings most
·sembling the individual's obtained ratings for the given occasion.
1us, they represent estimates of the amount of each factor that the
·rson has on that occasion.

As is well known, the regression procedure for estimating factor
·ores generates an intermediate set of values called the *factor score*
efficients. These coefficients provide a simple way of estimating any
·dividual's factor scores from his data. For each factor, the coefficients
·scribe a weighted linear combination of the individual's observed
·m ratings that gives the best estimate of that individual's factor

score on that factor. If a person has high ratings on those items that count strongly toward the particular factor, he/she obtains a high score on that factor. With three-way data, our method of computing the factor score coefficients is the same as is used in two-way factor analysis, that is, we simply take the generalized inverse of the factor loading matrix. However, our method of applying these coefficients differs in two respects from the standard procedure for two-way factor analysis: (a) we apply the coefficients separately to the subject's data on each occasion, and thus compute several sets of factor scores for each individual; (b) we apply the coefficients directly to the *uncentered raw data* to recover information about factor means.

In many applications, and particularly in longitudinal analysis, it would be very useful to be able to compare factor score means across groups or occasions. Because there has been some controversy about the proper way to handle changes in factor means when analyzing longitudinal data (e.g., Bentler, 1973, discusses problems with various approaches), it may be useful to explain and justify the approach we advocate (and which is used in Chapter 5). We remove any information on changes in factor means before performing the PARAFAC analysis and then recover the information at the time of estimating factor scores. Recall that the first step in computing item covariances (or, in Chapter 5, sums of deviation cross-products) involves centering the data across persons (i.e., removing the mean from each column of each of the data matrices according to the formula $\overset{*}{x}_{ijk} = x_{ijk} - \bar{x}_{i.k}$). Naturally this removes from the resulting covariances any information concerning mean changes in the factor scores across occasions (or in different subsamples if these correspond to different levels of k). This is desirable because it avoids possible "contamination" of within-occasion covariances by the effects of any cross-occasion (or cross-subsample) variance of the factor means that is not simply proportional to within-occasion changes in factor variances (as might occur with certain sex or cohort effects).

It can be shown that the recovered item loadings are *not affected by* this centering (aside from avoidance of possible "contamination," as mentioned). However, centering across persons *does* affect the factor scores. If we applied the factor score coefficients to person-centered data, we would get person-centered factor scores, that is, each factor score would represent a person's deviation from the average person score on that factor for that occasion and subsample (for occasion k we would obtain $\overset{*}{f}_{jsk} = f_{jsk} - \bar{f}_{.sk}$). To recover "raw" factors scores, that is scores that include the mean component, we apply the factor score coefficients directly to the raw, uncentered data. We can then study changes in factor means across times or subsamples by comparing the ieans of these factor scores. (Because the loadings for items are not ffected by centering, except as noted above, they provide an appropriate description of uncentered as well as centered data. Con-iquently, the factor score coefficients obtained from such loadings are lso applicable to uncentered as well as centered data. Artificial additive constants in the data might introduce small additive constants into ie factor scores, but as long as these constants do not change appreciably over time they should not affect the differences in factor means of roups or occasions.) We believe this approach will generally solve the roblems noted by Bentler (1973) and others regarding the treatment ' mean factor changes in longitudinal factor analysis.

PECIAL ASSUMPTIONS UNDERLYING PARAFAC ANALYSIS F LONGITUDINAL DATA

In addition to the usual assumptions of factor or component analysis ʾ.g., that scores are linearly decomposable into factors plus error), ʾrtain further assumptions about the behavior of factors across time re required for PARAFAC analysis of longitudinal data. It is impor-int to consider the various special assumptions or limitations that iay be implied by using particular forms of the PARAFAC model. One in then evaluate the advantages and disadvantages of PARAFAC ɔmpared to various other factor analytic approaches to longitudinal ata.

actor Loading Invariance

Only one set of variable or item loadings is obtained by PARAFAC nalysis of the three-way data. These are the a_{is} values of Eqs. 2 or 4. ɔnsequently, it is implicit in the PARAFAC model that the pattern of ʾadings of variables on a given factor remains unchanged from one ːcasion to the next. In other words, the factorial content of variables is ssumed to remain constant across occasions of measurement. This rovides a desirable base of common comparison across occasions, but ₊ seldom exactly true with variables that span long time periods. For ːample, this assumption may not be strictly valid for the type of ʾrsonality data that we have been taking as an example; the meaning ʾ some items—their interpretation in terms of underlying traits—may iffer when used to describe a 40-year-old, compared to their meaning hen applied to an adolescent. For any longitudinal data set being ɔnsidered for PARAFAC analysis, the researcher must decide how ʾrious this problem is, that is, whether the probable changes in facto-

rial content of the variables would be so great as to render useless th
PARAFAC approximation in terms of constant factorial compositio
across time. Some flexibility here seems appropriate, however. Unles
it is reasonable to assume that one's variables measure at leas
roughly the same thing across time periods, then not only PARAFA
but most other types of longitudinal analysis or comparison becom
almost impossible.

It is often useful to obtain empirical information on the stability (
factorial content of items across occasions by doing separate two-wa
factor analyses in the individual occasions or three-way analyses o
earlier versus later subsets of the data. For example, these method
were employed to check the appropriateness of the PARAFAC analys
of Q-sort items described in Chapter 5.

The Nature of Factor Score Changes

We have chosen an interpretation of PARAFAC in which th
changes across time are attributed to changes in the person loadings (
"factor scores" of individuals, rather than to changes in the variable (
item loadings (i.e., the w_{ks} is taken to multiply the f_{js} rather than th
a_{is}). Other interpretations are possible, but this one seems to us to k
the most appropriate for the particular personality example we hav
been considering. Having adopted this convention, let us consider wha
limitations are imposed on the patterns of factor score change when th
PARAFAC-CANDECOMP model is applied to different types of data

We have already seen how the direct application of PARAFAC 1
raw-score matrices imposes the limitation that factor score changes k
proportional across occasions, that is, $f_{jsk} = f_{js} w_{ks}$. This strictest mod
does not even allow for shifts of the factor means across time excep
those proportional to changes in factor standard deviations. If one su
pects that other, additive baseline shifts may be present, the data ca
easily be made suitable for PARAFAC analysis by centering the dat
for each occasion across persons before performing the factor analysi
(This removes any baseline shifts in factor scores and restores th
required proportionality of factor changes. If the data are otherwis
appropriate for direct PARAFAC, the centering will not affect the for
of the extracted *variable* loadings and will only remove the means fro
the extracted person loadings. Information on baseline shifts in th
factor means can be recovered, if desired, by factor score estimatio
procedures described above.)

Because of the assumption of system-variation in the direct applica
tion of PARAFAC to raw data matrices, this kind of application shou

be restricted to data in which system-variation is likely to be present (e.g., longitudinal growth data, economic system data, physiological measurements, or data where the third mode represents various experimental conditions designed to alter systematically the relative influence of the underlying factors; for examples see Harshman *et al.*, 1977; Meyer, 1980). For such data, however, direct PARAFAC has advantages over the indirect approach involving covariances. The direct approach allows oblique solutions if they provide a better fit to the data, whereas indirect analysis via covariances always gives orthogonal factors—unless the more general model PARAFAC2 is used[3] (see the following for further discussion of this point). The direct approach also yields three distinct sets of loadings rather than two, removing the need for estimating "factor scores."

When system variation is not likely to be found, a more indirect application of PARAFAC is warranted. If PARAFAC is applied to covariance matrices computed from the data rather than to the score matrices themselves, there are no restrictive assumptions imposed concerning the patterns of changes in factor scores *across occasions.* The data can follow object or system variation, or any intermediate pattern (Harshman, 1972a). Furthermore, although the separate computation of covariances on each occasion necessarily removes any information concerning mean changes in the factor scores across occasions, this information can be recovered. In fact, it is possible to estimate the specific object-variation pattern of each person's changes in factor scores across time. (See discussion of factor scores in the preceding.) Nonetheless, one restrictive assumption about factor scores is implied by using PARAFAC to analyze covariances, that is, that the factor scores for the different factors are orthogonal across persons within each occasion.

Orthogonal versus Oblique Factors

In dealing with the "obliqueness" of factors and of correlations among factors, it is necessary to specify which mode of the three-way data set is being considered. For example, two factors can vary in a

---

[3]A generalization of the PARAFAC model allows oblique factors to be extracted from three-way sets of covariance matrices. This model, called PARAFAC2 (Harshman, 1972a, 1976), has only been implemented in an experimental program that is not fully perfected. It is also more expensive to use because, at this point, it requires substantially more computer time. To avoid additional complications that would have been introduced by considering the PARAFAC2 model as well as PARAFAC, only PARAFAC was used in these initial longitudinal investigations.

correlated manner across persons and yet vary independently across occasions. Traditionally, those doing factor analysis of personality data have been concerned with the independence or correlation of factors *across persons*. To them, "oblique" factors were ones that had correlated factor scores. With our more general three-way model, we might want to consider the orthogonality or obliqueness of factors in any of the three modes; in terms of the personality score example, we might consider the independence of person loadings, occasion loadings, or variable loadings.

When PARAFAC is applied directly to the three-way raw data (or centered data) matrix, the factor loadings that emerge may be either oblique or orthogonal in any or all of the three modes. The results in a particular case will be uniquely determined by the structure of the three-way data itself. But in the analysis of covariances, one of the three modes "disappears" from the data. In the personality score example, the person mode disappears because covariances among items are computed across persons. The remaining two modes (variables and occasions, in our example) are still free to display orthogonal or oblique patterns of factor loadings, but to use the simple form of Eq. 4 for analysis of covariances, it is necessary to assume that the factor loadings are orthogonal in the mode that "disappeared."

We are involved in a trade-off of restrictions. In terms of our personality score example, the analysis of covariances allows us to relax the restriction that the variation of factor scores *across time* follow the system-variation pattern but imposes a new restriction of orthogonality on the variation of factor scores *across persons* on any one given occasion (i.e., for n persons we assume that $\sum_{j=1}^{n} (f_{jsk}) (f_{jtk}) = 0$, if $s \neq t$). (This restriction can be relaxed; see Footnote 3, p. 455.)

Although the restriction to orthogonality across persons is probably not exactly appropriate for most data sets, it will often serve as a reasonable simplifying assumption, particularly for the purposes of an initial investigation. When, for the "true" factors, the factor scores would actually have been correlated, then the solution obtained by analysis of covariances will provide a best orthogonal approximation to those factors. (In practice, however, factor score estimates obtained for these "orthogonal" factors may still be slightly correlated.) Unless the "correct" factors are strongly correlated across persons, this orthogonality restriction usually produces only a modest shift in the loadings that does not substantially alter interpretation of the factors. For object-variation data such as the personality score example, the trade-off of restrictions involved in covariance analysis is a worthwhile one.

Assumptions about Error Terms: Factor versus Component Analysis

When we set forth the equations defining the PARAFAC model for raw data (Eq. 2) and covariance matrices (Eq. 4) there were no specifications of the properties of the error terms e_{ijk}. Two approaches to these terms are possible, one corresponding to a three-way generalization of common factor analysis and the other to a three-way generalization of principal component analysis. Requiring that the error terms be uncorrelated across tests and persons results in a three-way form of common-factor analysis. Alternatively, specifying that these errors are simply the (correlated) residuals from a least-squares fitting of the q factors produces what is technically a three-way form of principal components analysis. For raw-data factoring, only the component-like analysis is currently programmed. However, for analysis of covariances, program options exist to implement either approach.[4] If the diagonals of the covariance matrices are left unaltered in the process of analysis, then a principal-components-like solution is obtained. If, on the other hand, the program option to iterate on the diagonal is selected, so that the diagonal cells are continually re-estimated in the course of the analysis, a common-factor type of solution is obtained. For large covariance matrices such as were analyzed in Chapter 5, it makes little difference which approach is taken. Because the diagonals constitute a very small percentage of the total data, the changes in their values that result from iteration have very little effect on the values of the factor loadings. (However, when employing the common-factor model, we should speak of our subsequently obtained person loadings as "factor score estimates" rather than "factor scores.")

Linear Independence of Factor Variations across Time

There is an additional assumption which is not necessary for the factor model of Eq. 2 or Eq. 4 to be appropriate, but which *is* necessary if one is to interpret the PARAFAC factors as "explanatory" and meaningful without rotation. The patterns of change of factor "size" or variance across time must be distinct for each factor. As discussed in the section on uniqueness these distinct patterns of change across time are

---

[4]A portable FORTRAN computer program for PARAFAC may be leased from Scientific Software Associates, 48 Wilson Avenue, London, Ontario, Canada N6H 1X3. Or, write to Richard A. Harshman, Department of Psychology, University of Western Ontario, London, Ontario, Canada N6A 5C2.

the clues that allow PARAFAC to resolve the factors. Loosely speaking, factors can be correlated across time, but should not be perfectly correlated. (In fact, variations in a factor generally should not be perfectly predictable from any linear combination of the variations in other factors. For a more precise statement of the required conditions for uniqueness, see Harshman, 1972b; Kruskal, 1976, 1977.)

Because the potential for a unique solution is one of the most important advantages of a PARAFAC analysis, the user should (a) make an effort before the analysis to ensure that the required distinct patterns of changes in the factor variance across time will be present in the data collected, (b) verify these distinct changes after the analysis by examining the occasion loadings, and (c) check the reliability of the factor orientations by performing additional split-half or "jack-knifing" analyses.

SUMMARY AND CONCLUSION

New methods of factor analysis may have great value for analysis of longitudinal data (as well as many other kinds of "three-way" data). They allow the entire three-way longitudinal data set to be entered into the analysis, without the usual requirement of "collapsing" the data into a two-way array. Because a more complete set of information is available to the analysis, a more complete and accurate description of the data can emerge from the analysis. For example, factor loadings for *occasions* as well as for variables, and factor scores for persons, can all be obtained from the same analysis.

In this discussion we have focused on the PARAFAC-CANDECOMP model for three-way factor analysis. This approach offers a particularly important advantage over two-way factor analysis, specifically, unique solutions. The additional information present in the three-way data (i.e., the pattern of variation of factors across time, as well as across variables and individuals) is used to remove the rotational ambiguity present in two-way factor analysis. Provided that (a) the factors show distinct patterns of variation across time, (b) the data are appropriate for the PARAFAC model, and (c) the solution is stable (e.g., across split-halves of the data), then the PARAFAC-determined factor axes have an empirical justification considerably stronger than any available in conventional two-way factor analysis: any rotation of those factors would reduce their ability to simultaneously fit all of the data matrices across the successive time periods.

When using the PARAFAC-CANDECOMP procedure for three-way

factor analysis, it is important to keep in mind certain general assumptions implied by the model, along with the special assumptions involved in its application to longitudinal data. These considerations can be summarized as follows: investigators must be able to assume that the factorial content of their variables is relatively constant across time (i.e., that approximately the same factors are present on the different occasions), and that the major systematic differences across occasions arise from changes in the relative importance of the factors from one occasion to the next. When these assumptions are appropriate, the PARAFAC-CANDECOMP method of three-way factor analysis can be a powerful way to uncover meaningful factors and study their changes across time.

Appendix B

Item Listing of Adult Core Q Sort

SPECIFIED 9-POINT DISTRIBUTION ($N = 100$)
5, 8, 12, 16, 18, 16, 12, 8, 5
$r = 1 - \text{Sum } d^2/864$

1. Is critical, skeptical, not easily impressed.
2. Is a genuinely dependable and responsible person.
3. Has a wide range of interests. (*N.B.:* Superficiality or depth of interest is irrelevant here.)
4. Is a talkative individual.
5. Behaves in a giving way toward others. (*N.B.:* Regardless of the motivation involved.)
6. Is fastidious.
7. Favors conservative values in a variety of areas.
8. Appears to have a high degree of intellectual capacity. (*N.B.:* Whether actualized or not. Originality is not necessarily assumed.)
9. Is uncomfortable with uncertainty and complexities.
10. Anxiety and tension find outlet in bodily symptoms. (*N.B.:* If placed high, implies bodily dysfunction; if placed low, implies absence of autonomic arousal.)
11. Is protective of those close to him. (*N.B.:* Placement of this item expresses behavior ranging from over-protection through appropriate nurturance to a laissez-faire, under-protective manner.)
12. Tends to be self-defensive.
13. Is thin-skinned; vulnerable to anything that can be construed as criticism or an interpersonal slight.
14. Basically submissive.
15. The "light touch" as compared to the "heavy touch."
16. Is introspective. (*N.B.:* Introspectiveness per se does not imply insight.)
17. Behaves in a sympathetic or considerate manner.

18. Initiates humor.

19. Seeks reassurance from others.

20. Has a rapid personal tempo.

21. Arouses nurturant feelings in others of both sexes.

22. Feels a lack of personal meaning in life. (Uncharacteristic end means zest.)

23. Extrapunitive; tends to transfer or project blame.

24. *Prides* self on being "objective," rational. (Regardless of whether person is really objective or rational.)

25. Tends toward overcontrol of needs and impulses; binds tensions excessively; delays gratification unnecessarily.

26. Is productive; gets things done. (Regardless of speed.)

27. Shows condescending behavior in relations with others.

28. Tends to arouse liking and acceptance in people.

29. Is turned to for advice and reassurance.

30. Gives up and withdraws where possible in the face of frustration and adversity.

31. Is satisfied with physical appearance.

32. Seems to be aware of the impression he/she makes on others.

33. Is calm, relaxed in manner.

34. Over-reactive to minor frustrations; irritable.

35. Has warmth; is compassionate.

36. Is negativistic; tends to undermine and obstruct or sabotage.

37. Is guileful and deceitful, manipulative, opportunistic.

38. Has hostility toward others. (*N.B.:* Basic hostility is intended here; mode of expression is to be indicated by other items.)

39. Thinks and associates to ideas in unusual ways; has unconventional thought processes. (Either pathological or creative.)

40. Is vulnerable to real or fancied threat, generally fearful.

41. Is moralistic. (*N.B.:* Regardless of the particular nature of the moral code.)

42. Reluctant to commit self to any definite course of action; tends to delay or avoid action. (Uncharacteristic end indicates quick to act.)

43. Is facially and/or gesturally expressive.

44. Evaluates the motivation of others in interpreting situations. (*N.B.:* Accuracy of evaluation is not assumed. *N.B.:* Again, extreme placement in one direction implies preoccupation with motivational interpretations; at the other extreme, the item implies a psychological obtuseness. S does not consider motivational factors.)

45. Has a brittle ego-defense system; has a small reserve of integration; would be disorganized and maladaptive when under stress or trauma.

46. Engaged in personal fantasy and daydreams, fictional speculations.

47. Tends to feel guilty. (*N.B.:* Regardless of whether verbalized or not.)

48. Aloof, keeps people at a distance; avoids close interpersonal relationships.

49. Is basically distrustful of people in general; questions their motivations.

50. Is unpredictable and changeable in behavior and attitudes.

51. Genuinely values intellectual and cognitive matters. (*N.B.:* Ability or achievement are not implied here.)

52. *Behaves* in an assertive fashion in interpersonal situations. (*N.B.:* Item 14 reflects underlying submissiveness; this refers to overt behavior.)

53. Tends toward undercontrol of needs and impulses; unable to delay gratification.

54. Emphasizes being with others; gregarious.

55. Is self-defeating.

56. Responds to humor.

57. Is an interesting, arresting person.

58. Enjoys sensuous experiences (including touch, taste, smell, physical contact).

59. Is concerned with own body and the adequacy of its physiological functioning. (Body cathexis.)

60. Has insight into own motives and behavior.

61. Creates and exploits dependency in people. (*N.B.:* Regardless of the techniques employed, e.g., punitiveness, overindulgence. *N.B.:* At the other end of the scale, item implies respecting and encouraging the independence and individuality of others.)

62. Tends to be rebellious and nonconforming.

63. Judges self and others in conventional terms like "popularity," "the correct thing to do," social pressures, etc.

64. Is socially perceptive of a wide range of interpersonal cues.

65. Characteristically pushes and tries to stretch limits; sees what he can get away with.

66. Enjoys esthetic impressions; is esthetically reactive.

67. Is self-indulgent.

68. Is basically anxious.

69. Is bothered by anything that can be construed as a demand. (*N.B.:* No implication of the kind of subsequent response is intended here.)

70. *Behaves* in an ethically consistent manner; is consistent with own personal standards.

71. Has high aspiration level for self.

72. Overconcerned with own adequacy as a person, either at conscious or unconscious levels. (*N.B.:* A clinical judgment is required here; number 74 reflects subjunctive satisfaction with self.)

73. Tends to perceive many different contexts in sexual terms; eroticizes situations.

74. Is consciously unaware of self-concern; feels satisfied with self.

75. Has a clear-cut, internally consistent personality. (*N.B.:* *Amount* of information available before sorting is not intended here.)

76. Tends to project his own feelings and motivations onto others.

77. Appears straightforward, forthright, candid in dealings with others.

78. Feels cheated and victimized by life.

79. Tends to ruminate and have persistent, preoccupying thoughts (either pathological or creative).

80. Interested in members of the opposite sex. (*N.B.:* At opposite end, item implies *absence* of such interest.)

81. Is physically attractive, good-looking. (*N.B.:* The cultural criterion is to be applied here.)

82. Has fluctuating moods.

83. Able to see to the heart of important problems.

84. Is cheerful. (*N.B.:* Extreme placement toward uncharacteristic end of continuum implies gloominess.)

85. Is self-pitying (whiny).

86. Handles anxiety and conflicts by repressive or dissociative tendencies.

87. Interprets basically simple and clear-cut situations in complicated and particularizing ways.

88. Is personally charming.

89. Compares self to others. Is alert to real or fancied differences between self and other people.

90. Is concerned with philosophical problems; e.g., religion, values, the meaning of life, etc.

91. Is power-oriented; values power in self or others.

92. Has social poise and presence; appears socially at ease.

93a. *Behaves* in a masculine style and manner.

93b. *Behaves* in a feminine style and manner. (*N.B.:* If subject is male, 93a applies; if subject is female, 93b is to be evaluated. *N.B.:* Again, the cultural or subcultural conception is to be applied as a criterion.)

94. Expresses hostile feelings directly.
95. Tends to proffer advice.
96. Values own independence and autonomy.
97. Is emotionally bland; has flattened effect.
98. Is verbally fluent; can express ideas well.
99. Is self-dramatizing; histrionic.
100. Does not vary roles; relates to everyone in the same way.

Appendix C

Item Listing of Adolescent Core Q Sort

SPECIFIED 9-POINT DISTRIBUTION ($N = 104$)

6, 9, 13, 15, 18, 15, 13, 9, 6

$r = 1 -$ Sum d ^{2}/976

1. Is critical, skeptical.

2. Behaves in a dependable and responsible way.

3. Has a wide range of interests. (*N.B.:* Superficiality or depth of interest is irrelevant here.)

4. Is a talkative individual.

5. Behaves in a giving way toward others. (*N.B.:* Regardless of the underlying motivation involved, be it genuine or not.)

6. Is fastidious in behavior and appearance. (*N.B.:* As opposed to *sloppy.*)

7. Favors status quo of the world as he/she perceived it.

8. Has a high degree of intellectual capacity. (*N.B.:* Whether actualized or not.)

9. Is uncomfortable with uncertainty and complexities.

10. Anxiety and tension find outlet in bodily symptoms. (*N.B.:* If placed high, implies bodily dysfunction; if placed low, implies absence of autonomic arousal.)

11. Is protective of those close to him. (*N.B.:* Placement of this item expressed behavior ranging from over-protection through appropriate nurturance to a laissez-faire, under-protective manner.)

12. Tends to be self-defensive, blame avoidant.

13. Is thin-skinned; sensitive to anything that can be construed as criticism or an interpersonal slight.

14. Genuinely submissive.

15. Is skilled in social techniques of imaginative play, pretending, and humor.

467

16. Is introspective; self-observing; concerned with self as an object. (*N.B.:* Introspectiveness per se implies neither insight nor narcissism nor brooding.)

17. Behaves in a sympathetic or considerate manner. (*N.B.:* Regardless of the motivation involved.)

18. Behaves in a dependent fashion.

19. Seeks reassurance from others.

20. Has a rapid personal tempo; behaves and acts quickly.

21. Arouses nurturant feelings in others.

22. Feels a lack of personal meaning in life.

23. Extrapunitive; tends to transfer or project blame.

24. Prides self on being "objective," rational.

25. Tends toward overcontrol of needs and impulses; binds tensions excessively; delays gratification unnecessarily.

26. Is productive; gets things done.

27. Shows condescending behavior in relations with others. (*N.B.:* Extreme placement toward uncharacteristic end implies simply an *absence* of condescension, not necessarily qualitarianism or inferiority.)

28. Tends to arouse liking and acceptance in others.

29. Is turned to for advice and reassurance.

30. Gives up and withdraws where possible in the face of frustration and adversity. (*N.B.:* If placed high, implies generally defeatist; if placed low, implies *counteractive.*)

31. Is comfortable with own physical appearance.

32. Aware of the impression he makes on others; accurately perceives his social stimulus value.

33. Is calm, relaxed in manner.

34. Reactive to minor frustrations; irritable.

35. Has warmth.

36. Is negativistic; tends to undermine and obstruct or sabotage.

37. Is guileful and deceitful, manipulative, opportunistic.

38. Has hostility toward others. (*N.B.:* Basic hostility is intended here; mode of expression is to be indicated by other items.)

39. Thinks and associates to ideas in unusual ways; has unconventional thought processes.

40. Behaves as if generally fearful in manner and approach, anticipating real or fancied threats.

41. Is judgmental in regard to human conduct. (*N.B.:* Regardless of the ideological nature of the moral code.)

42. Reluctant to commit self to any definite course of action; tends to delay or avoid action.

43. Is facially and/or gesturally expressive.

44. Evaluates the motivation of others in interpreting situations. (*N.B.:* Accuracy of evaluations is not assumed. *N.B.:* Again, extreme placement in one direction implies pre-occupation with motivational interpretation; at the other extreme, the item implies a psychological obtuseness; S does not consider motivational factors.)

45. Disorganized and maladaptive when under stress or trauma; has a small reserve of integration.

46. Engages in personal fantasy and daydreams; fictional speculations.

47. Has a readiness to feel guilty. (*N.B.:* Regardless of whether verbalized or not.)

48. Keeps others at a distance; avoids close interpersonal relationships.

49. Is basically distrustful of people in general.

50. Is considered unpredictable and changeable in behavior and attitudes. (*N.B.:* Behavioral lability is intended here; not long range predictability.)

51. Genuinely values intellectual and cognitive matters. (*N.B.:* Ability or achievement are not implied here.)

52. *Behaves* in an assertive fashion. (*N.B.:* Item 14 reflects underlying submissiveness; this refers to overt behavior.)

53. Various needs tend toward relatively direct and uncontrolled expression; unable to delay gratification.

54. Emphasis being with others; gregarious. (*N.B.:* Genuineness of quality is not of concern here.)

55. Is self-defeating in regard to his own goals.

56. Responds to humor, wit, and jokes. (*N.B.:* Item 15 refers to the quality and refinement of the humorous orientation.)

57. Is an interesting, arresting person; has individuality. (*N.B.:* The *sorter's* judgment is required here rather than judgment by peers.)

58. Enjoys sensuous experiences (including touch, taste, smell, physical contact).

59. Is concerned with own body and the adequacy of its physiological functioning.

60. Has insight into own motives and behavior.

61. *Perceives* self as the crucial and causative agent in determining the occurrences in his life. (*N.B.:* Opposite end implies life and consequences are seen as impersonally or fortuitously determined.)

62. Tends to be rebellious.

63. Values self and others in terms set by his cultural group, like "popularity," presumed adolescent norms, social pressures, etc.

64. Is socially perceptive of a wide range of interpersonal cues.

65. Characteristically pushes and tries to stretch limits; sees what he can get away with.

66. Enjoys esthetic impressions; is esthetically reactive.

67. Is explicitly self-indulgent; considers satisfaction of own desires as of paramount importance. (*N.B.*: As opposed to asceticism.)

68. Is concerned with physical appearance.

69. Is touchy and sensitive to anything that can be construed as a demand from others. (*N.B.*: No implication of the kind of subsequent response is intended here.)

70. Has shifting standards, depending on group and situation pressures.

71. Has high aspiration level for self as adult. (*N.B.*: Goal is self-defined.)

72. Is affected.

73. Tends to construe or define many different contexts in sexual terms; eroticizes situations.

74. Feels satisfied with self.

75. Has a clear-cut, internally consistent personality. (*N.B.*: *Amount* of information available before sorting is not intended here.)

76. Tends to project his own feelings and motivations onto others.

77. Behaves in a straightforward, forthright fashion in dealings with others.

78. Self-pitying; feels cheated and victimized by life.

79. Tends to ruminate and have persistent, preoccupying thoughts.

80. Becomes emotionally involved with members of the opposite sex. (*N.B.*: At low end implies inability to relate to members of opposite sex.)

81. Is physically attractive; good-looking. (*N.B.*: The cultural criterion is to be applied here.)

82. Has fluctuating moods.

83. Comfortable with the decisions he has made.

84. Is cheerful. (*N.B.*: Extreme placement toward uncharacteristic end of continuum implies gloominess.)

85. Communicates through nonverbal behavior, expresses attitudes and feelings through the context of behaviors. (*N.B.*: Item 43 refers to facial and gestural expressiveness per se.)

86. Handles anxiety and conflicts by attempting to exclude them from awareness.

87. Interprets basically simple and clear-cut situations in complicated and particularizing ways.

88. Becomes emotionally involved with members of the same sex.

(*N.B.:* Placement at low end implies inability to relate to members of same sex.)

89. Compares self to others, whether favorably or unfavorably; is alert to real or fancied differences between self and other people. (*N.B.:* Regardless of the reaction subsequent to the comparison.)

90. Is explicitly concerned with philosophical problems, e.g., religion, values, the meaning of life, death, etc.

91. Is power or status oriented; values power or status in self or others.

92. Has social poise and presence with others.

93a. *Behaves* in a masculine style and manner.

93b. *Behaves* in a feminine style and manner. (*N.B.:* If subject is male, 93a applies; if S is female, 93b is to be evaluated. *N.B.:* Again, the cultural or subcultural conception is to be applied as a criterion.)

94. Expresses hostile feelings directly.

95. Tends to proffer advice.

96. Values own independence and autonomy.

97. Is emotionally bland. (*N.B.:* At high end, implies flattened affect; at low end, implies extreme and deep emotionality.)

98. Is verbally fluent, articulate. (*N.B.:* Talkativeness per se is expressed by Item 4.)

99. Is self-dramatizing; histrionic.

100. Does not vary roles; relates to others in the same way.

101. Questing for meaning, self-definition, or redefinition.

102. Initiates humor, wit, and jokes. (*N.B.:* Item 15 refers to the quality and refinement of the humorous situation.)

103. Accepting of dependency in self; functions comfortably when dependent.

104. Is identifying and romanticizing of individuals and causes. (*N.B.: Irrespective* of nature or values of the cause or the individuals.)

References

Abeles, R. P., & Riley, M. W. *A life-course perspective on the later years of life: Some implications for research.* New York: Social Science Research Council Annual Report, 1976–77.

Abelson, H. I., Fishburne, P. M., & Cisin, I. *National survey on drug abuse.* Vol. I. National Institute on Drug Abuse, 1977.

Abraham, S., Johnson, C. L., & Carrol, M. D. Total serum cholesterol levels of adults 18–74 years of age, United States, 1971–74. Advance Data from Vital and Health Statistics, No. 7. DHEW, May 24, 1977.

Adorno, T. W., Frenkel-Brunswik, E., Levinson, D. J., & Sanford, R. N. *The authoritarian personality.* New York: Harper, 1950.

Andres, R., & Tobin, J. D. Aging, carbohydrate metabolism and diabetes. *Proceedings 9th International Congress of Gerontology,* 1972, **1,** 276–280.

Armstrong, J. D. The search for the alcoholic personality in understanding alcoholism. *Annals of the American Academy of Political and Social Science,* 1958, **135,** 40–47.

Atchley, R. C. The life course, age grading, and age-linked demands for decision making. In N. Datan & L. Ginsberg (Eds.), *Life-span developmental psychology: Normative life crises.* New York: Academic Press, 1975. Pp. 261–278.

Atkinson, J. W. (Ed.). *Motives in fantasy, action and society.* Princeton, New Jersey: Van Nostrand-Reinhold, 1958.

Back, K. W. Personal characteristics and social behavior theory and method. In R. H. Binstock & E. Thomas (Eds.), *Handbook of aging and the social sciences.* Princeton, New Jersey: Van Nostrand-Reinhold, 1976.

Baldwin, A. L. The effect of home environment on nursery school behavior. *Child Development,* 1949, **20,** 49–62.

Baltes, P. B., Cornelius, S. W., & Nesselroade, J. R. Cohort effects in developmental psychology: Theoretical and methodological perspectives. In W. A. Collins (Ed.), *Minnesota symposium on child psychology.* Vol. 11. Minneapolis, Minnesota: University of Minnesota, 1977.

Baltes, P. B., & Nesselroade, J. R. Cultural change and adolescent personality development: An application of longitudinal sequences. *Developmental Psychology,* 1972, **7,** 244–256.

Baltes, P. B., & Schaie, K. W. (Eds.) *Life-span developmental psychology: Personality and socialization.* New York: Academic Press, 1973.

Bane, M. J. *Here to stay: American families in the twentieth century.* New York: Basic Books, 1976.

Bardwick, J. The dynamics of successful people. In D. McGuigan (Ed.), *New research on women.* Ann Arbor, Michigan: University of Michigan Center for the Continuing Education of Women, 1974.

Barnett, R. J. *Roots of war.* New York: Penguin, 1973.

Barry, W. A. Marriage research and conflict: An integrative review. *Psychological Bulletin,* 1970, **73,** 41–54.

Bart, P. Depression in middle-aged women. In V. Gornick & B. K. Moran (Eds.), *Woman in sexist society.* New York: Basic Books, 1971.

Baumrind, D. Child care practices anteceding three patterns of preschool behavior. *Genetic Psychology Monographs,* 1967, **75,** 43–88.

Bayer, L. M., & Snyder, M. Illness experience of a group of normal children. *Child Development,* 1950, **21,** 93–120.

Bayer, L. M., Whissell-Buechy, D., & Honzik, M. P. Adolescent health and personality: Significance for adult health. *Journal of Adolescent Health Care,* 1980, **1,** 101–107.

Bayley, N. Mental growth in young children. *Yearbook of the National Society for the Study of Education,* 1940, **39,** Part II, 11–47.

Bayley, N. Consistency and variability in the growth of intelligence from birth to eighteen years. *Journal of Genetic Psychology,* 1949, **75,** 165–196.

Bayley, N. Data on the growth of intelligence between 16 and 21 years as measured by the Wechsler-Bellevue Scale. *Journal of Genetic Psychology,* 1957, **90,** 3–15.

Bayley, N. Learning in adulthood: The role of intelligence. In H. J. Klausmeier & C. W. Harris (Eds.), *Analyses of concept learning.* New York: Academic Press, 1966.

Bayley, N. Cognition and aging. In K. W. Schaie (Ed.), *Theory and methods of research on aging.* Morgantown, West Virginia: West Virginia University Library, 1968. Pp. 97–119.

Bayley, N. *Bayley Scales of Infant Development.* New York: The Psychological Corp., 1969.

Bayley, N., & Oden, M. H. The maintenance of intellectual ability in gifted adults. *Journal of Gerontology,* 1955, **10,** 91–107.

Bayer, L. M., & Snyder, M. M. Illness experience of a group of normal children. *Child Development,* 1950, **21,** 93–120.

Belloc, N. B., & Breslow, L. Relationship of physical health status and health practices. *Preventive Medicine,* 1972, **1,** 409–421.

Benedek, T., & Rubenstein, B. B. *The sexual cycle in women: The relation between ovarian function and psychodynamic processes.* Washington, D.C.: National Research Council, 1942.

Bennett, S. K., & Elder, G. H., Jr. Women's work in the family economy: A study of depression hardship in women's lives. *Journal of Family History,* **4** (2), 1979, 153–176.

Bensman, J., & Vidich, A. J. *The new American society.* Chicago, Illinois: Quadrangle Books, 1971.

Bentler, P. Assessment of developmental factor change at the individual and group level. In J. R. Nesselroade & H. W. Reese (Eds.), *Lifespan developmental psychology: Methodological issues.* New York: Academic Press, 1973. Pp. 145–174.

Bentler, P. M., & Weeks, D. G. Interrelations among models for the analysis of moment structures. *Multivariate Behavioral Research,* 1979, **14,** 169–186.

Bernard, J. *The future of marriage.* New York: Bantam, 1973.

Bernstein, I. *The lean years: A history of the American worker, 1929–1933.* Boston, Massachusetts: Houghton-Mifflin, 1970.

Birnbaum, J. Life patterns and self-esteem in gifted family-oriented and career-committed women. In M. Mednick, S. Tangri, & L. Hoffman (Eds.), *Women and achievement*. Washington, D.C.: Hemisphere, 1975.

Birren, J. E. Aging. I. Psychological aspects. In D. L. Sills (Ed.), *International encyclopedia of the social sciences*, Vol. I. New York: Macmillan, 1968. Pp. 176–186.

Blane, H. T. The personality of the alcoholic. In M. E. Chafets, H. T. Blane, & M. J. Hill (Eds.), *Frontiers of alcoholism*. New York: Science House, 1970.

Blau, P., & Duncan, O. D. *The American occupational structure*. New York: Wiley, 1967.

Blauner, R. *Alienation and freedom: The factory worker and his industry*. Chicago, Illinois: University of Chicago Press, 1964.

Block, J. *The Q-sort method in personality assessment and psychiatric research*. Springfield, Illinois: Thomas, 1961.

Block, J. Advancing the psychology of personality: Paradigmatic shifts or improving the quality of research. In D. Magnusson & N. S. Endler (Eds.), *Personality at the crossroads: Current issues in interactional psychology*. Hillsdale, New Jersey: Erlbaum (Wiley), 1977. Pp. 37–63.

Block, J., in collaboration with Haan, N. *Lives through time*. Berkley, California: Bancroft Books, 1971.

Block, J., von der Lippe, A., & Block, J. H. Sex-role and socialization patterns: Some personality concomitants and environmental antecedents. *Journal of Consulting and Clinical Psychology*, 1973, **41**, 321–341.

Blood, R. O., Jr., & Wolfe, D. M. *Husbands and wives*. New York: Free Press, 1960.

Blum, E. M., & Blum, R. H. *Alcoholism: A modern psychological approach*. San Francisco, California: Jossey-Bass, 1971.

Bock, R. *Multivariate statistical methods in behavioral research*. New York: McGraw-Hill, 1975.

Bradburn, N. J., & Caplovits, D. *Reports on happiness*. Chicago, Illinois: Aldine, 1965.

Bradway, K. P. IQ constancy on the Revised Stanford-Binet from the preschool to the junior high school level. *Journal of Genetic Psychology*, 1944, **65**, 197–217.

Bradway, K. P., Thompson, C. W., & Cravens, R. B. Preschool IQs after twenty-five years. *Journal of Educational Psychology*, 1958, **49**, 278–281.

Bray, G. (Ed.) *Proceedings of the Conference: Obesity in Perspective*. Fogerty International Center, NIH Bethesda Publication, DHEW, 1973.

Brim, O. G., Jr. Life-span development on the theory of oneself: Implications for child development. In H. Reese (Ed.), *Advances in child development and behavior*. Vol. 11. New York: Academic Press, 1976. (a)

Brim, O. G., Jr. Theories of the male mid-life crisis. *The Counseling Psychologist*, 1976, **6**, (1), 2–9. (b)

Brim, O., & Forer, R. A note on the relation of values and social structure to life planning. *Sociometry*, 1956, **19**, 54–60.

Brim, O. G., Jr., & Kagan, J. (Eds.) Constancy and change: A view of the issues. *Constancy and change in human development*. Cambridge, Massachusetts: Harvard University Press, 1980. Pp. 1–25.

Bronfenbrenner, U. The changing American child: A speculative analysis. *Journal of Social Issues*, 1961, **17**, 6–18.

Bronson, W. C. Early antecedents of emotional expressiveness and reactivity-control. *Child Development*, 1966, **37**, 793–810.

Bronson, W. C. Adult derivatives of emotional expressiveness and reactivity-control: Developmental continuities from childhood to adulthood. *Child Development*, 1967, **38**, 801–817.

Bronson, W. C. Stable patterns of behavior: The significance of enduring orientations for personality development. In J. P. Hill (Ed.), *Minnesota symposia on child psychology*. Minneapolis, Minnesota: University of Minnesota Press, 1968. Pp. 3–27.

Butler, R. The life review: An interpretation of reminiscence in the aged. *Psychiatry,* 1963, **26,** 65–76.

Cahalan, D. *Problem drinkers: A national survey*. San Francisco, California: Jossey-Bass, 1970.

Cahalan, D. Problem drinking among American men aged 21–59. Paper presented at the 30th International Congress on Alcoholism and Drug Dependence, Amsterdam September 1972.

Cahalan, D., Cisin, I. H., & Crossley, H. M. American drinking practices. Monograph of the Rutgers Center of Alcoholic Studies, No. 6. New Brunswik, New Jersey, 1969.

Cahalan, D., & Treiman, B. *Drinking behavior, attitudes and problems in San Francisco*. Berkeley, California: Social Research Group, 1976.

Callahan, D. Health and society: Some ethical imperatives. In *Doing better and feeling worse: Health in the United States, Daedalus. Proceedings of the American Academy of Arts and Sciences,* 1977, **106,** No.1, 23–33.

Campbell, A., Converse, P., & Rodgers, W. *The quality of American life: Perceptions, evaluations, and satisfactions*. New York: Russell Sage Foundation, 1976.

Cannon, C. Spirits of '77—Americans drink less. *Los Angeles Times,* April 21, 1977.

Carroll, J. D., & Arabie, P. Multidimensional scaling. In M. R. Rosenzweig & L. W. Porter (Eds.), *Annual review of psychology*. Palo Alto, California: Annual Review, 1980.

Carroll, J. D., & Chang, J. J. Analysis of individual differences in multidimensional scaling via an n-way generalization of 'Eckart-Young' decomposition. *Psychometrika,* 1970, **35,** 283–319.

Carter, H., & Glick, P. C. *Marriage and divorce: A social and economic study*. (rev. ed.) Cambridge, Massachusetts: Harvard University Press, 1976.

Cattell, R. B. "Parallel Proportional Profiles" and other principles for determining the choice of factors by rotation. *Psychometrika,* 1944, **9,** 267–283.

Cattell, R. B. *Factor analysis*. New York: Harper, 1952.

Cattell, R. B., & Cattell, A.K.S. Factor rotation for proprotional profiles: Analytical solution and an example. *British Journal of Statistical Psychology,* 1955, **8,** 83–92.

Caughey, J. W. *California*. Englewood Cliffs, New Jersey: Prentice-Hall, 1970.

Chafe, W. H. *The American women*. London and New York: Oxford University Press, 1972.

Charles, D. C. Ability and accomplishment of persons earlier judged mentally deficient. *Genetic Psychology Monograph,* 1953, **47,** 3–71.

Clausen, J. A. Adolescent antecedents of cigarette smoking: Data from the Oakland Growth Study. *Social Science and Medicine,* 1968, **1,** 357–382.

Clausen, J. A. Value transmission and personality resemblance in two generations. Paper presented at the Meetings of the American Sociological Association, Montreal, Canada, August 1974.

Clausen, J. A. The social world of middle age. *The International Journal of Aging and Human Development,* 1976, **7,** 99–106.

Cohen, J. *Statistical power analyses for the behavioral sciences*. New York: Academic Press, 1977.

Cohen, T., Giltman, L., & Lipschutz, D. Liver function studies in the aged. *Geriatrics,* 1960, **15,** 824–836.

Cohler, B. *Adult developmental psychology and reconstruction in psychoanalysis.* In G. Pollock & S. Greenspan (Eds.), *The course of life.* Washington, D.C.: U.S. Government Printing Office, 1980.

Coleman, J. *The adolescent society.* New York: Free Press, 1963.

Comrey, A. L. Tandem criteria for analytic rotation in factor analysis. *Psychometrika,* 1967, **32**, 143–153.

Corballis, M. C. A factor model for analyzing change. *British Journal of Mathematical and Statistical Psychology,* 1973, **26**, 90–97.

Coser, R., & Rokoff, G. Women in the occupational world: Social disruption and conflict. *Social Problems,* 1971, **18**, 535–554.

Crites, J. O., Bechtoldt, H. P., Goodstein, L. D., & Heilbrun, A. B., Jr. A factor analysis of the California Psychological Inventory. *Journal of Applied Psychology,* 1961, **45**, 408–414.

Cronbach, L. J., & Furby, L. How should we measure "change"—or should we? *Psychological Bulletin,* 1970, **74** (1), 68–80.

Cuber, J. F., & Harroff, P. *Sex and the significant Americans.* Baltimore, Maryland: Penguin, 1965.

Datan, N., & Ginsberg, L. (Eds.) *Life-span developmental psychology: Normative life crises.* New York: Academic Press, 1975.

Davidson, I., & Henry, J. B. (Eds.) *Todd-Sanford clinical diagnosis by laboratory methods.* (14th ed.) Philadelphia, Pennsylvania: Saunders, 1969.

Deutsch, H. *Psychology of women.* Vol. 1. New York: Grune & Stratton, 1944.

Deutsch, H. *Psychology of women.* Vol. 2. New York: Grune & Stratton, 1945.

Deutscher, I. The quality of postparental life: Definitions of the situation. *Journal of Marriage and the Family,* 1964, **26**, 52–59.

De Vries, H. A., & Adams, G. M. Comparison of exercise responses in old and young men: 1. The cardiac effort total body effort relationship. *Journal of Gerontology,* 1972, **27**, 344–348.

Dickinson, R. L., & Beam, L. *A thousand marriages.* Westport, Connecticut: Greenwood, 1970 (orig. pub. 1931).

Dohrenwend, B. S., & Dohrenwend, B. P. (Eds.) *Stressful life events.* New York: Wiley, 1974.

Douglas, P. H. The impact of recent social and economic changes upon the family. Child Welfare Pamphlets, No. 38, October 13. Iowa City, Iowa: State University of Iowa, 1934.

Douglas, P. H. Foreword to "Consumer Credit." *Annals of the American Academy of Political and Social Sciences,* 1938, **196**.

Douvan, E., & Adelson, J. *The adolescent experience.* New York: Wiley, 1966.

Duncan, B. Trends in output and distribution of schooling. In E. B. Sheldon & W. E. Moore (Eds.), *Indicators of social change.* New York: Russell Sage Foundation, 1968.

Durnan, J.V.G.A., & Rahaman, M. M. The assessment of the amount of fat in the human body from measurements of skin fold thickness. *British Journal of Nutrition,* 1967, **21**, 681–689.

Ebert, E., & Simmons, K. The Brush foundation study of child growth and development: I. Psychometric tests. *Monographs of the Society for Research in Child Development,* 1943, **8**, (2, Whole No. 35).

Eichorn, D. H. The Berkeley longitudinal studies: Continuities and correlates of behaviour. *Canadian Journal of Behavioral Sciences,* 1973, **5**, 297–320.

Eisdorfer, C. Intellectual and cognitive changes in the aged. In E. W. Busse & E. Pfeiffer (Eds.), *Behavior and adaptation in late life.* Boston, Massachusetts: Little, Brown, 1969. Pp. 237–250.

Elder, G. H., Jr. Occupational mobility, life patterns and personality. *Journal of Health and Social Behavior,* 1969, **10,** 308–323.

Elder, G. H., Jr. Marriage mobility, adult roles and personality. *Sociological Symposium,* 1970, (4), 31–54.

Elder, G. H., Jr. *Children of the Great Depression.* Chicago, Illinois: University of Chicago Press, 1974.

Elder, G. H., Jr. Historical change in life patterns and personality. In P. Baltes & O. Brim (Eds.), *Life-span development and behavior,* Vol. 2. New York: Academic Press, 1979.

Elder, G. H., Jr., & Rockwell, R. C. Economic depression and postwar opportunity in men's lives: A study of life patterns and health. In R. G. Simmons (Ed.), *Research in community and mental health: An annual compilation of research.* Greenwich, Connecticut: JAI Press, 1978. (a)

Elder, G. H., Jr., & Rockwell, R. C. Historical times in lives. In M. Kohli (Ed.), *Soziologie des lebenslaufes.* Darmstadt: Luchterhand, 1978. (b)

Epstein, C. *Women's place.* Berkeley, California: University of California Press, 1971.

Erikson, E. H. *Childhood and society.* New York: Norton, 1950.

Erikson, E. H. *Identity and the life cycle.* New York: International Universities Press, 1959.

Erikson, E. H. *Identity: Youth and crisis.* New York: Norton, 1968.

Erikson, E. H. *Life history and the historical moment.* New York: Norton, 1975.

Eshleman, J. R. *The family.* Boston, Massachusetts: Allyn & Bacon, 1978.

Eysenck, H. J. *The structure of human personality.* London: Methuen, 1970.

Eysenck, H. J. Personality and factor analysis: A reply to Guilford. *Psychological Bulletin,* 1977, **84,** 405–411.

Ezekiel, R. The personal future and Peace Corps competence. *Journal of Personality and Social Psychology Monograph Supplement,* 1968, **8,** No. 2, Part 2.

Faulkner, R. R. Coming of age in organizations: A comparative study of career contingencies and adult socialization. *Sociology of Work and Occupations,* 1974, **1,** 131–173.

Featherman, D. L. Schooling and occupational careers: Constancy and change in worldly success. In O. G. Brim, Jr. & J. Kagan (Eds.), *Constancy and change in human development.* Cambridge, Massachusetts: Harvard University Press, 1980. Pp. 675–738.

Feld, S. Feelings of adjustment. In I. Nye & L. Hoffman (Eds.), *The employed mother in America.* Chicago, Illinois: Rand-McNally, 1963.

Feldman, H. Marriage during the post-childrearing period. Unpublished manuscript. Cornell University, 1976.

Feldman, S. Impediment or stimulant? Marital status and graduate education. *American Journal of Sociology,* 1973, **78,** 982–984.

Feree, M. Working-class jobs: Housework and paid work as sources of satisfaction. *Social Problems,* 1976, **23,** 431–441.

Filene, P. G. *Him/her/self: Sex roles in modern America.* New York: Harcourt, 1974.

Finch, C. E., & Hayflick, L. *Handbook of the biology of aging.* Princeton, New Jersey: Van Nostrand-Reinhold, 1977.

Freedman, J. *Happy people.* New York: Harcourt, 1978.

Frenkel-Brunswik, E. Adjustments and reorientation in the course of the life span. In B. L. Neugarten (Ed.), *Middle age and aging: A reader in social psychology.* Chicago, Illinois: University of Chicago Press, 1968.

Freud, S. Sexual aetiology of the neuroses. *The collected works of Sigmund Freud.* Standard Edition, III. London: Hogarth (orig. publ. 1898).

Freud, S. On psychotherapy. *The collected works of Sigmund Freud.* Standard Edition, VII. London: Hogarth (orig. publ. 1905).

Friedan, B. *The feminine mystique.* New York: Norton, 1963.

Gandour, J. T., & Harshman, R. A. Crosslanguage differences in tone perception: A multidimensional scaling investigation. *Language and Speech,* 1978, **21,** Part 1, 1–33.

Glenn, N. D. Values, attitudes, and beliefs. In O. G. Brim, Jr. & J. Kagan (Eds.), *Constancy and change in human development.* Cambridge, Massachusetts: Harvard University Press, 1980, Pp. 596–640.

Glenn, N. W., & Weaver, C. N. A multivariate, multisurvey of marital happiness. *Journal of Marriage and the Family,* 1978, **40,** 269–282.

Glick, P. A demographer looks at American families. *Journal of Marriage and the Family,* 1975, **37,** 15–26.

Glick, P. C. Remarriage: Some recent changes and variations. *Journal of Family Issues,* 1980, **1** (4), 455–478.

Gloreg, A., & Roberts, J. Hearing levels of adults by age and sex, United States, 1960–1962. National Center for Health Statistics, Vital Health Statistics, Public Health Service Publ. No. 1000, Series 11, No. 11. Washington, D.C.: U.S. Government Printing Office, October 1965.

Gofman, J. W., Jones, H. B., Lindgren, F. T., Lyon, T. P., Elliott, H. A., & Stresower, B. Blood lipids and human atherosclerosis. *Circulation,* 1950, **2,** 161–178.

Gomberg, E. S. Etiology of alcoholism. *Journal of Consulting and Clinical Psychology,* 1968, **32,** 18–20.

Gomberg, E. S. Women and alcoholism. In V. Franks & V. Burtle (Eds.), *Women in therapy: New psychotherapies for a changing society.* New York: Bruner-Mazel, 1974. Pp. 169–190.

Goode, W. J. *Principles of sociology.* New York: McGraw-Hill, 1977.

Gordon, M. S. *Employment expansion and population growth: The California experience, 1900–1950.* Berkeley, California: University of California Press, 1954.

Gordon, T. Blood pressure of adults by age and sex (U.S. 1960–1962). Vital and Health Statistics, National Center for Health Statistics, Series II #4, DHEW, 1964.

Gough, H. G. A sociological theory of psychopaths. *American Journal of Sociology,* 1948, **53,** 359–366.

Gough, H. G. *Manual for the California Psychological Inventory.* Palo Alto, California: Consulting Psychologists Press, 1957.

Gough, H. G. Theory and measurement of socialization. *Journal of Consulting Psychology,* 1960, **24,** 23–30.

Gough, H. G. Appraisal of social maturity by means of the CPI. *Journal of Abnormal Psychology,* 1966, **71,** 189–195.

Gough, H. G. Scoring high on an Index of Social Maturity. *Journal of Abnormal Psychology,* 1971, **77,** 236–241.

Gough, H. G. Preface. In Megargee, E. (Ed.), *The California Psychological Inventory Handbook.* San Francisco, California: Jossey-Bass, 1972. Pp. xi–xv.

Gough, H. G., Devos, G., & Mizushima, K. Japanese validation of the CPI Social Maturity Index. *Psychological Reports,* 1968, **22,** 143–146.

Gough, H. G., & Quintard, G. A French application of the CPI Social Maturity Index. *Journal of Cross-cultural Psychology,* 1974, **5**, 247–252.

Gould, R. L. *Transformations: Growth and change in adult life.* London: Simon & Schuster, 1978.

Gove, W., & Tudor, J. Adult sex roles and mental illness. *American Journal of Sociology,* 1973, **78**, 812–835.

Greenstein, F. I. Personality and political socialization: The theories of authoritarian and democratic character. *The Annals of the American Academy of Political and Social Science,* 1965, **361**, 81–95.

Guilford, J. P. Will the real factor of extraversion-introversion please stand up? A reply to Eysenck. *Psychological Bulletin,* 1977, **84**, 412–416.

Gutmann, D. Parenthood: A key to the comparative study of the life cycle. In N. Datan & L. Ginsberg (Eds.), *Life-span developmental psychology: Normative life crises.* New York: Academic Press, 1975. Pp. 167–184.

Gutmann, D. The cross-cultural perspective: Notes towards a comparative psychology of aging. In J. Birren & K. W. Schaie (Eds.), *Handbook of aging psychology.* Princeton, New Jersey: Van Nostrand-Reinhold, 1977.

Haan, N. Proposed model of ego functioning: Coping and defense in relationship to IQ change. *Psychological Monographs,* 1963, **77**, (8), 1–23.

Haan, N. Coping and defense mechanisms related to personality inventories. *Journal of Consulting Psychology,* 1965, **29** (4), 373–378.

Haan, N. Personality organizations of well functioning younger people and older adults. *International Journal of Aging and Human Development,* 1976, **7**, 117–127.

Haan, N. *Coping and defending: Processes of self-environment organization.* New York: Academic Press, 1977.

Haan, N. Two moralities in action contexts. *Journal of Personality and Social Psychology,* 1978, **36** (3), 286–305.

Haan, N., & Day, D. Change and sameness in personality development: Adolescence to adulthood. *International Journal of Aging and Human Development,* 1974, **5**, 11–39.

Haggard, E. *Intraclass correlation and the analysis of variance.* New York: Holt, 1958.

Hamill, P. V. V., Drizd, T. A., Johnson, C. L., Reed, R. B., and Roche, A. F. NCHS growth curves for children birth—18 years, United States (*Vital and Health Statistics,* Series 11, No. 165, DHEW Publications No. [PHS] 78–1650). Washington, D.C.: Govt. Printing Office, 1977.

Harevan, T. Family time and historical time. *Daedalus,* Spring 1977, 57–70.

Harrison, T. R. *Principles of internal medicine* (7th ed.). New York: McGraw-Hill, 1974.

Harshman, R. A. Foundations of the PARAFAC procedure: Models and conditions for an "explanatory" multi-modal factor analysis. *UCLA Working Papers in Phonetics,* 1970, **16**, 86 pp. Reprinted by University Microfilms International, Ann Arbor, Michigan, Order No. 10, 085.

Harshman, R. A. PARAFAC2: Mathematical and technical notes. *UCLA Working Papers in Phonetics,* 1972, **22**, 30–47. Reprinted by University Microfilms International, Ann Arbor, Mich., Order No. 10, 085. (a)

Harshman, R. A. Determination and proof of minimal uniqueness conditions for PARAFAC1. *UCLA Working Papers in Phonetics,* 1972, **22**, 111–117. Reprinted by University Microfilms International, Ann Arbor, Michigan, Order No. 10, 085. (b)

Harshman, R. A. PARAFAC: Methods of three-way factor analysis and multidimensional scaling according to the principle of proportional profiles. Doctoral dissertation, UCLA, 1976. Published by University Microfilms International, Ann Arbor, Michigan, Order No. 76-25, 210.

Harshman, R. A., Ladefoged, P., & Goldstein, L. Factor analysis of tongue shapes. *Journal of the Acoustical Society of America,* 1977, **62,** 693-707.

Havens, E. Women, work and wedlock: A note on female marital patterns in the United States. *American Journal of Sociology,* 1973, **78,** 975-981.

Hetherington, E. M., & Feldman, S. E. College cheating as a function of subject and situational variables. *Journal of Educational Psychology,* 1964, **55,** 212-218.

Hicks, M. W., & Platt, M. Marital happiness and stability: A review of the research in the sixties. *Journal of Marriage and the Family,* 1970, **32,** 553-574.

Hill, R. *The family: A dynamic interpretation.* New York: Holt, 1951.

Hill, R. *Family development in three generations.* Cambridge, Massachusetts: Schenkman, 1970.

Holt, R. R. Revised edition of Rapaport, D., Gill, M. M, & Schafer, R. *Diagnostic psychological testing.* New York: International Universities Press, 1968.

Honzik, M. P. The constancy of mental test performance during the preschool period. *Journal of Genetic Psychology,* 1938, **52,** 285-302.

Honzik, M. P., Hunt, J. V., & Eichorn, D. H. Mental growth after age 18 years. Compte-Rendu de la XIIIe Reunion des Equipes Charges des Etudes sur la Croissance et le Developpement de l'Enfant Normal, Centre International de l'Enfance Press. Rennes, France, September, 1976.

Honzik, M. P., & Macfarlane, J. W. Personality development and intellectual functioning from 21 months to 40 years. In L. F. Jarvik, C. Eisdorfer, & J. E. Blum (Eds.), *Intellectual functioning in adults.* New York: Springer, 1973.

Honzik, M. P., Macfarlane, J. W., & Allen, L. The stability of mental test performance between two and eighteen years. *Journal of Experimental Education,* 1948, **17,** 309-324.

Horn, J. L., & Cattell, R. B. Age differences in fluid and crystallized intelligence. *Acta Psychologica,* 1967, **26,** 107-129.

Horn, J. L. & Donaldson, G. Cognitive development in adulthood. In O. G. Brim, Jr. & J. Kagan (Eds.) *Constancy and change in human development.* Cambridge, Massachusetts: Harvard University Press, 1980. Pp. 445-529.

Horn, J. L., and McArdle, J. J. Perspectives on mathematical/statistical model building (MASMOB) in research on aging. In L. W. Poon (Ed.), *Aging in the 1980s.* Washington, D.C.: American Psychological Association, 1980.

Huntington, E. H. *Unemployment relief and the unemployed.* Berkeley, California: University of California Press, 1939.

Inhelder, B., & Piaget, J. *The growth of logical thinking from childhood and adolescence.* New York: Basic Books, 1958.

Jaffa, A. S. *The California Preschool Mental Scale: Form A.* Berkeley, California: University of California Press, 1934.

Jessor, R., & Jessor, S. L. *Problem behavior and psychosocial development: A longitudinal study of youth.* New York: Academic Press, 1977.

Johnston, L. D., Bachman, J. G., & O'Malley, P. M. Drug use among American high school students, 1975-1977. National Institute on Drug Abuse, 1977.

Jones, H. E. Educational research at the Institute of Child Welfare. *Journal of Educational Research,* 1940, **34,** 158-159.

Jones, H. E., & Conrad, H. S. The growth and decline of intelligence: A study of a homogeneous group between the ages of ten and sixty. *Genetic Psychology Monographs,* 1933, **13,** 225-298.

Jones, M. C. Correlates and antecedents of adult drinking patterns. Paper presented at the Meeting of the Western Psychological Association, Honolulu, Hawaii, June 1965.

Jones, M. C. Personality correlates and antecedents of drinking patterns in adult males. *Journal of Consulting and Clinical Psychology,* 1968, **32**, 2–12.

Jones, M. C. Personality antecedents and correlates of drinking patterns in women. *Journal of Consulting and Clinical Psychology,* 1971, **36**, 61–69.

Jones, M. C., Bayley, N., Macfarlane, J. W., & Honzik, M. P. (Eds.) *The course of human development.* New York: Wiley, 1971.

Joreskog, K. G. Simultaneous factor analysis in several populations. *Psychometrika,* 1971, **36**, 409–426.

Joreskog, K. G., and Sorbom, D. Statistical models and methods for analysis of longitudinal data. In D. J. Aigner and A. S. Goldberger (Eds.), *Latent variables in socioeconomic models.* Amsterdam: North-Holland Publ., 1977.

Jung, C. G. *Modern man in search of a soul.* New York: Harcourt, 1933.

Jung, C. G. The stages of life. In J. Campbell (Ed.), *The portable Jung.* New York: Viking, 1971 (orig. publ. 1933).

Kagan, J. Perspectives on continuity. In O. G. Brim, Jr. & J. Kagan (Eds.), *Constancy and change in human development.* Cambridge, Massachusetts: Harvard University Press, 1980. Pp. 26–74.

Kagan, J., & Moss, H. *Birth to maturity.* New York: Wiley, 1962.

Kandel, D. B., & Lesser, G. C. *Youth in two worlds: United States and Denmark.* San Francisco, California: Jossey-Bass, 1972.

Kangas, J., & Bradway, K. Intelligence at middle age: A thirty-eight-year follow-up. *Developmental Psychology,* 1971, **5**, (2), 333–337.

Kannel, W. B. Some lessons in cardiovascular epidemiology. *American Journal of Cardiology,* 1976, **37**, 269.

Keller, M., & Efron, V. The prevalence of alcoholism. *Quarterly Journal of Studies on Alcohol,* 1955, **16**, 317–319.

Kemmerer, E. W. The prospect of rising prices from the monetary angle. *Annals of the American Academy of Political and Social Sciences,* 1936, **183**, 255–262.

Kerr, C., & Taylor, P. S. The self-help cooperatives in California. In *Essays in Social Economics.* Berkeley, California: University of California Press, 1935. Pp. 191–255.

Kidner, P. L. *California business cycles.* Berkeley, California: University of California Press, 1946.

Knupfer, G., Fink, R., Clark, W. B., & Goffman, A. S. Factors related to amount of drinking in an urban community. *Drinking Practices Study,* Report No. 6. Berkeley, California: State of California, Department of Public Health, 1963.

Knupfer, G., & Room, R. Age, sex and social class as factors in amount of drinking in a metropolitan community. *Social Problems,* 1964, **12**, 224–240.

Kogan, N. Creativity and cognitive style: A life-span perspective. In P. Baltes & K. W. Schaie (Eds.), *Life-span developmental psychology: Personality and socialization.* New York: Academic Press, 1973. Pp. 146–179.

Kohlberg, L. Continuities in childhood and adult moral development revisited. In P. Baltes & K. W. Schaie (Eds.), *Life-span developmental psychology: Personality and socialization.* New York: Academic Press, 1973. Pp. 180–207.

Kohn, M. L. Social class and parental values. *American Journal of Sociology,* 1959, **64**, 337–351.

Kohn, M. L. *Class and conformity: A study in values.* Homewood, Illinois: Dorsey Press, 1969.

Kohn, M. L. Reassessment, 1977. In *Class and conformity* (2nd ed.). Chicago, Illinois: University of Chicago Press. Pp. xxv–ix.

Kohn, M. L., & Schooler, C. Occupational experience and psychological functioning: An assessment of reciprocal effects. *American Sociological Review,* 1973, **38** (February), 97–118.

Kohn, M. L., & Schooler, C. The reciprocal effects of the substantive complexity of work and intellectual flexibility: A longitudinal assessment. *American Journal of Sociology,* 1978, **84,** 24–52.

Kreps, J. *Sex in the market-place: American women at work.* Baltimore, Maryland: Johns Hopkins, 1971.

Kris, E. *Psychoanalytic explorations in art.* New York: International Universities Press, 1952.

Kritchevsky, D. Lipid metabolism and aging. *Mechanisms of Aging and Development,* 1972, **1,** 275–284.

Kroonenberg, P. M., & de Leeuw, J. Principal component analysis of three-mode data by means of alternating least squares algorithms. *Psychometrika,* 1980, **45,** 69–97.

Kruskal, J. B. More factors than subjects, tests, and treatments: An indeterminacy theorem for Canonical Decomposition and Individual Differences Scaling. *Psychometrika,* 1976, **41,** 281–293.

Kruskal, J. B. Three-way arrays: Rank and uniqueness of trilinear decompositions, with application to arithmetic complexity and statistics. *Linear Algebra and Its Applications,* 1977, **18,** 95–138.

Lambo, T. A. Total health. *World health. The Magazine of the World Health Organization,* Geneva, Switzerland, December 1975.

Lessing, E. Demographic, developmental, and personality correlates of length of future time perspective. *Journal of Personality,* 1968, **36,** 183–201.

Leuchtenburg, W. E. The Great Depression. In C. Van Woodward (Ed.), *The comparative approach to American history.* New York: Basic Books, 1968.

Levinson, D. J., Darrow, C. M., Klein, E. B., Levinson, M. H., & McKee, B. The psychosocial development of men in early adulthood and the mid-life transition. In P. Ricks, A. Thomas, & M. Roff (Eds.), *Life history research in psychopathology,* Vol. 3. Minneapolis, Minnesota: University of Minnesota Press, 1974. Pp. 243–258.

Levinson, D. J. with Darrow, C. M., Klein, E. B., Levinson, M. H., & McKee, B. *The seasons of a man's life.* New York: Knopf, 1978.

Lisansky, E. S. The woman alcoholic. *Annals of the American Academy of Political and Social Sciences,* 1958, **325,** 73–81.

Lively, A. L. Toward a concept clarification: The case of marital interaction. *Journal of Marriage and the Family,* 1969, **31,** 108–114.

Livson, N. Developmental dimensions of personality: A life-span formulation. In P. B. Baltes & K. W. Schaie (Eds.), *Life-span developmental psychology: Personality and socialization.* New York: Academic Press, 1973.

Livson, N. & Day, D. Adolescent personality antecedents of completed family size: A longitudinal study. *Journal of Youth and Adolescence,* 1977, **6,** 311–323.

Livson, N., & Peskin, H. Prediction of adult psychological health in a longitudinal study. *Journal of Abnormal Psychology,* 1967, **72,** 509–518.

Livson, N., & Peskin, H. Perspectives on adolescence from longitudinal research. In D. Adelson (Ed.), *Handbook of adolescent psychology.* New York: Wiley, 1980.

Loevinger, J., Wessler, R., & Redmore, C. *Measuring ego development.* San Francisco, California: Jossey-Bass, 1970.

Lopata, H. *Occupation: Housewife.* London and New York: Oxford University Press, 1971.

Lowenthal, M. F., & Chiriboga, D. Transition to the empty nest. *Archives of General Psychiatry,* 1972, **256,** 8–14.

Lowenthal, M. F., Thurnher, M. F., & Chiriboga, D. *Four stages of life.* San Francisco, California: Jossey-Bass, 1975.

Lundberg, E. O. *Unemployment and child welfare: A study made in a middle-western and an eastern city during the industrial depression of 1921 and 1922.* Children's Bureau, Washington, D.C.: U.S. Government Printing Office, 1923.

Luria, Z. Recent women college graduates: A study of rising expectations. *American Journal of Orthopsychiatry,* 1974, **44**, 312–326.

Lynd, R. S., & Lynd, H. M. *Middletown in transition: A study in cultural conflicts.* New York: Harcourt, 1937.

Maas, H., & Kuypers, J. A. *From thirty to seventy.* San Francisco, California: Jossey-Bass, 1974.

Macfarlane, J. W. Studies in child guidance. I. Methodology of data collection and organization. *Monographs of the Society for Research in Child Development,* Vol. III, No. 6, 1938.

Macfarlane, J. W., Allen, L., & Honzik, M. P. A developmental study of the behavior problems of normal children between twenty-one months and fourteen years. *University of California Publications in Child Development,* 1954, **2**, 1–222.

Madsen, W. P. Value conflicts in cultural transfer. In P. Worchel & D. Byrne (Eds.), *Personality change.* New York: Wiley, 1964.

Manor, S. Geographic changes in U.S. employment from 1950 to 1960. *Monthly Labor Review,* 1963, **86**, 1–10.

McCall, R., & Appelbaum, M. Bias in the analysis of repeated-measure designs: Some alternative approaches. *Child Development,* 1973, **44**, 401–415.

McCarthy, J. A comparison of the probability of the dissolution of 1st and 2nd marriage. *Demography,* 1978, **15**, 345–359.

McCarthy, R. G. *Alcohol education for classroom and community.* New York: McGraw-Hill, 1964.

McClelland, D. C., Davis, W. N., Kalin, R., & Wanner, E. *The drinking man.* New York: Free Press, 1972.

McCord, W., & McCord, J. *Origins of alcoholism.* Palo Alto, California: Stanford University Press, 1960.

McGovern, J. R. The American woman's pre-World War I freedom in manners and morals. *Journal of American History,* 1958, **55**, 315–333.

McNemar, Q. *Psychological statistics* (4th ed.). New York: Wiley, 1969.

McWilliams, C. *California: The great exception.* Westport, Connecticut: Greenwood Press, 1971 (orig. pub. 1948).

Mead, G. *Mind, self and society.* Chicago, Illinois: University of Chicago Press, 1934.

Megargee, E. *The California Psychological Inventory handbook.* San Francisco, California: Jossey-Bass, 1972.

Meyer, J. P. Dimensions of causal attribution for success and failure: A multivariate investigation. Doctoral dissertation, Department of Psychology, University of Western Ontario. Published by University Microfilms International, Ann Arbor, Michigan, Order No. 03301-92, 1978.

Meyer, J. P. Causal attribution for success and failure: A multivariate investigation of dimensionality, formation, and consequences. *Journal of Personality and Social Psychology (Attitudes and Social Cognition Division),* 1980, **38**, 704–718.

Meyer, J. P., & Pepper, S. Need compatibility and marital adjustment in young married couples. *Journal of Personality and Social Psychology,* 1977, **35**, 331–342.

Miles, W. Presidential address, Meeting of the American Psychological Association, 1932.

Mischel, W. *Personality and assessment.* New York: Wiley, 1968.

Mischel, W. Continuity and change in personality. *American Psychologist*, 1969, **24**, 1012–1018.

Mischel, W. Toward a cognitive social learning reconceptualization of personality. *Psychological Review*, 1973, **80**, 252–283.

Mitchell, B. *Depression decade: From New Era through the New Deal, 1929–1940*. New York: Rinehard, 1947.

Mitchell, J. W., Jr., & Pierce-Jones, J. A factor analysis of Gough's California Psychological Inventory. *Journal of Consulting Psychology*, 1960, **24**, 453–456.

Moss, H. A., & Susman, E. J. Longitudinal study of personality development. In O. G. Brim, Jr. & J. Kagan (Eds.), *Constancy and change in human development*. Cambridge, Massachusetts: Harvard University Press, 1980. Pp. 530–595.

Mueller, C. W., & Pope, H. Marital instability: A study of its transmission between generations. *Journal Marriage and the Family*, 1977, **39**, 83–92.

Murray, H. A. *Explorations in personality*. New York: Oxford University Press, 1938.

Murstein, B. I., & Glaudin, V. The relationship of marital adjustment to personality: A factor analysis of the Interpersonal Check List. *Journal of Marriage and the Family*, 1966, **28**, 37–43.

Mussen, P. Some antecedents and consequents of masculine sex-typing in adolescent boys. *Psychological Monographs*, 1961, **75** (2, Whole No. 506).

Nardi, A. Person-perception research and perception of life-span development. In P. Baltes & K. W. Schaie (Eds.), *Life-span developmental psychology: Personality and socialization*. New York: Academic Press, 1973. Pp. 285–305.

Nelson, W. E. An introduction to the medical problems of infants and children. In Nelson, W. E. (Ed.), *Mitchell-Nelson textbook of pediatrics*. Philadelphia, Pennsylvania: Saunders, 1950. Pp. 1–13.

Nesselroade, J., & Baltes, P. Adolescent personality development and historical change: 1970–1972. *Monographs of the Society for Research in Child Development*, 1974, **39** (1, serial no. 154).

Neugarten, B. L. *Personality in middle and late life*. New York: Atherton Press, 1964.

Neugarten, B. L. The awareness of middle age. In B. L. Neugarten (Ed.), *Middle age and aging: A reader in social psychology*. Chicago, Illinois: University of Chicago Press, 1968.

Neugarten, B. L. Adaptation and the life cycle. *Journal of Geriatric Psychiatry*, 1970, **4**, 71–87.

Neugarten, B. L., & Datan, N. Sociological perspectives on the life cycle. In P. Baltes & K. W. Schaie (Eds.), *Life-span developmental psychology: Personality and socialization*. New York: Academic Press, 1973. Pp. 53–71.

Neugarten, B. L., & Gutmann, D. Age-sex roles and personality in middle age: A thematic apperception study. In B. L. Neugarten (Ed.), *Middle age and aging: A reader in social psychology*. Chicago, Illinois: University of Chicago Press, 1968.

Neugarten, B. L., & Moore, J. The changing age-status system. In B. Neugarten (Ed.), *Middle age and aging: A reader in social psychology*. Chicago, Illinois: University of Chicago Press, 1968.

Neugarten, B. L., Wood, V., Kraines, R. J., & Loomis, B. Women's attitudes toward the menopause. In B. L. Neugarten (Ed.), *Middle age and aging: A reader in social psychology*. Chicago, Illinois: University of Chicago Press, 1968.

Newman, F. B. The adolescent in social groups: Studies in the observation of personality. *Applied Psychology Monographs*, 1946, **9**, 1–94.

Nowlin, J. Duke Longitudinal Studies. Presented at the Conference on Longitudinal Studies of Adulthood and Aging. Univ. of Missouri, May, 1979.

Nuttall, R. L., & Costa, P. T. Drinking patterns as affected by age and by personality types. Paper read at the 28th Annual Scientific Meeting of the Gerontological Society, October, 1975. Abstract. *The Gerontologist,* 1975, **15,** Part II, 35.

Nydegger, C. Age and paternal behavior. Gerontology Society meetings, Louisville, Kentucky, October, 1975.

Nye, I. Marital interaction. In I. Ney & L. Hoffman (Eds.), *The employed mother in America.* Chicago, Illinois: Rand-McNally, 1963.

Offer, D, & Offer, J. B. *From teen-age to young manhood: A psychological study.* New York: Basic Books, 1975.

Ogburn, W. F. *American society in wartime.* Chicago, Illinois: University of Chicago Press, 1943.

Orden, S., & Bradburn, N. Working wives and marriage happiness. *American Journal of Sociology,* 1969, **74,** 392–407.

Owens, W. A. Age and mental abilities: A longitudinal study. *Genetic Psychology Monographs,* 1953, **48,** 3–54.

Owens, W. A. Age and mental abilities: A second adult follow-up. *Journal of Educational Psychology,* 1966, **57,** 311–325.

Parsons, T., & Bales, R. *Family socialization and interaction process.* Glencoe, Illinois: Free Press, 1955.

Pearlin, L. Sex roles and depression. In N. Datan & L. Ginsberg (Eds.), *Life-span developmental psychology: Normative life crises.* New York: Academic Press, 1975.

Pearlin, L. , & Johnson, J. S. Marital status, life strains and depression. *American Sociology Review,* 1977, **42,** 704–715.

Perron, R. *Modeles d' enfants, enfants modeles.* Paris: Presses Universitaires de France, 1971.

Perun, P. J., & Bielby, D. B. Midlife: A discussion of competing models. *Research on Aging,* 1979, **1,** 275–300.

Peskin, H. Multiple prediction of adult psychological health from preadolescent to adolescent behaviors. *Journal of Consulting and Clinical Psychology,* 1972, **38,** 155–160.

Peskin, H., & Gigy, L. Time perspective in adult transitions. Gerontology Society meetings, San Francisco, California, November, 1977.

Peskin, H., & Livson, N. Pre- and post-pubertal personality and adult psychologic functioning. *Seminars in Psychiatry,* 1972, **4,** 343–353.

Piaget, J. *Play, dreams and imitation in childhood.* New York: Norton, 1962.

Pineo, P. C. Disenchantment in the later years of marriage. *Marriage and Family Living,* 1961, **23,** 3–11.

Pinneau, S. R. *Changes in intelligence quotient: Infancy to maturity.* Boston, Massachusetts: Houghton Mifflin, 1961.

Plaut, T. F. *Alcohol problems: A report to the nation by the Cooperative Commission on the Study of Alcoholism.* London and New York: Oxford University Press, 1967.

Pleck, J. H. The male sex role: Definitions, problems, and sources of change. *Journal of Social Issues,* 1976, **32,** (3), 155–164.

Prather, J. *A valium a day keeps the tension away: Socio-psychological characteristics of minor tranquilizer users.* Paper presented to the Pacific Sociological Association, Sacramento, California, April 20–23, 1977.

President's Research Committee on Social Trends, *Recent social trends in the United States.* Vol. 1. New York: McGraw-Hill, 1933.

Progoff, I. *At a journal workshop.* New York: Dialogue House Library, 1975.

Pyles, (Honzik), M., Stolz, H. R., & Macfarlane, J. W. The accuracy of mothers' reports on birth and developmental data. *Child Development,* 1935, **6,** 165–176.

Quick, E., & Jacob, T. Marital disturbance in relation to role theory and relationship theory. *Journal of Abnormal Psychology,* 1973, **82**, 309–316.

Rabourn, R. E. A comparison of the Wechsler Bellevue I and the Wechsler Adult Intelligence Scale. Unpublished manuscript. Counseling Center, University of California, Berkeley, California, 1957.

Radloff, L. Sex differences in depression: The effects of occupation and marital status. *Sex Roles,* 1975, **1**, 249–265.

Rausch, H. L., Barry, W. A., Hentel, R. K., & Swain, M. A. *Communication, conflict, and marriage.* San Francisco, California: Jossey-Bass, 1974.

Ridley, J. D. The changing position of American women: Education, labor force participation, and fertility. In *The family in transition.* Fogerty International Center Proceedings No. 3. Washington, D.C.: U.S. Government Printing Office, 1969. Pp. 199–250.

Roberts, J., & Maurer, K. Blood pressure of youths 12–17 years. Vital and Health Statistics: Data from the National Health Survey, Series 11, No. 163. DHEW Publication No. (HRA) 77-1645, 1977. (a)

Roberts, J., & Maurer, K. Blood pressure levels of persons 6–74 years. Vital and Health Statistics: Data from the National Health Survey, Series 11, No. 203. DHEW Publication No. (HRA) 78-1648, 1977. (b)

Rollins, B. C., & Feldman, H. Marital satisfaction over the family life cycle. *Journal of Marriage and the Family,* 1970, **32**, 20–28.

Room, R. Drinking patterns in large U.S. cities: A comparison of San Francisco and national samples in the U.S.A. *Quarterly Journal of Studies on Alcohol,* 1972 (May), Supp. No. 6, 28–57.

Rosenthal, R., & Rosnow R. *Artifact in behavioral research.* New York: Academic Press, 1969.

Rossi, A. Barriers to the career choice of engineering, medicine or science among American women. In J. Mattfeld & C. Van Aken (Eds.), *Women and the scientific professions.* Cambridge, Massachusetts: MIT Press, 1965.

Rossi, A. Transition to parenthood. *Journal of Marriage and the Family,* 1968, **30**, 26–39.

Rossi, P. H. Trends in voting behavior research: 1933–1963. In E. C. Dreyer & W. H. Rosenbaum (Eds.), *Political opinion and electoral behavior.* Belmont, California: Wadsworth, 1966. Pp. 67–78.

Ryder, N. B. The family in developed countries. *Scientific American,* 1974, 123–132.

Safilios-Rothschild, C. Family sociology, or wives' family sociology? *Journal of Marriage and the Family,* 1969, **31**, 290–301.

Sampson, E. Psychology and the American ideal. *Journal of Personality and Social Psychology,* 1977, **35**, 767–782.

San Francisco Chronicle, September 22, 1972. P. 1.

Sands, R., & Young, F. W. Component models for three-way data: An alternating least squares algorithm with optimal scaling features. *Psychometrika,* 1980, **45**, 39–67.

Sattler, J. M. *Assessment of children's intelligence.* Philadelphia, Pennsylvania: Saunders, 1974.

Sawyer, J. On male liberation. *Liberation,* 1970, **15**, 32–33.

Schaeffer, E. S., & Bayley, N. Consistency of maternal behavior from infancy to preadolescence. *Journal of Abnormal and Social Psychology,* 1960, **1**, 1–6.

Schaeffer, E. S., Bell, R. Q., & Bayley, N. Development of a maternal behavior research instrument. *Journal of Genetic Psychology,* 1959, **95**, 83–104.

Schaie, K. W. A general model for the study of developmental problems. *Psychological Bulletin,* 1965, **64**, 92–107.

Schaie, K. W. A reinterpretation of age related changes in cognitive structure and functioning. In L. R. Goulet & P. B. Baltes (Eds.), *Life-span developmental psychology: Research and theory*. New York: Academic Press, 1970. Pp. 486–507.

Schaie, K. W., & Gribbin, K. Abilities, intelligence and cognitive studies. Conference on Longitudinal Studies of Adulthood and Aging. University of Missouri, St. Louis, 1979.

Schaie, K. W., Labouvie, G., & Beuch, B. Generational and cohort-specific differences in adult cognitive functioning. *Developmental Psychology*, 1973, **9**, 151–166.

Schaie, K. W., & Strother, C. R. The effect of time and cohort differences on the interpretation of age changes in cognitive behavior. *Multivariate Behavioral Research*, 1968, **3**.

Sears, D. O. Political behavior. In G. Lindzay & E. Aronson (Eds.), *The handbook of social psychology* (2nd ed.). Reading, Massachusetts: Addison-Wesley, 1969. Pp. 315–458.

Sears, P., & Barbee, A. *Career and life satisfaction among Terman's gifted women*. Unpublished paper, School of Education and Department of Psychology, Stanford University, 1976.

Selman, R. The relation of role taking to the development of moral judgment in children. *Child Development*, 1971, **42**, 79–92.

Selye, H. *The stress of life*. New York: McGraw-Hill, 1956.

Sheehy, G. *Passages: Predictable crises of adult life*. New York: Dutton, 1976.

Shock, N. W. Basal blood pressure and pulse rate in adolescents. *American Journal of Diseases of Children*, 1944, **68**, 16–22. (a)

Shock, N. W. Physiological changes in adolescence. *Yearbook of the National Society for the Study of Education*, 1944, **43**, Part I, 56–79. (b)

Shock, N. W. Some physiological aspects of development. *Review of Educational Research*, 1944, **14**, 413–426. (c)

Shock, N. W. Physiological responses of adolescents to exercise. *Texas Reports of Biological Medicine*, 1946, **4**, 368–386. (a)

Shock, N. W. Some physiological aspects of adolescence. *Texas Reports of Biological Medicine*, 1946, **4**, 289–310. (b)

Skolnick, A. Motivational imagery and behavior over twenty years. *Journal of Consulting Psychology*, 1966, **30**, 463–478. (a)

Skolnick, A. Stability and interrelationships of thematic test imagery over twenty years. *Child Development*, 1966, **37**, 389–396. (b)

Smart, R. G. *The new drinkers: Teenage use and abuse of alcohol* (Addictive Research Foundation Program Rep. Ser. No. 4). Toronto, Canada: The Addiction Research Foundation, 1976.

Smelser, N. J., & Almond, G. *Public higher education in California*. Berkeley, California: University of California Press, 1974.

Smuts, R. W. *Women and work in America*. New York: Columbia University Press, 1959.

Sofer, C. *Men in mid-career: A study of British managers and technical specialists*. London & New York: Cambridge University Press, 1970.

Srole, L., Langner, T. S., Michael, S. T., Kirkpatrick, P., Opler, M. K., & Rennie, T. A. C. *Mental health in the metropolis: The Midtown Manhattan Study*. New York: McGraw-Hill, 1962.

Starfield, B., & Pless, I. B. Physical health. In O. G. Brim, Jr. & J. Kagan (Eds.), *Constancy and change in human development*. Cambridge, Massachusetts: Harvard University Press, 1980. Pp. 272–324.

Stephenson, W. *The study of behavior*. Chicago, Illinois: University of Chicago Press, 1953.

Stewart, L. H., & Livson, N. Smoking and rebelliousness: A longitudinal study. *Journal of Consulting Psychology*, 1966, **30**, 225–229.

Stolz, H. R., & Stolz, L. M. *Somatic development of adolescent boys*. New York: Macmillan, 1951.

Straus, R., & Bacon, S. D. *Drinking in college*. New Haven, Connecticut: Yale University Press, 1953.

Stroud, J. *Careers of middle-aged women in work and family: Personal and social concomitants and antecedents*. Unpublished doctoral dissertation, University of California, Berkeley, California, 1977.

Sullivan, D. F. Conceptual problems in developing an index of health. (DHEW, Public Health Service Publication No. 1000, Series No. 17), 1966.

Suter, L, & Miller, H. Income differences between men and career women. *American Journal of Sociology*, 1973, **78**, 200–212.

Sutherland, E. H., Schroeder, H. G., & Tardella, C. L. Personality traits and the alcoholic. *Quarterly Journal of Studies on Alcohol*, 1950, **11**, 547–561.

Swanson, G. E. Family structure and the reflective intelligence of children. *Sociometry*, 1974, **37**, 453–490.

Syme, L. Personality characteristics and the alcoholic: A critique of current studies. *Quarterly Journal of Studies on Alcohol*, 1957, **18**, 288–302.

Tausky, C., & Dubin, R. Career anchorage: Managerial mobility aspirations. *American Sociological Review*, 1965, **30**, 725–735.

Tavris, C. Women: Work isn't always the answer. *Psychology Today*, September, 1976, p. 78.

Terman, L. M. *The measurement of intelligence*. Boston, Massachusetts: Houghton Mifflin, 1916.

Terman, L. M. *The intelligence of school children: How children differ in ability, the use of mental tests in school grading, and the proper education of exceptional children*. Boston, Massachusetts: Houghton Mifflin, 1919.

Tharp, R. G. Psychological patterning in marriage. *Psychological Bulletin*, 1963, **60**, 97–117.

Thernstrom, S. *The other Bostonians: Class and mobility in the American metropolis, 1880–1970*. Cambridge, Massachusetts: Harvard University Press, 1973.

Thomas, D. W., & Nishimoto, R. S. *The spoilage*. Berkeley, California: University of California Press, 1946.

Thurnher, M. Goals, values, and life evaluations at the preretirement stage. *Journal of Gerontology*, 1974, **29**, 85–96.

Timiras, P. S. *Developmental physiology and aging*. New York: Macmillan, 1972.

Todd, A. J. Limits on the changing functions of the family. In *Essays in social economics*. Berkeley, California: University of California Press, 1935. Pp. 301–320.

Tryon, C. McC. *U.C. Adjustment Inventory*. Vol. I. *Social and emotional adjustment*. Berkeley, California: University of California Press, 1939. (a)

Tryon, C. McC. Evaluation of adolescent personality by adolescents. *Monograph of the Society for Research in Child Development*, 1939, **4**, (Whole No. 23). (b)

Tucker, L. R. Implications of factor analysis of three-way matrices for measurement of change. In C. W. Harris (Ed.), *Problems in measuring change*. Madison, Wisconsin: University of Wisconsin Press, 1963. Pp. 122–137.

Tucker, L. R. Some mathematical notes on three-mode factor analysis. *Psychometrika*, 1966, **31**, 279–311.

Tuddenham, R. D. Studies in Reputation: III. Correlates of popularity among elementary school children. *Journal of Educational Psychology*, 1951, **42**, 257–276.

Tuddenham, R. D. Studies in reputation: I. Sex and grade differences in school children's evaluations of their peers. II. The diagnosis of social adjustment. *Psychological Monographs,* 1952, **66** (1, Whole No. 333).

Tuddenham, R. D., & Snyder, M. M. Physical growth of California boys and girls from birth to eighteen years. *University of California Publications in Child Development,* 1954, 1 (Vol. 2), 183–364.

Tuddenham, R. D., Blumenkrantz, J., & Wilkin, W. R. Age changes on AGCT: A longitudinal study of average adults. *Journal of Consulting and Clinical Psychology,* 1968, **32** (6), 659–663.

Ullman, A. D. First drinking experiences as related to age and sex. In D. J. Pittman & G. R. Snyder (Eds.), *Society, culture and drinking.* New York: Wiley, 1962. Pp. 259–266.

United States Department of Health, Education and Welfare. Health, United States, 1975. DHEW Publication No. (HRA) 76-1232, 1976.

Vague, J. Pathophysiology of adipose tissue. *Excerpta Medical Monographs,* 1969, Whole No. 19.

Vaillant, G. *Adaptation to life.* New York: Little, Brown, 1977.

van den Daele, L. Ego development and preferential judgment in life-span perspective. In N. Datan & L. Ginsberg (Eds.), *Life-span developmental psychology: Normative life crises.* New York: Academic Press, 1975. Pp. 51–88.

Vincent, C. E. Socialization data in research on young marrieds. *Acta Sociologica,* August, 1964.

Waldron, I., & Johnston, S. Why do women live longer than men? *Journal of Human Stress,* 1976, **1,** 19–30.

Watkins, M. P. Similarities between newlywed spouses (Assortative Marriage) with respect to specific cognitive abilities, socioeconomic status, and education. Doctoral dissertation, University of California, Berkeley, 1979.

Wechsler, D. *The measurement of adult intelligence.* Baltimore, Maryland: Williams & Wilkins, 1939, 1941, 1944.

Wechsler, D. *Manual for the Wechsler Adult Intelligence Scale,* New York: Psychological Corporation, 1955.

Wechsler, H., & McFadden, J. Sex differences in adolescent alcohol and drug use: A disappearing phenomenon. *Journal of Studies on Alcohol,* 1976, **37,** 1291–1301.

Weiss, J. The emergence of new themes: A contribution to the psychoanalytic theory of therapy. *International Journal of Psychoanalyses,* 1971, **52,** 459–467.

Werner, M., Tolls, R. E., Hultin, J. V., & Mellecker, J. Influence of sex and age on the normal range of eleven serum constituents. *Zeitschreft Klin. Chem. Biochem.,* 1970, **8,** 105–115.

Westin, J. *Making do: How women survived the 30s.* Chicago, Illinois: Follett, 1976.

Wilensky, H. Orderly careers and social participation. *American Sociology Review,* 1961, **26,** 521–539.

Wilensky, H. The moonlighter: A product of relative deprivation. *Industrial Relations,* 1963, 3, (October), 105–124.

Wohlwill, J. F. Cognitive development in childhood. In O. G. Brim, Jr. & J. Kagan (Eds.), *Constancy and change in human development.* Cambridge, Massachusetts: Harvard University Press, 1980. Pp. 359–444.

Women in the modern world. *Annals of the American Academy of Political and Social Sciences,* 1929, **143,** No. 232.

Wood, V. *Patterns of social role change and life styles of middle-aged women.* Unpublished doctoral dissertation, University of Chicago, Chicago, Illinois, 1963.

World Health Organization. *Constitution of the World Health Organization.* Public Health Report, 1946, **61,** 1268–1277.

Yarrow, M., Scott, P., deLeeuw, L., & Heinig, C. Child-rearing in families of working and non-working mothers. *Sociometry,* 1962, **25,** 122–140.

Yahraes, H. The effect of childhood influences upon intelligence, personality, and mental health. In *Mental Health Program Reports.* Washington, D.C.: Superintendent of Documents, U.S. Government Printing Office, 1969.

Index